THE ICSA HEALTH S DBOOK

THE ICSA

HEALTH SERVICE GOVERNANCE HANDBOOK

2ND EDITION

Claire Lea

icsa

The Governance Institute

First published 2015
Second edition 2017

ICSA Publishing
Saffron House
6–10 Kirby Street
London EC1N 8TS

Designed and typeset by Paul Barrett Book Production, Cambridge
Printed in Great Britain by Lightning Source, Milton Keynes, Buckinghamshire

British Cataloguing in Publication Data
A catalogue record for this book is available from the British Library.

ISBN 978-1-860727191

Contents

Dedication

'Love runs stronger than blood. Deeper than any name you could give me.'

Andrew Peterson, The Warden and the Wolf King

Preface

This is the second edition of the *ICSA Health Service Governance Handbook*, which has been compiled to update the handbook originally written in 2015. It will come as no surprise to NHS governance practitioners that there is plenty of new material and debate in the governance arena within the NHS, as well some intractable problems which have yet to be resolved. The intention is to create a one-stop publication which helps all those involved in the delivery of governance within the NHS, whether students or experienced practitioners, to grapple with these issues whilst providing clarity on the underlying principles of good governance. In this way it is hoped the handbook will support clear thinking about the issues of governance and assist in developing solutions for each circumstance we find ourselves grappling with.

The pace of change remains unchecked, with new guidance arriving almost monthly. This often leaves governance practitioners having to respond to new regulatory guidance on the basis of existing models and approaches to governance when new legislation may be required to fully deliver the level of collaboration being promoted. This handbook will attempt to highlight where these gaps are and the governance challenges that arise.

Students and experienced practitioners can be reassured, however, that the underlying principles remain constant – namely, ensuring that the appropriate checks and balances continue to be rigorous and adaptive, so those who have been entrusted with high levels of decision-making powers do so in the best interests of patients and the general public.

The wider debates that result from the decision to exit the European Union (EU) and the political climate across Europe and the US will challenge organisations including those in the NHS to address uncertainty and complexity in the immediate short term. Good governance for these organisations must continue to underpin decisions, and risk management will become of even greater importance to support that decision-making. Closer to home, the continuing austerity measures of the UK Parliament continue to impact on NHS services, despite the 'ring fencing' of NHS budgets, the impact on social care and welfare benefits continues to have a knock-on effect on the demand for NHS services.

Lessons learned from Mid Staffs, Morecambe Bay, Winterbourne, Shrewsbury and Telford, and Southern Healthcare continue to challenge boards on their patient safety and care record. Scandals elsewhere – such as the Jimmy Saville sexual abuse investigations and the failure of the authorities in Rotherham to act effectively against child sexual abuse – demonstrate more clearly than ever the impact of poor governance.

The introduction of the Well-Led Framework as a means of effective review for boards is to be welcomed, as it clearly sets out culture as a key component of good governance. Clear processes and auditing of performance will only deliver the high standards we expect of our NHS services if it is coupled with a commitment to an open, generous culture of continual improvement. I hope that this handbook will go some way to empowering NHS governance practitioners to be part of that culture.

My continued thanks go to ICSA: The Governance Institute, who have supported the production of this work. ICSA is the chartered membership and qualifying body for people working in governance, risk and compliance, including company secretaries. With over 120 years' experience of the skills, knowledge and experience required for governance professionals, ICSA is the home of good governance!

Thank you also to the NHS Providers who have also supported the development of the Health Service Governance module and who have continued to work with me to ensure that this handbook is as accurate as it can be at the time of publication. Thanks also to the many colleagues, both NHS and otherwise, who have shared their stories and experiences with me – your passion and dedication to improving the health service for patients is inspiring and makes all of this research worthwhile.

My final thanks go to my family, who endure the many hours of writing and disappearing into the office, whilst always remaining encouraging and supportive

Claire Lea
Director, Charis Consultants Limited
August 2017

Endorsements

I'm very pleased to introduce the second edition of this seminal work. Claire Lea has developed The *ICSA Health Service Governance Handbook* into the key go-to document for health and public service governance professionals, boards and advisors. The challenge for the future of public boards will be to work effectively with others, often mixing different cultures and use of language. It will be essential for all to understand the basics of good governance if they are to deliver the joint improvements in service delivery and budgeting required. GGI fully endorse this guidance as an essential addition to good governance knowledge, thinking and practice.

Dr John Bullivant FCQI, Chair
Good Governance Institute

Good governance provides ambitious, effective, prudent direction that helps deliver success over time. In delivering good corporate governance boards depend on the skills, knowledge and practical know-how of company secretaries. In the NHS chairs, chief executives and board directors, particularly non-executive directors, are finding an increasing need to turn individuals within their own organisation who are able to provide reliable corporate governance advice and to provide significant personal support in implementing it. That is most often the company secretary, so it is vital that company secretaries not only have the skills and knowledge required to deliver, but also access to up to date information on the nuts and bolts of corporate governance.

The ICSA Health Service Governance Handbook provides comprehensive guidance on governance in the NHS. It combines clarity and nuance and provides accurate coverage of the many complexities of today's NHS. Clearly it will be a significant source text those seeking to become qualified company secretaries, but just as importantly it is also a first rate point of reference for all of us who work in the field of governance in the NHS. We are delighted to endorse it.

NHS Providers

Acknowledgements

Figure 3.1: From *The health and care system explained*, licensed under the Open Government Licence v3.0.

Figure 3.2: From *The NHS Outcomes Framework 2013/14*, licensed under the Open Government Licence v3.0.

Figure 3.3: From 'The new structure of the NHS in England', © The Nuffield Trust

Figure 3.4: From 'The new structure of the NHS in England', © The Nuffield Trust

Figure 4.1: From *Six principles for engaging people and communities*, People and Communities Board of the Five Year Forward View, © National Voices 2016

Figure 4.2: From *Developmental reviews of leadership and governance using the well-led framework: guidance for NHS trusts and NHS foundation trusts*, NHSI, licensed under the Open Government Licence v3.0.

Figure 12.1: © NHS Providers

Figure 12.2: © NHS Providers

Figure 13.1: From *Good Governance Standard for Public Services*, 2004, image provided courtesy of Office for Public Management Limited, trading as OPM Group

Acronyms and abbreviations

A&E	Accident & Emergency
ABI	Association of British Insurers
ACC	Acute Care Collaboration
ACCA	Association of Chartered Certified Accountants
ACN	Accountable Clinical Network
ACO	accountable care organisation
ACP	accountable care partnership
ACS	Accountable Care System
AfC	Agenda for Change
AGM	annual general meeting
AGS	annual governance statement
AHA	area health authority
ALB	arm's-length body
AO	accounting officer/accountable officer
AQP	any qualified provider
ARG3	annual reporting guidance (NSH England)
ARM	Annual Reporting Manual
BAF	board assurance framework
BGAF	Board Governance Assurance Framework
BMA	British Medical Association
BME	black and minority ethnic
C&AG	Comptroller and Auditor General
CA 2006	Companies Act 2006
CA 2014	Care Act 2014
CCA 2004	Civil Contingencies Act 2004
CCG	clinical commissioning group
CCG ARM	Clinical Commissioning Group Annual Reporting Manual
CCG IAF	CCG Improvement and Assessment Framework
CEO	chief executive officer
CFO	chief financial officer
CFSMS	Counter Fraud and Security Management Service
CHAI	Commission for Healthcare Audit and Inspection
CHI	Commission for Health Improvement
CHRE	Council for Healthcare Regulatory Excellence
CIMA	Chartered Institute of Management Accountants
CIP	cost improvement plan
CIPFA	Chartered Institute of Public Finance and Accountancy

CJV	corporate joint venture
CMA	Competition and Markets Authority
COO	chief operating officer
COSO	Committee of Sponsoring Organizations of the Treadway Commission (US)
CPPIH	Commission for Patient and Public Involvement in Health
CQC	Care Quality Commission
CQUIN	Commissioning for Quality Improvement
CRO	chief risk officer
CSR	corporate social responsibility
CSU	commissioning support unit
DBS	Disclosure and Barring Scheme
DCLG	Department for Communities and Local Government
DDD	Director of Delivery and Development
DH	Department of Health
DHA	district health authority
DoF	director of finance
DoLS	Deprivation of Liberties Safeguards
DPA 1998	Data Protection Act 1998
DTR	Disclosure and Transparency Rules
ED	executive director
EHCH	enhanced health in care homes
ENDPB	executive non-departmental public body
EPLO	emergency planning liaison officer
ERA 1996	Employment Rights Act 1996
ERRA 2013	Enterprise and Regulatory Reform Act 2013
EU	European Union
5YFV	Five Year Forward View
FCA	Financial Conduct Authority
FOI	Freedom of Information
FOIA 2000	Freedom of Information Act 2000
FPC	family practitioner committee
FRC	Financial Reporting Council
FReM	Financial Reporting Manual
FSA	Financial Services Authority
FT	foundation trust
FT ARM	Foundation Trust Annual Reporting Manual
FT Code	NHS Foundation Trust Code of Governance
FTC	FT consolidation
FTGA	Foundation Trust Governors' Association
FTN	Foundation Trust Network
FTSU	Freedom To Speak Up
GAM	Group Accounting Manual (Department of Health)

GDPR 2016	EU General Data Protection Regulation 2016
GGI	Good Governance Institute
GMC	General Medical Council
GP	general practitioner
HEE	Health Education England
HFEA	Human Fertilisation and Embryology Authority
HFMA	Healthcare Financial Management Association
HMRC	Her Majesty's Revenue and Customs
HOSC	Health Overview and Scrutiny Committee
HPA	Health Protection Agency
HR	human resources
HRA	Health Research Authority
HRA 1998	Human Rights Act 1998
HRO	high reliability organisation
HSC	Health and Social Care (Northern Ireland)
HSCA 2012	Health and Social Care Act 2012
HSCIC	Health and Social Care Information Centre
HSE	Health and Safety Executive
HWB	health and wellbeing board
IAF	Improvement and Assessment Framework
ICAEW	Institute of Chartered Accountants in England and Wales
ICAS	Institute of Chartered Accountants of Scotland
ICGN	International Corporate Governance Network
ICO	Information Commissioner's Office
IFAC	International Federation of Accountants
IIA	Chartered Institute of Internal Auditors
IIRC	International Integrated Reporting Council
IMCA	Independent Mental Advocate Service
IPSIS	Independent Patient Safety Investigation Service
ISAP	Integrated Support and Assurance Process
IT	information technology
JHWS	Joint Health and Wellbeing Strategy
JSNA	Joint Strategic Needs Assessment
JV	joint venture
KLOE	key line of enquiry
KPI	key performance indicator
LGA	Local Government Association
LINk	Local Involvement Network
LLA	liability limitation agreement
LLP	limited liability partnership
LPDT Rules	Listing, Prospectus and Disclosure and Transparency Rules (Financial Conduct Authority)
MCA 2005	Mental Capacity Act 2005

MCP	Multispeciality Community Provider
MEP	Member of the European Parliament
MfA	manual for accounts (Department of Health)
MOU	memorandum of understanding
MP	Member of Parliament
MSFT	Mid Staffordshire NHS Foundation Trust
NAO	National Audit Office
NAPF	National Association of Pension Funds
NCVO	National Council of Voluntary Organisations
NDPB	non-departmental public body
NED	non-executive director
NHS	National Health Service
NHS Act 2006	National Health Service Act 2006
NHS FT ARM	NHS Foundation Trust Annual Reporting Manual
NHS TDA	NHS Trust Development Authority
NHSE	NHS England
NHSI	NHS Improvement
NHSLA	NHS Litigation Authority
NICE	National Institute for Health and Clinical Excellence
NMC	Nursing and Midwifery Council
NPSA	National Patient Safety Agency
NQB	National Quality Board
NSF	National Service Framework
NYSE	New York Stock Exchange
OECD	Organization for Economic Co-operation and Development
OHA	Occupational Health Assessment
OPM	Office for Public Management Ltd
OSC	overview and scrutiny committee
PA	personal assistant
PAC	Public Accounts Committee
PACS	Primary and Acute Care System
PCT	primary care trust
PEST factors	political and regulatory factors, economic factors, social and environmental factors and technology factors
PFI	private finance initiative
PHE	Public Health England
PHSO	Parliamentary and Health Service Ombudsman
PIDA 1998	Public Interest Disclosure Act 1998
PIE	public interest entity
PMO	programme management office
PPI	Patient and Public Involvement
PROM	patient reported outcome measure

QGF	Single Oversight Framework. The Framework replaced Monitor's Quality Governance Framework
QIPP	Quality, Innovation, Productivity and Prevention
RAF	Risk Assessment Framework
RCGP	Royal College of General Practitioners
RHA	regional health authority
SATCAR 2016	Statutory Auditors and Third Country Auditors Regulations 2016
SEC	US Securities and Exchange Commission
SHA	statutory health authority
SI	Statutory Instrument
SIC	statement on internal controls
SID	senior independent director
SLHT	South London Healthcare NHS Trust
SMT	Senior Management Team
SOCA	Serious Organised Crime Agency
Solace	Society of Local Authority Chief Executives
SOF	Single Oversight Framework
SOX	Sarbanes-Oxley Act
SPAMSOAP	Segregation of duties; Physical controls; Authorisation and approval; Management controls; Supervision; Organisation; Arithmetical and accounting controls; Personnel
STP	Sustainability and Transformation Plan
TSA	Trust Special Administrator
UK	United Kingdom
UK Code	UK Corporate Governance Code (Financial Reporting Council)
UECN	Urgent and Emergency Care Network
US	United States
VCSE	voluntary, community and social enterprise
VFM	value for money
VSM	very senior management

PART ONE

The governance landscape

1

Definitions and issues in governance

Defining governance

'Governance' refers to the way in which something is governed and to the function of governing. However, the term is so commonly used that it is often hard to define exactly what it means and its objectives. The governance of a country, for example, refers to the powers and actions of the legislative assembly, the executive government and the judiciary.

Governance is not an easy concept to understand. In the case of governing a country, it would be concerned with who has the power to rule and what the governors of the country should be trying to achieve. The government of a democratic country sets itself the objective of protecting its people and acting in their best interests, whatever these might be. Powers are shared between the legislative, executive and judiciary, but it is a matter of debate how these powers should be shared and exercised. In the UK, for example, there is healthy political debate about the respective powers of Parliament, the Prime Minister and the Cabinet, the UK law courts, and currently the powers of the government bodies and courts of the European Union (EU). In the case of governing an organisation, NHS or otherwise, governance would be concerned with how powers are shared and exercised by the directors, and how the holders of power in the organisation should be held accountable for what they do.

For the purposes of this handbook, specific definitions have been used to offer clarity about what is being referred to. These definitions may be used interchangeably in practice, but adhering to them within the handbook will enable the reader to distinguish between different landscapes in which governance needs to be understood. The defined meanings are as follows.

- **Governance:** the concepts of governance which are generally applicable regardless of landscape.
- **Corporate governance:** the governance applied to the corporate commercial business world, including public and private companies.
- **Health service governance:** the governance applied to NHS organisations.
- **Public sector governance:** the governance applied across the wider public sector including the NHS.

Health service governance operates on two levels:

1. the manner in which the government department (Department of Health (DH)) is held to account by the electorate for the way in which it manages the provision of healthcare
2. the way in which individual parts of the NHS are governed and to what purpose.

This handbook will focus on the aspects of health service governance concerned with the practices and procedures for governing the individual parts of the NHS. Such practices seek to ensure that these individual parts are run in such a way that they achieve their objectives and are in line with public sector values such as value for money (VFM), the Nolan Principles of Public Life, and providing universal and free healthcare benefits to all those in need. Those individual parts can be a NHS foundation trust (FT), NHS trust, clinical commissioning group (CCG), arm's-length body (ALB), accountable care organisation (ACO), accountable care partnership (ACP), commissioning support unit (CSU) and so on.

Membership and the balance of power

Companies and NHS organisations alike are legal entities or 'legal persons' established according to statutory obligations such as the Companies Act or Health and Social Care Act legislation. As legal persons, they can enter into contracts and make business transactions. They can own assets and owe money to others, and they can sue and be sued in law. However, decisions about what the company or organisation should do are taken by individuals in the company or organisation's name. There is a gap, therefore, between the legal entity and its owners (members). This gap is 'bridged' by the individuals who act on the entity's behalf. Governance is the foundation of that 'bridge'.

- The citizens of a country, even in a democracy, have relatively few powers. Power is in the hands of the legislative (Parliament) and the executive (the government). Similarly, shareholders have relatively few powers, and these are restricted mainly to certain voting rights. Power is in the hands of the board of directors, or perhaps just one or two individual directors on the board.
- Just as a country has citizens, a company has members. The members of a company are its owners, the 'equity' shareholders. The membership of large companies changes constantly, as investors buy and sell the company's shares.
- For large companies, the main issue with corporate governance is the relationship between the board of directors and the shareholders, and the way in which the board exercises its powers. The relationship between the shareholders and the board can be described as a 'principal–agent' relationship. In some companies, other stakeholders may have significant influence.
- For NHS organisations, the members are a wide and diverse range of stakeholders. Health service governance is concerned with how powers are shared

and exercised by different groups to ensure that the objectives of health provision for the general public, the political direction being given by the DH, and other interest groups such as employees, suppliers and the local community are balanced and managed.

In health service governance, the idea of membership is more complex because of the range and diversity of stakeholders. Whilst an FT will have a clear membership structure, the members are not, strictly speaking, the owners of the trust. Instead, they are the recipients of the health services provided, who might be seen as 'proxy shareholders' on behalf of the general public. Further complications arise as the FT is still required to consider the views of the community it serves, regardless of whether they are members and is also required to consider the views of its other stakeholders such as employees, trade unions, local authorities, clinical commissioning groups and NHS England.

CCGs also have a membership structure, comprising all of the general practices in their constituency. Even so, CCGs are also required to consider the wider views of its other stakeholders, including those organisations, which provide the services they commission. For other parts of the NHS structure (e.g. NHS trusts, CSUs, ACOs) there is no established membership structure but there is an equivalent variety of stakeholders. It is this variety of stakeholders and the different levels of influence that they are able to exercise within the NHS that makes health service governance an interesting and challenging subject.

The study of governance within the NHS is complicated by the overuse of the term 'governance'. The role of the governance practitioner or NHS company secretary is also made more complex (and potentially more interesting) by the way in which the term 'governance' is used so widely. In the NHS there is quality governance, information governance, data governance, board governance – to name just a few.

At times this handbook will refer to these other areas of governance to ensure that the breadth of the role of the NHS governance practitioner or company secretary is fully considered. Such references will specifically highlight the type of governance that is being referred to (e.g. quality governance).

The interests of stakeholders

Health service governance as set out by this handbook is defined as the process, practices and procedures by which power is shared and exercised by the board of directors (and the council of governors in FTs or governing body in a CCG) and how the holders of power in the organisation should be held accountable for what they do.

Guidelines and constraints in both the public and private sector include behaving in an ethical way and in compliance with laws and regulations. This framework of law, regulation and guidance puts in place boundaries for those who exercise this power and authority to run the organisation on behalf of stakeholders. These are the groups with an interest in how an organisation acts; they include the communities in which the organisation operates, customers, the DH, employees, the general public, patients, sector regulators and suppliers. The aim of health service governance should be to monitor and control management to ensure that it runs the organisation in the interests of these stakeholders.

Health service governance can therefore be defined as a process for monitoring and control to ensure that management runs the organisation in the interests of stakeholders. The numerous stakeholders and the variety of their roles will be explored in Chapter 2.

Corporate comparisons

Companies in the private sector – which are mostly governed in accordance with the interests of the shareholders – provide a useful comparison with healthcare organisations. Primarily, the objective of a company in the private sector is maximising the wealth of its owners (the shareholders) subject to various guidelines and constraints. However, it can be argued that they should also be governed in the interests of all its major stakeholders, not just its owners. This argument is particularly relevant to large companies whose activities have a big impact on the economy and society, where regard must be given to other groups or individuals with an interest in what the company does.

Principles of corporate governance are, therefore, based on the view that a company should be governed in the interests of the shareholders, and possibly also in the interests of other stakeholder groups. The board ought to use its powers in an appropriate and responsible way, and should be accountable in some ways to the shareholders (and perhaps other stakeholders).

The work of Lord Hutton and the Ownership Commission, set out in its March 2012 *Report on Plurality, Stewardship and Engagement*, raises interesting questions about the responsibilities of companies to consider the interests of a wider group of stakeholders. The Commission was established following the 2008 banking crisis and the expenses scandal in government where the balancing of interests has proven to be a key factor. Another recent example was that of the successful takeover of Cadbury by Kraft.

CASE STUDY: Kraft

Kraft, the world's second-largest food maker with annual revenues of $42 billion, appealed directly to UK-listed Cadbury's shareholders after the Cadbury's board rejected its proposal. US-based Kraft stressed it was committed to working towards a recommended transaction and to maintaining a constructive dialogue. Cadbury put out a statement, confirming it had received an 'unsolicited' proposal from Kraft that was conditional on financing and due diligence.

'The board of Cadbury reviewed the proposal with its advisers and rejected it', it said. 'The board is confident in Cadbury's standalone strategy and growth prospects as a result of its strong brands, unique category and geographic scope and the continued successful delivery of its Vision into Action plan. The board believes that the proposal fundamentally undervalues the group and its prospects.'

However, the final offer proved to be too attractive for the shareholders, and the board was required to act in their best interests even though it did not believe the takeover was in the interests of a wider group of stakeholders.

The relationship between the board of directors and its variety of stakeholders, and the way in which the board exercises its powers, has been a significant distinction between corporate governance and health service governance. This distinction, however, is lessening as corporate commercial organisations are being challenged to consider a wider group of stakeholders, e.g. the 2016 UK government Green Paper outlining proposals for corporate governance reform – including a suggestion to have employees represented on boards. It is suggested that the measure will be voluntary rather than mandatory. One of the government's proposals to strengthen employee representation at board level is for company boards to create stakeholder advisory panels, which could also be consulted on the company's executive remuneration policy and annual remuneration report. Another suggestion is to have designated non-executive directors (NEDs) on boards to ensure that the voices of key interested groups – especially employees – are heard at board level. The consultation closed in February 2017 and at the time of writing is still under consideration.

ICSA: The Governance Institute and the Investment Association intend to publish joint guidance on corporate governance later in 2017 following the release of the Green Paper. The joint project aims to help boards improve their engagement with employees and other stakeholders, and help identify different approaches to stakeholder engagement. The guidance will cover:

- the ways in which companies can identify NEDs with relevant stakeholder experience;
- methods by which boards can collate the views of their key stakeholders; and
- how training and induction can be used to enhance directors' understanding of their duties and the interests of, and impact on, different stakeholders.

This guidance may provide further resources for NHS organisations to consider in their board composition and when engaging with key stakeholders.

Health service governance principles are based on the view that the organisation should be governed in such a way that balances the requirements of a wide variety of stakeholders. The board is required to use its powers in an appropriate and responsible way, and is accountable in different ways to each of the stakeholders.

Why is governance important?

Regardless of sector, governance is a key issue as it regulates the power and decision-making of a small group of people who have been given a large responsibility for the stewardship of the assets of a third party.

In the context of the NHS, this stewardship involves both public assets and healthcare services. The outcome of decisions really can be a matter of life and death, as well as a matter of severe financial loss. As a result, NHS organisations have clear aims that have been set out in the NHS Constitution. They should be governed in such a way that they move towards the achievement of these aims.

Although NHS organisations and companies exist as legal persons, in reality each organisation is the organised, collective effort of many different individuals. They are controlled by boards of directors or governing bodies in the interests of their stakeholders. The interests of the board and the stakeholders ought to coincide, but in practice they may be in conflict with each other. The challenge of good health service governance is to find a way in which the interests of a wide variety of stakeholders and the directors can all be sufficiently satisfied. This is also a challenge for companies, but the major concern rests largely on balancing the interests of the board of directors and the shareholders.

Governance and management

It is important to recognise the difference between the governance of any organisation and its management.

Powers to manage the affairs of an NHS organisation are given to the board of directors or to the governing body in the case of a CCG. The term 'board' or 'board of directors' will be used for both, with the distinguishing aspects of the governance of a CCG highlighted (see Chapter 13 for more on CCGs).

Most powers are delegated to a chief executive officer (CEO) or managing director, and further delegated to executive directors (EDs) and executive managers. The board of directors should retain some powers and responsibilities, with certain matters reserved for board decision-making rather than delegated to the management team (see Chapter 5).

The board of directors should be responsible for monitoring the performance of the management team. However, the board of directors itself is not responsible for day-to-day management. It is responsible for governing the organisation. Responsibilities for governance go beyond management, and governance should not be confused with management. Even so, it is probably true to say that when a senior executive manager is 'promoted' to the board, he or she may consider the position of an ED to be recognition of his or her senior executive position. However, the promotion of an executive manager to the board creates new responsibilities for governance that are not related to management. The ED ought to think as a member of the board in performing his or her duties as a director, rather than as a senior executive.

This structure – where there is an effective single board that is collectively responsible for controlling the organisation or company, with no one individual having unfettered powers of decision-making – is known as the unitary board. When an ED becomes a board member, he or she takes on part of the collective responsibility for ensuring the achievement of corporate aims and objectives, and must not solely contribute to discussions and decisions in the light of his or her particular executive function.

It is important to note that CCGs have not been established on the basis of a unitary board. Instead, the *Good Governance Standard for Public Services* (2004), upon which CCG governance is based, presupposes a form of leadership that is not based on the principle of a unitary board. This is in stark contrast to most other NHS organisations (e.g. FTs) for whom the unitary board is a core principle of governance.

The purpose of the unitary board principle is to ensure that the interests of all stakeholders are properly considered and balanced. This is explored in more detail in Chapter 5.

Principles of good corporate governance

Several concepts apply to sound corporate governance in all countries where international investors invest their money. Many of these are ethical in nature and the King III Code describes them as the 'overarching corporate governance principles'. These are:

- fairness
- accountability
- responsibility
- transparency.

King IV has now also been published and builds on the ethics of King III – see Chapter 4. These principles are directly applicable to an understanding of health service governance and are set out here with examples from both corporate and health service governance.

Fairness

Fairness refers to the principle that all shareholders should receive equal consideration. For example, minority shareholders should be treated in the same way as majority shareholders. This concept might seem straightforward in the UK, where the rights of minority shareholders are protected to a large extent by company law. In some countries, however, larger shareholders and the board of directors often disregard minority shareholder rights. There should also be fairness in the treatment of stakeholders other than shareholders.

The NHS Constitution sets out a number of rights and pledges that underpin the principle of fairness such as:

- the right to access
- the right to drugs
- the right to complain
- staff rights.

Accountability

Decision-makers who act on behalf of an organisation should be accountable for the decisions they make and the actions they take. In a company, the board of directors should be accountable to the shareholders (the company's owners). Shareholders should be able to assess the actions of the board of directors and the committees of the board, and have the opportunity to query and challenge them. In an NHS organisation, a variety of stakeholders provide that level of accountability.

One problem with accountability is deciding how the board of directors should be accountable, and in particular over what period of time. According to the financial theory for companies, if the objective of a company is to maximise the wealth of its shareholders, this will be achieved by maximising the financial returns to shareholders through increases in profits, dividends, prospects for profit growth and an increasing share price. It might therefore follow that directors should be held accountable to shareholders on the basis of the returns on shareholder capital that the company has achieved. However, there is little consensus about the period over which returns to shareholders and increases in share value should be measured. Performance can be measured over a short term of one year, over a longer period of five or ten years, or even longer.

In practice, it is usual to measure returns over the short term and assess performance in terms of profitability over a 12-month period. In the short term, however, a company's share price may be affected by influences unrelated to the company's underlying performance, such as excessive optimism or pessimism in the stock markets. In the short term, it is also easier to soothe investors with promises for the future, even though current performance is not good. It is only when a company fails consistently to deliver on its promises that investor confidence ebbs away.

If company performance were to be solely judged by the return to shareholders over a 12-month period, the directors would focus on short-term results and short-term movements in the stock market price. Short-termism is easy to criticise, but difficult to disregard in practice if performance targets ignore the long term. Directors should really be looking after the underlying business of the company and its profitability over the longer term.

The problem of accountability remains, however. Even if it is accepted that company performance should not be judged by short-term financial results and share price movements, how can the board be made accountable for its contribution to longer-term success?

By way of contrast, accountability for an NHS organisation can be measured in a number of ways. These include:

- Regulators: Care Quality Commission (CQC), NHS Improvement (NHSI).
- Commissioners: NHS England (NHSE), CCGs, general practitioners (GPs).
- Political scrutiny: DH, overview and scrutiny committees, Health and Wellbeing boards, Healthwatch.
- Public opinion: Friends and Family Test, patient surveys, Patient Choice agenda, national staff surveys.

Short-termism is also an issue for NHS organisations, as changes in government policy often drives the form of accountability practiced by the regulators, commissioners and political scrutiny. The views expressed by public opinion can also focus on very local issues that need to be balanced against wider healthcare changes for the public benefit.

The NHS Constitution sets out that the NHS is accountable to the public, communities and patients that it serves. The government ensures that there is always a clear and up-to-date statement of NHS accountability for this purpose (see Chapter 2).

Responsibility

The board of directors is given authority to act on behalf of the company. A further principle of corporate governance is that the board should accept full responsibility for the powers that it is given and the authority that it exercises. A board of directors should understand what its responsibilities are, and should carry them out to the best of its abilities.

Accountability goes hand-in-hand with responsibility. The board of directors should be made accountable to the shareholders for the way in which it has carried out its responsibilities. Similarly, executive management should be responsible for the exercise of powers delegated to them by the board of directors, and should be made accountable to the board for their achievements and performance.

Within the NHS there are a number of mechanisms for delegating responsibility, such as the scheme of delegation and standing financial instructions. The role of the board committees is to oversee and scrutinise these delegated powers, and to provide assurance to the board that responsibility is being taken appropriately by the EDs.

Transparency

Transparency means openness. In the context of corporate governance, this is a willingness by the company to provide clear information to shareholders and other stakeholders about what the company has done and hopes to achieve, without giving away commercially sensitive information. It might be useful to think of openness in terms of its opposite – being a 'closed book' and refusing to divulge any information whatsoever.

Transparency should not be confused with 'understandability'. Information should be communicated in a way that is understandable, but transparency is concerned more with the content of the information that is communicated. A principle of good governance is that stakeholders should be informed about what an organisation is doing and plans to do in the future, and about the risks involved in its business strategies.

Transparency in NHS organisations is set out by the requirements of the Freedom of Information Act 2000 (FOIA 2000) and the requirements of openness set out in the Nolan Principles of Public Life. The NHS Constitution also requires that the system of responsibility and accountability for making decisions in the NHS should be transparent and clear to the public, patients and staff. The development of a 'duty of candour' is the most recent development in the NHS which underpins the principle of transparency (see Chapter 3).

Key issues in governance

Good governance should promote the best long-term interests of the organisation. It requires an effective board of directors, with an appropriate balance of skills and experience, and well-motivated individuals as directors. The composition of the board, its functions and responsibilities, and its effectiveness, are therefore core issues in governance.

At the heart of the debate about corporate governance lie conflicts of interest (and potential conflicts of interest) between shareholders, the board of directors as a whole, individual board members, and possibly also a number of other stakeholder groups. Directors may be tempted to take risks and make decisions aimed at boosting short-term performance. Many shareholders are more concerned with long-term performance, the continuing survival of their company and the value of their investment. If a company gets into financial difficulties, professional managers can move on to another company to start again, whereas shareholders suffer a financial loss.

Similar conflicts of interest arise in health service governance, such as pressure to conceal financial or performance information, inadequate risk management processes and poor communication with key stakeholders. For example, one stakeholder group may have a particular focus on an area of service delivery while directors have to manage the wider provision of healthcare services. Directors often have to manage the competing interests of patient groups, regulators, and the financial decisions contained within government policy. Directors also have to consider their own careers within the NHS, managing the performance requirements of the regulators and any consideration of a longer-term strategy for the particular body for whom they are responsible.

Transparent reporting and auditing

The board of directors or EDs may try to disguise the true performance of the organisation by giving less than honest statements or 'dressing up' publicly available information on performance, quality, safety and finances. 'Window-dressed' information makes it difficult for stakeholders to reach a reasoned judgment about the performance of an organisation, and subsequently assess whether public funding is being correctly managed and expended on key areas of service delivery.

Concerns about misleading published accounts in the corporate commercial world in the 1980s and early 1990s provided an impetus to the movement for better corporate governance in the UK. Accounting irregularities in a number of companies led to a tightening of accounting standards, although the problems of window dressing are unlikely ever to disappear completely. Concerns about financial reporting in the US emerged with the collapse of Enron in 2001, which filed for bankruptcy after 'adjusting' its accounts. This was followed by similar problems at other US companies, including telecommunications group WorldCom (which admitted to fraud in its accounting), Global Crossing and Rank Xerox. It was also suggested that incomprehensible or misleading accounts contributed to the global banking crisis, with banks such as Lehman Brothers (which collapsed in 2008) possibly using questionable accounting practices to disguise the true state of their financial position.

Throughout the peak of the banking crisis of 2007–2009, when Britain's financial system looked at its most vulnerable, the Co-operative Bank portrayed itself as a cut above the rest, offering ethical values untouched by the bonus culture for EDs and the high levels of debt that infected so many other banks. Yet, in 2013, the Co-operative Group hit the headlines when its governance shortfalls became public leading to significant losses resulting from a capital shortfall and controversy about its former chair Paul Flowers.

More recently, the collapse of BHS into administration in 2016, leaving 11,000 employees facing an uncertain future and 20,000 current and future pensioners facing substantial cuts to their entitlements, has raised significant concerns. According to the Work and Pensions Select Committee, BHS encapsulated many of its ongoing concerns about the regulatory and cultural framework in which business operates, including the ethics of business behaviour; the governance of private companies; the balance between risk and reward; mergers and acquisitions practices; the governance and regulation of workplace pension schemes; and the sustainability of defined benefit pensions.

The governance issues at stake in these examples are the balancing of short- and long-term returns and the extent to which the directors in each case were aware of these situations, and if they knew about the problems why shareholders were not informed much sooner. It is now widely accepted that the directors of a company should be responsible for giving an assurance to their shareholders that they consider their company to be a going concern that will not collapse within the next 12 months.

CASE STUDY: Enron

Enron was founded in 1985 with the merger of two US natural gas pipelines. In the 1990s it diversified into selling electricity and other activities; by 2000 it was one of the world's largest companies when measured by reported annual revenue. Both its board of directors and its audit committee appeared to be highly competent.

However, although investors and regulators were not aware of it at the time, the rapid growth in the reported assets and profits of Enron was attributable largely to misleading accounting practices. It inflated the value of its reported assets (sometimes recording expenses as assets) and it kept liabilities off its balance sheet by establishing 'special purpose entities'. It also anticipated profits by becoming the first non-financial services company to adopt 'mark to market' accounting techniques. This enabled it to earn profits on long-term contracts 'up front' as soon as the contract started. In one case it claimed a large profit on a 20-year contract agreed with Blockbuster Video in 2000, and continued to claim the profit even after the project failed and Blockbuster pulled out of the deal.

Senior management were rewarded on the basis of annual earnings and were highly motivated to continue reporting large increases in profits, regardless of the longer-term consequences. Investors began to have doubts about the reliability of Enron's reported profits in 2001. A 'whistleblower' (see Chapter 17) reported her concerns to the chief executive officer, but her allegations of dubious accounting practices were ignored. However, in October 2001 Enron was eventually forced to announce that it would be re-stating its accounts for 1997–2000 to correct accounting violations. The US Securities and Exchange Commission (SEC) announced an investigation into the company and the stock price collapsed. There were also doubts about whether Enron had sufficient liquidity (cash) to remain in business for long. Its debt was downgraded to junk bond status and in December 2001 the company filed for bankruptcy.

The company's auditors were Arthur Andersen, one of the 'big five' global accounting firms. The firm – in particular its Houston office – took extraordinary measures to protect its client. When the SEC investigation was announced in 2001, Andersen staff attempted to cover up evidence of negligence in its audit work by destroying several tonnes of documents, as well as many emails and computer files. The firm, especially the Houston office, was accused of losing its independence from Enron and over-relying on income from the non-audit work that it did for the company. Arthur Andersen was charged with obstructing the course of justice by shredding the documents and destroying the files. Although a guilty verdict was subsequently overturned by the Supreme Court, this was too late to save the firm from the loss of its major clients and collapse.

Several Enron employees were brought to trial for financial crimes. Andrew Fastow, a former chief financial officer (CFO), was found guilty of crimes including fraud, money laundering, insider trading and conspiracy. Two former chief executive officers, Kenneth Lay and Jeffrey Skilling, were charged with a range of financial crimes and brought to trial in 2006. Both were found guilty: Skilling was imprisoned and Lay died before sentence was passed.

Transparent reporting and auditing is vital for NHS organisations and it is subject to a high level of scrutiny. It must be remembered that the financial position of an NHS organisation is closely linked to its performance targets and its level of activity. While there is some guidance on how targets should be measured so correct financial data can be collated, the pressure to reach performance targets can lead to irregularities in the measurement of target data.

CASE STUDY: Whistleblowing

An NHS finance director took a leading teaching hospital to an employment tribunal over claims he was sacked for 'whistleblowing' over fiddled statistics for cancelled operations.

The director queried why a senior executive had instructed a junior member of staff to record the number of weekly cancelled operations as zero, instead of the recorded number, in a form sent to the DH to help determine the hospital's performance rating. It emerged that the figure zero had been entered for a number of weeks, during which time a number of operations were believed to have been cancelled on the day of the operation for non-clinical reasons – though no such cancellations were ever recorded.

The hospital had been under pressure because of its poor record on cancelled operations, and evidence of improvement would have gained it a greater share of a large performance fund made available by the DH.

CASE STUDY: Monitoring arrangements

A trust's financial position deteriorated significantly over a three-month period, so that instead of a modest surplus the trust was forecasting a significant deficit. When the deterioration became apparent, the trust failed to raise the matter promptly or notify Monitor, the regulator at the time, of risks associated with its recovery plan. The Monitor Compliance Framework requires trusts to report any material, actual or prospective changes that may affect their ability to comply with any aspect of their authorisation.

The trust submitted a re-forecast plan to Monitor, setting out a recovery in the following quarter. This largely relied on a significant reduction in staff costs. However, given the record of the trust in consistently overspending on pay, Monitor was not convinced that the recovery plan would be delivered.

Furthermore, the re-forecast showed a significant liquidity risk in the medium term that the board had neither put in place contingencies against nor taken any steps to mitigate. Overspend on pay had been reported to every board meeting over a protracted period, but plans to deal with the overspend were not due to take effect until the following financial year and the trust failed to identify that the situation would not be remedied in the short term.

There was no evidence that the level of challenge in the boardroom on financial issues was sufficient in the light of the level of financial deterioration. Despite the urgent need to improve the financial situation, Monitor noted that evidence suggested that the board was not sufficiently engaged in holding the executive to account for delivery of improvements and had tolerated slippage in delivery and extended timelines. The trust remained under enhanced monitoring arrangements until it was deemed to no longer be in breach of its terms of authorisation.

Exercise of board-level power

Most decision-making powers in an organisation are held by the board of directors. The governance debate continues to be about the extent to which professional managers, acting as board directors, exercise those powers in the interests of their principal stakeholders (and any other organisational stakeholders), and whether the powers of directors should be restricted.

Key issues include:

- the structure of the board of directors
- the role of independent NEDs
- the responsibilities of the board of directors
- the duties of directors.

Risk management

In the corporate world, investors typically expect higher rewards to compensate them for taking higher business risks. If a company makes decisions that increase the scale of the risks it faces, profits and dividends are usually expected to increase. A further issue in corporate governance is that the directors might take decisions intended to increase profits without giving due regard to the risks. In some cases, companies may continue to operate without regard to the changing risk profile of their existing businesses. When investors buy shares in a company, they have an idea of the type of company they are buying into, the nature of its business, the probable returns it will provide for shareholders and the nature of its business and financial risks. Directors, on the other hand, are rewarded on the basis of the returns the company achieves – profits or dividend growth – and their remuneration is not linked in any direct way to the risk aspects of their business. Some companies are also guilty of poor procedures and systems, so that the risk of breakdowns, errors and fraud can be high.

Good governance therefore requires an organisation to control its 'business risk' by having effective internal controls for managing operational risks. As a result, risk management is now recognised as a key ingredient of sound corporate governance.

Risk management is just as crucial in health service governance. Not only does it set out to protect public assets and the use of taxpayers' money, it also protects the quality of the healthcare services being delivered. Risk management is explored in more detail in Chapter 15.

Stakeholder engagement

Another issue in corporate governance is communication between the board of directors and the company's shareholders. Shareholders, particularly those with a large financial interest in a company, should be able to voice their concerns to the directors and expect to have their opinions heard. Small shareholders should at least be informed about the company, its financial position and its plans for the future – even if their opinions carry comparatively little weight.

In health service governance it is an explicit aspect of government policy that stakeholders are to be involved in the design and delivery of their own healthcare. Therefore, it is vital that NHS organisations provide public information about their services and future plans. Providing opportunities for the views and opinions of stakeholders to be heard is a key driver within health service governance. Better-informed boards of directors will make better healthcare decisions. In addition, the increased focus on patient choice results from research in the UK and overseas that treatments are more effective if patients choose, understand and control their own care. Patient choices now include the right to choose a GP, which hospital to go to and the right to be involved in decisions about their own healthcare.

This right to choose, combined with the introduction of 'internal market' or 'quasi-market' policies, has led to a greater degree of information about the performance of individual GPs, consultants and hospitals. This has introduced the commercial concepts of marketing and market share, and a much greater awareness of costs, efficiency and accountability.

Further, the introduction of the FOIA 2000 provided a clear procedure for all public bodies to respond to requests for information about their organisations. In addition, the requirements to make NHS annual accounts, reports from regulators (such as NHSI and the CQC), national NHS surveys (staff and patient surveys) and the introduction of Quality Accounts for all providers of healthcare services, all serve to ensure a greater transparency in the relationships with NHS stakeholders.

Corporate social responsibility and the NHS

Ethical conduct is a major governance issue. There is a growing recognition that organisations need to consider social and environmental issues for commercial and governance reasons, as well as purely ethical reasons. Stakeholders expect organisations to have regard to social and environmental issues, while the financial risks from government regulation to protect the environment continue to grow. A sustainable healthcare system is achieved by delivering high quality care and improved public health without exhausting natural resources or causing severe ecological damage.

In the NHS, sustainable development is often referred to as good corporate citizenship. This means using NHS organisations' corporate powers and resources in ways that benefit, rather than damage, the social, economic, and physical environment. How the NHS itself behaves can impact on people's health and on the wellbeing of society, the economy and the environment. Behaving as a good corporate citizen can save money, benefit population health and can help reduce health inequalities. Many measures that improve health also contribute to sustainable development and vice versa.

Sustainability reporting is increasingly required within NHS organisations' annual reports and Quality Accounts.

A brief history of corporate governance

To best understand the principles of health service governance it is important to understood the developments in corporate governance over time. These developments now underpin much of what currently exists in health service governance.

What seems clear from each development is that processes and systems only go so far. References are repeatedly made to behaviour and culture as the foundation stones of good governance.

The Cadbury Code

The *Report of the Committee on the Financial Aspects of Corporate Governance* was published in 1992, and was described as 'a landmark in thinking on corporate governance'. The report included a Code of Best Practice known as the Cadbury Code.

Whilst the terms of reference for the Committee were primarily focused on financial governance, concerns about the principles and values behind good corporate governance also meant that its findings went further than just financial governance. The Code also made recommendations relating to the structure and effectiveness of boards, internal controls and accountability to shareholders. Sir Adrian Cadbury's statement, following the review, makes interesting reading for health service governance practitioners:

> 'Corporate governance is concerned with holding the balance between economic and social goals and between individual and communal goals. The governance framework is there to encourage the efficient use of resources and equally to require accountability for the stewardship of those resources. The aim is to align as nearly as possible the interests of individuals, corporations and society.'

The significant legacies of the Cadbury Code include a voluntary system of good practice with the principles of openness, integrity and accountability at its heart and self-regulation based on 'comply or explain'.

The Greenbury Report

On the recommendation of the Cadbury Committee, a second committee was set up to review progress on corporate governance in UK listed companies. This committee issued the Greenbury Report in 1995, which focused mainly on directors' remuneration. At the time, the UK press was condemning 'fat cat' directors, particularly those in newly privatised companies.

The Greenbury Report issued a Code of Best Practice covering directors' remuneration. Its major recommendations included:

- the remuneration committee should be made up of entirely NEDs
- there should be an annual remuneration report for shareholders included within the annual report and accounts
- remuneration (and any other benefits) should be linked to performance (both by the company and the individual director).

The Combined Code

A further committee on corporate governance, chaired by Sir Ronald Hampel, was set up in 1995 to review the recommendations of the Cadbury and Greenbury Committees. Its final report was published in 1998. The report covered a number of governance issues, such as:

- the composition of the board and role of directors
- directors' remuneration
- the role of shareholders (particularly institutional shareholders)
- communications between the company and its shareholders
- financial reporting, auditing and internal controls.

The Hampel Report also suggested that its recommendations should be combined with those of the Cadbury and Greenbury Committees into a single code of corporate governance. This suggestion led to the publication of the original 1998 Combined Code on Corporate Governance (Combined Code), which applied to all UK listed companies. Interestingly, the Hampel report makes it clear that:

> 'Good corporate governance is not just a matter of prescribing particular corporate structures and complying with a number of hard and fast rules. There is a need for broad principles. All concerned should then apply these flexibly and with common sense to the varying circumstances of individual companies.'

The Combined Code was updated in 2003 to take account of the Higgs and Smith reports (see below), as well as in 2006 and 2008. It became the UK Corporate Governance Code in 2010.

The Turnbull Guidance

A committee was set up in 1998 to provide guidance on the board's responsibilities for internal control and risk management. This committee produced the Turnbull Report. This was revised and re-named *Internal Control: Guidance to Directors* (2005) by the Financial Reporting Council (FRC) in 2005, then amalgamated with the 2009 Going Concern guidance notes into the *Guidance on Risk Management, Internal Control and Related Financial and Business Reporting* in 2014.

The Turnbull Report defined an internal control system as 'the policies, processes, tasks, behaviours and other aspects of an organisation' that, taken together:

- help it to operate effectively and efficiently: these operational controls should allow the organisation to respond in an appropriate way to significant risks to achieving the organisation's objectives (this includes the safeguarding of assets from inappropriate use or from loss and fraud and ensuring that liabilities are identified and managed)
- help it to ensure the quality of external and internal financial reporting (financial controls)
- help to ensure compliance with applicable laws and regulations, and also with internal policies for the conduct of business (compliance controls).

The Higgs Report and *Improving Board Effectiveness*

Corporate governance issues remained in the spotlight in the UK in 2003 with two influential reports published in that year.

The Higgs Report, commissioned by the government, considered the role and effectiveness of the chair and independent NEDs. This was updated in 2010 following a review on behalf of the FRC by ICSA. Amended guidance was issued with the title *Improving Board Effectiveness*. In a similar vein to Cadbury and Hampel, Higgs was at pains to point out that people, behaviour and culture were the key to good governance, not a process of box-ticking exercises.

Work is underway on updating this guidance document and the FRC will consult on changes, alongside the Code, in autumn 2017.

The Smith Report and the *FRC Guidance on Audit Committees*

Further work and more detailed guidance on the role of the audit committee was commissioned by the FRC in 2003. The ensuing report was originally called the

Smith Report (after the name of the committee chair) but is now called the *FRC Guidance on Audit Committees*. It was revised in 2005, 2008, 2012 and 2016.

To assist audit committees looking to put their external audit out to tender, the FRC provided *Audit Tenders: Notes on Best Practice* in February 2017.

The Walker Report

The global financial markets and world economy were badly damaged by the banking crisis that emerged in 2007 and 2008. In the US, Lehman Brothers collapsed and other banks and brokerage firms were taken over to prevent their collapse. In the UK, the Northern Rock bank collapsed in 2007 while Royal Bank of Scotland was virtually nationalised in 2008. At the same time, the government acquired a major stake in Lloyds TSB Bank after Lloyds had agreed to take over another ailing bank, HBOS.

Recognition of governance problems in UK banks led to a review by Sir David Walker. Some recommendations of the Walker Report were included by the FRC in the 2010 UK Corporate Governance Code.

The Davies Report

In 2010, Lord Davies of Abersoch initiated a review into boardroom diversity at the request of the UK Government, publishing a report entitled *Women on Boards* in 2011.

The review rejected the imposition of a mandatory quota system, instead recommending voluntary targets and reporting requirements. In May 2011, the FRC began consulting on possible amendments to the UK Corporate Governance Code that would require companies to publish their policy on boardroom diversity, report against it annually and to consider the board's diversity when assessing its effectiveness (among other factors). These were added to the Code in 2012.

Lord Davies issued an updated report in 2015, which detailed progress that had been made and set out five next-step recommendations. The key recommendation was increasing the voluntary target for women's representation on Boards of FTSE 350 companies, to a minimum of 33%, to be achieved by 2020.

NHSI has declared that it is committed to achieving the goal of 50/50 gender balance on all NHS boards by 2020.

The UK Corporate Governance Code

The FRC has reviewed and amended the Combined Code regularly, and in June 2010 issued a significantly revised version under the new name of the UK Corporate Governance Code.

In September 2011, the FRC announced that it intended to consult on proposed further changes to the Code in relation to audit committees and audit re-tendering. In October 2011, the FRC announced that changes resulting from the Davies Report would also be implemented in a revised version of the Code. This revised version was issued in 2012, which also took account of the findings of the

Walker Report. A further update to the Code was carried out in September 2014, which included a number of significant changes on remuneration, going concern and risk management reporting and stakeholder engagement guidance.

The most recent version of the UK Corporate Governance Code was published in June 2016 and applies to reporting periods beginning on or after 17 June 2016. The update to the Code was required in order to comply with the new EU regulations on statutory audit. The new Code is accompanied by updated guidance on audit committees, the revised ethical standards of 2016 and revised auditing standards of 2016. The impact of the new guidance for audit committees will be assessed in Chapter 17, Audit. The full text of the 2016 Code is available in the appendices to this handbook.

In February 2017, the FRC then announced a fundamental review of the UK Corporate Governance Code, prior to a formal consultation in the autumn of 2017. The review will take account of the FRC's work on corporate culture and succession planning, and the issues raised in the government's Green Paper and the Business, Energy and Industrial Strategy (BEIS) Select Committee inquiry mentioned above.

The FRC also now publishes an annual report called *Developments in Corporate Governance and Stewardship*. The latest 2016 report can be accessed on the FRC website.

Alongside the updated Code in 2016, the FRC issued three related documents:

- the *Guidance on Risk Management, Internal Control and Related Financial and Business Reporting*
- *the Guidance for Directors of Banks on Solvency and Liquidity Risk Management and the Going Concern Basis of Accounting*
- the *International Standard on Auditing (UK) 570 (Revised June 2016): Going Concern* which requires auditors to consider and report on narrative disclosures (including risks), the going concern basis of accounting (and material uncertainties relating thereto) and the longer term viability statement and the risk management disclosure.
- *FRC: Corporate Culture and the Role of Boards (2016).* The FRC embarked on the culture coalition project in 2015 to gain a better understanding of how boards were currently addressing culture, to encourage discussion and debate, and to identify and share good practice to help companies. The FRC report (2016) seeks to address how boards and executive management can steer corporate behaviour to create a culture that will deliver sustainable good performance. The report looks at the increasing importance which corporate culture plays in delivering long-term business and economic success and doing so it focuses on the role of the board in shaping, monitoring and overseeing culture.

The UK Stewardship Code

The UK Stewardship Code was published in 2010 and subsequently reviewed in 2012 building on the findings of the Kay Review (2012). Whereas the UK Corporate Governance Code is concerned with governance by companies, the Stewardship Code is for institutional investors that are share owners or that manage shareholdings for other financial institutions such as pension funds. The Code aims to enhance the quality of engagement between institutional investors and companies, so that institutional shareholders contribute positively to the governance of the companies in which they invest.

In 2016 the FRC assessed signatories to the Stewardship Code based on the quality of their Code statements. Tiering distinguishes between signatories who report well and demonstrate their commitment to stewardship, and those where reporting improvements are necessary. The tiering exercise has improved the quality of reporting against the Code, promoted best practice and resulted in greater transparency in the UK market.

Governance and UK law

The Companies Act 2006 (CA 2006) introduced statutory duties of directors (similar to the duties that existed previously in common law and equity), and contained a requirement for quoted companies to be more accountable to shareholders by publishing a strategic business review (known as a business review until 2013) in narrative form each year. Under new regulations in 2013, the CA 2006 now requires the remuneration report to be split into three components:

- a statement from the chairman of the remuneration committee
- a policy report
- an annual report on remuneration.

It also introduces a binding shareholder vote on the policy report and the content of the annual report on remuneration (which remains subject to an annual advisory vote) is substantially different from the previous requirements. It now includes the 'single figure' for each director and a number of other new requirements.

Some aspects of corporate governance have also been transposed into UK law from the EU Directives.

Amendments to the Fourth and Seventh EU Company Law Directives approved in 2006 included a requirement for quoted companies to include a corporate governance statement in their annual reports, and amendments to the Eighth Company Law Directive in 2008 requires 'public interest entities' (including listed companies) to have an audit committee consisting of independent NEDs and to publish an annual corporate governance statement. The new EU Accounting Directive effective from 1 January 2016 introduced a wide range of amendments to the CA 2006, particularly in relation to the small companies regime such as revised accounting thresholds and reporting exemptions. It is likely that these directives will be fully incorporated into UK law following Brexit, however, this is still to be finalised in the Brexit negotiations.

Corporate governance in other countries

The UK is seen as a leading country in the development of a corporate governance framework, but there have been similar developments in many other countries. For many countries, particularly developing countries, good corporate governance is seen as an essential basic requirement for attracting foreign investment capital.

In South Africa, the King Committee developed a code of corporate governance. This was revised and strengthened in 2002, 2009 and again in 2016 (King III and IV, see Chapter 4). On an international basis, recommended principles on corporate governance have been published by the Organization for Economic Co-operation and Development (OECD) in 1999, then updated in 2004, with the latest revision being in 2015 when they sought to addresses challenges such as the increasing complexity of the investment chain, the changing role of stock exchanges and the emergence of new investors, investment strategies and trading practices.

Although the US appeared to show little concern for better corporate governance throughout the 1990s, the situation changed dramatically with the collapse of Enron and other major companies in 2001. The New York Stock Exchange (NYSE) proposed recommendations for change, and statutory provisions on corporate governance were introduced in 2002 with the Sarbanes-Oxley Act (SOX). However, the adequacy of corporate governance provisions in the USA (and the UK) continues to be questioned following the banking crisis in 2007–2009 and subsequent examples of poor governance such as the Co-operative Bank, Tesco and BHS.

Governance in the public and voluntary sectors

The public sector includes central government, state government (in some countries) and local government, state-run health and education services and many other regulatory and advisory bodies. While many of the principles of good corporate governance can be applied to the governing bodies of the public sector, there are also significant differences. For example, public bodies are not profit-making and are not accountable to shareholders.

The public sector has therefore adapted principles of good governance to its own specific circumstances, and to some extent the definition of 'governance' for the public sector differs in some ways from 'governance' of companies.

In the UK, the Chartered Institute of Public Finance and Accountancy (CIPFA) and Solace (the Society of Local Authority Chief Executives) published a governance framework in 2016 aimed at local government bodies called *Delivering Good Governance in Local Government*. This sets out principles of governance that local government bodies are encouraged to adopt and apply to their own particular circumstances. The framework defines governance as:

'[H]ow local government bodies ensure that they are doing the right things, in the right way, for the right people, in a timely, inclusive, open, honest and accountable manner. It comprises systems and processes, and cultures and values, by which local government bodies are directed and controlled and through which they account to, and engage with, and, where appropriate, lead their communities.'

Interestingly, given the demands in the NHS for joint or collaborative governance arrangements, the guidance states – 'The development of combined authorities and devolution deals, together with elected mayors, brings about the chance to design governance structures from the bottom up. It provides the opportunity to ensure that the core principles of good governance, covering openness and stakeholder engagement, defining outcomes, monitoring performance and demonstrating effective accountability, are integrated and embedded in new structures and that mechanisms for effective scrutiny are established.

New responsibilities and the development of innovative collaborative structures and ways of working provide challenges for governance such as ensuring transparency and, in particular, over managing risk. Whether working with other authorities, public sector bodies, the third sector or private sector providers, councils must ensure all joint arrangements follow the principles of good governance and are managed and reviewed with sufficient rigour.'

Nolan's Principles of Public Life

A key development for the governance of the UK public sector was the Nolan Committee on Standards in Public Life. The Committee was set up in 1995 in response to concerns that the conduct of some politicians was unethical – in particular, allegations over MPs taking cash for putting questions to Parliament.

While the Committee focused on MPs, its terms of reference also covered government departments and non-departmental public bodies (NDPBs). The Principles were originally intended as guidelines for individuals who were involved in public affairs and public bodies, whether as paid employees or as non-paid members of governing bodies. They are now considered to have much wider relevance and have formed the basis in the UK for developing governance guidelines for both the public sector and the voluntary sector.

The Committee on Standards in Public Life undertook a review of best practice in promoting good behaviour in public life, and in January 2013 it published its Fourteenth *Report of the Committee on Standards in Public Life. Standards matter: A review of best practice in promoting good behaviour in public life.* The report amended the definitions of the seven Nolan principles as shown in Table 1.1. Public sector boards and their members should adhere to these Seven Principles of Public Life.

Table 1.1: The Seven Principles of Public Life

Principle	Revised description
Selflessness	Holders of public office should act solely in terms of the public interest.
Integrity	Holders of public office must avoid placing themselves under any obligation to people or organisations that might try inappropriately to influence them in their work. They should not act or take decisions in order to gain financial or other material benefits for themselves, their family, or their friends. They must declare and resolve any interests and relationships.
Objectivity	Holders of public office must act and take decisions impartially, fairly and on merit, using the best evidence and without discrimination or bias.
Accountability	Holders of public office are accountable to the public for their decisions and actions and must submit themselves to the scrutiny necessary to ensure this.
Openness	Holders of public office should act and take decisions in an open and transparent manner. Information should not be withheld from the public unless there are clear and lawful reasons for so doing.
Honesty	Holders of public office should be truthful.
Leadership	Holders of public office should exhibit these principles in their own behaviour. They should actively promote and robustly support the principles and be willing to challenge poor behaviour wherever it occurs.

The standards for NHS board members

In July 2011, the Council for Healthcare Regulatory Excellence was commissioned to advise the Secretary of State for Health on standards of personal behaviour, technical competence and business practices for members of NHS boards and CCG governing bodies in England. These standards were issued by the Professional Standards Authority in November 2012.

The standards include implementing a transparent and explicit approach to the declaration and handling of conflicts of interest, with good practice requiring the maintenance and publication of a register of interest for all board members. Board meeting agendas should include an opportunity to declare any conflicts at the start of the meeting.

There is a distinct similarity between the Nolan Principles and the NHS board standards, as seen in Table 1.2.

Table 1.2: The Seven Principles of Public Life and NHS board standards

The Seven Principles of Public Life	Standards for NHS Board members
Selflessness	Responsibility
Integrity	Integrity
Objectivity	Respect
Accountability	Professionalism
Openness	Openness
Honesty	Honesty
Leadership	Leadership

The Good Governance Standard for Public Services

The Independent Commission for Good Governance in Public Service was established by the Office for Public Management (OPM) and CIPFA in partnership with the Joseph Rowntree Foundation.

The role of the Commission was to develop a common code and set of principles for good governance across all public services in the UK. In 2004 it published the *Good Governance Standard for Public Services*, a guide for everyone concerned with governance in the public services that applies to all organisations that work for the public using public money. Its application therefore extends from public sector bodies to all private sector organisations that use public money to work for the public. NHS England has advocated adherence with the *Good Governance Standard* as the guidance for health service governance for CCGs.

In justifying the need for the application of good governance principles and practice in the public service sector, the Commission has commented that good governance encourages public trust and participation, whereas bad governance fosters low morale and adversarial relationships.

The *Good Governance Standard* builds on Nolan's Principles and consists of six main principles, each with supporting principles, together with guidelines on how these might be applied in practice. It is useful to look at these and compare them with the principles that apply to good governance in the commercial sector. There are many similarities between these principles and those that should apply in corporate governance to companies (as described earlier in this chapter).

These are general principles, and individual public sector bodies can develop their own codes of governance that are consistent with and based on these principles. The six main principles and their supporting principles are as follows:

1. Focusing on the organisation's purpose and on its outcome for citizens and users of the organisation's services.

- Being clear about the purpose of the organisation and its intended outcomes for citizens and service users. It is suggested that the concept of 'public value' may be useful in helping organisations to identify their purpose and intended outcomes.
- Making sure that users receive a high-quality service.
- Making sure that taxpayers receive VFM.

2. Performing effectively in clearly defined functions and roles.

- Being clear about the functions of the organisation's governing body. It is recommended that the governing body should describe in a published document its approach to achieving each of its stated functions. This document can then be used as a basis for measuring actual performance and achievements by the governing body. Functions could include, for example, 'scrutinising the activities and performance of the executive management' and 'making sure that the voice of the public is heard in discussions and decision-making'.
- Being clear about the responsibilities of the non-executive and the executive governors; these will differ. Many governing bodies consist of both executives and non-executive members (who may be unpaid for their services). However, they should have equal status in discussions on policy and strategy. The framework recommends that the roles of CEO and chair of the governing body should not be held by the same individual.
- Making sure that these responsibilities are properly carried out.
- Being clear about the relationship between the governors and the public, so that both sides in this relationship know what to expect from the other.

3. Promoting values for the whole organisation and demonstrating good governance through behaviour.

- Putting the values of the organisation into practice. The governing body should take the lead in doing this.
- Individual governors behaving in ways that uphold and exemplify effective governance.

4. Taking informed and transparent decisions and managing risk.

- Being rigorous and transparent about how decisions are taken by the governing body. There should be clearly defined levels of delegation within the organisation. The governing body should not be concerned with matters that are more properly delegated to management. It should also be clear about what the objectives of its own decisions are.
- Using good quality information, advice and support.
- Making sure that an effective risk management system is in operation.

5. Developing the capacity and capability of the governing body to be effective.

- Making sure that governors have the skills, knowledge and experience to perform well.
- Developing the capabilities of individuals with governance responsibilities.
- Striking a balance in the membership of the governing body between continuity and renewal.
- The creation and refreshing of a governing body is similar in many respects to similar guidelines in corporate governance, although in the public sector, some governors may be elected representatives.

6. Engaging stakeholders and making accountability real.

- Understanding formal and informal accountability relationships.
- Taking an active and planned approach to dialogue with and accountability to the public.
- Taking an effective and planned approach to accountability to staff.
- Engaging effectively with institutional stakeholders. Institutional stakeholders in the public sector are very different from institutional shareholders in the corporate world. In local government, for example, institutional stakeholders include bodies representing local people. Engagement with stakeholders should help to improve the accountability of the public sector body to the public.

Good Governance: a code for the voluntary and community sector

The development of codes and rules for corporate governance and public sector governance has also influenced the voluntary sector. For example, the National Council of Voluntary Organisations (NCVO) adapted Nolan's Seven Principles of Public Life into a code of conduct for charity trustees. In addition, the Charity Commission's Statement of Recommended Practice requires larger charities to include a statement on risks in their annual report.

There are an increasing number of examples of poor governance in the voluntary and charity sector, e.g. the collapse of Kids Company amid allegations of financial mismanagement; the suicide of Olive Cooke, a victim of aggressive charity fundraising mailings; and the controversy concerning Age UK's deal to help market an e.ON energy tariff to older people, for which it received £6m in commission. These exposes have led to a decline in public confidence in charities and so charities and other bodies have tried to improve their standards of governance as a way of retaining public confidence in what they are doing;

Good Governance: a code for the voluntary and community sector (2nd edition) was published in October 2010.

A revised code was issued in July 2017 and renamed as the Charity Governance Code (July 2017). The new code sets out seven principles, namely, organisational purpose; leadership; integrity; decision-making, risk and control; board effectiveness; diversity; openness and accountability. Its premise is that charity boards must be able to maintain a strategic focus, commit to board development and stay true to the organisation's charitable purposes. New features within the Code include:

- an expectation that the board will review its own performance and that of individual trustees, including the chair, every year, with an external evaluation for larger organisations every three years
- that no trustee should serve more than nine years without good reason and that term limits are important for accountability
- boards to recruit a diverse range of trustees with the skills and experience required to lead a charity
- boards to involve stakeholders in key decisions and operating with the presumption of openness
- emphasis on the role of the chair and vice chair in supporting and achieving good governance
- increased oversight for large charities when dealing with subsidiary companies, registers of interests and third parties such as fundraising agencies or commercial ventures
- board evaluation of a charity's impact by measuring and assessing results, outputs and outcomes.'

In addition, an independent regulator – the Fundraising Regulator – was established in 2016 following the Etherington review of fundraising self-regulation (2015), to strengthen the system of charity regulation and restore public trust in fundraising. Its role as regulator is to:

- Set and promote the standards for fundraising practice (the Code of Fundraising Practice and associated rulebooks) in consultation with the public, fundraising stakeholders and legislators.
- Investigate cases where fundraising practices have led to significant public concern.
- Adjudicate complaints from the public about fundraising practice, where these cannot be resolved by the charities themselves.
- Operate a fundraising preference service to enable individuals to manage their contact with charities.
- Where poor fundraising practice is judged to have taken place, recommend best practice guidance and take proportionate remedial action.

Arguments for and against governance regimes

There are differences of opinion about the benefits of governance, and whether these justify the costs of compliance with governance regulations. It is therefore useful to consider just what the benefits of good governance might be, and what the arguments are against having laws or codes of governance practice.

The main arguments in favour of having a strong governance regime are as follows:

- Good governance will eliminate the risk of misleading or false reporting, and will prevent organisations from being dominated by CEOs or chairs.
- Stakeholders will be better protected by reducing the risks of scandals, and promoting fairness, accountability, responsibility and transparency in organisations.
- Organisations that comply with best practice in governance are more likely to achieve success. Good governance and good leadership and management often go hand-in-hand. Badly governed organisations may be very successful, and well-governed organisations may fail; however, the probability is greater that badly governed organisations will be less successful and more likely to fail than well-governed ones.
- Well-governed organisations will often develop a strong reputation and so will be less exposed to reputation risk (see Chapter 15) than organisations that are not so well governed. Reputation risk can have an adverse impact on stakeholders such as employees, patients and suppliers.
- Good corporate governance encourages a longer-term view of success and enables longer-term planning.

The main arguments against having a strong governance regime for organisations focus on costs, benefits and value:

- For many organisations, compliance with a code of governance is a box-ticking exercise as they adopt the required procedures and systems without considering what the potential benefits might be. The only requirement is to comply with the 'rules' and put a tick in a box when this is done. Governance requirements therefore create a time- and resource-consuming bureaucracy of governance practitioners, and divert the attention of the board of directors from more important matters.
- Good governance is likely to reduce the risk of scandals and unexpected organisational failures. However, it could be argued that the current regulations or best practice guidelines are far too extensive and burdensome.
- When regulations and recommended practice become burdensome, there is an inevitable cost, in terms of both time and money, in achieving compliance. It could be argued that less regulation is better regulation. However there has not yet been an authoritative assessment of the costs of governance compliance with the benefits of better governance systems.
- Organisations that are obliged to comply with governance regulations or best practice are at a competitive disadvantage to rival organisations from countries or regimes where governance regulation is weaker. This is one of the criticisms of widening the number of providers of healthcare beyond that of NHS organisations. If they are not subject to the same level of scrutiny and regulation then the playing field is not level.

- The connection between good governance and good performance (due to good leadership and management) has not yet been proven or demonstrated.

Summary

Governance is a wide-ranging and far-reaching subject. To be a well-versed health service governance practitioner requires an understanding of history, law, specific technical knowledge, politics, health policy and a robust understanding of human behaviour. This diversity and complexity makes for a fascinating area of work despite its connotations of checklists and tick-box exercises. It offers an intriguing insight into how an organisation can plan for its long-term success and then takes steps to deliver that success in a fast-paced changing external environment.

Any type of effective consideration of a subject benefits from clarity around the scope of the subject-matter, and governance – specifically health service governance – is no different. This handbook aims to provide that clarity and then to offer practical guidance on the practice of governance – enabling practitioners to 'walk the talk'. As a consequence, the following chapters will set out the rules and practices relevant to the chapter heading and also offer insights to what this means in practice. Since much of the basis for health service governance result from guidance from outside of the NHS, this will also be made clear so that the reader can differentiate between various sources.

2

Definitions and issues in health service governance

Defining health service governance

It is essential that there is a good understanding of what health service governance is, and what it is intended to achieve.

The NHS often faces times of uncertainty with short- and long-term policy competing for attention. This is particularly true with the significant changes introduced by the Health and Social Care Act 2012 (HSCA 2012) and now more recently by the Five Year Forward View (2014) (5YFV), the introduction of Sustainability and Transformation Plans (STPs) and the development of new models of care (covered in Chapter 14). Good governance is vital for NHS organisations as they face another series of major changes and will be key to ensuring that there is effective leadership, responsible stewardship of public assets and services and public accountability.

Health service governance is not a product in itself. Instead, it is foundational to the delivery of 'high quality for all' as envisaged in 2008's Darzi report (covered in more detail later).

Health service governance – a definition

There have been numerous attempts to define corporate governance. The classic definition has been provided by the UK Corporate Governance Code and it can be adapted for health service governance as follows:

> 'Health service governance is the system by which NHS organisations are directed and controlled. Boards of directors or governing bodies are responsible for the governance of their organisations. The stakeholders' role in governance is to appoint the directors and the auditors and to satisfy themselves that an appropriate governance structure is in place. The responsibilities of the board or governing body include setting the organisation's strategic aims, providing the leadership to put them into effect, supervising the management of the business and reporting to stakeholders on their stewardship. The actions of the board or governing body are subject to laws, regulations and the stakeholders in general meeting.'

Governance can, therefore, be defined as a system that allows organisations to be effective in the delivery of their strategic aims. The strategic aims for the NHS are set out in the NHS Constitution, which attempts to clarify the expectations of the taxpayer into rights and pledges that should be delivered (see later in this chapter). As a consequence, health service governance has to create a system that enables effective delivery of those healthcare rights and pledges, tailored for the local communities in which it is delivered by the individual parts of the NHS. The Constitution provides an overriding strategy that is then underpinned at a local level by each NHS organisation as it actively considers its own specific local strategy.

Why does health service governance matter?

The importance of good governance is often only highlighted in circumstances where an organisation has failed or is in crisis. It tends to be seen in organisations where the separation between stakeholder interests and management is wider. This is a significant risk for NHS organisations; government spending on healthcare for 2016/17 is budgeted at £120.4 billion and yet the recipients of the healthcare provided are often very distant from the holders of the healthcare budget. Health service governance in NHS organisations therefore must be resilient enough to hold NHS organisations to account for the responsibility of managing this expenditure. The separation between NHS stakeholders and Parliament is vast, and it is only through the health service governance regimes of the individual parts of the NHS that NHS stakeholders can exercise the relatively limited powers they have to hold the boards of directors to account.

The consequences for the NHS when health service governance goes wrong are often catastrophic for the patients and families involved, as well as very public. Sadly, there have been a number of cases where the poor health service governance has led to tragedy, e.g. Mid Staffordshire NHS Foundation Trust, University Hospitals of Morecambe Bay NHS Foundation Trust, Southern Health NHS Foundation Trust and Shrewsbury and Telford Hospital NHS Trust.

CASE STUDY: Bristol Royal Infirmary

In the early 1990s, it became clear to the parents of very sick children who had been treated at Bristol Royal Infirmary between 1984 and 1995 that the rate of death or brain damage in or after heart surgery was abnormally high. In 1998 – following an earlier, separate enquiry by the General Medical Council – the Health Secretary Frank Dobson announced a public inquiry into events at Bristol under the chair of Sir Ian Kennedy. The inquiry, which reported back in 2001, found a number of significant governance failings including:

- unsafe arrangements for caring for the children
- no requirement for consultants to keep their skills and knowledge up to date
- no agreed standards of care
- no openness about clinical performance
- no systematic mechanism for monitoring the clinical performance of healthcare professionals or hospitals.

CASE STUDY: Dr Harold Shipman

Dr Harold Shipman, a general practitioner (GP) in Hyde (near Manchester), was convicted at Preston Crown Court on 31 January 2000 of the murder of 15 of his patients and of one count of forging a will. He was sentenced to life imprisonment. Following the trial, a public inquiry was set up that reported over the next five years.

The inquiry identified a number of significant gaps in governance processes that enabled Dr Shipman to continue to murder his patients over a long period of time without detection. Among other issues, these included the need to share information about complaints and concerns raised; the requirement to investigate them systematically; and the importance of establishing strong governance processes and culture.

Mid Staffordshire NHS Foundation Trust

Mid Staffordshire NHS Foundation Trust was at the centre of one the largest healthcare scandals in recent times. The scandal came to light because of an investigation by the Healthcare Commission into the operation of Stafford Hospital. The Commission had been first alerted by the high mortality rates in patients admitted as emergencies. When the foundation trust (FT) failed to provide what the Commission considered to be an adequate explanation, a full-scale investigation was carried out between March and October 2008. Subsequent reports and inquiries led to full public inquiry chaired by Robert Francis QC. His final report was published on 6 February 2013, making 290 recommendations and calling for a 'fundamental culture change' across the health and social care system to put patients first at all times. It called for action across six core themes:

- culture
- compassionate care
- leadership
- standards
- information
- openness, transparency and candour.

Robert Francis QC commented:

> 'Whilst the executive and non-executive board members recognised the problems, the action taken by the board was inadequate and lacked an appropriate sense of urgency. The trust's board was found to be disconnected from what was actually happening in the hospital and chose to rely on apparently favourable performance reports by outside bodies such as the Healthcare Commission, rather than effective internal assessment and feedback from staff and patients. The trust failed to listen to patients' concerns, the board did not review the substance of complaints and incident reports were not given the necessary attention.'

The government's initial response in March 2013, entitled *Patients First and Foremost*, set out a radical plan to prioritise care, improve transparency and to ensure clear action and clear accountability where poor care was detected. The government instigated a number of immediate significant changes after the publication of the inquiry report to improve inspection; increase transparency; emphasise compassion, standards and safety; increase accountability for failure; and build capability. The key changes included:

- The Care Quality Commission (CQC) appointed three Chief Inspectors of hospitals, adult social care and primary care.
- The Chief Inspector of Hospitals began a first wave of inspections of 18 trusts.
- The CQC consulted on a new system of ratings with patient care and safety at its heart and on a new set of fundamental standards that must underpin all care in the future: the inviolable principles of safe, effective and compassionate care.
- Legislation to introduce a responsive and effective failure regime looking at quality as well as finance is progressing through Parliament.
- NHS England published guidance to commissioners, *Transforming Participation in Health and Care (September 2013)*, on involving patients and the public in decisions about their care and their services.

A further paper, *Hard Truths – The Journey to Putting Patients First* was published in January 2014 and provided a detailed response to the 290 recommendations the inquiry made across every level of the system. The NHS Constitution was revised as a result of the Francis Report (see below). There were also a further six independent reviews that the government had commissioned to consider some of the key issues identified by the Inquiry:

- *Review into the Quality of Care and Treatment Provided by 14 Hospital Trusts in England*, led by the NHS Medical Director in NHS England, Professor Sir Bruce Keogh KBE. Expert inspections of hospitals with the highest mortality rates revealed unacceptable standards of care. Eleven hospitals were placed into 'special measures' to put them back on a path to recovery and then to excellence.

- *The Cavendish Review: An Independent Review into Healthcare Assistants and Support Workers in the NHS and social care settings* (July 2013) by Camilla Cavendish set out how the training and support of healthcare and care assistants could be improved so that patients receive compassionate care in both NHS and social settings.
- *A Promise to Learn – A Commitment to Act: Improving the Safety of Patients in England* (August 2013) by Professor Don Berwick described a partial loss of focus on quality and safety as primary aims, inadequate openness to the voices of patients and carers, insufficient skills in safety and improvement, inadequate staffing for patients' needs, and a very unhelpful complexity and lack of clarity and cooperation amongst regulatory agencies.
- *A Review of the NHS Hospitals Complaints System: Putting Patients Back in the Picture* (October 2013) by Rt Hon Ann Clwyd MP and Professor Tricia Hart focused on four areas for improvement, namely: the quality of care; the way complaints were handled; independence in the complaints procedures; and whistle-blowing.
- *Challenging Bureaucracy* (2013) led by the NHS Confederation.
- *Report of the Children and Young People's Health Outcomes Forum 2014/15* (March 2015), co-chaired by Professor Ian Lewis and Christine Lenehan.

Some of the key actions that followed the publication of Hard Truths included:

- All hospitals to clearly set out how patients and their families can raise concerns or complain, with independent support available from local Healthwatch or alternative organisations.
- Trusts to report on complaints data and lessons learned quarterly, and the Ombudsman to significantly increase the number of cases considered.
- The passing of the Care Act 2014 which led to a statutory and professional duty of candour, a new fit and proper person's test and the introduction of a new criminal offence applicable to care providers that supply or publish certain types of false or misleading information. This is covered in more detail later.
- All arm's-length bodies and the Department of Health (DH) were to sign a protocol to minimise bureaucratic burdens on trusts by aligning their regulatory requirements.

The consequences for Mid Staffordshire NHS Foundation Trust were that on 1 November 2014 the services previously managed by Mid Staffordshire NHS Foundation Trust were transferred to the management of University Hospitals of North Midlands NHS Trust and the Royal Wolverhampton NHS Trust. Both the County Hospital (formerly Stafford Hospital) and Cannock Chase Hospital remain open.

While poor governance within the NHS is unlikely to lead to its complete disappearance (unlike a corporate body), it is likely to lead to the continual pressure to move towards greater centralisation of control by the government. Political opinions will differ as to whether this is in the best interests of the recipients of a publicly funded healthcare system. Lessons in good practice have generally resulted from such misconduct and poor decision-making. However, it is the reputation of the NHS and patient care that repeatedly suffers as a consequence in the meantime.

Common themes in poor governance

Aspects of poor governance include:

- a board of directors that fails to perform its duties properly, perhaps because it is dominated by one or more individuals, or because it fails to carry out its appointed tasks;
- a poor relationship between the board and the main stakeholders;
- failure to deliver the appropriate returns or services required by either statute or by regulators;
- ineffective systems of risk management, and exposure to errors and fraud due to inadequate internal control systems;
- inappropriate remuneration and reward systems for directors and senior executives;
- misleading performance reporting to regulators and stakeholders; and
- unethical business practices.

Therefore, a key issue in governance continues to be the relationship between the board of directors, its main stakeholders (such as patients, staff and the DH) and other important stakeholders. The following quote from the NHS Providers and Beachcroft LLP publication *The Foundations of Good Governance: A Compendium of Best Practice* is illuminating:

> 'Governance is sometimes regarded as an obscure subject, not necessarily visible in its own right, but it becomes a high-profile reputation issue when it is found lacking. At its core, delivering good governance is about strong, dynamic leadership and it should not be the preserve of "governance specialists" or experts, nor should it be driven by compliance with processes alone. Corporate governance is about leadership and is the system by which all board-led organisations across the public and private sectors are directed and controlled including NHS foundation trusts and NHS trusts.'

The NHS Constitution

The *NHS Constitution for England* is a formal constitution, which lays down in one document the objectives of the NHS, the rights and responsibilities of the various parties involved in healthcare in England and the guiding principles that govern the service.

The following are required by law to take account of the NHS Constitution in their decisions and actions:

- the Secretary of State for Health
- all NHS bodies, including clinical commissioning groups (CCGs), NHS trusts and NHS FTs
- all private and voluntary sector providers supplying NHS services
- local authorities in the exercise of their public health functions.

The Constitution was first published on 21 January 2009 and was one of a number of recommendations in Lord Darzi's 2008 report *High Quality Care for All*. This set out a ten-year plan to provide the highest quality of care and service for patients in England. These rights and responsibilities had previously evolved in common law, through UK or EU law, or were policy pledges by the NHS and government. They have now been written into the Constitution. Under the Health Act 2009, all providers and commissioners of NHS care are under a legal obligation to have regard to the NHS Constitution in all their decisions and actions. The Constitution enables the NHS to remain true to fundamental principles and values which are as relevant now as they were when the NHS was founded, and which continue to enjoy strong support from the public.

There are legally binding requirements for revising and updating the Constitution, which guarantee that the principles and values that underpin the NHS are subject to regular review and recommitment. These requirements also mandate that any government which seeks to alter the principles or values of the NHS – or the rights, pledges, duties and responsibilities set out in the Constitution – has to engage in a full and transparent debate with the public, patients and staff. The latest version of the Constitution was published in July 2015.

To accompany the updated NHS Constitution, the DH also publish a Handbook to the NHS Constitution, which explains the rights, pledges and responsibilities set out in the NHS Constitution in more detail.

The Constitution is based on seven key principles, which guide the NHS in all it does. They are underpinned by core NHS values that have been derived from extensive discussions with staff, patients and the public.

Principles of the NHS

1. The NHS provides a comprehensive service, available to all

It is available to all irrespective of gender, race, disability, age, sexual orientation, religion, belief, gender reassignment, pregnancy and maternity or marital or civil partnership status. The service is designed to improve, prevent, diagnose and treat both physical and mental health problems with equal regard. It has a duty to each and every individual that it serves and must respect their human rights. At the same time, it has a wider social duty to promote equality through the services it provides and to pay particular attention to groups or sections of society where improvements in health and life expectancy are not keeping pace with therest of the population.

2. Access to NHS services is based on clinical need, not an individual's ability to pay
NHS services are free of charge, except in limited circumstances sanctioned by Parliament.

3. The NHS aspires to the highest standards of excellence and professionalism
It provides high quality care that is safe, effective and focused on patient experience; in the people it employs, and in the support, education, training and development they receive; in the leadership and management of its organisations; and through its commitment to innovation and to the promotion, conduct and use of research to improve the current and future health and care of the population. Respect, dignity, compassion and care should be at the core of how patients and staff are treated not only because that is the right thing to do but because patient safety, experience and outcomes are all improved when staff are valued, empowered and supported.

4. The patient will be at the heart of everything the NHS does
It should support individuals to promote and manage their own health. NHS services must reflect, and should be coordinated around and tailored to, the needs and preferences of patients, their families and their carers. As part of this, the NHS will ensure that in line with the Armed Forces Covenant, those in the armed forces, reservists, their families and veterans are not disadvantaged in accessing health services in the area they reside. Patients, with their families and carers, where appropriate, will be involved in and consulted on all decisions about their care and treatment. The NHS will actively encourage feedback from the public, patients and staff, welcome it and use it to improve its services.

5. The NHS works across organisational boundaries
It works in partnership with other organisations in the interest of patients, local communities and the wider population. The NHS is an integrated system of organisations and services bound together by the principles and values reflected in the Constitution. The NHS is committed to working jointly with other local authority services, other public sector organisations and a wide range of private and voluntary sector organisations to provide and deliver improvements in health and wellbeing.

6. The NHS is committed to providing best value for taxpayers' money
It is committed to providing the most effective, fair and sustainable use of finite resources. Public funds for healthcare will be devoted solely to the benefit of the people that the NHS serves.

7. The NHS is accountable to the public, communities and patients that it serves

The NHS is a national service funded through national taxation, and it is the government which sets the framework for the NHS and which is accountable to Parliament for its operation. However, most decisions in the NHS, especially those about the treatment of individuals and the detailed organisation of services, are rightly taken by the local NHS and by patients with their clinicians. The system of responsibility and accountability for taking decisions in the NHS should be transparent and clear to the public, patients and staff. The government will ensure that there is always a clear and up-to-date statement of NHS accountability for this purpose.

Values of the NHS

These values have been developed with patients, public and staff with the intention that they should inspire passion in the NHS and that should underpin everything it does. Individual NHS organisations are expected to develop and build upon these values, tailoring them to their local needs – however, these NHS values provide common ground for co-operation to achieve shared aspirations at all levels of the NHS.

Working together for patients

Patients come first in everything we do. We fully involve patients, staff, families, carers, communities, and professionals inside and outside the NHS. We put the needs of patients and communities before organisational boundaries. We speak up when things go wrong.

Respect and dignity

We value each person – whether patient, their families or carers, or staff – as an individual, respect their aspirations and commitments in life, and seek to understand their priorities, needs, abilities and limits. We take what others have to say seriously. We are honest and open about our point of view and what we can and cannot do.

Commitment to quality of care

We earn the trust placed in us by insisting on quality and striving to get the basics of quality of care – safety, effectiveness and patient experience – right every time. We encourage and welcome feedback from patients, families, carers, staff and the public. We use this to improve the care we provide and build on our successes.

Compassion

We ensure that compassion is central to the care we provide and respond with humanity and kindness to each person's pain, distress, anxiety or need. We search for the things we can do, however small, to give comfort and relieve suffering. We find time for patients, their families and carers, as well as those we work alongside. We do not wait to be asked, because we care.

Improving lives
We strive to improve health and wellbeing and people's experiences of the NHS. We value excellence and professionalism wherever we find it – in the everyday things that make people's lives better as much as in clinical practice, service improvements and innovation. We recognise that all have a part to play in making ourselves, patients and our communities healthier.

Everyone counts
We maximise our resources for the benefit of the whole community, and make sure nobody is excluded, discriminated against or left behind. We accept that some people need more help, that difficult decisions have to be taken – and that when we waste resources we waste others' opportunities.

Patient rights and pledges provided by the Constitution

The Constitution grants patients 'rights', which are intended to be legally enforceable and also makes other non-binding 'pledges'. These are set out in Table 2.1.

Table 2.1: Patient rights and pledges

Access to healthcare	
Rights	**Pledges**
■ Free of charge. ■ Never refused on unreasonable grounds. ■ Appropriate, meets need and reflects preferences. ■ Assessed by the local NHS to meet locally assessed needs. ■ Obtainable from any UK NHS provider or with pre-approval from any European Economic Area or Swiss public provider. ■ Non-discriminatory. ■ Within maximum waiting times, or for the NHS to take all reasonable steps to offer a range of suitable alternative providers if this is not possible.	■ Access to healthcare will be convenient and easy to access within defined waiting times. ■ Make decisions in a clear and transparent way, so that patients and the public can understand how services are planned and delivered. ■ Transfers from one provider to another will be as smooth as possible and that patients will be involved in all relevant discussions.

Quality of care and environment	
Rights	**Pledge**
■ Treatment with a professional standard of care, by appropriately qualified and experienced staff and an organisation that meets required levels of safety and quality. ■ Cared for in a clean, safe, secure and suitable environment. ■ Provision of suitable and nutritious food and hydration to sustain good health and wellbeing. ■ Patients can expect NHS organisations to monitor, and make efforts to improve, the quality of healthcare they commission or provide.	■ Identify and share best practice in quality of care and treatments.

Nationally approved treatments, drugs and programmes	
Rights	**Pledge**
■ Drugs and treatments that have been recommended by the National Institute for Health and Clinical Excellence (NICE) for use in the NHS, if their doctor says they are clinically appropriate for them. ■ Expect local decisions on funding of other drugs and treatments to be made rationally following a proper consideration of the evidence. If the local NHS decides not to fund a drug or treatment that you and your doctor feel would be right for you, the local NHS must explain that decision. ■ Receive the approved vaccinations under an NHS-provided national immunisation programme.	■ To provide screening programmes as recommended by the UK National Screening Committee.

Respect, consent and confidentiality	
Rights	**Pledges**
■ To be treated with dignity and respect in accordance with your human rights. ■ To be protected from abuse and neglect, and care and treatment that is degrading. ■ Able to accept or refuse treatment that is offered, and not to be given any physical examination or treatment without valid consent. Lack of capacity requires consent to be obtained from a person who is legally able to act, or the treatment must be in the patient's best interests. ■ To be given information about the test and treatment options available, what they involve and their risks and benefits. ■ To access personal health records and to have any factual inaccuracies corrected. ■ To privacy and confidentiality and to expect the NHS to keep confidential information safe and secure; to be informed about how the information is used. ■ To request that confidential information is not used beyond their own care and treatment and to have their objections considered, and where their wishes cannot be followed, to be told the reasons including the legal basis.	■ To ensure those involved in a patient's care and treatment have access to their health information so they can care for them safely and effectively. ■ Admission to hospital will not require shared sleeping accommodation with patients of the opposite sex, except where appropriate. ■ To anonymise the information collected during the course of treatment and use it to support research and improve care for others. ■ Where identifiable information has to be used, to give patients the chance to object wherever possible. ■ To inform patients of research studies in which they may be eligible to participate. ■ To share with them any correspondence sent between clinicians about their care.

Informed choice	
Rights	**Pledges**
■ Choose their own GP practice, and to be accepted by that practice unless there are reasonable grounds to refuse.	■ To inform patients about the healthcare services available locally and nationally.

Informed choice *continued*	
Rights	**Pledges**
■ Express a preference for using a particular doctor within their GP practice, and for the practice to try to comply. ■ Access to transparent, accessible and comparable data on the quality of local healthcare providers, and on outcomes, as compared to others nationally. ■ Make choices about the services commissioned by NHS bodies and to information to support these choices.	■ To offer easily accessible, reliable and relevant information to enable patients to participate fully in their own healthcare decisions and to support them in making choices. This includes information on the quality of clinical services where there is robust and accurate information available.

Involvement in one's own healthcare and in the NHS	
Rights	**Pledges**
■ To be involved in planning and making decisions about one's own health and care with one's care provider or providers, including one's end of life care, and to be given information and support to enable one to do this. Where appropriate, this right includes one's family and carers. This includes being given the chance to manage one's own care and treatment, if appropriate. ■ To an open and transparent relationship with the organisation providing the care, including being told about any safety incident relating to the care which, in the opinion of a healthcare professional, has caused, or could still cause, significant harm or death. Patients must be given the facts, an apology, and any reasonable support needed. ■ To be involved, directly or through representatives, in the planning of healthcare services, the development and consideration of proposals for changes in the way those services are provided, and in decisions to be made affecting the operation of those services.	■ To provide the information needed for patients to influence and scrutinise the planning and delivery of NHS services. ■ To work in partnership with patients, their family, carers and their representatives. ■ To involve patients in discussions about planning their care and to offer them a written record of what is agreed if they want one. ■ To encourage and welcome feedback on a patients' health and care experiences and use this to improve services.

Complaint and redress	
Rights	**Pledges**
■ To have any complaint made about NHS services acknowledged within three working days and to have it properly investigated. ■ To discuss the manner in which the complaint is to be handled, and to know the period within which the investigation is likely to be completed and the response sent. ■ To be kept informed of progress and to know the outcome of any investigation into a complaint, including an explanation of the conclusions and confirmation that any action needed in consequence of the complaint has been taken or is proposed to be taken. ■ To take a complaint to the independent Parliamentary and Health Service Ombudsman or Local Government Ombudsman, if patients are not satisfied with the way their complaint was dealt with by the NHS. ■ To make a claim for judicial review if they think they have been directly affected by an unlawful act or decision of an NHS body. ■ To compensation where patients have been harmed by negligent treatment.	■ To ensure patients are treated with courtesy and receive appropriate support throughout the handling of a complaint, and the fact that they have made a complaint will not adversely affect their future treatment. ■ To ensure that when mistakes happen or if a patient is harmed while receiving health care they receive an appropriate explanation and apology, delivered with sensitivity and recognition of the trauma experienced, and know that lessons will be learned to help avoid a similar incident occurring again. ■ That the organisation will learn lessons from complaints and claims and will use them to improve NHS services.

Patient and public responsibilities

The NHS Constitution recognises that patients can make a significant contribution to their own, and their family's, good health and wellbeing, and take personal responsibility for it. The Constitution sets out key responsibilities as follows:

- Register with a GP practice – the main point of access to NHS care as commissioned by NHS bodies.
- Treat NHS staff and other patients with respect and recognise that violence, or the causing of nuisance or disturbance on NHS premises, could result in prosecution. Abusive and violent behaviour could result in a patient being refused access to NHS services.
- Provide accurate information about health, condition and status.

- Keep appointments or cancel within reasonable time. Receiving treatment within the maximum waiting times may be compromised otherwise.
- Follow the course of treatment agreed upon, and talk to the clinician if this is difficult.
- Participate in important public health programmes such as vaccination.
- Ensure that those closest to a patient are aware of their wishes about organ donation.
- Give feedback – both positive and negative – about their experiences and the treatment and care received, including any adverse reactions. Feedback will help to improve NHS services for all.

Staff rights and responsibilities

The Constitution applies to all staff doing clinical or non-clinical NHS work – including public health – and their employers. It covers staff wherever they are working, whether in public, private or voluntary sector organisations. Staff have extensive legal rights, embodied in general employment and discrimination law. These are summarised in the Handbook to the NHS Constitution *Handbook to the NHS Constitution*. In addition, individual contracts of employment contain terms and conditions giving staff further rights.

In addition to these legal rights, there are a number of pledges that the NHS is committed to achieve. Pledges go above and beyond the legal rights. They are not legally binding but represent a commitment by the NHS to provide high-quality working environments for staff. The NHS pledges to:

- Provide a positive working environment for staff and to promote supportive, open cultures that help staff do their job to the best of their ability.
- Provide all staff with clear roles and responsibilities and rewarding jobs for teams and individuals that make a difference to patients, their families and carers and communities.
- Provide all staff with personal development, access to appropriate education and training for their jobs, and line management support to enable them to fulfil their potential.
- Provide support and opportunities for staff to maintain their health, wellbeing and safety.
- Engage staff in decisions that affect them and the services they provide, individually, through representative organisations and through local partnership working arrangements. All staff will be empowered to put forward ways to deliver better and safer services for patients and their families.
- To have a process for staff to raise an internal grievance.
- Encourage and support all staff in raising concerns at the earliest reasonable opportunity about safety, malpractice or wrongdoing at work, responding to and, where necessary, investigating the concerns raised and acting consistently with the Employment Rights Act 1996.

The Constitution also sets out the key responsibilities for NHS staff. These duties are:

- To accept professional accountability and maintain the standards of professional practice as set by the appropriate regulatory body applicable to the profession or role.
- To take reasonable care of health and safety at work for themselves, their team and others, and to co-operate with employers to ensure compliance with health and safety requirements.
- To act in accordance with the express and implied terms of the contract of employment.
- Not to discriminate against patients or staff and to adhere to equal opportunities and equality and human rights legislation.
- To protect the confidentiality of personal information that they hold.
- To be honest and truthful in applying for a job and in carrying out that job.

The Constitution also includes expectations that reflect how staff should play their part in ensuring the success of the NHS and delivering high-quality care.

Overall the NHS Constitution is a key strategic document for understanding the parameters by which all of the individual parts of the NHS are required to function. In addition to this and in the light of the current financial, access and quality demands being placed on the NHS the other key document which is driving the strategic direction is the Five Year Forward View.

The Five Year Forward View and Dalton Review

Following the introduction of the new structure under the HSCA 2012, the findings of the Francis Review and the Nicholson Challenge (saving £15–20 billion through efficiency savings from 2011 to 2014), the NHS faced a major crisis relating to both the quality and safety of treatment and the ongoing funding of the NHS to meet the growing demands and activity. The Five Year Forward View (5YFV) published in October 2014 by the NHS leadership bodies – NHS England (NHSE), NHS Improvement (NHSI), Public Health England (PHE), Health Education England (HEE) and the CQC, set out three underpinning principles for change for the NHS, namely closing three gaps in healthcare:

- the health and wellbeing gap
- the care and quality gap
- the funding and efficiency gap.

The 5YFV built on the findings of the Dalton Review commissioned by the Secretary of State in February 2014 to explore options for providers of NHS care and to 'reduce variations in clinical standards, financial performance and patient safety'. The principle guiding the Dalton Review was that all patients should expect to receive the same high standards of care, no matter where or in what setting. The review aimed to encourage boards to explore how new organisational models could help safeguard an organisation's ability to provide safe and high-quality care. It made recommendations for boards and national bodies, in order for the necessary changes to be made quickly and easily. New organisational models explored by the review included those in Table 2.2.

Table 2.2: Organisational models

Collaborative models	Bring together two or more organisations voluntarily to pool resources and achieve better outcomes, e.g. federation or joint venture
Contractual models	More formalised agreements with performance and quality standards agreed as part of the arrangement, e.g. service level chains and management contracts
Consolidation models	Change of ownership with new organisation coming in to being potentially providing different services, e.g. integrated care organisations, mergers & acquisitions, multi-site trust and foundation groups
Other options	Buddying, informal partnering and clinical/strategic networks, mutual social enterprises

Led by the Salford Royal Foundation Trust chief executive Sir David Dalton, the review also identified five key themes for the pace of transformational change that is required within the NHS as follows:

1. One size does not fit all.
2. Quicker transformational and transactional change is required.
3. Ambitious organisations with a proven track record should be encouraged to expand their reach and have greater impact.
4. Overall sustainability for the provider sector is a priority.
5. A dedicated implementation programme is needed to make change happen.

In the future, it suggested, organisations are likely to operate more than one organisational form for their service portfolio. It recommends that trust boards consider whether a new organisational form may be most suited to support the delivery of safe, reliable, high-quality and economically viable services.

The Dalton Review did not set out the any of the governance detail required for these new models or organisational forms, nor did it set out a clear governance framework for boards and governing bodies to proceed with such transformation. Instead, it stated that a procurement framework must be developed to allow credentialed organisations to register for management contract and/or acquisition opportunities with stronger trusts acting as 'system architects', which would be encouraged to develop innovative organisational models and to codify and spread their success elsewhere.

The Dalton Review saw the overall sustainability of the provider sector as a priority and encouraged the DH and system regulators to create single, unified process with standardised documentation to support future transactions as providers moved towards new models of care. It was clear, however, that trust boards and CCG governing bodies were to be responsible for ensuring the sustainability of the local health economy as opposed to their individual organisation.

The 5YFV picked up on these themes and was equally committed to exploring new models of care; consequently less focus was placed on providers achieving FT status as it had become apparent that the FT process alone could not meet the significant challenges faced by the NHS sector. Indeed, it might be said that the FT process itself set provider trusts working competitively against each other and did not encourage collaboration and working across the health economy.

Between January and September 2015, 50 vanguards were selected to take a lead on the development of new care models which would act as the blueprints for the NHS moving forward and the inspiration to the rest of the health and care system. There were five vanguard types:

- integrated primary and acute care systems – joining up GP, hospital, community and mental health services
- multispecialty community providers – moving specialist care out of hospitals into the community
- enhanced health in care homes – offering older people better, joined up health, care and rehabilitation services
- urgent and emergency care – new approaches to improve the co-ordination of services and reduce pressure on A&E departments
- acute care collaborations – linking local hospitals together to improve their clinical and financial viability, reducing variation in care and efficiency.

In terms of closing the funding and efficiency gap, the 5YFV forecast that the NHS would have a £30 billion gap in funding by 2020/21 if current demand trends continued, the NHS has received flat real term funding and no further efficiencies were delivered. It went on to project that the NHS would need in the range of £8 billion to £21 billion real term growth annually by 2020/21, depending on demand and efficiency assumptions.

The 5YFV also called for a radical programme of health prevention and public health measures, alongside a review of the provision of social care and its associated funding, particularly for frail older people.

Carter Review (2016)

In June 2014, Lord Carter was asked to carry out a review by the Secretary of State as part of the aim to make the NHS safer and more efficient to ensure that the NHS would get the best value from its £102 billion annual budget and to help the NHS implement a seven-day service. Lord Carter's final report (February 2016) concluded that addressing unwarranted variation in use of resources across acute non-specialised hospitals could save up to £5 billion by 2020/21. The review recommended key measures, such as moving to e-rostering systems; adopting 'model hospital' standards; prioritising the role of procurement; and working more closely with neighbouring hospitals. NHSI were tasked with implementing the recommendations and Lord Carter was appointed as a non-executive director (NED) of NHSI. These recommendations also formed part of the STP process that was underway under 5YFV.

Delivering the Five Year Forward View

In December 2015, *Delivering the Forward View: NHS Planning Guidance: 2016/17–2020/21* outlined a new approach to help ensure that health and care services were built around the needs of local populations. To do this, every health and care system in England was required to produce a multi-year STP, showing how local services would evolve and become sustainable over the next five years – ultimately delivering the 5YFV vision of better health, better patient care and improved NHS efficiency.

The King's Fund was clear, however, that fundamental changes to how health services were commissioned, paid for and regulated would be required to deliver the vision of the NHS 5YFV.

As a result, local health and care systems came together in January 2016 to form 44 STP 'footprints' which are required to deliver plans based on the needs of local populations to drive genuine and sustainable transformation in patient experience and health outcomes of the longer term. The footprints have been locally defined, based on natural communities, existing working relationships and patient flows, and they take account of the scale needed to deliver the services, transformation and public health programmes required, along with how they best fit with other footprints. STPs were delivered in June 2016 with an intended implementation date of autumn 2016 onwards.

In order to support the extent of transformation required, the King's Fund argued for a transformation fund to provide financial support through the transition which was established under the jurisdiction of NHSE for each year of Parliament with the value of the fund in 2016/17 at £2.1 billion rising to £3.4 billion by 2020/21. Access to the STF was conditional on providers agreeing to financial control totals for 2016/17 that allowed provider trusts to return to aggregate financial balance. These control totals were part of the new financial oversight regime that NHSI put in place for 2016/17.

Governance issues for STPs and new models of care

Interestingly, from a governance perspective, STPs' footprints are not statutory bodies, but collective discussion forums that aim to bring together health and care leaders to support the delivery of improved health and care based on the needs of local populations. They do not replace existing local bodies or change local accountabilities.

The challenges for governance going forward will relate to clear accountability structures for the new models of care and the identification and management of the risks that are created by these new configurations with a range of partners. NHS Providers set out key questions about governance and accountability in these emerging structures that need urgent answers in its joint report with *Hempsons: New care models: Lessons learned so far and tips for moving forward (2016)*. These include:

- What happens if an STP footprint develops plans that require an individual provider to sacrifice its individual interests for the greater good of the local system as a whole – how is that reconciled to the provider's board, its NEDs and its governors' statutory duties?
- What happens if some parts of an STP agree to a plan but others don't? How far and when is it reasonable for the interests of an individual provider to be trumped by the needs of a wider local system?
- How much and what delivery will be put through STP footprints, and by when?
- How will accountability actually work if money and delivery is allocated, managed or measured at the level of a local system rather than an individual institution?

Chris Hopson, CEO of NHS Providers, states:

> 'If we are to move to new care models, adopt new integrated organisational forms and deliver services effectively across a wider geographic footprint, then we have to ensure the governance of service delivery and the accountability for that service delivery remain robust and effective. This means maintaining our investment in good corporate governance by organisations, but also developing a more robust approach to governance between organisations and being clearer on lines of accountability at the local system level.'

Many STPs are underpinned by some form of shared governance arrangements to take forward their planned changes and to support joint decision-making and accountability.

Most of the published STPs set out a delivery structure which, with variations, typically includes a strategic board and delivery board supported by a programme management office (PMO). These boards are generally fed by either workstream groups, sector groups or local area groups. The extent to which the key enablers of workforce, estates and IT are included is largely consistent, although the resource allocated to the PMO is mixed (ranging from some full-time teams to those working on it in addition to their day jobs). Some plans explicitly distinguish groups as decision-making, operational or advisory. However, they do not generally include details about how the governance structures will work in practice and how they will need to evolve as the STP progresses.

Many STPs have developed or are developing a memorandum of understanding (MOU), which is signed up to by individual boards and provides a clear model for accountability. *Governing for transformation: STPs and governance* (NHS Providers and Hempsons) provides a template MOU covering scope and clarity of purpose; agreed principles; governance for decision-making; disagreements and disputes; opting out; risk and assurance; and resources.

CASE STUDY: The Greater Manchester Health and Social Care Strategic Partnership Board

The Greater Manchester Health and Social Care Strategic Partnership Board oversees the region's health and care devolution plans, and brings together 37 local authority and NHS organisations from across the footprint. The board sets the vision, strategy and direction, and is supported by an executive. The governance arrangements also include primary care representation on the partnership board and executive. In addition there is a joint commissioning board, an NHS provider trust federation board, a provider forum and a primary care advisory group. Representation by other national bodies and the voluntary sector is included where appropriate.

The new models of care such as integrated care organisations (also known as accountable care organisations or accountable care partnerships), joint ventures, mergers & acquisitions, etc. do have governance frameworks in existence elsewhere outside of the NHS sector. The idea of the Dalton Review was to borrow these models and adapt them to the NHS sector.

The NHS Confederation has suggested that following key governance issues need to be considered for STPs:

- Accountability: Who will be accountable for the delivery of STPs? Most STPs have been organised by consensus and collaboration, wholly appropriate for developing plans, but not for implementation. At present NHSE and NHSI are clear that each board or governing body retains authority over the decision for each individual organisation that is part of the STP and that each board or governing body has a responsibility to the wider health economy, not just the performance of their individual part. This raises interesting questions when financial and performance targets are still set for each individual organisation not pooled for the STP. STPs also require full engagement with local authorities whose governance arrangements are completely different to that within the NHS.

- Patient and public engagement: How are the needs of patients and the public kept at the heart of STPs? Involvement with clinicians, CCG lay members, NEDs, FT governors, patient forums and by having wider engagement with local politicians and the public will be essential. Early involvement in STP planning and delivery will bring long-term benefits and there is evidence that already plans have progressed too far without this engagement and the reputation of the STPs and their leadership risk being damaged, perhaps fatally.
- Local government: How are the right relationships being built within STPs? STPs are about integration – social care and health integration, closer collaboration of CCGs, and bringing together responsibility for the commissioning and provision of services within innovative arrangements. As such, building relationships across the NHS and local government within each footprint is paramount for STP delivery. This integration will require careful thought and open debate as it will combine different forms of governance, e.g. unitary board and cabinet decision-making.
- Balancing the tension between making decisions quickly and openly and transparently. There is an inherent tension between making decisions quickly to speed up transformation and making the right decisions openly and transparently, with the support of the main stakeholders in the system. Governance structures will need to be streamlined but absolutely require good communication channels that support feedback gathering and information dissemination.
- The clinical voice: How can STPs preserve the clinical voice? It is essential for implementation that clinical input and the clinical voice sits equally alongside the managerial input and voice to drive service transformation and improvement.
- Independent scrutiny: What role will lay members, NEDs and FT governors have in delivering STPs? Each STP footprint has been left to determine its governance form and despite this flexibility it will be essential to ensure that independent challenge should be represented throughout the decision-making process to ensure that scrutiny, transparency and decision-making remains firmly in the interest of the public and patients.
- Audit and assurance: What assurance processes will be available to support that independent scrutiny? Effective assurance systems that include risk management and internal controls will need to be developed for the STPs. Where there are new models of care being used that are recognised forms of organisational structure, such as joint venture, then using their existing governance may be sufficient. However, there may also be a need for different central government policy and/or legislation to enable these new forms to develop.

The King's Fund in its publication Delivering sustainability and transformation plans (February 2017) makes the following observation which sets out clearly the challenges that may lie ahead for STPs and illustrates the consequences where there are poor governance arrangements:

> 'STPs are a conscious "workaround" by national bodies of the complex and fragmented organisational arrangements that are the legacy of the Health and Social Care Act 2012. They rely on the willingness of NHS leaders at a local level to collaborate with their peers in the best interests of the populations they serve. STPs have no basis in statute, and their proposals need to be endorsed and supported by the boards of the NHS organisations involved as they move from planning to implementation.
>
> There is an ever-present risk that these proposals will be challenged by those who oppose them through judicial review and other means. Were this to happen, it would introduce further delays to the implementation of planned changes. All the more important therefore that their governance and decision-making processes are formalised to align the ambition to collaborate in STPs with the sovereignty, accountability and legal duties of the boards of NHS organisations and local authorities '

The King's Fund goes on to recommend that the HSCA 2012 be revisited to amend those sections that are not aligned to the 5YFV and STPs, in particular the aspects of anti-competitive rules and to acknowledge the formal role of STPs.

And as a small aside, the recent report – Health and social care integration – from the National Audit Office (NAO) in February 2017 contends that at a national level there are also significant governance concerns:

> 'The Department of Health, the Department for Communities and Local Government and their partners have set up an array of initiatives examining different ways to transform care and create a financially sustainable care system. However, the Integration Partnership Board receives updates on progress of the Better Care Fund only, with no reporting from other integration initiatives. The ministerial Health and Social Care Integration Implementation Taskforce did not meet regularly and has now been disbanded. The lack of comprehensive governance is leading to uncoordinated effort across central bodies and the Department of Health has now initiated a review of governance arrangements.'

The increasing focus on working with partners across health and social care required by STPs, creates a tension for providers as they continue to work on organisational performance as part of wider system performance. This is increasingly being recognised in the guidance being published. The NHSI's Developmental reviews of leadership and governance using the Well-Led Framework: Guidance for NHS trusts and NHS Foundation Trusts (June 2017) maintains its focus on organisations because this is the statutory basis for service provision, but it has increased the emphasis on working proactively with partners. It recommends that many of the principles of good governance at organisational level are also applicable at system level and the guidance encourages local system partners to use the framework for development opportunities within STPs if it is appropriate.

Summary

Despite the uncertainty of the future success of STPs and whether they can deliver the widespread transformation required to deliver ongoing sustainability, there are key health service governance principles which need to be enshrined to guide the governance structures going forward for the STPs and their new models of care.

All healthcare bodies are bound to act within the constraints of best practice – both in the process, practices and procedures by which power is shared and exercised by those who make up the controlling mind of the organisation – and in how the holders of power in the organisation should be held accountable for what they do. Health service governance is key to ensuring that there is effective leadership, responsible stewardship of public assets and services and public accountability.

Whether you credit the phrase 'with great power comes great responsibility' to Voltaire in nineteenth-century France, Franklin D Roosevelt in 1945 or to the uncle of the comic book character Spider-Man, the intention remains the same. Those who exercise power are required to be held to account for the decisions they make. Health service governance provides a framework of law, regulation and guidance to put in place boundaries for those who exercise this power and authority with regard to the world's largest publicly funded health service.

3 The structure of the NHS

The NHS

Health service governance is the governance that is applied to National Health Service (NHS) organisations. Therefore, it is useful to clarify the structure and guiding principles of the NHS.

The NHS is the shared name of three of the four publicly funded healthcare systems in the United Kingdom (UK). They provide a comprehensive range of health services, the vast majority of which are free at the point of use to residents of the UK.

The NHS in England was created by the National Health Service Act 1948 (NHS Act 1948), which created an NHS for both England and Wales. Responsibility for the NHS in Wales was passed to the Secretary of State for Wales in 1969, leaving the Secretary of State for Social Services solely responsible for the NHS in England.

The English NHS is the only system officially called the NHS, the others being NHS Scotland and NHS Wales. The Northern Irish equivalent to the NHS is called Health and Social Care (HSC). Each system operates independently and is politically accountable to the relevant government: the Scottish Government, the Welsh Government, the Northern Ireland Executive or the UK Government (for the English NHS).

Despite their separate funding and administration, there is no discrimination when a resident of one country of the UK requires treatment in another – although a patient will often be returned to their home area when they are fit to be moved. The financial and administrative consequences are dealt with by the organisations involved and no personal involvement by the patient is required.

The NHS in England has agreed a formal Constitution, which lays down in one document the objectives of the NHS, the rights and responsibilities of the various parties involved in healthcare in England (patients, staff and trust boards) and the guiding principles that govern the service. It was first published on 21 January 2009 as part of a ten-year plan to provide the highest quality of care and service for patients in England. Previously, these rights and responsibilities had evolved in common law or through UK or European Union (EU) law, or were policy pledges by the NHS and government. These have now been written into the Constitution.

In summary, the guiding principles of the NHS are as follows.

- The NHS provides a comprehensive service, available to all irrespective of gender, race, disability, age, sexual orientation, religion, belief, gender reassignment, pregnancy and maternity or marital or civil partnership status.
- Access to NHS services is based on clinical need, not an individual's ability to pay (except in exceptional circumstances sanctioned by Parliament).
- The NHS aspires to the highest standards of excellence and professionalism to provide high-quality care that is safe, effective and focused on the patient experience.
- The NHS aspires to put patients at the heart of everything it does.
- The NHS works across organisational boundaries and in partnership with other organisations in the interest of patients, local communities and the wider population. The NHS is an integrated system of organisations and services bound together by the principles and values reflected in the Constitution.
- The NHS is committed to providing best value for taxpayers' money and the most effective, fair and sustainable use of finite resources.
- The NHS is accountable to the public, communities and patients that it serves.

The Department of Health (DH) is the government department responsible for policy in health and social care matters. It is responsible for the NHS in England, along with a few elements of the same matters that are not otherwise devolved to the Scottish, Welsh or Northern Irish governments. The DH then delegates powers to the various authorities and boards established to oversee and scrutinise the provision of healthcare. This structure was altered radically in 2013 by the Health and Social Care Act 2012 (HSCA 2012).

The Statement of Accountability

The Statement of Accountability describes how the NHS in England currently works and who is responsible for its different parts. It is required by the NHS Constitution. In May 2013, a revised Statement of NHS Accountability for England was published in *A Guide to the Healthcare System in England,* to bring it into line with the revisions made to the NHS Constitution in April 2013. Despite the transformational changes being required through the Five Year Forward View (5YFV) (see Chapter 2), the Statement of Accountability has not yet been updated as there is no new legislation to enable these new models or governance arrangements.

The NHS is a system of organisations responsible for organising and providing a comprehensive health service. The funding for running the NHS is granted to the DH by Parliament out of national taxation. There is therefore a continuous thread of accountability to the government running throughout the NHS.

The Secretary of State for Health is accountable to Parliament, and through Parliament to the voters, for the promotion of a comprehensive health service and for the use of public money. Any decision taken by ministers about health policy can be scrutinised by Members of Parliament. The Health Select Committee and the Public Accounts Committee provide a scrutiny function holding the government to account for the delivery of health policy and effective use of resources. Other Select Committees perform similar functions in other policy areas. It is the role of the DH to support the Secretary of State in discharging their duties.

The Secretary of State for Health is a politician, and is the Cabinet minister responsible for health in England. They have a duty to promote a comprehensive health service in England and ministerial responsibility to Parliament for the provision of the health service. The Secretary of State has a number of further legal duties, particularly in relation to improving the quality of services and reducing health inequalities. They must also keep the performance of the health service under review and lay before Parliament a published report on this performance annually. They are responsible to Parliament for the provision of the health service and they work through the DH to provide strategic direction for the NHS (as well as the wider health and care system), and hold all of the national bodies to account for their operational and financial performance, thereby ensuring that the different parts of the system work properly together. They take decisions on national health, public health and social care policy, advised by the civil servants who make up the DH.

The DH's purpose is to help people live better for longer. It leads, shapes and funds health and care in England, making sure people have the support, care and treatment they need, with the compassion and dignity they deserve. The DH, on behalf of the Secretary of State, acts as 'system steward' – it is the only body with oversight over the whole health and care system, and it works to ensure the system operates effectively to meet the needs of people and their communities. This stewardship role has several main aspects. These are as follows:

- Setting national priorities which reflect what patients, service users and the public value. The DH sets ambitions and priorities for the NHS and health care system, through the outcomes frameworks and the Mandate (explained later). It also supports the delivery of ministerial ambitions, priorities and policies; and does this through obtaining information and intelligence, and appropriate monitoring.
- Securing and allocating resources to meet priorities and deliver services. The DH secures and distributes resources for the NHS, and the health and care system, by securing public funding for the NHS, public health and social care from HM Treasury through the Spending Review process. It is an important stakeholder and shareholder in NHS provider organisations, and is a key source of funding for capital investment. It can also secure additional sources

of funding, e.g. through existing prescription and dental charges, and directly allocates resources to local authorities for public health.

- Sponsoring national health and care system bodies by supporting them and holding them to account for the delivery of their role. 'Sponsorship' means the DH ensuring organisations are delivering their functions, meeting their statutory duties, and using public money efficiently and effectively. The specifics of the relationships between the DH and its sponsored bodies are set down in 'framework agreements'.
- Fostering relationships, collaborating with patient organisations, and ensuring the system works well together. This involves ensuring all health and care bodies, and other bodies, work effectively together and with common purpose, whilst recognising their own unique roles and autonomy in deciding how to carry out their defined functions. The DH also works with other government departments on health matters.
- Creating and updating the policy and legislative frameworks within which the health and care system operates. It oversees an effective regulatory framework that ensures all organisations and professionals meet essential standards of quality and safety.
- Accounting to Parliament and the public for the effectiveness of the health and care system. This includes supporting ministerial accountability to Parliament and the public for the effectiveness of the health and care systems, the effective use of resources voted by Parliament, and the discharge of Secretary of State's legal duties. Ultimately, the Secretary of State has powers to remove the chairs of the major national health bodies from office and (in the case of significant failure to exercise their functions properly) powers of direction, which could force an organisation to undertake or cease a particular course of action. Failure to comply with such a direction could result in the function being carried out by another body. The DH is accountable to Parliament and the public. It does not lead on the day-to-day running and organisation of health services.

Whilst the DH remains responsible for the health and care legislative framework and ministers continue to be ultimately accountable, most day-to-day operational management in the NHS takes place at arm's length from the DH since HSCA 2012. With the exception of the remaining special health authorities, all organisations in the NHS have their own statutory functions conferred by legislation, rather than delegated to them by the Secretary of State.

The Statement of Accountability sets out a number of areas of focus within the NHS structure, namely:

- providing care
- commissioning care
- improving public health
- empowering people and local communities
- supporting the health and care system

- education and training
- safeguarding patients' health.

The individual parts of the NHS that make up this NHS structure are set out in Figure 3.1, which shows the main organisations that now make up the healthcare system in England.

Providing care

The provision of healthcare by NHS is divided into two sections: primary and secondary care.

Primary care

Providers of 'primary care' are the first point of contact for physical and mental health and wellbeing concerns in non-urgent cases. These include general practitioners (GPs), dentists, opticians, and pharmacists (for medicines and medical advice). For urgent cases, patients can visit a provider of urgent care, such as an accident and emergency department. Health care professionals within GP practices aim to resolve problems locally, including through services provided by the practice. If a condition requires more specialised treatment, or further investigation, patients may be referred to another healthcare provider. These could be based in a hospital, or in the community. Patients are entitled (where possible) to choose between different types of care and providers of their care. They should be supported to make the choice that is best for them.

Community-based care is becoming the preferred means of providing care for the majority of longer-term and mild to moderate conditions. This enables people to keep their normal routine, staying close to family and friends. Hospital services remain a key part of the NHS, such as for specialised, surgical or emergency care.

Secondary care

Providers of secondary care are those bodies that provide acute healthcare. This can be either elective care or emergency care. Elective care means planned specialist medical care or surgery, usually following referral from a primary or community health professional such as a GP. Most of these services are provided by 'NHS bodies', which are part of the public sector.

There are, however, also many other types of organisation involved in providing NHS care, including providers from the independent sector or voluntary sector. For example, pharmacies tend to be independent sector organisations, and most GPs and dentists have traditionally worked as contractors for the NHS, either individually or in partnerships. The third sector includes organisations such as local community groups, voluntary groups, registered charities, social enterprises and co-operatives. All organisations contracted to provide NHS services must meet the NHS's required levels of care. Not all provider organisations, however, will have a board as such; for example, GP practices are unlikely to have

Figure 3.1: The health and care system from April 2013

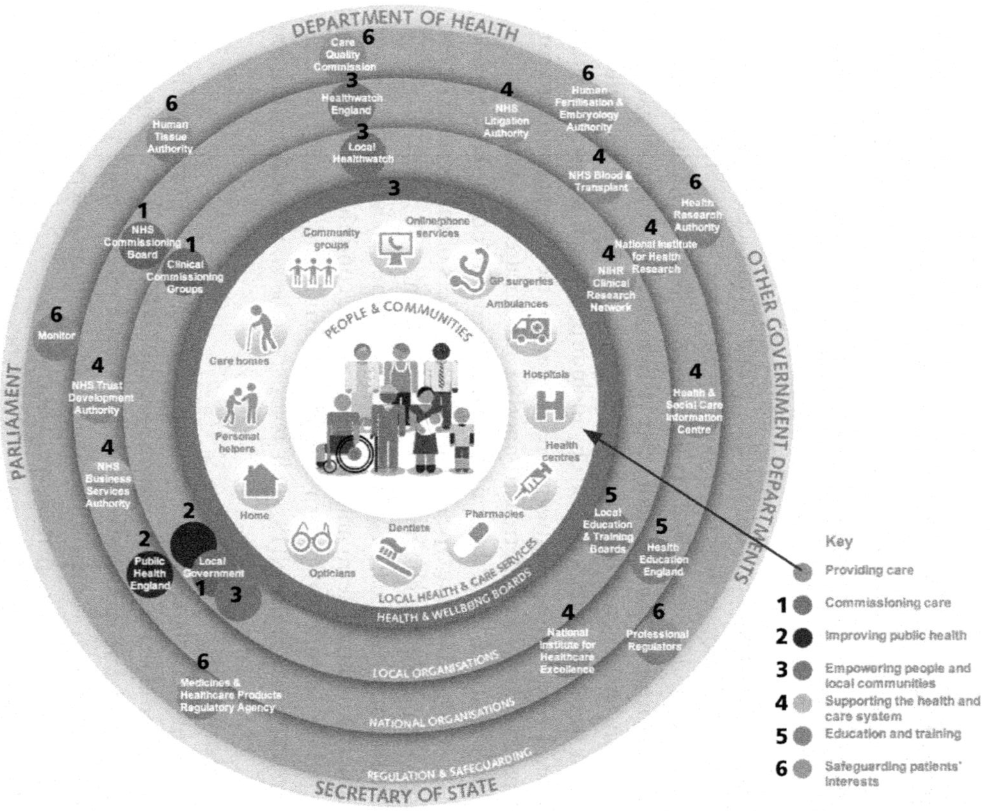

Source: www.gov.uk/government/publications/the-health-and-care-system-explained/the-health-and-care-system-explained

boards. Every organisation, however, will have a person or people who are legally accountable for the service they are providing.

The majority of NHS services, such as hospitals, belong to either an NHS trust or NHS foundation trust (FT). Until recently it has been the government's ambition that all NHS trusts will ultimately become NHS FTs. Each trust can have multiple sites, meaning one or more hospitals often belong to a single trust. However with the developments of new care models and the proposed transformation work of the Sustainability and Transformation Plans (STPs) (see Chapter 2) this may not now be the case and non-FTs may well find themselves involved in joint ventures, mergers & acquisitions or other collaborative models of working (see Chapter 14). The secondary care sector is regulated by NHSI which is the operational name for the organisation that brings together Monitor and the NHS Trust Development Authority. It has incorporated Monitor's role to 'authorise' new FTs. In order to become an FT, NHS trusts had to demonstrate that they were well led and able to provide good quality services for patients on a sustainable basis, achieving an overall rating of 'Good' or 'Outstanding' from the Chief Inspector of Hospitals. There is more information on these ratings in the section below on the Care Quality Commission (CQC). The STP process, which was covered in more detail in Chapter 2, will incorporate similar standards for NHS trusts, but may require these trusts to become part of an FT or a different type of organisation as set out in the Dalton Review in December 2014.

Foundation trusts

In NHS FTs, the board of directors is directly accountable to their local population through their membership and council of governors. The public, patients, service users, their families and carers, and staff can join their local FT as members. Members elect governors to represent them. In an FT, the council of governors oversees the organisation's board, holding the board to account for the performance of their organisation. These are covered in more detail in Chapter 12.

> **CASE STUDY: CASE STUDY: A FT**
>
> Heart of England NHS Foundation Trust provides over 40 different healthcare services and is based across four sites: Birmingham Heartlands Hospital; Solihull Hospital; Good Hope Hospital; and Birmingham Chest Clinic. The services provided by the trust include: general medical, surgical and accident and emergency services, as well as specialist services, such as cardiology, dermatology, orthodontics, paediatrics, radiology, and speech and language therapy.

NHS trusts

In NHS trusts the board is accountable to the Secretary of State for Health via NHS Improvement (NHSI). The services and hospitals that are currently NHS trusts are included within the 5YFV STPs. Such trusts will be required to become part of the footprints within their respective STPs, which may or may not include FT status (see Chapter 12).

As of April 2017, there were 153 FTs with a number of mergers & takeovers completed during 2014–2017 and 80 NHS trusts. NHSI has incorporated Monitor's role to 'authorise' new FTs. In order to become an FT, NHS trusts had to demonstrate that they were well led and able to provide good quality services for patients on a sustainable basis, achieving an overall rating of 'Good' or 'Outstanding' from the Chief Inspector of Hospitals. There is more information on these ratings in the section below on the Care Quality Commission (CQC). The STP process, which was covered in more detail in Chapter 2, will incorporate similar standards for NHS trusts, but may require these trusts to become part of an FT or a different type of organisation as set out in the Dalton Review in December 2014.

Commissioning care

The NHS is funded by taxation with a fixed budget available to spend on services for the whole population. The challenge faced by the NHS is how to spend that budget in a way that results in the best possible outcomes for individual patients and delivers value for money for the public. This planning and purchasing of NHS services is undertaken by organisations (or individuals) known as commissioners. They are responsible for assessing the reasonable needs of their populations and using their buying power as purchasers to secure services that are affordable and of the highest quality. They can buy services from any provider that meets NHS standards of care and prices. As part of their role, commissioners have to work together with providers to determine the services needed for local areas.

Clinical commissioning groups

Given the complexity and scale of the healthcare system, it is more efficient to plan and commission healthcare at a population level, such as for a town and its surroundings or a metropolitan borough. All GP practices are required to be a member of a clinical commissioning group (CCG). In order to plan their commissioning decisions, local authorities and CCGs (coming together through health and wellbeing boards (HWBs)) use Joint Strategic Needs Assessments (JSNAs), and Joint Health and Wellbeing Strategies (JHWSs) to agree local priorities for local health and care commissioning. CCGs are held to account by their regulator NHS England (NHSE) and NHSE has a statutory duty (under the HSCA 2012) to conduct an annual assessment of every CCG. The framework for this and further detail on the structure and governance arrangements for CCGs can be found in Chapter 13.

NHS England

As it is not appropriate to commission some services locally, NHSE (known in HSCA 2012 as the NHS Commissioning Board) commissions these services, which are more appropriate to commission at a national level. These include specialised services (such as those for rare diseases), offender healthcare and some services for members of the armed forces. NHSE is also responsible for commissioning primary care, including GP services.

In addition to commissioning services itself, NHSE also has responsibility for ensuring the overall system of commissioning NHS-funded services works well. This involves working on plans to improve commissioning for specific conditions (such as dementia) or patient groups (such as children's services). NHSE provides information and resources for CCGs, and holds them to account for how they carry out their commissioning activities and improve the healthcare outcomes that matter locally.

NHSE is an executive non-departmental public body. It works under its mandate from the government to improve the quality of NHS care and health outcomes, reduce health inequalities, empower patients and the public and promote innovation. Its key responsibilities include:

- authorisation and oversight of CCGs and support for their ongoing development;
- the direct commissioning of primary care, specialised health services, prison healthcare and some public health services (including, for a transitional period, health visiting and family nurse partnerships); and
- developing and sustaining effective partnerships across the health and care system.

NHSE was originally established with 27 area teams but in its Organisational Change Programme 2014/15 these were integrated into the four existing regional teams: London; Midlands and East; North; and South, each maintaining a local presence. The regions cover healthcare commissioning and delivery across their geographies and provide professional leadership on finance, nursing, medical, specialised commissioning, patients and information, human resources, organisational development, assurance and delivery. The regional teams work closely with organisations such as CCGs, local authorities, HWBs as well as GP practices.

NHSE is one single organisation with senior clinical leadership at all levels operating to a common model. It has one board, composed of the following:

- the chair of the board (appointed by the Secretary of State);
- eight other members (appointed by the Secretary of State) who, together with the chair, are the non-executive members of the board; and
- the chief executive and three other executive members.

In the NHS 5YFV, NHSE set out its vision for the future. This is set out in more detail in Chapter 2. Overall the NHSE has been set the objective of ensuring that any proposals for major service change meet four tests:

1. strong public and patient engagement;
2. consistency with current and prospective need for patient choice;

3. a clear clinical evidence base; and
4. support for proposals from clinical commissioners.

If the relevant local authority does not consider the proposed changes to be in the best interests of the local population, they can refer the matter to the Secretary of State.

NHSE is operationally independent from the DH, with the Secretary of State setting out what the government expects from NHSE in the Mandate. The Mandate, a legally binding annual publication by the SoS setting out NHSE's objectives, highlights the areas of health and care where the government expects to see improvements in the NHS and contains a number of objectives which NHSE must seek to achieve. The Mandate is intended to provide the NHS with stability to plan ahead; it is set for a number of years at a time. The Secretary of State refreshes it every year, albeit not during the year without the agreement of NHSE (except in exceptional circumstances or after a General Election). It is the main way in which the Secretary of State holds NHSE to account for the NHS commissioning system.

The Mandate 2016/17 set out objectives to 2020, which centred on the 5YFV and seven-day working in the NHS. This mandate was refreshed for 2017/18. It also sets an overarching objective for NHSE to improve outcomes for people using the NHS, in particular to improve against all indicators (or measures) in the NHS Outcomes Framework. The NHS Outcomes Framework sets out the outcomes and corresponding indicators used to hold NHSE to account for improvements in quality. It was developed in partnership between clinicians and stakeholders.

From 2016/17 onwards, NHS England introduced a comprehensive, rigorous and transparent new approach to CCG ratings. CCGs are rated in 29 areas, underpinned by 60 indicators, all made available to patients for the first time on the myNHS website. These ratings follow the same structure as the CQC rating structure of:

- Outstanding
- Good
- Requires Improvement
- Inadequate.

This approach has been updated again in line with the *NHS Operational Planning and Contracting Guidance* for 2017–2019 which is built out of the STPs and which sets out the CCG Improvement and Assessment Framework (CCG IAF) which will be used as a central framework for public accountability of the NHS. The CCG IAF has been designed to supply performance indicators for adoption in STPs as markers of success. More detail on the CCG IAF is contained in Chapter 13.

Commissioning support units

Commissioning support units (CSUs) provide commissioning support services to NHS commissioners, including local CCGs, NHSE, acute trusts and local government.

Commissioning support is NHS money spent on non-clinical services. While CSUs do not provide direct patient care or treatment, the five CSUs across England play a key role in helping commissioners to improve patient care and achieve savings, releasing resources for reinvestment in frontline clinical services. The units are designed to provide commissioning support services that enable clinical commissioners to maximise resources and focus their clinical expertise and leadership on securing the best outcomes for patients and driving up quality of NHS patient services.

CSU specialist support services include:

- contract management and negotiation
- business intelligence
- information governance
- financial management
- human resources (HR), estates and IT
- service transformation and redesign
- healthcare procurement and market management
- non-clinical purchasing
- communications and patient engagement
- bespoke services such as individual funding request management, infection prevention, governance and quality.

CSUs are not geographically defined. In some cases, customers are local or regional clinical commissioners, and in others they include CCGs in other parts of England. Some CSUs also provide services to NHSE, local government, and acute trusts. In addition to specialist business support services, CSUs work in partnership with NHSE, commissioners, acute and community health and social care providers to develop new services and improve existing services through innovation in technology, data intelligence, clinical pathway design, patient experience initiatives and patient information campaigns.

Currently governed by NHSE, CSUs were planned to be become autonomous organisations in 2016 as fully established, self-sustaining entities in a competitive market. There is at present no update on progress to achieve this.

Local authorities

Local authorities (or councils) have a wide range of duties and responsibilities regarding the health of their populations. These extend beyond the NHS into both public health and social care. Since 1 April 2013, local government has led the public health system at local level. The changes under the HSCA 2012 also mean that local authorities in England have a statutory duty to take steps to improve the health of the people in their area as well as other public health functions and in order to improve their work, CCGs and local authorities have, for example, the freedom to commission services together. The relevant local authorities are:

Figure 3.2: The NHS commissioning structure

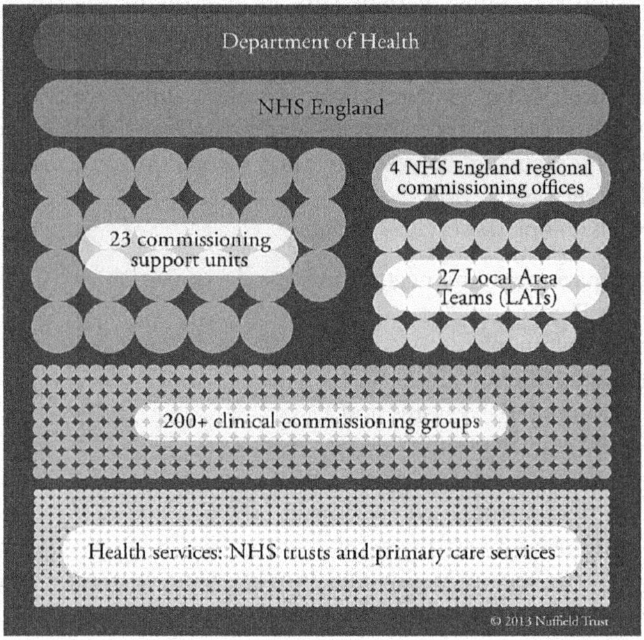

Source: © Nuffield Trust

- county councils
- unitary authorities, including metropolitan district councils
- London boroughs and the Common Council of the City of London
- the Council of the Isles of Scilly.

With these new functions comes the responsibility for a range of services that were previously commissioned and provided by NHS bodies. This does not mean that local authorities are now NHS bodies. However, when they are undertaking their public health functions, they are an important part of the comprehensive health service and, like NHS bodies, must have regard to the NHS Constitution.

Local authorities also commission social care for their local populations based on local criteria and national minimum standards. Unlike NHS care, state-funded social care is means tested. The DH has responsibility for national adult social care policy, and has committed to changing how care is paid for (subject to legislation) with the overall aim of a sustainable and fair partnership between the government and individual for care costs. The Adult Social Care Outcomes Framework defines national priorities for the social care sector, and includes indicators that enable the public and other stakeholders to assess the performance of services. The Department for Education has responsibility for national children's social care policy.

Upper tier and unitary local authorities in England have, by law, powers to review and scrutinise any matter relating to the planning, provision and operation of the health service (including public health) in its area. This enables scrutiny of the quality of services provided locally and proposals put forward for significant changes to those services, such as re-organising stroke care in an area. Every upper tier and unitary local authority area in England has arrangements with a Local Healthwatch organisation to support patient and public involvement activities in its area.

Local authorities also have the responsibility for improving the public health of the people in their area. This includes the planning and provision of public health services, such as smoking cessation, and considering the public health effects through the planning of other linked services, such as education, housing, social care and transport. Local authorities are supported in this work by Public Health England (PHE).

One of the criticisms of a number of STPs is that they have not included the local authorities sufficiently for this engagement to occur and consequently this is having an impact on the ability of the STP to deliver.

Figure 3.2 sets outs the commissioning structure within the NHS.

Improving public health

Whilst responsibilities for improving health lie with both providers and commissioners, PHE has a key responsibility in this area with regard to local authorities.

Public Health England

PHE is an operationally independent executive agency of the DH, which supports local authorities in their duty to improve public health and has national responsibility for protecting the public against major health risks. NHSE also commissions some national public health services. PHE makes comparative data available to help drive improvements and reports annually on progress against the public health outcomes set out in the Public Health Outcomes Framework.

Empowering people and local communities

Overview and Scrutiny Committees

The public's opinion can influence local health services through the overview and scrutiny committees of local authorities. Overview and scrutiny committees (OSCs) are made up of elected local councillors, supported by council officials. They allow democratically elected community leaders to voice the views of their constituents and require local NHS bodies to listen and respond.

OSCs have the power to scrutinise the operation and planning of local health services. All councillors, except for leaders and cabinet members, are able to be members of overview and scrutiny committees. They review the policies made by the council and its partners. They can refer decisions back to the cabinet or decision-maker for reconsideration if they have concerns. This power to scrutiny includes the right to scrutinise and make reports to NHS bodies, require officers of NHS bodies to attend scrutiny committee meetings when requested (often called the Health Overview and Scrutiny Committee (HOSC)), ask for information about the planning and provision of services from NHS bodies and require them to respond to their recommendations. Where scrutiny committees have concerns about substantial changes being proposed by NHS bodies, if they were not considered to be in the interests of local health services, they can refer decisions back to the NHS. If these are not satisfactorily resolved, they can be referred to the Secretary of State.

As such the HOSC has held NHS bodies to account for the quality of their services through these powers. Under HSCA 2012, local authorities were no longer required to have overview and scrutiny committees to discharge health scrutiny functions but they continue to have such functions, which they are able to discharge in various ways. For example, local authorities may choose to continue to operate their prior HOSCs, or may choose to put in place other arrangements such as appointing committees involving members of the public. HSCA 2012 also provided that the requirements for an NHS body to consult the local authority overview and scrutiny committee and to require officers of NHS bodies to attend before the committee to answer questions will also potentially include CCGs, NHSE and other providers of health services, including independent sector providers.

Although local authorities are no longer required to have such committees as the means by which they discharge their scrutiny function, in practice most have retained them.

If there is a HOSC, then it should be involved early on in discussions about any reconfiguration of health services and should take a view about whether changes are in the interests of local health services. For example, it can examine the proposal in the light of councillors' knowledge of their local area and make recommendations about how the people who use services, particularly vulnerable groups, can be informed about changes to services. It should also assess the impact of such changes after implementation.

Instead of the HOSC, the HWBs created by HSCA 2012 were set up to operate differently from these existing local authority scrutiny committees because, for the first time, officers (such as the director of adult social services, the director of children's services and the director of public health), CCGs and the local Healthwatch will have the same statutory status as councillors.

Health and wellbeing boards

The HWBs encourage work to improve local health and wellbeing outcomes, including (where appropriate) more joined-up working across the NHS, public health, social care and other services.

The boards have very limited formal powers. They are constituted as a partnership forum rather than an executive decision-making body. In most cases,

HWBs are chaired by a senior local authority elected member. The board must include a representative of each relevant CCG and local Healthwatch, as well as local authority representatives. The local authority has considerable discretion in appointing additional board members. Most have chosen not to invite providers to become formal members, though many engage with providers in other ways.

HWBs assess the current and future health and social care needs of the local community through JSNAs. JSNAs are based on a principle of analysing the available evidence on the local community's health and social care needs. This includes engaging and working with a wide range of local stakeholders such as patient groups, voluntary organisations and the public. Using the JSNA, HWBs jointly agree strategic priorities for local health and social care services in JHWSs. Taken together, JSNAs and JHWSs are intended to form the basis of commissioning plans across local health and care services (including public health and children's services) for CCGs, NHSE and local authorities. Boards are under a statutory duty to involve local people in the preparation of JSNAs and the development of JHWSs.

Guidance has been published to support HWBs, including:

- *New Partnerships, New Opportunities (November 2011)*: a resource to assist setting up and running health and wellbeing boards; and
- *Operating Principles for Health and Wellbeing Boards (October 2011)*: a resource to help board members consider how to create really effective partnerships across local government and the NHS.

A progress report published in March 2016, The force begins to awaken, a third review of the state of health and wellbeing boards concludes that a significant number of HWBs were beginning to play a genuine leadership role across local health and care systems, however their potential remained unfulfilled. Ironically this improvement in the performance of some HWBs coincided with the emergence of a more top down approach by NHSE with the introduction of sustainability and transformation plans, which introduced an alternative focus for system leadership across a larger geographical footprint. The STP approach represents a significant extension of central control over local decision-making with the necessary implications for the partnership and collaborative dynamic intended to be fulfilled by HWBs.

HWBs in their entirety remain accountable to communities, service users and overview and scrutiny committees. All board members also have incentives to deliver on shared objectives to improve efficiency.

The Parliamentary and Health Service Ombudsman

The Parliamentary and Health Service Ombudsman (PHSO or 'the Ombudsman') is an independent crown servant appointed by the Queen. The Ombudsman's role is to independently investigate complaints that individuals have been treated unfairly or have received poor service from government departments and other public organisations and the NHS in England. Although the service has separate parliamentary and health functions, both come under the same Ombudsman. The Ombudsman can look at complaints about the actions of providers of NHS care, as well as commissioners, and also at complaints about the DH, NHSE, the CQC and NHSI.

The Ombudsman is accountable to Parliament through the Public Administration and Constitutional Affairs Committee. In law, the Ombudsman is a corporation sole and has a personal jurisdiction. This is not consistent with modern requirements of good governance and in January 2013, the Ombudsman established a unitary board, which combined and replaced the previous executive and advisory boards. The board is chaired by the Ombudsman and is the top-level decision-making body in the organisation. In addition, an executive team has been established which is responsible for the day-to-day management of PHSO and is accountable to the board for implementing its decisions. The executive team is chaired by the chief executive. The Ombudsman has the right to disagree with the board's decisions – reflecting their statutory accountability – but will do so only as a last resort and will put their reasons in writing to the board. The Ombudsman is independent of the NHS. Advised by HM Treasury, contractual responsibility for the chief executive officer (CEO) to be the Accountable Officer with executive responsibility for effective control arrangements was established. This enables the Ombudsman, as Accounting Officer, to have a separate, accountable person charged with stewardship of public money. The CEO carries principal responsibility for the use of resources against strategic and annual plans.

The Ombudsman had already set out principles which were intended to promote a shared understanding of what is meant by good complaint handling and to help public bodies in the Parliamentary and Health Service Ombudsman's jurisdiction deliver first-class complaint handling to all their customers. The Francis report prompted the Prime Minister and the Secretary of State for Health to commission a review of NHS hospital complaints handling, co-chaired by the Rt Hon Ann Clwyd and Professor Tricia Hart, which endorsed these principles.

Following the publication of this review, the PHSO suggested that NHS organisations use the option of self-referral for the most serious cases to the PHSO for independent investigation. This allows the PHSO to play its part in delivering justice, discovering what went wrong and ultimately helping the NHS to restore public trust in what is such a key public service.

From April 2016, the Independent Patient Safety Investigation Service (IPSIS) will offer support and guidance to NHS organisations on investigations into the most serious complaints and carry out some investigations itself.

For local authority services and for services paid for by local authorities, patients can take their cases to the Local Government Ombudsman. The DH established an independent review in 2013 to consider the handling of concerns and complaints; this recommended legislative changes to provide for a single Local Government Ombudsman in England, presiding over an integrated process for handling complaints against bodies within the jurisdiction of the Local Government Ombudsman Service.

Figure 3.3: Ways the public can influence health and social care services

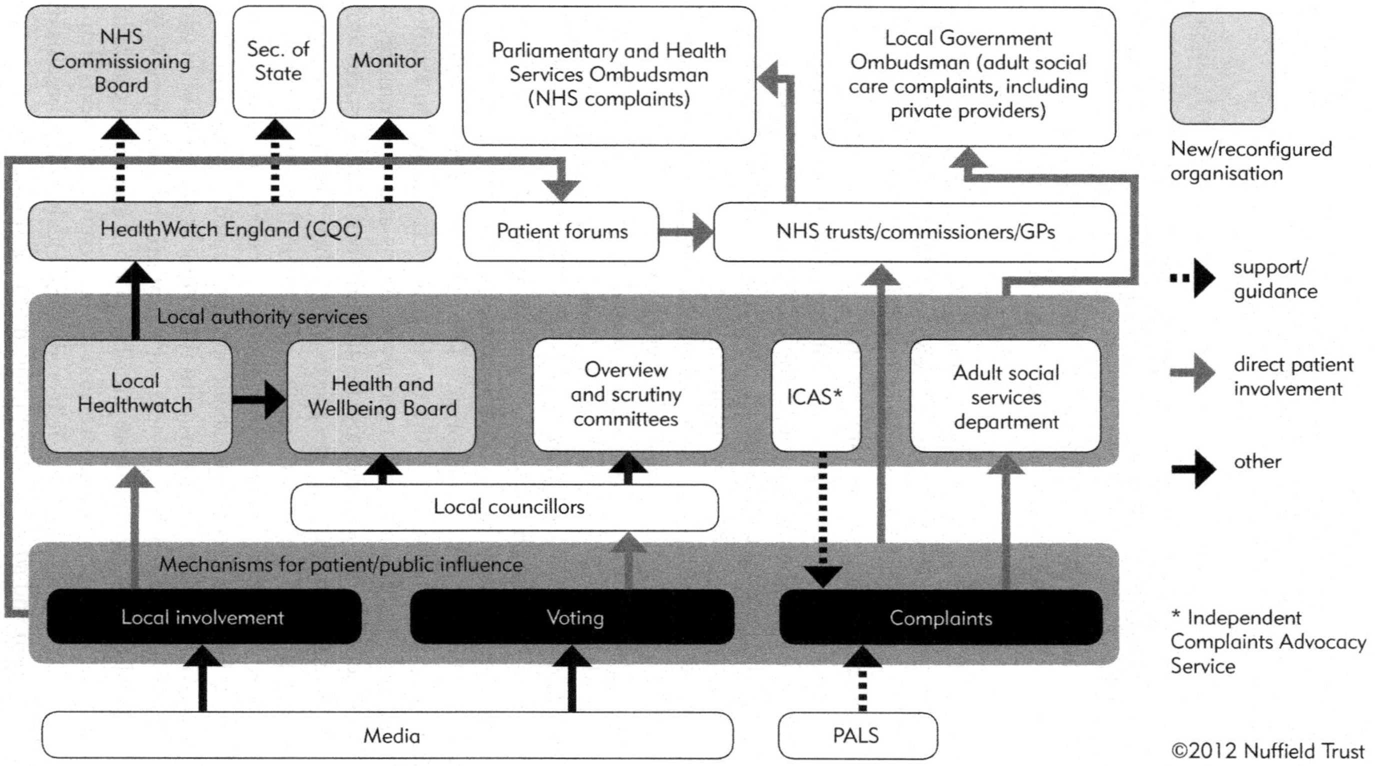

Source: © Nuffield Trust

Figure 3.3 sets out how members of the public can influence their health and social care services.

Healthwatch England and Local Healthwatch

The Healthwatch network consists of two connected levels:

- Healthwatch England works at the national level and supports local Healthwatch organisations. It takes local experiences of health and care and uses them to influence national policy with CQC, NHSE, Monitor and local authorities.
- A local Healthwatch organisation covers every local authority area in England. They take the experiences that people have of local care and use them to help shape local services.

Healthwatch England is the consumer champion for both health and social care, and has a role in gathering people's views on their local health and care services. When established, the organisation was hosted by the CQC but reported directly to the DH. However in January 2016, after the departure of its first chief executive, it was announced that a new national director would be appointed who would report to the chief executive of the CQC. Interestingly this new national director is still expected to criticise the workings of the CQC where appropriate, despite the conflict created by reporting to the CQC CEO.

Healthwatch's role is to provide national leadership, support and advice to local Healthwatch organisations and to ensure that the collective voice of patients has a direct route into the CQC's decision-making processes operating independently from the CQC. NHSE can escalate concerns about health and social care services raised by local Healthwatch, users of services and members of the public to the CQC. Healthwatch England is also able to provide advice and information (which could include making recommendations and reports) to the Secretary of State, NHSE, NHSI and local authorities. The recipients of Healthwatch England's advice are required in law to respond to Healthwatch England in writing.

The aim of local Healthwatch is to give citizens and communities a stronger voice to influence and challenge how health and social care services are provided within their area. They enable people to share their views and concerns about their local health and social care services to help build a picture of where services are doing well and where they can be improved. Local Healthwatch can also alert Healthwatch England to concerns about specific health and care providers, as well as provide people with information about their choices and what to do when things go wrong – including supporting people who want to complain about NHS services.

Local Healthwatch organisations are able to enter and view certain health and social care premises, produce reports and make recommendations that influence the way services are designed and delivered. Local Healthwatch organisations provide information and advice to the public about local services, and pass on views to Healthwatch England. They can also make recommendations to Healthwatch

England and the CQC. If a local Healthwatch organisation sends a report or recommendation to a specified provider or commissioner of a local health or social care service, the provider or commissioner is legally obliged to respond to the local Healthwatch organisation in writing.

The Local Government Association (LGA) and the DH jointly published a document in 2013 to help local Healthwatch audiences understand the legal requirements that have been set out in regulations. *Local Healthwatch Regulations Explained* aims to explain and provide clarity in relation to the following issues:

- layperson and volunteer involvement in local Healthwatch
- restrictions on activities of a political nature.

Supporting the health and care system

Special health authorities

Special health authorities are health authorities that provide a health service to the whole of England, not just to a local community. They have been set up to provide a national service to the NHS or the public under section 9 of the NHS Act 1977. They are independent, but can be subject to ministerial direction in the same way as other NHS bodies.

NHS Improvement

From 1 April 2016, NHSI was established, which is the operational name for an organisation that incorporates:

- NHS Trust Development Authority (NHS TDA) (regulator for NHS trusts)
- Monitor (regulator for FTs)
- Patient Safety
- the National Reporting and Learning System
- Advancing Change Team
- Intensive Support Teams.

NHSI is led by a unitary board consisting of non-executive and executive directors, although it needs to be recognised that both the statutory organisations of NHS TDA and Monitor remain in existence. The NHS TDA was established as a special health authority in June 2012 and Monitor was established as an executive non-departmental public body of the DH.

NHSI is responsible for overseeing FTs, NHS trusts and independent providers that provide NHS-funded care. It offers the support these providers need to give patients consistently safe, high quality, compassionate care within local health systems that are financially sustainable. By holding providers to account and, where necessary, intervening, it aims to help the NHS to meet its short-term challenges and secure its future. It works closely with NHSE and CQC to ensure alignment and collaboration of support and accountability.

NHSI has set five themes as its strategic objectives. These are in line with Implementing the Forward View. These themes are:

- Leadership and improvement capability
- Quality
- Finance and use of resources
- Operational performance
- Strategic change.

Licensing regime

The statutory obligations of Monitor and TDA, however, continue within NHSI. Therefore, NHSI must ensure the operation of a licensing regime over all eligible NHS providers in line with Monitor's main duty to protect and promote patients' interests by ensuring that health care services are provided effectively, efficiently and economically, while the quality of services is maintained or improved. It has also assumed Monitor's responsibility with respect to:

- Regulating prices: NHSI is responsible for designing a pricing methodology and calculating the efficiency requirements for the sector. This will then be used to set prices in agreement with the NHSE.
- Enabling integrated care and preventing anti-competitive behaviour: NHSI's role as the sector regulator will be to work with others, particularly commissioners, to remove any barriers and consider how to enable integrated care provision where this is in the interests of patients.
- Supporting service continuity: NHSI will support commissioners to ensure that, in the rare event of the failure of a healthcare provider, patients could continue to access the care that they need.

NHSI now oversees the provision of all provider licenses. These have been required by all providers of healthcare services for the purposes of the NHS since April 2014, unless they qualify for one of the following exemptions:

- providers that are not required to register with the CQC
- small providers of NHS-funded healthcare services whose annual turnover from providing NHS services is less than £10 million
- providers of primary medical and dental services
- providers of NHS continuing healthcare and NHS-funded nursing care
- NHS trusts (which will only be licensed when they are authorised as NHS foundation trusts).

Whilst NHS trusts are exempt from the requirement to apply for and hold the licence, directions from the Secretary of State require NHSI to ensure that NHS trusts comply with conditions equivalent to the licence as it deems appropriate. This includes giving directions to an NHS trust where necessary to ensure compliance.

The exemptions don't apply (apart from the exemption for NHS trusts) if the provider provides essential NHS-funded services designated by a commissioner as commissioner requested services. Two criteria have to be met in order to be granted a licence:

- registration with the CQC
- directors or governors must meet the CQC fit and proper persons test.

The types of services provided determine the conditions that need to meet as a licensee. There are a number of universal requirements of all licensees:

- General conditions: There are nine general conditions such as providing and publishing information, paying fees, fit and proper persons requirements, and a requirement for providers to be registered with the CQC.
- Integrated care condition: This allows the regulator to take action if the provider acts in a way that is detrimental to the delivery of integrated care.
- Choice and competition conditions: This requires providers to notify patients when they have a right of choice of provider, and to tell patients where they can find information about the choices they have; it also aims to prevent anti-competitive behaviour that is not in the interests of patients.
- Pricing conditions: This requires providers to comply with the national tariff and to provide the regulator with information on costing.

The additional requirements for licensees who supply commissioner requested services is the continuity of services conditions which require providers to meet certain conditions, so that if they get into very serious financial difficulty the regulator can step in and ensure the services can continue to be provided on a sustainable basis. There are additional conditions for FTs which are set out in Chapter 12.

NHSI can take action such as making sure the provider takes corrective action and, in certain circumstances, can impose a fine:

- if a licence condition or a requirement to provide information is breached
- if NHS services are provided without holding a licence when required to have one.

There is no requirement on providers to re-register every year. Instead, they have to complete a simple annual self-certification that confirms their continued eligibility to hold an NHS provider licence. Indeed for the first time in 2017, NHS Trusts have been required to self certificate on conditions G6(3) and FT4(8) of the licence.

The introduction of the 5YFV, which requires collaboration and cross-system working has resulted in NHSI and NHSE having to consider how the pricing mechanism will support such a collaborative system and the impact on choice and competition which are governed by specific rules laid down by Parliament, such as the Competition Act 1998 and the Procurement, Choice and Competition Regulations 2013.

Regulatory framework

To deliver the statutory obligations of both NHS TDA and Monitor, NHSI intends to work closely, alongside providers, with national partners to create the conditions for providers to flourish and has developed a single definition of success. At the same time, the NHSI must also hold provider boards to account, and intervene if necessary.

During 2016/17, NHSI introduced a Single Oversight Framework (SOF) based on the principle of earned autonomy and that segments providers according to the extent to which they meet the single definition of success. The single definition of success will incorporate:

- Quality, i.e. CQC's quality assessment, and five key questions (safe, effective, caring, responsive and well-led), supplemented with real-time information. Success will represent a CQC rating of 'Good' or better.
- Finance and use of resources, i.e. NHS Improvement and CQC are co-developing a methodology for assessing providers' use of resources. This will reflect the recommendations of the Carter Review.
- Operational performance, which will focus on the delivery of a small number of core NHS standards and targets for acute, mental health, community and ambulance trusts. This may include A&E waiting times, referral to treatment times, cancer treatment times, ambulance response times, access to mental health services and progress on implementation of seven-day services.
- Leadership and improvement capability which will build on existing governance tools like the Well-Led Framework to set out a single, shared system view on what good leadership looks like.
- Strategic change which will require the development in conjunction with partners on the 5YFV board of an assessment tool to assess how well trusts are delivering the strategic changes set out in the 5YFV. This will include new care models, based on areas' sustainability and transformation plans and, where relevant, devolution.

Under the SOF providers will be segmented based on how closely they meet the NHSI single definition of success. Higher performing providers will be allowed greater freedoms, including fewer data and monitoring requirements and simpler processes for transactions. More challenged providers will be given more direct and tailored support to help stabilise and improve their performance.

Segmentation is not intended to give an overall assessment of a provider's performance, for which the CQC's rating is the benchmark; nor does it determine the specifics of the support package needed, which is tailored by teams working with the provider in question. NHSI propose segmenting the sector into four, depending on the extent of any issues identified in the oversight process:

1. No potential concerns identified across the five themes – lowest level of oversight.

2. Triggering criteria of concern in one or more of the five themes – but not in breach of licence (or equivalent for NHS trusts) and/or formal licence action not needed.
3. Serious issues – the provider is in actual/suspected breach of the licence (or equivalent for NHS trusts).
4. Critical issues – the provider is in actual/suspected breach of its licence (or equivalent for NHS trusts) with very serious/complex issues (e.g. including providers requiring major intervention on multiple issues to return to sustainable performance).

The SOF has replaced Monitor's Risk Assessment Framework and governance and finance risk ratings, as well the NHS TDA's Assessment Framework. The board of directors is the first line of regulation in provider trusts (i.e. both FTs and NHS trusts), and NHSI requires board's to submit an annual plan and regular financial and operational reports. If NHSI considers that problems are developing then it will ensure that the provider trusts has an action plan in place and will monitor progress against that plan. NHSI has assumed all of NHS TDA's and Monitor's powers to intervene in a provider trust in the event of failings in its healthcare standards, as judged by the CQC, or other aspects of its leadership that result in a significant breach of its licence conditions.

NHSI assesses a breach or a potential breach of the governance and continuity of service licence conditions through a risk-based system of regulation. This determines the intensity of the monitoring undertaken at each provider trust. Its intervention powers are broad, ranging from closing a specific service – if there are serious concerns about it – and requiring a board either to take or not take a specific action(s), to requiring a board to obtain external advice on a particular issue or – in extreme cases – removing any or all of the directors (or governors in the case of an FT) and appointing replacements.

In the most serious cases, where intervention by NHSI cannot resolve the breach, a provider trust could be dissolved after consultation. If this were to happen, the Health and Social Care (Community Health and Standards) Act 2003 provides mechanisms to ensure that NHS patients and users continue to receive high-quality treatment.

Reporting and planning requirements

The framework divides the information NHSI may routinely request into four broad categories:

- annual submissions (plans, statutory reporting requirements of the licence holder, and other annual requirements specified in the licence)
- in-year submissions (financial and other service performance information submitted during the year, generally quarterly)
- exception reports (other information that may have material implications for a licence holder's compliance, but which are not routinely requested by NHSI)

- other information from provider trusts (such as the Well-Led Framework reviews).

Annual Submissions

The *NHS Operational Planning and Contracting Guidance 2017–2019* is joint guidance from NHSE and NHSI for the annual planning process. For the first time the guidance covers two financial years and is underpinned by a two-year tariff and two-year NHS Standard Contract. This is intended to support the STP process and, from April 2017, each STP (or agreed population/geographical area) will have a financial control total that is also the summation of the individual organisational control totals. All organisations will be held accountable for delivering both their individual control total and the overall system control total. It will be possible to flex individual organisational control totals within that system control total, by application and with the agreement of NHSE and NHSI. Plans will need to demonstrate:

- how they will be delivering the nine 'must-dos' for the health economy:
  - STPs
  - finance
  - primary care
  - urgent and emergency care
  - referral to treatment times and elective care
  - cancer
  - mental health
  - people with learning difficulties
  - improving quality in organisations;
- how they support delivery of the local STP with credible milestones and deliverables;
- how they intend to reconcile finance with activity and workforce to deliver their agreed contribution to the relevant system control total;
- robust, stretching and deliverable activity plans which are directly derived from their STP;
- how local independent sector capacity should be factored into demand and capacity planning from the outset, and local independent sector providers engaged throughout;
- the planned contribution to savings;
- how risks have been jointly identified and mitigated; and
- the impact of new care models.

CCG and provider plans will need to be jointly agreed by NHSE and NHSI, with a clear expectation that they must be fully aligned in local contracts.

In-year submissions

In-year reporting is designed to measure and assess the trusts actual performance against its annual plan. Trusts are monitored depending on their segmentation;

for most trusts, in-year reporting includes a quarterly submission to NHSI and other exception or ad hoc reports. Segment 1 or 2 trusts may be asked to make six-monthly reports to NHSI, while segment 3 or 4 trusts may have to report each month. The reports cover the trust's financial performance – including income and expenditure, a statement of financial position and cash flow performance – and its performance against national access and outcomes standards (e.g. waiting times and 18-week referral to treatment times).

NHSI reviews the performance against the trust's annual plan and looks at the board's assessment of its compliance with its licence or equivalent requirements (NHS trusts). If there is a significant difference between the in-year submissions and the annual plan, the board will have to explain why and what it is doing to address the difference. Each quarter, NHSI publishes an overview of the whole provider sector's performance, using the information the trusts provide.

Exception reports

Exception reports are reports on issues that could affect the trust's ability to comply with its licence or equivalent. These must be sent to NHSI, even if it is not routinely requested. Examples of these issues might include:

- investigations being opened by other authorities
- patient safety incidents or 'never' events
- any significant reputational issues such as any adverse national press attention
- any change in the board.

NHSI intends to work closely with the CQC to align its approaches as they move towards a single combined assessment of quality and use of resources. This will impact on the revision of the Well-Led Framework as set out in Chapter 4. More detail on NHSI regulatory role is included later in the section on Special Measures on page 91.

NHS Litigation Authority

The NHS Litigation Authority (NHSLA) was established in 1995 as a special health authority as a not-for-profit part of the NHS. It provides indemnity cover for legal claims against the NHS, assists the NHS with risk management, shares lessons from claims and provides other legal and professional services for its members. As a Special Health Authority, the NHSLA is an arm's length body of the DH. It is an independent body, but can be subject to ministerial direction. The NHSLA has a unitary board consisting of a non-executive chair, four other non-executive members and four executive members, holding the offices of the CEO and accounting officer (AO), chief finance officer (CFO), and such other executive appointments as required by legislation. The Secretary of State appoints the chair, and other non- executive directors. The DH principal accounting officer appoints the chief executive. The chair, chief executive and other non-executive directors are responsible for appointing the executive directors.

In April 2017 the three main functions of the NHSLA were brought together under the umbrella name, NHS Resolution. The focus of NHS Resolution will be on prevention and learning and early intervention to avoid unnecessary court action. NHS Resolution will:

- Improve the experience for patients, families and healthcare staff, with support for candour and the learning which goes hand in hand with a claim for compensation.
- Resolve concerns and disputes fairly and effectively to deliver resolution in its broadest sense, which is about more than just money.
- Provide analysis and expert knowledge to the healthcare and civil justice systems, to drive improvement.
- Deliver in partnership, interventions and solutions that prevent harm, improve safety and save money.
- Expand its role of sharing learning through the development of interventions, in partnership with others, to improve patient safety and prevent future harm.

Its primary focus for the future is to resolve concerns fairly. It will also have a duty to use what it learns from claims to help prevent the same thing happening again.

The NHS Blood and Transplant Authority

The NHS Blood and Transplant Authority is responsible for the supply of blood, organs, plasma and tissues across the NHS. It was established by legislation in 2005.

National bodies

There are a number of other bodies or authorities involved in the provision or organisation of NHS services. They have responsibility for things that are most effectively carried out or coordinated at the national level. Some examples are as follows.

The National Institute for Health and Care Excellence (NICE) is the main source of evidence-based guidance and advice for health and social care practitioners, patients, service users and the public on the most effective way to prevent, diagnose and treat disease and ill health. NICE produces quality standards – concise sets of statements that describe what high-quality care looks like for a particular condition or patient group – which are used to drive up the quality of health and care services. In April 2013 it was established in primary legislation, becoming an executive non-departmental public body (ENDPB) as set out in HSCA 2012. At this time it also took on responsibility for developing guidance and quality standards in social care. As an ENDPB, it is accountable to the DH, but operationally it is independent of government. The NICE Board sets the strategic priorities and policies, but the day-to-day decision-making is the responsibility of the Senior Management Team (SMT).

The Medicines and Healthcare Products Regulatory Agency is responsible for ensuring that medicines and medical devices work and are acceptably safe. It was created by Parliament as an executive agency of the DH and is overseen by a unitary board consisting of the MHRA's chairman, nine non-executive directors and two executive members (chief executive and chief operating officer (COO)). The non-executive members are appointed by the Secretary of State following open competition.

The Human Fertilisation and Embryology Authority (HFEA) is the UK's independent regulator of treatment using eggs and sperm and of treatment and research involving human embryos. They set standards and issue licences to fertility clinics. It is an ENDPB, operating under the provisions in the Human Fertilisation and Embryology Act 1990, as amended. Under the 1990 Act, the HFEA is statutorily independent of government but works in partnership with the DH. It is led by a board made up of a non-executive chair appointed by the Secretary of State; a deputy chair and ten authority members, also appointed by the Secretary of State. The board appoints the chief executive, who is not a member of the board.

Education and training

Health Education England

Originally established as a Special Health Authority in 2012, Health Education England (HEE) is now a non-departmental public body (NDPB), as of 1 April 2015, under the provisions of the Care Act 2014. HEE is responsible for promoting high-quality training and education, undertaking national planning and leadership, allocating financial resources, monitoring outcomes and securing the required supply of qualified staff. Long-term national planning is needed because a medical student graduating today will still be providing care in 2050. The DH sets the HEE's direction and its expectations for the whole education and training system through a document called the Education Outcomes Framework. The DH holds the operationally independent HEE board of directors to account for HEE's performance.

Clinical senates

Clinical senates are advisory groups of experts from across health and social care. They are non-statutory bodies and do not have a legal duty to commission health services. There are 12 senates covering areas across England providing strategic clinical advice and leadership across a broad geographical area to CCGs, health and wellbeing boards and NHSE. Senates are formed by clinical leaders from across the healthcare system, as well as those from social care and public health. Patients and members of the public will also be involved. They work with strategic clinical networks, academic health science networks, local education and training boards and research networks to develop an alignment of these organisations to support improvements in quality.

Safeguarding patients' interests

Organisations providing NHS services are regulated to ensure they meet essential standards. The boards of organisations providing NHS care have the primary responsibility to ensure the care they provide is safe and high quality. Regulators exist to ensure providers are fulfilling their obligations to patients and the public.

The system of regulation is independent from the government and from the NHS itself. It exists to ensure that the care patients receive is safe and of acceptable quality. The regulators also make sure the bodies or healthcare professionals they regulate are sound and fit for purpose.

The 2013 Francis Report identified a lack of clarity about the roles of NHS regulatory organisations. In response, the government announced that the CQC would focus on assessing the level of quality of care for NHS FTs and NHS trusts whilst Monitor and the NHS TDA would focus on using their powers, where necessary, to intervene to resolve quality failings. There has been further alignment and clarification with the amalgamation of Monitor and the NHS TDA under the umbrella of NHSI.

Care Quality Commission

From April 2009, the safety and quality regulator for all health services has been the CQC, which is also responsible for the regulation of adult social care services. The CQC is responsible for assessing and making judgments as to the level of safety and quality of care provided by providers of health and social care. To make these assessments, CQC can look at information received from the provider itself, its patients, staff, and from other organisations, and also conducts its own inspections. Information is published on the CQC website.

Providers of healthcare (including hospitals, care homes, care delivered in the home, dentists, GPs, mental health and other specialist services such as hospices) must register with CQC in order to be able to carry on regulated activities, which include the provision of NHS-funded health services.

The CQC is a NDPB within the DH. The CQC board is the senior decision-making structure and it is accountable to the public, Parliament and the Secretary of State for Health. The DH and CQC agreed a Framework Document in 2010, which set out CQC's purpose, its governance and accountability, management and financial responsibilities and reporting procedures. It was last reviewed in 2014 and is due to be reviewed again in 2017 to take account of subsequent legislative changes.

The CQC's unitary board is made up of CQC's chair, non-executive members and executive members, including the chief executive and the three chief inspectors (namely, Hospitals, Adult Social Care and General Practice). It also includes the Chair of Healthwatch. All non-executive commissioners are public appointees, appointed by the Secretary of State.

The CQC's principal function in relation to healthcare is to:

- register healthcare providers (whether or not they provide services for the NHS);
- monitor compliance with registration requirements and, if necessary, use its enforcement powers to ensure all service providers meet those requirements;
- review and publish comparative information on organisations providing and commissioning healthcare, and undertake reviews or studies of particular types of care; and
- monitor the operation of the Mental Health Act 1983 and Mental Capacity Act 2005.

All healthcare providers are required to be registered with CQC and some of the emerging models of integrated care under STPs and the new vanguards as well as existing large and complex organisations now present challenges for CQC's current approach to registration. Their latest consultation Our next phase of regulation: A more targeted, responsive and collaborative approach (Cross-sector and NHS trusts) (December 2016) recognises that it needs to make sure that providers are clear about who has accountability for quality and that, where relevant, CQC adequately reflect the role of head office or board-level leadership when registering these types of organisation. The Next Phase consultation also recognises that the provider base is changing and so it is recommending just two assessment frameworks going forward, one for health care and one for adult social care. There will be additional sector-specific material such as core service inspection frameworks for acute hospitals.

The CQC have set out what good and outstanding care looks like and ensures that services meet fundamental standards below which care must never fall. These are:

- Person-centred care: Patients must have care or treatment that is tailored to them and meets their needs and preferences.
- Dignity and respect: Patients must be treated with dignity and respect at all times while they are receiving care and treatment.
- Consent: Patients (or anybody legally acting on their behalf) must give their consent before any care or treatment is given.
- Safety: Patients must not be given unsafe care or treatment or be put at risk of harm that could be avoided. Providers must assess the risks to the patient's health and safety during any care or treatment and make sure their staff have the qualifications, competence, skills and experience to keep patients safe.
- Safeguarding from abuse: Patients must not suffer any form of abuse or improper treatment while receiving care (e.g. neglect, degrading treatment, unnecessary or disproportionate restraint or inappropriate limits on their freedom).
- Food and drink: Patients must have enough to eat and drink to keep them in good health while they receive care and treatment.

- Premises and equipment: The places where patients receive care and treatment and the equipment used in it must be clean, suitable and looked after properly. The equipment used in a patient's care and treatment must also be secure and used properly.
- Complaints: Patients must be able to complain about their care and treatment. The provider of a patient's care must have a system in place so they can handle and respond to their complaint. They must investigate it thoroughly and take action if problems are identified.
- Good governance: The provider of a patient's care must have plans that ensure they can meet these standards. They must have effective governance and systems to check on the quality and safety of care. These must help the service improve and reduce any risks to the patient's health, safety and welfare.
- Staffing: The provider of a patient's care must have enough suitably qualified, competent and experienced staff to make sure they can meet these standards. Their staff must be given the support, training and supervision they need to help them do their job.
- Fit and proper staff: The provider of a patient's care must only employ people who can provide care and treatment appropriate to their role. They must have strong recruitment procedures in place and carry out relevant checks such as on applicants' criminal records and work history.
- Duty of candour: The provider of a patient's care must be open and transparent with them about your care and treatment. Should something go wrong, they must tell the patient what has happened, provide support and apologise.
- Display of ratings: The provider of a patient's care must display their CQC rating in a place where it can be seen. They must also include this information on their website and make the latest CQC report on their service available to them.

The regulatory aspect of the CQC's work is conducted through the inspections and CQC have now inspected every NHS healthcare provider using its core service inspection approach and will complete the first phase of inspections of most independent healthcare providers during 2017. The next phase approach is set out in its December 2016 consultation and CQC is proposing to focus their inspections on those core services where it has greatest concerns or where it believes quality might have improved. The new inspection approach will also assess the overall leadership of the trust based on the CQC's learning of the importance of leadership for the delivery of safe, high-quality care. This will include an assessment of how well trusts assure themselves that basic systems underpinning safe care are in place, for example learning from incidents. CQC's mixture of announced and unannounced inspections will continue and will still focus on the quality and safety of the care provided based on five key areas:

- safety
- effectiveness

- care
- responsiveness to people's need
- well-led.

From April 2017 the CQC will undertake more focused inspections on core services where there are concerns about the quality and safety of a service provided or where there have been perceived improvements in the quality of the service. In addition to the core services that the CQC selects to inspect (at least one core service will be inspected annually), the CQC will assess the overall leadership of the provider. This will include an assessment of how well the board assures itself that basic systems underpinning safe care are in place, e.g. learning from incidents. Comprehensive inspections will also continue and may happen at different times and will mostly be unannounced. Such inspections will only be carried out for newly registered providers or where there are significant concerns. The well-led focused inspection will be announced to ensure the appropriate interviews can be scheduled for designated trust employees.

Following each inspection the CQC will continue to publish an independent assessment of how the organisation performed. It will continue to rate services on a four-point scale of:

- Outstanding
- Good
- Requires Improvement
- Inadequate.

For planning purposes previous ratings will be used as a guide to setting maximum intervals for re-inspecting core services as follows:

- one year for ratings of Inadequate
- two years for ratings of Requires Improvement
- three and a half years for ratings of Good
- five years for ratings of Outstanding.

The CQC also reports annually to Parliament on how the health and social care systems are working overall. The State of Care in NHS Acute Hospitals 2014 to 2016 Report was published in March 2017 and captured the CQC learning from three years of inspections. Analysis of the ratings for acute non-specialist providers against financial performance shows a correlation between the ratings and provider deficits. Providers with higher CQC ratings tend to be better at balancing their budgets than those rated inadequate. Providers with better overall ratings tend to score better in the well-led domain. One of the main messages from the report was that effective leadership, which was values driven and had a strong culture of learning delivered high-quality care; this has led to a greater focus on the well-led domain aspect of the CQC approach.

The CQC is proposing a new single framework relating to well-led for all healthcare providers, developed jointly with NHSI as part of the commitment to promoting a single shared view of quality. As already mentioned there is a demonstrable link between leadership, culture and the delivery of safe, high-quality care, and the CQC's focus on well-led is intended to support and reinforce this link. The intention is to create a new Well-Led Framework for providers, building on the strengths of the previous version issued by Monitor and the NHS TDA, and to streamline it to cover system governance and leadership, leadership behaviours, promotion of an open and fair culture, and sustainability of high-quality, patient-centred care that supports learning and innovation. To support this single Well-Led Framework, the CQC and NHSI are also working together to recognise that effective use of resources is also fundamental to enable trusts to deliver and sustain high-quality services for patients. A joint consultation was published in parallel Consultation on the use of resources and well-led assessments (December 2016), which describes in detail how they intend to work together on these two aspects.

The CQC retains the power to inspect all registered healthcare providers and to suspend services, impose fines, prosecute or de-register organisations if it has evidence that suggests a serious problem that may be putting patients at risk. When a provider delivers a wide range of services or a more integrated model of care, the CQC will be able to bring specialist inspection teams together, and a single high-level process for each provider will enable this. The CQC also recognises that as services become larger and more complex, with a mix of service types delivered at different scales, it needs to consider how best to present its four-point score ratings at overall organisational level. The CQC may produce an organisational level rating for providers other than NHS trusts or FTs in the future.

As already mentioned above, this means that the assessment of leadership, through the CQC domain of well-led, will be of increasing importance for such new or complex models, given its significance for the sustainability, quality and safety of services. As such the other four domains will also have to be strengthened to encourage information sharing and co-ordinated care within and across services, organisations and local health economies. The CQC also wants to support providers that have taken over poor services because they want to improve them without penalising their organisational level rating and is consulting on this process to reduce any disincentives.

The CQC's Intelligent Monitoring is being replaced by a new Insight model. It will include a number of the indicators that were used previously along with a wider range of data sources. This will include qualitative information from people who use the services, relationship management, national partners and the new style provider information request.

In summary then, the overall provider rating will only be reviewed and updated following an organisation level well-led assessment and planned core service inspections. Reports will make clear whether a rating is based on the most recent or previous inspection. Aggregated ratings will be a combination of previously allocated and new ratings from recent on-site inspections. Providers will be required to display an updated grid.

Fit and proper persons and the duty of candour

Following the final report of the Mid Staffordshire NHS Foundation Trust Public Inquiry in February 2013, the government made a commitment to implement a statutory duty of candour. The August 2013 Berwick Review, entitled A Promise to Learn: A commitment to Act: Improving the Safety of Patients in England, recommended that, for serious incidents, CQC regulations should require that the patient or carer affected by a safety incident is notified and supported. However, the Berwick Review did not subscribe to an 'automatic' duty of candour, where patients were told about every error or near miss, as it was thought that this would lead to defensive documentation and large bureaucratic overheads that detracted from patient care. Following a consultation process by the CQC, The HSCA (Regulated Activities) Regulations 2014 came into force in October 2014 and set out both the statutory duty of candour and the 'fit and proper person' requirement for directors.

The contractual duty of candour had already been included in the NHS Standard Contract 2013/14, which required all providers to be open and honest with patients when things go wrong. The contractual duty imposed an obligation to report some adverse incidents, in restricted circumstances, to some patients and their families. It applied only to contracts for NHS and non-NHS providers of services to NHS patients. As with all duties which apply on a contractual basis, its terms were limited to those who signed the agreement. It did not apply to services commissioned under primary care contracts or to many private providers.

The duty of candour is now a statutory duty to be open and honest with patients (or 'service users'), or their families, when something goes wrong that appears to have caused or could lead to significant harm in the future. It applies to all health and social care organisations registered with the CQC in England. The key principles are:

- Care organisations have a general duty to act in an open and transparent way in relation to care provided to patients. This means that an open and honest culture must exist throughout an organisation.
- The statutory duty applies to organisations, not individuals, though it is clear from CQC guidance that it is expected that an organisation's staff cooperate with it to ensure the obligation is met.
- As soon as is reasonably practicable after a notifiable patient safety incident occurs, the organisation must tell the patient (or their representative) about it in person.
- The organisation has to give the patient a full explanation of what is known at the time, including what further enquiries will be carried out. Organisations

must also provide an apology and keep a written record of the notification to the patient.
- A notifiable patient safety incident has a specific statutory meaning: it applies to incidents where a patient suffered (or could suffer) unintended harm that results in death, severe harm, moderate harm or prolonged psychological harm. Severe and moderate harm definitions are derived from the National Patient Safety Agency (NPSA)'s Seven Steps to Patient Safety. Prolonged psychological harm means that it must be experienced continuously for 28 days or more.
- There is a statutory duty to provide reasonable support to the patient. Reasonable support could be providing an interpreter to ensure discussions are understood, or giving emotional support to the patient following a notifiable patient safety incident.
- Once the patient has been told in person about the notifiable patient safety incident, the organisation must provide the patient with a written note of the discussion, and copies of correspondence must be kept.

The thresholds for incidents can be confusing, as the threshold is lower for the doctor's ethical duty (any harm or distress caused to the patient) while the thresholds for the contractual and statutory duties are higher and slightly different (with the inclusion of prolonged psychological harm in the statutory duty).

More recently the National Quality Board has published its *National Guidance on Learning from Deaths* (March 2017) which sets out a framework for providers on identifying, reporting, investigating and learning from deaths in care. As a result of this publication, all providers are required to put the following recommendations in place:

- Regularly monitor, identify and review deaths in patients with a learning disability or mental health problem.
- Review the quality of investigations carried out by providers and implement improvements where necessary.
- Include learning from deaths in the provider's board report.
- Implement actions taken in response to learning from death.
- Further understanding in how families and carers can be involved in reviews and investigations.
- Update mortality review policy to include the recommendations outlined by the CQC.

The 'fit and proper person' requirement for directors was also introduced by the 2014 regulations and made it clear that directors and people in 'equivalent' positions of authority are personally responsible for the overall quality and safety of care. When a service is meeting the 'fit and proper person' requirement, its directors:

- will be of good character;
- with the necessary qualifications, skills and experience to be able to perform the role that they are appointed to;

- will supply information, such as certain checks and a full employment history; and
- will never have been responsible for, or involved in, any serious misconduct or mismanagement relating to any office or employment with a service provider.

More detail on this is provided in Chapter 6.

Special measures

Following the publication of the Francis Report, Sir Bruce Keogh led a review of 14 trusts (nine NHS FTs and five NHS trusts) that had high mortality rates. The Keogh Review identified significant problems relating to quality and safety and/or leadership in all 14 trusts. In July 2013, 11 of the 14 trusts were put into 'special measures'. This regime was new to the NHS and was set out in the *Guide to Special Measures* published jointly by the CQC, Monitor and NHS TDA.

Special measures apply to NHS trusts and FTs that have serious failures in quality of care and where there are concerns that existing management cannot make the necessary improvements without support. Special measures consist of a set of specific interventions designed to improve the quality of care within a reasonable time.

The CQC, through the Chief Inspector of Hospitals, will normally recommend that a trust is placed in special measures when an NHS trust or FT is rated 'Inadequate' in the well-led domain, i.e. there are concerns that the organisation's leadership is unable to make sufficient improvements in a reasonable timeframe without extra support, and 'Inadequate' in one or more of the other domains (safe, caring, responsive and effective).

When the NHSI receives a recommendation from the Chief Inspector to place an NHS trust or FT in special measures, the NHSI will consider the evidence that CQC provides to them alongside other relevant evidence. On the basis of the full range of information, the NHSI will make a decision whether the trust or FT will be placed in special measures.

The NHSI may also place a trust or FT into special measures without receiving a recommendation from the Chief Inspector, based on its own evidence. In these circumstances, the NHSI will always seek advice from CQC. An NHS trust or FT will not enter special measures until the NHSI formally makes that decision.

The NHSI will communicate its decision to the trust and then make a formal public announcement through a press release. The period of special measures begins when the NHSI formally and publicly announces that a trust is in special measures. It is intended that the usual period of time a trust remains in special measures will be a maximum of 12 months, although this may be extended in some circumstances.

The CQC will focus on identifying failures in the quality of care and judging whether improvements have been made. The NHSI will use their respective powers to support improvement in the quality of care provided.

Typically, providers will be subject to the following interventions, although their detailed application will vary according to the specific circumstances of the organisation.

- The NHSI will appoint an improvement director who will act on their behalf to provide assurance of the trust's approach to improving performance.
- In most cases, the NHSI will also appoint one or more appropriate partner organisations to provide support in improvement. Partner organisations are selected for their strength in the areas of weakness at the trust in special measures. The nature and amount of support from the partner will be tailored to the trust's requirements but will focus on addressing quality issues identified in the trust's action plan. Arrangements for this appointment will be set out in a memorandum of understanding between the NHSI and the partner ('buddy') organisation. Partner organisations will be reimbursed by NHSI for reasonable expenses and may receive an incentive payment.
- The NHSI will review the capability of the trust's leadership. If needed, this may lead to changes to the management of the organisation to make sure that the board and executive team can make the required improvements.
- The NHSI will require trusts in special measures to publish their progress against action plans every month on the NHS Choices and their own website, and to participate as required in national and local press conferences.

The CQC report Special measures: one year on gave an overview of the progress made by the 11 trusts that were placed in special measures. The Chief Inspector of Hospitals concluded that significant progress had been made at ten of the 11 trusts.

- Two had made exceptional progress and had been rated 'Good' overall.
- Three had made good progress. Although they still required further improvement, the Chief Inspector recommended they should exit special measures with ongoing support.
- The Chief Inspector recommended five trusts remain in special measures whilst ongoing improvement work was carried out.
- One trust had failed to make significant overall progress and continued in special measures for a further three years, only being rated as good in March 2017.

A provider will only come out of special measures if it has made the required improvements. This is usually expected to take place within one year, however, as can be seen by Medway and North Cumbria, for some providers it can take a number of years. It is for the relevant Chief Inspector to inspect the provider and judge whether improvements have been made and if it is delivering good enough care to exit special measures. The NHSI will only take a provider out of special measures after it has been re-inspected, is no longer rated as 'inadequate' in the 'well-led' domain and has made progress across the other four CQC domains. The NHSI must also be confident that improvements will be sustained.

An inspection and recommendation from the CQC Chief Inspector may result in a range of outcomes for a provider in special measures that includes:

- exit from special measures
- exit after an extension period
- continuing in special measures where the NHSI has concerns that the provider may not be able to sustain improvements without special measures in place. In this instance, special measures may run in parallel to processes which will consider longer-term solutions, such as a transaction such an acquisition or merger.

In some circumstances, a transaction may be the best means of securing longer-term improvements in the quality of care. In these circumstances, the resulting organisation (whether an acquiring parent organisation, new entity formed by merger, and so on) itself would not automatically be placed into special measures at the point of transaction. The resulting organisation would be assessed on its own merits and regulated accordingly by the CQC and the NHSI, which would take full account of the nature of the quality problems being taken on within the resulting organisation and how it, as a whole, was seeking to address them.

Since the original Keogh review and creation of special measures, a number of other providers have been placed in special measures due to quality issues. At the same time, the financial context has also led to a growing number of commissioners and providers being placed in 'financial' special measures. NHSI, in partnership with NHS England, is using a suite of measures for providers and commissioners to restore financial discipline and help ensure ongoing financial sustainability for the NHS. NHSI and NHSE placed several challenged NHS providers and commissioners in financial special measures in order to bring about swift improvement in their finances. As part of this each organisation undergoes a rapid financial review, and agrees a financial recovery plan. Specialist teams, led by a financial improvement director, oversee intensive, accelerated action to bring about financial improvement, including support from peer organisations where appropriate. Each organisation receives a package of support designed to achieve rapid financial improvement, whilst maintaining or improving quality. The support can include:

- ensuring that financial systems and controls operate effectively, so that money isn't being spent without proper checks and controls – including, for example, in the authorisation of agency and locum spend
- improving efficiency and productivity, including learning lessons from higher performing organisations
- improving the way workforce is managed and rotas planned to use permanent staff most effectively
- ensuring commissioners and providers charge and get paid appropriately for the work carried out.

In order to leave financial special measures, organisations have to demonstrate rapidly that they are returning to financial discipline, which includes developing a robust financial recovery plan. Once out of financial special measures, NHSI and NHSE continue to work extremely closely with each organisation to ensure that the improvements are lasting and that recovery plans are carried out properly. Organisations in financial special measures are expected to maintain, and where necessary, improve standards of quality during and after their financial recovery. NHSI published Criteria for exit from financial special measures in February 2017.

By May 2017 there were nine trusts in financial special measures and 15 trusts in quality special measures.

The Human Tissue Authority

The Human Tissue Authority is an independent watchdog set up in 2005 following events in the 1990s that revealed a culture in hospitals of removing and retaining human organs and tissue without consent. The legislation that established the Authority not only addressed this issue but also updated and brought together other laws that related to human tissue and organs. It protects the public's interest by licensing and inspecting organisations that store and use human tissues and organs for purposes such as research, patient treatment, transplantation, post-mortem examination, teaching and public exhibitions. It was created by Parliament as an executive agency of the DH and is overseen by lay and professional members appointed by the government.

Professional regulators

There are a number of regulatory bodies that are responsible for the regulation of healthcare professionals. An example is the General Medical Council (GMC), which regulates doctors, and the Nursing and Midwifery Council (NMC), which regulates nurses and midwives.

The professional regulators are independent bodies responsible to Parliament that register and regulate the training and practice of health professionals. They safeguard the safety and the quality of the care that patients receive from health professionals. This includes dealing with concerns about misconduct raised by patients, their families or other professionals. Professional regulators certify new practitioners and ensure that they maintain standards and remain fit to practice.

Health professionals can be reported to the relevant professional regulator and guidance is available on the website of the Council for Healthcare Regulatory Excellence (CHRE), which provides an oversight role on professional regulation.

Other examples include:

- doctors (GMC)
- nurses and midwives (NMC)
- dental teams (General Dental Council)

Figure 3.4: NHS regulatory relationships

Regulating and monitoring the quality of services

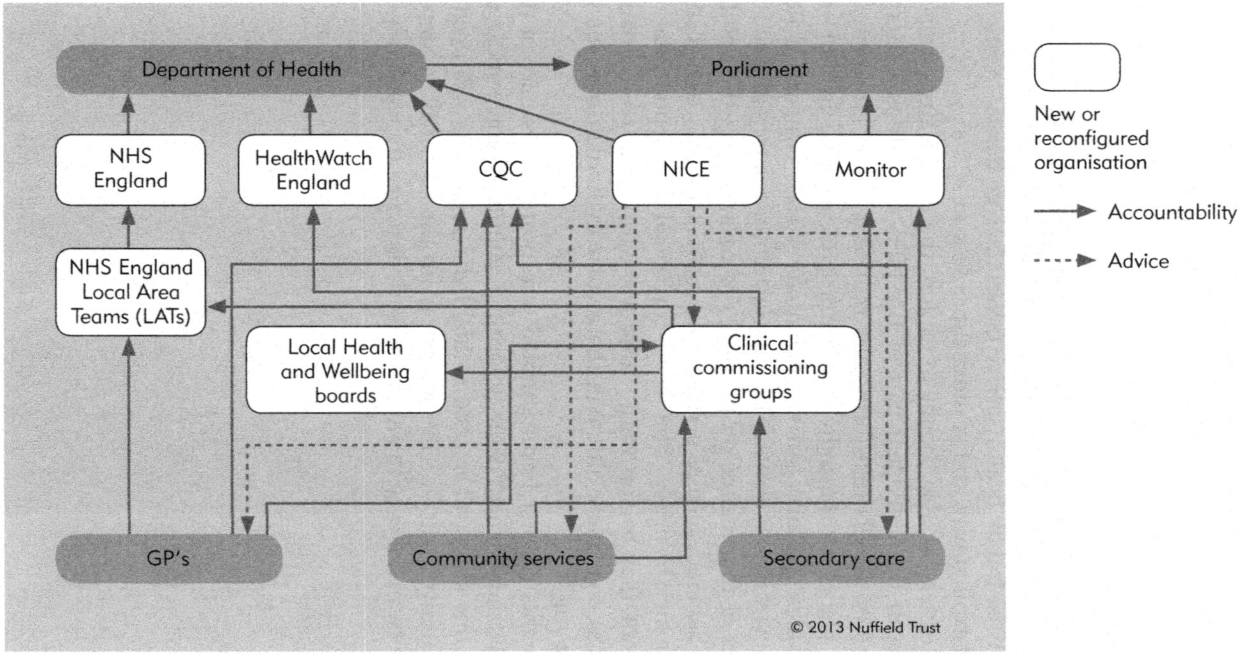

Source: © Nuffield Trust

- optical professionals (General Optical Council)
- pharmacists (General Pharmaceutical Council)
- chiropractors (General Chiropractic Council)
- osteopaths (General Osteopathic Council) and
- health, psychological and social work professionals (Health and Care Professions Council).

Figure 3.4 illustrates the regulatory relationships within the NHS.

Summary

This chapter has included a number of figures in an attempt to demonstrate the inter-relationships that exist within the NHS landscape. Every single part of the structure is bound by health service governance guidance – sometimes in a very direct and explicit way, and at other times less so.

The chapter has also sought to explore the complexity of relationships that exist between the individual part of the NHS as well as setting out the clear accountability models that form each individual part. This complexity and the burden it places on the individual parts is clearly and helpful explored in the NHS Providers member survey in January 2017 – Impact of Regulation in a Shifting Environment outlines how the current regulatory regime is operating and the impact of that regime on provider organisations on their ability to manage increased demand, restore performance against targets, transform services and achieve financial balance. The report confirmed a perception that the regulatory environment may be starting to improve, with better co-ordination and alignment across regulators, although the regulatory burden remains high and is in fact increasing.

Whilst this chapter has attempted to capture the essence of that landscape, there are further changes planned for the regulatory framework in the light of the 5YFV. As this chapter has tried to highlight, regulators will need to align their approach to oversight of STPs as set out in the recent Next steps on the NHS five year forward view, with any framework designed for regulation and oversight.

4

The law and other regulatory frameworks

Governance and the law

To a certain extent, best practice in both health service governance and corporate governance is imposed on organisations by the law or other regulations. There are two different approaches to establishing a system of best practice in governance. One approach is to establish voluntary principles and guidelines, and invite (or expect) organisations to comply with them.

A second approach is to establish laws and other regulations for governance that organisations must obey. In practice, many countries combine both of these approaches by establishing legal and regulatory requirements alongside voluntary principles and codes of conduct.

There is no corporate governance law in any country: rather, some aspects of corporate governance are regulated by sections of different laws. Other aspects of governance are not regulated by law at all, or are regulated only partially. Even in the US, where there is greater emphasis on regulation of corporate governance, many elements of 'best practice' in corporate governance are voluntary.

Similarly, there is no health service governance law for the NHS. Different aspects of public law and national legislation regulate some aspects of health service governance; there is also a raft of guidance and voluntary codes that have been established for use within the NHS.

It is inevitable that some aspects of health service governance practice are regulated by law, and that organisations should be required to comply with 'best practice'. Regulations on health service governance may be found in:

- healthcare law
- laws on patient and public involvement
- laws on transparency of information, mental capacity, human rights, bribery, corporate manslaughter etc.
- company law.

Healthcare law

The *National Health Service Act 1948* established the NHS in 1948. Since that time, there have been significant amendments and additions to the legislation, which has resulted in a fragmented and piecemeal approach to NHS healthcare law. Rather than list each amendment and addition since 1948, this section sets out the main items of legislation that result in the current form and structure of the NHS.

The *NHS Reorganisation Act 1973* provided for lines of authority from NHS providers up to the Secretary of State through the creation of 90 area health authorities (AHAs), which managed both hospitals and community health services. The AHAs were also given joint planning responsibilities with the local authorities. Beneath the AHAs were District Management Teams, which managed hospitals and family practitioner committees (FPCs) that took responsibility for administering contracts for general practitioners (GPs), dentists, pharmacists and opticians. The AHAs were under the supervision of 14 regional health authorities (RHAs), which operated from 1974 to 1996.

The *National Health Service Act 1977* set out the obligations of the Secretary of State to promote a comprehensive health service. The Secretary of State's national responsibilities were delegated to special heath authorities such as the National Blood Authority and National Institute for Health and Clinical Excellence (NICE), whilst their local responsibilities were delegated to AHAs. RHAs on behalf of the Secretary of State carried out the management of these functions.

The *Health Services Act 1980* abolished the AHAs and District Management Teams and replaced them with district health authorities (DHAs) in 1982.

The *National Health Service and Community Care Act 1990* set out how the NHS should assess and provide for patients based on their needs, requirements and circumstances. It established the split between 'purchasers' (health authorities and some family doctors, under the GP fundholding scheme), who were given budgets to commission healthcare; and 'providers' (acute hospitals, organisations providing care for the mentally ill, people with learning disabilities and the elderly, and ambulance services). The Act introduced the concept of the internal market and established the relationship between the purchasers and the providers as a contractual one. These contractual relationships operated at a common law level but were not judicially enforceable. As a result of the internal market, the state became an 'enabler' rather than a supplier of health and social care provision. The functions of NHS trusts (the 'providers') were partly determined by the 1990 Act and partly through each individual trust's establishment order. The Act also set out key statutory financial obligations such as the obligation to break even, to carry out functions effectively, efficiently and economically, and to hold a public meeting at which the annual report and audited accounts were presented.

The *NHS Trusts (Membership and Procedures) Regulations 1990* set out the composition of the board for NHS trusts, the criteria for appointment and tenure of the chair and non-executive directors (NEDs). It sets out the rules regarding the meetings and proceedings of NHS trusts and the appointment procedures for executive directors (EDs). It was updated by regulations in 1998 amending the size and composition of the board and in 2014 allowing existing NHS chairs or non-executive director to hold additional non-executive positions within other NHS organisations.

The *Health Authorities Act 1995* abolished regional health authorities, district health authorities and family health services authorities and established a single tier of health authorities.

The *Health Act 1999* abolished GP fund-holding in England, Wales and Scotland. The Act amended the National Health Service Act 1977 to make provision for the establishment of new statutory bodies in England and Wales, to be known as primary care trusts (PCTs), and provided for NHS trusts in Scotland to take on additional functions.

The *Health and Social Care Act 2001* was designed to deliver many of the aspects of the NHS Plan 2000 that required changes to primary legislation. The Act provided for a new form of trust, care trusts, to provide closer integration of health and social services. It outlined a new delivery system for the NHS, which provided for the commissioning of health and social care by care trusts under partnership arrangements. It also strengthened the arrangements for public and patient involvement in the NHS by providing for local authority OSCs (Oversight and Scrutiny Committee), whose role was to scrutinise the NHS and to represent local views on the development of local health services. It also created a duty on NHS organisations to have arrangements for involving patients and the public in decision-making about the operation of the NHS. In addition, it legislated for:

- the establishment of the Healthcare Commission;
- regulations to be made about complaints procedures in both health and social services; and
- the Health Service Ombudsman to consider complaints about the handling of NHS complaints by any person or NHS body.

The *National Health Service Reform and Health Care Professions Act 2002* provided for amendment of the structural framework of the NHS. The Act renamed health authorities as statutory health authorities (SHAs) and conferred most of their functions onto PCTs. NHS resources were to be allocated directly to the PCTs by the Secretary of State. Service planning would be undertaken by the PCTs, with the SHAs providing the performance management function for the health services provided within their boundaries. The Act also provided for the creation of an independent 'Patients' Forum' for every NHS trust and PCT in England, to perform an inspection, monitoring and representation role on behalf of patients and the public. The national Commission for Patient and Public Involvement in Health (CPPIH) was created to oversee this.

The *Health and Social Care (Community Health and Standards) Act 2003* provided for the establishment of NHS foundation trusts (FTs) that have the right to enter into legally enforceable contracts. The Act also established a new regulatory body for healthcare – the Commission for Healthcare Audit and Inspection (CHAI). It also repealed the statutory 'duty of quality' for services commissioned and provided by all NHS trusts, for which trust chief executives are accountable, established in the Health Act 1999 but restated the duty as: 'It is the duty of each NHS body to put and keep in place arrangements for the purpose of monitoring and improving the quality of health care provided by and for that body.' This duty was further reinforced by the principles of the NHS Constitution.

The *Directions to NHS bodies on Counter Fraud Measures 2004* set out that each NHS organisation must take all necessary steps to counter fraud in the NHS in accordance with the Directions and according to:

- the NHS Counter Fraud and Corruption Manual;
- the policy statement 'Applying appropriate sanctions consistently' published by the Counter Fraud and Security Management Service (CFSMS), now known as NHS Protect; and
- having regard to guidance or advice issued by NHS Protect.

Each NHS organisation must require its chief executive and director of finance to monitor and ensure compliance with these Directions and must cooperate with NHS Protect to enable the CFSMS efficiently and effectively to carry out its counter-fraud functions. Each NHS organisation must also designate a person to undertake specific responsibility for the promotion of counter fraud measures; in the case of an NHS trust this is to be one of the trust's NEDs and in the case of an NHS body other than an NHS trust, it must be one of that organisation's non-officer members.

The *National Health Service Act 2006 (NHS Act 2006)* redefined the structure of the NHS in England by consolidating much of the existing legislation concerning the health service. The consolidation repealed and re-enacted in its entirety the National Health Service Act 1977, which was itself a consolidation. It also incorporated provisions from:

- National Health Service and Community Care Act 1990;
- Health Authorities Act 1995;
- Primary Care Act 1997;
- Health Act 1999;
- Health and Social Care Act 2001;
- National Health Service Reform and Health Care Professions Act 2002;
- Health and Social Care (Community Health and Standards) Act 2003; and
- Health Act 2006.

The *Local Government and Public Involvement in Health Act 2007* reformed the existing arrangements (Patients' Forums) for patient and public involvement in the provision of health and social care services with the creation of Local Involvement Networks (LINks).

The *Health and Social Care Act 2008* established the Care Quality Commission (CQC), a single, integrated regulator for health and adult social care to replace the Healthcare Commission (health and adult social care regulator in England), the Commission for Social Care Inspection (social care regulator) and the Mental Health Act Commission (monitoring of Mental Health Act 1983).

The *Health Act 2009* set out the framework for how the NHS Constitution would operate, including a new legal duty on providers of NHS services in England and other relevant bodies to have regard to the Constitution; and a duty on the Secretary of State to consult on, review and re-publish the Constitution at least every ten years, and to report on its impact. The Act also placed a duty on NHS providers to produce Quality Accounts and gave the Secretary of State power to set out in regulations the content (including locally agreed elements), format and timing of Quality Accounts (see Chapter 16).

The Health Act 2009 also amended Chapter 5A of the NHS Act 2006 to introduce a special administration process. This made provision for the appointment of a Trust Special Administrator (TSA) over an NHS trust, where the Secretary of State considered it in the interests of the health service.

The key objective of a TSA appointed to an NHS trust is to develop and consult locally on a draft report and make recommendations to the Secretary of State in a final report about what should happen to the trust and the services it provides to ensure the continued provision of key services (location specific services). The legal framework sets out a maximum period of 120 working days for completion of the process (unless extended by order of the Secretary of State), by which time the Secretary of State must make a final decision on the future of the NHS trust following the TSA's recommendations.

With many hospitals facing significant financial difficulties as a result of a variety of complex factors, it is vital, both politically and socially, that NHS services are maintained. The Department of Health (DH) assesses NHS trusts according to their performance against a set of financial and quality indicators. If clinical or financial performance is below the required standard and does not improve then the Regime for Unsustainable Providers could be triggered under Chapter 5A of the NHS Act 2006 as the only way in which the DH can take decisive action to deal with NHS trusts that are either unsustainable in their current form or significantly failing to make progress towards attaining FT status.

The *Health and Social Care Act 2012 (HSCA 2012)* extended this regime to include FTs. It enables NHS Improvement (NHSI) to appoint a TSA where the FT is, or is likely to become, unable to pay its debts. The legal framework applicable to FTs is very similar to NHS trusts, although the timetable is longer to enable NHSI to be consulted (a period of 150 days, unless extended). The framework is different from an ordinary administration under general insolvency legislation in that its main objective is to protect patients and staff from failing services and secure the continued provision of patient services.

Since its inception, the regime has been used only twice – in relation to South London Healthcare NHS Trust (SLHT) and Mid Staffordshire NHS Foundation Trust (MSFT).

CASE STUDY: South London Healthcare NHS Trust

SLHT was formed on 1 April 2009 by merging three hospitals. At the time of the merger, these hospitals had a combined deficit of £21.3 million.

Following the merger, SLHT ran up debts of more than £150 million to become the most financially challenged trust in the NHS. As well as inheriting the financial difficulties of its three predecessor hospitals, six private finance initiative (PFI) schemes operated across the three main sites, adding to its deficit. As a result, SLHT was judged by the DH to be 'not financially viable in its current form' and the first ever TSA was appointed on 16 July 2012.

In accordance with the statutory timetable, on 1 February 2013 the Secretary of State for Health, Jeremy Hunt, made the final decision on the future of SLHT (following on from the recommendations made by the TSA). Ultimately, it was decided that:

- SLHT should be dissolved and its services transferred to other providers, including King's College Hospital NHS Foundation Trust, Lewisham and Greenwich NHS Trust and Oxleas NHS Foundation Trust;
- all vacant or poorly utilised premises should be vacated and sold where possible; and
- the DH should pay the excess costs of the PFI buildings at the Queen Elizabeth and Princess Royal Hospitals, and write off the accumulated debt of SLHT so that the other providers were not saddled with historic debts. The DH also agreed to negotiate an appropriate level of transitional funding to cover implementation.

Importantly, it was also decided that services at Lewisham hospital would be downgraded. This was significant because Lewisham hospital was part of the neighbouring Lewisham Healthcare NHS Trust and did not fall within the remit of SLHT.

The London Borough of Lewisham and a local campaign group called Save Lewisham Hospital applied for judicial review of the TSA's recommendations to scale back services offered at their local hospital and of the Secretary of State's decision to accept those recommendations. The judicial review application was brought on the basis that each NHS trust is a separate legal entity and that the Secretary of State had appointed the TSA only in relation to SLHT.

Both the High Court and the Court of Appeal held that the powers of a TSA appointed over an NHS trust were confined to that particular trust. The TSA's final report and the Secretary of State's decision were held to be *ultra vires* to the extent that they made recommendations about or affected the services provided by Lewisham Healthcare NHS trust at Lewisham hospital.

In his leading judgment, Lord Justice Sullivan held that:

> 'If Parliament wishes a TSA appointed in respect of a particular trust to make recommendations for action, not merely in relation to that Trust, but in relation to any trust within all or part of the region in which the trust is located, then it must expressly say so.'

As a result of the judicial review proceedings, amendments to Chapter 5A of the NHS Act 2006 were proposed in the passage of the CA 2014.

The HSCA 2012 introduced significant reforms to the structure of the NHS and continued to drive through the implementation of the split of provider/commissioner relationships. It was brought into force by commencement orders. A commencement order is a Statutory Instrument (SI) which is designed to bring into force the whole or part of an Act of Parliament. Different parts of an Act may be brought into force at different times.

The *Care Act 2014* (CA 2014) sets out a new framework of local authority duties in relation to the arrangement and funding of social care, along with a number of changes to the regulation of social care providers. Whilst primarily aimed at local authorities, the Act has some key implications for NHS organisations due to the growing integration of health and social care.

In particular, the CA 2014 places a specific duty of candour on health and social care providers registered with the CQC (see Chapter 3). A statutory duty of candour must always be one of the registration requirements placed on CQC-registered providers. The duty of candour itself, along with the fit and proper persons test are set out in the Health and Social Care Act 2008 (Regulated Activities) Regulations 2014.

The CA 2014 also reforms the law relating to care and support for adults and the law relating to support for carers. It sets out a clear legal framework for how local authorities and other parts of the system should safeguard adults from abuse or neglect, provides for additional care standards and established and made provision for Health Education England (HEE) and the Health Research Authority (HRA).

Phase 2 of this Act relating to social care funding reform was due to come into force in 2016 but was delayed until 2020 following a letter to Parliament In July 2015.

The CA 2014 has also introduced extensions to the special administration timetable to give greater time for the TSA to publish their draft report, extend the consultation period and create an obligation for the TSA to consult:

- other NHS trusts and NHS FTs affected by wider recommendations, their staff and their commissioners;
- any local authority in whose area the trust in administration and other affected trusts are located; and
- any Local Healthwatch organisation in the area of any local authority.

The CQC gained a greater role in dealing with quality and safety failure in FTs by requiring also that NHSI appoint a TSA where the CQC is satisfied that there is a serious failure by an NHS FT to provide services that are of sufficient quality. It also requires NHSI to consult more widely with the CQC in various situations, such as before publishing guidance. In addition, TSAs may not provide draft reports to NHSI without obtaining a statement from the CQC stating that it considers that the recommendations would achieve the sufficient safety and quality of the services.

Laws on patient and public involvement

The HSCA 2012 introduced significant amendments to the NHS Act 2006, especially with regard to how NHS commissioners will function. These amendments included two complementary duties for CCGs with respect to patient and public participation.

The first duty requires CCGs and NHS England (NHSE) to promote the involvement of patients and carers in decisions which relate to their care or treatment. It requires CCGs to ensure that they commission services which promote involvement of patients across the full spectrum of prevention or diagnosis, care planning, treatment and care management.

The second duty places a requirement on CCGs and NHSE to ensure public involvement and consultation in commissioning processes and decisions. A description of these arrangements must be included in a CCG's constitution. It requires the involvement of the public, patients and carers in:

- the planning of commissioning arrangements, which might include consideration of allocation of resources, needs assessment and service specification
- any proposed changes to services which may impact on patients.

CCGs must make arrangements to secure that individuals to whom the services are being or may be provided are involved (whether by being consulted or provided with information or in other ways) in accordance with section 14Z2 of the NHS Act 2006.

There are two other relevant aspects to section 14Z2. Subsection 3 requires all CCGs to include in their constitution a description of their public engagement arrangements and a statement of the principles that they will follow in when implementing them. Subsection 4 empowers NHSE to publish guidance on compliance with this section, which CCGs must have regard to.

Section 13Q of the Act applies to NHSE and contains effectively identical provisions to section 14Z2. Section 242 of the Act contains the same obligations with regard to patient and public involvement for NHS trusts and FTs. Any NHS body considering a change of the services it commissions or provides must be aware of these obligations. The proposals under consideration must have an impact on the manner in which the services are delivered to users of those services or the range of health services available to those users for the sections to apply.

In summary, any significant commissioning decision or reconfiguration of provision will be caught by these statutory requirements. Whilst the statute does not insist on 'consultation', it seeks to make sure that service users are 'involved'. In practice, some form of consultation exercise will be required for any significant proposed change to services to comply with this duty. The biggest area of application and challenge for NHS organisations currently are the requirements and methods of public involvement in the development of Sustainability and Transformation Plans (STPs).

The most recent NHSE guidance *Engaging People* (September 2016) outlines the requirement for public involvement in relation to STPs. It suggests:

- using lay representatives and establishing patient reference or advisory groups;
- considering and carrying out formal consultation with enough time for the public to make their views heard; and
- testing options with local councils and other important stakeholders, where possible by building on the work of existing bodies such as health and wellbeing boards (HWBs).

It claims that many local health systems were already publishing summaries of their proposals for patients and the public, with others expected to do so later this year. Relevant organisations such as hospital trusts were also advised to devote a public board meeting in full to discussing proposals.

The Saving STPs – Achieving Meaningful Health and Social Care Reform Review by Reform (February 2017) paints a different picture, however, as do many of the comments on the NHSE website. The Reform review reports that 'in some STPs, the involvement of local authorities has been minimal. They spoke of concerns from local authorities that they are not being treated as equal partners, partly due to their much smaller budgets'. The review cites NHSE instructing local leaders not to make their STPs public and to reject Freedom of Information (FOI) requests until proposals were formally approved. Whilst this is understandable in the very early stages to allow space to discuss proposals, it has led to insufficient public involvement in the process.

Nevertheless *Engaging People* states 'involving people, communities and stakeholders in developing plans is the right thing to do to ensure that the plans and their implementation are robust and meet the needs of people and communities'. It recommends that STP partners build on the Six Principles for Engaging People and Communities (June 2016), in order to work with the knowledge, skills and experience of people in their communities, working in co-production to improve access and outcomes.

The six principles were developed by the People and Communities Board, National Voices, in conjunction with the new models of care 'vanguard' sites, to give practical support to services as they deliver the 'new relationship with people and communities;' set out in the Five Year Forward View (5YFV) (see Chapter 2). These 'six principles' set out the basis of good person-centred, community-focused health and care and are set out in Figure 4.1.

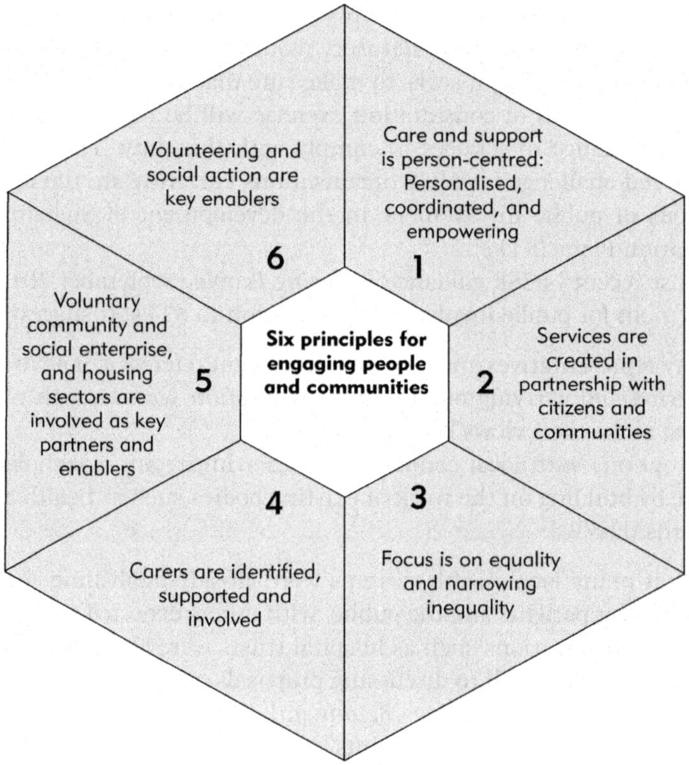

***Figure 4.1**: Six principles for engaging people and communities: putting them into practice*

Six principles acknowledges that the evidence is increasingly clear that better engagement –which means involvement and co-production – is not a nice-to-have, it is core business. In fact, there is a growing body of knowledge and practice that demonstrates that engagement is doable and has real impact. However, NHSE recognises that there is a long way to go.

CCGs, local authorities, NHS trusts, FTs and NHSE all have separate, but similar, obligations to consult or otherwise involve the public. Joint public involvement exercises are encouraged by Engaging People as 'they reduce the burden on patients and the public. They are likely to have wider reach into communities, help ensure a joined-up approach across the STP footprint, and save time and money'. Where joint exercises are developed, local partners will need to:

- ensure clarity about roles and responsibilities between the different organisations involved;
- ensure they understand and have taken account of the governance and assurance requirements for their constituent organisations of the STP, and have reflected these requirements in their timetable;

- consider how the constituent organisations should discharge their involvement duties with regard to the changes that are being consulted on; and
- ensure consistent messages about the case for change and the options for change that are being proposed.

Engaging People suggests an ongoing dialogue with patients, volunteers, carers, clinicians and other staff, citizens, the local voluntary and community sector, local government officers and local politicians, including those representing HWBs and scrutiny committees and MPs. It also suggests engaging people who live outside the STP footprint area but access health and care services within it.

The guidance recognises that working with existing networks helps to maximise efficiency and effectiveness. Such networks will include CCG lay members; voluntary, community and social enterprise (VCSE) networks; trust NEDs and governors; community networks and neighbourhood fora; Healthwatch; HWBs; Strategic Clinical Networks and Senates; Academic Health Science Networks; and local councillors.

And finally, the guidance recognises that it is essential that STP partners involve staff from constituent organisations, working through the internal communication channels available (including with unions). In particular, it recognises that clinicians should be involved in the case for change, based on the best available evidence. Clinicians can be powerful advocates and play an important role in communicating the need for change and potential solutions to a wider community.

Engaging People recommends that the method of engagement should be appropriate to the nature of the engagement exercise and the appropriate audience. For example, online methods can often be useful, but may be inaccessible for older people from more disadvantaged socio-economic groups.

As a general rule, the greater the extent of changes and number of people affected, the greater the level of activity that is likely to be necessary to achieve an appropriate and proportionate level of public involvement. However, the nature and extent of public involvement, including the length of consultation required always depends on local circumstances.

Whichever methods of involvement are used, it is essential that the approach is documented and agreed through governance structures, and that there is an audit trail of the activity that has taken place, including questions raised and the response to them. This strengthens proposals, highlights likely areas of concern, and provides evidence in the event of subsequent challenge.

Engaging People is clear that a formal public consultation is not needed for every service change. However, it is likely to be needed should substantial changes to the configuration of health services in a local area be proposed, such as hospital closure, or significant service change. It is therefore necessary to include consideration of the need for public consultation, and how this can be undertaken if required, in the overall STP.

Engaging People outlines the basic consultation principles as fairness and proportionality. These are set out in the Gunning Principle (resulting from the case *R v London Borough of Brent ex parte Gunning* (1985)), providing a helpful overview of what constitutes a fair consultation process:

- Consultation must take place when the proposal is still at a formative stage: consultation cannot take place on a decision that has already been made. Decision makers can consult on a 'preferred option' (of which those being consulted should be informed) and even a 'decision in principle' as long as they are genuinely open to influence.
- Sufficient reasons must be put forward for the proposal to allow for intelligent consideration and response: those being consulted should be made aware of the basis on which a proposal for consultation has been considered and will be considered thereafter, including any criteria to be applied or factors to be considered.
- Adequate time must be given for consideration and response: there is no automatically required time frame within which the consultation must take place unless statutory time requirements are prescribed. A rationale must be set out for any departure from that expected timeframe.
- The product of consultation must be conscientiously taken into account: decision-makers must properly consider the material produced by the consultation.

The Cabinet Office's latest statement of 'Consultation Principles' (January 2016) echoes many of these issues:

> 'Consultations are also a good way for departments to publicise an issue and demonstrate that they are open to ideas and discussion. Too often though consultations continue to be accused of being too short, not inclusive enough, not publicised, not feeding back and, worst of all, being nothing but a fig leaf for a decision that has already been made.
>
> The same accusations are also made of local consultations as well – those run by schools, the NHS and others. Poor consultation also continues to be an area of successful legal challenge as well. There is a whole set of case law out there where consultations have been challenged and, in many instances, have had to be re-run.'

A public body that fails to involve patients and the public leaves itself open to a challenge by way of judicial review. It may not lawfully be able to take decisions and thus implement the changes until consultation has occurred. The courts may also award legal costs against the NHS body.

Judicial review is a process by which a decision of the Secretary of State or an NHS body can be challenged, on the basis that it is unlawful. This right is derived from administrative law and does not just apply to the failure to involve. It is not a right of appeal and is concerned primarily with how decisions are made, rather than the merits of the decision itself. A decision might be unlawful if:

- the decision-maker does not have power to make the decision, or is using their power improperly;
- the decision is irrational;
- the procedure followed by the decision-maker was unfair or biased;
- the decision was in breach of the Human Rights Act 1998; or
- the decision breaches EU law.

If an application for judicial review is successful, the court has six possible remedies:

- Quashing orders: the original decision is struck down and the public body has to take the decision again.
- Prohibiting orders: the public body is forbidden from doing something unlawful in the future.
- Mandatory orders: the public body is ordered to do something specific which it has a duty to do.
- A declaration: on the way to interpret the law in future, for example.
- An injunction: this is usually a temporary remedy until the full application for judicial review is heard.
- Damages: whilst rare, this may be available for example, where there has been a breach of an individual's rights under the Human Rights Act 1998.

The duty to involve arises whether the changes in health service provision are required in response to financial pressures, clinical requirements or other reasons, or a combination of two or more factors. Changes made to comply with DH policy decisions are also subject to the duty to consult. The legal duty to consult both patients and the wider public falls both on the commissioner of health services and on to those providing services. The courts have ruled that, even where a commissioner was simply implementing DH policy, the provision of services was still the commissioner's responsibility and therefore it had an obligation to consult.

Finally, the *Local Authority (Public Health, Health and Wellbeing Boards and Health Scrutiny) Regulations 2013* remove the requirement for local authorities to have a Health Overview and Scrutiny Committee as the means by which they discharge their scrutiny function – although most have retained them. Even so, under regulation 23, NHSE, CCGs, and public and independent sector providers of NHS services must consult with the local authority about any proposals for a 'substantial' development or variation of the health service in the authority's area. Whilst substantial is not defined, it would be advisable for an NHS body to tell the local authority when it is proposing to consult. If the local authority ultimately disagrees with the decision of the NHS body, it is entitled to refer the matter up to the Secretary of State for a final decision.

CASE STUDY: Save our Surgery

The case of *R (on the application of Save our Surgery Ltd) v Joint Committee of Primary Care Trusts* [2013], related to specialist centres for paediatric cardiac surgery.

It was held that lawful consultation requires that:

- it is undertaken at a time when proposals are still at a formative stage;
- it must include sufficient reasons for particular proposals to allow those consulted to give intelligent consideration and an intelligent response;
- adequate time must be given for this purpose;
- the product of the consultation must be conscientiously taken into account when the ultimate decision is taken.

Healthwatch England is a key player for patient and public involvement under HSCA 2012, not least in its role as the independent consumer champion that gathers and represents the views of the public about health and social care services in England. Local Healthwatch organisations were established in April 2013 and have taken over the work previously done by the LINks, but with additional functions (see Chapter 2).

Local Healthwatch has to be representative of its local community as laid out in HSCA 2012. This includes ethnic groups, different users of services and carers.

Other UK law

There are several other specific pieces of UK legislation with a wide remit that are directly applicable to the NHS.

The *Employment Rights Act 1996 (ERA 1996)* protected employees from detriment if the reason for the employee's action arises from certain cases of whistleblowing – informing on improper practices of employers – where this amounts to a protected disclosure. The whistleblowing legislation is complex. The main principles are as follows:

- a dismissal is automatically unfair if the reason for it is that the employee made a protected disclosure;
- the ERA 1996 sets the parameters of what constitutes a protected disclosure, as well as the manner of the permissible disclosure by the worker; and
- different degrees of protection apply depending upon whether the disclosure was made internally within the employer's organisation, or externally to a third party.

A protected disclosure includes the disclosure of any information by a worker that in their reasonable belief tends to show that:

- a criminal offence has been, is about to be or is likely to be committed;
- a person has failed or is about to fail, to comply with a legal obligation imposed upon them, including an obligation imposed upon them by a contract of employment;
- the health and safety of any person has been or is being or is likely to be endangered;
- a miscarriage of justice has occurred, is occurring or is likely to occur;
- the environment has been or is being or is likely to be damaged; or
- information tending to show that one of the above matters has been, or is likely to be, deliberately concealed.

It is not necessary for the worker to show that the act concerned has or will occur. A reasonable belief is sufficient. It is immaterial whether the act has taken place in the UK or elsewhere. The court determines the state of the employee's disclosure by reference to the date of his or her dismissal or detriment, not the date on which the disclosure was made.

Where a worker is victimised by the employer as a result of making a protected disclosure, a claim can be brought to an employment tribunal. Dismissals or selection for redundancy for making a protected disclosure are automatically unfair. The worker does not have to have been employed for a minimum period of time to make a claim. There is no limit on the compensation that can be awarded. Employment tribunals can award interim relief in unfair dismissal claims.

The *Public Interest Disclosure Act 1998 (PIDA 1998)* protects the public by protecting individuals from workplace reprisals for raising a genuine concern, whether a risk to patients or other wrongdoing. The Act's tiered disclosure regime – promoting internal and regulatory disclosures – encourages workplace accountability and self-regulation.

PIDA 1998 protects the public by providing a remedy for individuals who suffer a detriment by any act or any deliberate failure to act by their employer for raising a genuine concern, whether it be a risk to patients, financial malpractice, or other wrongdoing. The Act's tiered disclosure regime promotes internal and regulatory disclosures, and encourages workplace accountability and self-regulation.

Under PIDA 1998, workers who act honestly and reasonably are given automatic protection for raising a matter internally. In the NHS an internal disclosure can go up to the highest level and includes going to the responsible Minister at the DH. Protection is also readily available to individuals who make disclosures to prescribed regulators, such as CQC and NHSI.

In certain circumstances, wider disclosures (e.g to an MP or the media) may also be protected. A number of additional tests apply when going wider, including:

- whether it is an exceptionally serious concern;
- whether the matter has already been raised;

- whether there is good reason to believe that the individual will be subject to a detriment by his or her employer if the matter were raised internally or with the appropriate regulator;
- whether disclosure was reasonable given all the circumstances.

The Act covers all workers, including temporary agency staff, persons on training courses and self-employed staff who are working for and supervised by the NHS. It does not cover volunteers. PIDA 1998 also makes it clear that any clause in a contract that purports to gag an individual from raising a concern that would have been protected under the Act is void. Where an individual is subjected to a detriment by their employer for raising a concern or is dismissed in breach of PIDA 1998, they can bring a claim for compensation under PIDA 1998 in an employment tribunal. Awards are uncapped and based on the losses suffered.

The *Human Rights Act 1998* came into force in the UK in October 2000. All public bodies (such as courts, police, local governments, hospitals, publicly funded schools, and others) and other bodies carrying out public functions have to comply with the Convention rights. The Act sets out the fundamental rights and freedoms that individuals in the UK have access to.

The *Freedom of Information Act* 2000 (FOIA 2000) created a public 'right of access' to information held by public authorities. The full provisions of the Act came into force on 1 January 2005. The Act led to the renaming of the Data Protection Commissioner (set up to administer the Data Protection Act 1998 (DPA 1998)), who is now known as the Information Commissioner. The Office of the Information Commissioner oversees the operation of the Act. It requires public authorities to have an approved publication scheme, which is a means of providing access to information that an authority proactively publishes. The Information Commissioner's Office (ICO) has developed and approved a model publication scheme that all public authorities must adopt.

The scheme:

- sets out the types of information that must be routinely published
- explains the way the information is provided
- states what charges can be made for providing information and
- commits the authority to providing and maintaining a guide to the information provided, how it is provided and any charges.

All public authorities should have adopted the model publication scheme and produced a guide to information using either definition documents or template guides to information provided by the ICO.

The definition documents for the main public sectors give sector-specific guidance on the type of information that authorities are expected to publish and list in their guide to information. The template guides to information are for smaller authorities and are downloadable guides that can be printed off, completed and used without further modification. They have been produced for local councils, schools and NHS practitioners.

The FOIA 2000 means that public authorities must disclose official information when people ask for it (unless there is a good legal reason not to), and they must reply within 20 working days.

This model publication scheme for NHS organisations gives examples of the kinds of information that they are expected to provide to meet their commitments under the model publication scheme. They are required to make the information available unless:

- they do not hold the information
- the information is exempt under one of the FOI exemptions or Environmental Information Regulations (EIRs) exceptions, or its release is prohibited under another statute
- the information is archived, out of date or otherwise inaccessible or
- it would be impractical or resource-intensive to prepare the material for routine release.

FOI requests may be refused if:

- it would cost too much to comply
- the request is vexatious or repeated or
- the information is exempt from disclosure under one of the exemptions in the Act.

If any of these criteria apply then the requester must be sent a written refusal notice.

The Act also recognises that there may be valid reasons for withholding information by setting out a number of exemptions from the right to know, some of which are subject to a public interest test. There are 23 exemptions in the FOIA 2000, divided as follows:

- Those that apply to a whole category (or class) of information, for example:
  - information about investigations and proceedings conducted by public authorities
  - court records
  - trade secrets.
- Those that are subject to a 'prejudice' test, where disclosure would, or would be likely to, prejudice, for example:
  - the interests of the UK abroad
  - the prevention or detection of crime
  - the activity or interest described in the exemption.

Information covered by one or more of the exemptions does not have to be disclosed. However, the decision has to be made as to whether the information should nevertheless be released in the public interest. This is called the 'public interest test' and involves considering the circumstances of each case with the exemption that covers the information. The information must be released unless the public interest in maintaining the exemption outweighs the public interest in releasing it.

Under the FOIA 2000, an authority must apply the public interest test separately to each exemption. When the test does apply, these are called qualified exemptions. Those to which the test does not apply are called absolute exemptions.

There are also exemptions for personal information.

- If personal information relates to the applicant, the request must be dealt with as a 'subject access request' made under the DPA 1998.
- If the information requested relates to a third party, a decision on whether to release it must be based on whether releasing it would contravene the DPA 1998.

When refusing a request for information, it is not possible to withhold an entire document because some of the information contained within it is exempt. A redacted version of the document must be provided along with a refusal notice stating why some of the information cannot be released. When refusing a FOI request, the exemption or exemptions applied must be set out, why they have been applied and, where appropriate, the public interest factors for and against disclosure fully explained.

CASE STUDY: Model Publication Scheme for NHS organisations

Who we are and what we do

- Organisational information, structures, locations and contacts
- How we fit into the NHS structure
- Organisational structure
- Lists of and information relating to organisations with which the authority works in partnership
- Senior staff and management board members
- Location and contact details for all public-facing departments

What we spend and how we spend it

- Financial information relating to projected and actual income and expenditure, procurement, contracts and financial audit.
- Annual statement of accounts
- Budgets and variance reports
- Financial audit reports
- Standing financial instructions
- Capital programme
- Staff and board members' allowances and expenses
- Staff pay and grading structures
- Funding (including endowment funds)

- Procurement and tendering procedures
- Details of contracts currently being tendered
- List and value of contracts awarded and their value
- What are our priorities and how are we doing

Strategies and plans, performance indicators, audits, inspections and reviews.

- Annual Report
- Annual business plan
- Targets, aims and objectives
- Strategic Direction document (five year)
- Performance against targets (KPI)/performance
- Clinical
- CQC reviews
- Audit reports
- Service user surveys

How we make decisions

- Decision-making processes and records of decisions for at least the current and previous three years.
- Board papers – agenda, supporting papers and minutes
- Patient and public involvement (PPI) strategy
- Public consultations (e.g. concerning closures/variations of services)
- Internal communications guidance and criteria used for decision-making (i.e. process systems and key personnel)

Our policies and procedures

- Current written protocols, policies and procedures for delivering services and responsibilities.
- Policies and procedures relating to the conduct of business and the provision of services
- Policies and procedures relating to human resources (including Race, Disability, Age and Gender, Equal Opportunities)
- Policies and procedures relating to recruitment and employment
- Standing financial procedures
- Standing orders
- Complaints and other customer service policies and procedures
- Data protection/information governance/Caldicott Guardian
- Estate management
- Charging regimes and policies

List and registers

- Any information currently required by law to be held in publicly available registers.
- List of main contractors/suppliers
- Assets registers and Information Asset Register
- Any register of interests kept in the authority
- Register of Gifts and Hospitality provided to board members and senior personnel
- Disclosure Log

The services offered

- Information about the services offered, including leaflets, guidance and newsletters.
- Clinical services provided and/or commissioned
- Non-clinical services
- Services for which the authority is entitled to recover a fee together with those fees
- Patient information leaflets and other booklets and newsletters
- PALS (Patient Advice and Liaison Service)
- Advice and guidance

The *Mental Capacity Act 2005 (MCA 2005)* received Royal Assent in April 2005 and was fully implemented in October 2007. It provides a clear legal framework for people who lack capacity, and their family and carers, to be involved as far as possible in decisions about their care. It sets out five key principles, as well as procedures and safeguards, which are:

- a person must be assumed to have capacity unless it is established that he or she lacks capacity
- a person is not to be treated as unable to make a decision unless all practicable steps to help him or her to do so have been taken without success
- a person is not to be treated as unable to make a decision merely because he or she makes an unwise decision
- an act done, or decision made, under this Act for or on behalf of a person who lacks capacity must be done, or made, in his or her best interests and
- before the act is done, or the decision is made, regard must be had to whether the purpose for which it is needed can be as effectively achieved in a way that is less restrictive of the person's rights and freedom of action.

These principles of the MCA 2005 apply whether the decisions are life-changing or everyday matters. The underlying philosophy is to ensure that individuals are empowered to make decisions where possible and where this is not possible, that any decision made or action taken is made in their best interests. The MCA Code of Practice also describes the role of the Independent Mental Advocate Service (IMCA) set up under the Act. This service provides support for those particularly vulnerable individuals who lack capacity and have no family or friends so that their views are represented to those working out their best interests.

Deprivation of Liberties Safeguards (DoLS) are an amendment to the MCA 2005. They apply In England and Wales only. The MCA 2005 allows restraint and restrictions to be used – but only if they are in the person's best interests. Extra safeguards are needed if restrictions and restraints used deprive a person of their liberty – these are called DoLS. DoLS can only be used if the person will be deprived of his or her liberty in a care home or hospital, and then the care home or hospital must ask the local authority if they can deprive the person of his or her liberty.

The *Corporate Manslaughter and Corporate Homicide Act 2007* came into effect on 6 April 2008 and disposed of the need the need to identify a single individual as the 'controlling mind'. This means a trust can be prosecuted as a corporate body.

The *Equality Act 2010* legally protects people from discrimination in the workplace and in wider society. It replaced previous anti-discrimination laws with a single Act, making the law easier to understand and strengthening protection in some situations. It sets out the different ways in which it is unlawful to treat someone. The intention of the public sector duty is to ensure that a public authority must, in the exercise of its functions, have due regard to three main aims:

- eliminating discrimination, harassment, victimisation and any other conduct that is prohibited by or under the Equality Act;
- advancing equality of opportunity between persons who share a relevant protected characteristic and persons who do not share it; and
- fostering good relations between persons who share a relevant protected characteristic and persons who do not share it.

Section 1 of the *Bribery Act 2010* makes it an offence for a person to offer, promise or give a financial or other advantage to another person in one of two cases:

- Where the intention is to bring about the improper performance by another person of a relevant function or activity or to reward such improper performance.
- Where the intention is that the acceptance of the advantage offered, promised or given in itself constitutes the improper performance of a relevant function or activity.

Section 7 of the Bribery Act also creates a new offence which can be committed by commercial organisations that fail to prevent persons associated with them from bribing another person on their behalf. An organisation that can prove it has adequate procedures in place to prevent persons associated with it from committing bribery will have a defence to the section 7 offence. A 'relevant commercial organisation' is defined at section 7(5) as a body or partnership incorporated or formed in the UK irrespective of where it carries on a business, or an incorporated body or partnership that carries on a business or part of a business in the UK irrespective of the place of incorporation or formation. The key concept here is that of an organisation that 'carries on a business' and so is directly applicable to NHS organisations.

The Modern Slavery Act 2015 is designed to tackle slavery in the UK. All businesses with a turnover In excess of £36 million are required to publish an annual statement setting out the steps they have taken to ensure that slavery and human trafficking do not exist in supply chains. The NHS role is twofold – it must review its own supply chains; and also it must ensure that its policies, procedures and training in safeguarding are updated to include slavery and human trafficking. In October 2016, the Independent Anti Slavery Commission published its annual report 2015/16 saying: 'The NHS has a significant role to play in controlling modern slavery and supporting victims. But to do this we need to ensure staff understand that modern slavery exists and we need to ensure that staff are confident and able to both recognise the signs and symptoms of both victim and perpetrators and know what to do.'

NHS organisations also have statutory responsibilities under the *Health and Safety at Work Act 1974*, the *Management of Health and Safety at Work Regulations 1999* and a number of other health and safety regulations (e.g. *Reporting of Injuries, Diseases and Dangerous Occurrences Regulations 1995*, *Noise at Work Regulations 1989*, *Manual Handling Operations Regulations 1992* and the *Control of Substances Hazardous to Health Regulations 2002*).

There have also been a number of EU Directives that have related to the NHS. For example, the *EU Clinical Trials Directive 2001* authorised and regulated the conduct of clinical trials, as trials are often conducted in multiple sites across a number of European countries. A revision of this Directive during 2014 introduced changes to speed up the process for authorising new clinical trials and reduce the administrative burden associated with the conduct of these studies. The new EU Directive takes the form of a Regulation, meaning that it will apply directly in each member state of the EU without the need to be transposed into national law, and thereby will ensure the rules are consistent throughout the EU The new EU Regulation is expected to apply from 2016.

EU General Data Protection Regulation 2016 (GDPR 2016) comes into force in May 2018. Many of the GDPR's main concepts and principles are much the same as those in the current DPA 1998. The government has confirmed that the UK's decision to leave the EU will not affect the commencement of the GDPR.

The GDPR will apply to organisations that fall into two broad definitions: 'controllers' and 'processors'. The definitions are similar to those defined in the DPA 1998 in that controllers say how and why personal data is processed, and processors act on the controller's behalf. The GDPR requires organisations to demonstrate compliance by design. This means ensuring there are adequate systems, contractual provisions, documented decisions about processing, and training in place. The GDPR stipulates that any data that can be used to identify an individual is considered to be personal data. It can include things such as genetic, mental, cultural, economic or social information, and IP addresses. Organisations will need to ensure they are explicit when seeking consent and detail how they will use the information. An individual's silence or inactivity will generally no longer be considered as consent. It also requires the appointment of a data protection officer (specifically including public bodies), the imposition of privacy impact assessments, adequate systems to manage data breaches, not holding data longer than necessary, not changing the use of the data and compliance with the right to be forgotten.

Company law and other legislation

While the NHS is not governed by UK company legislation, it provides a useful backdrop for understanding health service governance. In the UK, the main item of company legislation is the *Companies Act 2006* (CA 2006). This includes regulations relating to:

- the preparation and auditing of annual financial statements, for approval by the shareholders;
- the powers and duties of directors;
- other disclosures to shareholders, such as the requirement for companies to publish an annual business review;
- the disclosure of information about directors' remuneration;
- general meetings of companies, and shareholder rights to call a general meeting; and
- shareholder voting rights at general meetings, including the right to re-elect directors.

The impact of this legislation has been felt in health service governance and is covered throughout this handbook.

A number of EU company law directives also have relevance for the NHS. A proposal for a new or amended EU Directive is initiated by the European Commission in Brussels. Legislation is then agreed by the European Council and the European Parliament in a process known as the 'co-decision procedure'. When a directive has been agreed, its contents must be implemented by all EU member states within a stated timeframe, either in a law or other regulation, if suitable legislation does not already exist. EU Directives on company law have included a requirement for companies to publish an annual business review. Several directives have also been passed affecting companies whose shares are traded on a regulated exchange, including:

- a directive relating to shareholder rights
- requirements to publish an annual corporate governance statement

- requirements to have an audit committee
- requirements to introduce measures that provide for the independence and ethical conduct of their external auditors.

Companies become insolvent for reasons unconnected with corporate governance. Occasionally, however, the directors of a company may allow it to continue in business when they are aware that it is insolvent and will be unable to pay its creditors or employees. In the UK, the CA 2006 includes provisions that make fraudulent trading a criminal offence; in addition, the *Insolvency Act 1986* makes wrongful trading a civil offence.

As discussed earlier, the insolvency framework for NHS organisations is different from an ordinary administration under general insolvency legislation in that its main objective is to protect patients and staff from failing services and secure the continued provision of patient services. The NHS statutory provisions also provide an alternative corporate insolvency procedure for companies to ensure that patients receive uninterrupted services if a provider becomes insolvent.

Money-laundering regulations are also in place to protect the UK financial system. Money laundering is the process of disguising the source of money that has been obtained from serious crime or terrorism, so that it appears to come from a legitimate source. Companies are often used for the purpose of money laundering, which is a criminal offence in most countries, and the owners or directors of the companies concerned are often involved in the money laundering activity themselves. If an organisation is covered by the regulations, it must put in place certain controls to prevent it being used for money laundering by criminals and terrorists. These include:

- appointing a 'nominated officer'
- checking the identity of customers
- keeping all relevant documents
- report any suspicious activity to the Serious Organised Crime Agency (SOCA).

Whilst NHS organisations are not specifically covered by the regulations, a number of its suppliers will be such as external and internal audit, counter fraud, and law firms.

Compulsory regulation and voluntary best practice

There are aspects of organisations where laws are essential to protect the interests of stakeholders such as employees or shareholders. For example, employment laws are needed to give protection to employees against unfair treatment by employers. Legal requirements for organisations to prepare annual financial statements and have them audited, and the duties of directors are in place to protect stakeholders. There may be different views about the extent of regulation that is required; however, the need for some regulation seems unquestionable.

Best practice in health service governance has some connection with ethical business practice. Some aspects of behaviour may be considered unethical but legal. Laws are required to prevent or punish activities that are considered so unethical that they should be illegal. Bribery is an example of behaviour that has been tolerated in the past but which is now accepted as illegal by most countries.

Regulation may be needed to address public concerns and maintain public confidence in the governance system. This has probably been most evident in the US. The Sarbanes-Oxley Act (SOX) of 2002 was a response to public outrage against the many corporate scandals that emerged after the collapse of Enron. Public fury against the banks following the financial crisis in 2007–2008 continues to prompt demands for legislative action that would affect the governance of banks.

Advantages of voluntary regulation of governance issues

It is difficult to devise a set of rules that should apply to all organisations in all circumstances. Rules that are appropriate for one organisation might not be appropriate for another whose circumstances are very different. Although a voluntary system of governance (such as the corporate governance system in the UK) places an expectation on organisations to comply with the guidelines, it also allows them to breach the guidelines if it seems appropriate and sensible to do so.

As a general rule, governance issues become greater as an organisation gets bigger. A voluntary code of best practice in governance can be targeted at the largest organisations; smaller organisations can then choose whether they want to model their own governance systems on parts of the code for the larger organisations. Governance practices can therefore be adapted to the circumstances of the organisation.

In corporate governance, however, there may be a risk that companies will migrate to those countries where the rules are less onerous if different countries have their own corporate governance regulations. Indeed, governments may compete to offer a corporate governance regime that is more attractive in their country than in other countries in order to attract foreign companies. Excessive regulations may deter companies from becoming a listed company, particularly if the rules for listed companies are stricter than the rules for private companies.

In practice, good governance is a combination of regulation and voluntary best practice. In some countries there is more emphasis on regulation and in others there is greater reliance on voluntary codes of practice for large organisations. However, unless law regulates governance, it is probable that standards of governance will vary substantially between organisations.

Voluntary governance frameworks

A voluntary code of governance is issued by an authoritative national or international body and contains principles or best practice in governance that major companies (listed companies) or organisations are encouraged to adopt and apply.

The principles may consist of main principles with associated supporting principles, and for each principle, there may also be provisions or recommendations about how the principle should be applied in practice. Voluntary codes of corporate governance have been adopted in many countries (e.g. in all the countries of the Commonwealth and all the countries of the EU).

There is no statutory requirement for organisations to apply the principles or provisions of a voluntary code. However, a well-established code should attract the support of the significant organisations in that sector, and this develops an expectation that others should adopt the code unless their circumstances are such that non-compliance with some of the code's provisions is a more sensible option.

Although voluntary, organisations may be required to adopt the code of governance, or to explain their non-compliance with any aspect of the code and their reasons for non-compliance in their annual report and accounts. For example, NHSE advocates that CCGs adhere to the *Good Governance Standard for Public Services 2004*. This requirement, common in many countries, is known as 'comply or explain'.

The purpose of a voluntary code is to raise standards of governance. It is principles-based, because there is a recognition that the same set of rules is not necessarily appropriate in every way for all organisations, and that there will be situations where:

- non-compliance with provisions in the code is desirable, given the circumstances that the organisation faces; and
- implementing a principle of best practice is not always best achieved by following the detailed provisions or recommendations in the code, and some flexibility should be allowed.

It is also recognised that a code cannot provide detailed guidelines for every situation and circumstance. The preface to the UK Corporate Governance Code in 2010 points out:

> 'It seems that there is almost a belief that complying with the Code in itself constitutes good governance. The Code, however, is of necessity limited to being a guide only in general terms to principles, structure and processes. It cannot guarantee effective board behaviour because the range of situations in which it is applicable is much too great for it to attempt to mandate behaviour more specifically than it does.'

'Comply or explain' and 'apply or explain'

The UK Corporate Governance Code explains:

> 'The "comply or explain" approach is the trademark of corporate governance in the UK. It has been in operation since the Code's beginnings and is the foundation of its flexibility. It is strongly supported by both companies and shareholders and has been widely admired and imitated internationally. The

> Code is not a rigid set of rules. It consists of principles (main and supporting) and provisions.'

The UK Code recognises that an alternative to following a provision may be justified in particular circumstances if good governance can be achieved by other means. A condition of doing so is that the reasons for it should be explained clearly and carefully to shareholders, who may wish to discuss the position with the company and whose voting intentions may be influenced as a result.

In providing an explanation, the company should aim to illustrate how its practices:

- are consistent with the principle to which the particular provision relates;
- contribute to good governance; and
- promote delivery of business objectives.

It should set out the background, provide a clear rationale for the action it is taking, and describe any mitigating actions taken to address any additional risk and maintain conformity with the relevant principle. Where deviation from a particular provision is intended to be limited in time, the explanation should indicate when the company expects to conform with the provision.

The UK Code makes it clear that satisfactory engagement between company boards and investors is crucial to the health of the UK's corporate governance regime. In this way both companies and shareholders have responsibility for ensuring that 'comply or explain' remains an effective alternative to a rules-based system. It recognises that there are practical and administrative steps to be taken to improve interaction between boards and shareholders, but it also makes it clear that there is scope for an increase in trust, which could generate a virtuous upward spiral in attitudes to the Code and in its constructive use.

A similar approach has been taken with some voluntary codes in the NHS. NHSI requires FTs to comply with the *FT Code of Governance* or to explain any non-compliance. The same is true of the UK Listing Rules, which require listed companies to comply with the UK Corporate Governance Code.

There is a view that the word 'comply' encourages organisations to follow the provisions of a code in all its details without considering the principles that underpin the code. This may encourage a box-ticking approach, and a view that the detailed provisions must be followed without considering whether the provisions might be appropriate or finding a suitable way of applying the governance principles in the actual circumstances.

For this reason, some countries have adopted governance codes that espouse an 'apply or explain' approach. South Africa in its fourth iteration of *King Code*, the governance code for South Africa has now moved on to 'apply and explain'. King IV has 17 basic principles,

> '16 of which can be applied by any organisation and all are required to substantiate a claim that good governance is being practised. The required explanation

> allows stakeholders to make an informed decision as to whether or not the organisation is achieving the four good governance outcomes required by King IV. Explanation also helps to encourage organisations to see corporate governance not as an act of mindless compliance but something that will yield results only if it is approached mindfully with due consideration of the organisation's circumstances.'

'Apply and explain' is a less prescriptive approach but this has been balanced by a greater emphasis on transparency with regards to how the judgement was exercised when considering the recommendations contained in King IV.

- 'Apply' – all principles are phrased as aspirations and ideals that organisations should strive for in their journey to wards good governance and realising the governance outcomes. The principles are basic and fundamental to good governance and application is therefore assumed.
- 'Explain' – explanation should be provided in the form of a narrative account, with references to practices that demonstrate application of the principle. The explanation should address which recommended or other practices have been implemented and how these achieve or give effect to the principle.

The detail of information provided in the narrative should be guided by materiality and should enable stakeholders to make an informed assessment of the quality of an organisation's governance.

The UK Corporate Governance Code also recognises the dangers of a 'box-ticking' mentality with 'comply or explain' and stresses that it is not intended to be a set of rules:

> 'The Code is not a rigid set of rules ... It is recognised that [non-compliance with a provision] may be justified in particular circumstances if good governance can be achieved by other means.'

Likewise, the introduction to the *FT Code of Governance* makes it clear that some FTs may decide that the provisions are disproportionate or less relevant in their case. Therefore, they should actively consider how to adopt the approach in the code in their particular circumstances.

It should be noted that some principles and recommendations have become legislation (such as with Bribery Act 2010) and the practices required by the legislation then become mandatory.

Codes for health service governance

Governance in the public sector, and specifically in the NHS, is the subject of several reports. Some of the more prominent reports are as follows.

- *The Nolan Principles on Public Life* (1995): covered in detail the standards of behaviour and principles in public life with particular focus on appointment on merit, with an independent element on all selection panels recommended as the way forward for public bodies (see Chapter 1).

- *The Intelligent Board* (2006): looked at board level information needs and information flow.
- *The Integrated Governance Handbook* (2006): looked in detail at the processes and information requirements of sound governance.
- *Taking it on Trust* (2009): examined how the boards of NHS trusts and FTs in England assure themselves that internal controls are in place and operating effectively.
- *The Healthy NHS Board: Principles for good governance* (2013): set out the principles of high-quality governance, and is supported by a regularly updated digital compendium, which puts the principles in an operational context.
- *The NHS Foundation Trust Code of Governance* (2014): set out the governance arrangements for FTs.
- *Developmental Reviews of Leadership and Governance using the Well-Led*
- *Framework* (2017): the purpose of this framework is to support NHS provider organisations in gaining assurance that they are well led.
- *UK Corporate Governance Code*: a corporate framework of governance that underpins much of healthcare governance.
- Financial Reporting Council *(FRC) Guidance for Boards and Committees*: practical guidance for effective meetings.

The Intelligent Board

This report set out a set of principles and model framework for structuring information to support strategy development and oversight of business delivery and effectiveness. It also suggests practical ways in which boards might use the framework proposed.

The report outlines:

- the information challenge, including discussion of the growing pressure on boards to raise their game and the need to improve the information they receive and how they use it;
- intelligent information for the board, including some key principles that should govern information for the board, together with a proposed framework and minimum data set for reviewing trust performance, supporting decision-making and considering strategy; and
- putting the framework into practice by improving the structure of agendas for the board, developing a 'dashboard' of routine performance indicators and informing the annual cycle of board meetings.

The report was followed by the Intelligent Board series of publications, which includes guidance for mental health trusts, ambulance trusts and clinical commissioners, outlines practical, focused advice for NHS board members on the kind of information they should be using to understand and oversee their organisations' performance.

All the reports in the series are based on the following Intelligent Board principles.

- All information should cover locally defined priorities as well as national 'must do' requirements.
- All information should focus on outcomes, not systems and processes.
- All information should be available in a timely and understandable format.
- All information should be clearly and simply presented.
- All information should be forward-looking, presenting trends and anticipating future issues.
- All information should allow internal comparison between services and make use of external benchmarks.
- All information should provide interpretation and analysis as well as information.
- All information should provide a level of detail that is appropriate to the board's governance role.

The Integrated Governance Handbook

The idea of integrated governance was developed by Professor Michael Deighan and Dr Roger Moore with support from Sir William Wells, Professor Sir Ian Kennedy and Bill Moyes. It was first introduced to the NHS in a paper entitled 'Developing Integrated Governance', published by the NHS Confederation in May 2004.

The handbook was published in 2006 by the DH to ensure that the basic building blocks of integrated governance were in place, with rollout and implementation planned over the following two years. The chief concern that the integrated governance sought to address was the risk of boards governing in silos (e.g. clinical governance, research governance, quality governance, information governance) by moving to an integrated agenda that would enable boards to meet their responsibilities.

Integrated governance is defined as: 'systems, processes and behaviours by which trusts lead, direct and control their functions to achieve organisational objectives, safety and quality of service and in which they relate to patients and carers, the wider community and partner organisations'.

The NHS chief executive at the time, Sir Nigel Crisp, said in issue 245 of the *Chief Executive Bulletin*:

> 'Integrated governance provides the umbrella for all NHS governance approaches. It combines the principles of corporate/financial accountability and it moves towards a single risk sensitivity process which covers all the trust's objectives, supported by a coordinated source of collecting information and subject to coordinated inspection.'

Integrated governance emphasises the critical importance of the board defining, within the overall goals established for the NHS, its own purpose and strategic direction, with clarity of purpose, objective setting and planning of the board's annual cycle of business. The handbook also focused on quality as the driver of change, examined the critical role of clinical governance at the heart of the integrated governance agenda, and covered the legal implications for boards and what they should to do to plan the journey towards good governance.

Integrated governance required an examination of a number of key areas:

- the need for boards to take account of a wide range of NHS requirements in determining overall priorities and drawing up annual operational plans;
- a review of assurance arrangements, with particular reference to the Standards for Better Health (now superseded by the CQC);
- the 'intelligent' information required by boards integrating a wide range of perspectives, including finance, human resources, information systems, research and, most importantly, clinical governance;
- the key role of the Board Assurance Framework, which should complement the strategic priorities identified during the annual business planning cycle; and
- the simplification of committee structures and supports in order to ensure they had clear terms of reference and understood the actions and behaviours expected of them.

It was envisaged that the board would take corporate responsibility for all aspects of strategy setting, performance management and quality assurance, as a result of being assured that the appropriate systems were in place to manage the identified risks.

In particular, the handbook suggested a consideration of the 'company secretary' role within health organisations and a development of the role of the audit committee to scrutinise and streamline committee structures and agendas, ensuring all risks (activity, quality and resources) were anticipated, aligned and integrated.

The key task for integration was an examination of the role of the audit committee to ensure that it scrutinised all the sub-committees reporting to the board. At the time, some boards had more than 40 committees (some, of course, were subcommittees) but they reported either through the audit committee or directly to the board. This was unworkable and did not allow non-executives to fulfil their strategic role. The handbook proposed a phased transition to the following structure:

The handbook recommended that boards should be served by the following main standing committees:

- audit
- remuneration and review
- appointments.

Other committees that boards might find useful included:

- risk compliance and assurance
- clinical governance
- health and safety.

This required a change in board meeting reporting structure to ensure that agendas were robust enough to deal adequately with the business from many of the committees that no longer existed. It also relied upon the strengthened audit committee clarifying much of the work prior to it being placed on the board's agenda.

The handbook set out a direction of travel for health service governance, which was subsequently updated and revised by a further publication entitled *Integrated Governance: A guide to risk and joining up the NHS reforms* in 2011. This outlined a governance development programme that clarifies:

- the purpose and behaviours of the board;
- the board structures and systems; and
- the review and improvement process.

It also set out a number of exercises for board development.

Taking it on Trust

The Audit Commission report *Taking it on Trust* was published in April 2009. It examined the rigour with which NHS trust boards operated the processes available to them and obtained the assurance they need.

The report highlighted discrepancies between trust declarations of compliance with Standards for Better Health (now superseded by the CQC) and subsequent Healthcare Commission inspections; differences between the Statement on Internal Controls (now known as the Annual Governance Statement (AGS)) and core standards declarations; and some major failures in patient care, such as that at Maidstone and Tunbridge Wells NHS Trust and Mid Staffordshire NHS Foundation Trust. There were significant gaps between the processes on paper and the rigour with which they were applied.

The report said that the introduction of FTs had generally reinvigorated governance process. It resulted in the recruitment of non-executives with a greater knowledge of effective risk management and board challenge, drawn from private sector experience. However, the report was critical of assurance processes that had become 'a paper chase' rather than a critical examination of the effectiveness of the trust's internal controls and risk management arrangements.

The report recommended that NHS trusts should:

- ensure that their strategic aims and objectives are clearly defined and few in number so they can be widely understood and clearly cascaded throughout the organisation, and that their strategic risks are identified and aligned to their strategic objectives;

- review their risk management arrangements – including the way in which risks are reported to the board and consider how best to promote and demonstrate the value of risk management work to staff;
- ensure they have systems in place to comply with all statutory, regulatory, clinical and contractual requirements;
- consider cascading the Statement of Internal Control (now the AGS) through the organisation by sub-certification by managers, allied with a more effective compliance function, performance information and performance management;
- review how they identify and then evidence assurances on the operation of controls and how these are then evaluated;
- review and increase the assurances they receive from sources other than internal audit, including clinical audit, and in doing so, ensure that their full portfolio of risk is covered;
- maximise the assurance obtained from internal audit by reviewing the scope of internal audit plans and improving its commissioning;
- better align clinical audit programmes to key strategic and operational risks to maximise the assurance provided by the clinical audit function;
- strengthen their compliance mechanisms and distinguish them more clearly from internal audit, which should review the effectiveness of the compliance framework;
- ensure they have robust arrangements for assuring the quality of their data and by developing systematic and formalised review programmes for their data, including checking accuracy back to records; and
- develop policies and guidance on data quality and assurance processes, including defining and allocating responsibility for data quality, to promote consistency and improve awareness of board members.

CASE STUDY: Maidstone and Tunbridge Wells NHS Trust

In the autumn of 2005, Maidstone and Tunbridge Wells NHS Trust suffered a significant outbreak (150 cases) of Clostridium difficile (C. difficile) infection, although it went unrecognised at the time. In April 2006 a second outbreak (258 cases) occurred and was recognised and reported to the SHA (NHS South East Coast) and the Health Protection Agency (HPA). The SHA arranged for an investigation by the Healthcare Commission.

The Commission's report was published in October 2007. As well as analysing the problem and the management of C. difficile specifically, the report also made general comments and criticisms about the leadership and governance of the trust.

One of the central issues was the role of the chair and the NEDs, and their ability to govern. The non-executive board members had struggled to gain a true understanding of what was going on in the organisation, and had also struggled to hold the chief executive and senior managers and clinicians of the trust to account in the period covered by the report. The report stated that the board could have been in a position to ensure the trust managed emergent control of infection issues better than they did if the non-executives had been better advised.

Other issues included the board not providing clear leadership to the organisation as a whole, in its culture and approach to its core business. Board members were reported as being remote and preoccupied with finance and targets.

It was also clear that the board was given information, rather than asking for it. Most information came with a recommendation only that it be noted. The reports to the board on nursing and cleanliness issues were long, academic and did not make clear the success or otherwise of the solutions relied on, such as the nursing quality assurance framework. There was no lack of information or data, but there was an apparent lack of analysis about what it showed. All information appeared to have been given the same weight.

The trust had an assurance framework throughout, but it was mostly not serviceable and not capable of identifying the primary risks at board level. There was no evidence in the minutes that the chair and non-executives made sufficient attempts to clarify what they were being told, to consider the implications, or to identify the decisions that may be required of them.

The Commission estimated that about 90 patients 'definitely or probably' died as a result of the infection.

The Healthy NHS Board: principles for good governance

This 2013 guidance is a refreshed edition of the original guidance, published in 2010. The 2013 guidance was influenced by the Francis Report, and starts from the premise that there is a strong relationship between leadership capability and performance, which is well demonstrated by evidence. It sets out that good leadership leads to a good organisational climate; in turn, good organisational climates lead to sustainable, high-performing organisations via improved staff satisfaction and loyalty.

The report sets out the principles that will allow NHS board members to understand the:

- collective role of the board including effective governance in relation to the wider health and social care system;
- activities and approaches that are most likely to improve board effectiveness;
- contribution expected of them as individual board members.

The guidance is primarily intended for boards of NHS trusts and FTs, but with some interpretation it is also relevant for organisations operating at a national level. While CCGs, as membership organisations, have developed very specific governance arrangements and are not therefore the primary focus of this guidance, the general principles outlined are relevant to them. It offers a framework that will help them to place reliance on the effective governance of provider organisations.

The guidance sets the three key roles of an effective board as:

- formulating strategy for the organisation;
- ensuring accountability by holding the organisation to account for the delivery of the strategy; being accountable for ensuring the organisation operates effectively, with openness, transparency and candour, and by seeking assurance that systems of control are robust and reliable; and
- shaping a positive culture for the board and the organisation.

These are underpinned by three building blocks that allow boards to exercise their role – namely, that boards:

- are informed by the external context within which they must operate;
- are informed by, and shape, the intelligence that provides trend and comparative information on how the organisation is performing together with an understanding of local people's needs, market and stakeholder analyses; and
- prioritise engagement with key stakeholders and opinion formers within and beyond the organisation. The emphasis here is on building a healthy dialogue with, and being accountable to patients, the public, and staff, governors and members, commissioners and regulators.

The three roles of the board and the three building blocks all interconnect and influence one another. The guidance also sets out clear boundaries for the various roles within the board and outlines an established role for a company secretary.

CASE STUDY: Barking, Havering and Redbridge University Hospitals NHS Trust

The trust had experienced frequent changes to its board. A new chief executive had been in place since February 2011, followed by a medical director (following a number of years where non-permanent staff had provided this function). A number of new NEDs had also been appointed and an interim chair had been in place since 2010.

At the time of CQC registration, the trust had a high number of 'conditions' placed on it to require improvements in care. A series of unannounced inspections in 2010/11 resulted in some of these being lifted, but also resulted in warning notices being issued to the trust (in March, June and July 2011) on staffing levels and maternity care.

> The CQC concluded its investigation into the quality and safety of care at the trust. One of the findings of that investigation was that trust governance systems were weak and health service governance was underdeveloped. Governance systems had recently changed, but lines of communication in the new structure were unclear and there was a risk of duplication or issues being missed. The trust was reliant on external reviews to identify issues, and while it held extensive performance information, this was not used to drive change. There was a lack of learning from incidents, with investigations identifying recurring themes.

NHS Foundation Trust Code of Governance

The NHS Foundation Trust Code of Governance (the FT Code) was first published in 2006 and was revised in 2010. It was updated again in December 2013, following the significant regulatory change as a result of HSCA 2012. The Code builds on the approach, principles and provisions of the UK Corporate Governance Code (and the Combined Codes before it) to bring best practice from the private sector to the NHS.

The legal framework for FTs has been described as being closer to that of a commercial company than that of other trusts. As such, it adopted a much more 'commercial' approach to their regulation. FTs must comply with the NHS provider licence, reporting requirements and the Audit Code used by NHSI. Each FT needs to develop individual standing orders, giving authority to each organisation's standing financial instructions, schemes of delegation and matters reserved for the board.

FTs are created as legal entities as public benefit corporations by the NHS Act 2006. The legislation constitutes FTs with a new governance regime that is fundamentally different from NHS trusts. FT boards of directors have more autonomy to make financial and strategic decisions. They also have a framework of local accountability through members and a council of governors, which has attempted to central control from the Secretary of State (see Chapter 12).

The provisions of the FT Code, as best practice advice, do not represent mandatory guidance and accordingly non-compliance is not in itself a breach of NHS Foundation Trust Condition 4 of the NHS provider licence (also known as the 'governance condition'). However, trusts should note the relevant statutory requirements that have been highlighted within the FT Code.

The FT Code sets out best practice principles and structures and processes (through its provisions), but also makes clear that ultimately only directors and governors can demonstrate and promote the effective board behaviour that is needed to guarantee good corporate governance in practice. The emphasis on governance can be demonstrated from the example of Derbyshire Healthcare NHS Foundation Trust, which was authorised in 2011 after having been unsuccessful in two earlier assessments.

CASE STUDY: Derbyshire Healthcare NHS Foundation Trust

The trust first came to the regulator Monitor in 2007 and subsequently requested a deferral, which was agreed and imposed a number of conditions that would need to be resolved before assessment could recommence. These included concerns about the board's capacity to deliver the business plan, and a less than satisfactory working capital report. When assessed again in 2008, Monitor were still not satisfied that the trust's board was able to deliver the business plan, or that the trust was financially viable in the medium term.

Monitor recommended that, among other actions, the trust re-examine the skill mix of the NEDs and how any gaps on the board could be addressed. The trust returned to Monitor for assessment in September 2010.

The actions the trust had taken in the intervening period, following Monitor's recommendations, were evident. A new chair had been appointed, along with four new NEDs. A new finance director had been recruited from an existing FT, and a director of business strategy role had been created. The appointee brought in-depth knowledge of commissioning and an effective working relationship with the local PCT.

Significant time had been committed to board development activities, focusing heavily on the principles of good governance and the characteristics of high-performing boards. Monitor observed board meetings and held individual meetings at the trust, and the board was clearly very capable. The executive and non-executive teams worked effectively together, which was apparent throughout the assessment process, and from the outset the integrated business plan had been developed and owned jointly. The trust also demonstrated that it was very focused on quality.

Mike Shewan, Chief Executive of Derbyshire Healthcare NHS Foundation Trust said:

> 'From day one, Monitor's assessment team was very clear about their expectations and gave us every opportunity to provide the evidence they were looking for. We had learned a lot about the process from our previous assessments and had developed a keen awareness of what Monitor would be looking for. We knew that we needed to be operating as a FT board before we became a FT, and so spent a lot of time developing our board and a strong governance structure. We knew that a high performing unitary board was key to our success, not only in order to achieve FT status, but to continue to deliver in the future.'

The trust's commitment to improving the board and strengthening organisational capacity, based on feedback from Monitor's assessment process, meant that it was authorised as a FT on 1 February 2011.

Source: Monitor Annual Report and Accounts, 2010/2011

The FT Code explains that satisfactory engagement between the board of directors, the council of governors, members and patients is crucial to the effectiveness of FTs' corporate governance approach. It outlines that both directors and governors have a responsibility for ensuring that 'comply or explain' remains an effective alternative to a rules-based system and a key aspect of this is ensuring improved interaction between directors, governors, members and – crucially – patients, communities and the public.

The FT Code does impose some specific disclosure requirements upon FTs, which are similar to the requirements set out by the UK Listing Authority for listed companies. To meet the requirements of 'comply or explain' each trust must comply with each of the provisions of the Code (which in some cases will require a statement or information to be required in the annual report) or, where appropriate, explain in each case why the trust has departed from the Code.

In addition, the FT Code also requires a trust, when it opts not to comply with a provision, to explain how its approach still reflects the principles of the FT Code relating to that provision. The form and content of this part of the statement are not prescribed, the intention being that trusts should have a free hand to explain their governance policies in the light of the principles, including any special circumstances applying to them which have led to a particular approach.

Although compliance with the provisions in the FT Code is on a 'comply or explain' basis, it also clearly identifies any relevant statutory requirements that fit closely with the Code. In the first instance, boards, directors and governors should ensure they are meeting the specific governance requirements described in HSCA 2012 (see Chapter 12).

Key aspects of the FT Code are set out in more detail in Chapter 12. In essence, the Code adopts a similar structure to the UK Corporate Governance Code with a series of Main Principles, supported by a series of supporting principles, under the following broad headings:

Section A: Leadership

A.1 The role of the board of directors
A.2 Division of responsibilities
A.3 The chair
A.4 Non-executive directors
A.5 Governors

Section B: Effectiveness

B.1 The composition of the board
B.2 Appointments to the board
B.3 Commitment
B.4 Development
B.5 Information and support
B.6 Evaluation

B.7 Re-appointment of directors and re-election of governors
B.8 Resignation of directors

Section C. Accountability
C.1 Financial, quality and operational reporting
C.2 Risk management and internal control
C.3 Audit committee and auditors

Section D. Remuneration
D.1 The level and components of remuneration
D.2 Procedure

Section E. Relations with stakeholders
E.1 Dialogue with members, patients and the local community
E.2 Co-operation with third parties with roles in relation to NHS FTs

Developmental Reviews of Leadership and Governance using the Well-led Framework: Guidance for NHS trusts and NHS foundation trusts

This guidance was published June 2017 following a full consultation on the previous Well-Led Framework (2015). The intention was to create a new Well-Led Framework for all NHS providers, building on the strengths of the earlier version issued by Monitor and the NHS Trust Development Authority (NHS TDA), and to streamline it to cover system governance and leadership, leadership behaviours, promotion of an open and fair culture, and sustainability of high quality, patient-centred care that supports learning and innovation. To support this single Well-Led Framework, the CQC and NHSI have also worked together to recognise that effective use of resources is also fundamental to enable trusts to deliver and sustain high-quality services for patients..

It is intended that trusts will assure themselves of their leadership and governance through a range of different means, such as external governance reviews (including peer review or consultancy support), advice from professional bodies, and feedback and guidance from regulators; these will be supported by self-reviews, internal audit, CQC inspections and board development programmes. Such developmental reviews reflect the regulators' view of good practice. Developmental well-led reviews will be conducted on a 'comply or explain basis', meaning that trusts should be able to give a robust explanation if they use alternative means to assure themselves. As these reviews are for development purposes, trusts need only feed back that a review has been completed and if it identified any material governance concerns. Trusts' approach to learning from past developmental reviews, and planning for future reviews, would be a source of evidence that would be considered in CQC's regular trust-level well-led assessments.

1 Is there the **leadership capacity and capability** to deliver high-quality, sustainable care?	2 Is there a clear **vision** and credible **strategy** to deliver high-quality, sustainable care to people, and robust plans to deliver?	3 Is there a **culture** of high-quality, sustainable care?
4 Are there clear responsibilites, **roles** and systems of accountability to support good governance and management?	**Are services well led?**	5 Are there clear and effective processes for managing **risks**, issues and **performance**?
6 Is appropriate and accurate **information** being effectively processed, challanaged and acted on?	7 Are the **people** who use services, the public, **staff** and **external partners engaged** and involved to support high-quality sustainable services?	8 Are there robust system and process for **learning**, continuous **improvement** and **innovations**?

Figure 4.2: The eight KLOEs for the Well-led Framework

The depth and breadth of the areas for investigation can be shaped through the trust's self-assessment and/or initial findings of an independent review team at the start of the process. The developmental reviews are intended to complement CQC's trust-level well-led reviews. They will be greater in scope and depth, forward-looking, preventative and focused on improvement. They aim to identify early any factors which may lead to future failings and provide insight into areas for further development

The new Well-Led Framework is based on eight key lines of enquiry (KLOEs) as shown in Figure 4.2.

Each of the framework's KLOEs is supplemented by characteristics of good organisations, and detailed descriptions of good practice. The framework sets out the questions that providers and reviewers should ask of themselves under each KLOE. For read-across with the CQC's assessment process, the guidance also includes the prompts that CQC inspection teams use to assess each KLOE. During a developmental review, the self-review should be presented to the external facilitator for comments and further discussion. The reviewer will then agree areas for further scrutiny with the board.

Each of the KLOEs should be rated using a scheme that allows prioritisation of findings and escalation of concerns, informed by the good practice examples in the framework. Each judgment should be backed up by evidence where appropriate. Rating will aid prioritisation and ensure that issues are brought to the attention of the board. Boards should ensure that their approach facilitates continuous improvement rather than a compliance mindset. The reviews should not be about 'meeting a bar', but rather about prioritising improvement actions.

The guidance also contains appendices setting out how to scope a developmental review, commissioning an external facilitator and carrying out a developmental review. The review is likely to include:

- a desktop review of documents
- board and committee observations
- a board self-assessment
- a board skills inventory
- focus groups with internal and external stakeholders
- one-to-one interviews with board members, the trust secretary, lead governor, clinical leads and local stakeholders
- a peer practice assessment
- stakeholder surveys.

Choosing an external facilitator is the provider's responsibility. As well as the skills and experience needed to address specific areas of focus arising from self-review, the provider must ensure their supplier can take a holistic view of the organisation, connecting findings from different parts of the review and supporting action-planning, including suggesting appropriate interventions.

Providers should also ensure reviewers are suitably independent of the board. This includes avoiding using reviewers who have done audit or governance-related work for the provider in the previous three years, unless there are suitable safeguards against conflict of interest (i.e. information barriers).

Providers are also encouraged to consider involving peer reviewers as part of their external facilitation team, where appropriate, to make use of and enhance leadership and governance capability in the NHS.

The UK Corporate Governance Code

The first version of the UK Corporate Governance Code (the Code) was produced in 1992 by the Cadbury Committee. It is a particularly relevant document for FTs, as a significant similarity exists between the FT Code and the UK Corporate Governance Code. Chapter 1 outlines the changing emphasis in the UK Code. Even so, paragraph 2.5 is still the classic definition of the context of the Code:

> 'Corporate governance is the system by which companies are directed and controlled. Boards of directors are responsible for the governance of their companies. The shareholders' role in governance is to appoint the directors and the auditors and to satisfy themselves that an appropriate governance structure is in place. The responsibilities of the board include setting the company's strategic aims, providing the leadership to put them into effect, supervising the management of the business and reporting to shareholders on their stewardship. The board's actions are subject to laws, regulations and the shareholders in general meeting.'

Corporate governance is, therefore, about what the board of a company does and how it sets the values of the company. It is to be distinguished from the day-to-day operational management of the company by full-time executives. The Code has been updated regularly and the most recent version was published in September 2014.

The main principles of the Code (April 2016 version) can be summarised as follows:

Section A: Leadership

- Every company should be headed by an effective board, which is collectively responsible for the long-term success of the company.
- There should be a clear division of responsibilities at the head of the company between the running of the board and the executive responsibility for the running of the company's business. No one individual should have unfettered powers of decision.
- The chair is responsible for leadership of the board and ensuring its effectiveness on all aspects of its role.
- As part of their role as members of a unitary board, NEDs should constructively challenge and help develop proposals on strategy.

Section B: Effectiveness

- The board and its committees should have the appropriate balance of skills, experience, independence and knowledge of the company to enable them to discharge their respective duties and responsibilities effectively.
- There should be a formal, rigorous and transparent procedure for the appointment of new directors to the board.
- All directors should be able to allocate sufficient time to the company to discharge their responsibilities effectively.
- All directors should receive induction on joining the board and should regularly update and refresh their skills and knowledge.
- The board should be supplied in a timely manner with information in a form and of a quality appropriate to enable it to discharge its duties.
- The board should undertake a formal and rigorous annual evaluation of its own performance and that of its committees and individual directors.
- All directors should be submitted for re-election at regular intervals, subject to continued satisfactory performance.

Section C: Accountability

- The board should present a fair, balanced and understandable assessment of the company's position and prospects.

- The board is responsible for determining the nature and extent of the principal risks it is willing to take in achieving its strategic objectives. The board should maintain sound risk management and internal control systems.
- The board should establish formal and transparent arrangements for considering how they should apply the corporate reporting, risk management and internal control principles and for maintaining an appropriate relationship with the company's auditors.

Section D: Remuneration

- Executive directors' remuneration should be designed to promote the long-term success of the company. Performance-related elements should be transparent, stretching and rigorously applied.
- There should be a formal and transparent procedure for developing policy on executive remuneration and for fixing the remuneration packages of individual directors. No director should be involved in deciding his or her own remuneration.

Section E: Relations with shareholders

- There should be a dialogue with shareholders based on the mutual understanding of objectives. The board as a whole has responsibility for ensuring that a satisfactory dialogue with shareholders takes place.
- The board should use general meetings to communicate with investors and to encourage their participation.

The Code's function should be to help boards discharge their duties in the best interests of their companies. In recent reviews of the Code, the FRC has focused on changing its 'tone' by making limited but significant changes to signal the importance of the general principles which should guide board behaviours. The Corporate Governance Reform: Green Paper (November 2016) asked for views on:

- executive pay
- employee and customer voice
- corporate governance in large private businesses.

The Combined Code, which was replaced by the UK Corporate Governance Code in 2010, used to have a section that was addressed specifically to institutional shareholders, and dealt with the responsibilities of institutional investors for good corporate governance. This has now been replaced by a separate UK Stewardship Code.

FRC Guidance for Boards and Board Committees

The FRC issues guidance and other publications to assist boards and board committees in considering how to apply the UK Corporate Governance Code to their particular circumstances. These publications cover:

- board effectiveness
- the role of audit committees
- risk management, internal control and related financial and business reporting
- audit tendering.

This guidance is explored in greater detail in Chapters 2 and 5, as they are key to an understanding of board and committees effectiveness.

Other codes

The OECD Corporate Governance Principles

In 1999, the Organization for Economic Co-operation and Development (OECD) issued a number of non-binding principles on corporate governance, which were reviewed and amended in 2004.

The OECD Principles are intended to serve as a reference point for countries to use when evaluating their legal, institutional and regulatory provisions for corporate governance. They offer guidance and suggestions for stock exchanges, investors, companies and other bodies involved in developing good corporate governance practices.

Unlike national codes of corporate governance, the OECD Principles do not contain any detailed provisions about how the principles should be applied in practice. They are simply a set of main principles and supporting principles, with some additional explanations or 'annotations'. The principles deal with six aspects of governance:

- ensuring the basics for an effective corporate governance framework
- the rights of shareholders and key ownership functions
- the equitable treatment of shareholders
- the role of stakeholders in corporate governance
- disclosure and transparency
- the responsibilities of the board.

The OECD Principles begin with a statement that the corporate governance framework should:

- promote transparent and efficient markets
- be consistent with the rule of law
- clearly articulate the division of responsibilities among different supervisory, regulatory and enforcement authorities.

In the UK these basics are probably accepted as 'normal' for public companies, but it is a useful reminder that this is not necessarily the case at all times or in all countries.

The King IV Code

The 2016 King IV Code is the corporate governance code for South Africa. It is distinctive because it adopts a 'stakeholder inclusive' approach to corporate governance. In taking this approach, King IV includes some aspects of governance that are not found in other voluntary codes such as the UK Code such as the 'apply and explain' outlined earlier.

> 'Corporate governance for the purposes of King IV is defined as the exercise of ethical and effective leadership by the governing body towards the achievement of the following governance outcomes:
>
> - Ethical culture
> - Good performance
> - Effective control
> - Legitimacy'.

The objectives of King IV are to:

- Promote good governance as integral to running an organisation and delivering governance outcomes.
- Broaden the acceptance of the King IV by making it accessible across a variety of sectors.
- Reinforce corporate governance as a holistic and interrelated set of arrangements to be understood and implemented in an integrated way.
- Encourage transparent and meaningful reporting to stakeholders.
- Present corporate governance as concerned with not only structure and process but also with ethical consciousness and conduct.

Summary

Best practice in both health service governance and corporate governance is found in the combination of legal and regulatory requirements alongside voluntary principles and codes of conduct. The key issue at stake here is to prevent the tsunami-like wave of regulations, codes and guidance from obliterating the core principles of good governance.

To paraphrase the UK Corporate Governance Code, such frameworks are limited to being a general guide to principles, structure and processes. They cannot guarantee effective board behaviour because the range of situations in which they apply are too great for them to attempt to more specifically mandate behaviour.

PART TWO

The board's role and directors' responsibilities

5

The board's structure and its committees

Introduction

An efficient and effective board is a key requirement of good governance. The board should have a clear idea of its responsibilities, and should fulfil these to the best of its abilities. There should be a suitable balance of skills, experience and power on the board. As a consequence, the role and composition of a board, and the duties and responsibilities of directors and committees, will be important. The ability to identify the characteristics of an effective board, and compare these with the actual practice of boards, is also important.

This chapter concentrates on the structures and processes of the board, while boardroom behaviours and practice will be covered in more detail in Part 3. For the purposes of this chapter, reference to the board should be taken to include a clinical commissioning group's (CCG) governing body unless expressly set out otherwise.

The board is sometimes referred to as the 'controlling mind' of an organisation or as its 'head'. Though an organisation is not a person in the human sense, it does have characteristics, which support the use of these terms, such as entering into contractually binding arrangements. As the head of the organisation, the board has governance responsibilities to control and lead, while being held to account for delivering the organisation's strategic objectives.

Another way of looking at this is to say that the board acts as the agent for the organisation and exercises powers on its behalf. These powers are delegated to the board under the constitutional documents that establish the organisation, such as statutory instruments, core constitutions or standing orders. Underpinning all of this is the expectation that the board is collectively responsible for its actions, and that the individual members of the board make their decisions in the best interests of the organisation.

Governance responsibilities of the board

Responsibilities set out in NHS regulation or guidance

It is important to distinguish between the different organisations as there are different guidelines set out for each. These are as follows.

Foundation trusts

According to paragraph 18A of Schedule 7 to the National Health Service Act 2006 (NHS Act 2006) (as inserted by Health and Social Care Act 2012 (HSCA 2012)) the duty of the board, and of each director individually, is to act with a view to promoting the success of the corporation so as to maximise the benefits for the members of the corporation as a whole and for the public. This mirrors the duty as set out in the Companies Act 2006 (CA 2006) for companies. This is also set out in the FT Code, which goes on to say that 'every NHS FT should be headed by an effective board of directors. The board is collectively responsible for the performance of the NHS FT'.

Clinical commissioning groups

The duty of the governing body is to ensure that the CCG has made appropriate arrangements for ensuring that the CCG complies with its obligations to exercise its functions effectively, efficiently and economically. It also has a duty to ensure that it complies with relevant generally accepted principles of good governance. Section 14L of NHS Act 2006, as inserted by section 25 of the HSCA 2012, sets out the duties of the governing bodies of CCGs:

- promoting the NHS Constitution in the securing of health services;
- securing continuous improvement in the quality and safety of health services and in the quality of the experience undergone by patients;
- securing continuous improvement in quality of primary medical services;
- reducing inequalities between patients with respect to their ability to access health services, and with respect to the outcomes achieved for them;
- promoting the involvement of patients, their carers and representatives in relation to their health service;
- enabling patients to make choices with respect to aspects of health services provided to them;
- obtaining appropriate professional health service advice to enable it effectively to discharge its functions;
- promoting innovation in the provision of health services;
- promoting research on matters relevant to health services;
- promoting education and training for the persons connected with the provision of health services; and
- securing health services that are provided in an integrated way to improve quality, reduce inequalities of access or outcome.

NHS trust boards

According to the Department of Health (DH), NHS trust boards have six key functions. They are held accountable for these by the DH on behalf of the Secretary of State. These are:

- to set the strategic direction of the organisation within the overall policies and priorities of the government and the NHS, define its annual and longer-term objectives and agree plans to achieve them;
- to oversee the delivery of planned results by monitoring performance against objectives and ensuring corrective action is taken when necessary;
- to ensure effective financial stewardship through value for money, financial control and financial planning and strategy;
- to ensure that high standards of health service governance and personal behaviour are maintained in the conduct of the business of the whole organisation;
- to appoint, appraise and remunerate senior executives; and
- to ensure that there is effective dialogue between the organisation and the local community on its plans and performance and that these are responsive to the community's needs.

The *Healthy NHS Board* (see Chapter 4) states that 'the purpose of NHS boards is to govern effectively and in doing so build patient, public and stakeholder confidence that their health and healthcare is in safe hands'.

It goes on to say that 'in unitary NHS boards, all directors are collectively and corporately accountable for organisational performance'.

Responsibilities according to the UK Code

The board of directors is the key decision-making body in an organisation. Therefore, an organisation should have an effective board of directors dedicated to ensuring that it achieves its objectives. The UK Code states as one of its main principles 'every company should be headed by an effective board, which is collectively responsible for the long-term success of the organisation'.

The introduction of the phrase 'long-term' into this principle in 2010 recognised that the board should not focus on short-term achievements, if these are inconsistent with longer-term success. The UK Code also states that the role of the board should be to:

- provide entrepreneurial leadership of the company within a framework of prudent and effective controls which enables risk to be assessed and managed;
- set the company's strategic aims;
- ensure that the necessary financial and human resources are in place for the company to meet its objectives and review management performance;
- set the company's values and standards and ensure that its obligations to its shareholders and others are understood and met.

The preface to the UK Code states:

> 'One of the key roles for the board includes establishing the culture, values and ethics of the company. It is important that the board sets the correct "tone from the top". The directors should lead by example and ensure that good standards of behaviour permeate throughout all levels of the organisation.

> This will help prevent misconduct, unethical practices and support the delivery of long-term success.'

The board should not get involved with operational matters (except in its monitoring role), with the responsibility delegated to executive management. The UK Code also states that all directors must act in what they consider to be the best interests of the company, without specifying what those 'best interests' are or might be.

The South African King IV corporate governance code identifies the distinct roles and responsibilities of the board and management as follows:

> '[The governing body should] steer the organisation and set its strategic direction, on the basis of which management will develop the strategy which is to be approved by the governing body. To give effect to the organisation's strategy, management formulates policy and operational plans, also to be approved by the governing body. Management then, implements and executes strategy in accordance with policy and plans, which are overseen and supervised by the governing body. The governing body finally ensures that there is accountability for organisational performance through, among others, reporting and disclosure. The latter in turn forms the basis for reviewing strategic direction, which starts the business cycle anew.'

King IV goes on to describe the key governance areas of ethics, risk, compliance, remuneration and stakeholder relationship.

Responsibilities according to the FRC Guidance on Board Effectiveness

The Financial Reporting Council (FRC) *Guidance on Board Effectiveness* (2011) states that an effective board is one that:

- provides direction for management;
- demonstrates ethical leadership, displaying and promoting throughout the company behaviours consistent with the culture and values it has defined for the organisation;
- creates a performance culture that drives value creation without exposing the company to excessive risk of value destruction;
- makes well informed and high-quality decisions based on a clear line of sight into the business;
- creates the right framework for helping directors meet their statutory duties under the CA 2006, and/or other relevant statutory and regulatory regimes;
- is accountable, particularly to those that provide the company's capital; and
- thinks carefully about its governance arrangements and embraces evaluation of their effectiveness.

The guidance adds that a board that demonstrates that it has suitable governance policies and systems in place is much more likely to generate trust and support among its shareholders and other stakeholders. It also goes on to look at effective decision-making in boards, as this is an important board activity. The guidance sets out that the board should have clear policies about what matters need a board decision or approval, and the processes required for each type of decision. Good decision-making can be improved by giving directors sufficient time to prepare for meetings, allowing sufficient time for issues to be discussed at board meetings, and making clear to executives what action they must take to implement board decisions.

The guidance also recognises that, even with suitable policies and procedures, the quality of decision-making by the board can be impaired by:

- a dominant personality or group of directors on the board, which can inhibit contributions from other directors;
- insufficient attention to risk along with treating risk as a compliance issue rather than as part of the decision-making process;
- failure to recognise the value implications of running the business on the basis of self interest and other poor ethical standards;
- a reluctance to involve non-executive directors (NEDs), or of matters being brought to the board for sign-off rather than debate;
- complacent or intransigent attitudes;
- a weak organisational culture; and
- inadequate information or analysis.

The guidance suggests that boards may wish to consider extra measures to reduce the risk of flawed decisions, such as describing in board papers the process that has been used to arrive at and challenge proposals prior to presenting them to the board. This allows directors not involved in the project to assess the appropriateness of the process as a precursor to assessing the merits of the project itself. It might also be appropriate to put in place additional safeguards to reduce the risk of distorted judgments by:

- commissioning an independent report;
- seeking advice from an expert;
- introducing a 'devil's advocate' to provide challenge;
- establishing a sole purpose sub-committee; or
- convening additional meetings.

The guidance notes that some boards favour separate discussions for important decisions; for example, separating discussions about concepts, proposals for discussion and proposals for decision. This gives executive directors (EDs) more opportunity to put their case at the earlier stages, and all directors the opportunity to share concerns or challenge assumptions well in advance of the point of decision.

Board structures

Unitary boards

Organisations are based around a unitary board structure in many countries. The unitary board consists of both EDs and NEDs under the leadership of the chair. A unitary board makes collective decisions and is accountable to the shareholders or major stakeholders. It is commonly accepted governance practice that the NEDs in a listed organisation should be independent, although this is not a legal requirement.

In the NHS, the concept of a unitary board has not always been well understood or implemented. In 2006, the *Integrated Governance Handbook* illustrates several dangers of not using a unitary board structure:

> 'To date, NHS boards have performed in a diverse manner by separating out the roles of the various directors, i.e. finance, medical, nursing etc, and the non-executive director/lay individual input. The result of this is that, if the board takes a decision, it is often deemed to be the decision of, say, the finance director or HR director, rather than being a corporate decision. Board corporacy is paramount. Each decision or agreement entered into in the boardroom is a fully accepted corporate decision. If a decision around finance is taken and the information brought to the board clarifies the debate, if there are implications say, one month after the decision, the responsibility is of the corporate whole, rather than just the finance director.'

There is a clear move away from the unitary board structure for the CCGs that were established in 2012. NHS England (NHSE) advocates adherence with the Good Governance Standard for Public Services (2004) as the guidance for best practice in governance, which presupposes a form of leadership not based on the principle of a unitary board. This is in stark contrast to most other NHS organisations (such as FTs) for whom the unitary board is a core principle of governance.

The purpose of the unitary board principle was to ensure that the interests of all stakeholders were properly considered and balanced. As such, CCGs are unlikely to operate in a way that is entirely consistent with the major codes of practice that set out best practice in corporate governance for the NHS – including the UK Corporate Governance Code, King IV, the Higgs Report and the FT Code.

The concept of the unitary board is reinforced within the governance structure of the NHS FT, even though there may appear to be a two-tier board structure with a council of governors and a board of directors. The FT Core Constitution and the FT Code make it clear that the concept of the unitary board refers to the fact that NEDs and EDs share the same liability within the board of directors. All directors, executive and non-executive, have the responsibility to constructively challenge the decisions of the board and help develop proposals on priorities, risk mitigation, values, standards and strategy.

The *Healthy NHS Board* adds:

> 'A key strength of unitary boards is the opportunity provided for the exchange of views between executives and NEDs, drawing on and pooling their experience and capabilities. Boards are "social systems". The most effective boards invest time and energy in the development of mature relationships and ways of working.'

One of the threats to the principle of the unitary board is the increasing emphasis on the role of the NED. The role of independent scrutiny and constructive challenge undertaken by the NED role can create a tension with their responsibility to provide a strategic oversight and to act collectively alongside the executive board members. Executive directors are not excused from providing scrutiny and challenge, it's just that they cannot be classed as independent.

For example, it has been seen as good practice for NEDs to meet (at least) annually as a group without the chair or executives present, and also for board committees to be made up solely of NEDs; if not managed correctly, this can divide a unitary board. There is also a further threat, particularly rife in the NHS, which is the increasing requirement for NEDs to be 'champions' for specific areas of management concern, e.g. for whistleblowing or infection control or learning from deaths. This blurs the boundary between governance and management, and between the roles of the NED and the executive board member.

Having said all that, the concept of a unitary board is still common practice within the NHS and continues to be the subject of a considerable amount of board development.

Two-tier boards

Some countries, including Germany and Austria, have two-tier boards. A two-tier structure usually consists of a supervisory board and a management board.

The management board is responsible for managing the organisation. It is led by the chair of the management board, normally the chief executive officer (CEO), and its members are appointed by the supervisory board. The management board consists entirely of EDs. It develops strategy for the organisation in co-operation with the supervisory board, and is responsible for implementing the agreed strategy. It also has responsibility for risk management and for the preparation of the annual financial statements (which are examined by the auditors and the supervisory board). The chair of the management board reports to the supervisory board chair.

The supervisory board is responsible for general oversight of the organisation and of the management board. Members are normally elected by shareholders, except in public companies with more than 500 employees where a minimum proportion of the supervisory board must consist of employee representatives. The supervisory board consists entirely of NEDs. The chair leads the supervisory board, which advises the management board and must be involved in decision-making on all fundamental matters affecting the organisation. These include 'decisions or measures which fundamentally change the asset, financial or earnings situations of the enterprise' (German Corporate Governance Code). The audit committee consists entirely of supervisory board members. In Germany, supervisory board members include:

- representatives of trade unions and/or the organisation's employees
- representatives of major shareholders
- former executives of the organisation.

Supervisory board NEDs are therefore not necessarily independent, particularly employee representatives. It can therefore be difficult to reconcile the differing views of employee representatives and representatives of major shareholders without antagonising the executives on the management board.

On the other hand, if there are a large number of former executives on the supervisory board, there is a risk that it could take a lenient view of management activities. In addition, some independent supervisory board directors might well be senior managers of other companies, where they are management board members. These individuals might therefore sympathise with the views of the management board.

The success of corporate governance in a two-tier structure depends on a functional relationship between the supervisory board and the management board. The chair of the supervisory board plays a key role. They are responsible for making sure that the two boards work well together. The most powerful individuals in the organisation are the chair of the supervisory board and the CEO. If the relationship between these two works well, the chair will effectively speak for the management at meetings of the supervisory board.

The German Corporate Governance Code states that 'the management board and supervisory board co-operate closely to the benefit of the enterprise' and the management board should discuss the implementation of strategy regularly with the supervisory board.

Criticisms of the two-tier board structure

The main concerns are as follows.

- Supervisory boards are too big, having up to 20 members. German supervisory boards include a large number of employee representatives, and large numbers can result in inefficient meetings.
- It has been common to appoint retired former managers of the organisation to the supervisory board, and these individuals might be tempted to retain some influence over the actions and operational decisions of their successors. This is not the purpose of a supervisory board. On the other hand, if former managers are appointed to the supervisory board, it will benefit from their knowledge and experience of the business. In Germany former managers are

now prohibited from 'moving upstairs' to the supervisory board for at least two years, unless the move receives the support of at least 25% of shareholders, because it is thought a former executive will not be sufficiently independent immediately after retiring.

- Companies with more than 500 employees are required to have workers' or trade union representatives on the supervisory board. Companies with more than 2,000 employees are required to have an even greater percentage of employee representatives on the supervisory board. This requirement is an enforcement of the principle of 'co-determination', embodied in German law, that the workers as well as the management and owners should determine the future of their companies. Unfortunately, workers' representatives can lack the competence to consider strategic issues or are not independent from the organisation. In some instances, worker members of a supervisory board opposing planned initiatives by the organisation have been accused of leaking confidential information to the press.
- Concerns about information leaks can damage communications between supervisory and management boards.

The German Corporate Governance Code suggests that, the unitary board system and two-tier board system are becoming similar in practice because of intensive interaction between the management and supervisory boards. The German Code also suggests that the two types of board structure are equally successful. Developments in some German companies in recent years also suggest that the supervisory boards of large German companies are becoming more responsive to the interests of their shareholders.

The 2009 Walker Report on UK bank corporate governance considered whether unitary boards contributed to the scale of the financial crisis in 2007–2009 and whether a two-tier board structure might be more suitable for large banks. Its conclusions were fairly critical of the two-tier structure:

> 'In practice, two-tier structures do not appear to assure members of the supervisory board of access to the quality and timeliness of management information flow that would generally be regarded as essential for non-executives on a unitary board. Moreover, since, in a two-tier structure, members of the supervisory and executive boards meet separately and do not share the same responsibilities, the two-tier model would not provide opportunity for the interactive exchange of views between executives and NEDs, drawing on and pooling their respective experience and capabilities in the way that takes place in a well-functioning unitary board.'

Matters reserved for the board

Regardless of structure, the board of directors must meet sufficiently regularly to discharge its duties effectively. In addition the board should have a formal schedule of matters specifically reserved for decision by the board of directors which will ensure that the main decision-making powers belong to the board of directors. Although the board delegates many of the operational decision-making responsibilities to executive management, it should retain the most significant decisions and these are recorded in the Matters Reserved for the Board. A key aspect of governance is therefore the nature of the decisions the board reserves for itself (rather than delegating them to executive management).

The UK Code does not specify which matters should be reserved by the board, but states simply in a provision that 'there should be a formal schedule of matters reserved for its decision'. It then states that the annual report should include a statement of how the board operates, a high-level statement of the types of decision that it reserves for its own decisions and the types of decision that it delegates to executive management.

Example statement – Marks and Spencer plc 2016 annual report
Role of the Board and its committees

The Board is responsible for the stewardship of the Company, overseeing its conduct and affairs to create sustainable value for the benefit of its shareholders. In performing this task, the Board recognises that to be successful over the long-term it has a wider duty to care for the interests of employees, customers and the communities in which the Company operates, and whose support is required to create sustainable value.

The Board discharges some of its responsibilities directly and discharges others through its Board Committees and through management. The Terms of Reference of the Board and its Committees are included in our Governance Framework.

The Board agrees, and has collective responsibility for, the strategy of the Company. For M&S, our strategy is understood to mean the development of specific actions aimed at satisfying the needs of our target customer groups across the product categories and in the territories in which we choose to operate. The articulation of our strategy will include agreement on how our physical and intellectual property and the skills of our people should be used, developed and enhanced to create competitive advantage for the Company.

The Board delegates to executive management, the execution of the Company's strategy and the day-to-day management and operation of the Company's business.

The Board is responsible for overseeing, guiding and holding to account management in carrying out these responsibilities. The Board is responsible for ensuring that appropriate values, ethics and behaviours for the conduct of the Company are agreed and that appropriate procedures and training are in place to ensure that these are observed throughout the Company. The Board has discussed and agreed the key values of Inspiration, Innovation, Integrity and In Touch and these underpin the required values, ethics and behaviours.

Clear Terms of Reference outline the full schedule of matters reserved for the Board's decision and that of its key committees.

The Board is responsible for:

- Ensuring leadership through effective oversight and review. Supported by its principal committees – Audit, Remuneration, and Nomination – the Board sets the strategic direction and aims to deliver sustainable shareholder value over the longer term.
- Overseeing the implementation of appropriate risk assessment systems and processes to identify, manage and mitigate the principal risks of the Company's business. Much of this work is delegated to the Audit Committee.
- Effective succession planning at Board level and for assessing the processes in place to ensure that there is appropriate succession planning amongst senior management. Much of this work is delegated to the Nomination Committee.

In addition to the other matters referred to in its framework, the Board is responsible for specific matters relating to strategy, finance, risk management, internal control and audit, legal, reputation and public company management. These, along with the individual roles of the Board members, are covered by the 'Schedule of Matters Reserved to the Board' in the Marks and Spencer Group plc Governance Framework, and can be found at www.marksandspencer.com/thecompany.

ICSA: The Governance Institute's Guidance Note on matters that should be reserved for the board is consistent with the provisions of the UK Code. The list of items in the Guidance Note includes decisions relating to matters such as:

- approval of annual operating and capital expenditure budgets;
- approval of the annual report and accounts;
- approval of formal communications with shareholders;
- approval of major contracts and investments;
- approval of policies on matters such as health and safety, corporate social responsibility (CSR) and the environment approval of strategy;
- changes in corporate or capital structure;
- compliance with legal and regulatory requirements;
- oversight of operations (including accounting, planning and internal control systems); and
- performance review.

The company secretary may be given the task of preparing and maintaining the list of matters to be reserved for the board (for board approval), and reminding the board whenever necessary that certain decisions should not be delegated.

Although this guidance is not specifically aimed at NHS boards, it contains best practice, which NHS boards should actively consider. Though the formal powers of an NHS organisation are vested in its board, the NHS Code of Accountability allows the board to delegate some of its business to board committees and to the executive.

The board approach to delegation should be consistently set out in:

- its standing orders, which specify how the organisation conducts its business;
- its standing financial instructions, which detail the financial responsibilities, policies and procedures adopted; and
- its scheme of reservation and delegation. This sets out which responsibilities and accountabilities remain at board level and which have been delegated to committees and to the executive, together with the appropriate reporting arrangements that ensure the board has oversight.

The ICSA guidance notes do offer a sample matters reserved for both a FT board of directors and council of governors. A thorough understanding of the matters reserved for the board must underpin a board's approach to delegation. Its schemes of delegation must be subject to regular board review to ensure that the distribution of functions and accountabilities is accurately and appropriately described, and remains appropriate despite changes in the organisation.

Size and composition of the board

The effectiveness of a board of directors depends on its size and composition.

Size

The typical size of a board of directors varies with the size of the organisation and/or the industry or business sector in which it operates. In addition, the average size of boards in listed companies varies between different countries.

A board should not be any larger than it needs to be. Large boards are more difficult to manage, because there are more individuals involved, and board meetings can be very long and time consuming. On the other hand, a board should be large enough for its members to collectively have the knowledge, skills and experience to make effective decisions.

The UK Code suggests that the board should be sufficiently large to avoid a situation in which it becomes over-reliant on one or two individuals, for example as chairmen of board committees (nominations, remuneration, audit and risk committees). It states:

> 'The board should be of sufficient size that the requirements of the business can be met and that changes to the board's composition and that of its committees can be managed without disruption, and should not be so large as to be unwieldy.'

The Walker Review identified that where board membership exceeded 8–12 directors, the risk known as 'group-think' – the phenomenon of a group exhibiting thought processes whereby they seek to minimise conflict and reach consensus without critically testing, analysing and evaluating ideas – increases.

The *Healthy NHS Board* suggests that:

> 'NHS boards should not be so large as to be unwieldy, but must be large enough to provide the balance of skills and experience that is appropriate for the organisation. The number of directors is defined in the trust's establishment order, or in a FT's constitution. The composition of the board should achieve a balance between continuity and renewal. Chairs and non-executive directors (NEDs) of NHS trusts serve a maximum of 10 years in the same NHS post (or two three-year terms for FTs) to ensure this balance. Within this period, any second reappointment must be through open competition. The composition of the board should achieve a balance between continuity and renewal.'

Composition

The composition of a board of directors depends partly on its size. In the UK, the board of a large public company commonly consists of a:

- chair
- possibly a deputy chair
- the CEO
- the senior independent director (SID, who may also be the deputy chair)
- EDs
- NEDs.

Collectively, the members of the board should have sufficient skills and experience to provide effective leadership for the organisation. This suggests that they should have a variety of different backgrounds and expertise.

There should also be a suitable balance of power so that one individual or a small group of individuals is unable to dominate the board and its decision-making. In countries such as the UK, it is considered appropriate to appoint independent NEDs to a board, because they act as a counter-balance to EDs who may give priority to their own interests above those of the shareholders (and other stakeholders). They also have skills and experience that EDs do not have, because they come from a different background and so are able to contribute different ideas and views to board discussions and decision-making. As they do not have a strong personal financial interest in the organisation, NEDs are more easily able to represent the interests of the major stakeholders (typically shareholders) and to act (where required) as a restraint on executive management.

These principles relating to board composition are set out in the UK Code as follows:

> 'The board and its committees should have the appropriate balance of skills, experience, independence and knowledge of the company to enable them to discharge their respective duties and responsibilities effectively.'

> 'The board should include an appropriate combination of executive and non-EDs (and in particular independent non-executive directors) such that no individual or small group of individuals can dominate the board's decision-taking.'

The UK Code sets out different requirements for large listed companies – where at least one half of the board, excluding the chair, should be independent NEDs – and for smaller companies (those outside the FTSE 350). Smaller companies should appoint at least two independent NEDs.

Guidelines about the composition of a unitary board differ between countries. The King IV Code, for example, recommends that the majority of directors should be NEDs and the majority of NEDs should be independent, but also adds that there should be at least two executive directors on the board – the CEO and chief finance officer (CFO) (finance director).

NHS board composition

The principle that there should be sufficient independent NEDs to create a suitable balance of power is also reflected in the FT Code. However there is a distinction between NEDs and the role of lay members on a CCG governing body which is explored in Chapter 13.

In the NHS, the composition of the board is clearly dictated either by:

- the Trust Membership and Procedure Regulations (SI 1998/1975);
- in FTs, by Schedule 7 to the NHS Act 2006; or
- in CCGs by section 14L of the NHS Act 2006 as inserted by section 25 of the HSCA 2012.

The detail of the composition for FTs and CCGs are set out in Chapters 12 and 13 respectively.

The composition for NHS Trusts is as follows:

- The maximum number of directors of an NHS trust shall be 12 excluding the chair and the minimum not less than eight.
- The EDs of an NHS trust shall include the chief officer of the trust; the chief finance officer of the trust; a medical or dental practitioner and a registered nurse or registered midwife.
- There will be a trust chair (appointed by NHS TDA), up to seven NEDs (appointed by the NHS TDA), and up to five EDs (but not exceeding the number of non-officer members) including the chief executive and the director of finance.

Board committees

One aspect of best practice in governance is that the board should decide that the EDs be excluded from the decision-making or monitoring responsibilities for some issues.

This is achieved by delegating certain responsibilities to committees of the board. A board committee might consist entirely or mostly of NEDs, and have the responsibility for dealing with particular issues and making recommendations to the full board. The full board is then usually expected to accept and endorse the recommendations of the relevant board committee. Despite this, the committees only have delegated authority from the board; they do not have the capacity to act independently.

According to the Walker Review, the optimum size for a sub-committee is between five and nine members. It states 'at five a group becomes more of a team, at seven thinking is optimised; above nine the ability of the cognitive limit of the group is exceeded'.

Three standing committees are recommended by the UK Code:

- an audit committee
- a nomination committee
- a remuneration committee.

Guidance for the NHS can be found in the DH publication *The Intelligent Board*, which recommended that all NHS trusts should have an audit committee, a nomination committee and a remuneration (and terms of service) committee as part of their governance arrangements. All report to the board of directors.

Nowadays, the model standing orders for NHS Trusts requires an audit committee as well as a remuneration and terms of service committee. In line with its role as a corporate trustee, the board should also establish a charitable funds committee. This enables it to administer any funds held in trust either as charitable or non-charitable funds, in accordance with any statutory/legal requirements or best practice required by the Charity Commission.

The FT core constitution for FTs requires the board to establish:

- a committee consisting of the trust chair, the chief executive and the other non-EDs to appoint or remove the other EDs (nomination committee); and
- a committee of NEDs to decide the remuneration and allowances, and the other terms and conditions of office, of the chief executive and other EDs (remuneration committee).

According to the FT Code, FTs may choose to have two nomination committees, one dealing with NEDs and one dealing with EDs. Where an NHS FT has two nomination committees, the nomination committee responsible for the appointment of NEDs should consist of a majority of governors. If only one nominations committee exists, when nominations for non-executives are being discussed – including the appointment of a chair or a deputy chair – there should be a majority of governors on the committee and also a majority of governors on the interview panel. The core constitution also requires the FT to establish a NED committee as an audit committee to perform monitoring, reviewing and other functions. It also requires the council of governors to approve the appointment of all NEDs, including the trust chair.

CCGs are required by statute to appoint an audit committee and the remuneration (see section 14M(1) of the NHS Act 2006, as inserted by section 25 of HSCA 2012). The NHS England guidance *Towards Establishment: Creating responsive and accountable clinical commissioning groups* also recommends that CCGs consider the establishment of a quality committee to:

- provide assurance on the quality of services commissioned; and
- to promote a culture of continuous improvement and innovation with respect to safety of services, clinical effectiveness and patient experience.

Some boards might establish other committees. For example, an organisation might have an environment committee if its business activities are likely to have important consequences for the environment – especially if it involves an exposure to government regulation, the law and public opinion. The Walker Review recommended that all banks and life assurance companies establish a risk committee with responsibility for 'oversight and advice to the board on the current risk exposures to the entity and future risk strategy'. In practice, most NHS organisations also have a board committee, which covers quality assurance, governance and/or risk.

Boards should ensure that they delegate authority to committees in line with their constitutional documents, set out clear terms of reference for them – including the composition and quoracy requirements – and provide a clear statement of the remit of the committee. These committees do not absolve the board of its responsibility in their respective areas of scrutiny: rather, they should support the board in carrying out its responsibilities of strategic leadership and holding to account.

The three main committees (audit, nomination and remuneration) are set out in detail in later chapters. Here is a brief summary of their functions.

The audit committee

The FRC *Guidance on Audit Committees* (2016) states that the 'audit committee has a particular role, acting independently from the executive, to ensure that the interests of shareholders are properly protected in relation to financial reporting and internal control'. The guidance contains recommendations about the conduct of the audit committee's relationship with the board, with the executive management and with internal and external auditors:

> 'The essential features of these interactions are a frank, open working relationship and a high level of mutual respect. The audit committee must be prepared to take a robust stand, and all parties must be prepared to make information freely available to the committee, to listen to their views and to talk through the issues openly.'

At times, it may be necessary for the committee to challenge the position of the external auditors or other professional advisers. The committee should comprise a minimum of three independent NEDs and have clear terms of reference. The chair of the board may only be a member of the committee in smaller companies, and even then may not chair the committee. These principles are reflected in the *NHS Audit Committee Handbook,* published by the Healthcare Financial Management Association (HFMA). The HFMA handbook says the audit committee plays a key role by:

> 'critically reviewing and reporting on the relevance and robustness of the governance structures and assurance processes on which the board places reliance. In particular, this requires the committee to understand and scrutinise the organisations overarching framework of governance, risk and control'.

The HFMA handbook stipulates that the chair of the board should not chair the audit committee nor be a member of the committee. It also specifies that at least one member of the committee should have 'recent and relevant financial experience' (in line with the FRC guidance mentioned above).

The audit committee should summarise its work during the year, submitting an annual report to the board promptly after the year-end but before it considers the organisation's annual report and statutory declarations. The UK Code also provides that a separate section of the annual report should describe the work of the committee. This deliberately puts the spotlight on the audit committee and gives it an authority that it might otherwise lack.

The FRC *Guidance on Audit Committees 2016* has introduced additional requirements, which are set out in more detail in Chapter 17.

The nomination committee

This committee gained a higher profile after the publication of the Higgs Report, which resulted in the UK Code recommending that all listed companies should establish a nomination committee. Its remit covers the review of the structure, size and composition of the board, including:

- the oversight of the board's succession planning requirements for both EDs and NEDs (and the company secretary);
- the identification and assessment of potential board candidates; and
- making nominations to the board for its approval as appropriate.

The committee should comprise the chair, the CEO and the NEDs, all appointed by the board. The majority of its members must be independent NEDs. The chair of the board should chair the committee, except when it is dealing with the appointment of a successor chair: the SID should chair the committee in this instance.

These guidelines are largely followed by NHS organisations in their standing orders or constitutional documents.

The remuneration committee

This committee received an increased profile following the publication of the Kay Review and the stirrings of the 'Shareholder Spring' in 2012 when investors refused to back multi-million pound bonuses for executives when coupled with extremely poor corporate performance.

There has been a greater emphasis on public disclosure of executive remuneration, and a culture change of shareholders refusing to accept severance pay arrangements. Changes in 2013 to the CA 2006 saw increased levels of reporting on remuneration in the annual report and greater voting powers for shareholders. More recently the consultation on employee representation on boards may also impact remuneration levels for senior managers and directors.

The Enterprise and Regulatory Reform Act 2013 underlines the importance of boards and investors engaging on directors' remuneration. The UK Code recommends that the committee determines an appropriate balance between fixed and performance-related, and immediate and deferred, remuneration; that performance conditions should be relevant, stretching and designed to promote the long-term success of the company; and that incentives should be compatible with risk policies and systems. The committee should also consider whether the directors should be eligible for annual bonuses and/or benefits under long-term incentive schemes.

The UK Code states that the committee should comprise at least three independent NEDs (although two is permissible for smaller companies). In addition to the independent NEDs, the chair of the board may also be a member of the committee if they were considered independent on appointment as chair, but may not chair the committee. ICSA's model terms of reference for the remuneration committee states that it is good practice for the company secretary to act as secretary to the committee, although this is not a provision in the UK Code.

Under the UK Code, companies are required to publish a remuneration report which includes three sections:

- a statement from the chair of the remuneration committee covering key decisions and changes made to remuneration in the year;
- a forward-looking remuneration policy report; and
- an annual report on remuneration which includes both how the policy has been implemented in the year under review and how it will be implemented in the forthcoming year.

Shareholders also have a binding vote on the policy report, in addition to an annual advisory vote on the annual remuneration report. HM Treasury also requires NHS organisations to provide a remuneration report in a prescribed format within their annual report and accounts.

Table 5.1: Summary of the UK Code's recommendations regarding membership of board committees

Nominations committee	Audit committee	Remuneration committee
Chair should be the chair of the board	Chair should be an independent NED	Chair should be an independent NED
Majority of members should be independent NEDs	All independent NEDs – in large companies, at least three, in smaller companies two	All independent NEDs – in large companies, at least three, in smaller companies two
If the board chair is the company chair, he should not act as chair when the committee is considering a successor	In smaller companies, the chair of the board may also be a member of the audit committee (but not chair of the committee), in addition to the independent NEDs – but only if he was independent on appointment to the chair	The chair of the board may be a member of the committee if they were considered independent on appointment as chair, but may not chair the committee
	At least one member of the committee should have recent and relevant financial experience	

Protecting the independence and effectiveness of board committees

As a way of protecting the independence and improving the effectiveness of board committees, the UK Code recommends that consideration should be given to the benefits of ensuring that committee membership is refreshed when deciding the chairship and membership of board committees (membership rotation). It adds that undue reliance should not be placed on particular individuals.

In addition, the only individuals who are entitled to attend meetings of the nomination, remuneration and audit committees are the chair and members of the committee, although other individuals may attend at the invitation of the committee.

Governance checklist

- ✓ Does the board act as the controlling mind of the organisation?
- ✓ Does it provide strategic and entrepreneurial leadership?
- ✓ Are there prudent and effective controls to manage the principal risks faced by the organisation?

- ✓ Do EDs and NEDs fulfil their roles individually and collectively within a unitary board structure?
- ✓ Are the statutory board committees properly constituted?
- ✓ Do they provide effective oversight in their respective areas?
- ✓ How does assurance flow from committee to board and between committees?
- ✓ Are the board committees properly constituted with delegated powers and clear terms of reference?
- ✓ Does the board make the appropriate public disclosures about its work and the work of its committees?

Summary

The unitary nature of the board is a key issue in understanding the governance arrangements for the board. There is a distinct difference for governing bodies of CCGs, which are not established as unitary boards. On all boards, however, the distinct roles for EDs and NEDs (lay members in CCGs) must be recognised, while at the same time maintaining collective responsibility. The board acts as the 'controlling mind' or head of the organisation: checks and balances need to be in place to make sure that it is held fully to account by stakeholders for the decisions that it takes.

In order to further understand the dynamics of the board the following chapters will explore the individual duties and powers of directors and the specific roles played by board members.

6

Directors' duties and liabilities

Introduction

It is an accepted governance tenet that boards have a collective responsibility for the way they act and make decisions. However, the individual directors who make up the board also have key duties and responsibilities as a consequence of their roles – and they will be liable for certain outcomes that result from the actions and decisions of the board. There is extensive legal precedent on this subject which cannot be covered in detail in this handbook. However, the information collected here will form the basis of a good understanding for those individuals who take on a director role within an NHS organisation.

As set out in Chapter 5, the directors act as agents of the organisation, binding the organisation in its relationships with a number of third parties. They can do this with 'actual authority' or 'apparent authority' (the directors represented to the third party that they had the authority to act on behalf of the organisation).

This power to act is constrained by the duties that are expected of those directors. These duties stem from two sources – common law and statute. The duties enshrined in common law should be considered for directors of NHS organisations. As far as the legislation is concerned, a 'company' means a company formed and registered under the companies' legislation. NHS organisations that are organisations created by statutory instrument – not registered companies – are not bound by this legislation. Even so, it is good practice to have an understanding of the general principles of the companies' legislation and the nature of the original common law duties.

A distinction should be made between the powers and duties of EDs as board members and their responsibilities as managers of the organisation. Managers have neither powers nor duties to bind the organisation. The relationship they have with the organisation (including their authority and responsibilities) is established by their contract of employment and by the law of agency.

Who can be a director?

Anyone can become a director under companies legislation, with a few exceptions. The following cannot be a company director:

- someone who is disqualified by the company's own articles of association (the rules relating to the running of the company)
- an undischarged bankrupt
- someone disqualified by a court order
- the company's auditor.

If someone effectively acts as a director, even without the title, they may still legally be seen as a director. The law on a director's duties and liabilities also specifically includes a person who is classed as a 'shadow director'; this is anyone who, despite not officially being a 'director', regularly attends board and strategy meetings and upon whose advice the directors are accustomed to act. This could apply to a lawyer or accountant (or a foundation trust (FT) governor acting outside their role!) who advises a company's directors and whose guidance the directors usually take.

NHS directors

The 'fit and proper persons' test for NHS directors was introduced under the Health and Social Care Act 2008 (Regulated Activities) Regulations 2014. This means the CQC will assess whether directors are:

- of good character
- have the necessary qualifications, skills and experience
- are able to perform the work that they are employed for
- can supply information, such as certain checks and a full employment history.

The 'fit and proper person' requirement for directors will have a wider impact, in both the scope of its application and the nature of the test. It makes it clear that individuals who have authority in organisations that deliver care are responsible for the overall quality and safety of that care and, as such, can be held accountable if standards of care do not meet legal requirements.

It will apply to all directors and 'equivalents'. This will include executive directors (EDs) and non-executive directors (NEDs) of NHS trusts and FTs and members of clinical commissioning group (CCG) governing bodies. It will be the responsibility of the healthcare provider and, in the case of FTs and CCGs, the chair, to ensure that all directors meet the fitness test and do not meet any of the 'unfit' criteria. For NHS trusts, NHS Improvement (NHSI) is responsible for ensuring NEDs meet the criteria.

In addition to the usual requirements of good character, health, qualifications, skills and experience, the regulation bars individuals who are prevented from holding the office of director (e.g. under a directors' disqualification order). It also excludes from office people who:

> 'have been responsible for, been privy to, contributed to or facilitated any serious misconduct or mismanagement (whether unlawful or not) in the course

of carrying on a regulated activity, or discharging any functions relating to any office or employment with a service provider.'

In addition, a director will fail the 'fit and proper person' test if:

- they are an undischarged bankrupt
- are the subject of a bankruptcy order or an interim bankruptcy order or
- have an undischarged arrangement with creditors.

Directors will also be unfit if they are included on any barring list preventing them from working with children or vulnerable adults or are prohibited from holding the position under any other law. This means that a person subject to a disqualification order under the Company Directors' Disqualification Act 1986 or under the Charities Act would not meet the 'fit and proper' person requirement in relation to a registered provider that was a company or charity respectively.

The CQC will require the chair of the board or NHSI to confirm that the fitness of all new directors has been assessed in line with the regulations and to declare to the CQC in writing that they are satisfied that they are fit and proper individuals for that role.

The standing orders of an NHS organisation may also include grounds upon which a person is disqualified from office. These include:

- people who have received a prison sentence or suspended sentence of three months or more in the last five years;
- people who are the subject of a bankruptcy restriction order or interim order;
- anyone who has been dismissed (except by redundancy) by any NHS body;
- in certain circumstances, those who have had an earlier term of appointment terminated;
- anyone who is under a disqualification order under the Company Directors' Disqualification Act 1986;
- anyone who has been removed from trusteeship of a charity;
- in most circumstances, civil servants within the Department of Health (DH), or members/employees of the Care Quality Commission (CQC);
- a member of the council of governors or a chair or member of the governing body of a clinical commissioning group – or an employee of such group or a member of the local authority's overview and scrutiny committee;
- a person who is the spouse, partner, parent or child of a member of the board of directors (including the chair) of the trust;
- a person whose tenure of office as a chair or as an officer or director of a health service body has been terminated on the grounds that their appointment is not in the interests of the health service, for non-attendance at meetings, or for non-disclosure of a pecuniary interest;
- a person who has had their name removed or been suspended from any list prepared under the National Health Service Act 2006 (NHS Act 2006) who

has otherwise been suspended or disqualified from any healthcare profession, and has not had the suspension lifted or qualification reinstated; and

- anyone who has previously been or is currently subject to a sex offender order and/or required to register under the Sexual Offences Act 2003, or has committed a sexual offence prior to the requirement to register under current legislation.

The powers of directors

The powers of the board of directors are set out in an organisation's constitution. In UK companies, formed under the UK Companies Act 2006 (CA 2006), this means the articles of association. These are similar to, for example, a CCG's or FT's constitution or NHS trust's standing orders. Article 3 of the model articles of association states:

> 'Subject to the articles, the directors are responsible for the management of the company's business, for which purpose they may exercise all the powers of the company.'

The shareholders may instruct the directors what they should do (or should not do), but only by passing a special resolution in general meeting. A special resolution of the shareholders cannot invalidate what the directors have already done. Article 5 allows the directors to delegate any of the powers conferred on them under the articles to any person (such as the chief executive officer (CEO)) or committee (such as to an audit committee) as they think fit.

In health service governance, the powers of the board of directors are set out in their governing document. For example, FTs have a written constitution, which has to be approved by NHSI. This is then further defined by:

- the schedule of matters reserved for the board
- the scheme of delegation
- standing orders
- standing financial instructions.

These will be covered in more detail later in this chapter.

The duties of directors to their organisation

Directors act as agents of their organisation. They have certain duties, which are to the organisation itself – not to its shareholders, its employees or any person external to the organisation, such as the general public. Although an organisation is a legal person in law, it is not human. Since the relationship between directors and the organisation is by its very nature impersonal, it might be wondered just what 'duty' means.

The concept of duty is not easy to understand, and it is helpful to make a comparison with the duties owed by other individuals or groups.

Examples of individuals owing a duty to something inanimate are uncommon, although personnel in the armed forces have a duty to their country. It is more usual to show loyalty to something inanimate than to have a duty. For example, individuals might be expected to show loyalty to their country and they might voluntarily show loyalty to their sports team, group of friends or work colleagues. Arguably, solicitors have a duty to their profession to act ethically, although the solicitors' practice rules in the UK specify that solicitors owe a duty of care to their clients. Similarly, doctors have a duty to act ethically, but their duty is to their patients. Duty is normally owed to individuals or a group of people. It might therefore be supposed that directors should owe a duty to their shareholders and possibly to the organisation's employees, but this is not the case.

- Accountability and responsibility should not be confused with duty.
- Directors have a responsibility to use their powers in ways that seem best for the organisation and its shareholders or major stakeholders.
- They should be accountable to the 'owners' of the organisation, for the ways in which they have exercised their powers and/or the performance of the organisation.
- They have duties to the organisation.

If a person is guilty of a breach of duty, there should be a process for calling them to account. There might be an established disciplinary procedure, for example, in a court or before a judicial panel, with a recognised set of punishments for misbehaviour.

The common law duties of directors

Until the CA 2006 came into force, the main legal duties of directors to their organisation were duties in common law – a fiduciary duty and duty of skill and care to the organisation.

The CA 2006 has now written the common law duties of directors into statute law. It states that these general duties 'are based on certain common law rules and equitable principles as they apply to directors, and have effect in place of those rules and principles as regards the duties owed to an organisation by a director' (CA 2006, s. 170). The Act goes on to state that the statutory general duties should be interpreted in the same way as the common law rules and equitable principles.

Fiduciary duty of directors

'Fiduciary' means given in trust, and the concept of a trustee (as established in US and UK law) is applicable. The directors hold a position of trust because they make contracts on behalf of the organisation and also control its property. Since this is similar to being a trustee of the organisation, a director has a fiduciary duty to the organisation (not its shareholders).

If a director were to act in breach of their fiduciary duty, legal action could be brought against them by the organisation. In such a situation, 'the organisation' might be represented by a majority of the board of directors, a majority of the shareholders or a single controlling shareholder.

A director would be in breach of their fiduciary duty in carrying out a particular transaction or series of transactions in any of the following circumstances:

- The transaction is not in any way incidental to the business of the organisation. For example, the CEO of a building construction organisation might decide to trade in diamonds and lose large amounts of money in these diamond-trading transactions.
- The transaction is not carried out *bona fide* (in good faith) with honesty and sincerity.
- The transaction has not been made for the benefit of the organisation but for the personal benefit of the director or an associate. A director has a fiduciary duty to avoid a conflict of interest between him or herself personally and the organisation, and must not obtain any personal benefit or profit from a transaction without the consent of the organisation. In other words, it would be a breach of fiduciary duty for a director to make a secret profit from a transaction by the organisation in which he has a personal interest.

CASE STUDY: Fiduciary duty

An organisation wishes to buy some land and has identified a property for which it would be prepared to pay a large sum of money. The CEO secretly sets up a private organisation of his own to buy the property, and then sells this on to the organisation of which he is CEO, making a large profit in the process.

The actions of the CEO are breach of fiduciary duty, because his actions have not been *bona fide* and he has made a secret profit at the expense of the organisation. Under the CA 2006, these actions would be a breach of statutory duty.

Director's duty of skill and care

Directors are also subject to a duty of skill and care to the organisation. A director should not act negligently in carrying out his or her duties, and could be personally liable for losses suffered by the organisation as a consequence of such negligence.

The standard of skill and care expected of a director is the higher of the skill that he or she has or the skill that would objectively be expected of a director of the particular organisation. In the case *Re D'Jan of London* [1993] (covered later in this chapter) the judge ruled that the common law duty of care was the equivalent to the statutory test applied by section 214 of the Insolvency Act 1986. This statutory test refers to what would be expected of 'a reasonably diligent person' having both:

- the general knowledge, skill and experience that may reasonably be expected of a person carrying out the same functions as are carried out by that director in relation to the organisation; and
- the general knowledge, skill and experience that that director has.

A director is expected to show the technical skills that would reasonably be expected from someone of his or her experience and expertise. If the finance director of a scientific research organisation is a qualified accountant, he or she would not be expected to possess the technical skills of a scientist, but would be expected to possess some technical skill as an accountant.

However, the duty of skill and care does not extend to spending time in the organisation. A director should attend board meetings if possible, but at other times is not required to be concerned with the affairs of the organisation. This requirement is perhaps best understood with NEDs, who might visit the organisation only for board or committee meetings. The duties of a director are intermittent in nature and only arise from time to time, such as when the board meets. If a director holds an executive position in the organisation, a different situation arises, because he is an employee of the organisation with a contract of service. This contract might call for full-time attendance at the organisation or on its business. However, this requirement arises out of his or her job as a manager, not out of his or her position as a director.

It is also not a part of the duty of skill and care to watch closely over the activities of the organisation's management. Unless there are particular grounds for suspecting dishonesty or incompetence, a director is entitled to leave the routine conduct of the organisation's affairs to the management. If the management appears honest, the directors may rely on the information they provide. It is not part of their duty of skill and care to question whether the information is reliable, or whether important information is being withheld.

A board of directors might make a decision that appears ill-judged or careless. However, the courts in the UK are generally reluctant to condemn business decisions made by the board that appear, in hindsight, to show errors of judgment. Directors can exercise reasonable skill and care, but still make bad decisions.

For a legal action against a director to succeed, an organisation would have to prove that serious negligence had occurred. It would not be enough to demonstrate that some loss could have been avoided if the director had been a bit more careful.

CASE STUDY: Dorchester Finance Co Ltd v Stebbing [1989]

In the UK legal case *Dorchester Finance Co Ltd v Stebbing* [1989], a company brought an action against its three directors for alleged negligence and misappropriation of the company's property. The company (Dorchester Finance) was in the money-lending business and it had three directors, S, H and P. Only S was involved with the company full-time; H and P were NEDs who made only rare appearances. There were no board meetings. S and P were qualified accountants and H, although not an accountant, had considerable accountancy experience. S arranged for the company to make some loans to persons with whom he appears to have had dealings. In the loan-making process he had persuaded P and H to sign blank cheques that were subsequently used to make the loans. The loans did not comply with the Moneylenders Acts and they were inadequately secured. When the loans turned out to be irrecoverable, the company brought its action against the directors.

It was held that all three directors were liable to damages. S, as an ED, was held to be grossly negligent. P and H, as NEDs, were held to have failed to show the necessary level of skill and care in performing their duties, even though it was accepted that they had acted in good faith at all times.

Wrongful trading and the standard of duty and care

The standard of duty and care required from a director has been partly defined in a number of UK legal cases relating to wrongful trading. Under the Insolvency Act 1986, directors may be liable for wrongful trading by the organisation when they allowed the organisation to continue trading but knew (or should have known) that it would be unable to avoid an insolvent liquidation. When such a situation arises and an organisation goes into liquidation, the liquidator can apply to the court for the director to be held personally liable for negligence. The duty of a director under the Insolvency Act was used in the case of *Re D'Jan of London [1993]* to illustrate a director's general duty of skill and care.

CASE STUDY: Re D'Jan of London [1993]

An insurance broker completed a fire insurance proposal form with an incorrect answer, but a director of the company (D'Jan) applying for the insurance policy signed the form. The company premises burnt down, and the insurance company, on discovering the mistake on the proposal form, repudiated all liability under the policy. The company went into insolvent liquidation. The liquidator brought an action against the director who had signed the proposal form, alleging a failure to exercise reasonable care to the company.

The court found that although it would be unreasonable to expect a director to read every word of every document that he or she signed, in this case the form consisted of a few simple questions that the director was the best person to answer. The director was therefore guilty of a breach of duty of care, although, in this particular case, was exonerated on other grounds.

When there is a question about the extent of the director's duties and responsibilities, a significant factor could be the level of reward that the director was entitled to receive from the company. *Prima facie*, the higher the rewards, the greater the responsibilities should be expected.

The statutory duties of directors

NHS organisations are not registered companies but organisations created by statutory instrument. As such, they are not bound by the CA 2006. Good practice, however, would require an understanding of the general principles of the Act, which are set out here.

The duties of directors were introduced into UK statute law by the CA 2006 (ss. 171–177). These consist of a duty to:

- act within powers
- promote the success of the organisation
- exercise independent judgment
- exercise reasonable care, skill and diligence
- avoid conflicts of interest
- not accept benefits from third parties
- declare any interest in a proposed transaction or arrangement.

Duty to act within powers

A director must act within his or her powers in accordance with the organisation's constitution and should only exercise these powers for the purpose for which they were granted. If a director acts outside his or her powers to make a contractual agreement with a third party, the organisation is still liable for any obligation to the third party, provided that the third party has acted in good faith.

Directors should also ensure that they comply with the organisation's constitution. For example, when a group of directors meets, it must be clear whether the meeting is a full board meeting, a meeting of a board committee or an unofficial meeting of directors. Unless the meeting is a formal board meeting, the directors would be acting outside their powers if they took a decision on a matter that is reserved for decision-making by the board.

Duty to promote the success of the organisation

A director must act, in good faith, in the way he or she considers would be most likely to 'promote the success of the organisation for the benefit of its members as a whole'. The Act does not define 'success', but the term is likely to be interpreted as meaning 'increasing value for shareholders'. However, in so doing, a director must also have regard, among other matters, to the:

- likely long-term consequences of any decision;
- interests of the organisation's employees;
- need to foster the organisation's relationships with its customers, suppliers and others;
- impact of the organisation's operations on the community and the environment;
- desirability of the organisation maintaining its reputation for high standards of business conduct; and
- need to act fairly as between members of the organisation.

The Act does not create a duty of directors to any stakeholders other than the shareholders (members), but it requires directors to consider the interests of other stakeholders in reaching their decisions. The Act specifically mentions employees, customers, suppliers and the community.

FT directors now have the same responsibility to promote the success of the corporation so this particular duty is directly applicable to FTs.

Duty to exercise independent judgment

A director must exercise independent judgment. However, this requirement does not prevent a director from acting in a way authorised by the organisation's constitution (such as accepting resolutions passed by the shareholders in general meeting) or from acting in accordance with an agreement already entered into by the organisation that prevents the director from using discretion. The requirement for independent judgment does not prevent a director from taking advice and acting on it.

The ICSA Guidance on *Directors' General Duties* (2015) comments as follows on this duty.

- A director should ensure that they do not allow personal interests, for example in a particular contract, to affect their independent judgment in the interest of the company. A director should ideally excuse themselves from any meeting at which a decision is to be taken in respect of their own property or interest.
- Importantly, where someone is an ED, they must not promote a collective executive line, but should give the board the benefit of their own independent judgment, including their appreciation of the risks involved in a particular course of action.
- This duty does not prevent a director from exercising their power to delegate, but they must still exercise their own judgment in deciding whether to follow the action suggested by that person(s).

- Similarly, a director would not be prevented by this duty from seeking legal or other professional advice but, ultimately, the director's final judgment would need to be independent.
- A director associated with a major shareholder should set any 'representative' function aside and make decisions on their own merits. This is of particular importance in joint venture situations where there may be constraints imposed by joint venture agreements. However, the Act states that this duty is not infringed by a director acting in accordance with an agreement duly entered into by the company that restricts the future exercise of discretion by its directors, or in a way authorised by the company's constitution.
- Likewise, a director who is a family representative in the business may consult their family but must understand that they will make the final decision.
- A director of a subsidiary would need to take into account the interests of the parent company and the other subsidiaries, but not insofar as this would prejudice the solvency of the subsidiary itself. This might apply, for instance, in relation to a transfer of assets within a group.

Duty to exercise reasonable care, skill and diligence

This is similar to the common law duty of care. For example, if a NED had an accounting qualification, they would be expected to exercise more active scrutiny of the accounts (such as on the appropriateness of accounting policies) than a director without such a qualification.

Duty to avoid conflicts of interest

A director has a duty to avoid conflicts of interest with the interests of the organisation. However, this duty is not breached if the director declares to the board their interest in a transaction and the interest is authorised/approved by the board.

In the commercial world, it is inevitable that many directors will have a potential conflict of interest with their organisation (whether direct or indirect). For example, one organisation might be planning to trade with another organisation in which one of its directors is a shareholder. In such a situation, the director concerned is required to declare their interest in the proposed contract and must not make a secret profit.

A director or a connected person might have a material interest in a transaction undertaken by the organisation. For example, the organisation might award a contract to a firm of building contractors to rebuild or develop a property owned by the organisation, and the director or their spouse might own the building organisation.

A director might also have a direct or indirect interest in a contract (or proposed contract) with the organisation. For example, the director might be a member of another organisation with which the organisation is planning to sign a business contract. Such a contract is not illegal, although the organisation can choose to rescind it should it wish to do so.

If a director has an interest in a contract with the organisation and has failed to disclose it, and has received a payment under the contract, they will be regarded as holding the money in the capacity of constructive trustee for the organisation (and so is bound to repay the money).

The CA 2006 recognises three situations in which an actual or potential conflict of interests may arise.

- A conflict of interest may arise in a situation where the organisation is not a party to an arrangement or transaction, but where the director might be able to gain personally from 'the exploitation of any property, information or opportunity'. For example, a director might pursue an opportunity for their personal benefit that the organisation might have pursued itself.
- A conflict of interest may arise about a proposed transaction or arrangement to which the organisation will be a party. If a director has a direct or indirect personal interest in any such transaction or arrangement, they must disclose their interest to the board of directors before it is entered into by the organisation. An example would be a proposal to acquire a target company in which a director owns shares.
- A third type of conflict of interest arises with existing transactions or arrangements in which the organisation is already a party. It can be a criminal offence for a director not to make or update their declaration of interest in an arrangement or transaction to which the organisation is a party.

This is key principle for NHS directors. There are specific guidelines for NHS directors to follow with regard to conflicts of interest, in line with the Nolan principles, which are set out in the NHS Code of Conduct and Accountability (covered later in this chapter).

Duty not to accept benefits from third parties

A director must not accept benefits from a third party unless they have been authorised by the shareholders or cannot reasonably be regarded as creating a potential conflict of their interest. Clearly, accepting a bribe from a supplier in return for awarding a supply contract would be a breach of this duty. It would also be illegal to accept lunch or dinner from the same supplier or customer every week, accepting an all-expenses-paid holiday or accepting frequent invitations to 'hospitality' events. On the other hand, it should be within the law to accept an invitation to a day out to tennis at Wimbledon or an invitation to dinner to celebrate the successful completion of a project.

Many listed companies already have strict policies on the acceptance of gifts and corporate hospitality, especially from other companies that are or might be about to tender for business with the organisation. A policy might include a requirement for a director to obtain clearance from another director before accepting any such benefits, and for all instances of gifts or hospitality to be recorded in a register.

The Bribery Act 2010 sets out that an organisation may be liable for failing to prevent a person from bribing on its behalf, but only if that person performs business services for it. It contains a full defence for an organisation that shows it had adequate procedures in place to prevent bribery. It is important to note that guidance on the Act specifically sets out that while hospitality is not prohibited by the Act, facilitation payments are classed as bribes.

The Bribery Act is applicable to NHS organisations and there are a number of steps that they can consider. These include:

- carrying out a bribery and corruption risk assessment;
- putting in place anti-bribery procedures that are proportionate to the identified risks;
- ensuring that when proportionate anti-bribery procedures are put in place, the principles outlined in the guidance are taken into account (top-level commitment, due diligence, communication and training, and monitoring and review);
- being clear that NHS organisations and their employees, contractors and agents are covered by corporate liability for bribery;
- taking steps to make their trust employees and contractors aware of the standards of conduct expected of them, particularly in known risk areas such as procurement; and
- recording any steps taken, as they provide the defence against corporate liability under the Act.

Duty to declare interests in proposed transactions with the organisation

This duty is linked to the duty relating to conflicts of interest. A director must declare the nature and extent of their interest to the other directors, who may then authorise it. The NHS Code of Conduct and Accountability also covers this for NHS directors.

A director may have a personal interest in a proposed transaction with the organisation. For example, a director may own a building that the organisation wants to buy or rent; or a director may be a major shareholder in another organisation that is hoping to become a supplier or customer. Proposed transactions do not necessarily create a conflict of interest, but they must, nevertheless, be declared and subject to approval by the rest of the board. If a conflict of interest would arise from the proposed transaction, the director must take measures to ensure that the conflict is avoided.

Other statutory duties

Directors' responsibilities to third parties

Although the duty of directors is to their organisation, a breach of that duty could also affect outsiders. When the directors make a contract with an outsider, the contract is binding on the organisation when it is made according to its constitutional documents. However, the directors might exceed their powers in making the contract, for example, because they should have obtained stakeholder approval first, but failed to do so. Contracts entered into without proper authority are known as 'irregular contracts' and might seem to be void.

The main provision of UK company law is that an irregular contract is binding on an organisation when an outsider, acting in good faith, enters into the contract and the board of directors has approved the contract. The directors will be liable to the organisation for any loss suffered. This rule means that irregular contracts do not affect third parties (outsiders). Instead, when they occur, they would be a corporate governance problem.

Related party transactions and the UK Disclosure and Transparency Rules for listed companies

In listed companies, the requirements of UK law are reinforced by the UK Disclosure and Transparency Rules, which include a section on related party transactions. In broad terms, a related party means a substantial shareholder of the organisation, a director of the organisation, a member of a director's family or an organisation in which a director or family member holds 30% or more of the shares. A related party transaction is a transaction between an organisation and a related party, other than in the normal course of business and results in a disclosure being made to the stock market and the shareholders. The effect of the rules should be to prevent directors or major shareholders of UK listed companies from obtaining a personal benefit from any non-business transaction with their organisation, unless the shareholders have given their approval.

The NHS Code of Conduct and Accountability covers this for directors and stakeholders of NHS organisations.

Borrowing powers of directors

In the UK, there is no restriction in law on how much the directors can borrow on behalf of their organisation unless the constitutional documents include a specific restriction. As far as the law is concerned, the borrowing powers of companies are limited only by what lenders are prepared to make available to them. Conceivably, the directors could therefore put the investment of their shareholders at risk by borrowing more than the organisation can safely afford.

FTs are also free to borrow from banks and other private sector lenders to improve the facilities and equipment available to patients. They are, however, subject to statutory controls – unlike voluntary or private providers of healthcare – which give NHSI powers to set limits on the amount they can borrow.

Duty to break even

Although the break-even duty is a statutory requirement for NHS trusts, all NHS bodies including FTs are expected to operate a balanced budget ensuring that total expenditure does not exceed total income.

Paragraph 2(1) of Schedule 5 to the NHS Act 2006 states: 'Each NHS trust must ensure that its revenue is not less than sufficient, taking one financial year with another, to meet outgoings properly chargeable to revenue account.' This is known as the 'breakeven duty'. NHS trusts and CCGs should normally plan to meet this duty by achieving a balanced position on their income and expenditure accounts each and every year. The breakeven duty includes the phrase 'taking one financial year with another'. This provides some flexibility on the time-scale for matching income with those costs whose incidence is uneven and when managing the recovery of an NHS trust with serious financial difficulties.

An agreement was reached in 1997 with the Treasury and the Audit Commission that the duty will be assumed to have been met if expenditure is covered by income over a rolling three-year period. Exceptionally, the breakeven duty is assumed to be met if the cumulative deficit being recovered is covered by subsequent surpluses over a four- or five-year period.

2013/14 saw a threefold increase in the number of NHS organisations being reported to the Secretary of State for Health for failing to meet their statutory break-even duty, with 20 trusts failing (compared with only five trusts for 2012/13). In addition, 24 CCGs – 11% of all CCGs – were also referred to the Secretary of State as a result of financial concerns in that period. By the end of 2015/16 the position had deteriorated further with the NHS provider sector overall reporting a deficit of £2.45 billion – £461 million worse than planned and 157 out of 240 providers (65%) reporting a deficit position.

Where an NHS trust or CCG is recovering a cumulative deficit position, the organisation would be required to produce and agree a robust recovery plan with either the NHSI or the NHS England (see the section on financial special measures in Chapter 3).

Duty to improve quality

The Health Act 1999 (and 2003) introduced a statutory 'duty of quality' for services commissioned and provided by all NHS trusts, for which trust chief executives are accountable. The DH expected this duty of quality to be discharged, at trust level, through the implementation of clinical governance. The relevant section was repealed by the Health and Social Care (Community Health and Standards) Act 2003 but was restated as:

> 'It is the duty of each NHS body to put and keep in place arrangements for the purpose of monitoring and improving the quality of health care provided by and for that body.'

This duty was further reinforced by the principles of the NHS Constitution.

Liability of directors

The starting point for considering the liabilities of individual directors is to understand the role of the board and the corporate nature of the specific NHS organisation (NHS trust, CCG or FT). Any such organisation will be a corporate entity in its own right and will take decisions as such. As noted earlier, this has implications for the role of directors, who are collectively responsible for all decisions.

The corporate nature of the organisation will mean that, in most instances, even if a decision is open to criticism, individual directors will not be legally liable. There are also specific statutory protections where they are acting in good faith (see Public Health Act 1875, s. 265). This section covers the circumstances where such personal liability can arise.

Criminal liability

An individual who, in the course of their activities as a director, commits a criminal offence will carry personal responsibility and liability. Perhaps more significantly, a director can be held to have committed a criminal offence where the offence arises under statute that includes explicit provision to hold a director liable. Examples are the Health and Safety at Work Act, the Environmental Protection Act and the Data Protection Act.

Prior to the Corporate Manslaughter Act 2007 coming into force, it was possible for a corporate entity, such as a company, to be prosecuted for a wide range of criminal offences, including the common law offence of gross negligence manslaughter. However, in order for the corporate entity to be guilty of the offence, it was also necessary for a senior individual who could be said to embody the company (also known as a 'controlling mind') to be guilty of the offence. The new law was wider, meaning a corporate entity can be convicted if it can be proven that there was a gross breach of duty of care by senior management, instead of just one individual.

Civil liability to third parties

Civil liability, which generally relates to the payment of compensation, can arise in either contract or tort. Liability in contract will only occur if the contract is entered into in the personal name of the director rather than that of the trust or where a contract entered into by the trust is found to be *ultra vires* and the director has given a personal warranty or representation that the trust has appropriate powers. Directors therefore need to be careful about what assurances they give about the powers of the organisation.

The more usual risks are for the individual to have a claim in tort made against them, most commonly in relation to either negligence or defamation. A tort can be defined as a wrongful act resulting in injury to another's person, property, or reputation, for which the injured party is entitled to seek compensation where there has been no contractual relationship. Negligence arises where an individual acts without due care towards a person to whom they owe a duty of care, and causes foreseeable loss. Usually, as with clinical negligence claims, the claim is pursued against the trust, not the individual, and the NHS Litigation Authority will provide cover. Indeed, the Liabilities to Third Parties Scheme includes cover for directors similar to that available in the commercial market by way of directors' and officers' liability insurance.

Defamation is a potential risk, and while some degree of protection is afforded where public officers are acting honestly and in the course of their business, there are risks if they step outside the strict parameters of the role.

A potential threat is misfeasance in public office. In practice this is very rare and requires the establishment of deliberate malice, targeting the individual or a limited class of people who has/have suffered loss.

Claims by the NHS organisation

A final area of risk is that of claims by the NHS organisation itself. All directors owe a duty of care and skill to the NHS organisation, and breaches could give rise to claims. There is a material difference in this matter between the position of EDs and NEDs (or lay members). The latter are protected by the terms of the standard HM Treasury indemnity, unless they have been reckless. However, EDs could in theory be the subject of claims, even if they have only been negligent.

Although there are some high-profile corporate cases, such as Equitable Life, in practice claims against the directors for negligently carrying out their duties are rare. It does, however, underline the need for directors to use care and skills in carrying out their role. Where a matter is outside their competence, they may want to consider whether they need independent advice.

A further area of claim by an NHS organisation would be for breach of fiduciary duty or for repayment of benefits improperly received. This can arise in two main ways. The first is where a director abuses their position to make private gain. This could occur where a director arranged for a contract with a company in which they had an interest, without declaring the relevant interest. In such circumstances the trust can call for an account of the proceeds.

Secondly, and perhaps more commonly, situations may arise where the auditors call into question officers' severance or retirement packages. Irrespective of the propriety of the individual's conduct, if the award of the package was outside the powers of the NHS organisation or decided upon improperly, it can be clawed back.

Indemnity

As indicated above, directors have a degree of protection against claims. Non-executives will typically have the benefit of the Treasury approved wording (HSG 1999/104):

> 'A chair or non-executive member or director who has acted honestly and in good faith will not have to meet out of his or her own personal resources any personal civil liability that is incurred in the execution or purported execution of his or her board function. Save where the person has acted recklessly.'

This indemnity may be extended to members of those committees that have delegated powers to make decisions or take actions on behalf of NHS boards. This covers the director for acts carried out in good faith in the execution or purported execution of the functions of the trust, short of recklessness. It does not cover criminal liability, and no indemnity could do so.

There is some doubt about the position where the director is in fact acting outside the powers of the organisation, particularly where to enforce the indemnity would be to allow a collateral enforcement of an *ultra vires* obligation against the trust.

Executive directors will generally be indemnified in relation to claims against them arising from third parties, but difficult issues can arise when staff make allegations of harassment, and trusts will need to tread carefully in such cases.

NHS Code of Conduct and Accountability

Unsurprisingly, the duty to avoid conflicts of interest, not to accept benefits from third parties and to declare any interest in a proposed transaction or arrangement are very clearly set out in the Code of Conduct and Accountability for NHS organisations. Given the scale and magnitude of the procurement of contracts and services within the NHS, there is clearly a significant need to regulate the behaviour of both the board and NHS staff in regard to managing conflicts of interests.

The NHS Code of Conduct and Accountability (third revision, April 2013) is quite clear in that NHS boards should act in a way that protects the interest of the NHS in the way they undertake their business.

- Accountability: Everything done by those who work in the NHS must be able to stand the test of parliamentary scrutiny, public judgments on propriety and professional codes of conduct.
- Probity: There should be an absolute standard of honesty in dealing with the assets of the NHS: integrity should be the hallmark of all personal conduct in decisions affecting patients, staff, and suppliers, and in the use of information acquired in the course of NHS duties.
- Openness: There should be sufficient transparency about NHS activities to promote confidence between the NHS organisation and its staff, patients and the public.

Public service values matter in the NHS. Those who work in it have a duty to conduct NHS business with probity. They have a responsibility to respond to staff, patients and suppliers impartially, to achieve value for money from the public funds with which they are entrusted and to demonstrate high ethical standards of personal conduct. The Code makes it clear that chairs and board directors should act impartially and should not be influenced by social or business relationships. Where there is a potential for private interests to be material and relevant to NHS business, the relevant interests should be declared and recorded in the board minutes, and entered into a register, which is available to the public. When a conflict of interest is established, the board director should withdraw and play no part in the relevant discussion or decision.

It is vital that NHS board directors should set an example to their organisation in the use of public funds and the need for good value in incurring public expenditure. The use of NHS monies for hospitality and entertainment, including hospitality at conferences or seminars, should be carefully considered. All expenditure on these items should be capable of justification as reasonable in the light of the general practice in the public sector. NHS boards should be aware that expenditure on hospitality or entertainment is the responsibility of management and is open to be challenged by the internal and external auditors and that ill-considered actions can damage respect for the NHS in the eyes of the community.

NHS boards should also have an explicit procedure for the declaration of hospitality and sponsorship offered by, for example, suppliers. Their authorisation should be carefully considered and the decision should be recorded. NHS boards should be aware of the risks in incurring obligations to suppliers at any stage of a contracting relationship.

NHS boards should ensure that staff have a proper and widely publicised procedure for voicing complaints or concerns about maladministration, malpractice, breaches of this code and other concerns of an ethical nature. This has been developed further in whistleblowing procedures, which are set out in more detail in Chapter 17.

The Healthy NHS Board also reinforces the importance of NHS boards acting, and being seen to act, with integrity and in the best interests of the organisation:

> 'Probity requires that the board maintains an up-to-date register of board members' interests. Board agendas should include an opportunity for board members to declare conflicts of interests that may relate to specific agenda items so that they can be managed appropriately.'

For NHS FTs, there is also a requirement for the board of directors to adopt appropriate standards of conduct and to be open and transparent in their decision-making and the manner in which conflicts of interest are managed. This was clarified further in section 152 of HSCA 2012 as follows:

> 'The duties that a director of a public benefit corporation has by virtue of being a director include in particular
>
> a) a duty to avoid a situation in which the director has (or can have) a direct or indirect interest that conflicts (or possibly may conflict) with the interests of the corporation;

> b) a duty not to accept a benefit from a third party by reason of being a director or doing (or not doing) anything in that capacity.
>
> This duty is not infringed if the situation cannot reasonably be regarded as likely to give rise to a conflict of interest, or the matter has been authorised in accordance with the constitution, or if acceptance of the benefit cannot reasonably be regarded as likely to give rise to a conflict of interest.
>
> If a director of a public benefit corporation has in any way a direct or indirect interest in a proposed transaction or arrangement with the corporation, the director must declare the nature and extent of that interest to the other directors. And if a declaration under this section proves to be, or becomes, inaccurate or incomplete, a further declaration must be made. Any declaration required by this section must be made before the corporation enters into the transaction or arrangement. The section did not require a declaration of an interest of which the director was not aware or where the director was not aware of the transaction or arrangement in question.'

Conflicts of interest are a major governance issue for CCGs. NHSE provided guidance for CCGs in *Managing Conflicts of Interest: Revised Statutory Guidance for CCGs* (2016). This will be covered in more detail in Chapter 13. However, the core of the issue is neatly summarised in the below quote from the September 2011 briefing paper on managing conflicts of interest by the Royal College of General Practitioners (RCGP) and NHS Confederation.

> 'If conflicts of interest are not managed effectively by CCGs, confidence in the probity of commissioning decisions and the integrity of clinicians involved could be seriously undermined. However, with good planning and governance, CCGs should be able to avoid these risks.'

CCGs need to provide clear guidance to their members and employees on what might constitute a conflict of interest, providing examples that are likely to arise. They should also highlight the following points to members and employees:

- a perception of wrongdoing, impaired judgment or undue influence can be as detrimental as any of them actually occurring;
- if in doubt, it is better to assume a conflict of interest and manage it appropriately rather than ignore it;
- financial gain is not necessary for a conflict to exist.

Governance checklist

- ✓ Are the directors aware of the extent of their authority and powers and the purposes for which they have been granted?
- ✓ Are directors aware of the boundaries set out in the matters reserved for the board and in the standing orders/standing financial instructions?
- ✓ Are directors aware of the implications of the common law and statutory duties that could be the benchmark their actions are judged against?
- ✓ Are board members provided with sufficient and accurate information and advice for them to exercise reasonable care, skill and diligence?
- ✓ Does that information enable them to make decisions which will fulfil their function – for example, promoting the success of the corporation in a FT?
- ✓ Are the directors confident in identifying potential conflicts of interest, how to declare them and how to manage them?

Summary

This chapter makes it clear that the individual directors who compose the board have key duties and responsibilities as a consequence of the role. Consequently, they will be liable for certain outcomes that result from the actions and decisions of the board. Directors need to have a clear understanding of these duties and liabilities: this should form a key part of their induction and ongoing development as board members.

PART THREE

The effective board and its officers

7

Maintaining an effective board

Introduction

This chapter deals with governance issues relating to the effectiveness of the board (and again this should be taken to include the governing body of a clinical commissioning group (CCG)). Board performance and operation has been highlighted in a number of NHS publications but the key guidance can be found in *The Healthy NHS Board* (2013) and the *Well-Led Framework* (2014).

This area has also been subject to intense scrutiny following the Francis Inquiry Report of February 2013, the subsequent government responses and independent reviews. The guidance is intended to support NHS boards in gaining assurance on their effectiveness in carrying out their role of setting strategy, leading the organisation and overseeing operations, and being accountable to stakeholders in an open and effective manner.

Though such guidance is helpful in setting out clear processes and procedures, it is important to recognise the vital interplay of the different roles, personalities and relationships around the board table. Defining an effective board merely in terms of its processes and procedures, without recognising that behaviours and culture are the essential ingredients, is a recipe for poor governance and failing organisations.

In the corporate sector a similar realisation is dawning – the global financial crisis and other governance failings of large organisations (e.g. BHS, Volkswagen, Tesco) have demonstrated that, as the old saying goes, 'culture eats strategy for breakfast'! This had also been apparent during the failed corporate mergers and restructures of the 1980s and 1990s and yet the lesson had failed to be learned.

The latest Financial Reporting Council (FRC) study *Corporate Culture and the Role of Boards* (2016) explores the relationship between corporate culture and long-term business success in the UK. Sir Winfried Bischoff, Chairman of the FRC, writes:

> 'There needs to be a concerted effort to improve trust in the motivations and integrity of business. Rules and sanctions clearly have their place, but will not on their own deliver productive behaviours over the long-term. This report looks at the increasing importance which corporate culture plays in delivering long-term business and economic success.'

It is now accepted that stakeholders and society in general have a vested interest in healthy corporate values, attitudes and behaviours that lead to sustainable growth and long-term economic success. The study also asks stakeholders and investors to consider their behaviours too, so that they 'engage constructively to build respect and trust, and work with companies to achieve long term value'.

Consequently the role of the nomination committee in recruitment and appointment, as well as ongoing high-quality board development and regular evaluation, are crucial for the life of the effective board.

Good boardroom practice

Boardroom practice describes the way in which a board conducts its procedures and reaches its decisions.

The FRC *Guidance on Board Effectiveness*, issued in 2011, states:

> 'An effective board develops and promotes its collective vision of the company's purpose, its culture, its values and the behaviours it wishes to promote in conducting its business. In particular it:
>
> - provides direction for management;
> - demonstrates ethical leadership, displaying – and promoting throughout the company – behaviours consistent with the culture and values it has defined for the organisation;
> - creates a performance culture that drives value creation without exposing the company to excessive risk of value destruction;
> - makes well informed and high-quality decisions based on a clear line of sight into the business;
> - creates the right framework for helping directors to meet their statutory duties under the Companies Act 2006, and/or other relevant statutory and regulatory regimes;
> - is accountable, particularly to those that provide the company's capital; and
> - thinks carefully about its governance arrangements and embraces evaluation of their effectiveness.'

The guidance continues to say:

> 'An effective board should not necessarily be a comfortable place. Challenge, as well as teamwork, is an essential feature. Diversity in board composition is an important driver of a board's effectiveness, creating a breadth of perspective among directors, and breaking down a tendency towards "group think".'

The key findings of the FRC's corporate culture study are set out below:

> 'Recognise the value of culture: A healthy corporate culture is a valuable asset, a source of competitive advantage and vital to the creation and protection of

long-term value. It is the board's role to determine the purpose of the company and ensure that the company's values, strategy and business model are aligned to it. Directors should not wait for a crisis before they focus on company culture.

Demonstrate leadership: Leaders, in particular the chief executive, must embody the desired culture, embedding this at all levels and in every aspect of the business. Boards have a responsibility to act where leaders do not deliver.

Be open and accountable: Openness and accountability matter at every level. Good governance means a focus on how this takes place throughout the company and those who act on its behalf. It should be demonstrated in the way the company conducts business and engages with and reports to stakeholders. This involves respecting a wide range of stakeholder interests.

Embed and integrate: The values of the company need to inform the behaviours which are expected of all employees and suppliers. Human resources, internal audit, ethics, compliance, and risk functions should be empowered and resourced to embed values and assess culture effectively. Their voice in the boardroom should be strengthened.

Align values and incentives: The performance management and reward system should support and encourage behaviours consistent with the company's purpose, values, strategy and business model. The board is responsible for explaining this alignment clearly to shareholders, employees and other stakeholders.

Assess, measure and engage: Indicators and measures used should be aligned to desired outcomes and material to the business. The board has a responsibility to understand behaviour throughout the company and to challenge where they find misalignment with values or need better information. Boards should devote sufficient resource to evaluating culture and consider how they report on it.

Exercise stewardship: Effective stewardship should include engagement about culture and encourage better reporting. Investors should challenge themselves about the behaviours they are encouraging in companies and to reflect on their own culture.'

Interestingly this line of approach, which is also adopted in the King IV Code, is also beginning to have more profile in health service governance. The *Well-Led Framework* (2014) clearly sets out capacity and culture as a domain for evaluation in a board's self-effectiveness. But more on this later.

The role of the chair

The Association of British Insurers (ABI) *Report on Board Effectiveness* (2012) makes it quite clear that the chair has a key role to play in the effective board. While the report found no 'one size fits all' approach to the role, with different chairs having different approaches based on what is best for the individual company and board, it did find a significant amount of consensus about the role and responsibilities of the chair.

The report emphasised a number of aspects to the role of the chair on the following five themes:

- creating the right board dynamic and having the right people around the boardroom table;
- helping to set the board agenda, ensuring the board has the right information and is debating the right issues;
- managing the board's relationship with the executives and in particular the chief executive;
- being an ambassador for the company; and
- being fully engaged in the business and understanding what is happening on the ground.

The NHS Leadership Model from the NHS Leadership Academy describes nine behaviours which together contribute towards strong and effective NHS leaders. NHS Improvement (NHSI) expects board members to demonstrate this range of behaviours and the highest standards of conduct required to contribute effectively in this board level role:

- Inspiring shared purpose
- Leading with care
- Evaluating information
- Connecting our service
- Sharing vision
- Engaging the team
- Holding to account
- Developing capability
- Influencing for results
- Championing the standards of public life.

The role of the chair is covered in more detail in Chapter 8.

Board meetings

A basic requirement of an effective board is that there should be regular board meetings. The UK states simply that the board should meet sufficiently regularly to discharge its duties effectively and there should be a formal schedule of matters reserved for the board.

The agenda for board meetings is a governance issue in the sense that the chair decides what the board will discuss when they set the agenda. Although directors can raise matters as 'any other business', most of the time at board meetings is spent in discussion of the items listed on the agenda. It is therefore important that the agenda should include all matters reserved for board decision, whenever they arise. The company secretary can assist the chair by providing advice and reminders.

To contribute effectively to board discussions, directors must be provided with relevant information. They should receive relevant documents in advance of a board meeting, so that they have time to read them and think about the issues they deal with. The UK Code states that 'the board should be supplied in a timely manner with information in a form and of a quality sufficient to enable it to discharge its duties'.

The chair has the responsibility for ensuring that directors receive the information that they need in sufficient time. The UK Code states that management has an obligation to provide the required information, but that the directors should ask for clarification or additional information if required.

The *Intelligent Board* report states that 'every member of the board needs sufficient information at a high enough level to be confident that the organisation is well run, but not so much information that it becomes difficult to tell what is important' and that 'good governance is underpinned by intelligent information'.

Such information enables the board to:

- set an appropriately challenging, but achievable, strategic direction;
- identify the strategic issues that require discussion or decision, and distinguish these issues from operational detail;
- provide constructive challenge;
- ensure taxpayers are receiving value for money (VFM);
- identify trends in performance;
- enable comparisons with the performance of similar organisations;
- understand the needs, views and experiences of users and non-users from all backgrounds and communities;
- ensure users are receiving a high-quality service;
- anticipate the potential impact of key policy, technological and socioeconomic developments; and
- assure themselves that the organisation is complying with standards and other regulatory requirements.

All information should:

- be clearly and simply presented, including graphic overviews as well as brief commentary;
- be updated in a timely manner;
- direct the board's attention to significant risks, issues and exceptions; and
- provide a level of detail appropriate to the board's role.

Information flows should be both formal and informal. Information is provided formally in documents or files, but this is supplemented by informal communication by e-mail, telephone or face-to-face conversation. Whether providing information formally or informally, the company secretary should ensure that there are good information flows between the board and its committees, between committees and between executive directors (EDs) and non-executive directors (NEDs).

Decision-making

One critical requirement for an effective board is well-informed and high-quality decision-making. This does not happen by accident. Boards can minimise the risk of poor decisions by investing time in the design of their decision-making policies and processes, including the contribution of committees.

The FRC guidance outlines that:

'good decision-making capability can be facilitated by:

- high quality board documentation;
- obtaining expert opinions when necessary;
- allowing time for debate and challenge, especially for complex, contentious or business critical issues;
- achieving timely closure; and
- providing clarity on the actions required, and timescales and responsibilities.'

Boards should be aware of factors that can limit effective decision-making, such as:

- a dominant personality or group of directors on the board, which can inhibit contribution from other directors;
- insufficient attention to risk, and treating risk as a compliance issue rather than as part of the decision-making process, especially in cases where the level of risk involved in a project could endanger the stability and sustainability of the business itself;
- failure to recognise the value implications of running the business on the basis of self-interest and other poor ethical standards;
- a reluctance to involve NEDs, or of matters being brought to the board for sign-off rather than debate;
- complacent or intransigent attitudes;
- a weak organisational culture; or
- inadequate information or analysis.

Most complex decisions depend on judgment, but the judgment of even the most well-intentioned and experienced leaders can, in certain circumstances, be distorted. Some factors known to distort judgment in decision making are conflicts of interest; emotional attachments; and inappropriate reliance on previous experience and previous decisions. For significant decisions, therefore, a board may wish to consider extra steps, for example:

- describing in board papers the process that has been used to arrive at and challenge the proposal prior to presenting it to the board, thereby allowing directors not involved in the project to assess the appropriateness of the process as a precursor to assessing the merits of the project itself; or
- where appropriate, putting in place additional safeguards to reduce the risk of distorted judgments by, for example, commissioning an independent report,

seeking advice from an expert, introducing a devil's advocate to provide challenge, establishing a sole purpose sub-committee, or convening additional meetings. Some chairs favour separate discussions for important decisions (e.g. concept, proposal for discussion, proposal for decision). This gives EDs more opportunity to put the case at the earlier stages, and all directors the opportunity to share concerns or challenge assumptions well in advance of the point of decision.

Boards can benefit from reviewing past decisions, particularly those with poor outcomes. A review should not focus just on the merits of the decision itself but also on the decision-making process.

Support

As well as receiving relevant and timely information, directors should be given access to independent professional advice, at the organisation's expense, when they consider this necessary in order to fulfil their duties as director. For example, a director might ask to consult a lawyer for advice on a matter where the legal position is not clear.

NEDs and possibly also EDs may also need administrative support or advice on routine matters. Board committees should be provided with sufficient resources to carry out their duties, and all directors should have access to the advice and assistance of the company secretary.

Board behaviour

There is a general consensus among recently published reports and reviews in both corporate and health service sectors that the quality of governance depends ultimately on the culture and behaviour of individuals, and consequently the ability of procedures and regulation to provide good governance is limited.

The Walker Report argued that both character and culture of the board members are important for an effective board. It commented that:

> 'Board conformity with laid-down procedures ... will not alone provide better corporate governance overall if the chair is weak, if the composition and dynamic of the board is inadequate and if there is unsatisfactory ... engagement with its owners.'

The report went on to argue that the main weaknesses in the boards of banks had been caused by behavioural factors and a failure to challenge.

> 'The sequence in board discussion on major issues should be: presentation by the executive, a disciplined process of challenge, decision on the policy or strategy to be adopted and then full empowerment of the executive to implement. The essential "challenge" step in the sequence appears to have been missed in many board situations and needs to be ... clearly recognised and embedded for the future.'

Back in 2004, the NHS Confederation published *Effective Boards in the NHS*, which identified the behaviour and culture of a board as key determinants of the board's performance. From the interviews, the research identified four characteristics of effective boards:

- a focus on strategic decision-making
- board members who trust each other and act cohesively/behave corporately
- constructive challenge by board members of each other
- effective chairs who ensure meetings have clear and effective processes.

Some boards appeared to be too trusting, with little constructive challenge or debate about strategic issues. Reasons for this lack of challenge included the desire to present a united public face in public meetings. The report recommended that the perceived differences between non-executive and executive roles needed to be addressed, as challenge should not be seen as the preserve of non-executives scrutinising the executive team. The report concluded that a culture that enables board business to be conducted in a sharp and focused manner was required at board level, making clear what decisions are required of the board and what action will follow as a result of the decisions.

John Deffenbuaugh, author of, 'It's the people in the boardroom' in the *British Journal of Healthcare Management* 2012, Vol 18, No 7 writes:

> 'The current economic and geopolitical environment means that board effectiveness must be increased. This will not be tackled by further structural and process improvement in board operations, but rather by addressing the key relationship issues that underpin decision-making ... First, there is the range of "hats" that board members wear. There are three of these: the individual; the expert; the corporate player ... the second dimension explores the relationship among the "groups" within the board ... the chair, chief executive, non-executives and EDs.'

Deffenbuaugh (2015) goes on to describe the behaviour of board members as 'the how' of the challenge function:

> 'I have worked with boards where challenge has been inappropriate. I have seen executives suit up with armour in advance of a board meeting because their expectation is that they will be challenged in a manner that borders on the unprofessional. I have observed instances where a robust challenge may have been merited due to performance issues, but was carried out in a way that became counterproductive.'
>
> ('Effective challenge on a unitary board', *British Journal of Healthcare Management* 2015 Vol 21 No 11)

As far back as 2002, Jeffrey Sonnenfeld argued that the behaviour of individual board members rather than the structures of the board were key determinants of organisational performance ('What makes boards great', *Harvard Business*

Review, September 2002). Sonnenfeld argued that good board governance cannot be legislated for but can only be built over time. Consequently it is the balance between challenge and support in the relationship between executives and non-executives that is key to effective behaviours and the building of trust is therefore a significant factor for success in an effective challenge function.

Sonnenfeld went on to highlight that great boards:

- Create a climate of trust and candour
- Foster a culture of open dissent
- Use a fluid portfolio of roles
- Ensure individual accountability
- Evaluate the board's performance.

Building on this analysis, *The Healthy NHS Board* identified boards as 'social systems'. It summarised the techniques and practices that support and hinder the effectiveness of these social systems (see Table 7.1).

Table 7.1: Techniques and practices that support and hinder boards

Ways of working that support good social processes	Ways of working that obstruct good social processes
Building a crystal clear understanding of the roles of the board and individual board members	Board members behaving in a way that suggests a 'master–servant' relationship between non-executive and executive
Actively working to develop and protect a climate of trust and candour	Executive directors only contributing in their functional leadership area rather than actively participating across the breadth of the board agenda
Building cohesion by taking steps to know and understand each other's backgrounds, skills and perspectives	Demonstrating an unwillingness to consider points of view that are different from individual directors' starting positions
Encouraging all board members to offer constructive challenges	Challenge primarily coming from non-executive directors, rather than all directors feeling empowered to challenge one another in board meetings
Sharing corporate responsibility and collective decision-making	Challenging in a way that is unnecessarily antagonistic and not appropriately balanced with appreciation, encouragement and support
Ensuring that neither chair nor chief executive power and dominance act to stifle appropriate participation in board debate	Working in ways that don't demonstrate overall confidence in the executive and that feed individual anxiety and insecurity about capability

In 2009, ICSA: The Governance Institute submitted a report, entitled *Boardroom Behaviours,* to Sir David Walker, who was reviewing the corporate governance issues that contributed to the 2007–2009 banking crisis in the UK.

The ICSA report suggested that the corporate governance problem was partly attributable to inappropriate 'boardroom behaviours' and that behavioural problems were only a part of the problem of ineffective governance. However, insufficient attention had been given to the problem and there should be better guidance to directors on how to improve board behaviours.

The report suggested that best practice in boardroom behaviour is characterised by:

- a clear understanding of the role of the board
- the appropriate deployment of knowledge, skills, experience and judgment
- independent thinking
- the questioning of assumptions and established orthodoxy
- challenge, which is constructive, confident, principled and proportionate
- rigorous debate
- a supportive decision-making environment
- a common vision
- the achievement of closure on individual items of board business.

The report commented that:

> 'Despite the importance of these ... considerations, it is remarkable that there is practically no guidance in the Code on the main drivers of, and factors affecting, boardroom behaviours ... To improve on existing standards of behaviour in the boardroom, directors need to develop a greater awareness of, and commitment to, "fit for purpose" governance as the means by which the board can collectively agree the business objectives of the company and a strategy for their implementation by executive management.'

Boardroom Behaviours also provided an outline of the guidance that might be useful to directors about boardroom behaviours:

- All directors, including EDs, need to improve their performance in these important areas of boardroom behaviours. The process of achieving this for NEDs can be made more effective by giving them greater exposure to the organisation's operations.
- A knowledgeable board is a function of board balance and there may be insufficient balance if the board is shrunk to just two EDs (chief executive officer (CEO) and finance director) in order to achieve a majority of NEDs without making the board too big.
- Diversity of board membership is necessary to provide sufficient independent challenge.
- High standards of performance evaluation are needed to increase the effectiveness of a board.

- At the moment the remuneration of EDs appears to focus on maximising short-term 'value' rather than pursuing the goal of a sustainable business. Remuneration arrangements should give more emphasis to the behaviours of directors in the boardroom, working in the long-term interests of the organisation.
- In terms of developing a wider perspective of the business, directors should look 'forward and out, as well as backwards and in'.
- The board should lead by example, 'evidenced by high levels of visibility and integrity, strong communications, and demanding expectations'.
- Practical issues, such as the timely circulation of board papers, 'can have a disproportionate effect on the quality of decision-making'.

The ICSA research project *Mapping the Gap: Highlighting the disconnect between governance best practice and reality in the NHS* (July 2011) was initiated to examine the degree to which trust boards in the NHS understood issues of governance, and the extent to which actual boardroom behaviour reflected guidance on best practice.

The resulting report stated that respondents rated constructive challenge in the top three contributors to sound decision-making, but that the boardroom behaviours observed suggests that more challenge was required to improve discussions and decisions. The project further identified that, on average, respondents saw board trust and collective behaviours as a minimal contributory factor in an effective board. However, in the meetings observed there were a number of behaviours that did not suggest that all board members were fully engaging with the business to be transacted. Examples of poor boardroom behaviour included:

- using electronic devices
- conversing with colleagues
- interrupting
- reading non-board papers
- arriving late
- fidgeting
- exchanging knowing looks/raising eyebrows/rolling eyes.

Directors need to see best practice in governance as a 'business facilitator' and not a 'business killer'. The pursuit of best practice in governance should be seen as a way of achieving competitive advantage, because it strengthens the process and quality of decision-making by the board. Directors also need to be aware that failure to perform at a satisfactory level can have negative consequences, and directors need to be aware of their duties and potential liabilities. Failure to provide best practice in governance, and failure to perform at a satisfactory level, creates a risk to the reputation of boards of directors and individual directors.

Deffenbauagh (2015) goes on to outline two final dimensions to effective board behaviour within the NHS. First is the way in which the challenge function is carried out on a CCG governing body where lay members will naturally challenge around their specific remit and the half way position occupied by general practitioner (GP) governing body members in their representative and lobbying role. This is picked up further in Chapter 13.

The second dimension is the role of women and those from diverse backgrounds on boards. Deffenbauagh quotes Roger Kline's paper The *'Snowy White Peaks' of the NHS* (2014) which explores the links between good diversity management and improved service delivery. Kline states that 'the case for an inclusive and diverse leadership at trust board level – and indeed across the NHS – is now a convincing one'. In London, the proportion of trust board members from a BME (black and minority ethnic) background is 8%, which has declined from 9.6% almost a decade ago – this in a city where 41% of staff and 45% of the population are from a BME background. Kline also reports that the proportion of women in London on trust boards is 40%, which is well below that of the NHS workforce (77%) or the population as a whole (51%) – women are especially under-represented at chair and chief executive level.

Ruth Sealy of Cranfield University in *The Female FTSE Board Report* (2015) has reported on the better governance resulting from more gender diverse boards – enhanced independence, better induction, more accountable, better self-evaluation, more awkward questions, improved innovation and decision-making processes, improved stakeholder relations – all of which affect organisation performance. This supports the findings of the Davies Report, which is set out in more detail later in this chapter.

Appointments to the board

The appointment of the chair and NEDs for NHS trusts is overseen by NHSI.

Foundation trust (FT) chairs and NEDs are appointed by the council of governors and will be covered in Chapter 12. The appointment processes for CCGs will be covered in Chapter 13 as they are quite distinct to the procedures illustrated here.

The NHSI is responsible for around 650 chair and non-executive appointments to NHS trusts and around 60 NHS charitable trustees. The Secretary of State for Health has the power to make these appointments, but has delegated this to the NHS Trust Development Authority (NHS TDA), which is now under the umbrella of NHSI.

The main functions of the NHSI in this regard are to:

- appoint, re-appoint and, where necessary, terminate the appointment of chairs and non-executives of NHS trusts;
- ensure chairs and non-executives receive relevant and appropriate training;
- ensure through annual performance review that chairs and non-executives are supported and developed in their role and feel valued;

- ensure chairs and non-executives receive all necessary support through mentoring programmes;
- ensure that overall NHS boards add value to the NHS locally and more widely.

NHSI follows *The Government's Governance Code* (December 2016) which sets out the regulatory framework for public appointments processes within the Commissioner's remit. NHSI must comply with the following principles of the Code:

- **Selflessness:** Ministers, when making appointments, should act solely in terms of the public interest.
- **Integrity:** Ministers, when making appointments, must avoid placing themselves under any obligation to people or organisations that might try inappropriately to influence them in their work. They should not act or take decisions in order to gain financial or other material benefits for themselves, their family or their friends. They must declare and resolve any interests and relationships.
- **Merit:** All public appointments should be governed by the principle of appointment on merit. This means providing ministers with a choice of high-quality candidates, drawn from a strong, diverse field, whose skills, experiences and qualities have been judged to meet the needs of the public body or statutory office in question.
- **Openness:** Processes for making public appointments should be open and transparent.
- **Diversity:** Public appointments should reflect the diversity of the society in which we live and appointments should be made taking account of the need to appoint boards which include a balance of skills and backgrounds. Public appointment competitions which are open and/or have not completed on the day notified should continue to run to completion under the previous Code of Practice published by the Commissioner for Public Appointments.
- **Assurance:** There should be established assurance processes with appropriate checks and balances. The Commissioner for Public Appointments has an important role in providing independent assurance that public appointments are made in accordance with these Principles and this Governance Code.
- **Fairness:** Selection processes should be fair and impartial and each candidate must be assessed against the same criteria for the role in question.

NEDs hold a statutory office under the National Health Service Act 2006 and their appointment does not create any contract of service or contract for services between the individual and the NHS trust. Chairs and non-executives are not employees. Her Majesty's Revenue and Customs (HMRC) has determined that the nature of the appointment means that the status of chairs and non-executives is 'employment-like' and their remuneration is taxable under Schedule E and subject to Class 1 NI contributions but it is not pensionable. Non-executive board members are also eligible to claim allowance for travel and subsistence costs incurred necessarily on NHS business in line with rates set centrally within the Department of Health (DH). The legislation governing the payment of chairs and non-executives of boards means that they can only be paid remuneration at the levels determined by the Secretary of State. This includes any work on any of the organisation's committees.

At present, the NHSI engages and supports NHS trusts throughout the entire recruitment and selection process. It works with the trust's nomination committee (covered later in this chapter) to conduct a full recruitment campaign, including developing a job description and person specification, advertising the post and supporting the interview process. The NHSI's Appointments Committee makes the final appointment decision based on the recommendation of the selection panel that assesses the merit of each application received.

The NHSI rules state that, in most circumstances, civil servants within the DH, members/employees of the Care Quality Commission (CQC), chairs and members of the governing body of a CCG, and employees of such a group are ineligible as a NED of an NHS trust. The National Health Service Trusts (Membership and Procedure) Amendment Regulations 2014 removed the disqualification which prevents a person being appointed as chair or NED of an NHS trust where they are (a) a chair, NED or member of certain health service bodies; (b) providers or performers of primary health services; or (c) an employee of such health service bodies or of such performers or providers.

NHSI has a duty to ensure that the chairs and non-executives it appoints meet the requirements of the 'fit and proper persons' regulations. Consequently a number of checks may be undertaken to ensure that these requirements are met. They include:

- Disclosure and Barring Scheme (DBS) checks
- Occupational Health Assessment (OHA)
- Photographic proof of ID
- Proof of qualifications, where appropriate
- Search of insolvency and bankruptcy register
- Search of disqualified directors register
- Check with relevant regulators, where appropriate.

Suspension or removal from office

The NHSI has principles and processes that it will use to establish whether and how a chair or NED of an NHS trust should be suspended or removed from office. The policy incorporates three separate but interconnected pathways:

- seeking resignation
- suspending the office holder
- terminating the appointment.

Where there is clear evidence supporting the removal of an NED from office, the individual may choose to resign or a resignation may be actively sought. This is the preferred course of action in most cases. As these posts are public appointments, information about those appointed and removed is in the public domain. Resignation enables the person to be removed from office with dignity and in a managed way that normally meets the needs of both the individual and the organisation. However, there are circumstances when this would not be appropriate or in the public interest.

If the circumstances associated with an appointee's removal from office are actually or potentially so damaging that it would not be in the public interest for them to be able to take up another non-executive role in the NHS, it might be more appropriate to pursue the suspension and/or termination of appointment procedures.

If the office holder submits their resignation during the course of a suspension or termination procedure, the NHSI reserves the right to continue with the procedure. This includes completing any investigation until a conclusion is reached, which may then form part of the person's formal appointment record.

When an appointment to an NHS trust is terminated, an automatic disqualification period lasting two years applies. The NHSI may specify a longer period, such as potentially indefinitely in serious cases. The appointee may apply to the NHSI to reduce the period of disqualification.

Regulation 9 of the NHS Trusts (Membership and Procedure) Regulations 1990 sets out the grounds on which a NED appointment may be terminated with immediate effect. They are:

(i) If they are, or become, disqualified for appointment.
(ii) If it is considered that it is not in the interests of the health service that they should continue to hold office.
(iii) If they do not attend a meeting of the trust for a period of three months.
(iv) If they do not properly comply with the requirements of the regulations with regard to pecuniary interests in matters under discussion at meetings of the trust (e.g. a failure to disclose such an interest).
(v) If they fail to disclose a non-pecuniary conflict of interest.
(vi) If they are appointed following a nomination from a university or local authority and they cease to hold a post with the nominating body.

The following list also provides examples of matters which may indicate that it is no longer considered to be in the interests of the health service that a NED continues in office. It is not intended to be exhaustive or definitive; NHSI will consider each case on its merits, taking account of all relevant factors.

- If they are found to be an unfit person as set out in the Health and Social Care Act 2008 (Regulated Activities) Regulations 2014.
- If an annual appraisal or a sequence of appraisals is unsatisfactory.

- If they no longer enjoy the confidence of their chair, other board members, the public or local community or NHSI in a substantial way.
- If (as chair) they fail to ensure that the board monitors the performance of the trust in an effective way.
- If they fail to meet agreed objectives.
- If there is a breakdown in essential relationships (e.g. between them and the chair, them and the chief executive, them and NHSI, or between them and other members of the board).
- If they fail to apply The Nolan Principles of Public Life.
- If they fail to comply with the letter and/or principle of the trust's internal policies and procedures, as applicable.
- If an investigation into allegations of wrong doing results in a finding against them.
- If a capability or other board effectiveness review indicates that they are not making a full contribution to the board.
- If a chair has reviewed the contribution of the trust's non-executive directors and identified performance issues and/or skills gaps.

If a NED is disqualified from continuing as a chair or NED on any of the grounds set out above, they should immediately give notice in writing to NHSI. They are also required to declare immediately if they have ever been arrested, have any pending prosecutions or convictions (including driving offences) or if they have accepted any police cautions.

Appointments in the corporate sector

Corporate governance is less prescriptive than health service governance when it comes to appointments, although it is an accepted principle of good corporate governance that the power over board appointments should rest with the whole board. Under UK corporate governance, new appointments can be made to the board at any time during the year, but each newly appointed director must offer themselves for re-election at the next annual general meeting (AGM). The company chair and the board committees chairs are appointed by the board. These appointments are not subject to shareholder approval at the next AGM.

Recommendations about new appointments should not belong exclusively to the chair and/or the CEO. Appointments should be made on merit and against objective criteria; however, in practice, criticism has been expressed about the way in which most appointments are made, particularly appointments of NEDs. This criticism centres on the fact that most NED appointments come from a fairly small circle of successful businessmen, many of whom know each other, whereas the net should be cast much wider and individuals from more diverse backgrounds should be chosen.

The UK Code states that there should be 'a formal, rigorous and transparent procedure for the appointment of new directors to the board'. The procedure of identifying candidates for a directorship should be rigorous, and candidates should be investigated thoroughly before the directorship is offered. It goes on to say that appointments should be made on 'merit' and 'against objective criteria'. However, it does not specify what these 'objective criteria' should be.

The procedure should be transparent so that shareholders and other stakeholders are able to see what is happening (what type of person the company is looking for and why a particular individual has been appointed). A formal procedure involves the nomination committee.

The Davies Report

Perhaps somewhat controversially, the UK Code also states that appointments to the board should be made 'with due regard to the benefits of diversity on the board, including gender'. This reflects the widely expressed concern that the boards of major UK companies are dominated by middle-aged to older white males with a commercial or financial background and that there are not enough directors with different attributes, talents and experience to provide boards with an appropriate balance. The relative shortage of female board directors has been well-publicised in the Davies Report, *Women on Boards* (February 2011).

The report made a strong case for greater diversity on boards, recommending in particular that there should be a greater proportion of women on the boards of FTSE 350 companies. Its general argument in favour of greater diversity was that diverse and balanced boards: 'are more likely to be effective boards, better able to understand their customers and stakeholders, and to benefit fresh perspectives, vigorous challenge and broad experience. These in turn lead to better decision-making'.

The report rejected the view, for example, that directors (and particularly NEDs) should have had experience of financial responsibilities before their appointment: 'although there is a real need for financial literacy, financial responsibility ... can be taught and should not be a pre-requisite for appointments'.

The report recommended a voluntary business-led strategy to bring about a culture change at the heart of business. Chapter 1 sets out the reviews in 2013 and 2015. NHSI has declared that it is committed to achieving the goal of 50/50 gender balance on all NHS boards by 2020.

Nomination committees

The role of the nomination committee in FTs and CCGs will be covered in Chapters 12 and 13 (respectively), as they are quite distinct to the procedures that follow here. However, best practice as to composition and process should be used as a useful benchmark as far as possible.

Chapter 5 has already set out the background for the nomination committee, along with its basic role and composition. The committee membership is appointed by the board and is usually made up of at least three members, including the chair and a majority of independent NEDs and is free of any conflict of interest. The chair of the committee should be the chair or vice-chair of the board of directors or an independent NED. Members conflicted on any aspect of an agenda presented to the committee are required to declare their conflict and withdraw from discussions. The committee makes its recommendations on board appointments and succession planning issues to the whole board.

It is important to note that a nomination committee does not have the authority to make new appointments; it simply carries out the search and makes the recommendation. Appointing new directors is a matter for the board, therefore the whole board should make decisions.

It is also important to note that the need for a new board appointment, or a replacement for an existing board member (succession planning), is not necessarily decided by the nomination committee. The chair has responsibility for ensuring that the composition of the board is appropriate. The need for a new NED may also emerge from the annual review of board performance, if an existing NED has not been performing as well as expected or if a gap is identified in the range of skills and experience that the board needs. The chair is also responsible for ensuring that there is succession planning for board positions and may therefore ask the nomination committee to identify potential successors.

If the chair of the board is the chair of the nomination committee, they should not chair the committee when it is dealing with the succession to the role of chair.

The existence of a majority of NEDs should ensure that the chair and CEO do not dominate the appointments process. The committee should consider new appointments to the board and make recommendations to the full board. The full board should then reach a decision about offering a position to the individual concerned so that final responsibility for board appointments remains with the board as a whole.

The main duties of the nomination committee

For NHS trusts, the work of the nomination committee in the appointment of NEDs is supported and underpinned by the NHSI. In general though, the main role of the nomination committee is to:

- regularly review the structure, size and composition (including the skills, knowledge and experience) required of the board compared to its current position, and make recommendations to the board with regard to any changes;
- give full consideration to succession planning for all board members in the course of its work, taking into account the challenges and opportunities facing the trust, and what skills and expertise are therefore needed on the board of directors in the future;
- before any appointment is made by the board of directors, evaluate the balance of skills, knowledge and experience on the board, and, in the light of this evaluation, prepare a description of the role and capabilities required for

a particular appointment. In identifying suitable candidates the committee shall:
  - use open advertising or the services of external advisers to facilitate the search
  - consider candidates from a wide range of backgrounds
  - consider candidates on merit and against objective criteria, taking care that appointees have enough time available to devote to the position;
- review the job descriptions of the director role as required;
- keep under review the leadership needs of the organisation, with a view to ensuring the continued ability of the organisation to deliver services effectively;
- keep up-to-date and fully informed about strategic issues and commercial changes affecting the trust and the environment in which it operates; and
- review annually the performance evaluation process for EDs ensuring it is fit for purpose.

The committee shall also make recommendations to the board of directors concerning:

- formulating plans for succession for EDs;
- membership of the audit and remuneration committees, in consultation with the chairs of those committees;
- any matters relating to the continuation in office of any ED at any time including the suspension or termination of service.

The committee also ensures that the full range of eligibility checks have been performed and references taken and found to be satisfactory.

This is based on the principal duties of the nomination committee, which were summarised in the suggestions for good practice in the Higgs Report. These have been adopted in the NHS; a further useful document is the ICSA guidance note *NHS Foundation Trust Non-Executive Directors Nomination Committee*.

The UK Code requires that a separate section of the annual report should describe the work of the nomination committee, including the process it used in relation to appointments that were made during the year. An explanation should be given if neither the services of an external search consultancy ('headhunters') nor advertising were used in making the appointment of chair or NED. If the vacancy was not advertised nor a headhunter used, this would suggest that the appointment was made of a person that the nomination committee already knew or who was recommended privately: this would be contrary to the requirement for a formal, rigorous and transparent appointment procedure. Executive directors may be appointed from within the organisation, so the requirement applies only to the appointment of a chair or NED.

Criteria for appointment

The UK Code includes several provisions about criteria for appointment to the board that are reflected in health service governance for NHS organisations.

- The search for board candidates should be conducted, and appointments made on merit, against objective criteria and with due regard for the benefits of diversity on the board, including gender.
- The nomination committee should evaluate the balance of skills, experience, independence and knowledge on the board and, in the light of this evaluation, prepare a description of the role and capabilities required for a particular appointment.
- On initial appointment, the chair should meet the criteria for independence.
- For the appointment of a chair, the nomination committee should prepare a job specification, including an assessment of the time required and recognising the need for the chair's availability in times of crisis.
- The departing chair should not chair the nomination committee when it is meeting to consider the appointment of the successor to the role of chair.
- A proposed new chair's other significant commitments should be disclosed to the board before an appointment is made, and included in the annual report (subsequent changes should also be disclosed and reported).

In the NHS, the requirement to openly advertise all NED appointments under the auspices of the NHSI has gone some way to addressing issues of ethnicity and gender. The Equality Act 2010 also imposes a duty on public bodies to achieve equal opportunities in the workplace and in wider society. The Act is supported by specific duties, which require public bodies to publish relevant, proportionate information demonstrating their compliance with the equality duty and to set themselves specific, measurable equality objectives. NHS trusts must set objectives that eliminate unlawful discrimination, harassment and victimisation, advance equality of opportunity and foster good relations.

Practical aspects of board appointments: time commitment

In practice, a nomination committee is likely to carry out its responsibilities by:

- using a firm of headhunters to find individuals outside the firm who might be suitable for appointment (as NED, CEO, finance director, and so on);
- vetting the candidates put forward by the headhunters;
- making a selection and recommendation to the full board.

When an individual is appointed to the company board, the appointment may be for a fixed term. This is usually the case with NEDs: in the UK, NEDs are typically appointed on a fixed three-year contract, which may then be renewed at the end of each term. Executive directors are commonly appointed for an indeterminate length of time, subject to a minimum notice period (typically six months in the NHS). At present, the more usual term of office being offered to NEDs by the NHSI is two years (four years for chairs), due to the uncertainty about the sustainability of such trusts as they have no clear trajectory to attain FT status.

The UK Code states that 'all directors must be able to allocate sufficient time to the company to discharge their responsibilities effectively'. Executive directors are full-time appointments, so the problem of time commitment is not usually significant for them (unless the executive is also appointed as NED for another organisation). The main problem is ensuring that the chair and NEDs give sufficient time to the company. More time will probably be required from the chair than from a NED, and some NEDs (such as the chair of the audit committee) will be expected to commit more time than others.

When the nomination committee prepares a job description for the position, this should include an estimate of the time commitment expected. A NED should undertake that they will have sufficient time to meet what is expected of them. This undertaking could be written into the NED's letter of appointment.

Governing the NHS (June 2003) had this to say about likely time commitments.

> 'In our view a [NHS] non-executive serving on a board, which is properly focused on its governance responsibilities and which is properly supported by papers and information from the executive team, should be able to fulfil the role in 2.5 days per month. This may be regarded as the minimum acceptable commitment. Clearly some individuals will be able to give more time to the organisation and where this is helpful we are not suggesting that it should be discouraged. However, these additional duties should not be regarded as an extension or part of their board role or cross the boundaries set out above.'

NED posts are usually advertised as a minimum time commitment of 2.5 days per month, and a commitment for an NHS chair of 2-3 days per week. If an individual who is proposed to the board as chair or NED has significant time commitments outside the organisation, this should be disclosed to the board before the appointment is made.

An organisation should also protect itself against the risk that an ED is unable to commit sufficient time to the organisation because of NED appointments with other organisations. The UK Code states that the board should not allow one of its own EDs to take on more than one NED post in a FTSE 100 company, or the chair of a FTSE 100 company.

Accepting an offer of appointment as an NED

The formal procedures for appointing a new NED are the same for the appointment of an ED, with the exception of the close involvement of the NHSI. In addition, a newly appointed NED is likely to be less familiar with the organisation than a senior executive manager and they should not accept an appointment unless they are satisfied that there are no matters of concern.

An individual should only be willing to accept an appointment as NED if:

- the organisation does not use unethical business practices and has a good reputation;

- the organisation is a going concern and is not in financial difficulties;
- they can commit to the role the time that the organisation expects;
- the individual believes that they can contribute positively to the effectiveness of the board;
- there is no risk that the directors of the organisation could be held liable for any breach of duty, or that there is sufficient directors' and officers' liability insurance as protection against this risk;
- the fee that the organisation has offered is adequate.

As ICSA has commented: 'by making the right enquiries, asking the right questions and taking care to understand the replies, a prospective director can reduce the risk of nasty surprises and dramatically increase the likelihood of success'.

Guidance from ICSA on the due diligence that a prospective NED should undertake recommends asking questions about:

- the business (e.g. its nature and size, and the organisation's market share, financial performance and financial position);
- governance and stakeholder relations – who the major stakeholders are, and about the structure of the board of directors and its committees;
- the role that the NED would be expected to perform, including membership of board committees. The prospective NED should be satisfied that they have the necessary qualities or experience to make an effective contribution to the work of the organisation's board;
- the organisation's risk management systems and controls; and
- ethical issues, and whether there are any ethical matters that might give cause for concern.

NHS NEDs may also want to ask questions about the impact of any health reform legislation. Answers to many of these questions can be obtained from published documents that are available to the general public, in paper form or on a website. These include the annual report and accounts of the organisation, the organisation's constitution, standing orders, any quality accounts, sustainability report or social and environmental report that the organisation publishes, regulator inspection reports or reviews and press reports about the organisation.

Terms of engagement

If a prospective NED decides to accept the offer of the appointment, terms of engagement should be agreed with the organisation (either with the board as a whole or its nomination committee). The terms that must be agreed are as follows.

- The initial period of tenure in office.
- Time commitment: the organisation must indicate how much time the NED is expected to commit to the organisation, and the NED should make this commitment. This should be included in the formal letter of appointment.

Typically, NEDs of listed companies are expected to commit between 15 and 30 days each year, and possibly more for a committee chair. NHS NEDs are expected to commit a minimum of 30 days each year, with more for a committee chair.

- Remuneration: the annual remuneration of the NED should be agreed. This is usually a fixed annual fee. It is generally considered inappropriate for NEDs, including the chair, to be remunerated on the basis of incentive schemes linked to organisation performance, because this would undermine their independence.

The terms of engagement should be set out in a formal letter of appointment. As well as including details of the role that the NED will be required to perform (including initial membership of board committees), the expected time commitment, the tenure and the remuneration, the letter of engagement should also:

- specify that the NED should treat all information received as a director as confidential to the company;
- indicate the arrangements for induction;
- give details of directors' and officers' liability insurance that will be available;
- indicate the need for an annual performance review process for directors;
- state what organisation resources will be made available to the NED (e.g. desk, computer terminal and telephone).

A sample letter of appointment for a NED can be found on the ICSA's website (www.icsa.org.uk).

Succession planning

The key positions on the board of directors are the chair of the board and the CEO. The individuals holding these positions will retire or resign at some time, perhaps because the individual has reached retirement age or has come to the end of a fixed-term contract.

The board of directors should try to ensure a smooth succession, with a replacement lined up to take the place of the departing individual. In the case of a departing CEO, the successor might be an existing executive manager who has been groomed for the role. In the case of a departing chair, the successor might be an external appointment. A smooth succession is desirable to avoid disruptions to the organisation's decision-making processes or changes in policy or direction. The succession can also be planned well in advance, so that the newly appointed individuals will have an opportunity to learn about their new role before the actual succession occurs.

The FRC *Guidance on Board Effectiveness* states that while 'EDs may be recruited from external sources, companies should also develop internal talent and capability'. Initiatives might include middle management development programmes, facilitating engagement from time to time with NEDs, and partnering and mentoring schemes.

The positions of chair and CEO (and director of finance or CFO) are important. It is undesirable to have vacancies in these positions for more than a short period. Ideally, the successor should be in place for immediate appointment. This is why succession planning should be carried out in advance.

Succession planning should be delegated to the nomination committee. If the board of a listed company intends to breach the governance code by appointing the current CEO as the next chair, it would be advisable for a suitable representative of the board (such as the chair of the nomination committee or the SID) to discuss the reasons for their choice with major shareholders and representative bodies of the institutional shareholders. These discussions should take place well in advance of any final decision about the appointment.

There should also be succession planning for NEDs. As stated above, NEDs are typically appointed in the UK for a fixed period of three years, but it is now a requirement of the UK Code that directors of FTSE 350 companies should stand for re-election annually. The three-year contract may be extended at the end of that time for another three years and so on. Over time, however, a NED will lose some of their independence as they become more engaged with the organisation. Chapter 10 sets out that a NED is generally considered 'not independent' under the UK Code if they have been with the organisation for nine years or more. The FT Code stipulates six years as the threshold. Interestingly, the NHSI is currently having to consider terms of office beyond six years. It is re-appointing existing office holders as it is proving increasingly difficult to attract new candidates for the some of the more challenged NHS trusts under their care.

The FT Code and the UK Code both include a provision that any term beyond six years for a NED should be subject to particularly rigorous review. The board should be continually refreshed, and this is achieved by appointing a new NED when the three-year term of an existing NED reaches its end. In the case of a FTSE 350 company where a NED has performed poorly, this may be achieved by not supporting their annual re-election.

The nominations committee may recommend the re-appointment of a NED at the end of their first year term, but should be more inclined to terminate the appointment after six years, when the second three-year term ends. Any term of office beyond six years should be subject to annual review.

Refreshing board membership

The FT Code and the UK Code state that there should be 'progressive refreshing of the board'. Succession planning as outlined above, in terms of horizon scanning for the right skills and experience to manage the future challenges the board will face, is one way of refreshing the board. However, the nomination committee should also be aware of when a vacancy is expected to arise and should plan in advance to appoint the type of person it considers would improve the balance of skills and experience on the board. In addition, there has been increasing pressure for board appointments to be regularly reviewed under a process of annual re-election.

The financial crisis in banking between 2007 and 2009 led to a re-assessment of the UK Code, when it was argued that some or all of the board should be subject to annual re-election. Annual re-election increases the accountability of the directors to the shareholders and also gives more power to the shareholders, who are able to threaten to vote against a director at the next AGM (instead of possibly having to wait up to three years before having the opportunity).

After extensive consultation. the UK Code now requires:

- annual re-election of directors of FTSE 350 companies;
- annual re-election of all NEDs who have served longer than nine years on the board;
- the same recommendations as before for directors of other companies subject to the UK Code: all other directors to be subject to re-election at the first AGM following their appointment and re-election subsequently at intervals of no more than three years.

The UK Code also requires that, when the board proposes a NED for election at an AGM, they should present reasons why the directors believe that the individual should be appointed. When a director is proposed for re-election, the chair should confirm to the shareholders that following a formal performance evaluation of the individual, they have concluded that the individual's performance continues to be effective and the individual remains committed to the role.

The requirement for the board to ensure planned and progressive refreshing means that re-election of current directors, particularly NEDs, should not be an automatic process. As indicated earlier, plans to refresh the board with new NEDs should be a part of succession planning.

Induction and training of directors

Induction of new directors

The induction of directors is a process by which new directors familiarise themselves with the business, its services and how it operates. New directors need induction in order to become effective contributors to the board decision-making process. The need for induction is more important for NEDs than for EDs, particularly internally appointed EDs, who should be familiar with much of the business before their appointment to the board. However, newly appointed EDs may not be familiar with all the responsibilities and duties of being a director, and may also need induction to make them more aware of what will be expected of them in their new role.

In the NHS, the Healthcare Financial Management Association (HFMA) and NHS Providers provide structured inductions for new chairs, NEDs and CCG lay members around key issues. It includes:

- an introduction to NHS board roles
- sessions on structures, roles, patient safety and individual liabilities
- an introduction to their governance responsibilities; including risk assurance, financial obligations and the board role in delivering a safe and high-quality service.

The UK Code states that all directors should receive an induction on joining the board and that 'to function effectively, all directors need appropriate knowledge of the organisation and access to its operations and staff'.

The chair is responsible for ensuring that new directors receive 'full, formal and tailored' induction. Although there is no specific reference to the company secretary, the chair will probably ask the company secretary to arrange for each director to receive a personalised induction programme. The aim should be to make the director an effective member of the board quickly. An induction programme may therefore focus initially on providing essential information and familiarity with the organisation, such as visits to key sites, meetings with senior management and staff and providing copies of previous board meetings and copies of any current strategy documents. Over time, further induction may then be provided.

Reading is an effective way for an individual to absorb new information quickly, and the company secretary might therefore wish to give a new director a selection of documents as an induction pack.

Training and professional development

Directors should keep their knowledge and skills up to date so they can continue to perform effectively. The organisation should ensure this is provided. The appropriate training and personal development for each individual director will depend on the director's personal situation. All directors may need training or updating when there is a change in an important aspect of the law or when new regulations are introduced that affect the organisation's operations or its governance. Members of board committees may need to be updated or may need to acquire greater in-depth knowledge of matters affecting the work of their committee. Directors may need to be informed about an important new service or product or an important new acquisition for the organisation.

Reflecting as it does the UK Code, the FT Code states that:

> 'The chair should ensure that the directors continually update their skills and the knowledge and familiarity with the organisation required to fulfil their role both on the board and on board committees. The organisation should provide the necessary resources for developing and updating its directors' knowledge and capabilities.'

Meanwhile, the FRC *Guidance on Board Effectiveness* states:

> 'Non-executive directors should devote time to developing and refreshing their knowledge and skills, including those of communication, to ensure that they continue to make a positive contribution to the board. Being well-informed about the company, and having a strong command of the issues relevant to the business, will generate the respect of the other directors.'

The chair, as part of their annual appraisal, should assess the particular training and development needs for each individual director. Each director should also be able to make suggestions about the type of training or development that might be suitable for them personally. The UK Code includes a provision that the chair should agree a personalised approach to training and development with each director. This should be reviewed regularly. The obvious time to do this is during the annual performance review of the director.

Performance evaluation of the board, its committees and individual directors

Requirement for annual evaluation

A possibly contentious issue in both corporate and health service governance is the extent to which the performance of directors should be monitored and assessed, and what form such assessments should take.

In the UK, a requirement for company directors to undergo formal performance appraisals each year was introduced into the UK Code in 2003. Both the FT Code and the UK Code state as a main principle that the board should undertake a 'formal and rigorous annual evaluation of its own performance and that of its committees and individual directors'. The evaluation should consider the 'balance of skills, experience, independence and knowledge of the organisation on the board, its diversity, including gender, how the board works together as a unit, and other factors relevant to its effectiveness'.

Evaluation of individual directors should aim to show whether each director continues to contribute effectively and demonstrates commitment to the role (such as in terms of time spent carrying out director's duties, attendance at board and committee meetings, and on other duties). The evaluation of performance is particularly important for NEDs. Executive directors commit all or most of their time to the organisation and should be fully familiar with the business and the organisation's operations. In contrast, NEDs spend only a part of their time with the organisation, even though they make up the membership of key committees of the board – the audit and remuneration committees in particular. There is a possibility that NEDs will lose some of their enthusiasm for the organisation, and may get into a habit of missing meetings and spending less time with the organisation than expected. In some cases, a director may fail to keep up to date with an important area of his supposed expertise.

The FRC *Guidance on Board Effectiveness* states that 'evaluation should be bespoke in its formulation and delivery' and provides a non-exhaustive list of areas that might be considered, such as:

- the mix of skills, experience, knowledge and diversity on the board, in the context of the challenges facing the organisation;
- clarity of, and leadership given to, the purpose, direction and values of the organisation;
- succession and development plans;
- how the board works together as a unit, and the tone set by the chair and the CEO;
- key board relationships, particularly chair/CEO, chair/senior independent director (SID), chair/company secretary and executive/non-executive;
- effectiveness of individual NEDs and EDs;
- clarity of the senior independent director's role;
- effectiveness of board committees and how they are connected with the main board;
- quality of the general information provided on the organisation and its performance;
- quality of papers and presentations to the board;
- quality of discussions around individual proposals;
- process the chair uses to ensure sufficient debate for major decisions or contentious issues;
- effectiveness of the secretariat;
- clarity of the decision processes and authorities;
- processes for identifying and reviewing risks; and
- how the board communicates with, and listens and responds to, stakeholders.

Originally, the UK Code did not make any recommendation about how the performance evaluation of the board, its committees and individual directors should be carried out, or who should do it. It became established practice, however, that (except for the performance review of the chair themselves) the chair should organise the performance review process and should be closely involved in it.

One approach is for the chair to carry out the reviews personally, possibly with advice and assistance from the company secretary. Alternatively, the chair may be responsible for deciding on the process that should be used for the performance review, and should act on the findings of the review, but may hand the responsibility for conducting the review to the SID. Organisations may also use the services of specialist external consultants.

The respective chapters for the chair, EDs and NEDS set out the performance evaluation process for each role respectively. In addition, the processes for these roles in FTs and CCGs are set out in Chapters 12 and 13 respectively.

The FT Code and the UK Code requires that the board should state in the organisation's annual report how the performance evaluation of the board, its committees and individual directors has been carried out. In addition, the FT Code requires the outcomes of the evaluation of the EDs to be reported to the board of directors, and for the chief executive to take the lead on the evaluation of the EDs.

Board evaluation – what does it mean to be well-led?

In the UK, the potential value of external consultants has been recognised, and the UK Code 2016 states that for the evaluation of the board as a whole, the evaluation of the board of FTSE companies should be 'externally facilitated' at least every three years. In other words, the company should use specialist external consultants at least once every three years, and where the company uses external consultants, it should make a statement of whether the consultants have any other connection with the company.

This is echoed in the FT Code and was formalised in *Developmental Reviews of leadership and governance using the well-led framework: guidance for NHS Trusts and NHS FTs* was published June 2017. The 2017 version aligns the view of a well-led organisation with CQC's assessments and ratings and with the NHSI expectations under the Single Oversight Framework. The Framework replaced Monitor's Quality Governance Framework (QGF) and the Board Governance Assurance Framework (BGAF), which were effectively incorporated within this framework.

The guidance recognises that in-depth, regular and externally facilitated developmental reviews of leadership and governance are good practice across all industries. Such reviews should identify the areas of leadership and governance of organisations that would benefit from further targeted development work to secure and sustain future performance, rather than assessing current performance. The external input is vital to safeguard against the optimism bias and group think to which even the best organisations may be susceptible. The guidance recommends that all providers carry out externally facilitated, developmental reviews of their leadership and governance using the Well-Led Framework every three to five years, according to their circumstances.

The structure of the framework (key lines of enquiry (KLOEs) and their characteristics) is wholly shared with the CQC, and underpins CQC's regular regulatory assessments of the well-led question. This means that information prepared for regulation can also be used for development, and vice versa. The main elements of the framework are also reflected in NHS England's (NHSE) *Improvement and Assessment Framework for CCGs*.

However, while CQC's regulatory assessments are primarily for assurance, developmental reviews are primarily for providers themselves to facilitate continuous improvement.

As John Coutts of NHS Providers writes:

> '[Previously] meeting targets was a reasonable measure of the quality of trust leadership because compliance was an indication that boards could effect change within their organisations where their lesser colleagues might struggle.
>
> It makes sense therefore, to move towards using [the Well-Led] framework to judge the quality of leadership rather than compliance with arbitrary and sometimes unattainable targets.'

This is a move in the right direction as previously the assessment of board effectiveness was largely determined using national access and quality targets to produce a governance risk rating. Recognising that a board's leadership and performance must also be assessed for its contribution to strategy and culture and as well as holding the executive to account for the day-to-day performance of the organisation aligns health service governance with the similar movement in corporate governance (e.g. FRC study in corporate culture).

Whilst the specific detail of the 2017 framework has already been set out in Chapter 4, essentially the aligned framework sets out a clear expectation of what 'good' looks like for any well-led NHS organisation.

It is encouraging to see that the guidance has moved away from a checklist approach: recognising that a mechanical 'ticking off' of each item is unlikely to lead to better performance. Much more important to the development of leadership and good governance is the attitude of organisational leaders to the review process, the connections they draw between the framework's different areas, and their judgments about what needs to be done to continually improve. Consequently, providers are encouraged to engage with the review processes openly and honestly, selecting an external facilitator to provide tailored support and prioritise actions arising from reviews. Providers are also encouraged to make more use of peer review, to utilise and enhance skills within the NHS, draw on learning from others and share learning back with the system. This is how providers, individually and together, will gain the greatest benefit from these reviews.

To assess the performance of the board, a comparison should be made between what the board should be expected to achieve, and what it has actually achieved. One way of doing this may be to provide answers to a set of questions about performance, possibly through discussions at a special board meeting.

Questions that may provide a useful basis for assessment of board performance are set out below:

- Does the board have any specific performance objectives (e.g. in terms of business performance or quality measures)? How well has the board performed against any such targets?
- What has the board contributed to the development of strategy and what has it done to oversee the implementation of strategy and achievement of strategy targets?

- What has the board contributed to ensuring that the organisation has a robust and effective risk management system?
- Is the board concerning itself with the appropriate issues? Is the list of matters reserved for the board suitable or should it be amended?
- Is the board an appropriate size and is the mix of members suitable (in terms of spread of experience, knowledge, skills and/or background)? Are changes needed?
- How well does the board communicate with patients, the public, management, employees and other stakeholders?

Questions may also be asked about the effectiveness of boardroom practice:

- Do board members receive relevant and clear information in good time for board meetings and decision-making? Is the amount and quality of this information adequate?
- Have there been sufficient board meetings in the past year?
- Are the board meetings too short to be effective or too long?

Evaluation of board committees

Board committees should be evaluated in a similar way to the board as a whole. For each committee, there should be a comparison between what the committee is responsible for doing and what it has actually done. For example:

- Has the nomination committee been successful in identifying suitable individuals for board appointments?
- Have any individuals been appointed to the board who, in retrospect, were not as good as originally thought?
- Has the nomination committee done any succession planning and if so, how good have its plans been?
- Has the committee made clear recommendations to the board, and has the board acted on its recommendations?
- Is the committee an appropriate size and is the mix of members suitable? Are changes needed?
- Have there been enough committee meetings during the past year?

Similar questions can be asked about the remuneration and audit committees as well as any other committees established by the board.

Using the results of a performance review

To obtain practical value from an annual evaluation of the board, its committees and its individual directors, the board should be prepared to act on its findings whenever performance is not considered to be as good as it should be. The chair has the responsibility for acting to deal with poor performance.

The UK Code makes the following provisions for how the performance review should be used:

> 'The chair should act on the results of the performance evaluation by recognising both the strengths and weaknesses of the board and, where appropriate, proposing new members to be appointed to the board or seeking the resignation of directors.'

In the preface to the UK Code 2016, the chair of the FRC stated: 'Chairs are encouraged to report personally in their annual statements how the principles relating to the role and effectiveness of the board have been applied.' The recommendation is that the chair of an organisation should recognise their personal responsibility for performance and effectiveness of the board, and an organisation should not simply disclose its procedures for assessing performance in a 'boiler plate' fashion.

The chair may also consider the need for changes to the composition of board committees and may ask for the resignation of a committee chair. Some improvements may be achieved by changing board procedures (such as holding meetings more frequently or changing the dates of meetings to give management more time to prepare the information required).

Although the chair has the primary responsibility for acting on the results of the annual performance review, the FRC guidance *Improving Board Effectiveness* states that: 'The results of a board evaluation should be shared with the board as a whole and fed back, as appropriate, into the board's work on composition, the design of induction and development, and other relevant areas.'

Problems with performance reviews

The performance evaluation of the board and its directors is recognised in the UK as a valuable tool for the assessment of the effectiveness of the board, and stakeholders have shown an interest in obtaining information about the evaluation process. They want to know that an evaluation has taken place, but they also need assurance that the evaluation process is of a suitable quality standard and rigour. This is one reason why the UK Code introduced a requirement for external consultants to be used at least every three years.

Stakeholders would also like to know more about the action that has been taken following an annual performance review, because they want assurance that the review is being used to improve the effectiveness of the board. However, it may be difficult to provide as much information about the performance review, especially the review of individual directors, without compromising the confidentiality of the exercise.

Conflicts of interest

The board of directors of an NHS organisation has a legal obligation to act in the best interests of that organisation, in accordance with the governing document, and to avoid situations where there may be a potential conflict of interest. As such, there are requirements for board members to register personal financial interests that may be perceived as conflicting with that overriding duty.

In February 2017, NHSE issued new guidance *Managing Conflicts of Interest in the NHS*. This guidance:

- introduces common principles and rules for managing conflicts of interest
- provides simple advice to staff and organisations about what to do in common situations
- supports good judgment about how interests should be approached and managed.

The guidance came into force on 1 June 2017 and is applicable via the statutory guidance to CCGs issued by NHSE (see Chapter 13), NHS trusts and FTs and NHSE itself. It includes a model policy for voluntary adoption by such organisations. Organisations may adopt their own policy instead, but it must meet the standards in the guidance as a minimum.

The *Healthy NHS Board* reinforces the importance of NHS boards acting – and being seen to act – with integrity and in the best interests of the organisation:

> 'Probity requires that the board maintains an up-to-date register of board members' interests. Board agendas should include an opportunity for board members to declare conflicts of interests that may relate to specific agenda items so that they can be managed appropriately.'

Under section 152 of the Health and Social Care Act 2012 (HSCA 2012), boards in NHS FTs (see Chapter 6) are also required to adopt appropriate standards of conduct, as well as being open and transparent in their decision-making and the manner in which conflicts of interest are managed.

It is, therefore, essential that there are clear and robust systems in place for identifying and managing real and potential conflicts of interest of board members to protect the reputation and tangible assets of the NHS organisation, as well as the reputation of individual board members.

The Companies Act 2006 (CA 2006) defines conflict of interest as arising when the interests of directors, or 'connected persons', are incompatible or in competition with the interests of the organisation. Such situations present a risk that directors may make decisions based on these external influences, rather than the best interests of the organisation. The Act goes on to define 'connected persons' (see below).

What are conflicts of interest?

The NHSE guidance (2017) defines a conflict of interest as:

> 'A set of circumstances by which a reasonable person would consider that an individual's ability to apply judgement or act, in the context of delivering, commissioning, or assuring taxpayer funded health and care services is, or could be, impaired or influenced by another interest they hold.'

A conflict of interest may be actual, where there is a material conflict between one or more interests or potential where there is the possibility of a material conflict between one or more interests in the future. The guidance recommends caution as staff may hold interests in which they cannot see potential conflict but others may see it differently. It will be important, therefore, for them to exercise judgment and to declare such interests, as there is a risk of implied improper conduct.

Interests can arise in a number of different contexts. A material interest is one, which a reasonable person would take into account when making a decision regarding the use of taxpayers' money because the interest has relevance to that decision. Such interests fall into the following categories:

- Financial interests: where an individual may get direct financial benefit (over and above the agreed remuneration and terms of their service package) from the consequences of a decision they are involved in making. This is the most easily recognisable form of conflict of interest. Examples include the award of a contract to a company or other business with which a director is involved, and the sale of assets at below market value to a director.
- Indirect interests: where an individual has a close association with another individual who has a financial interest, a non-financial professional interest or a non-financial personal interest who would stand to benefit from a decision they are involved in making. For example, when a close relative of a director benefits from the decision. Directors will also benefit indirectly if their financial affairs are bound with those of the relative in question through the legal concept of 'joint purse', as would be the case if the relative were the spouse, partner, dependent child of the director, or directly connected in some other way
- Non-financial professional interests: where an individual may obtain a non-financial professional benefit from the consequences of a decision they are involved in making, such as increasing their professional reputation or promoting their professional career. For instance, to gain some other intangible benefit or kudos, or awarding contracts to friends or personal business contacts.
- Non-financial personal interests: where an individual may benefit personally in ways which are not directly linked to their professional career and do not give rise to a direct financial benefit, because of decisions they are involved in making in their professional career. For example, directors may have competing loyalties between the trust to which they owe a primary duty and some other person or entity which could inhibit free discussion resulting in decisions or actions that are not in the interests of the trust.

The guidance provides additional examples for each of these types of interests. It recognises that a benefit may arise from the making of gain or avoiding a loss and explains that associations may arise through relationships with close family members and relatives, close friends and associates, and business partners and that a common sense approach should be applied to these terms.

It would be unrealistic to expect staff to know of all the interests that people in these classes of association might hold. However, if staff do know of material interests (or could be reasonably expected to know about these) then these should be declared. The guidance also distinguishes between staff generally and those who are more likely than others to have a decision-making influence on the use of public monies because of their role. Board and governing body members are clearly decision-making staff for the purposes of the guidance as are:

- members of advisory groups which contribute to direct or delegated decision making on the commissioning or provision of taxpayer-funded services;
- those at Agenda for Change band 8d and above;
- administrative and clinical staff who have the power to enter into contracts on behalf of their organisation;
- administrative and clinical staff involved in decision-making concerning the commissioning of services, purchasing of good, medicines, medical devices or equipment, and formulary decisions.

This guidance is comparable to the companies legislation requirements which defines a 'connected person' to a director (at section 252(2) of the CA 2006) as:

'a) members of the directors' family (section 253 defines these as spouse or civil partner; any other person with whom the director lives as a partner in an enduring family relationship, the directors' children or step-children, a partners' children or step-children under 18 years of age; and the directors' parents);
b) a body corporate with which the director is connected;
c) a person acting in their capacity as a trustee of a trust – (i) the beneficiaries of which include the director or a person who by virtue of (a) or (b) is connected with them, or (ii) the terms of which confer a power on the trustees that may be exercised for the benefit of the director or any such person, other than a trust for the purposes of an employees' share scheme or pension scheme;
d) a person acting in their capacity as a partner – (i) of the director, or (ii) of a person who by virtue of (a) to (c) is connected with that director;
e) a firm that is a legal person under the law by which it is governed and in which – (i) the director is a partner, (ii) a partner is a person who by virtue of (a) to (c) is connected with the director, or (iii) a partner is a firm in which the director is a partner or in which there is a partner who by virtue of (a), (b) or (c) is connected with the director.'

Decisions made under a conflict of interest may be legally challenged and could result in personal liability for the director. The aim of a conflict of interest policy, therefore, is to protect both the organisation and the individuals involved from any appearance of impropriety.

Declaration of interests

Having interests is not in itself negative, but not declaring them or managing them is – consequently where there is potential for an interest to be material and relevant to NHS business, then the relevant interest should be declared and recorded in a register of interests. The company secretary must maintain the Register of Directors' Interests and ensure that arrangements have been made for staff interest to be recorded within the organisation as appropriate.

Once recorded, then appropriate action needs to be taken and the NHSE guidance includes the following possibilities:

- deciding that no action is warranted
- restricting an individual's involvement in discussions and excluding them from decision making
- removing an individual from the whole decision-making process
- removing an individual's responsibility for an entire area of work
- removing an individual from their role altogether if the conflict is so significant that they are unable to operate effectively in the role
- keeping an audit trail of the actions taken.

The guidance outlines situations with associated principles and rules, which may give rise to a possible conflict of interest. These are:

- gifts
- hospitality
- outside employment
- shareholdings and other ownership interests
- patents
- loyalty interests
- donations
- sponsored events
- sponsored research
- sponsored posts
- clinical private practice.

Hospitality & gifts policy and associated registers

A hospitality & gifts policy is intended to assist all employees of an NHS organisation (and this includes all board members) in following the NHS guidance and relevant legislation on the giving and receipt of hospitality or gifts. This covers both the receipt and delivery of hospitality and gifts. Any hospitality, gifts or benefits accepted should be entered on the hospitality & gifts register by means of a standardised form. Each employee has a personal responsibility to declare hospitality and gifts in accordance with the policy.

Under the Prevention of Corruption Acts 1906 and 1916, it is an offence for employees corruptly to accept any gifts or consideration as an inducement or reward for; doing, or refraining from doing, anything in their official capacity; or showing favour or disfavour to any person in their official capacity. Under the 1916 Act, any money, gift or consideration received by an employee in public service from a person or organisation holding or seeking to obtain a contract will be deemed to have been received corruptly unless the employee proves to the contrary.

Under NHS Standing Orders and European Commission Directives on Public Purchasing for Works and Supplies, there is a requirement for fair and open competition between prospective contractors or suppliers.

Circular HSG (93) 5, 'Standards of Business Conduct for NHS Staff' (January 1993) provides guidelines for NHS employers and employees. This sets out that NHS employers are responsible for ensuring the guidelines are brought to the attention of all employees, and that machinery is put in place to ensure they are effectively implemented. A hospitality policy is intended to fulfil these requirements by providing clear guidance to employees and by establishing a hospitality register.

The NHS guidance also sets out that it is the responsibility of staff to ensure that they are not placed in a position which risks, or appears to risk, conflict between their private interests and their NHS duties. This applies to both staff who commit resources directly (ordering of goods or services) or indirectly (by policy development).

Examples of hospitality, gifts or benefits where a declaration may be necessary include the following:

- meals and drinks
- crates and bottles of wine or spirits
- tickets for sporting events/theatre, etc.
- events where the cost of accommodation is paid for by a research company
- national and international seminars where the placement has been paid for by the company organising the seminar
- sponsored golf events
- lecture trips (national and international)
- site visits to prospective suppliers of goods and services where hospitality, gifts or benefit is provided or loaned
- gifts of equipment by drug companies.

The above list is not exhaustive, but it will give an indication of the types of items that may need to be declared. The NHSE guidance (2017) stipulates that low cost branded promotional items from suppliers valued at more than £6 in total must be declared. Gifts of cash or vouchers to individuals from patients or families should always be declined and gifts of over £50 can only be accepted on behalf of the organisation (e.g. to the organisations' charitable funds). Modest gifts under a value of £50 do not, however, need to be declared, but multiple gifts over a 12-month period should be declared if the total value exceeds £50.

Hospitality (meals, refreshments, accommodation, tickets etc.) may only be accepted where there is a legitimate business reason and it is proportional to the event itself. If the value is under £25 then it does not need to be declared, however if the meal and/or refreshments are valued at more than £75 then it should be refused unless senior approval is given. All other hospitality must be declared and recorded. However, the recipient should not allow themselves to reach a position whereby they might be deemed by others to have been influenced in making a business decision as a consequence of accepting such hospitality.

Where it is not easy to decide whether the hospitality or gift should be accepted or not, advice should be sought from the line manager.

Outside employment

The NHS relies on staff with good skills, broad knowledge and diverse experience. Many staff bring expertise from sectors outside the NHS, such as industry, business, education, government and beyond. The involvement of staff in these outside roles alongside their NHS role can therefore be of benefit, but their existence should be well known so that conflicts can be either managed or avoided. Staff should declare any existing outside employment on appointment, and any new outside employment when it arises.

Shareholding and other ownership interests

Staff should declare, as a minimum, any shareholdings and other ownership interests in any publicly listed, private or not-for-profit company, business, partnership or consultancy which is doing, or might be reasonably expected to do, business with their organisation. There is no need to declare shares or securities held in collective investment or pension funds or units of authorised unit trusts.

Clinical private practice

Service delivery in the NHS is done by a mix of public, private and not-for-profit organisations. The expertise of clinicians in the NHS is in high demand across all sectors and the NHS relies on the flexibility that the public, private and not-for-profit sectors can provide. It is therefore not uncommon for clinical staff to provide NHS-funded care and undertake private practice work either for an external company, or through a corporate vehicle established by themselves.

Existing provisions in contractual arrangements make allowances for this to happen and professional conduct rules apply. However, these arrangements do create the possibility for conflicts of interest arising. Therefore, these provisions are designed to ensure the existence of private practice is known so that potential conflicts of interest can be managed.

Clinical staff should declare all private practice on appointment, and/or any new private practice when it arises including:

- where they practise (name of private facility)
- what they practise (specialty, major procedures)
- when they practise (identified sessions/time commitment).

In situations where a conflict of interest arises NHS commitments must take precedence over the private work.

Managing conflicts of interest

Interests must be declared as soon as they become apparent and any change in interests should be declared as soon as it is recognised.

The register of interests (directors) is maintained by the company secretary who formally records the declarations of interests made by members of the board. These details must be kept up-to-date by means of at least an annual review of the register in which any changes to interests declared during the preceding months will be incorporated. The register is available to the public and to the trust's internal and external auditors and should be published on the trust's website, to ensure compliance with Information Commissioner's Office Publication Scheme. The details of the interests of board members must be published in the trust's annual report.

If a board member has an actual or potential interest, the chair should consider the following approaches and ensure that the reason for the chosen action is documented in minutes or records:

- Requiring the member to not attend the meeting
- Ensuring that the member does not receive meeting papers relating to the nature of their interest
- Requiring the member to not attend all or part of the discussion and decision on the related matter
- Noting the nature and extent of the interest, but judging it appropriate to allow the member to remain and participate
- Removing the member from the group or process altogether.

Any interest that arises during the course of a meeting should be declared immediately, and should be recorded in the relevant minutes. When a conflict of interest is established, the person should withdraw and play no part in the relevant discussion or decision.

The default response should not always be to exclude members with interests, as this may have a detrimental effect on the quality of the decision being made. An example is the need for clinical involvement, when clinicians may hold and represent a diversity of interests. Good judgment is required to ensure proportionate management of risk. The composition of groups should be kept under review to ensure effective participation.

An interest should remain on the register(s) for a minimum of six months after the interest has expired. Organisations should retain a private record of historic interests for a minimum of six years after the date on which it expired. Sanctions for the failure to declare a conflict of interests could include:

- Disciplinary sanctions – verbal, written or dismissal
- Professional regulatory sanctions – fitness to practise
- Civil sanctions - misfeasance in public office
- Criminal sanctions – fraud, bribery and corruption.

The Bribery Act 2010

The Bribery Act 2010 came into force in July 2011 and made it a criminal offence for commercial organisations to fail to prevent bribes being paid on their behalf. NHS organisations are included within the definition of 'commercial'. Therefore, if any NHS organisation fails to take appropriate steps to avoid (or at least minimise) the risk of bribery taking place it could face large fines and even the imprisonment of the individuals involved and those who have turned a blind eye to the problem. The Act makes it a criminal offence to give or offer a bribe or to request, offer to receive or accept a bribe, whether in the UK or abroad (the measures cover bribery of a foreign public official), and for a director, manager or officer of a business to allow or turn a blind eye to bribery within the organisation.

The Act also introduces a corporate offence of failure to prevent bribery by persons working on behalf of a commercial organisation. However, organisations will have a defence against prosecution if they can show that they have adequate procedures in place to prevent bribery.

Guidance from the Ministry of Justice describes six guiding principles that set out the approach that organisations should take to prevent bribery occurring in their organisation. These are as follows.

- **Proportionate procedures:** designed to prevent bribery by anyone associated with the organisation and should be proportionate to the level of bribery risk to the organisation.
- **Top-level commitment:** senior management teams must show a commitment to preventing bribery, and promote a culture that does not tolerate acts of bribery.
- **Risk assessment:** an assessment of both internal and external risks of bribery to the organisation should be carried out regularly and documented.
- **Due diligence:** there must be effective due diligence procedures in place in respect of those involved in the organisation or carrying services out on behalf of the organisation.
- **Communication:** the organisation's stance on bribery should be clearly communicated to all employees and all those carrying out services on behalf of the organisation. This should include appropriate training.
- **Monitoring and review:** there should be an ongoing review process that regularly monitors the effectiveness of the procedures in place to prevent bribery.

These principles can be implemented by updating existing documentation, for example:

- updating policies and procedures by adding an anti-bribery statement to the organisation's employee handbook/intranet – this should be adequately communicated to all staff;
- amend whistleblowing policies to make specific reference to bribery, and encourage disclosure of bribery offences;
- training/presentations to make employees aware of the strengthened legislation around 'bribery', particularly in relation to corporate hospitality and the organisation's policy on business conduct (or similar);
- updating/adding a clause on bribery to employment contracts;
- ensuring all employees are under an express obligation to report any potential acts of bribery, including where an employee has personally committed an act of bribery;
- ensuring recruitment checks are robust;
- adding bribery to the matters covered by a disciplinary policy; and
- reviewing remuneration structures so that they comply with the new law where applicable.

Governance checklist

- ✓ Does the board perform the leadership functions expected of an effective board?
- ✓ Does it develop strategy, promote behaviours consistent with the culture and values it has defined for the organisation?
- ✓ Is there an effective process in place to allow the organisation to make well informed and high-quality decisions based on a clear line of sight into the business?
- ✓ Does the board know what the balance of skills, experience, knowledge and personality it requires currently and in the medium to long term? Does it have that balance?
- ✓ What consideration has the board given to equality and diversity with regard to its own composition?
- ✓ Is the nomination committee actively involved in developing the recruitment and appointment process for new board members? Is there a focus on competencies rather than experience?
- ✓ Is there an open and positive interplay between the nomination and remuneration committees?
- ✓ Is there a clear and informative report from the nomination committee in the annual report?

- ✓ Are the terms of reference for the nomination committee available publicly and subject to regular review?
- ✓ Does the board have a succession plan and is it kept under regular review?
- ✓ What plans does the board have for annual self-evaluation of itself, its committees and individual directors?
- ✓ How are external assessors for evaluation appointed so that their independence is assured?

Summary

There is a fine balance to be maintained in assessing the effectiveness of a board. There should be quantitative evidence of outcomes achieved and processes followed, yet there must also be a more subjective and qualitative approach which considers the individual skills, experience and personalities that are represented in the board. How do these people work together to make a cohesive unit?

This chapter has sought to demonstrate that there is guidance to outline best practice in processes and procedures though at the same time posing questions or challenges about behaviour and culture, which each board and each individual board member must consider in its or their own development.

As John Deffenbaugh says in his 2012 *British Journal of Healthcare Management* article, 'It's the people in the boardroom': 'In a world requiring a high-performing board, the knowledge derived from this insight to behaviour and relationships can enable the individual components to meld into an effective decision-making body.'

8

The chair of the board

Introduction

Although this chapter explores the role of the chair of the board, it should be also be considered in the light of the next chapter and the role of the chief executive officer (CEO). This is because these are the two most powerful roles within the board: there needs to be a clear distinction between the roles and a clear understanding by the individuals fulfilling them how they are meant to complement and work together.

Much of the friction in board relationships is centred upon this key dynamic; effective boards often demonstrate what the dynamic should be and vice versa. Much of what follows here can also be applied to the role of board committee chairs. Obviously, the focus here on the role of the chair must not distract from the underlying principle of the unitary board, with the chair having the same duties and responsibilities of every other board director. However, the role of the chair in creating the right team dynamic for a disparate group of board directors with varied and strongly held views to reach agreement on strategic direction and corporate objectives is absolutely crucial.

As the Financial Reporting Council (FRC) *Guidance on Board Effectiveness* states: 'good boards are created by good chairs': therefore, the role warrants further examination here.

The role of the chair

Whereas the CEO is responsible for the executive management, the chair's responsibilities relate primarily to managing the board of directors, and ensuring that the board functions effectively. To do this, a chair needs to ensure that the board discusses relevant issues in sufficient depth, with all the information needed to reach a decision, and with all the directors contributing to the discussions and decision-making.

The UK Code states that:

- 'The chair is responsible for leadership of the board and ensuring its effectiveness on all aspects of its role.'

- 'The chair is responsible for setting the board's agenda and ensuring that adequate time is available for discussion of all agenda items, in particular strategic issues.'
- 'The chair should also promote a culture of openness and debate by facilitating the effective contribution of non-executives in particular and ensuring constructive relations between executive and NEDs [non-executive directors].'
- 'The chairman is responsible for ensuring that the directors receive accurate, timely and clear information. The chairman should ensure effective communication with shareholders.'

These principles emphasise the role of the chair in trying to ensure that all directors, in particular NEDs, contribute effectively to board discussions. There is always a risk that individuals who do not work full-time for the organisation may have difficulty in challenging the views of full-time executive directors (EDs). The chair should make sure that this does not happen.

The FRC *Guidance on Board Effectiveness* states that: 'the chair creates the conditions for overall board and individual director effectiveness'. It emphasises that an effective chair is a team-builder, developing a board whose members communicate effectively and enjoy good relationships with each other. They should develop a close relationship of trust with the CEO, giving support and advice while still respecting the CEO's responsibilities for executive matters. They should also ensure the effective implementation of board decisions, provide coherent leadership for the organisation and understand the views of the stakeholders.

The FRC guidance also provides a detailed list of matters for which the chair is responsible, which includes:

- setting the board agenda, which is primarily focused on strategy, performance, value, creation and accountability, and ensuring that issues relevant to these areas are reserved for board decision;
- making certain that the board determines the nature, and extent, of the significant risks the organisation is willing to embrace in the implementation of its strategy, and that there are no 'no go' areas that prevent directors from operating effective oversight in this area;
- making certain that the board has effective decision-making processes and applies sufficient challenge to major proposals;
- encouraging all board members to engage in board and committee meetings by drawing on their skills, experience, knowledge and, where appropriate, independence;
- fostering relationships founded on mutual respect and open communication between the NEDs and the executive team;
- developing productive working relationships with all EDs, and the CEO in particular, providing support and advice while respecting executive responsibility;

- taking the lead on issues of director development, including through induction programmes for new directors and regular reviews with all directors; acting on the results of board evaluation; and
- ensuring effective communication with all stakeholders and, in particular, that all directors are made aware of the views of those who provide the organisation's capital.

The NHS Improvement (NHSI) role description for an NHS trust chair sets out that they are accountable to the Secretary of State through the NHSI, for giving leadership to the NHS trust board and ensuring the trust provides high-quality, safe services, and value for money (VFM) within NHS resources. It goes on to set out in the chair's role in the following areas:

- Formulate plans and strategy
- Ensure accountability
- Shape culture and capability
- Engagement.

The NHSI guidance then sets out the key responsibilities of the chair as to:

- provide leadership to the board, the trust, the other non-executives, the CEO and EDs; and ensure the effectiveness of the board in all aspects of its role and agenda; including directing the organisation towards achieving the government's objective of all trusts achieving foundation trust (FT) status;
- ensure the provision of accurate, timely and clear information to the board and directors to meet statutory requirements;
- ensure effective communication with the board, staff, patients and the public in a changing healthcare environment;
- arrange the regular evaluation of the performance of the board, its committees and individual non-executives, directors, and the CEO;
- plan and conduct board meetings with the CEO;
- facilitate the effective contribution of NEDs and ensure constructive relations within the organisation and between executive and NEDs, and
- share and use relevant expertise of all members of the board.

In particular, the chair will:

- proactively direct and manage the development of major board decisions, ensuring that 'due process' has been applied at all stages of decision-making and full and complete consideration has been given to all options during the process;
- hold the CEO to account for the effective management and delivery of the organisation's strategic aims and objectives;
- ensure the board develops and oversees strategies, which will result in tangible improvements to the health of the population and clinical services;

- ensure the board establishes clear objectives to deliver agreed strategies and regularly review performance against these objectives;
- ensure the board maintains its responsibility for the effective governance of the organisation by making the best use of resources including the development of effective risk and performance management processes;
- ensure the board, and the organisation, observe the Secretary of State's policies and priorities, including the requirements of the Codes of Conduct and Accountability;
- be aware of relevant, regulatory and central government policies;
- play a key role in building strong partnerships with the local authorities, local health economy, and other stakeholders in the community and nationally, including regulators such as NHSI and the Care Quality Commission (CQC). For FTs this includes developing an effective council of governors and promoting harmonious relations with the board;
- ensure that the interests of all stakeholders, and influence of all advisers, are fairly balanced;
- provide the leadership needed by the board to shape the organisation; develop a culture which supports the values of the NHS, and ensure the organisation values diversity in its workforce and demonstrates equality of opportunity in its treatment of staff and patients and in all aspects of its business;
- be an ambassador for the trust with national, regional and local bodies; be knowledgeable and aware of local issues, and recognise the trust's role as a major local employer; and
- where necessary, assist in the appointment of executives and non-executives and ensure systems of support and appraisal.

The NHSI guidance goes on to set out the board level behaviours expected of a chair. These have already been covered in Chapter 7.

Independence of the chair

As a general rule, the chair should be independent when first appointed. This is a provision of the UK Code for listed companies and of the FT Code. See Chapter 13 for a discussion about independence in CCG appointments.

It follows that the CEO of an organisation should not subsequently become the chair, as a former CEO will not be independent (although the King IV Code states that a former CEO should not become chair for at least three years after ceasing to be CEO, believing that this is sufficient time in which to become independent). If, exceptionally, it is proposed that the current CEO should become the chair when the existing chair retires, shareholders should be consulted first. The UK Code also states that the reasons for appointing a former CEO as chair should be explained to shareholders both at the time of the appointment and in the next annual report and accounts.

A governance problem with 'promoting' the CEO to become the chair is that the incoming CEO may find it difficult to run the organisation as they wish because the former CEO is still on the board, monitoring what they are doing. Even so, there have been several cases where a CEO has gone on to become the chair without any serious protest from shareholders or investor groups.

The National Association of Pension Funds (NAPF)'s *Corporate Governance Policy and Voting Guidelines* (2011) also recommend that if the chair is not independent on appointment, the organisation should consult its shareholders and explain why it considers the appointment desirable. The shareholders should then consider the case on its merits.

The chair's commitments

A problem with non-executive chairs – as with NEDs generally – is that the individual may not have enough time to devote to the role because of a large number of other commitments. For example, the chair of a large company may also be the chair of another organisation, without enough time to fulfil either of these roles adequately.

Chairs need to be able to demonstrate that they have sufficient time to perform their role to the standards expected. NAPF's *Corporate Governance Policy and Voting Guidelines* state that where a chair has 'multiple appointments', investors will require a 'compelling explanation' of how they will be able to handle all the various appointments without any detriment to the organisation. The Walker Report suggested that the chairs of large banks would need to spend about two-thirds of their time with the organisation.

The UK Code is less specific on the amount of time that a chair should commit to the organisation. However, a provision of the Code is that, when a chair is appointed, the nomination committee (see also Chapter 7) should prepare a job description including an assessment of the amount of time commitment that should be expected and recognise the need for the chair to make himself or herself available in a time of crisis.

The chair's other commitments should be disclosed to the board before their appointment and included in the next annual report and accounts. If there are changes to the time commitment required from or provided by the chair, these should be disclosed to the board and reported in the next annual report and accounts.

The FT Code also sets out that the board of directors should not agree to a full-time ED taking on more than one non-executive directorship of an NHS FT or another organisation of comparable size and complexity, nor the chair of such an organisation.

The criteria for independence are set out in Chapter 7; the same criteria should be applied to the chair (on appointment) as it is to other NEDs. However, circumstances may change, so the independence of NEDs should be kept under review.

Behaviours of an effective chair

The report *What Makes an Outstanding Chair* by Directorbank Group set out the following as key characteristics of an effective chair.

1. **Integrating the board's collective thinking.** This is possible when a chair excels at seeking and sharing information; building ideas into concepts; analysing and considering multiple perspectives and different alternatives; and can subvert their individual needs for commitment to a common goal.
2. **Empathy and promoting openness in board members.** The ability to listen at multiple levels is critical to successful chairship and team dynamics. Listening to what is not being said is as critical as listening to the words that are spoken. Only with this ability can a chair engender deep trust and respect.
3. **Facilitating interaction.** This requires that a chair's behaviour move seamlessly depending upon who needs to be in the conversation, rather than 'managing' the process. It requires that skills and expertise (authority) are valued and respected regardless of hierarchy or power dynamics.
4. **Developing others.** Undertaking active coaching, mentoring and development of talent within the board, in particular with new board members.
5. **Communicating complex messages succinctly.** Effective communication, through written and spoken means, reduces the cognitive load on the board, freeing more time for analysis, exploration and learning.
6. **Collaborating across boundaries.** The ability to identify boundaries and successfully navigate across and within them is critical to creating a culture of collaboration and efficiency.
7. **Continuous improvement.** Good behavioural objectives include continuous evaluation against internal and external benchmarks. The continual focus on improvement is as much a mindset as a behaviour.

The report goes on to say that outstanding chairs, according to the directors they work with and by their own admission, are good all-round communicators; they listen in a non-judgmental and non-condemnatory way, taking views from all the board members, though remaining impartial and effectively drawing together the differing opinions around the table. Perhaps most importantly of all, they listen.

On the contrary, an 'ineffective chair is marked out by factors such as a tendency to dominate; weakness in keeping the board on course and making decisions; poor communication and listening skills; insufficient interest or involvement in the business; and poor leadership abilities'.

What makes a top chair? published by Hunter Healthcare in 2015 sets out key skills and attributes for the NHS.

> 'Good chairs understand their role in helping their trusts embrace a large cultural shift [as required by the duty of candour]. They lead by example; they are a critical but supportive friend of the chief executive and make sure they do not get dragged into the detail. The new duty of candour places even more

> weight on the shoulders of NHS trust chairs. There is no hiding from mistakes and top chairs recognise this and use candour as a driver for improvement. Above all, chairs need to understand that success is about relationships, whether this involves creating the right environment for an effective board meeting, or helping clinicians understand management processes. The best chairs understand this and will invest time in developing and nurturing their board members.'

The report goes onto cite the following as key characteristics – courage, strength and agility, curiosity, tenacity, approachability, emotional resilience and integrity. Good communication skills were also seen as key alongside an ability to listen effectively.

The appointment and evaluation of the chair

In an FT, the responsibility for appointing the chair lies with the council of governors and this is set out in more detail in Chapter 12. For CCGs, the appointment of the chair is an appointment from amongst the members of the governing body. More details are provided in Chapter 13. For NHS trusts, the appointment of the chair is carried out by NHSI.

The UK Code states that the NEDs, led by the senior independent director (SID), should be responsible for the performance evaluation of the chair, 'taking into account the views of executive directors'. However, for some organisations, the actual performance review of the chair may be conducted for the NEDs by external consultants.

The chair's performance should be assessed by comparing their responsibilities with their achievements, and asking whether they have been successful in providing the board leadership that should be expected of them.

In an FT, the responsibility for the performance evaluation of the chair lies with the council of governors and this is set out in more detail in Chapter 12. For CCGs the evaluation of the chair is carried out by the lay members of the governing body. Further details are provided in Chapter 13.

Overall responsibility for the NHS trust chair appraisal process rests with the chair of the NHSI. As there are 80 NHS trust chairs to appraise, it is not possible for the NHSI chair to conduct all NHS trust chair appraisals personally. Therefore, some of this activity is delegated to directors of the NHSI.

The initial assessment for all appraisals will be prepared by the relevant Director of Delivery and Development (DDD) within the NHSI. This will inform the appraisal meetings that will be undertaken either by the NHSI chair, the DDD or the NHSI NED allocated to that region. At the end of the appraisal exercise, when all of the appraisals are complete, the chair of the NHSI will review all of the appraisal reports to ensure that the exercise has been conducted in a way that is fair and consistent. The final appraisal form will be copied to the chair and a copy put on their personal record by the NHSI. In the event of a disagreement between the chair and the appraiser on any element of the appraisal, including the overall assessment, further discussions will take place between the chair and appraiser. If, however, it is not possible to reach agreement, the appraisal will stand as drafted by the appraiser but the chair will be invited to provide comments that will be held on file with the appraisal.

The level of remuneration for NHS chairs is generally considerably lower than that of chairs in the private sector. For NHS trusts, the Secretary of State sets the level of remuneration. All NHS trusts are allocated to one of three remuneration bands, dependent on their turnover. These bands are available on the NHSI website.

Separating the role of chair and chief executive officer

The report from Directorbank Group makes it clear that:

> 'The success of a chair undoubtedly hinges first and foremost on the relationship the chair has with the CEO. This is a relationship which should be centred on honesty, trust and transparency, and the success of this relationship is based on mutual understanding by both parties of the distinction between their two roles. One of the main faults identified in chairs deemed to be ineffective is their failure to comprehend that they are not there to run the business; that their role is instead to coach, support and guide.'

As leader of the management team and leader of the board of directors, the CEO and chair are the most powerful positions on the board of directors. It is important, therefore, for the proper functioning of the organisation that the chair and CEO work well together. Acting in alliance, the chair and CEO can dominate the board and its decision-making, particularly if the chair also has executive responsibilities in the organisation's management.

More specifically, the *NHS Healthy Board* report sets out some pointers for chairs and chief executives. The chair should not:

- be too operational, interfere with details of management
- exceed part-time hours
- take specific strategic decisions alone
- adopt a bullying, macho 'hire and fire' culture.

Chief executives should not:

- be too controlling or autocratic towards the chair
- get too involved in NED role (e.g. no consultation on shaping board agendas)
- break the fundamental rule of 'no surprises'
- be too entrenched in the organisation.

Table 8.1 sets out the key distinctions in role for the chair and CEO.

Table 8.1: Distinctions between NHS chair and CEO roles

	Chair	CEO
Formulate strategy	Ensures board develops vision, strategies and clear objectives to deliver organisational purpose	Leads strategy development process
Ensure accountability	Holds CEO to account for delivery of strategy	Leads the organisation in the delivery of strategy
	Ensures board committees that support accountability are properly constituted	Establishes effective performance management arrangements and controls
		Acts as accountable officer
Shape culture	Provides visible leadership in developing a positive culture for the organisation, and ensures that this is reflected and modelled in their own and in the board's behaviour and decision-making	Provides visible leadership in developing a positive culture for the organisation, and ensures that this is reflected in their own and the executive's behaviour and decision-making
	Board culture: leads and supports a constructive dynamic within the board, enabling contributions from all directors	
Context	Ensures all board members are well briefed on external context	Ensures all board members are well briefed on external context
Intelligence	Ensures requirements for accurate, timely and clear information to board/directors (and governors for FTs) are clear to executive	Ensures provision of accurate, timely and clear information to board/directors (and governors for FTs)
Engagement	Plays key role as an ambassador, and in building strong partnerships with: ■ patients and public ■ members and governors (FTs) ■ clinicians and staff ■ key institutional stakeholders ■ regulators.	Plays key leadership role in effective communication and building strong partnerships with: ■ patients and public ■ members and governors (FTs) ■ clinicians and staff ■ key institutional stakeholders ■ regulators.

Source: *The NHS Healthy Board*

When the same person holds the position of both chair and CEO, there is a possibility that they could become a dominant influence in decision-making in the organisation. As leader of the executive management team, a chair-cum-CEO may be reluctant to encourage challenges from NEDs about the organisation's performance or to question management proposals about future business strategy.

In some countries (including the US), it is common to find organisation leaders who are both chair and CEO, although separation of the roles has become more common there. The UK Code states as a principle that the roles should be separated:

> 'There should be a clear division of responsibilities at the head of the organisation between the running of the board and the executive responsibility for the running of the organisation's business. No one individual should have unfettered powers of decision.'

The UK Code therefore states that the roles of chair and CEO should not be performed by the same individual. In addition, the division of responsibilities between the chair and CEO should be set out clearly in writing, to prevent one of them from encroaching on the area of responsibility of the other. The FT Code makes a similar statement.

When an individual holds the positions of chair and CEO, they could exercise dominant power on the board, unless there are strong individuals on the board, such as a deputy chair or a SID, to act as a counterweight. If the individual also has a domineering or bullying personality, the situation will be even worse, because a chair-cum-CEO who acts in a bullying manner will not listen to advice from any board colleagues, and the board would not function as an effective body.

There is even a risk that the individual will run the organisation for their own personal benefit rather than in the interests of the shareholders/stakeholders. The only way to prevent a chair-cum-CEO from dominating an organisation is to have an influential group of directors capable of making their opinions heard. However, it is important to distinguish between the position of 'unfettered power' that is created when the roles of chair and CEO are combined and given to one individual and the ability to act in a dominant or tyrannical way, possibly out of self-interest.

Combining the two roles increases the risk that the organisation and its board will be dominated by a tyrannical individual, but this does not happen every time.

CASE STUDY: Marks & Spencer

In the UK, Mr Luc Vandevelde was appointed as chair and CEO of Marks & Spencer in 2004, at a time when its business operations were in difficulty and the share price was falling sharply. This appointment attracted some criticism but appears to have been a successful short-term measure. By 2002, the organisation's fortunes had improved to the point where he relinquished the position of CEO and announced his intention to become part-time chair.

When in 2008 the then-CEO, Sir Stuart Rose, was also appointed as organisation chair for a limited period until a successor to the role of CEO could be appointed this, given the previous appointment of Vandevelde, attracted strong criticism from institutional investors. Legal & General publicly criticised the decision by Marks & Spencer to appoint Sir Stuart Rose as executive chair, saying it was an arrangement that made it difficult to appoint a successor to Sir Stuart as CEO.

However, shareholders could not prevent the appointment of the new chair because this was a decision of the board. Shareholders were able, however, to vote on the re-election of Sir Stuart Rose as director at the AGM in 2008, and 22% of shareholders either opposed his re-election or abstained in the vote.

CASE STUDY: Monitor's governance

Dr Bill Moyes was executive chair of Monitor, the independent regulator for NHS FTs, from its establishment January 2004 until January 2010. It was the board's view that the regulator's corporate governance principles, the stature and experience of the members of the board of director, and a culture of open communication were conducive to board effectiveness with a combined chair and CEO position.

The board agreed separate objectives for the chair and chief executive elements of his role and that he would be separately appraised on the chair and chief executive aspects of his role by the deputy chair and the SID.

Following Dr Moyes' departure, the role was separated. Monitor was chaired by Steve Bundred and Dr David Bennett was appointed as an Interim CEO. Following the departure of Mr Bundred in March 2011, Dr Bennett was appointed as chair while continuing as interim CEO. In February 2014 the National Audit Office published its report *Monitor: Regulating NHS Foundation Trusts*, which reported that Monitor's governance had not been good practice in that the same person acted as both chair and chief executive for nearly three years. It recommended that the Department of Health (DH) appoint a permanent chair of Monitor as soon as possible as an independent chair was needed to boost the capacity of Monitor's senior team, hold the executive management to account and strengthen Monitor's accountability to Parliament. Baroness Hanham was appointed in September 2014 and subsequent appointments maintained the separation of the two roles.

There might occasionally be situations where it is appropriate for the same person to be both chair and CEO. When an organisation gets into business or financial difficulties, for example, there is an argument in favour of appointing a single, all-powerful individual to run the organisation until its fortune has been reversed.

The combination of the roles of chair and CEO might have been necessary in the short term to give an organisation strong leadership to get it through its difficulties.

CASE STUDY: Transition from trust to foundation trust

A chair of an NHS trust had served a three-year term of office and was one year into her second three-year term when the trust was authorised as an FT. At the date of authorisation the chair was offered the remaining two years of her term of office which she accepted. At the end of that second term of office the council of governors agreed that while they would be happy to appoint the chair for a further term of three years, the appointment had to be subject to open competition. The role was advertised, candidates interviewed, and the chair was re-appointed for a further three-year term.

At the end of the third term of three years, the company secretary advised that since the FT Code now set out a six-year term of office any further terms of office would be for one year and would have to be subject to open competition. The chair refused to accept this, claiming that her previous term of office before the trust became an FT did not count and that she had only served five years. The trust's lawyers advised the chair similarly and the governor-led nomination committee was advised accordingly. When the position was made clear, the chair refused to stand for a further term of office and resigned.

The chair and the company secretary

Though the role of the company secretary is set out more fully in Chapter 11, it is worth highlighting the key dynamics in the relationship between these two roles. The essential criterion is a relationship of mutual trust, with the chair having full confidence in the company secretary and vice versa.

In particular, there are a number of key areas where the two roles will work very closely together. The first is governance. The company secretary should be responsible for advising the board through the chair on all governance matters (UK Code). This should include the evaluation of the board and the periodic review of governance processes, including the effectiveness of board committees.

A second area where the chair and company secretary need to work together is on the development and implementation of training and development programmes for board members, which may include both individual training and board development sessions. Though this remains the chair's responsibility, in practice this is often delegated to the company secretary.

A further area is that of obtaining a good flow of information within the board and its committees, and between senior management and the NEDs. The UK Code sets this out as a responsibility of the company secretary under the direction of the chair. Other areas of work might include agenda planning, quality control of board papers; overseeing the production of accurate minutes; induction programmes for all board members and for FTs; and supporting the work of the council of governors.

The chair and the senior independent director

In anticipation of the potential for problems arising between shareholders, the chair and the CEO, the UK Code requires that the board of directors of large companies should nominate an independent NED as the senior independent director (SID), whom shareholders could approach to discuss problems and issues when the normal communication route through the chair has broken down. In addition, if the chair fails to pass on the views of the institutional shareholders to the NEDs, there should be another channel of communication that could be used instead.

The role of the SID has also been taken up by the FT Code and has been adopted as good practice in NHS trusts. The lay members in a CCG governing body have a similar role in particular, the lay member for governance. The FT board of directors appoints one of the independent NEDs to be the SID in consultation with the council of governors. The SID is then available to members and governors if they have concerns which contact through the normal channels of chair, CEO or finance director have failed to resolve or for which such contact is inappropriate. Both the UK Code and the FT Code state that the SID may also be the deputy chair. In NHS trusts, the board appoints the SID and they are available to all stakeholders where concerns cannot be addressed through the normal channels. In the NHS, the SID often has a key role to play in the organisation's whistleblowing procedures.

Having a SID is a key element of an effective board. The FRC *Guidance on Board Effectiveness* sets this out quite clearly, making a distinction between the role of the SID in 'normal times' and when the board is undergoing 'a period of stress'.

At normal times, the role of the SID is to:

- provide support for the chair
- ensure that the views of other directors, particularly the other NEDs, are conveyed to the chair
- ensure that the views of the shareholders, particularly matters that concern them, are conveyed to the rest of the board
- ensure that the chair is giving sufficient attention to succession planning
- carry out the annual review of the performance of the chair, in conjunction with the other NEDs (see Chapter 6).

At times of stress for the board, the role of the SID should be to take the initiative to resolve the problem, working with the other directors and stakeholders and/or the chair, as appropriate. Examples of problems where intervention by the SID may be appropriate include situations where:

- there is a dispute between the chair and the CEO;
- shareholders or the NEDs have expressed serious concerns that are not being addressed by the chair or CEO;
- the strategy pursued by the chair or CEO is not supported by the rest of the board;
- there is a very close relationship between the chair and the CEO;
- decisions are being taken without the approval of the board;
- succession planning is being ignored.

Issues where intervention may be required should be considered when defining the responsibilities of the SID and should be set out in writing. The FRC guidance makes it clear that the SID should work alongside the chair and other board directors, but requiring intervention by the SID will also mean at times acting to challenge custom and practice and demonstrating significant people skills to find a solution.

Critics of the SID concept argue that the chair should be able to resolve difficulties between an organisation and its shareholders/stakeholders, and the position of SID should therefore be superfluous. Opening up the possibility of an additional channel of communication for shareholders/stakeholders is perhaps more likely to undermine organisation–stakeholder relationships than improve them.

However, the International Corporate Governance Network (ICGN)'s *ICGN Global Corporate Governance Principles* put forward reasons why a 'lead independent director' or independent deputy chair is necessary:

- If the chair is the CEO or former CEO, or was for another reason not independent when first appointed, the SID should provide independent leadership for the board, and should have a key role in setting the agenda for board meetings and acting as spokesman for the independent members of the board.
- Even when the chair was independent when first appointed, the role inevitably brings them closer than the NEDs over time to the views of the CEO and executive management.
- The SID should provide leadership to the independent members of the board when this situation creates a problem.

The ICGN Principles also recognise the role of the lead independent director as an alternative conduit for communication with the shareholders/stakeholders.

Although not specifically set out in the UK Code, in the event that the chair had to be removed, it would be the SID's job to lead that process. In the NHS, this would also involve NHSE or NHSI.

Under the UK Code a further responsibility of the SID is to chair the annual meeting of NEDs, without the chair's presence, and to appraise the chair's performance as well as any other meeting as appropriate. In the NHS, this will happen to some extent but will be bound by the specific appraisal structures for NHS trusts, FTs and CCGs.

The role of the SID is most effective when there is a strong working relationship between the chair and SID, which is often why the SID will also be appointed as the deputy chair.

CASE STUDY: Benefits of a SID
At a board meeting of a well-established FT, which was being held in private session, the chair proposed that a significant donation be made to a local charity that was working alongside one of the healthcare areas delivered by the trust.

The chair was an aggressive person, who bullied and dominated the people working with them; and they often attempted to run the trust regardless of the role of the CEO. The chair was also a trustee of the charity in question. They apparently made no clear distinction between their own private activities and the public sector.

It was only the concerted effort of the SID, in conjunction with the finance director, that enabled the board to turn down the request.

The chair and stakeholders

The dissemination of information about the performance of the board and the organisation to stakeholders is important and the chair has a key role to play in that dissemination. This may be through the formal route of publicly available information or more informal meetings to discuss issues with key stakeholders.

The annual report

From a formal perspective, the Preface to the UK Code encourages chairs to report personally in their annual statements how the principles of the Code relating to the role and effectiveness of the board have been applied. This is one way in which the chair is held to account in a very public and personal way for their ability to oversee the role and effectiveness of the board. There is also a requirement for the annual board evaluation to be set out in the annual report, including the evaluation of the board committees and its individual directors. External evaluation should also be declared in the annual report.

From an informal perspective, regular briefing meetings or board to boards with key stakeholders are another useful way of engaging with stakeholders at which the chair will play a vital role. For NHS organisations this is a key role for the chair as such meetings can help to support the development of an active and collaborative local health economy.

The annual meeting

The chair also has a key role to play in the organisation's annual meeting. For companies this will be the annual general meeting with its institutional and individual shareholders in attendance; for NHS trusts this will mean the annual public meeting.

The NHS Trusts (Public Meetings) Regulations 1991 require NHS trusts to present their audited accounts, annual reports and any report on the accounts to a public meeting on or before 30 September in every year. They also provide that an NHS trust shall hold a public meeting to consider an auditor's report other than a report on the audited accounts as soon as practicable, and in any event not later than three months after the date on which the NHS trust received that report.

Governance checklist

✓ Does the chair have the necessary personal attributes to create the right conditions for the board and its directors to be effective?
✓ What leadership, decision-making and governance skills does the chair possess?
✓ Does the process for appointing and appraising a new chair follow the best practice outlined here?
✓ Does the chair set the board agenda and chair meetings effectively?
✓ Do the chair and the CEO work together effectively? Do they complement each other's roles and personalities?
✓ Is the company secretary available to the chair and do they work together effectively? Is there a clear delegation of tasks to the company secretary from the chair?
✓ Is there evidence of high quality, timely information, access to external advice, successful induction programmes and effective annual evaluation?
✓ Has a SID been appointed with a clearly defined role and with the necessary personal attributes to deal with potentially conflicted situations?
✓ Has the chair developed clear lines of communications, both formal and informal, with key stakeholders ?

Summary

According to the Directorbank Group annual survey *Life in the Boardroom 2013*:

> 'The role of the chair and NED has never been more important nor more challenging and, though the financial rewards are generally not comparable to those for executive roles, the ideal non-executive is one who does not need the position for money and has chosen the company as much as vice versa.'

The survey – which also looks at chair and NED remuneration – commented on the levels of remuneration within the public sector:

> 'The public sector is paying substantially less than listed companies; and for many small public sector organisations no fees are paid. We suspect this is

> an area for concern – it is difficult to insist on the highest standards of competence, contribution, conduct and performance when directors are not paid a fair reward. If people are paid fairly, then they expect to be held to account. With increasing pressure on costs and value for money in the public sector, this problem can only grow.'

These comments are very perceptive given the current challenges faced by NHS organisations, both financially and reputationally. The NHS organisations with largest challenges and the most fraught relationships with stakeholders will need to be able command the kind of leadership from their chairs set out here as prerequisites. Consequently, the need for effective selection and appointment processes is hugely important, as is clarity on how the role of the chair complements other key roles within the board.

9

Executive directors

Introduction

Executive directors (EDs) combine their role as director with their position within the executive management of the organisation. Non-executive directors (NEDs) perform the functions of director, only without any executive responsibilities. The interests of EDs are therefore likely to differ from those of NEDs.

The focus in this chapter on the role of the chief executive officer (CEO) and EDs must not distract from the underlying principle of the unitary board. As discussed in Part Two, EDs have the same responsibilities and duties as NEDs; these extend to the entire business of the organisation, not just their own specific portfolio.

The role of executive directors

Unlike NEDs, EDs are full-time employees of the organisation, with executive management responsibilities as well their responsibilities as directors. Management is responsible for running the business operations and is accountable to the board of directors and the CEO.

For the EDs, there is a tension between their role as members of the board, 'one step down from the stakeholders' and their role as senior operational directors, 'one step up from management'.

This can manifest in different ways. There will be times when individual EDs and/or the CEO are held to account for their executive performance by fellow EDs, acting alongside NEDs as a unitary board. This can raise tensions – especially if the CEO is being held to account – and highlights the critical role of the chair in maintaining an effective board.

On the other hand, EDs and the CEO may want to present a united front to the rest of the board to justify what the management team has done and achieved, or what it would like to do. However, if the EDs come together with a united opinion, this raises doubts in their ability to provide effective challenge in discussions on strategy. Independent NEDs should not have this problem, which is why they should be more effective in providing effective challenge in board discussions, encouraged by the chair.

The issues for EDs are, therefore, that they may be inclined to support the views of the CEO on all matters, including strategy, and they may mistrust the NEDs as 'outsiders' who do not know much about the organisation and its business.

In recognition of this problem, the Financial Reporting Council (FRC) *Guidance on Board Effectiveness* suggests that EDs should see themselves as representatives of the shareholders (for NHS, read stakeholders) rather than as executive managers who are responsible and accountable to the CEO. The chair should encourage this attitude among the EDs, partly through ensuring that they receive appropriate induction and training for their role as a board member.

The FRC guidance goes on to say that EDs should have a detailed knowledge of the organisation and its business, and should apply this knowledge when making judgments about organisational strategy. However, they should also recognise that constructive challenge from NEDs is an essential part of good governance, and they should welcome and encourage such challenges. For an effective board, the EDs and NEDs must work constructively together.

ICSA: The Governance Institute's guidance note *The Governance Challenge for the NHS Executive Director* sets this out quite neatly by suggesting EDs ask 'which hat am I wearing?' to retain an appropriate balance between the varying roles for which they are being paid. These include:

- leadership and management of their particular section or department;
- being a member of the senior operational management of the organisation;
- wider leadership and management responsibility within the operational environment;
- ensuring the organisation remains focused on delivering its core business objectives;
- governance and strategic responsibility from the board perspective.

The 'governance role' is different to the 'management role'. An ED's governance role along with the other members of the board is to:

- ensure that sufficient assets are aligned against the operational objectives being set though also guarding, maintaining and nurturing those same assets;
- debate, determine and set the strategy for the organisation; and
- monitor progress towards its fulfillment.

In contrast, the management role is to utilise the assets of the organisation in the fulfilment of the operational objectives of the organisation and to deliver the strategy determined by the board. The Foundation Trust Network (FTN)'s publication *New Voices, New Accountabilities: A guide to wider governance in foundation trusts* states:

> 'Boards of directors will increasingly have to operate as corporate entities, not sounding boards, in a world of contestable service provision ... Executive

directors must make the transition from operating as functional heads of service to members of a corporate board, bearing the full weight of the fiduciary responsibility that falls on their shoulders and contributing fully to the strategic decision-making of the trust.'

The appointment of executive directors

The nomination committee and the appointment committee have a key role to play in the appointment of EDs, as discussed in Chapters 5 and 7. The CEO will bring recommendations to the committees on succession planning and appointment, but the board will delegate the responsibility for appointment to these committees (which are essentially composed of NEDs). The key principle about the appointment of EDs is that it is the responsibility of the chair and the NEDs, acting under the remit of these two committees. The exception worth noting relates to the appointment of the CEO, which is covered below.

Induction of an executive manager as an executive director

The induction process for new ED who is already an executive manager of the organisation needs a specific focus. A senior executive of the organisation should already be familiar with many aspects of the organisation's operations (although their induction might include visits to parts of the organisation they have not worked with before).

An executive manager 'promoted' to the board is more likely to lack knowledge and experience about being a director and governance, although some larger organisations try to give their senior executives experience as a director by allowing them to take a position as a NED in another organisation.

An induction programme for an ED may therefore need to focus on matters such as:

- the role of the board, including matters reserved for the board and oversight of management;
- the powers and duties of directors, and the rights of shareholders/stakeholders (the new director should be given a copy of the organisation's constitutional documents);
- the role of board committees and their membership;
- the role of the board in monitoring risk and internal control (see also Chapter 16);
- membership of the board and its committees, how the board operates and the role of the company secretary;
- frequency of board meetings;
- what the new director will be expected to contribute;
- who the major shareholders/stakeholders are and their relationship with the organisation;

- compliance with governance requirements;
- the potential liabilities of directors;
- directors' liability insurance;
- organisation policy on public involvement and sustainability;
- arrangements for monitoring the performance of board members.

NHS Providers now offer a ED induction programme which was developed following requests from new board EDs for a deeper understanding of their board role as part of a unitary board and of the wider context within which the role is set. The programme includes:

- Understanding the developing NHS environment and what that means for the leadership of foundation trusts and trusts
- Governance, risk and assurance in the provider sector
- What your chief executive expects of you
- The Care Quality Commission (CQC) and regulation
- NHS Improvement (NHSI) – the way forward
- Your board role vs your ED role
- Working with commissioners
- Your responsibilities and accountabilities.

For listed companies, the law relating to fair dealing by directors (insider dealing) and the Model Code on share dealing by directors should also be set out in any induction programme.

This list is not exhaustive, although in some cases it might be considered too long. The main point is that an executive manager appointed as a director needs to learn about the differences in the roles of manager and director, and that they have not been appointed as a director simply to be a 'high level' executive of the organisation.

The role of the chief executive officer

The FRC *Guidance on Board Effectiveness* says the CEO is the most senior ED on the board, with responsibility for proposing strategy to the board and for delivering the strategy as agreed.

Consequently, the CEO's relationship with the chair is a key relationship that can assist board effectiveness. The CEO leads the executive team, is responsible for the executive management of the organisation's operations and is the senior executive to whom all other executive managers report. Other executive managers might also be directors of the organisation, but the CEO is answerable to the board for the way the business is run and its performance

The CEO has, with the support of the executive team, primary responsibility for setting an example to the organisation's employees and communicating to them the expectations of the board in relation to the organisational culture, values and behaviours. The CEO is also responsible for supporting the chair to make certain that appropriate standards of governance permeate through all parts of the organisation and will make certain that the board is made aware, when appropriate, of the views of employees on issues of relevance to the business.

In order to improve the standard of boardroom discussion, the CEO should also act as a spokesperson for the executive team in board discussions, explain the views of the executive team to the rest of the board and explain in a balanced way any differences of opinion within the executive team.

The UK Code states that the differing responsibilities of the chair and the CEO should be set out in writing and agreed by the board. Particular attention should be paid to areas of potential overlap.

The role of the accountable/accounting officer in the NHS

At a macro level, the Department of Health (DH) accounting officer (AO), as principal AO, has overall responsibility in government for the proper and effective use of resources as voted by Parliament for the health and care system, including the NHS.

The majority of resources are allocated annually to NHS England (NHSE). Its CEO, as AO, is responsible for the effective use of these resources. There is a robust system in place to allow the AO to discharge their responsibilities by providing assurance about the commissioning of NHS care and the provision and regulation of services. This system entails the appointment of accountable officers (for NHS trusts and CCGs) and AOs (for foundation trusts (FTs)).

For NHS trusts, the accountable officer is the CEO. He or she is accountable to Parliament via the DH AO and the Secretary of State for Health. The NHSI AO is responsible for the appointment of accountable officers for each NHS trust.

In clinical commissioning groups (CCGs), the accountable officer is either the chief officer or the chief clinical officer (CCO). They are accountable to Parliament via NHSE's AO (the CEO, as designated in the Health and Social Care Act 2012 (HSCA 2012)) and the Secretary of State. In NHS FTs, AOs are directly responsible to Parliament.

The accountable officer memorandum for chief executives of NHS trusts sets out the responsibilities as follows:

- ensuring there are effective management systems in place to safeguard public funds and assets and assisting in the implementation of corporate governance;
- ensuring value for money (VFM) is achieved from the resources available to the trust;
- ensuring the expenditure and income of the trust has been applied to the purposes intended by Parliament and conform to the authorities which govern them;
- ensuring effective and sound financial management systems are in place; and

- ensuring annual statutory accounts are prepared in a format directed by the Secretary of State, with the approval of HM Treasury, to give a true and fair view of the state of affairs as at the end of the financial year. This should include the income and expenditure, recognised gains and losses and cash flows for the year.

The CCG accountable officer is responsible for ensuring that the CCG fulfils its duties to exercise its functions effectively, efficiently and economically – thus ensuring improvement in the quality of services and the health of the local population though maintaining value for money. They will ensure that the regularity and propriety of expenditure is discharged, and that arrangements are put in place to ensure that good practice is embodied (as identified through the head of the National Audit Office, the Comptroller and Auditor General). They will also ensure that funds are safeguarded through effective financial and management systems.

The CCG accountable officer, working closely with the chair of the governing body, will ensure that proper constitutional, governance and development arrangements are put in place to assure the members of the CCG's ongoing capability and capacity to meet its duties and responsibilities. This will include arrangements for the ongoing development of its members and staff. The individual who takes on the accountable officer role for a CCG will be proposed by the governing body of the CCG and formally appointed to the role by NHSE in accordance with the NHSE guidance *CCG Guidance on Senior Appointments including Accountable Officer* (2017). In circumstances where the lead clinician undertakes the accountable officer role, they will be known as the CCO. When a manager undertakes the role, the individual will be known as the chief officer. The accountable officer may not be the chair of the governing body or the chief finance officer (CFO). The involvement of NHSE does not create an employment relationship between the accountable officer and NHSE, instead the accountable officer is an employee of the individual CCG.

Each FT has an AO, who has responsibilities for ensuring regularity, propriety and value for money, including signing the trust's accounts, annual governance statement and annual report. The National Health Service Act 2006 designates the CEO of an NHS FT as the AO. *The NHS Foundation Trust Accounting Officer Memorandum* (2015) sets out the role as responsibility for the overall organisation, management and staffing of the NHS FT and for its procedures in financial and other matters, and ensuring:

- there is a high standard of financial management in the NHS FT as a whole;
- the NHS FT delivers efficient and economical conduct of its business and safeguards financial propriety and regularity throughout the organisation and
- financial considerations are fully taken into account in decisions on NHS FT policy proposals.

The FT AO has a particular responsibility to see that appropriate advice is tendered to the board and to the council of governors on all matters of financial propriety and regularity and, more broadly, as to all considerations of prudent and economical administration, efficiency and effectiveness. The NED-led appointments committee appoints the AO and the appointment is approved by the council of governors.

In all three settings, if the board or the chair is contemplating a course of action which the accountable/accounting officer considers would infringe the requirements of propriety and regularity, they should set out their objections (and the reasons for it) in writing to the chair and the board. If the decision is still taken to proceed, a written instruction to take the action in question should be issued. The audit committee, which has specific terms of reference and delegated powers to inquire into matters of propriety and regularity, should receive a copy of the objections.

If the board is contemplating a course of action which affects the responsibility for obtaining VFM from the organisation's resources, then the accountable/ accounting officer should draw the relevant factors to the attention of the board. If the accountable/accounting officer is overruled, despite clear advice to the contrary, then the accountable/accounting officer should refer their concerns to their appointing body. In all such cases, the accountable/accounting officer should, as a board member, vote against the course of action rather than merely abstain from voting.

The accountable officer, together with the director of finance, is responsible for ensuring that the accounts of the trust presented to the board for approval are prepared under principles and in a format directed by the Secretary of State with the approval of HM Treasury (as set out in the NHS Finance Manual and in 'The role of the director of finance in the NHS' – EL(94)18). These accounts must disclose a true and fair view of the trust's income and expenditure; cash flows; gains and losses; and of its state of affairs. The accountable officer will sign these accounts, along with the director of finance/CFO, on behalf of the board.

In FTs, the CEO, as the AO, should sign and date the statement of financial position and annual report after adoption by the board as evidence of this. As AO, the CEO should also sign the foreword to the accounts, the annual governance statement and the remuneration report. Once the annual report and accounts have been approved by the external auditors, the AO or director of finance must sign a certificate which states that the FT consolidation (FTC) schedules are consistent with the annual accounts.

The role of the director of finance or chief finance officer

NHS trusts and FTs are required to have a director of finance (DoF) on the board and CCGs are required to have a CFO on their governing body.

Though financial management is the corporate responsibility of the board, and the individual responsibility of the CEO/CO as the accountable officer, the DoF has both a professional and corporate role as a board member. The DoF ensures that systems are in place so that the organisation is properly governed in terms of financial transactions, financial reporting, financial performance, financial planning and in securing value for money. They also must also maintain assurance processes to ensure that internal controls and checks are working properly (such as engagement with clinical and non-clinical staff holding delegated financial budgets). These systems also include ensuring that 'treasury management' systems are in place to manage cash flow and liquidity.

The key responsibilities for finance directors are to provide business and commercial advice for the board as well as financial governance and assurance, and to fulfil their corporate responsibilities as a board member. A key requirement for NHS organisations is sustainable financial viability; the DoF has to involve and inform the board in assessing all the options in terms of strategic financial risk, including a 'worst case' scenario.

The DoF should be a professional accountant, and as such is required to behave with confidentiality, integrity, objectivity, professional competence and due care as mandated in the International Federation of Accountants (IFAC)'s Code of Ethics. They must also comply with professional quality standards, especially those relating to professional ethics, continuing professional development, and national and international external reporting requirements. The conduct and behaviour of a DoF must be within the law and, as a professional accountant, they also have a 'public interest' role. However, as a board member, the DoF's contribution is not, and should not be, limited to finance as a specialist area.

The National Health Service (Clinical Commissioning Groups) Regulations 2012 require that the CCG's governing body must also include an employee who has a professional qualification in accountancy and the expertise or experience to lead the financial management of the CCG, to be known as the CFO. If the governing body's membership includes two or more individuals of that description, the CCG must designate one of them as the CFO. They should be an individual with a recognised professional accounting qualification, as well as significant experience and skills. The CFO cannot be the chair of the governing body nor may they undertake the accountable officer role. The role may, however, be combined with that of chief operating officer (COO) in circumstances where a CCG has a COO (for instance, in CCGs where the clinical leader is also the accountable officer). In these circumstances, the role is known as 'chief finance and operating officer'.

Other executive director roles

There are several other key ED roles that are an important part of an NHS board.

The roles of medical director and director of nursing (or chief nurse or executive nurse) are mandatory roles for a legitimately constituted board. Again, as board members, these roles should not be limited to their areas of professional expertise and they are required to contribute across the breadth of the organisation.

In a CCG, the lead clinician is the individual recognised by the CCG as the clinical voice of its members. This individual is either the chair of the governing body or undertakes the role of accountable officer as chief clinical officer. In circumstances where a CCG chooses to appoint a clinician to the chair of the governing body and nominate a clinician for the role of the accountable officer, then the CCG should identify one of them to be known as the lead clinician.

The remuneration of executive directors

The remuneration of EDs and other senior executives in the corporate sector is a contentious issue, partly because of the amounts paid to top executives in some companies and partly because remuneration for senior executives has generally risen by a much larger percentage than increases in pay for other employees.

While remuneration packages should be sufficient to attract and retain executives of a suitable calibre, they should not be excessive. Such packages should also reward executives for successful performance, in both the short term and the longer term, because pay incentives are expected to encourage executives to perform better. A further area of concern to the corporate sector (and to the NHS) is the payment of large 'rewards for failure'. Contracts of employment for senior executives should try to minimise the risk of these severance payments when a senior director fails to perform to a satisfactory standard and is dismissed.

The remuneration committee is the critical mechanism for governing executive remuneration.

Remuneration in the corporate sector

This has become very much a hot topic and a concerted focus of government and industry discussion. Total pay for the CEOs of FTSE 100 companies quadrupled between 1998 and 2015, according to the Department for Business, Energy and Industrial Strategy (BEIS) analysis, largely due to the growth in annual bonus payments and long-term pay incentives. It far outstripped growth in average pay in the UK in the same time period. According to the High Pay Centre, in 1998 the ratio of average FTSE 100 CEO pay to the average pay of full-time employees in the UK was 47:1. This ratio increased to 132:1 in 2010 and stood at 160:1 in 2017.

The remuneration of EDs and senior executives was not seen as a major problem of corporate governance until the 1990s in the UK and early 2000s in the US. A sense that something might be wrong began when the general public, alerted by the media, criticised some top executives for being paid far more money than they were worth and investment institutions criticised directors for receiving ever-increasing rewards even when their company performed badly.

In many listed companies in the UK during the 1980s and early 1990s, the CEOs and executive chairs were involved in deciding their own remuneration package. Concern about remuneration has grown in other countries, particularly with regard to the banking crisis in 2007–2009 and the high rewards earned by senior bankers in spite of the large amounts of public funds provided to prevent banks from financial collapse.

As can be seen from the statistics above, the remuneration of top corporate executives rose rapidly regardless of company performance, the effects of global recession, and at a faster annual rate than the remuneration of other company employees. This seemed counter to the principle of good corporate governance that remuneration should be linked to some extent to company performance, so that a director will earn more if the company does well, but less if it does badly.

Government reforms in 2013 introduced new shareholder controls and oversight over executive remuneration. The reforms gave shareholders a binding vote on pay policies (at least once every three years) and an annual advisory vote on the actual pay awards made to directors under the shareholder-approved pay policies. They also introduced greater clarity in the reporting of executive pay. There are concerns, however, that these reforms have not had sufficient impact.

The Government Green Paper on Corporate Governance Reform (November 2016) includes a section on further reforms to executive remuneration and sets out the following options for further discussion:

- Make all or some elements of the executive pay package subject to a binding shareholder vote
- Introduce stronger consequences for a company losing its annual advisory vote on the remuneration report
- Require or encourage quoted company pay policies to (a) set an upper threshold for total annual pay (from all elements of remuneration), and (b) ensure a binding vote at the annual general meeting (AGM) where actual executive pay in that year exceeds the threshold
- Require the existing binding vote on the executive pay policy to be held more frequently than every three years
- Strengthen the Corporate Governance Code to provide greater specificity on how companies should engage with shareholders on pay, including where there is significant opposition to a remuneration report.

The Enterprise and Regulatory Reform Act 2013 (ERRA 2013) contains amendments to the Companies Act 2006 relating to quoted companies' disclosure of directors' remuneration and shareholder approval of quoted company directors' remuneration reports. The key changes made by ERRA are:

- the directors' remuneration report must include a forward-looking remuneration policy report;

- shareholders have been given a new binding ordinary resolution vote on the remuneration policy report (and retain their existing advisory ordinary resolution vote on the implementation report);
- any subsequent changes to the remuneration policy must be agreed by shareholders and, even if no changes are made to the remuneration policy, it must be must be approved by shareholders at least every three years;
- if shareholders did not approve the advisory vote on the implementation report at the company's previous AGM, the remuneration policy must be put to shareholders at the next AGM;
- all remuneration and loss of office payments to directors must be consistent with the approved remuneration policy; and
- unless a payment has been separately approved by shareholders in advance, any unauthorised payment is held on trust by the party that received it (usually this will be the director him or herself). Directors who authorised the payment will be liable for any loss to the company unless they can demonstrate that they acted honestly and reasonably.

A directors' remuneration report in the new format must be put to shareholders in the first financial year to begin on or after 1 October 2013. Though these regulations apply to companies, not to NHS organisations, the principles they contain are applicable and should still be considered by NHS boards.

NHS remuneration

NHS organisations are subject to a greater level of remuneration regulation than the corporate sector, but pay levels for senior management have still come under close public scrutiny – especially as all public sector wage rises have been capped at an average of 1% for two years from April 2013.

On 2 June 2015, the Secretary of State wrote to the chairs of all NHS trusts, FTs and CCGs urging restraint over very senior managers (VSM) pay and announcing a range of initiatives, including:

- a requirement for ministers to see all proposals for VSM pay above £150,402 before appointments are confirmed (£150,402 being the salary of the Prime Minister);
- the development of a national framework for VSM pay in the NHS; and
- the introduction of a limit on the daily rate payable to an off-payroll interim VSM and request for rigorous compliance with Her Majesty's Treasury guidance on off-payroll engagements.

The Secretary of State set out their expectation that there should be no significant difference in the terms and conditions of senior leadership teams and those working on the front-line and their view that it is not acceptable that some senior managers experience high levels of pay, with year-on-year increases, as a matter of course.

The work on a national VSM pay framework was undertaken by the DH and it will be published in 2017. In the meantime, NHSI requires all NHS trusts to seek approval via NHSI, DH, the Secretary of State and Her Majesty's Treasury before confirming VSM salaries at appointment or any individual/group VSM pay increase (outside of any nationally recommended cost of living increase). FTs must seek the opinion of the same. This process covers on-payroll appointments (substantive and fixed term) for VSM roles:

1. in NHS ambulance and community trusts, however, reference should also still be made to the DH's Pay Framework for Very Senior Managers in Strategic and Special Health Authorities, Primary Care Trusts and Ambulance Trusts (June 2013) until this is replaced by the new pay framework
2. in all other NHS trusts and in all NHS foundation trusts where the annual salary is £150,402 or above (irrespective of whether the new salary is an increase or not);
3. in acting-up arrangements, promotions/pay-rises for individuals already in post and earning £150,402 or above, and NHS secondments and conversion of off-payroll interims into on-payroll arrangements
4. for directors who by virtue of their qualifications and the requirements of the post are eligible to be on the standard NHS consultant contract
5. chief executives or executive directors who plan to resign and take their pension benefits when they reach pensionable age, and then return to work.

There are established pay ranges for all such appointments in the NHS, examples for a CEO are given in Table 9.1.

Table 9.1: Pay ranges for CEOs

Chief executives	Lower quartile	Median	Upper quartile
Small acute NHS trusts and foundation trusts (£0–£200 million turnover) *	£141,000	£167,500	£182,500
Medium acute NHS trusts and foundation trusts (£200–400 million) *	£160,000	£182,500	£202,500
Large acute NHS trusts and foundation trusts (£400–£500 million)	£190,000	£197,500	£230,000
Very large acute NHS trusts and foundation trusts (£500 million +)	£195,000	£225,000	£267,500

* Specialist trusts can apply for a 15% premium

The framework when published will be informed by the Rose Review (June 2015). Sir Stuart Rose, the former Chairman of Marks & Spencer, was commissioned by the Secretary of State to review the NHS leadership challenge and identified the following three areas of concern:

1. Vision: There is a lack of One NHS Vision and of a common ethos.
2. People: The NHS has committed to a vast range of changes; however, there is insufficient management and leadership capability to deal effectively with the scale of challenges associated with these.
3. Performance: There is a need for proper overall direction of careers in management across the medical, administrative and nursing cadres.

Consequently, CCGs, NHS trusts and NHS FTs are no longer free to determine their own rates of pay for VSMs – CEOs, EDs and others with board-level responsibility who report directly to the CEO.

VSM pay in DH arm's-length bodies (ALBs) such as NHSE, Monitor, the CQC and the NHSI is subject to two national pay frameworks, one set in 2006 and the other in 2012. Performance-related pay is available to VSMs within ALBs on either of the existing national pay frameworks, although it is currently restricted by the government to the top 25% of performers and to a maximum of 5% of reckonable pay.

Pay data for CCGs analysed by e.reward.co.uk in 2015 identified that more than two-fifths (43%) of chief officers in CCGs servicing the largest populations (more than 500,000 people) collected pay above the £120,000 to £130,000 recommendations. These decisions were taken despite strong encouragement from NHSE to make lower pay awards to senior executives. NHSE had proposed three pay ranges for chief officers and CFOs, based on the population sizes of CCGs (see Table 9.2).

Table 9.2: CCG pay ranges

CCG level	Population size	Pay range for chief officer	Pay range for CFO
Level 3	At or over 500,000	£120k–£130k	£95k–£110k
Level 2	150,000 to 499,000	£105k–120k	£85k–£95k
Level 1	149,000 or below	£90k–£105k	£75k–£85k

Source: NHSE

All other posts within the NHS are governed by the Agenda for Change system, which allocates posts to set pay scales using a job evaluation scheme. All FTs have the freedom to use local terms and conditions when setting pay for all employees. However, in practice, all but one (Southend University Hospital NHS Foundation Trust) has continued to be guided by VSM and to operate Agenda for Change for their staff.

CASE STUDY: Southend University Hospital NHS Foundation Trust

Southend University Hospital NHS Foundation Trust took the decision to opt out of the nationally negotiated Agenda for Change agreement, balloting staff in March 2006 to gain their consent.

The vast majority of employees have opted for local terms, agreed annually between management and unions. The trust has set pay levels that are on a par with Agenda for Change, but has also introduced enhancements to other conditions. Retaining local terms has helped the trust to remain competitive as an employer, and has kept its staff both committed and engaged. The trust has also introduced a bonus scheme linked to operational performance.

A compromise agreement is a specific type of contract, regulated by statute, between an employer and its employee (or ex-employee) under which the employee receives consideration, often a negotiated financial sum, in exchange for agreeing that they will have no further claim against the employer as a result of any breach of a statutory obligation by the employer.

As the financial position of the NHS tightens due to the economic climate, more attention will be paid to the level of ED remuneration within the NHS. The lessons learned from the corporate sector should offer useful insights to health service governance in this area. In addition, the remuneration levels that are on offer in the corporate sector will also influence NHS remuneration levels, as suggested by the response of the NHS Confederation:

> 'NHS organisations are large and complex in nature and require the right managerial skills to be led effectively. A large city hospital could have a budget of between £500 million and £1 billion and employ as many as 10,000 staff – comparable to many FTSE 250 companies. Because of the challenging nature of a chief executive's role, NHS boards must consider a range of factors, including pay, to encourage the best candidates in to these positions. The NHS is looking to involve more clinical staff in top management positions. Given that a number of hospital doctors will be paid more than NHS chief executives, this factor must be taken into consideration when making a decision on pay.'
>
> *David Stout, Deputy CEO, NHS Confederation*

Public attitudes

Public attitudes about remuneration within the NHS are somewhat contradictory – a fact which was recognised, although not specifically, in the Hutton Review of Fair Pay (2011) in the public sector (covered in more detail later):

> 'Success [of the public sector] would be a fundamental building block in supporting economic growth and social well-being, but it cannot be done without motivated, high calibre public servants, along with managers to lead them.

> But while the British public is very sympathetic to front line delivery staff, it is hostile to the public sector managers responsible and accountable for the effective deployment of resources – and even more hostile to their pay. In the eyes of some, they are the quintessential "burdens" on the rest of us.'

The review set out that some of this public reaction is quite reasonable, since public sector managers have also benefited from significant earnings growth at the top remuneration levels, particularly in the early 2000s. However, some balance is required. As the Hutton interim report demonstrated, only £1 of every £100 earned by the top 1% of earners in the UK is earned by public sector employees.

Even so, the perception remains that the public sector is no less awash with 'fat cats' than the private sector; indeed, in one poll, a quarter of respondents thought that public sector executives earned more than their private sector counterparts. Regardless, Hutton maintains that: 'the public has the right to know that pay is deserved, fair, under control and designed to drive improving public sector performance'.

Rewards for failure

In the UK, there was institutional investor concern, supported by widespread media coverage, about large remuneration packages for senior corporate directors where the size of the reward did not seem sufficiently linked to performance, and large severance payments (payments on dismissal) to outgoing senior executives who had been ousted from their job following poor company performance.

High severance payments to unsuccessful directors were seen as 'rewards for failure'. Following the global banking crisis of 2007–2009, there was also widespread criticism of remuneration in banks, whereby top executives and traders received large bonuses even though their bank may have been close to collapse or in need of government financial support to remain in business.

Similar problems of rewards for failure have been seen in the NHS and raises very clear issues of health service governance.

CASE STUDY: *Gibb v Maidstone and Tunbridge Wells NHS Trust [2010]*

In *Gibb v Maidstone and Tunbridge Wells NHS Trust [2010]*, G was employed as the trust's CEO with a basic annual salary of £150,000 and an entitlement to six months' notice. Following outbreaks of the 'super bug' C. difficile at hospitals managed by her, there were a significant number of deaths and widespread public anger and anxiety.

G left the trust under a compromise agreement that agreed to pay her around £250,000 including around £75,000 pay in lieu of notice and a compensation payment of £175,000. The compensation payment, which had been agreed, was challenged by G's successor as being *ultra vires* (i.e. beyond the powers of the NHS trust to award). G issued proceedings against the trust to recover the £175,000. The High Court found that the £175,000, which had been agreed under the compromise agreement, was irrationally generous and was therefore outside of the trust's powers to award. It held that G was not therefore entitled to recover the £175,000. The trust had failed to ensure that it did not reward for failure, and the £175,000 was over and above any contractual or statutory entitlement that G may have had.

The court also held that she was not entitled to any other lesser payment (such as compensation for unfair dismissal). While G could have claimed for unfair dismissal, she had not done so. G therefore failed to recover the £175,000, which had been an agreed payment under the compromise agreement. G was out of time to bring a claim for unfair dismissal, but if she had still been within time, she could have issued proceedings against the trust. The NHS trust was a public body, so it was clearly of relevance to those involved in the public sector. The trust had failed to follow specific guidance for NHS bodies in assessing compensation and had acted outside its authority.

A compromise agreement is a specific type of contract, regulated by statute, between an employer and its employee (or ex-employee) under which the employee receives consideration, often a negotiated financial sum, in exchange for agreeing that they will have no further claim against the employer as a result of any breach of a statutory obligation by the employer.

The problem of inappropriate remuneration policies for senior executives is now well recognised both within the NHS and the corporate sector, but a satisfactory solution has not necessarily been found. However, a distinction should be made between the unethical 'corporate greed' of some senior executives, and a reasonable desire by senior executives to be well remunerated for what they do. Similarly, it is important to make the distinction between high rewards that are justified by performance, and high rewards that are earned in spite of poor performance.

Why is remuneration a governance issue?

Remuneration of senior executives is a governance issue for several reasons.

- Excessive remuneration for senior executives that is not clearly linked to good performance breaches the requirement for economy, efficiency and effectiveness which underpins the NHS.
- Executives should not be rewarded for failure.
- Large organisations need to attract and retain talented professionals to provide them with effective leadership. Top executives are attracted and retained by the remuneration packages they are offered.
- Organisations need effective boards and senior executive management. Remuneration incentives can be used to motivate executives to perform better

and to achieve better results, however, remuneration incentives should be designed carefully to align the interests of the organisation and executives as much as possible, in both the short term and the longer term.

- The remuneration of senior executives may antagonise employees (and employee representatives), when it appears that senior executives are paid excessive amounts in comparison with their own pay. A sense that benefits or rewards are unfairly distributed could lead to industrial unrest within the organisation.

A further reason relates to the stability and continuity of the board. A study by Income Data Services in february 2016 found while median salary levels had flat-lined, boardroom turnover across all parts of the NHS was running at high levels. Overall, the attrition rate stood at around 30% with some variations according to country and trust type. In fact turnover in non-FT boardrooms was 35% in the year to March 2015 and 27% in foundation trusts. This contrasts with March 2012 when board turnover levels were around 25% and this was considered substantial because they followed the initial stages of change that resulted from the newly introduced Health and Social Care Bill 2011. Additionally, Will Hutton identified in his 2011 review on fair pay that there were real concerns about director tenure in the NHS, where the average tenure of NHS acute trust chief executives was just two years and four months, compared with the average tenure for FTSE 100 chief executives at 5.9 years. He went on:

> 'Such short tenures not only compare unfavourably with the private sector (average tenure for FTSE 100 chief executives is currently 5.9 years), but are also not conducive to successful management: business management research suggests that most chief executives need an average of 30 months to complete their learning curve upon taking up a new role.'

This is backed up by research by the King's Fund in 2015 that found that the average tenure of an NHS provider chief executive was just two and a half years.

Principles of executive director remuneration

Principles of remuneration are now included in the corporate governance codes of many countries. In a system of good governance, the remuneration of directors and key senior executives should be sufficient to attract and retain individuals of a suitable calibre. At the same time, the structure of an individual's remuneration package should motivate the individual towards the achievement of performance that is in the best interests of the organisation and its stakeholders, as well as those of the individual.

The UK Corporate Governance Code states as a principle that:

> 'Levels of remuneration should be sufficient to attract, retain and motivate directors of the quality required to run the company successfully, but a

company should avoid paying more than is necessary for this purpose. A significant proportion of executive directors' remuneration should be structured so as to link rewards to corporate and individual performance.'

It is widely accepted that senior executives should be able to earn a high level of remuneration in return for the work they do and the responsibilities they carry. If a company does not offer an attractive package, it will not attract individuals of the required calibre. It is also generally accepted that the level of remuneration should be linked in some way to satisfactory performance. If an executive performs well, they should receive more rewards than if they perform only reasonably well.

The central issue for good corporate governance is concerned with the link between pay and performance. In the corporate sector the remuneration package should include a performance-related element. If the director successfully achieves predetermined levels of performance, they will be rewarded accordingly. There could be some debate as to how much remuneration should be performance related, but there is a view that a substantial part of a director's total potential remuneration should be linked to performance. Linking remuneration, wholly or in part, to performance is not an easy task, however, as the following shows.

- Unsuitable measures of performance may be selected, so that although the individual executive succeeds in achieving targets that earn high rewards, the organisation does not obtain a comparable benefit.
- Many performance measures are based on the short term, possibly linked to annual results. This may not be in the interests of the organisation's longer-term development and performance.
- Remuneration systems are normally designed to provide the reward after the performance has been made. This time delay means that if the organisation has poor results in the current year after having done well in the previous year, an executive may be paid high remuneration (for the previous year) at a time the organisation is doing badly.

The UK Code requires that the responsibility for setting the remuneration of EDs (and possibly other senior executives) should be delegated by the board to a remuneration committee. The remuneration committee is explained in more detail later in this chapter; however, an appendix to the UK Code sets out provisions for the design of the performance-related elements of a remuneration package that the remuneration committee should apply. These provisions offer a useful insight into how incentive schemes may be structured and approved.

If it is not an easy task for corporate governance, then it becomes even more difficult for health service governance. As this handbook has already demonstrated, there is significant diversity and complexity amongst stakeholders and their objectives for NHS organisations. Finding suitable measures of performance is a challenge that was highlighted in the Hutton Review (see below). For health service governance, a key principle relates to the public scrutiny and transparency of the remuneration package and the accountability of the ED.

Hutton Review of fair pay in the public sector

The Hutton Review was published in March 2011 and sets out a new Fair Pay Code for senior pay, to be adopted by all organisations delivering public services, on a 'comply or explain' basis based on the principle of fairness as due desert – namely, reward should be proportional to the weight of each role and each individual's performance. The Code also required pay levels to be set according to a fair process, though recognising that an organisation's success derives from the collective efforts of the whole workforce.

The review also set out 12 recommendations to the government that together form the framework for fairness.

1. **Using pay multiples to track executive pay against that of all employees:** the government should not cap pay across public services, but should require that from 2011–2012 all public service organisations publish their top to median pay multiples each year to allow the public to hold them to account.
2. **Informing the public debate through annual Fair Pay Reports:** to support citizen accountability, the government should commission the Senior Salaries Review Body to publish annual Fair Pay Reports, starting from 2011–2012.
3. **Re-calibrating the pay** of non-departmental public body chief executives.
4. **From disclosure to explanation – ensuring complete transparency over executive roles and remuneration:** to enable citizens to understand executive remuneration and the nature of executive responsibilities, from 2011–2012 the government should require that all organisations delivering public services disclose in precise numbers the full remuneration of all executives, alongside an explanation of the responsibilities of each role and of how executives' pay reflects individual performance.
5. **Enabling citizen analysis of executive pay:** from 2011–2012, the government should require public organisations to submit executive pay data through an online template, and make this data available on data.gov.uk, to allow citizens to access and analyse this data and thus have the information required to hold public service organisations to account.
6. **Abandoning arbitrary benchmarks for public service pay:** once this framework of recommendations is in place, the government should refrain from using the pay of the Prime Minister or other politicians as a benchmark for the remuneration of senior public servants, whose pay should reflect their due desert and be proportional to the weight of their roles and their performance.
7. **Preventing rewards for failure through earn-back pay for senior public servants:** to allow pay to vary down as well as up with performance, all public service executives should have an element of their basic pay that needs to be earned back each year through meeting pre-agreed objectives with excellent performers who go beyond their objectives eligible for additional pay.

8. **Extending earn-back pay** to high performing middle managers.
9. **Sharing the rewards of greater productivity:** to prevent executives monopolising the rewards of productivity increases, and allow all employees who have contributed to share the benefits, government departments should identify ways of offering gainsharing schemes linked to achievement of the efficiency aspects of their business plans.
10. **Opening up opportunities for future generations of public service leaders:** to increase the supply of candidates for top positions and reinforce public service management as a career, the government should facilitate greater opportunities for managers to move across different public services.
11. **A Fair Pay Code:** to embed fairness principles and ensure fair process in executive remuneration, all public service organisations should adopt the Fair Pay Code proposed by this Review. Government departments should by July 2011 bring forward proposals for the application of this code to all bodies and sectors in which they have an interest.
12. **Tracking pay multiples across the economy:** to make tracking pay multiples normal practice across the economy, as part of its commitment to improve corporate reporting, the government should require listed companies to publish top to median pay multiples in their annual reporting from January 2012.

The component elements of executive directors' remuneration

The remuneration package for a senior executive in the corporate sector is likely to consist of a combination of: a fixed-pay element – remuneration received regardless of performance, such as a fixed salary and payments made into a salary related pension scheme – and a variable pay element. This might consist of performance-related incentives, which might be tied to short-term performance such as an annual bonus, and longer-term incentives such as share option awards. In addition, executives might enjoy a number of other perks such as free private medical insurance, a company car and the use of a company plane or apartment.

The major issue for the corporate sector in negotiating a remuneration package with an executive is deciding on the balance between the fixed and the variable elements, and to agree on measures of performance as the basis for deciding on how much the performance-related payments should be. Short-term incentives are based on annual performance targets. Long-term incentives may be awarded each year, but are linked to performance over a longer period of time, typically three years (or longer). Another problem in deciding a remuneration package is to find a suitable balance between short-term and longer-term incentives.

Admittedly, this is less of an issue for the NHS, where a senior executive remuneration package usually consists of a fixed salary and a final salary-related pension. The FTN Remuneration Survey of executive pay confirms this, although some FTs are now adding a car allowance or lease car to their remuneration packages.

There is also evidence that some FTs offer a performance-related pay scheme in connection with the achievement of trust corporate objectives. These schemes, however, are still in their infancy and small in number.

The remuneration committee

It is a well-established principle of 'best practice' in governance that there should be a formal procedure for deciding on remuneration for directors and senior executives, and no individual should be involved in setting their own remuneration. This is made clear in the UK Code. This means that EDs should not be involved in setting their remuneration packages (although they can negotiate with the individuals who make the decision) and NEDs should not decide their fees.

The remuneration of EDs was recognised as an important governance issue in the UK in the 1990s with the work of the Greenbury Committee, whose recommendations were subsequently incorporated into the UK governance code in 1998. Health service governance has adopted these principles, either in the constitution of an FT or the founding regulations and statutory instruments of other NHS organisations. It is worth, therefore, considering the provisions of the UK Code as they underpin the provisions of health service governance. Specimen terms of reference for NHS Remuneration Committees can be found on the ICSA website.

The requirement for a remuneration committee

The UK Code states that 'the board should establish a remuneration committee ... [which] should make available its terms of reference, explaining its role and the authority delegated to it by the board'.

The remuneration committee is responsible, therefore, for both developing remuneration policy and for negotiating the remuneration of individual directors. Although these two matters are related, they are different. According to the UK Code the remuneration committee in the corporate sector should consist entirely of independent NEDs. In larger companies, the committee should consist of at least three members, and in smaller companies (i.e. companies below the FTSE 350) at least two members. The company chair may be a member of the committee, but not the committee chair, provided that they were considered to be independent on appointment as company chair. The remuneration committee should have delegated responsibility for setting the remuneration for all EDs and the chair (including pension rights and any compensation payments or severance payments). The remuneration committee should also recommend and monitor the level and structure of remuneration for senior management. The definition of 'senior management' is a matter for the board to decide, but it will normally include the first level of management below board level.

The UK Code also states as a supporting principle that the remuneration committee should consult with the chair and/or the CEO about their proposals for the remuneration of the other EDs. This is to ensure that the remuneration committee receives advice about the performance of EDs from individuals who know about their contributions to the management team and to the work of the board.

The remuneration committee may ask for advice from other sources, including other senior executives and is responsible for deciding whether to appoint remuneration consultants to advise it. If executives or senior managers are involved in giving advice to the remuneration committee, the committee should take care to recognise and avoid any conflicts of interest. The committee should keep the chair well informed about its decisions on remuneration policy and the remuneration of individual directors, because the chair should be the point of contact for shareholders/stakeholders who want to ask questions about remuneration or make their opinions known to the organisation.

The specific requirements for a remuneration (and terms of service) committee for are set out more fully in Chapter 5.

The principal duties of the remuneration committee

A list of duties of the remuneration committee were at one time included as an annex to the UK Corporate Governance Code, and they are now set out in ICSA's guidance note on the terms of reference for a remuneration committee. Typically, the duties of a remuneration committee in the corporate sector are as follows.

- The committee should determine and agree with the main board the remuneration policy for the CEO, the chair of the board and any other designated executive managers. This policy should provide for executive managers to be given appropriate incentives for enhanced performance.
- To maintain and assure their independence, the committee should also decide the remuneration of the company secretary.
- The committee should decide the targets for performance for any performance-related pay schemes operated by the organisation.
- It should decide the policy for and scope of pension arrangements for each ED.
- It should ensure that the contractual terms for severance payments on termination of office are fair to both the individual and the organisation, that failure is not rewarded and that the director's duty to mitigate losses is fully recognised.
- Within the framework of the agreed remuneration policy, it should determine the remuneration package of each individual ED, including any bonuses, incentive payments and share options.
- It should be aware of and advise on any major changes in employee benefit structures throughout the organisation or group.
- It should agree the policy for authorising expense claims from the chair and CEO.

- It should ensure compliance by the organisation with the requirements for disclosure of directors' remuneration in the annual report and accounts.
- It should be responsible for appointing any remuneration consultants to advise the committee.
- In the annual report, it should report the frequency of committee meetings and the attendance by members.
- It should make available to the public its terms of reference, setting out the committee's delegated responsibilities. Where necessary these should be reviewed and updated each year.

NHS remuneration committees are also required to declare the relationship between the remuneration of the highest-paid director in their organisation and the median remuneration of the organisation's workforce in its annual report in line with the Hutton Fair Pay Review.

Evaluation and appraisal of executive directors

Both the FT Code and the UK Code state as a main principle that the board should undertake a 'formal and rigorous annual evaluation of its own performance and that of its committees and individual directors'. This includes the EDs in their board member roles. The performance of individual EDs as executive managers is not dealt with by a governance code, because individual executive performance is not a governance issue. For governance purposes, the evaluation of performance relates to performance as a director.

Good workforce management would require the EDs to undergo an annual appraisal with the CEO as their line manager in respect of the portfolio of management responsibilities that they undertake. However, this appraisal should also take into account the board level responsibilities that they carry and the chair of the board should be asked to participate in this aspect of their appraisal.

The chair of the board will appraise the CEO and this appraisal will also include both their management and board role responsibilities. The remuneration committee should then consider the appraisals of the EDs in considering any annual pay review decisions.

Use of remuneration consultants

Companies and NHS organisations often use remuneration consultants, who give advice to the remuneration committee on remuneration packages, including basic salary levels for senior executives. Consultants should not be given responsibility for deciding remuneration; this responsibility should remain with the remuneration committee of the board. Consultants may use competitive pay data to recommend a basic package for senior executives. Competitive pay data is simply information about the rewards that are being paid to senior executives in other top companies. It is essential that there is a robust tendering exercise for the appointment of such consultants in order to demonstrate their independence and objectivity.

A supporting principle in the UK Code is that the remuneration committee should benchmark its position on remuneration to comparative organisations, but it should exercise caution in making this judgment 'in view of the risk of an upward ratchet of remuneration levels with no corresponding improvement in performance'. If a UK-listed company does use the services of remuneration consultants, it should make available a statement of whether they have any other connection with the organisation. This statement may help to indicate that the consultants are independent and can provide objective advice.

Practice and process

There is no set requirement for the frequency of meeting of the remuneration committee; however, it needs to meet at least annually to approve the remuneration report for the annual report and accounts. Other meetings are likely in order to consider the remuneration policy required by ERRA 2013, any annual reviews of executive remuneration, and decisions on individual EDs as they are appointed. It is routine practice for non-members to be invited to attend the committee as required by the business of the meeting (e.g. the CEO, director of workforce or employment lawyer). The company secretary (or someone from the company secretary's department) should act as secretary to the remuneration committee, because it is the company secretary's responsibility to ensure that the board and its committees are properly constituted and advised. The company secretary can also play a role as intermediary and co-ordinator between the committee and the main board.

The FRC *Guidance on Board Effectiveness* makes it clear that whilst the board may make use of a committee to assist its consideration of remuneration, it still retains responsibility for, and makes the final decisions on, all of these areas. The chair should ensure that sufficient time is allowed at the board for discussion of these issues and for allowing the remuneration committee to report on its activity and decisions. As with all board committees the effectiveness of the committee and its terms of reference should be reviewed annually.

Severance payments

Most EDs have employment contracts with their organisation that provide for an annual review of their remuneration and a minimum period of notice in the event of dismissal. When an organisation decides to dismiss a director, it is bound by the terms of the employment contract. There are various reasons why an individual might leave the company – for instance, they might be regarded as having failed to do a good job, and someone else should do the job instead. In this instance a high severance payment would be seen as 'rewarding failure'. Alternately, there may have been a disagreement or falling out between directors, resulting in one or more directors being asked to leave; in this instance any severance payment needs to be fair and not calculated to prevent whistleblowing disclosures or reputational damage.

The employment contract of a director might provide for the payment of compensation for loss of office. Alternatively, an organisation might be required to give the individual a minimum period of notice, typically one year or six months in the UK. If an individual is asked to leave, they might be paid for the notice period without having to work out the notice. In addition, the individual may be entitled to further bonus payments under the terms of their remuneration package – in spite of being considered a failure in the job.

Shareholder concerns, and the wider public concern in regard to public sector organisations, arise particularly where the severance payment is paid even though an individual is being dismissed for having performed badly. In the past, severance payments have been high for executives who have been seen to have failed. A large compensation payment can seem annoying, because it seems that the individual is being rewarded for failure. Large severance payments reduce company profits and returns to shareholders and in the public sector are viewed as the improper use of public sector monies.

The UK Code contains two provisions about employment contracts and compensation for termination of office.

- When negotiating the terms of appointment of a new director, the remuneration committee should consider what compensation commitments the organisation would have in the event of early termination of office. More specifically, the aim should be to avoid rewarding poor performance. The committee should 'take a robust line' on reducing the amount of compensation to reflect a departing director's obligation to mitigate losses.
- Notice periods in the employment contract of an ED should be set at one year or less. If it is necessary to offer a longer notice period to a director coming into the organisation from outside, the notice period should subsequently be reduced to one year or less 'after the initial period'.

Remuneration committees should consider whether the organisation should retain an entitlement to reclaim bonuses if performance achievements are subsequently found to have been materially mis-stated. Contracts of employment should not provide for compensation payments to senior executives in the event of a change of control over the organisation (a takeover).

Remuneration committees should also ensure that the benefits of mitigation are obtained when an individual is dismissed. This should include a contractual obligation of the dismissed individual to mitigate the loss incurred through severance by looking for other employment. The contract should provide for the severance payment to be reduced in circumstances where the individual finds alternative employment.

NHS Employers published *Guidance for Employers within the NHS* in December 2013 to assist NHS employers in handling special severance payments. Originally designed to cover senior managers, the guidance also outlined the process for issuing a special severance payment to any employee. Though it made clear that employers needed to take legal and audit advice in each particular situation, the guidance summarised the considerations employers need to make when considering terminating the employment of an individual with a special severance payment.

HM Treasury define a 'special severance payment' as one paid to employees, contractors and others above normal statutory or contractual requirements when leaving employment in public service whether they resign, are dismissed or reach an agreed termination of contract. The guidance also referred to Chapter 5 of the NHS Financial Manual (losses and special payments) and the HM Treasury guidance *Managing Public Money*.

The process requires all NHS organisations to obtain agreement from the relevant national body to make a special severance payment before presenting a paper to the HM Treasury for approval (see Table 9.3).

Table 9.3: Bodies that approve special severance payments

Organisation type	National body
NHS trust	NHSI
NHS FT	NHSI
Clinical commissioning group	NHSE
ALB/special health authority	DH

The guidance sets out the following questions to help inform NHS organisations in their decision-making.

- Is it appropriate to terminate the individual's employment? Severance should not be used as an option if it is primarily to avoid formal performance management action, disciplinary processes, unwelcome publicity or reputational damage.
- What is the appropriate method of termination? For example, in cases involving performance or misconduct issues, generally the capability or disciplinary procedures are appropriate and should be utilised as appropriate.
- Have all the circumstances of the case been considered, including the scope for potential litigation and the consequences of this?
- Is this arrangement in the public interest? Consider:
  - why the severance payment is in the public interest
  - why it represents value for money
  - how it represents the best use of public funds.
- Have the NHSI or NHSE (as applicable) been informed? The employer should inform their contact at the relevant body at the earliest opportunity.

The guidance also recommends that any specific process requirements should be clarified with the appropriate national body according to Table 9.3 (the NHSI for FTs and NHS trusts and NHSE for CCGs).

Once the above steps have been taken and the employer is satisfied that termination of the employee's employment, together with making a severance payment, is in the best interests of the employer and represents value for money, then a proposal for the remuneration committee, as appropriate and in line with its terms of reference, should be prepared containing the business case for the severance payment.

This document should be created in order to take legal effect and should be marked as such. In addition to the preparation of the proposal, the following steps should be taken:

- written advice from the trust's auditors and legal advisers should be taken on the proposed business case and severance payment. Advice should also be sought on the proposal and, if appropriate, a settlement agreement should be drafted; and
- the legal advice about the draft proposal, together with the audit advice and the proposal itself, should be put before the remuneration committee of the employer for approval.

In the event the remuneration committee approves the business case, further approval should be sought from NHSE or NHSI (as applicable). If a settlement agreement is to be used, the approving body and HM Treasury will need to be assured that it does not include a confidentiality clause that prohibits an individual raising a concern covered under the Public Interest Disclosure Act 1998 (PIDA 1998). If the appropriate national body approves the business case, it will seek HM Treasury approval on behalf of the employer.

The remuneration committee, operating in accordance with its terms of reference, should satisfy itself that it has the relevant information before it to make a decision and should conscientiously discuss and assess the merits of the business case. It should then consider the payment or payment range being proposed and address whether it is appropriate, taking into account the issues set out under initial considerations. The committee should only approve such sum or range which it considers value for money, the best use of public funds and in the public interest. A written record must be kept summarising its discussions and its decision (remembering that such a document could potentially be subject to public scrutiny in various ways – such as by the Public Accounts Committee (PAC)).

It is only once all of the above steps have been taken, and the necessary approvals received, that the employer should enter into the appropriate agreement to terminate the employee's employment and make the severance payment.

In addition the Small Business, Enterprise and Employment Act 2015 legislated that highly paid public sector executives who receive redundancy payments only to return to work within a year will need to repay some or all of their redundancy payment. In brief, the Act mean that individuals earning more than £100,000 who take a new job in the same part of the public sector within 12 months of being made redundant will have to repay all or some of their redundancy payment. The proposals will mainly affect NHS and local government administrators, many of whom have taken redundancy payments only to go back into the public sector. The precise amount of the repayment will be pro-rated depending on the length of time between exit and re-employment. The legislation will require the old employer to inform the individual of their obligation to repay the exit payment. Any new employer would be unable to engage with the individual until recovery arrangements for the money have been agreed.

HM Treasury has said that it intends to include the following payments related to loss of employment within the scope of this policy:

- redundancy payments, both voluntary and compulsory
- voluntary exit payments
- discretionary payments made to buy out actuarial reductions in pensions
- *ex gratia* payments such as special severance payments
- payments representing the value of fixed-term contracts
- payments made to facilitate a dismissal on the grounds of efficiency.

Disclosure of directors' remuneration details

Directors' remuneration report

Under ERRA 2013, companies are required to publish a remuneration report which includes three sections:

- a statement from the chair of the remuneration committee
- a forward-looking remuneration policy report (not subject to audit)
- an annual report on remuneration (audited) which includes both how the policy has been implemented in the year under review and how it will be implemented in the forthcoming year.

Shareholders have a binding vote on the policy report at least every three years, or whenever any changes are made, in addition to an annual advisory vote on the annual remuneration report. The report must set out the total remuneration of individual executive members disclosed as a single figure in the financial statements (including base pay, bonuses, dividend equivalents, pensions etc). The Act does not, however, make a distinction between executive and NEDs and information about both must be included in the report.

The remuneration report must be approved by the board and signed on its behalf. A copy must be circulated to shareholders in the same way as the annual report and accounts, and it is normal for the remuneration report to be included in the same document. The auditors must state whether in their opinion the report has been prepared properly in their audit report (see Chapter 17). For companies, a signed copy of the report must also be filed with the Registrar of Companies, in the same way as the annual accounts, directors' report and auditors' report.

The remuneration committee should also be available at the annual general meeting to assist in answering any questions put to the board on any aspect of the remuneration report or generally on remuneration principles and practice.

Items to be included in the committee chair's statement include the key messages on remuneration, the context in which decisions were taken and any major changes during the year. This places the chair of the remuneration committee in the spotlight with regard to the organisation's approach to executive remuneration.

The remuneration policy must include an explanatory table, with detailed notes, setting out the approach taken to directors' remuneration in the period covered by the policy. This must be supplemented with a bar chart showing illustrative scenarios. It must also include a section on the approach to remuneration for new directors recruited to the board, as well as details of the policy on payments for loss of office. An explanation of the extent to which the views of employees' and shareholders have taken into account is also required.

The annual report then sets out how the remuneration policy was implemented in the previous financial year. A new requirement in this report is the obligation to include a single total figure for the remuneration of each director. The aim is to provide comprehensive disclosure on all types of remuneration – fixed and variable elements, as well as pension provision – in a consistent format. There is also a focus on including a breakdown of payments for loss of office. Any such payment, in addition to being included in the annual report, will also need to be published on the company's website 'as soon as practicable' after the payment has been agreed. These details will need to be kept available until the next annual report is published.

The NHS FT annual reporting manual (NHS FT ARM) and the NHS Finance Manual both require a similar report to be made in the organisation's annual report. This report should include all exit packages, including those paid to senior managers.

Governance checklist

- ✓ Are the EDs aware of their wider role as a board member? Does their induction and ongoing development support them in their board role?
- ✓ Does the CEO or chief officer enhance board effectiveness by ensuring high standards of board/committee reporting?
- ✓ Is there evidence of the CEO implementing board decisions and lead on delivering best practice in governance across the organisation?
- ✓ Is the DoF an effective partner with the CEO with the required professional and corporate experience to both support and challenge the CEO?

- ✓ Does the remuneration committee have the necessary skills for its role and is it sufficiently independent of the EDs?
- ✓ Is there evidence of the committee eliciting the appropriate professional advice as and when required?
- ✓ If remuneration consultants are retained, then has there been a robust rendering process to ensure their independence and objectivity?
- ✓ Has the committee determined a coherent policy on director's remuneration, which is regularly reviewed to ensure it remains 'fit for purpose' and in line with best practice?
- ✓ Does the committee apply the policy to its decisions, taking account of appropriate benchmarking information?
- ✓ Do the EDs' employment contracts address issues relating to rewards for failure on termination?
- ✓ Does the committee fulfil its responsibilities with regard to the reporting requirements on remuneration?
- ✓ Does the committee make itself available at the annual meeting or on other occasions for scrutiny and challenge by the shareholders/stakeholders?

Summary

The matter of executive remuneration will continue to be a contentious issue both in the corporate and public sector. Ongoing debate and discussion continues to surround shareholder voting on executive remuneration in the annual round of corporate AGMs. And there are still further changes being considered as set out in the government's 2016 Green Paper.

It is clear that the greater degree of regulation in the NHS, combined with the attitude of largely well-motivated public servants – including senior managers – is currently providing control and restraints on NHS ED remuneration. Public perception is unlikely to reflect this, however, therefore boards and their remuneration committees will continue to have to balance the need to attract high calibre appointments, the morale of the wider workforce and the reputation of their organisation.

10

Non-executive directors

Introduction

A non-executive director (NED) is a member of the board of directors without executive responsibilities in the organisation. NEDs should be able to bring judgment and experience to the deliberations of the board that the executive directors (EDs) on their own would lack.

To be effective, a NED has to understand the organisation's business, but there appears to be general consensus that the experience and qualities required of a NED can be obtained from working in other industries or in other aspects of commercial and public life. NEDs may therefore include individuals who:

- are EDs in other public companies
- hold NED positions and chair positions in other public companies
- have professional qualifications (e.g. partners in firms of solicitors)
- have experience in government, as politicians or former senior civil servants.

NEDs are expected not only to bring a wide range of skills and experience to the deliberations of the board, particularly in the area of strategy and business development, but also to ensure that there is a suitable balance of power on the board. A powerful chair or CEO might be able to dominate other EDs, but in theory at least, independent NEDs should be able to bring different views and independent thinking to board deliberations. Decisions taken by the board should therefore be better and more in keeping with the aims of good corporate governance.

CASE STUDY: The Bristol Royal Infirmary Enquiry

The Bristol Royal Infirmary Enquiry (July 2001) stated that:

> 'In our view, non-executive directors have a crucial role to play in representing the public interest in the conduct of the Trust's affairs. They must be people with a high level of ability and experience in the leadership and management of organisations ... they should have a commitment to public service.'

Lessons for NEDs that resulted from the Bristol Enquiry were as follows:

- Non-executive directors can be prevented from exerting their authority by 'not being let in on issues' at senior executive level.
- Lack of sound knowledge about trust activity can lead to an inability to challenge chief executives' or EDs' views.
- Role objectives may not be clarified and communicated. There was:
  - a variation in the roles played by non-executives on the board
  - variation in what was expected of non-executives
  - a lack of clarity and direction for the role.

The role and effectiveness of NEDs has been the subject of much scrutiny and challenge since the publication of the Higgs Report in 2003, with doubts being expressed at the level of balance they are able to bring to the board. The role of the NED was also considered as part of the Walker Review (2009), following the banking crisis. The review found firmly in favour of the NED role, stating that the NED contribution was materially helpful in financial institutions that had weathered the storm better than others.

In broad terms, the role of the NED, under the leadership of the chair is:

- to ensure that there is an effective executive team in place
- to participate actively in the decision-taking process of the board
- to exercise appropriate oversight over execution of the agreed strategy by the executive team.

The appointment, induction and evaluation of non-executive directors

The appointment of the chair and NEDs for NHS trusts is overseen by NHS Improvement (NHSI) as set out in Chapter 7; foundation trust (FT) chairs and NEDs are appointed by the council of governors (see Chapter 12). The appointment processes for clinical commissioning group (CCGs) are covered in Chapter 13. Even so, the best practice guidance set out below benchmarks best practice for those fulfilling the role of NED in all types of NHS organisation.

Induction for non-executive directors

The Financial Reporting Council (FRC) *Guidance on Board Effectiveness* provides useful guidance on induction of NEDs.

> 'A NED should, on appointment, devote time to a comprehensive, formal and tailored induction that should extend beyond the boardroom. Initiatives such as partnering a NED with an executive board member may speed up the process of him or her acquiring an understanding of the main areas of business

activity, especially areas involving significant risk. The director should expect to visit, and talk with, senior and middle managers in these areas.'

The chair is responsible for making sure that all NEDs have such a tailored induction programme, although in practice this is often undertaken and overseen by the company secretary. In the NHS, Healthcare Financial Management Association (HFMA) provides a structured induction for new chairs, NEDs and CCG lay members around key issues. It includes an introduction to NHS board roles, including sessions on structures, roles, patient safety and individual liabilities and an introduction to their governance responsibilities, including risk assurance, financial obligations and the board role in delivering a safe and high-quality service.

Evaluation of non-executive directors

Both the FT Code and the UK Code state as a main principle that the board should undertake a 'formal and rigorous annual evaluation of its own performance and that of its committees and individual directors'.

The UK Code states that: 'Individual evaluation should aim to show whether each director continues to contribute effectively and to demonstrate commitment to the role (including commitment of time for board and committee meetings and any other duties).'

Chairs of NHS trusts are responsible for ensuring that NEDs receive performance appraisals at least annually. Trusts can determine the approach to appraisal that is most relevant to their own circumstances. An NHSI good practice guide to appraisal, as well as copies of the chair and non-executive role descriptions and behaviour frameworks, are also available to support an effective appraisal and appointment process.

NHS trusts should retain copies of NED appraisal forms, and share copies with those who have been appraised. This meets the requirement of the Office of the Commissioner of Public Appointments that all performance reviews must be formally recorded in the event of an investigation into a complaint. These copies may be needed to support future re-appointments, as evidence of poor performance. The NHSI does not intend to collect NED appraisals routinely, but may request them as and when required.

The key board level competencies for a NED set out by the NHSI are:

- **Patient and community focus:** a high level of commitment to patients, carers and the community, and to tackling health inequalities in disadvantaged groups.
- **Strategic direction:** the ability to think and plan ahead, to develop a clear vision and enthuse others, balancing needs and constraints.
- **Holding to account:** the ability to accept accountability for board performance, and probe and challenge constructively.
- **Effective influencing and communication:** a high level of ability to gain support and influence, political acumen.

- **Team working:** be committed to working as a team member self belief and drive – the motivation to improve NHS performance and confidence to take on challenges.
- **Intellectual flexibility:** the ability think clearly and creatively, make sense of complexity and clarify it for other people.
- **Application of standards of public life**: uphold the highest standards of conduct set out in *The Seven Principles of Public Life* (see Chapter 2).

Key questions for independent NED evaluation include the following.

- How many board meetings has the director attended, and how many times have they been absent?
- How well prepared has the individual been for meetings (e.g. have they read the relevant papers in advance)?
- What has been the quality of contributions of the individual to board meetings (e.g. on strategic development and risk management)?
- Has the individual shown independence of character, or have they tended to go along with the opinions of certain other board members?
- How many board committee meetings has the director attended and how many have they missed?
- What has the individual contributed to committee meetings?
- Has the time commitment of the director been sufficient? Has the time commitment been as much as expected, or as much as stated in the director terms of appointment?
- Does the NED continue to show interest in and enthusiasm for the organisation?
- Are there reasons why the director may no longer be considered independent?
- Does the director communicate well with the other directors and with senior executives of the organisation?

The performance evaluation of NEDs in FTs is carried out by the council of governors and is set out in more detail in Chapter 12. The performance evaluation of CCG general practitioner (GP) members, lay members, secondary care and nurse members is carried out by the governing body: more details on this can be found in Chapter 13.

Non-executive directors and the UK Corporate Governance Code

The UK Code has largely incorporated the recommendations from the Higgs Report on the role and effectiveness of NEDs. Key among them are:

- NEDs should 'constructively challenge and help develop proposals on strategy'

- NEDs should also scrutinise the performance of management in meeting agreed goals or targets of performance, and they should monitor the reporting of performance (to ensure that this is honest and not misleading)
- NEDs should satisfy themselves about the integrity of the financial information produced by the organisation, and that the financial controls and systems of risk management are 'robust and defensible'
- NEDs should be responsible for deciding the remuneration of EDs
- NEDs should have a significant role in the appointment (and where necessary removal) of EDs and in succession planning for the major positions on the board.

The UK Code recognises there are matters that the NEDs should discuss without EDs being present, and a provision of the UK Code is that the chair should hold meetings with the NEDs without EDs being present. In addition, NEDs should meet at least once a year to discuss the performance of the chair, without the chair and led by the senior independent director (SID) (see Chapter 8). They should also meet on other occasions if this is considered necessary or appropriate.

FRC Guidance on Board Effectiveness and the role of NEDs

The FRC *Guidance on Board Effectiveness* makes the following recommendations on the role of NEDs.

- A NED should, on appointment, devote time to a comprehensive, formal and tailored induction and should devote time to developing and refreshing their knowledge and skills.
- NEDs need to make sufficient time available to discharge their responsibilities effectively.
- Their letter of appointment should state the minimum time that the NED will be required to spend on the organisation's business, and indicate the possibility of additional time commitment when the organisation is undergoing a period of particularly increased activity, such as an acquisition or takeover, or as a result of some major difficulty with one or more of its operations.
- NEDs should insist on receiving high-quality information sufficiently in advance so that there can be thorough consideration of the issues prior to, and informed debate and challenge at, board meetings. High-quality information is that which is appropriate for making decisions on the issue at hand – it should be accurate, clear, comprehensive, up-to-date and timely; contain a summary of the contents of any paper; and inform the director of what is expected of them on that issue.

The Walker Report on the role of NEDS in banks

The Walker Report (2009) suggested that the role of NEDs is crucial to the effectiveness of a board in formulating and implementing business strategy. The report included the following comments.

- Stakeholders have a right to expect that there should be a material input from the NEDs in a unitary board to decisions on strategy and oversight of strategy implementation. It should also be expected that when there is such shared decision-making between EDs and NEDs, the organisation should perform better in general and over time than if strategy were determined exclusively by the executive management. This expectation appeared to have been justified by the banking crisis in the US and Europe.
- NEDs should provide a 'disciplined but rigorous challenge on substantive issues'. This should be seen as the norm, not an exception, and if any NED has insufficient strength of character to participate in providing a challenge, their continued suitability to remain as a board member should be thrown into question.

The Walker Report did add a note of caution on the extent NEDs should challenge the executive team, however:

> 'This does not, of course, mean open season for challenge to the executive team. Appropriate balance will only be achieved where the ED expects to be challenged, but where the board debate surrounding such challenge is conducted in a way that leaves the executive team with a sense of having drawn benefit from it.'

The 'inherent tension'

The Cadbury Report – published in 1992 – first raised the issue of the balance for the NED role between monitoring the performance of the executive team against the contribution to the strategic direction of the organisation.

In a heavily regulated sector like the NHS, this can be a particularly challenging balance to achieve. This was covered again in 1998's Hampel Report, which noted that though NEDs are normally appointed to the board primarily for their contribution to the development of the company's strategy, there was also a general acceptance that NEDs should have both a strategic and a monitoring function.

This dual role was supported by the Higgs Report, which recommended that the NED role should not be forced to decide between these two perspectives. For the NED role to be overly concerned with monitoring would be for the NED to take on 'an alien policing influence on the board' whereas being overly concerned with identifying the strategic direction could lead to the NED over-identifying with the executive team.

Keeping these two aspects of the role in 'tension' is what helps NEDs provide a valuable contribution. Though the FRC *Guidance on Board Effectiveness* has overtaken the Hampel and Higgs reports, these reports still offer helpful insights and demonstrate the balance between the role of monitoring and providing strategic direction very clearly. For example, Higgs listed the key elements of the NED role as follows.

- **Strategy:** NEDs should constructively challenge and contribute to the development of strategy.
- **Performance:** NEDs should scrutinise the performance of management in meeting agreed goals and objectives and monitor the reporting of performance.
- **Risk:** NEDs should satisfy themselves that financial information is accurate and that financial controls and systems of risk management are robust and defensible.
- **People:** NEDs are responsible for determining appropriate levels of remuneration of EDs and have a prime role in appointing, and where necessary removing, senior management and in succession planning.

Independence of non-executive directors

NEDs are either independent or non-independent. A NED is not independent if their opinions are likely to be influenced, in particular by the senior executive management of the organisation or by a major stakeholder. What follows is an exploration of the importance of independence and the criteria for making that judgment.

Though this applies directly to CCGs, NHS trusts and FTs alike, the implications are somewhat different for CCGs as they are essentially membership organisations. These are explored more fully in Chapter 13.

Independent NEDs are supposed to bring an independent view to the deliberations of the board. However, they are in a difficult position as they are legally liable in the same way as EDs. For example, they owe the same fiduciary duties to the organisation, as well as an obligation to exercise the duty of skill and care. As fellow directors, they might also be reluctant to blow the whistle on their executive colleagues. If they have been selected and appointed by the chair or the CEO, they will be less likely to ask tough questions about the way the organisation is being run.

The UK Code does not suggest that all NEDs should be independent. Non-independent NEDs are permissible, although the majority of the total board should consist of independent NEDs. If there are NEDs on the board who are not considered independent, this could create problems with the size and composition of the board. It may be considered necessary to appoint independent NEDs to act as a counterbalance to the NEDs who are not independent.

The FT Code states that:

> 'The board of directors should identify in the annual report each non-executive director it considers to be independent. The board should determine whether the director is independent in character and judgement and whether there are relationships or circumstances which are likely to affect, or could appear to affect, the director's judgement. The board of directors should state its reasons if it determines that a director is independent notwithstanding the

existence of relationships or circumstances which may appear relevant to its determination.'

What is meant by 'independent'? It is easier to answer this question by specifying what is not independent. A NED is not independent if their opinions are likely to be influenced by someone else, in particular by the senior executive management or by a major stakeholder. The independence of an NED could be challenged, for example, if the individual concerned:

- has a family connection with the CEO – a problem in some family controlled public companies
- until recently used to be an ED in the organisation
- until recently used to work for the organisation in a professional capacity (e.g. as its auditor or corporate lawyer)
- receives payments from the organisation in addition to their fees as an NED.

A person cannot be independent if they personally stand to gain, or otherwise benefit substantially, from income from the organisation (in addition to their fee as a NED) or from the organisation's reported profitability and movements in its share price.

A NED cannot be properly independent if, for example, they accept a fee from the organisation for consultancy work. Consultancy involves the individual in the operational aspects of the organisation, and by implication puts them on the side of the executive team. Nor can an individual be independent if they have been awarded a large number of share options by the company. Holding share options gives the individual a direct interest in the share price of the company around the time the options can be exercised. They might therefore favour decisions that improve the reported profitability of the company in the short term, because good financial results are likely to be good for the share price.

Occasionally, NEDs are appointed to represent the opinions of a major stakeholder (e.g. the appointment of a NED from a related university or dental school in NHS teaching hospitals). In such cases, the individual can be expected to voice the wishes of the stakeholder, and so could not be regarded as independent.

To ensure that NEDs should not rely for their tenure in office on one or two individuals, the UK Code recommends that they should be selected through a formal process. EDs cannot be independent. Not only are they involved in the running of the organisation's operations and report (and are accountable) to the chief executive officer (CEO) for this aspect of their work, they also rely on the organisation for most (if not all) of their remuneration.

Criteria for judging independence

The UK Code, and as quoted above, the FT Code, both require the board to identify in the annual report each NED it considers to be independent. Although this is a matter for the board's judgment, both codes set out the circumstances in which independence would usually be questionable.

- The director has been an employee of the organisation within the last five years.
- The director has a material business relationship with the organisation (or has had such a relationship within the last three years). This relationship might be as a partner, shareholder, director or employee in another organisation that has a material business relationship with the organisation.
- The director receives (or has received) additional remuneration from the organisation other than a director's fee, is a member of the organisation's pension scheme or participates in the organisation's share option scheme or a performance-related pay scheme.
- The director has close family ties with any of the organisation's advisers, directors or senior employees.
- The director has cross-directorships or has significant links with other directors through involvement in other companies or organisations. A cross-directorship exists when an individual is a NED on the board of Organisation X and an ED on the board of Organisation Y, when another individual is an ED of Organisation X and an NED on the board of Organisation Y.
- The director represents a significant shareholder or stakeholder.
- The director has served on the board for more than nine years since the date of his first election (six in the case of FTs).

These criteria of independence should be applied to the chair (on appointment) as well as other NEDs. Circumstances may change, and the independence of NEDs should be kept under review.

Independence of serving directors

There is a general view that the independence of a NED is likely to diminish over time as the NED becomes more familiar with the organisation and executive colleagues. The risk is that the NED will take more of the views of executive colleagues on trust and will be less rigorous in their questioning. This is noted in the UK Code, the King IV Code and the FT Code.

There will be circumstances where NEDs, having served their full terms, may exceptionally remain on the board. Indeed, the UK Code is pragmatic in its approach to the nine-year rule. If the board considers that a director is still independent even after nine years' service, they may still be considered 'independent' for the purposes of the corporate governance provisions.

The FT Code takes a similar approach, although restricting the length of tenure to six years, stating that:

> 'Any term beyond six years (e.g. two three-year terms) for a NED should be subject to particularly rigorous review, and should take into account the need for progressive refreshing of the board. NEDs may in exceptional circumstances serve longer than six years (e.g. two three-year terms following authorisation of the NHS FT), but subject to annual re-appointment. Serving more than six years could be relevant to the determination of a NED's independence.'

Barriers to being an effective non-executive director

There are differing views about the effectiveness of NEDs. The accepted view is that NEDs bring experience and judgment to the deliberations of the board that EDs on their own would lack.

An alternative view is that the effectiveness of NEDs can be undermined by lack of knowledge about the business operations of the organisation, insufficient time spent with the organisation, the weight of opinion of the EDs on the board and that NED involvement leads to delays in decision-making.

Insufficient knowledge

The quality of decision-making depends largely on the quality of information available to the decision-maker. The UK Code states that the board as a whole should be 'supplied in a timely manner with information in a form and of a quality appropriate to enable it to discharge its duties'. However, the senior executives in an organisation control the information systems, and so control the flow of information to the board. It is quite conceivable, for example, that the CEO and other EDs might have access to management information that is withheld from the board as a whole, or that is presented to the board in a distorted manner. Lacking the 'insider knowledge' of EDs about the business operations, and having to rely on the integrity of the information supplied to them by management and the EDs, restricts the scope for NEDs to make a meaningful contribution to board decisions.

Insufficient time

NEDs often have executive positions in other companies and organisations, where most of their working time is spent. As a general rule, NEDs do not have an office at the organisation headquarters and may spend at most two to three days per month on the organisation's business. A further criticism of NEDs is that some individuals hold too many NED positions, with the result that they cannot possibly give sufficient time to any of the organisations concerned. It could be argued, for example, that an individual cannot be an effective NED of an organisation if they are also the CEO of another public organisation and hold four or five other NED positions in other organisations.

The UK Code states that all directors should be able to allocate sufficient time to the organisation to discharge their responsibilities effectively. Although this principle of the code applies to all directors, the main concern is with NEDs (since EDs are usually full-time employees) and in particular the chair. The UK Code requires that when a chair or NED is appointed, the nomination committee should prepare a job specification that includes an assessment of the expected time commitment and in particular for the chair, recognising the need to be available to the organisation in times of crisis. When a NED or a new chair is appointed, the letter of appointment should set out the expected time commitment. In addition, the Code requires all new chair or NED appointments to disclose any other significant commitments they already have.

Overriding influence of executive directors

Yet another criticism of NEDs is that if a difference of opinion arises during a meeting of the board, the opinions of the EDs are likely to carry greater weight, because they know more about the organisation. NEDs may be put under pressure to accept the views of their ED colleagues. This potential problem provides an argument for the role of a strong SID, to ensure that the opinions of the independent NEDs are properly considered.

Delays in decision-making

It may be argued that NEDs delay decision-making within an organisation. Major decisions should be reserved for the board; therefore, to implement an important new strategy initiative it may be necessary to call a board meeting. The time required to hold the meeting, giving the NEDs sufficient time to reach a well-informed opinion about the matter, may delay the implementation of the proposed strategy. It has also been argued that NEDs may be conservative in outlook, whereas the board of directors needs to be 'entrepreneurial'.

One counter-argument is that when a major new strategy or initiative is proposed, it should be given full and careful consideration before a decision is made. NEDs, with their range of skills and experience, can contribute positively to this decision-making process.

The effectiveness of non-executive directors

The Higgs Report of 2003 is helpful in identifying the behaviours and attitudes that will make for an effective NED.

> 'Non-executive directors should constantly seek to establish and maintain confidence in the conduct of the company. They should be independent in judgement and have an enquiring mind. To be effective, non-executive directors need to build a recognition by executives of their contribution in order to promote openness and trust. To be effective, non-executive directors need to be well-informed about the company and the external environment in which it operates, with a strong command of issues relevant to the business. A non-executive director should insist on a comprehensive, formal and tailored induction. An effective induction need not be restricted to the boardroom, so consideration should be given to visiting sites and meeting senior and middle management. Once in post, an effective non-executive director should seek continually to develop and refresh their knowledge and skills to ensure that their contribution to the board remains informed and relevant.'

Another aspect to the effectiveness of the NEDs is to ensure that there is a diversity of background and experience. This encourages a diverse range of views to be expressed in consideration of proposals being brought to the board. Being less closely involved in the day-to day running of the organisation enables NEDs to bring a fresh perspective to the discussion – highlighting shareholder/stakeholder concerns is a vital role that NEDs can play. This supports the board in avoiding the 'group-think' tendencies that can develop in any group that works closely together.

The rigour that the NEDs bring to the independent scrutiny and challenge of board decisions is equally important; it is therefore essential that NEDs have the necessary people skills. Exercising influence rather than a 'command and control' role requires very particular interpersonal skills of diplomacy and persuasion.

The Walker Review highlighted that NEDs sitting on the boards of highly complex businesses needed to ensure that they had the right mix of industry-specific experience as well as a diverse range of other backgrounds to ensure there was an external critique of the business being considered. It further recognised that:

> 'Even where the NED composition on the board is well balanced between financial industry experience and deep experience from elsewhere, the effectiveness of the overall NED contribution will be enhanced by a combination of appropriate induction and, thereafter, regular training programmes, adapted to the needs of the individual director; and dependable access for NEDs to support from within the company, for example from a dedicated capability in the company secretariat and greater time commitment.'

Non-executive director remuneration

The level of remuneration appropriate for any particular NED role should reflect the likely workload, the scale and complexity of the business and the responsibility involved.

Where a NED has extra responsibilities (such as membership or chairship of board committees), the total remuneration should reflect these. The Higgs Report recommended that NED fees should be clearly built up using an annual fee, meeting attendance fees (to include board committee meetings) and an additional fee for the chairship of committees (typically a multiple of the attendance fee) or role as senior independent director. In addition, organisations should expect to pay additional reasonable expenses in addition to the director's fee to cover related costs incurred by their NEDs (such as travel and administrative costs). Any significant support of this kind should be agreed in advance.

The principle that individuals should not decide their own remuneration applies to NEDs as well as to EDs. This means that a remuneration committee should not decide the fees of the NEDs. In the corporate sector, deciding the remuneration of the NEDs should be the responsibility of the chair and the EDs (or the shareholders if required by the articles of association). Where permitted by the articles, the board may delegate this responsibility to a committee which might include the CEO. A provision in the UK Code is that the level of remuneration for NEDs should reflect the time commitment and responsibilities of the role.

NEDs are not employees. They receive a fee for their services, not a salary. In the UK corporate sector, it is usual for NEDs to receive a fixed annual fee, typically in the region of £20,000 to £60,000 (or possibly more), for attending board meetings, some committee meetings and general meetings of the company. This is substantially less in the health service sector, although the annual NED fees are increasing in larger FTs.

CASE STUDY: Royal Free London NHS Foundation Trust

The Royal Free London NHS Foundation Trust established a set of principles to support the council of governors in setting the remuneration element of non-executive terms and conditions. These were as follows:

- **Competitive:** NED remuneration should be competitive with comparable trusts on a comparative workload basis/the trust should be able to attract at least as good NEDs as other comparable trusts.
- **Value for money (VFM):** the total cost of the non-executive team should be demonstrably good value for taxpayers' money in comparison to comparable trusts.
- **Aligned with role:** the remuneration structure should be appropriate to the role of the NEDs in independently holding the executive team to account.
- **Effective team working:** the structure of remuneration for non-executives should encourage behaviour which leads to effective team working.

The NHS Providers 2015 Remuneration Survey of chairs and NEDs revealed average annual NED remuneration in FTs of £13,000 and in NHS trusts of £6,000. The average for all chairs was £40,000, with an average monthly time commitment of 11 days. The difference in fees is tied to the size of trust turnover or number of staff in the trust, as these are usually the indicators used to benchmark individual trusts when assessing the level of non-executive fees.

The remuneration for chairs and NEDs in NHS trusts is set by the Secretary of State and overseen by the NHSI. In FTs, the council of governors decides their remuneration. This provides the same protection as in the corporate sector, preventing individuals from setting their own remuneration. However, in CCGs the fees for GP members, lay members, secondary care and nurse members are set by the CCG itself. The CCG remuneration committee therefore needs to set clear parameters to ensure that individuals are not allowed to participate in decisions about their own fees. This is explored further in Chapter 13.

In the corporate sector, NEDs may receive other forms of remuneration or reward from the organisation alongside the basic fee (such as payment for additional services); however, this can raise questions about their independence. For example, a NED might be paid additionally as a 'consultant' to the company. No matter how genuine and useful these consultancy services are, they put the NED's independence at risk because executive management decides the size of a consultancy fee. Management also decides whether to extend or renew a consultancy agreement. This kind of arrangement is very unusual in the NHS.

The UK Code makes specific provisions about performance-related rewards for NEDs, including the award of share options to NEDs.

- As a general rule, the remuneration of NEDs should not include share options or any other performance-related reward.
- In exceptional cases, share options may be granted. However, the approval of the shareholders should be obtained in advance, and if the NED subsequently exercises options to acquire shares in the company, these shares should be held until at least one year after the NED leaves the board.
- Holding share options could affect the determination of whether or not the NED is independent.

Resignation

Some of those who responded to the consultation for the Higgs Report described the resignation of a NED as being the ultimate sanction at their disposal. Higgs believed that resignation should be regarded very much as a last resort once other efforts to resolve problems have failed. Indeed, NEDs may be constrained from resigning by their fiduciary duty to act in the organisation's best interests. Where NEDs have real concerns about the way in which an organisation is being run or about a course of action proposed by the board, the first step should be to raise their concerns with the chair and their fellow directors. NEDs should, as a matter of course, ensure that their concerns are recorded in the minutes of the board meeting if they cannot be resolved.

If the NED feels that resignation is the only course of action left, a written statement should be provided to the chair, for circulation to the board, setting out the reasons for resignation. Higgs also recommended that a NED should explain their reasons for resigning when they leave in other circumstances.

Governance checklist

- ✓ Do the NEDs contribute to the strategic direction of the organisation, the performance of management, review the risk management system and both appoint and set the remuneration of the EDs?
- ✓ Are the NEDs provided with timely and sufficient information and resources to fulfil their role?
- ✓ Do the NEDs have the right attributes, skills and diversity of experience to provide sufficient and credible challenge to board debate and discussion? Do they have the intellectual capacity to test management proposals and the right influencing skills to suggest alternatives where appropriate?
- ✓ Are at least half of the board members judged to be independent, taking account of the criteria in the UK code?
- ✓ Do the NEDS have clear terms of appointment in writing, which include independence, time commitment, duties, and fees?
- ✓ Is there a comprehensive and formal induction programme on appointment tailored to the needs of the individual?
- ✓ Is there ongoing development for each NED based on the findings of the annual evaluation process?
- ✓ Do the NEDs give sufficient commitment to such development activities and acknowledge the value of engaging in them?

Summary

The role of the NED is a vital link in the chain of governance and a key part of the principle of the unitary board. In balancing the tension between monitoring and setting strategy, the NED acts as an important check and balance to the power and authority of the executive team. It is important for the board to understand the nature of the role and for the chair to develop a good working relationship between the NEDs and the EDs on the board. Clarity as to the independence of each individual NED will provide a robust framework in which to manage any potential conflicts of interest that might arise.

11

The company secretary

Introduction

> 'All directors should have access to the advice and services of the company secretary, who is responsible to the board for ensuring that board procedures are complied with.'
>
> *Financial Reporting Council (FRC), UK Corporate Governance Code (2012) (UK Code)*

This is repeated in the King IV Code, which suggests that even for those companies not required by the Companies Act 2006 (CA 2006) to employ a company secretary, it is good practice to do so.

With the spotlight firmly fixed on corporate governance issues in the banking sector in recent times, the profile of the company secretary has been increasing. The All Party Parliamentary Corporate Governance Group commissioned research into the role and their report in May 2012, *Elevating the Role of the Company Secretary*, highlighted the important role that the company secretary can play in ensuring effective corporate governance. The report recognised that there was a potential for the administrative duties laid on the company secretary to undermine the potential to be seen as a high-level adviser to the board; this was also affected by the use of the term 'secretary' in the title, with a common suggestion that an alternative of corporate governance director be used.

A recurring theme of the review was the unique position of the company secretary as the interface between the board and management. The review considered that this could be developed further, so that the company secretary could coach management to help them understand the expectations of, and value brought by, the board. Interestingly, the review went on to consider that company secretaries might make good non-executive directors (NEDs) due to their insights from observing and advising a number of boards during their career.

In 2013, ICSA: The Governance Institute worked with Henley Business School to explore how company secretaries help organisations create trust through governance, and the skills and knowledge that they need. The key findings of the study, *The Company Secretary – Building Trust through Governance*, published in November 2014:

> 'illustrate how high-performing company secretaries ultimately help build trust, which results in good governance. Many company secretaries acknowledge that their individual discretion, freedom of choice, personal morals and ethics are important in positively impacting corporate judgement. Other respondents note how effectiveness is achieved through more than fixed administrative capabilities or technical knowledge'.

The study was also clear about some of the challenges that are faced by company secretaries. These included:

- being considered 'traitors' by the executive team
- supporting chairs exhibiting poor performance
- acting as the third person in a chief executive officer (CEO)–chair relationship
- becoming the pivotal contact for insurmountable problems
- maintaining independence from other executives and board members.

The role of the company secretary is less developed within the NHS. Therefore, this chapter will outline the role within the corporate sector to give a richer and more diverse picture of the role, before looking at its development within the NHS.

The skills and knowledge required to be a company secretary

The Henley/ICSA study identified three broad areas of skills and knowledge required by a company secretary:

- technical expertise
- commercial and business acumen
- social skills and emotional intelligence.

Company secretaries need technical expertise in law, governance codes and an understanding of financial issues. They need commercial experience in decision-making, problem-solving, analytical skills, attention to detail and ability to get things done properly. Finally, but just as importantly, they need interpersonal skills and relationship management skills including judgment, diplomacy, tact and discretion – along with adaptability and patience.

Company secretaries also need to be incredibly resilient, as without the authority of a board member position they need to be able to challenge and remain independent of the individual board members while at the same time building good working relationships. Anecdotally, it was once said that the best person to take on the role is someone who has already retired or who is not dependent upon their monthly salary from the organisation, as they can then challenge the chair or CEO when required, without fear of jeopardising their career.

Before setting out specific responsibilities of the company secretary, it is important to note that the most effective company secretary:

- is regarded by the board as its trusted adviser
- can be seen as the board's chief of staff
- wins the confidence of and acts as a confidential sounding board to the chair and other directors on issues of concern.

Company secretaries provide, where appropriate, a discreet but challenging voice in relation to board deliberations and decision-making, drawing in particular on their professional experience and historical knowledge of the organisation. They also keep under review legislative, regulatory and governance developments that may impact the organisation and ensures that the board is appropriately briefed on them.

The Henley/ICSA report went on describe the attributes of a company secretary as very similar and closest to the role of the chair. A good company secretary requires the leadership qualities of humanity, humility, high intelligence, an understanding of agendas, negotiation and a tough resilience to dealing with everyday issues.

The company secretary as an officer of the company

The secretary of a public limited company must be appropriately qualified. Under section 273 of the CA 2006, the board must be satisfied that the secretary has the 'requisite knowledge and experience to discharge the functions of the secretary of the company'. In addition, the CA 2006 states they must meet one or more of the following qualifications:

- be a member of any of the following bodies: ICSA; the Institute of Chartered Accountants in England and Wales (ICAEW); the Institute of Chartered Accountants of Scotland (ICAS); the Association of Chartered Certified Accountants (ACCA); the Institute of Chartered Accountants in Ireland; the Chartered Institute of Management Accountants (CIMA); or the Chartered Institute of Public Finance and Accounting (CIPFA);
- have held the office of company secretary of a public company for at least three out of the five years immediately before their appointment as secretary;
- be a barrister, advocate or solicitor called or admitted in any part of the UK; or
- be a person who appears to the directors to be capable of carrying out the functions of company secretary, because that person holds or has held a similar position in another body or is or was a member of another body.

This contrasts significantly with the lack of any statutory qualification requirements for a company director. The appointment of a company secretary has to be notified to the registrar of companies, including confirmation of the person's consent to be appointed.

However, like the director, the company secretary is an officer of the company and as such owes fiduciary duties to the company and its shareholders. These duties include acting in good faith in the best interests of the company, avoiding conflicts of interest and not making secret profits from dealings for or on behalf of the company.

The CA 2006 imposes numerous obligations on companies regarding the conduct of their affairs. Most of these requirements are backed up by criminal sanctions so that, in the event of a breach, the company and every officer of it who is in default is liable to a fine and, in some cases, imprisonment. As an officer of the company, the company secretary can be prosecuted for these offences. For example, if the company becomes insolvent, the company secretary may also become liable under the Insolvency Act 1986, which allows an action in damages against any officer of a company for a misfeasance or breach of trust. Responsibility for ensuring compliance with these matters ultimately rests with the directors. However, by making the company secretary liable as an officer, the Act not only recognises that the directors usually rely on the company secretary in this regard, but also provides a strong indication that they should give the company secretary responsibility for (or an involvement in) these matters.

It is clear that, in view of their potential liabilities, the company secretary should not close their eyes to cases of non-compliance even if the directors have purported to make someone else responsible for those matters. At the very least, the company secretary should draw such cases to the attention of the directors and advise on the company's duties and obligations. The company secretary should be in a position to act independently and not be restricted by their reporting line within the company. The company secretary should also ensure that where certain of their responsibilities have been delegated, such tasks are properly executed, since they can still be held accountable in law for any failure by the company to comply.

The responsibilities of the company secretary

Whatever the type of organisation, company secretaries are in a unique position to fulfil an important role in governance. They are not members of the board of directors, and so do not have direct responsibility for governance and accountability to stakeholders. Without being a director, they know about what is taking place at board level in the organisation and can give advice and assistance – not only to the chair, but also to the board as a whole, board committees and individual directors.

Good governance relies on communication and the exchange of information, and the company secretary is able to help ensure that this happens. By attending board meetings and committee meetings, they should ensure that relevant information is passed from board to committee or from one committee to the board or another committee. By acting as a point of communication and contact for NEDs, the company secretary should also be able to contribute to the flows of information between NEDs and senior executive managers in the company. The company secretary should have a full understanding of governance requirements, and should be able to identify governance issues that arise and advise the board accordingly:

> 'The company secretary should be responsible for advising the board through the chair on all governance matters.' (UK Code)

The specific responsibilities of a company secretary for governance matters should be decided by the organisation. The ICSA guidance note *The Corporate Governance Role of the Company Secretary* (2013) provides a list of responsibilities relating to corporate governance divided into the following areas.

Specific responsibilities derived from the UK Code

Board composition and procedures:

- Establishing a formal schedule of matters reserved for decision by the board and a formal division of responsibilities between the chair and CEO.
- Scheduling board meetings, assisting with the preparation of agendas, providing guidance on board paper content, ensuring good and timely information flows within the board and its committees and between senior management and NEDs; recording board decisions clearly and accurately, pursuing follow-up actions and reporting on matters arising.
- Ensuring that appropriate insurance cover is arranged in respect of any potential legal action against directors.
- Ensuring board committees are constituted in compliance with the UK Code and that the committees have the appropriate balance of skills, experience, independence and knowledge of the company.
- Supporting the board and nominations committee on board succession planning and on the process for the appointment of new directors to the board.

Board information, development and relationships:

- Planning and organising director induction programmes which provide a full, formal and tailored introduction to the board and the business.
- Planning and organising director professional development programmes to refresh the directors' skills and knowledge.
- Arranging for major shareholders to be offered the opportunity to meet new directors.
- Facilitating good information flows between board members, the committees and senior management as well as fostering effective working between executives and NEDs.
- Establishing and communicating procedures for directors to take independent professional advice at the company's expense if required.

- Developing a proactive relationship with board members, providing a source of information and advice, and acting as the primary point of contact with NEDs.
- Supporting the process for the board to undertake formal annual evaluation of its own performance and that of its committees and individual directors.

Financial and business reporting:

- Having a detailed knowledge of, and advising on, the board's responsibility to present a fair, balanced and understandable assessment of the company's position and prospects in annual and interim reports plus other price-sensitive public reports and reports to regulators and that information required under statute.
- The company secretary should also ensure that the requirements of the Financial Conduct Authority (FCA)'s Listing, Prospectus and Disclosure and Transparency Rules (LPDT Rules) are met and be aware of the guidance available on these areas.

Risk management and internal control:

- Assisting the board in an annual review of the effectiveness of the company's risk management and internal control systems including financial, operational and compliance controls.

Audit committee and auditors:

- Ensuring that the audit committee is fully conversant with the UK Code principles around corporate reporting, risk management and internal control principles. This should include the relationship with the external auditors, in particular as regards audit quality, provisions of non-audit services, recommendations for appointment and renewal of auditors and putting the audit contract out to tender.
- Ensuring the implementation of and monitoring the effectiveness of the procedure for staff to raise concerns about possible improprieties in matters of financial reporting or other matters.

Remuneration:

- Ensuring that the remuneration committee is familiar with the UK Code principles and provisions on remuneration, including the provisions on the design of performance-related remuneration for EDs set out in Schedule A to the UK Code.
- Ensuring that grants of share options and other long-term incentive awards do not contravene the UK Code.
- Ensuring that the provisions in the directors' term of appointment in relation to early termination are in accordance with the UK Code.

- Ensuring that non-executive remuneration is determined in line with UK Code provisions and within the limits set by the articles of association.
- Ensuring that all new long-term incentive schemes and significant changes to existing schemes are submitted to shareholders for approval, in accordance with the Listing Rules.
- Ensuring compliance with the legal requirements in relation to directors' remuneration, including any necessary shareholder approvals, contributing to the drafting of the directors' remuneration report and ensuring its compliance with the full range of disclosure requirements.

Relationship with shareholders:

- Ensuring the board keeps in touch with shareholder opinion on a continuing basis.
- Managing relations with institutional investors on corporate governance issues and board procedures in accordance with the principles established in the UK Stewardship Code.
- Managing the convening and conduct of the annual general meeting (AGM) in line with statutory and regulatory requirements and the UK Code, and using it as an opportunity to communicate with retail investors.

Disclosure and reporting:

- Ensuring that the necessary disclosures on corporate governance and the workings of the board and its committees are included in the annual report. All companies with a premium listing of equity shares in the UK are required under the Listing Rules to report how they have applied the UK Code in the annual report and accounts.
- Ensuring that the requisite types of governance information are made available, as required (e.g. on the company's website).

The FRC *Guidance on Board Effectiveness* emphasises the role of the company secretary in supporting the board in the areas of director induction and development, as well as the delivery of high-quality information to the board and its committees. It states that the chair, directors and the company secretary who, together, set the agenda for the board's deliberations.

There is further guidance available in ICSA's *The Duties and Reporting Lines of the Company Secretary* (2013) which explains the role in more detail.

Responsibilities for statutory and regulatory compliance

Compliance with laws and regulations is a requirement of good governance. The company secretary is responsible for implementing procedures to help directors discharge their statutory duties as codified in the CA 2006, in particular their specific duties to promote the success of the company, taking account of a wide range of stakeholder interests and to avoid conflicts of interest. Guidance on these particular duties is available in the ICSA guidance note *Directors' General Duties* (2015).

The company secretary should be responsible for ensuring compliance with all the statutory and regulatory requirements relating to governance. For health service governance, these include the key pieces of NHS legislation and voluntary codes outlined in Chapter 4. For UK corporate governance, these include the requirements of the CA 2006, and the FCA's LPDT Rules.

The company secretary should also be responsible for ensuring proper disclosure of information. For example, these include quarterly disclosures to NHS Improvement (NHSI), the regulator for provider organisations in the NHS. In the case of companies, this includes the dissemination of regulatory news announcements to the stock market, such as trading statements and information about share dealings by directors.

The company secretary should also keep under review all legal and regulatory developments affecting the organisation's operations, and making sure that the directors are properly briefed about them.

In addition, in corporate governance, the Listing Rules require companies to comply with the Model Code, which sets out rules about when directors should not usually be permitted to buy or sell shares in the company. For example, directors should not deal in the company's shares during 'close periods' before an announcement of their financial results. The company secretary is responsible for making sure that directors understand the requirements of the Model Code and comply with them.

Corporate social responsibility (CSR)

The ICSA Guidelines refer to guidelines on corporate social responsibility (CSR) published by the Association of British Insurers (ABI) and National Association of Pension Funds (NAPF) on how to incorporate environmental, social and governance issues into investment decision-making. The ICSA Guidelines state that:

> '[T]he company secretary should share responsibility with relevant specialist functions for ensuring that the board is aware of current guidelines in this area and that it identifies and takes account of the significance of corporate responsibility issues in its stewardship and oversight of the company.'

The company secretary should therefore try to ensure that the interests of all important stakeholders are remembered when important business decisions are made, particularly those affecting employees.

Additional duties of the company secretary

In addition to the core duties above, the duties that the company secretary commonly undertakes in areas such as legal, accounting, financial services, personnel and HR, property, risk management, estates and facilities, pensions and insurance management must also be considered. Though these are not seen as core duties, these duties will frequently take up a substantial proportion of the company secretary's time and their importance should not be underestimated.

The professional background, previous work experience and general personal capabilities of the company secretary will generally dictate the nature and scope of these additional responsibilities, as will the nature of the company's business activities. For example, a lawyer is more likely to specialise in litigation and an accountant is more likely to manage a treasury function. A chartered secretary, being specifically trained for the role, is more likely to take on additional responsibilities such as property management, pensions and insurance matters.

The conscience of the company

In the context of business ethics and governance, the company secretary can be described as the 'conscience of the organisation'. There will often be situations where it is in the best short-term interests of an organisation to ignore best governance practice or even act in an unethical way. For example, the board of directors may want to 'window dress' the financial statements and make the performance of the organisation appear better than it really is, or an organisation may wish to bribe a government official in order to win a major contract.

The company secretary should speak out against bad governance and unethical practice, and remind the board and senior executives of the appropriate course of conduct and the principles of good governance that they should apply. As the Henley/ICSA report summarises: 'the company secretary has to have the trust of both the board and the executive while at the same time maintaining an independence to act in the "best interests of the organisation"'.

In order to act in this way, as a 'conscience' for the directors and senior executives, the company secretary must be independent-minded, and should not be under the influence of any other individual, such as the chair or CEO.

The independence of the company secretary

> 'You're not a member of [the] executive team, you're not a member of [the] board, you're the interface between board and executive, you've got to have independence.'
>
> *Co Sec 04 and 05, Private sector, Henley/ICSA Report (2014)*

The role of the company secretary in governance is such that it is essential to ensure his or her independence from undue influence and pressure from a senior board member. An ICSA guidance note, *The duties and reporting lines of the company secretary*, comments:

> 'The company secretary is a key member of the executive team appointed by the board of directors as an officer of the company with specific responsibility to the entity as a whole for its sound corporate governance and for the guidance

> of the board in its responsible and effective execution of its tasks. Boards of directors have a right to expect the company secretary to give impartial advice and to act in the best interests of the company. However, it is incumbent on boards of directors to ensure that company secretaries are in a position to do so, for example by ensuring that they are not subject to undue influence of one or more of the board of directors. If the board fails to protect the integrity of the company secretary's position, one of the most effective in-built internal controls available to the company is likely to be seriously undermined. The establishment of appropriate reporting lines for the company secretary will normally be a crucial factor in establishing that protection. It will also be important for NEDs to have access to the advice and services of the company secretary and for them to support the company secretary in his or her role.'

It is neither practical nor desirable in terms of line management for the company secretary to report on a day-to-day basis to all the directors. However, it is important not to lose sight of the ultimate line of authority when establishing these reporting lines. The company secretary is responsible to the board of directors collectively rather than to any individual director. The UK Code reinforces this by stating: 'both the appointment and removal of the company secretary should be a matter for the board as a whole'.

The ICSA *Guidance on the Appointment of the Company Secretary* (November 2014) recommends that the company secretary is responsible to the board and should be accountable to the board through the chair on all matters relating to corporate governance and their duties as an officer of the company (core duties). As the person elected by the directors to act as their leader, the chair is the person to whom the company secretary should report with respect to responsibilities which concern the whole board.

If, in addition to the core duties mentioned above, the company secretary has other executive or administrative duties, they should report to the chief executive or such other director to whom responsibility for that matter has been delegated by the board. The company secretary should not report to a director (except the chair) on any matter unless responsibility for that matter has been delegated to that director by the board.

A director who is authorised unilaterally to fix the company secretary's remuneration and benefits could gain undue influence. It is therefore recommended (particularly where the company secretary reports to the chair on all matters) that decisions on remuneration and benefits should be taken (or at least noted) by the board as a whole, or by the remuneration committee of the board on the recommendation of the chair or CEO. In this way, the company secretary is not dependent on one individual, or a small group of board members, for their role or remuneration. Where the company secretary has an additional reporting line to the chief executive or other director, the views of that director can be taken into account by the board or board remuneration committee when decisions are taken on the remuneration and benefits of the company secretary.

Similar recommended practice was included in King III (prior to King IV, which does not reference company secretaries), which stated that the board should appoint and remove the company secretary and empower the individual to enable them to fulfil their duties properly. It also recommended that the company secretary should have an 'arm's-length relationship' with the board, emphasising the requirement for independence.

Departures from these guidelines will reduce the ability of the company secretary to perform their core duties in accordance with the standards, which boards of directors should expect.

The company secretary and the in-house lawyer

Many of the governance duties of a company secretary have a legal aspect or involve compliance with regulations or a voluntary code of governance practice. It could be argued that an in-house lawyer working for the organisation could perform many of these tasks better, since corporate lawyers are specialists in company law and regulations. However, as stated previously, independence is a critical aspect of the governance role of the company secretary; to perform the task effectively, the company secretary needs to be as independent as it is possible for a full-time employee to be. The Henley report in November 2014 stated that 'there is a conflict of interest in the combined "Head of Legal (or General Counsel) and Company Secretary" role. The roles should be separate, as they can be incompatible'.

In their legal work, an in-house lawyer must at times consider the specific interests of the organisation and individual directors, and may be required to advise them on the most appropriate way of dealing with legal issues that arise. In performing this role, the lawyer will often have to 'take sides' to represent a particular interest. This would be inconsistent with the requirement to be independent when advising on governance issues.

It would therefore be inappropriate for the organisation's in-house lawyers to take on the governance that are usually given to the company secretary. An individual who has trained and qualified as a professional lawyer could be a suitable candidate to act as company secretary or take on governance responsibilities within the organisation, but only if two key conditions are applied:

- the qualified lawyer does no legal work for the organisation, and also
- the independence of the individual can be protected in the same way as for a company secretary, with the board as a whole responsible for appointing and dismissing them and deciding their remuneration.

Appointing a lawyer may increase the company secretary's responsibility and may make them responsible for some of the legal judgments, which is fundamentally not a company secretary role.

The development of company secretaries in the NHS

The *Integrated Governance Handbook* attempted to establish an equivalent role within the NHS and the authors had discussions with a number of FTSE 100 companies to look at the role of the company secretary, exploring, more importantly, whether these companies could exist without such an adviser. The evidence clearly pointed to the need for such integrated corporate support.

Foundation trusts (FTs) began to establish such a role in their corporate structures and guidance was included in the FT Code. The significance of the role is to ensure that, for the first time in the history of NHS boards, the board *per se* can confidently assure itself that at the end of the 12-month cycle it has full evidence and is fully appraised before signing off the Annual Governance Statement (AGS). The *Integrated Governance Handbook* also clarifies the point by stating that it is not necessary for the company secretary to be either an accountant or a lawyer.

The Good Governance Institute (GGI) have launched their latest research into the role – *The Role of the Company Secretary in the NHS* (July 2016). The research found wide variances in the seniority and scope of the role within the NHS and ultimately, concluded that the role of the company secretary in the NHS is under-appreciated and under-utilised, with a need for clearer guidance from the centre to improve awareness of the role and reaffirm its importance to the workings of the board.

It summarised the responsibilities of the role as follows:

1. Administrative function: The company secretary should ensure that all committees are properly serviced (including working with chairs to formulate agendas and business cycles), and should manage information flows between the board, its committees, and senior management.
2. Conscience of the organisation: The company secretary should be the interface between different elements of the board, the first point of contact for NEDs and governors, and a trusted advisor to board members, governors and senior management.
3. Governance: The company secretary should play a central role in governance – advising the board on all current governance matters: reviewing terms of reference and the annual cycle of business; managing the induction and development of board members and governors and enhancing board and committee structures (including co-ordinating effectiveness reviews).
4. Compliance: The company secretary should manage procedures to ensure compliance with any relevant regulatory and legal requirements.
5. Governors: In the case of NHS FTs, the company secretary should manage the governors, organise and attend the council of governors meetings (including the AGM) and endeavour to integrate the governors with the rest of the organisation in support of core values and goals.

It also supported the view that the company secretary should be accountable to the collective board in order to retain their position as a neutral, independent advisor. The management of the company secretary, as opposed to the accountability, is to an executive member of the board, usually the chief executive or director of corporate affairs.

The difficulty in establishing the role within the NHS has been the misapprehension that the role is purely a minute-taking and administrative role, which traditionally had been undertaken by the senior personal assistant (PA) with the organisation. The other common misapprehension has been that this is a role to be undertaken by the director of corporate affairs, which although they were often responsible for engagement with stakeholders and the annual disclosure and reporting functions, the role did not fully encompass the corporate governance and board advisory role.

There has also been some difficulty with the terminology for the role as the use of the word 'company' in the job title clashes with the public sector NHS. Accordingly, the role is sometimes referred to as board secretary, trust secretary or assistant to the board. There has also been some difficulty with establishing the board-level nature of the role through the Agenda for Change (AfC) job evaluation panels as the use of the word 'secretary' has also imbued the role with too much of an administrative flavour. As a result some posts are advertised on AfC pay bands, while others are advertised as very senior management (VSM) roles.

The creation of the lead governor role in FTs in 2011 demonstrates the limited understanding of the role of the company secretary and also possibly the senior independent director (SID). The lead governor role will be covered in more detail in Chapter 12 but, suffice to say, NHSI already had a direct line of contact with the council of governors through the company secretary and the SID for those situations where it would be inappropriate for NHSI to contact the chair, or vice versa.

As can be seen by the more extensive and wide-ranging role within the corporate sector that establishes the role as part of the executive team, there is significant scope within NHS organisations to adopt a similar board level role. A number of NHS trusts and FTs have recently established a board level role of director of governance, which has encompassed the role of company secretary. The caveat to this arrangement that the independence of the role must be maintained within a direct line of report to the chair for on all matters relating to corporate governance and their duties as an officer of the company. In addition, the appointment and removal of the company secretary should remain a matter for the board as a whole, not just the CEO as the line manager of the executive function carried out by the director of governance. The FT Code departs from this slightly by requiring the appointment and removal of the company secretary to be a joint matter for the chief executive and chair.

The other challenge for NHS organisations is to be clear where the boundaries lie between corporate governance and clinical governance. This too can create tensions for the role of the company secretary. The *Integrated Governance Handbook* helpfully set out the following points to establish the independence of the company secretary.

- The remuneration committee, as opposed to either the chair or the CEO, appoints the company secretary in order to ensure the neutrality of role.
- The company secretary is answerable to the board but will be line managed by the CEO in order to ensure personal development and accountability.
- The company secretary will also work closely with the chair, the CEO and the NEDs.
- The company secretary will be actively involved in or be a member of the executive team to ensure a full understanding of the organisation's business.
- The company secretary will not undertake executive activity in respect of having a specific role, but will be the neutral observer and adviser to the board or executive team.
- An NHS-based company secretary should have sufficient knowledge of the NHS to gain the respect of the doctors in the organisation but need not necessarily be a clinician.
- The company secretary should be appropriately qualified to carry out their role and should ideally be accredited by a professional body such as ICSA.

Whilst current legislation does not specify the need for CCGs to appoint a company secretary, good practice from the corporate sector and experience in FTs suggests that this is also a key role in the governance of an organisation. The company secretary could play a leading role in governance, supporting the chair as well as helping the governing body and committees to function effectively. They could also have a key role in ensuring good communication between the governing body, senior management and committees and helping to ensure compliance with legislation and regulations. It has been interesting to observe the profile of the company secretarial role in the new governing bodies, which have been established. In many cases, although a corporate secretary or head of corporate services seems to be in post, further research needs to be carried out to see whether these appointments are in line with the best practice set out here.

ICSA has worked alongside the NHS to produce a sample job description outlining the responsibilities of a FT secretary, set out below.

Core duties of an NHS foundation trust secretary

The following list includes both those duties, which are legal obligations as well as those which result from best practice. This is not a comprehensive list and the trust secretary will also need to refer to other pertinent legislation and regulation.

Board meetings – directors and governors:

- Facilitating the smooth operation of the FT's formal decision-making and reporting machinery.

- Organising board of directors and council of governors meetings along with those of their committees (e.g. audit, remuneration, nomination committees etc).
- Ensuring that there is proper and appropriate co-ordination of boards and committees and an effective flow of information.
- Formulating meeting agendas with the chair (and CEO) and advising management on content and organisation of memoranda or presentations for the meeting.
- Collecting, organising and distributing such information, documents or other papers for meetings.
- Ensuring that all meetings are minuted and that the minute books are maintained with certified copies of the minutes; and that action is taken on matters arising.
- Communicating board decisions to those required to implement them and ensure that actions and tasks assigned are managed appropriately and to the required timetable, reporting back as required.
- Ensuring that the board of directors and council of governors meetings and all board committees are properly constituted and provided with clear reference.
- Managing the FT HQ secretariat ensuring the effective running of the board's support system including the production of board and committee papers.

Annual members' meetings:

- Ensuring that an annual members' meeting is held in accordance with the requirements of the National Health Service Act 2006 (NHS Act 2006) and the FT's constitution.
- Preparing and issuing notices of meetings.
- Obtaining internal agreement to all documentation for circulation to members.
- Preparing directors and governors for any members' questions and helping them create briefing materials.
- Formally minuting those aspects of the meeting that are required to be recorded.

Constitution:

- Ensuring that the FT complies with its constitution, and drafting and incorporating amendments in accordance with correct procedures.
- To lead the process of non-financial compliance with the trust's constitution, including management of the public and staff membership and governance reporting requirements with NHSI.
- Review, propose and implement approved changes to the trust's constitution.

NHSI requirements:

- Establishing and monitoring procedures to ensure that the FT complies with the requirements of the NHS Act 2006 and its provider licence.

- Ensuring that the requirements of the compliance framework are fulfilled appropriately and in a timely manner.
- Submitting the annual risk assessment to NHSI.
- Ensuring quarterly submissions are accurate and timely.
- Acting as initial point of contact between the FT, NHSI and other regulators.

Statutory registers:

- Maintaining the following statutory registers and responding to appropriate requests concerning the information they contain:
  - members, including the constituency they belong to (and class, if relevant)
  - members of the council of governors
  - governors' interests
  - members of the board of directors
  - directors' interests.

Statutory returns:

- Ensuring that formal documentation is filed with appropriate bodies, as required, and to report certain changes regarding the FT:
  - annual report and accounts
  - amendments to the constitution
  - notices of removal or resignation of the auditors.

Annual report and accounts:

- Co-ordinating the preparation, publication, distribution and presentation of the annual report (including annual accounts), in consultation with the FT's internal and external advisers, and ensuring its presentation to Parliament.

Membership communications

- Communicating with the members (e.g. through circulars, newsletters); maintaining good general relations with members and other interested parties.
- In liaison with the communications team, co-ordinating communications with the FT's members.
- Establishing and monitoring the election processes for public and staff governors.
- Supporting the council of governors in reviewing and suggesting proposals for the membership development strategy.
- Ensuring that arrangements are made for the election of public and staff governors including:
  - establishing members entitlement to vote
  - obtaining the necessary declarations from candidates
  - arranging the distribution of candidates statements
  - arranging the issue of voting papers

- arranging for the returning of ballot papers and the counting of votes
- declaring the results of the elections.

Corporate governance:

- Continually reviewing developments in corporate governance.
- Facilitating the proper induction of directors and governors into their role.
- Advising and assisting the directors and governors with respect to their duties and responsibilities.
- Advising and facilitating board performance evaluations and any ongoing development matters resulting from that exercise.
- Counselling directors and governors when preparing presentations and memoranda.
- Ensuring the FT has a robust framework for compliance with corporate governance standards, the FT Code and recommended best practice.
- Maintaining and reviewing procedures for the sound governance of the FT and advising on developments in governance issues.
- Ensuring the FT has adequate insurance arrangements.
- Ensuring standing orders, including standing financial instructions, a scheme of delegation, and schedule of matters reserved for the board of directors and associated procedures are reviewed updated and properly discharged.

Non-executive director and governor development:

- Acting as a channel of communication and information for NEDs and governors.
- Advising the council of governors on an appropriate approach to reviewing board performance and facilitating an annual board evaluation for NEDs and facilitating any ongoing training highlighted.
- Management and development of the governors and their appropriate integration and interaction with the FT, including appropriate organisational development.
- Establishing arrangements for the review of effectiveness of the council of governors and developing ongoing development programme as appropriate.
- Arranging additional training and other support for directors and governors, as required.

Foundation trust seal:

- Ensuring the safe custody and proper use of any corporate seal(s).

Trust identity:

- Ensuring that all business letters, notices and other official publications of the FT show the name of the FT and any other information as required by statute.

General compliance:

- Monitoring and implementing procedures which allow for compliance with relevant regulatory and legal requirements.
- Providing advice on the impact of FT status on the terms and conditions of contracts with NHS bodies.
- Ensuring the FT implements the structures associated with the compliance and board assurance frameworks.
- Co-ordinating and submitting relevant information to other regulatory bodies, as required.
- Arranging for the FT to access a comprehensive legal service, where appropriate.
- Monitoring and reporting on compliance with the NHS Constitution.
- Ensuring any funds held in trust are used and managed appropriately.
- Reporting to the board of directors on any matters of non-compliance.

Subsidiary undertakings

- Ensuring that procedures are in place for the correct administration of any subsidiary undertakings and that correct information is given to the holding company
- Maintaining a record of the group's structure.

Acquisitions, disposals and mergers

- Participating as a key member of the FT's management team established to implement corporate acquisitions, disposals and mergers.
- Protecting the FT's interests by ensuring the effectiveness of all documentation.
- Ensuring that due diligence disclosures enable proper commercial evaluation prior to completion of a transaction.
- Ensuring that the correct authority is in place to allow timely execution of documentation.

Governance checklist

✓ Are the company secretary's role and reporting lines well defined and in line with best practice?

✓ Does the board understand and promote the role, utilising it to provide support to the board corporately and individual directors?

✓ Does the company secretary have the trust and confidence of the board and possess the necessary qualifications and personal attributes for the role?

✓ If the company secretary's role is combined with another executive role, has the board taken steps to ensure that conflicts of interest are addressed and the independence of the company secretary maintained?

✓ Does the board run efficiently, with high quality and timely information?

✓ Does the company secretary support the chair as leader of the board, supporting them with director induction, professional development, training and evaluation?
✓ Does the company secretary advise the board on all governance matters and in conjunction with the chair, periodically review the board and its committees to ensure they are fit for purpose?
✓ Does the company secretary take responsibility for the co-ordination of the annual report and accounts and provide quality input to the director's report, annual governance statement and other reports required to be published?
✓ Is the organisation's stakeholder management strategy in place and implemented by the company secretary?
✓ Does the company secretary manage and over see the provision of legal services to the organisation?

Summary

There are common issues for the role of the company secretary across both the corporate and public sectors – particularly the recognition of the value added to the organisation if the role is appropriately established at board level. Chairs and CEOs who have worked with high calibre company secretaries are perhaps the best advocates. The understanding of the role of NHS company secretaries still has some way to go in terms of profile and credibility, but the increasing recognition of the impact of poor governance on the quality and safety of healthcare is lending an impetus to the discussion and governance practitioners (regardless of job title) are increasingly be look upon to contribute at board level.

The Henley/ICSA report concluded that as every organisation is different and leadership teams are unique, there is a need to build discretionary capacity into the role of company secretary. However, it went on to make some broad recommendations for large and medium-sized organisations across all sectors.

- The company secretary role should be a direct, primary reporting line to the chair and is most effective as a standalone position.
- The secretariat needs to retain independence to rebalance power as required and demonstrate accountability.
- The profile of the company secretary role needs to be raised among other board members.
- Boards need to have more open internal dialogue, so that strategy can fully emerge and be openly understood.
- Mentoring and succession planning for company secretaries needs to improve to advance junior staff into the top roles.
- The broader ICSA-qualified professional is best placed to fulfil the needs of effective boards.

PART FOUR

Foundation trusts, clinical commissioning groups and new models of care

12 Foundation trusts

Foundation trusts and the NHS landscape

The introduction of foundation trusts (FTs) (often referred to as 'foundation hospitals') in 2006 represented a significant change in the way in which hospital services were managed and provided in England. FTs were part of the government's plan for creating a patient-led NHS. The aim of the reforms was to provide high-quality care, with devolved decision-making so that they were more responsive to the needs and wishes of patients and local communities. FTs were also at the leading edge of many of the other reforms and improvements that aim to create a patient-led NHS.

Whilst FTs are not, legally, subject to direction from the Secretary of State for Health, in recent times this has begun to shift quite significantly, with FTs coming under increasing levels of central control. The *NHS Planning Guidance* (December 2015) has made it clear that the core elements of the Health and Social Care Act 2012 (HSCA 2012) of competition and autonomy for FTs have now been set aside. Centrally it would seem that it has now been accepted that the widespread levels of deficits, which have resulted from focusing on quality and safety in the aftermath of the Francis Report and the deteriorating financial situation both within the health service and more widely across the economy could not be resolved by provider organisations alone. The planning guidance set out that creating a sustainable financing model would need all parts of the health economy (e.g. commissioners, providers (primary and secondary) and local authorities, working together). Consequently this change of policy and direction, at present being fulfilled by the Sustainability and Transformation Plan (STP) process, has led to a significant change with national bodies re-asserting control in order to get a strong grip on finances and performance. With the amalgamation of the NHS Trust Development Authority (NHS TDA) and Monitor into NHS Improvement (NHSI), both NHS trusts and FTs now have the same regulatory body, which again is another example of the diminishing distinction between FTs and NHS trusts.

It remains to be seen how the FT model will continue to operate under these changes, but for now it remains a legal form of body corporate that is set out in statute (i.e. public benefit corporation) which governance practitioners need to be aware of. As John Coutts of NHS Providers comments:

> 'The model has the advantage that all powers of the organisation rest with the board which allows proper corporate governance as practiced in the private sector rather than the watered down, often second guessed version that would seem to be finding favour at present. The strong link from boards through governors to the membership and the broader community facilitates strong local accountability promotes both vigilance in stewardship of vital public services and responsiveness to needs of those who use those services.'

The advantage of local accountability offered by the FT model is set out in the legally defined constitution FTs are obliged to adopt. It requires FTs to establish stronger connections with their local communities by encouraging people living locally to become members of the trust. The membership of each FT is therefore made up of local people (including patients and carers) and staff.

Members are able to stand as, and vote to elect, representatives to serve on the council of governors. Governors are responsible for representing the interests of the members and partner organisations in the local health economy in the running of the FT. The intention is that local communities and staff working on the front line can influence the management and provision of NHS services in their area. This allows FTs to direct their services more closely to the needs of their communities, with freedom to develop new ways of working so that hospital services more accurately reflect the needs and expectations of local people.

Governors are unpaid volunteers. Their voluntary role is entirely different to that of a director. Governors are not expected to undertake the above duties or to be ultimately responsible for the performance of the trust. The governor's role does include specific statutory duties, but the board of directors remains ultimately responsible for the trust's operations and performance.

The model envisages that FTs will be run locally, whilst remaining fully part of the NHS. They have been set up as public benefit corporations, with a primary purpose to provide NHS services to NHS patients and users according to NHS principles and standards – free care based on need and not ability to pay. This is a unique legal form based on the traditions of mutuality.

FTs are accountable to:

- their local communities through their members and governors
- their commissioners through contracts
- Parliament (each FT must lay its annual report and accounts before Parliament)
- the Care Quality Commission (CQC) (through the legal requirement to register and meet the associated standards for the quality of care provided)
- NHSI (as their regulator).

One of the potential disadvantages of the model is set out in the March 2011 memorandum to Parliament in response to HSCA 2012, where ICSA: The Governance Institute has commented as follows:

Figure 12.1: Foundation trust accountabilities

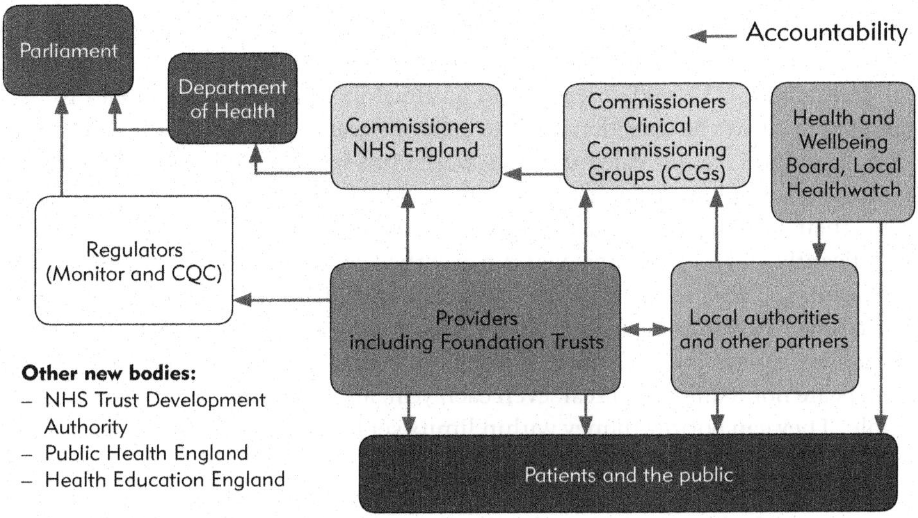

Source: NHS Providers

> 'Regardless of the freedoms proposed in the Bill (i.e. HSCA 2012), FTs still have to operate a governance framework unique within the UK economy and one that presents its own challenges and costs. The additional layer of governance inherent within the dynamic between the council of governors and the board of directors will impact on financial and non-financial resources. The dual nature of the decision-making process on specific areas of business development disadvantages FTs as their governance and accountability framework is more cumbersome operating an almost two-tier board approach.'

The two-tier governance structure of FTs referred to by ICSA does not mean the two-tier board structure common in Germany as outlined in Chapter 5. Rather, it refers to the council of governors' oversight role alongside the unitary role of the board of directors, which is unusual in British public services or in corporate models of governance. There is evidence that the structure has led to confusion and conflict, but there has also been a significant amount of development work to clarify the role and powers of the board and the council, and how they relate to one another.

Figure 12.1 outlines the FT accountabilities as set out in the legislation.

Foundation trusts, the law and the regulatory frameworks

The following paragraphs in the handbook outline the historic approach to the FT pipeline and the assessment process under the NHS TDA and Monitor. Since

1 April 2016, NHS TDA and Monitor have been brought together under the umbrella of NHSI.

FTs were established through the Health and Social Care (Community Health and Standards) Act 2003, consolidated into the National Health Service Act 2006 (NHS Act 2006). The other legislation outlined in Chapter 4 also applies to FTs, but should always be considered in the light of these two primary pieces of legislation. The 2006 Act provided that FTs would not be directed by government and that they would have greater freedom to decide, with their governors and members, their own strategy and the way services are run. Consequently, they had significantly greater freedoms over the way they conducted their finances. Unlike NHS trusts, FTs were able to build up operational surpluses, retain proceeds from asset sales, raise capital in the public and/or private sectors, and manage their organisations and their resources – free from central government control.

FTs are not required to break even each year, although they must be financially viable. They can borrow money within limits set by the regulator, retain surpluses and decide on service developments and innovations for their local community. The Prudential Borrowing Code, which determined the amount FTs could borrow, was repealed by HSCA 2012 with effect from 1 April 2013. This has, however, been significantly diminished as a consequence of the NHS *Planning Guidance* (2015) referred to above as it has established a planned health economy with centrally fixed control targets for individual parts of the NHS and where sustainability is achieved by moving money around local NHS organisations.

Becoming a foundation trust

In the government's July 2010 White Paper *Equity and Excellence: Liberating the NHS*, it was made clear that all NHS trusts would become, or become part of, a FT by 2014 and NHS trusts would be abolished. Failure to meet this deadline, or achieve a credible plan for transition, would result in the Secretary of State placing the NHS trust under a special administration regime.

In October 2012, the NHS TDA took over responsibility for the FT pipeline from the outgoing strategic health authorities (SHAs). The NHS TDA was given a fixed term of three years from 1 April 2013 to achieve this work, after which time it is expected that all trusts will have achieved FT status. This informally resets the deadline to achieve FT status to April 2016.

The Dalton review (see Chapter 2), published in December 2014, concluded that many of the 93 trusts that had not yet reached foundation status would 'not reach the required standards in their current organisational form'. It identified a number of organisational forms that had the potential to be adopted across the wider NHS: federations, joint ventures, service level chains, management contracts, integrated care organisations and multi-service chains or foundation groups. The Dalton Review recommended that the NHS TDA should publish its assessment of the capacity of each of the remaining 93 organisations' capacity to reach FT status, and the dates by which they could achieve FT status or another 'suitable organisational form'. It added that the Department of Health (DH) should hold the NHS TDA to account for 'meeting the trajectory and milestones for each of the 93 organisations'.

The introduction of the requirement for a full inspection by the Chief Inspector of Hospitals under CQC slowed the number of organisations moving through the FT assessment process significantly during 2013, as the new inspection regime was implemented. This was to ensure that quality of care, post-Francis, was truly embedded in the assessment process. A key part of the formal FT assessment process was a comprehensive inspection by CQC and aspirant trusts were required to achieve an overall rating of 'Good' or 'Outstanding' from the inspection in order to pass to the next stage of the FT assessment process. Trusts that met the CQC's requirements moved forward in the application process; this culminated in an assessment by the NHS TDA board on the organisation's readiness for FT status. If the NHS TDA board was satisfied that the trust was ready to proceed then it would offer its support, on behalf of the Secretary of State, for the organisation to move to Monitor for formal FT assessment.

The process of authorisation as an FT was designed to help equip NHS trust boards to meet future challenges more effectively by testing clinical quality, financial viability and governance arrangements, the latter being assessed by the Board Governance Assurance Framework. This framework consisted of a combination of self-assessment and independent assessment processes designed to ensure that boards were appropriately skilled and prepared to achieve FT authorisation. This has since been superseded by the Well-Led Framework (see Chapter 7 and later in this chapter).

There were some minor changes to the FT pipeline process in the NHS TDA 2015/16 Accountability Framework to reflect the implementation of the Well-Led Framework for NHS providers and the move to a system of independent financial review to replace historic due diligence. Six NHS trusts were authorised by Monitor as FTs in 2014/15 and six more in 2015/16. The residual 80 NHS trusts are now being required by NHSI to consider their futures in line with the requirements of the Sustainability and Transformation Plan (STP) process rather than the imperative to become an FT.

The provider licence

The HSCA 2012 also resulted in FTs becoming subject to the provider licence, the new licensing regime for health and adult social care, as set out in Chapter 2. This replaced the earlier system of issuing terms of authorisation. In addition to the new licence conditions for all regulated services, it included an additional four extra conditions for FTs, which are now monitored by NHSI:

- provision of information that the regulator has a duty to maintain on the register of NHS FTs;
- payment to the regulator in respect of any registration and related costs;

- an obligation to provide information requested by the advisory panel established by the regulator; and
- a condition that enables the regulator to continue its oversight of the governance of NHS FTs.

This fourth condition sets out the regulator's expectations that an FT has effective board and committee structures, reporting lines and performance and risk management systems. FTs did not need to apply for a licence, as the regulator agreed to license existing FTs from 1 April 2013.

Foundation trust Licence Condition 4 allows NHSI to use reasonable evidence, from disclosures made about NHS FTs, to determine if there is a risk of a breach of the licence condition and make a decision regarding intervention. The information NHSI will receive includes:

- a forward-looking disclosure on corporate governance (the corporate governance statement);
- a backward-looking disclosure on corporate governance (statement on compliance with the FT Code); and
- a backward-looking statement on internal control, risk and quality governance (the annual governance statement).

The regulatory framework

NHSI's Single Oversight Framework describes in detail how each FT's compliance with its licence is monitored. It sets out NHSI's approach to overseeing FTs' compliance with the governance and continuity of services requirements of their provider licence. It replaced the earlier Compliance Framework and Risk Assessment Framework from 1 October 2016. As set out in Chapter 3, NHSI is using a segmentation approach, where the level of support tailored to the needs of the provider as dictated by their segmentation. The legal basis for actions in relation to FTs remains unchanged, for example, an FT will only be in segments 3 or 4 where it has been found to be in breach or suspected breach of its licence.

The FT Code of Governance

Though the other health service governance codes and corporate governance codes set out in Chapter 4 set out best practice that FTs should consider, the primary governance code for an FT is the FT Code of Governance (FT Code). Key aspects of FT governance emphasised in the Code include:

- the unitary nature of the board of directors and the collective responsibility for all aspects of the performance of the FT, including financial performance, clinical and service quality, management and governance;
- the need for at least 50% of board members to be independent non-executives;
- a recommendation to appoint a senior independent director (SID);
- an emphasis on actively developing the effectiveness of the board of directors

through performance evaluation of the board, its committees and individual directors;

- clarification on the committee structure of the board of directors and the council of governors;
- clarification on the roles of the remuneration, audit and nomination committees, including a recommendation for a clear nominations process and for all members of the audit committee to be independent;
- a recommendation for evaluation of the board should be externally facilitated at least every three years. The evaluation now needs to be carried out against the Well-Led Framework;
- clarification of the need for high-quality information tailored to the board's duties and availability of access to external advice;
- a recommendation to appoint a secretary of the board of directors and the council of governors;
- the statutory duty of the council of governors to hold the non-executive directors (NEDs) individually and collectively to account for the performance of the board of directors;
- the role of a nominated lead governor;
- the duty of the board to take steps to ensure that governors are equipped with the skills and knowledge they need to discharge their duties appropriately;
- board meetings and the annual meeting to be open to the public, with members of the public only to be excluded for special reasons; and
- recommendations to be clear on the purpose and outcomes of the relationships of the FT with other stakeholders including members, patients, the local community, commissioners and other NHS and non-NHS bodies with an interest in the local health economy.

FTs are required to set out a complete set of disclosures in respect of the FT Code within their annual report and accounts.

Foundation trust model core constitution

Every FT has a constitution that has been approved by the regulator upon authorisation. The constitution will set out the governance arrangements for the FT. Although each FT's constitution will be unique, there are legal requirements that apply to all FTs set out in Schedule 7 to the NHS Act 2006. These requirements are set out in FT's model core constitution, on which all FT constitutions must be based. It sets out what the regulator considers 'otherwise appropriate', as set out in the publication, *Applying for NHS Foundation Trust Status: Guide for applicants*. All applicant trusts for FT authorisation were required to prepare their constitutions on the basis of this model core constitution.

The model core constitution also reflects the legislative changes implemented by the HSCA 2012. Additions or amendments to the model may be made, however, at authorisation, the regulator requires that any departure be in accordance with Schedule 7, are clearly indicated as a tracked change and are accompanied by an explanation for the intended departure from the model core constitution.

The constitution sets out that the principal purpose of the trust is the provision of goods and services for the purposes of the health service in England and that the trust does not fulfil this purpose unless, in each financial year, its total income from the provision of goods and services for the purposes of the health service in England is greater than its total income from the provision of goods and services for any other purposes. The constitution also covers:

- who may be a member
- the makeup of the council of governors and the board of directors
- how elections of governors will be carried out
- the statutory duties of the governors and directors
- the grounds and procedures for the disqualification and removal of members, governors and directors
- the requirement for open meetings of the council of governors and board of directors
- the management of conflicts of interests
- requirements for the disclosure of public documents and the statutory registers
- the management of mergers and significant transactions.

The constitution also includes a number of annexes as follows:

- the public constituency
- the staff constituency
- the patient constituency (if any)
- composition of the council of governors
- the model election rules
- additional provisions – council of governors
- standing orders – council of governors
- standing orders – board of directors
- further provisions
- annual members' meeting.

Any changes to the constitution after authorisation must have the approval of both the board and the council. Where the amendments relates to the powers or responsibilities of the governors, the constitution must also be approved by the members at member meeting. Amendments no longer need to be submitted to NHSI for approval.

Foundation trust board structure and its committees

The DH's *Guide to NHS Foundation Trusts* (2002) sets out that the governance of FTs was to be based on experience in other sectors, as the following extracts demonstrate:

> 'The new governance arrangements for NHS FTs have been modelled on cooperative societies and mutual organisations. These combine community ownership with accountability.
>
> NHS FTs will herald a new form of social ownership where health services are owned by and accountable to local people rather than central Government. In this way, much stronger connections will be established between providers of NHS services and their stakeholder communities ... In a similar way to becoming a member of a co-operative society or mutual organisation, the members of an NHS FT will become its owners, taking on responsibility for their local hospitals from national Government.'

The guidance for FTs establishes that they are to be accountable to their members. This accountability is underpinned by the aforementioned establishment of a council of governors in addition to the board of directors, as shown in Figure 12.2. As previously mentioned, this is not a two-tier board structure, and the FT Code reiterates the unitary board principle strongly. This structure is set out in the individual FT's constitution.

The HSCA 2012 set out a requirement that all FT board meetings be held in public. Boards need to decide which papers and minutes should be discussed in public session. The ability to meet in closed session is still available for confidential or commercially sensitive matters. Boards should strive to deal with as much business as possible in the public part of the meeting and should be guided by the exemptions in the Freedom of Information Act 2000 (FOIA 2000) in deciding where to draw the line with regard to information not in the public domain.

Board composition

Under the NHS Act 2006, the FT is to have a board of directors comprising both executive directors (EDs) and NEDs. The board must have a non-executive chair, [*] other NEDs; and [*] EDs ([*] denotes a number to be inserted at the trust's discretion). One of the EDs must be the chief executive officer (CEO) and they must be the accounting officer. One of the EDs must be the finance director. One of the EDs must be a registered medical practitioner or a registered dentist (within the meaning of the Dentists Act 1984). One of the EDs must be a registered nurse or a registered midwife.

The general duty of the board of directors, and of each director individually, is to act with a view to promoting the success of the corporation so as to maximise the benefits for the members of the corporation as a whole and for the public.

A FT board has the same role as that of any other unitary board: to set the strategic direction and to supervise the work of the executive to ensure that corporate objectives and performance targets are achieved. The board is directly accountable through the council of governors to trust membership and the wider community.

The authority of the board is derived from Schedule 7 to the NHS Act 2006, as amended by HSCA 2012. Schedule 7 states that the constitution must provide for

Figure 12.2: Foundation trust governance arrangements

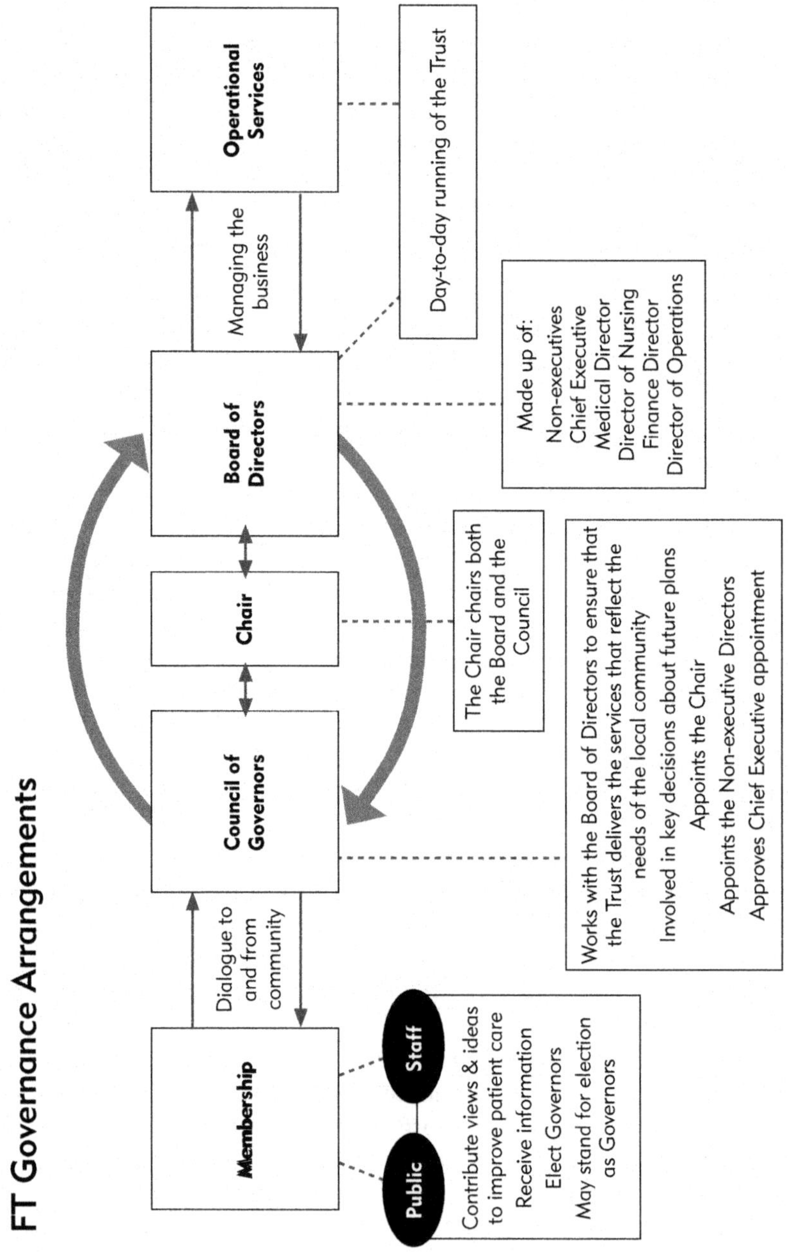

Source: NHS Providers

all the powers of the corporation (the FT) to be exercisable by the board directors on its behalf. Any of those powers may, however, be delegated to a committee of directors or to an ED.

The FT Code recommends that FTs have a schedule of matters reserved for board decision.

Board committees

Under Schedule 7, FT boards may only delegate authority to a committee of directors or to an ED. Committees that have formal memberships which include non-board members cannot have powers delegated to them by the board, and neither can individual NEDs.

FTs are required to establish an audit committee, a nomination committee and a remuneration committee. They may establish other committees as required, such as a quality assurance committee. The board must supervise the work of its committees and keep under review the need for each committee to exist. The committees are there to help the board gain assurance, not to deal with operational matters.

The FT Code allows for the establishment of separate NED and governor committees for both nomination and remuneration purposes – dealing with NED appointments and remuneration, and ED appointments and remuneration respectively. Where there is just one nomination and remuneration committee, the membership changes depending upon whether it is considering a NED or ED appointment.

The role of the nomination and remuneration committees for ED appointments/remuneration and the audit committee is in line with the details set out in Chapters 7, 10 and 17 respectively. The role of the nomination and remuneration committees for NED appointments is set out later in this chapter.

The Audit Code for Foundation Trusts (2011) gives the FT audit committee the responsibility for monitoring and ensuring the independence of the external auditors. If the external auditors provide non-audit services to the organisation, the annual report should explain how auditor independence and objectivity are safeguarded.

The auditors of an FT have a primary responsibility to the FT's council of governors. Such auditors may also be responsible to NHSI for the exercise of some functions, and will have responsibilities to the members of the FT, as well as the wider public, in the case of public interest reports.

Auditors of FTs are also required to review the organisation's compliance with the FT Code, and to obtain evidence to support the organisation's compliance statement (in the annual report and accounts) of its compliance with the code. In addition, external auditors of FTs are currently required to satisfy themselves that the quality report has been prepared according to the detailed guidance issued by NHSI.

Duties of a foundation trust director

The HSCA 2012 introduced into the NHS Act 2006 provisions on the duties of NHS FT directors. While some of these duties simply amount to a re-statement of the common law in this area, others are new and were intended to address concerns on the need for transparency in the conduct of the business of NHS FT boards. The changes are contained in section 152 of HSCA 2012 and are as follows.

- Section 152(1) lays down a general duty of the board, and of each director individually, to act with a view to promoting the success of the corporation so as to maximise the benefits for the members of the corporation as a whole and for the public.
- Section 152(2) lays down the duties of NHS FT directors to avoid conflicts of interest and duty, and not to accept benefits from third parties in connection with their directorship.
- Section 152(3) lays down the duty to declare any interest that a director may have in relation a proposed transaction with their FT and provides for exceptions to the duty.
- Section 152(4) lays down new requirements for an NHS FT board to send a copy of the agenda of its meeting to the council of governors prior to the holding the meeting to which the agenda relates, and send a copy of the minutes of its meeting to the council of governors as soon as practicable after the holding of the meeting to which those minutes relate.
- Section 15(5) lays down the duty of the board to ensure that the constitution of its NHS FT provides for board meetings to be open to members of the public. The provision permits exceptions to be provided for in an NHS FT's constitution in relation to this requirement.

In addition, directors have a role under HSCA 2012 in approving constitutional changes (alongside governors), and a duty to equip governors with the skills they need to do their job.

ICSA welcomed these new duties in its March 2011 memorandum to Parliament 'as [section 152(1) and (2)] makes explicit the step change from being a senior manager to being an ED, and brings the duties of FT directors in line with the private sector'.

The FT Code also specifies that directors on the board of directors, and governors on the council of governors, should meet the 'fit and proper' persons test described in the provider licence and required by the CQC.

Foundation trust council structure and its committees

The council of governors is made up of elected governors and appointed governors. Elected governors are those members elected by the membership to represent the staff, patient and public constituencies that make up the membership of a FT. The appointed governors are the representatives from certain key stakeholders, such as local authorities that commission services from the FT. These representatives are appointed to the council of governors to represent those stakeholder groups.

Members

Residents and patients in areas served by an FT with an interest in the wellbeing of their local hospital and health services can register as members of the organisation. Patients who do not live locally, and their carers, may also become members if provided for in the trust's constitution. Members of FTs do not receive any special treatment as NHS patients and users. They have the same access to NHS services as anyone who chooses not to become a member. The eligibility for membership of a FT is open to local residents, patients and carers and staff employed by the trust, in the terms provided in each trust's constitution. All FT members can expect to receive regular information about their local trust and be consulted on plans for future development.

The model constitution sets out that an FT membership will consist of two main groupings, namely staff and public members. In addition, a third grouping of members may be included to represent patient members. These groupings are known as constituencies. Within each constituency there may be a number of classes, which differentiate between geographical areas for public members or between staff categories for staff members. For the public constituency, the constitution must specify the area or areas; each of these areas must be an electoral area for the purposes of local government elections in England and Wales or an area consisting of two or more areas. The constitution may provide for automatic membership of the staff constituency by default.

If an FT decides to have a patient constituency then it may also divide those members into descriptions or classes of individuals. There must, however, be at least three such classes and one must comprise the carers of patients. The constitution may provide for automatic membership of the patients' constituency (if there is one) by default.

If automatic membership for the staff and/or patient constituency is within the constitution, the FT must consider how they will inform staff and/or patients that they are subject to automatic membership.

There is no limit on the number of people who can register as members, providing they meet the eligibility criteria. It is for FTs to ensure they have a representative membership and sufficient members so that they can mount credible election processes. Governance arrangements for FTs need to be reflective of local conditions and proposals that work best for them.

It is this membership body made up of local residents, patients and carers and staff employed by the trust, which are able to vote in the elections to appoint the council of governors of the FT. Each member, if nominated, can stand for election as a governor.

The FT Code sets out the key responsibilities of the council and the board in respect to members as follows.

The board should:

- Keep in touch with the opinion of members, patients and the local community in whatever ways are most practical and efficient. There must be a members' meeting at least annually.
- Ensure governors have the mechanisms in place to secure and report on feedback that will enable them to fulfil their duty to represent the interests of members and the public.
- Monitor how representative the trust's membership is and the level and effectiveness of member engagement and report on this in the annual report. This information should be used to review the trust's membership strategy, taking into account any emerging best practice from the sector.

Governors should:

- Seek the views of members and the public on material issues or changes being discussed by the trust.
- Provide information and feedback to members and the public regarding the trust, its vision, performance and material strategic proposals made by the trust board.

Elections

New model council election rules were published in August 2014. The new rules allow members to vote for FT governors using e-voting technology (internet, telephone or text), initially in tandem with paper-based voting. They also set out that the Independent Elections Arbitration Panel, rather than the regulator, would determine challenges to the conduct of FT elections.

NHS trusts that applied for FT status after 1 October 2014 had to use this version of the rules in their draft constitutions and hold their first elections in line with them. The rules make provision for both first-past-the-post and single transferable voting systems. The model election rules require candidates to declare membership of a political party, and they also set out a clear and strict timetable for the election proceedings. Section 60 of the NHS Act 2006 also requires persons standing for and voting in the elections to make a declaration setting out the particulars of their qualification to vote or stand as a member of the constituency (or class/area) for which the election is being held.

The constitution of each trust sets out a number of criteria for disqualification for standing as a governor. For example, a person cannot be an FT governor if they are bankrupt or have served a prison sentence of three months or more during the last five years. Other grounds include, in the case of an elected governor, ceasing to be a member of the constituency they represent or, in the case of an appointed governor, the sponsoring organisation withdrawing their sponsorship of them.

Governors may not stand for election if they have previously served as a governor of the trust for a total of six years (whether such years were served consecutively or not) or if they have within the preceding two years been dismissed, otherwise than by reason of redundancy or ill health, from any paid employment with a health service body. The following persons are also not eligible to stand:

- a director of the FT itself
- a governor, ED, NED, chair or CEO of another health service body or a body corporate whose business involves the provision of healthcare services, including (for the avoidance of doubt) those who have a commercial interest in the affairs of the trust.

Governors are elected for a maximum of a three-year term of office under Schedule 7 to the NHS Act 2006 but there is some debate about whether they should be allowed two or three terms of office. Some FT constitutions allow for two terms so that the six-year tenure is in line with the terms of office available to NEDs, whereas others allow for three terms of office (i.e. nine-year tenures so that they are in line with the UK Code recommendations for independence of NEDS and refreshing of the board).

The latter FTs would argue that the induction and development of governors is a costly exercise and so it is a better use of taxpayers' money. They also argue that the governors are at arm's length from the FT and therefore likely to stay independent of the FT longer. This obviously depends upon the individual governor and the time commitment they make to being a governor.

All elected governors should be submitted for re-election at regular intervals. The FT Code states:

> 'Elected governors must be subject to re-election by the members of their constituency at regular intervals not exceeding three years. The names of governors submitted for election or re-election should be accompanied by sufficient biographical details and any other relevant information to enable members to take an informed decision on their election. This should include prior performance information such as attendance records at governor meetings and other relevant events organised by the NHS FT for governors.'

Where a governor stands down mid-term, an election process for a by-election takes place meaning that the newly elected or appointed governor completes the existing term of office. The constitution will often allow for a vacancy to run until the next scheduled election process in order to minimise costs.

Council of governors

The duties of the council of governors are to hold the NEDs individually and collectively to account for the performance of the board of directors and to represent the interests of the members of the corporation as a whole and the interests of the public. The requirement for the council to hold the NEDs to account arises from the fact that they can appoint and remove the NEDs but not the EDs.

The council of governors is responsible for representing the interests of the local community in the management and stewardship of the FT, and for sharing information about key decisions with other FT members. It is not responsible for the day-to-day management of the organisation such as setting budgets, staff pay and other operational matters – the oversight of that management is a matter for the board of directors. However, the council of governors allows local residents, staff and key stakeholders to influence decisions about spending and the development of services.

The council of governors typically meets as a full council four or five times a year. The meetings are held in public and are open to all members and the general public. The council of governors is required to hold an annual members' meeting to receive the annual report and accounts and any report of the auditor. This meeting is often used to provide an overview of the year from the CEO.

FTs are allowed some local flexibility over the size and composition of their council of governors. However, every council must have the following.

Public governors

More than half of the members of the council are to be elected by members of the trust other than those who come within the staff constituency. Therefore, there must be a majority of public and patient governors.

Staff governors

At least three governors should represent staff.

Appointed governors

At least one member of the council of governors is to be appointed by one or more local authorities which covers the whole or part of an area specified in the constitution as a public constituency. If any of the trust's hospitals includes a medical or dental school provided by a university, at least one member of the council of governors is to be appointed by that university. An FT may also specify other organisations within its constitution as a partnership organisation who may also appoint a member of the council of governors.

The HSCA 2012 abolished the requirement for a primary care trust (PCT) governor and there is no requirement for a clinical commissioning group representative to be appointed as a governor. Trusts may wish to nominate a specified commissioner as an organisation for the purposes of appointing a governor.

The chair

The chair of the FT is responsible for leadership of both the board of directors and for the council of governors. The FT Code sets out that it is the chair's responsibility to ensure that the board and the council work together effectively, but that the governors also have a responsibility to make these arrangements work. The council should take the lead in inviting the CEO or other board members to their meetings, where they may raise questions about the affairs of the trust of the chair or other board members.

The lead governor

NHSI requires the council of governors appoint a lead governor who would lead the council of governors where it is not considered appropriate for the chair or another one of the NEDs to do so. These occasions are likely to be infrequent and require consultation with the SID, but one example may be a meeting discussing the appointment of the chair. The lead governor could also have a role in certain circumstances where it would not be appropriate for the chair to contact NHSI, or NHSI to contact the chair (e.g. in relation to appointment of the chair). Communication would instead take place between the lead governor and NHSI in such circumstances. Routine communication from NHSI to governors is disseminated through the FT secretary.

The main circumstances where NHSI will contact a lead governor are where the regulator has concerns as to the quality of the board leadership at an FT, which may lead to the use of its formal powers to remove the chair or NEDs. As the council of governors appoints the chair and NEDs, NHSI would want to consult with the governors as to the capacity and capability of these individuals to lead the trust, to rectify successfully any issues, and also for the governors to understand NHSI's concerns. The other situation where NHSI may wish to contact the lead governor is where it has concerns that the process for the appointment of the chair or other members of the board, or elections for governors, may not have complied with the FT's constitution, or alternatively may be inappropriate.

NHSI suggests: 'The lead governor should take steps to understand NHSI's role, the available guidance and the basis on which NHSI may take regulatory action. The lead governor will then be able to communicate more widely with other governors.'

The existence of a lead governor does not, in itself, prevent any governor from contacting NHSI directly if they feel it is necessary. The term lead governor is used to prevent confusion with the deputy. The council of governors should choose the lead governor, who should not deputise for the deputy chair of the board of directors.

The nomination committee

The council of governors has a similar committee structure to that of the board of directors to fulfil its role of appointing (or removing) the chair and other NEDs. The FT Code sets out that:

> 'The governors are responsible at a general meeting for the appointment, re-appointment and removal of the chair and the other NEDs. They should agree

with the nominations committee a clear process for the nomination of a new chair and NEDs. Once suitable candidates have been identified the nominations committee should make recommendations to the council of governors.'

The FT Code describes two scenarios for the role of the council of governors in the appointment of NEDs:

> 'In FTs there may be one or two nominations committees. If there are two committees, one will be responsible for considering nominations for EDs and the other for NEDs (including the chair) ... Where a FT has two nominations committees, the nominations committee responsible for the appointment of NEDs should consist of a majority of governors. If only one nominations committee exists, when nominations for non-executives, including the appointment of a chair or a deputy chair, are being discussed, there should be a majority of governors on the committee and also a majority governor representation on the interview panel.'

The chair or an independent NED should chair the nominations committee(s). At the discretion of the committee, a governor can chair the committee in the case of appointments of NEDs or the chair. A person may only be appointed as an NED or chair if they are a member of the public constituency (or the patient constituency, if there is one). Where the trust has a university medical or dental school, a person may be appointed as an NED if they exercise functions for that organisation.

Upon receiving a recommendation to appoint, the council of governors should consider the qualifications, skills and experience required: for the appointment of a chair; they should also consider the time commitment required. The FT Code stipulates that 'no individual, simultaneously while being a chair of an NHS FT, should be the substantive chair of another NHS FT'.

In accordance with the FT's constitution, appointment is by a majority of the governors attending the relevant meeting. Removal requires the approval of three-quarters of the members of the council of governors, not just those who attend the meeting.

Remuneration committee

The council of governors is also responsible for setting the remuneration of NEDs and the chair. The council of governors should consult external professional advisers to market-test the remuneration levels of the chair and other NEDs at least once every three years and when they intend to make a material change to the remuneration of a NED. Levels of remuneration for the chair and other NEDs should reflect the time commitment and responsibilities of their roles.

The council of governors may delegate the task of market testing to a remuneration committee consisting solely of governors. Chairing this committee would often be the responsibility of the lead governor if one has been appointed;

if not, the council of governors may appoint a chair. The committee then makes its recommendation back to the council of governors for decision.

CASE STUDY: Appointment of an FT chair

The council of governors and board of directors had worked collaboratively in the process of appointing a new chair. The nominations committee, consisting of the deputy chair and other non-executives had considered the make-up of the board and identified the key skills and experience required from the new appointment. They had made their recommendations to the governors nomination committee and these had been accepted.

The governors nomination committee, led by the deputy chair, appointed recruitment consultants to assist them with the search and consulted with executive and NEDs alike on the process for appointment.

The committee – again led by the deputy chair and supported by the company secretary, director of human resources (HR) and the recruitment advisers – conducted the interviews and offered an opportunity for the candidates to be met by members of the board, the wider council of governors and members of staff.

When it came to a decision to appoint, the committee was divided in its view as to the best candidate for the post. One candidate was very experienced but had demonstrable time constraints on their commitment to the trust, the other was less experienced but much more committed to the organisation. The committee agreed that both candidates were appointable and therefore invited the current CEO to offer her opinion as to which candidate would gain the support of the board. As a result the decision was taken to recommend the less experienced candidate to the council of governors for appointment as the new chair.

The EDs immediately rejected the decision of the committee and refused to support the proposal. The CEO demanded that the committee reconvene and reconsider its decision. The pressure on the committee was such that it subsequently decided not to appoint and to re-advertise the post. The committee complained to the regulator that the EDs had undermined their statutory duty to appoint the chair and the regulator formally reprimanded the EDs. The committee was advised to appoint an independent adviser to work with them on the new recruitment process.

The committee is required to make a report of its activities in the FT's annual report and accounts. This is in line with the reports required of FTs and NHS trusts; likewise, the report must also include the relationship between the remuneration of the highest-paid director in their organisation and the median remuneration of the organisation's workforce, in line with the Hutton Fair Pay Review.

Appointment of auditors

The council of governors should take the lead in agreeing with the audit committee the criteria for appointing, re-appointing and removing external auditors. The council of governors will need to work hard to ensure they have the skills and knowledge to choose the right external auditor and monitor their performance. However, they should be supported in this task by the audit committee, which provides information to the governors on the external auditor's performance as well as overseeing the FT's internal financial reporting and internal auditing.

As part of the appointment process, the FT is required to ensure the appointed auditors meet the criteria set out by NHSI. The auditors must agree the terms of engagement with the FT in a letter of engagement. The auditors must resign if they fail to meet, or have cause to believe that they will not be able to comply with, the criteria set out in the terms of authorisation at any point during their appointment. FTs must provide NHSI with details of their auditors on authorisation and whenever a change to the auditors is made. This information should include the name and address of the organisation. When an auditor's appointment ends, the auditor is required to write to the FT and to NHSI giving notice of resignation and setting out a statement of the circumstances or stating that there are none.

As an important independence point for FT auditors, no member of the audit team may be a member or governor of the FT (Audit Code 2011). The board of directors' audit committee should make recommendations to the council of governors about the appointment, re-appointment and removal of the external auditor, as well as the approval of the remuneration and terms of engagement of the external auditor. The council of governors may delegate the work involved to an auditor appointments committee, made up of governors and could be chaired by the chair of the audit committee, before making its recommendation to the council of governors for decision.

If the council of governors does not accept the recommendation, it should include in the annual report a statement from the audit committee explaining the recommendation and should set out reasons why the council of governors has taken a different position. When the council of governors ends an external auditor's appointment in disputed circumstances, the chair should write to NHSI informing it of the reasons behind the decision.

Approval of the appointment of the CEO

It is for the NEDs to appoint and remove the CEO; however, the appointment of a CEO does require the approval of the council of governors. The guide *Your Statutory Duties: A reference guide for NHS foundation trust governors* (first published by Monitor in October 2009; an updated version was published in August 2013 which reflects the new roles and responsibilities of governors as set out in the HSCA 2012) sets out a clear process for engaging with the council of governors to reduce the likelihood of the governors not giving their approval.

The NEDs should make sure that the governors are kept informed about the appointment process, ensuring that the governors are satisfied with the various stages of the process such as use of advertisements, the criteria for selection and how selection was carried out.

To give their approval, the council of governors needs to be confident that the appointment process has identified a candidate with sufficient experience to fulfil all essential aspects of the job description and that the process has been fair, open and transparent. The council of governors should receive a report setting out that due law and process has been followed, as well as detailing how the proposed candidate's skills and experience meet the agreed role and person specification. The primary responsibility for the appointment lies with the NEDs, and the council of governors should only withhold its approval with good cause.

If approval is withheld, the council of governors must set out their reasons to the chair and the other NEDs. The reasons for withholding approval must be justifiable, as there are likely to be financial consequences. The process, the decision and the reasons for the decision should be set out in the FT's annual report, whatever the outcome.

Duties, rights and powers of the foundation trust governor

According to ICSA's March 2011 memorandum to Parliament:

> 'Greater clarification is required to inform governors of their role, and potential liability, in those situations where a FT may be heading towards insolvency. Governors will also need to be aware of the powers they have available to prevent a course of action by directors they believe to be financially threatening to the long term existence of the FT, which does not sit within the definition of a "significant transaction".'

The statutory duties of FT governors are set out in the NHS Act 2006 and HSCA 2012. They are further expanded in the guidance *Your Statutory Duties: A Reference Guide for NHS Foundation Trust Governors*. It should be recognised that these publications set out the baseline in terms of duties, rights and powers; how these are fulfilled in practical terms is open to a great deal of local interpretation. There is also a great deal of helpful guidance on best practice set out in the Foundation Trust Network (FTN) and DAC Beachcroft publication *The Foundations of Good Governance – A Compendium of Good Practice* (2015). The following sections set out the statutory duties of governors, which are essential as an introduction to the role of the council of governors.

The NHS Act 2006 set out statutory duties of FT governors as:

- appoint and, if appropriate, remove the chair and NEDs
- decide the remuneration and other allowances of the chair and NEDs
- approve the appointment of the CEO

- appoint and, if appropriate, remove the trust's auditor
- receive the annual accounts, auditor report and annual report.

The HSCA 2012 sets out the general duty of the council of governors to hold the NEDs, individually and collectively, to account for the performance of the board of directors. It also has the general duty to represent the interests of the members of the trust as a whole and the interests of the public. HSCA 2012 also gave the council additional rights and powers to:

- require one or more of the directors to attend a governors' meeting for the purpose of obtaining information about the trust's performance of its functions or the directors' performance of their duties (and for deciding whether to propose a vote on the trust's or directors' performance);
- approve 'significant transactions' (i.e. at least half of the governors voting agree with the transaction). The trust may choose to include a description of 'significant transactions' in the trust's constitution;
- approve an application by the trust to enter into a merger, acquisition, separation or dissolution. In this case, approval means at least half of all governors agree with the application;
- to decide whether the trust's private patient work would significantly interfere with the trust's principal purpose (i.e. the provision of goods and services for the health service in England or the performance of its other functions);
- approve any proposed increases in private patient income of 5% or more in any financial year. Approval means at least half of the governors voting agree with the increase; and
- approve any amendments to the trust's constitution. Approval means at least half of the governors voting agree with the amendments.

In addition, HSCA 2012 created the following additional responsibilities.

- Before each board meeting, the board of directors must send a copy of the agenda to the governors. After the meeting, the board of directors must send a copy of the minutes to the governors. The trust must take steps to ensure that governors have the skills and knowledge they require to undertake their role.
- The regulator gains the power to establish a panel of persons to which a governor can refer questions as to whether the trust has failed or is failing to act in accordance with its constitution. The council must first approve the referral. Approval means at least half of the governors voting agree with the referral.
- The trust must hold annual members' meetings. At least one of the directors must present the trust's annual report and accounts to the members at this meeting.
- Where there has been an amendment to the constitution which relates to the powers, duties or roles of the council, at least one governor must attend the next annual members' meeting and present the amendment to the members.

Members have the right to vote on and veto these types of constitutional amendments.

The implications of these changes will require additional training and development for governors in their new role and a much more effective working relationship between the board of directors and council of governors. Care will also be required in the definition of 'significant transactions', otherwise FTs will find they regularly have to seek governor approval on more minor or less significant proposals. Judgment will have to be exercised where a number of minor transactions could in fact warrant the attention of the council of governors as collectively they represent a 'significant transaction'.

According to the FT Code:

'[G]overnors should use their voting rights to hold the NEDs individually and collectively to account and act in the best interest of patients, members and the public. If the council of governors does withhold consent for a major decision, it must justify its reasons to the chair and the other NEDs, bearing in mind that its decision is likely to have a range of consequences for the NHS FT. The council of governors should take care to ensure that reasons are considered, factual and within the spirit of the Nolan principles.'

NHS Providers has a developed a national governor training programme called GovernWell to support FTs in their statutory obligation to ensure that governors have the skills and knowledge they require to carry out their role.

Codes of conduct

The Stewardship Standard for Governors of NHS FTs was developed during 2012 amongst governance practitioners, as part of the North West Company Secretary Network hosted by Hill Dickinson. The standard is not copyrighted and is in free circulation.

This voluntary Stewardship Standard sets out good practice on engagement with FTs and provides an opportunity for the high-quality dialogue needed between councils and boards to underpin good governance. The standard describes actions that councils can take to ensure that they fulfil their statutory duties. For example, at least once every three years the council could seek independent assurance to satisfy themselves, to the extent possible, that the FT board is effective and that NEDs provide adequate oversight of the FT. This is in line with the requirements of the Well-Led Framework, which is set out in more detail later. It also suggests that governors could use a wide range of activities to listen to the views of their local communities and reflect them back to the FT, ensuring these views are considered by the board in the development of the FT's annual plan. It makes it clear that the principal relationships between governors and the board are via the chair and other NEDs, in relation to the board being held to account. Governors will depend upon the CEO and other EDs for information updates on a regular basis.

Appropriate application of the Stewardship Standard should assist governors to avoid taking on a role in which the council directs management, and therefore it ensures that governors do not unintentionally take on the role of shadow directors.

There are also several other locally determined codes of conduct and published guidance. For example, there is a sample code of conduct in the aforementioned FTN/Beachcroft publication *The Foundations of Good Governance – A Compendium of Good Practice* (2015).

Liabilities of the council

NHSI has recognised that governors may be concerned about the level of liability they are taking on, particularly when it exercises powers in relation to significant transactions. Governors may be concerned that they will be held responsible if a transaction damages the trust, financially or otherwise.

Though the NHS Act 2006, as amended, does not make explicit reference to governors' liability in this regard, the regulator has made it clear in its guidance on transactions that the governors' duty to 'hold the NEDs, individually and collectively to account for the performance of the board of directors' does not mean that governors are responsible for the decision itself, or the operational detail behind it. Responsibility for a decision remains with the board of directors, acting on behalf of the FT. FTs are not required to provide an indemnity for governors, or insurance to cover their service on the council of governors.

Maintaining an effective foundation trust board

The UK Corporate Governance Code states that the evaluation of the board of FTSE companies should be 'externally facilitated' at least every three years; in other words, the company should use specialist external consultants at least once every three years, and where the company uses external consultants, the company should make a statement of whether the consultants have any other connection with the company.

This is echoed in the FT Code and has been formalised in the Well-Led Framework issued originally by Monitor. NHSI's *Developmental reviews of leadership and governance using the well-led framework: guidance for NHS trusts and NHS foundation trusts* (June 2017) has taken this requirement further and requires reviews every three to five years (see Chapter 7). The framework is applicable to all provider trusts including FTs.

Though the framework does not directly require the engagement of the council of governors, some aspects of the review recognise that clear working arrangements between the council and the board are essential, particularly as there is a requirement for internal and external stakeholder engagement. FT boards may wish to involve their council of governors in designing the review process, and they could have sight of the findings as part of their assurance on board performance.

The chair of the board and the council

Under Schedule 7 to the NHS Act 2006, the chair is responsible for leadership of both the board of directors and the council of governors. The governors are also given a responsibility under the FT Code to make the arrangements between the board and the council work. The council should take the lead in inviting the CEO to their meetings and inviting attendance by other EDs as appropriate. In these meetings, other members of the council of governors may raise questions of the chair or the deputy chair, or any other relevant director present at the meeting about the affairs of the FT.

Though the council has a statutory duty to appoint the chair and NEDs, they also have a duty to hold the NEDs (including the chair) to account for the performance of the board. This means that there can be a blurring of the role of the chair, who would normally be responsible for appraising and managing the NEDs. Indeed, the appraisal and line management of NEDs has previously been the responsibility of the chair, and this presents a potential conflict for the chair in their dual role of chair of both bodies. The council is supported in this role by their power to require directors to attend a meeting to obtain information about their organisation's performance and that of its directors. FT chairs and governors will have to consider how they work together to hold the NEDs to account. There is also a clear role for the SID in supporting the council in holding the chair to account.

Under the existing powers they could, if they were dissatisfied with performance, remove the chair or the NEDs. This, however, must be handled sensitively and in accordance with the law. The council should in the first instance liaise informally with NHSI over its concerns after exhausting all informal and internal mechanisms, before moving to a formal dismissal proposal at a council meeting. The council will require the support of the lead governor, SID and company secretary in these circumstances.

The foundation trust company secretary

Most of the conversations around the role of the company secretary (see Chapter 11) are applicable to the FT company secretary. However, there are some specific aspects of the company secretary role that are critical for the FT model.

In the FT Code, NHSI recommends the 'appointment of a secretary to the board of directors and the board of governors' and states that 'a FT secretary has a significant role to play in the administration of corporate governance'. Ham and Hunt's 2008 report, *Membership Governance in NHS Foundation Trusts: A review for the Department of Health,* also argues that 'the company secretary has a key role in governance [for the FT]'.

Specific FT duties include establishing and monitoring procedures to ensure that the trust complies with:

- the requirements of the NHS Act 2006
- its licence conditions
- its constitution
- its standing orders.

Duties also include acting as the initial point of contact between the board of directors, the council of governors and the regulator as set out above. The role also involves supporting the chair in managing the potential conflicts and tensions created by the duality of their role. FT secretaries provide administrative and governance resources for the effective operation of both the board and the council, including any council committees or working groups.

The role also quite often includes ensuring that arrangements are in place for the board and council to communicate effectively with members through a variety of means, and supporting the governors in communicating and engaging with members. The other distinction for the company secretary role is in overseeing the effective arrangements for the election of public, patient and staff governors including by-elections, as required.

The FT Code requires that the appointment and removal of the FT secretary is a joint matter for the CEO and chair.

Foundation trust reporting requirements

FTs are required to follow NHSI's annual planning and reporting cycle. This is based upon the regulator's approach to overseeing an FT's compliance, particularly the provider licence's governance and continuity of services requirements. This approach is now set out in the Single Oversight Framework, which is applicable to both FTs and NHS trusts alike. The full details are set out in Chapter 3. However, it is important to factor in to planning timetables that under the FT Code, governors can 'expect to be consulted on the development of forward plans for the trust and any significant changes to the delivery of the trust's business plan'. The role of the governors is to ensure that the interests of the FT's members are considered when establishing the strategic direction for the FT.

Other reporting requirements include the annual report and accounts and the quality account. FTs must submit its annual report and accounts to NHSI and lay them before Parliament. They cannot be presented to the FT annual members' meeting until they have been laid before parliament. There is more detail on these requirements in Chapter 16.

Foundation trusts and significant transactions

An increasing number of FTs may plan transactions (including mergers, acquisitions, significant investments, joint ventures and divestments) as they seek to reorganise or respond to changes required within their STP.

'[W]hile integration remains the current "buzzword", it need not necessarily imply organisational integration through a transaction such as a merger or acquisition. Improved outcomes may equally be achieved through improved collaboration arrangements between partners. These arrangements may take the form of joint ventures, networks, chains or partnerships. In legal terms these arrangements can be set up either contractually through partners entering into one, a series of contracts with each other or through the creation of new corporate vehicles for service delivery which are jointly owned by the partners.'

New Care Models – Governance between organisations (Hempsons and NHS Providers)

NHSI issued guidance in August 2015 (*Guidance: Transactions involving new care models*) setting out what would constitute a significant transaction as far as new model of care might be concerned. It defined three particular aspects of new models of care that make them inherently risky and therefore subject to scrutiny by the regulator:

- New and innovative delivery models (e.g. creative solutions to deliver care may involve a number of NHS organisations and local authorities with varying cultures coming together to deliver integrated patient care).
- Unusual or unfamiliar legal structures (e.g. NHS parties may wish to utilise novel legal structures including setting up a new legal entity or jointly entering into an arrangement to deliver a new service).
- Outside core competencies/normal areas of business. As new models may make greater use of clinical networks across nearby sites, involve joint ventures between NHS organisations (e.g. to take on social services) or the delivery of specialist single services across a number of different providers, some organisations may begin to deliver services that are outside their historic competencies or normal course of business.

Consequently, NHSI would want to understand the issues including risk sharing arrangements (financial, clinical and demand management risks), potential exit provisions and associated costs and changes to workforce structures or terms and conditions. Having understood these aspects in more detail, NHSI would then determine whether there were any major risk factors associated with the transaction. NHSI would then consider whether it met the requirements to be classified as a significant transaction (defined and set out later in this section).

FTs contemplating a relevant transaction are required to engage with NHSI at an early stage of these discussions. The Competition and Markets Authority (CMA) reviews certain transactions involving one or more FTs (including mergers between an FT and an NHS trust) to determine whether the transaction is likely to have adverse effects on patients by reducing competition between providers. FTs can also approach the CMA for informal advice on whether the transaction is within its jurisdiction (seeking informal advice from the CMA will not automatically trigger a review of the transaction). To be reviewable, a transaction must meet certain thresholds. Broadly, these are:

- if the UK turnover of the acquired organisation exceeds £70 million; or
- if the merged organisation will supply or acquire at least 25% of particular goods or services in a substantial part of the UK and the merger increases that share.

For NHSI, a relevant transaction is one that meets one or more of the following categories:

- a transaction that could be reviewed by the CMA (under the Enterprise Act 2002) as set out above;
- a transaction that should be reported under the threshold set out for significant and/or material transactions. This includes most mergers or acquisitions as well as larger capital investment projects and property transactions, private finance initiative (PFI)-funded projects and potentially some major service contracts. Potential transactions should be reported if the ratio of the gross assets, income or consideration attributable to the transaction exceeds 10% of the FT's gross assets, income or total capital respectively. These will be classified as either 'material' or 'significant' according to the criteria; and/or
- a statutory transaction. These are defined in sections 56–57A of the NHS Act 2006 (as amended by the HSCA 2012). In essence, they are mergers or acquisitions involving one or more FTs, separations and dissolutions of FTs.

The March 2015 guidance *Supporting NHS Providers: Guidance on Transactions for NHS Foundation Trusts* makes it clear that FTs must satisfy NHSI's requirements before entering into any legally binding commitments related to transactions; these are summarised below.

- For material transactions, NHSI requires a board certification to be submitted to and agreed.
- For significant transactions, NHSI requires the opportunity to do a detailed review which will result in a transaction risk rating.
- For statutory transactions, in order to grant the formal application NHSI must be satisfied that the FT has undertaken the necessary steps to prepare for the transaction, including approval by the council of governors.

An FT can decide for itself what constitutes a 'significant transaction' and may choose to define this in its constitution. Alternatively, if the governors agree, FTs may choose not to give a definition, but this would need to be stated in the constitution. Examples of a definition include any proposed contract valued over a certain monetary threshold or over a certain percentage of the trust's annual turnover, or alternatively using non-monetary terms. If an FT defines some types of transaction as 'significant' in the terms of their constitution, then the FT will need the consent of more than half of the council of governors to proceed with the transaction. However, the consent of more than half of the governors will always be required for any merger, acquisition or separation of the FT. Unlike 'significant transactions', this is not an optional requirement and this means that, in practice, responsibility for signing off any merger or acquisition moves jointly to the directors and governors.

Where an FT is seeking to merge with or acquire an NHS trust, NHSI will normally have a role as vendor. In this instance, NHSI's responsibilities include:

- confirming to the Secretary of State that assurances are in place for various aspects of the transaction (including quality, sustainability and taxpayers' value for money (VFM));
- working with the NHS trust to ensure it has the necessary support to navigate the transaction processes;
- maintaining quality, operational and financial performance, board focus and risk management.

FT directors and governors must agree on a process for the approval of transactions by governors. Such a process might specify:

- the content and timing of information to be provided to governors
- at what point in the process governors will be asked to approve the transaction(s)
- how the views of members will be sought and stakeholders kept informed.

Responsibilities of directors and governors in transactions are shown in Table 12.1.

Governors should be provided with as much information as reasonably possible for them to be able to make an informed judgment. To ensure the governors have sufficient information, and are assured that the board has been through a thorough and comprehensive process before voting on the transaction, the governors' formal vote should take place after the finalisation of due diligence reports and soon after the board's approval.

This places the governors' vote shortly before completion in the process, after the full business case stage. The vote should, however, take place before the trust's formal application to NHSI (required for statutory transactions), since governor approval must be obtained before NHSI can grant the application.

Where a new organisation is formed as the result of a merger, the timings of making appointments to the new board of that organisation needs to be carefully considered, particularly where governors need to be elected in order for such appointments to be made. Transitional arrangements are likely to be required in FT constitutions to transition the various constituencies and ensure they are reflective of the patients served by the enlarged organisation.

Once the governors have approved a transaction and the chair has confirmed that it is not confidential, the council of governors should communicate the result to the FT members and the public. Governors are likely to need the FT's help to do so, for example, through its website or at an advertised drop-in session with the governors. The communication method should be agreed locally.

Table 12.1: Responsibilities of directors and governors in transactions

Executive directors	Non-executive directors	Governors
Executive directors should make proposals for the future of the organisation. They should work with governors by providing them with sufficient information on a proposed transaction for the purposes of considering their required approval. They should explain to governors why they believe the transaction is necessary and provide evidence to support their view.	NEDs should challenge the executives to justify their recommendations, deal with the risks involved and seek assurance that the executive directors' decisions are the right ones.	The council of governors must approve any statutory or significant transactions. Governors are responsible for satisfying themselves that the board of directors (that is, executive and NEDs collectively) has been thorough and comprehensive in reaching its proposal (that is, has undertaken proper due diligence) and that it has obtained and considered the interests of trust members and the public as part of the decision-making process. Provided appropriate assurance is obtained, governors should not unreasonably withhold their consent for a proposal to go ahead.

The material set out here around significant transactions will become increasingly important as STPs progress with their plans as it should be reasonably clear that STPs will involve some quite significant change for FTs and that their governors will need to be consulted. Substantial and open engagement with the council will be necessary to enable it to fulfil its statutory role of holding to account and representing members and the wider public. Such engagement will of course form part of a much wider public consultation process, but if that consultation is to be meaningful it must allow for the possibility of plans being changed by that consultation process. One of the very valid criticisms of many STPs has been limited engagement and consultation. FT boards would be wise to include the involvement of their council of governors sooner rather than later.

The foundation trust governance challenge

Despite the diminishing scope and freedom of FTs, nevertheless the governance structure is still the statutory form required for public benefit corporation and it would seem there is little political appetite at present to unpick the current structure. Understanding the challenges and tensions created by the governance structure of an FT will assist governance practitioners as they navigate STPs and the new models of care.

Balancing the tension in the foundation trust board's general duty

The HSCA 2012 says: 'The general duty of the board of directors, and of each director individually, is to act with a view to promoting the success of the corporation so as to maximise the benefits for the members of the corporation as a whole and for the public.' This has been taken by some to mean that FTs cannot engage in the collaborative processes under the STP umbrella since this might require the FT board to put the broader interest of patients and public in direct opposition to promoting the success of the corporation in the short term. However, it can also be argued that the long-term success of the STP will maximise benefits for patients and the public and this requires the board to take a broader approach.

Capacity and capability of governors

The HSCA 2012 significantly extended the role of the council of governors. This raises a number of questions around their capacity and capability; many governors are likely to require significant training to understand and be able to discharge their duties. The increased responsibilities may also reduce or limit the number of people who are willing to fill the role.

ICSA's March 2011 memorandum to Parliament states:

> 'Significant resources will have to be made available to governors in order to hold the board of directors to account and understand the competitive market when asked to vote on significant transactions. The requirements on governors are going to be onerous, and councils of governors will require at least some, if not all, of their number to have the financial and commercial skills to evaluate FT proposals in relation to mergers, acquisitions and other significant transactions ... There is also concern as to how governors can reconcile their role as representatives of the membership and play a significant part in the strategic decision making process.'

This challenge has become increasingly an issue as discussions progress on STPs, vanguards, new models of care etc. FTs can seize the opportunities for local accountability and community engagement that an active and functional council of governors can offer, however, it does take considerable resources (in terms of management time and capacity) to support and develop the council in this manner, which may not be prioritised by FT boards in the current financial context.

Independent panel

The HSCA 2012 established an independent panel to give 'authoritative' advice to governors in response to concerns about constitutional and governance issues.

The panel cannot answer operational questions or act as an independent arbitrator between the council of governors and board of directors. It recommends that governors should always seek to resolve questions internally with the trust chair and other NEDs before contacting the panel. The panel will only share information with the regulators if it believes a trust is at significant risk of breaching regulatory standards (those of NHSI or the CQC). In such cases the referring governors would also be asked to contact regulators directly in the first instance. The panel has also taken on the additional role of determining foundation trust election challenges, replacing the regulator who had previously performed this task. The panel is known as 'The Independent Elections Arbitration Panel' when performing this role and it is separate from the formal role of the panel as described above. FT members and candidates are able to make an application to challenge an election if the foundation trust has adopted the model election rules. To limit referrals to material areas of concern, referral of a matter to the panel requires the approval of more than half of the governors' council. This may mean that the FT will need to provide more ongoing support and advice to its council of governors.

Training and support for governors

The NHS Leadership Academy, working in partnership with the NHS Providers, commissioned the GovernWell programme as a one-stop national resource for FTs to develop their governors' knowledge and skills. In September 2014, the Foundation Trust Governors Association (FTGA) merged with NHS Providers in order to deliver a comprehensive governance support service for members. The merged organisation aims to support increased engagement with governors (as recommended by the Francis Report) through targeted support including development days, networking opportunities, enhanced policy support and high-quality member communications. This support will complement GovernWell, the national training programme for FT governors.

Who owns the foundation trust?

Ultimately, health service governance is concerned with the practices and procedures to ensure that the individual parts of the NHS are run in such a way that they achieve their objectives, as well as being in line with public sector values such as VFM and providing universal and free healthcare benefits to all those in need. This provides an interesting contrast to the objectives of a company in the private sector, where the aim is to maximise the wealth of its owners (the shareholders) subject to various guidelines and constraints and with regard to other groups or individuals with an interest in what the company does.

The question for FTs relates to ownership, and therefore who sets the objectives for the organisation. Who owns the NHS organisation and the healthcare services it provides? The governance structure of FTs has attempted to articulate the answer to this question: the FT is accountable to its members and therefore should be governed according to their interests.

The changes proposed by the HSCA 2012 reinforce this view by further empowering governors (the representatives of the members). This only emphasises the largest health service governance issue for FTs – how to establish an effective relationship between the members and their elected representatives.

It is not appropriate to liken the members of an FT to the shareholders of a listed company, as this does not reflect the complexity and breadth of the diversity of interests that are represented by FT members (although there are limited grounds for viewing the governors as proxy shareholders). In other words, the members authorise governors to speak and act for them in respect of the business of the FT. The challenge for FTs has been how to ensure that governors are aware of, and informed by, the healthcare concerns of their respective constituencies and the members they represent.

In addition, there are a considerable number of other arrangements that already exist to provide patient and public involvement and scrutiny of NHS decision-making, such as Healthwatch and local government overview and scrutiny committees. How do these work alongside the membership and council of governors?

Other governance issues faced by foundation trusts

- **Accountability:** governors must be accountable to their constituencies. If a governor is not representing the interests of the members who elected them, then there must be clear procedures about how such a governor might be removed. The constitution currently sets out grounds for disqualification, but these do not include failure to act in the interests of the members.
- **The dual role of the chair:** chairing both the board of directors and the council of governors will expose the chair to ongoing conflicts of interest. With the increasing power of the council of governors, the chair's role will be crucial and it will require high levels of interpersonal and listening skills.
- **The role of the company secretary:** a fundamental support for the chair in this role is the company secretary or FT secretary, who will require 'a sophisticated understanding of the political dynamics at play within the governance structure'. Equally, the secretary will be the senior manager to whom the governors and members relate. They will be a useful player in helping to manage the relationships between stakeholders, and act as an early warning for the chair when issues arise.

NHS Providers

NHS Providers plays a key role in supporting FTs in facing these challenges, as well as representing the views and common interests of FTs and those aspiring to FT status. It has established a track record as the national voice for the FT movement. It has an extensive programme of influencing, networking and learning events for members with a variety of member benefits and opportunities to get involved in their work.

Originally established as the Foundation Trust Network, NHS Providers has over 200 NHS organisations in membership – including nearly all of the authorised FTs, most of the NHS trusts, mental health and ambulance trusts and, more recently, community services providers. It is led by an elected board of trustees who are chairs and CEO of the member organisations and is an incorporated charity. Membership of the NHS Providers is open to all NHS Provider organisations, including FTs.

Governance checklist

- ✓ Is the board aware of how the FT's compliance with its licence is assessed by NHSI? In particular, does it understand the requirements of FT licence Condition 4?
- ✓ Does the board review the requirements of the FT Code to ensure it is compliant?
- ✓ Has the FT's constitution been properly approved by the board and council (and members if required)?
- ✓ Are the board and council confident that the terms of the constitution are in line with HSCA 2012 and that they are followed? How would they become aware of a breach of the constitution?
- ✓ Are all FT board meetings held in public?
- ✓ Are the statutory board and council committees properly constituted?
- ✓ Are the directors aware of their duties under HSCA 2012?
- ✓ How does the board keep in touch with members, patients and the local community?
- ✓ How do governors secure and report back on feedback that will enable them to fulfil their duty to represent the interests of members and the public?
- ✓ How representative is the trust's membership? Is the representation and effectiveness of member engagement report in the annual report?
- ✓ Have all governors been elected in accordance with the model election rules?
- ✓ Are the governors actively involved in developing the recruitment and appointment process for new NEDs?
- ✓ Are the governors aware of the extent of their authority and powers and the purposes for which they have been granted? Is there an induction and development programme for governors in place?
- ✓ When is the Well-Led Developmental Review scheduled?
- ✓ Does the board and council business programme allow for the FT reporting requirements to be considered in a timely manner?
- ✓ Has the FT defined a significant transaction?

Summary

The unique governance structure of FTs warrants a complete chapter of its own in this publication as each part of the structure – the membership, the council and the board – has its own specific role to play in an FT's governance arrangements. However, the closer working together of NHSI and the CQC means that many of the regulatory requirements are now the same for FTs and NHS trusts.

The original concepts for FTs – increased autonomy, freedom from central government and greater local accountability – are still yet to be fully achieved, rather they seem to be diminishing. The creation of FTs has not solved the financial or clinical sustainability challenges that the NHS faces. While the private income cap has been lifted, the complexity and immaturity of the new commissioning structures make it hard for FTs to plan and operate strategically despite NHSI's best efforts. The new direction of collaboration brought in by the STPs seems to completely cut through the concepts of provider/commissioner split and competitive market of earlier government policy. In addition, the regulatory burden continues to grow and the response to challenges such as A&E waiting times and financial deficits results in a somewhat hands-on management approach from the Secretary of State and NHSI. Consequently, FTs still continue to look towards their regulator and the DH rather than to the local population and its representatives.

13

Governance of clinical commissioning groups

Clinical commissioning groups and the NHS landscape

The Health and Social Care Act 2012 (HSCA 2012) moved responsibility for commissioning care to clinicians by introducing new statutory bodies called clinical commissioning groups (CCGs) which replaced primary care trusts (PCTs) from April 2013.

CCGs are responsible for commissioning secondary and community care services; they have a legal duty to support quality improvement in primary care. Most of the NHS commissioning budget is now managed by the 207 CCGs. These are groups of general practices which come together in each area to enable general practitioners (GPs), working with other health professionals, to commission services for their local communities. CCGs are different entities from previous NHS arrangements, with each GP practice being a member and clinicians leading commissioning decisions. The CCG is its member practices; the members are the authority and they appoint a governing body to act on their behalf.

The services that CCGs commission include:

- maternity services
- most community health services
- mental health and learning disability services
- planned hospital care
- rehabilitative care
- urgent and emergency care (including out-of-hours and Accident & Emergency (A&E) services).

CCGs are accountable to their public and patients, to NHS England (NHSE) (via the regional team) and to their member practices. HSCA 2012 and subsequent regulations require each member of a CCG (each GP practice) to appoint an individual to act on its behalf in dealings with the CCG. The intention is that this person has to be a GP or other healthcare professional. Most CCGs then have some form of member council that comprises either all practice representatives (in smaller CCGs) or locality representatives (in larger CCGs).

All CCGs are required to have a governing body that provides the challenge and assurance that their accountabilities are being effectively met. The NHSE regional teams play a role in holding CCGs to account and providing them with developmental support. CCGs are also supported by commissioning support units (CSUs), which are intended to have a commercial (rather than managerial) relationship with their CCG customers. CSUs are now procured by CCGs via the NHSE Lead Provider Framework.

CCGs have an important relationship with the health and wellbeing boards (HWBs) that have been established in local authorities. These boards are intended as a forum for strategic co-ordination and as a means of enhancing the accountability of the health system to the local population. CCGs have a legal obligation to consider the local needs and priorities identified by these boards, as laid out in their health and wellbeing strategies.

Commissioning decisions can impact on numerous services and over wide geographical areas. CCGs need to take this into account and they should seek to work together, developing collaborative commissioning arrangements when such complex decisions are to be made. Clinical senates will exist to help commissioners make the best decisions by considering the strategic impact of proposals. In addition, in order to plan their commissioning decisions, local authorities and CCGs (coming together through HWBs) will use Cs (JSNAs), and Joint Health and Wellbeing Strategies (JHWSs) to agree local priorities for local health and care commissioning.

Since their establishment, CCGs have entered into greater levels of collaboration ranging from informal collaboration to full mergers. This has become even more pressing as the Sustainability and Transformation Plans (STPs) have begun to encourage and foster new models of care. For example, in Birmingham and Solihull, three CCGs are 'setting out a path' to merge their organisations, reducing duplication of roles and functions and looking to reshape commissioning so that it works at the STP level and supports the commissioning of new models of care and at the same time reducing costs by more than £5 million. There are other integrated approaches to commissioning that are proposed between the NHS and local government, ranging from greater alignment between commissioners (both health and social care) to full integration and single commissioning agreements.

The role of NHS England and the regional team

For 2017/18, NHSE intends to measure progress through a new CCG Improvement and Assessment Framework. This replaces both the previous CCG assurance framework and CCG performance dashboard. Its relevance reaches beyond CCGs, because it's about how local health and care systems and communities can assess their own progress. The new framework provides a greater focus on assisting improvement alongside NHSE's statutory assessment function. It aligns with NHSE's Mandate and planning guidance, with the aim of unlocking change and improvement in a number of key areas. The approach aims to reach beyond CCGs, enabling local health systems and communities to assess their own progress from ratings published online.

The framework is intended as a focal point for joint work and support between NHSE and CCGs, and was developed with input from NHS Clinical Commissioners, CCGs, patient groups and charities. It draws together the NHS Constitution, performance and finance metrics and transformational challenges and will play an important part in the delivery of the Five Year Forward View (5YFV).

The framework has four domains of better health, better care, sustainability and leadership. These are:

- **Better health:** how the CCG is contributing towards improving the health and wellbeing of its population, and bending the demand curve.
- **Better care:** focusing on care redesign, performance of constitutional standards, and outcomes, including in important clinical areas.
- **Sustainability:** how the CCG is remaining in financial balance, and is securing good value for patients and the public from the money it spends.
- **Leadership:** the quality of the CCG's leadership, the quality of its plans, how the CCG works with its partners, and the governance arrangements that the CCG has in place to ensure it acts with probity, for example in managing conflicts of interest.

The framework indicators will form the main, but not the only, source of evidence to support the joint work between NHSE and CCGs. For example, NHSE will continue to conduct the nationally commissioned 360 degree CCG stakeholder survey. NHSE is clear that a critical factor in the success of the new framework will be the quality of the relationships between its regional teams and the CCGs. It states that there is a joint responsibility to help each other transform and sustain the NHS; and that the purpose of engendering mutual assistance and taking timely action where needed, should be as valuable as the formal act of annual assessment.

- NHSE has a statutory duty to conduct an annual performance assessment of every CCG. The annual assessment will be a judgment, reached by taking into account the CCG's performance in each of the indicator areas over the full year and balanced against the qualitative assessment of the leadership of the CCG. The intention of the CCG IAF is to empower CCGs to deliver the transformation necessary to achieve the 5YFV.
- The focus is therefore on practical support, rather than assurance and monitoring. However, some CCGs operate in very challenging environments, are dealing with legacy issues, or indeed, need to address internal weaknesses. A number of initiatives are in place such as success regimes, which aim to improve whole local health economies. NHSE introduced special measures for CCGs in 2015/16. Where NHSE has very grave concerns across the breadth of what a CCG does, this regime provides a structured approach for the CCG to improve its performance or capability, and to implement an intensive support package.

Clinical commissioning groups, the law and the regulatory frameworks

The CCG's overarching duty to involve patients and the public is outlined in Chapter 4. In addition, HSCA 2012's amendments to the National Health Service Act 2006 (NHS Act 2006) imposes further duties on the establishment of CCGs (in sections 25–28). In summary, these requirements are the duty of the CCG to:

- exercise its functions effectively, efficiently and economically
- obtain appropriate advice
- promote education and training
- promote integration
- promote the NHS Constitution
- promote innovation in the provision of health services (including innovation in the arrangements made for their provision)
- promote patient choice
- promote research on matters relevant to the health service, and the use in the health service of evidence obtained from research
- reduce inequalities in respect of access and outcomes
- secure continuous improvement in the quality of services provided or in the prevention, diagnosis or treatment of illness (quality is defined as the effectiveness and safety of the services, and the quality of the experience undergone by patients).

A CCG also has a general financial duty to:

- ensure its expenditure does not exceed the aggregate of its allotments for the financial year
- ensure its use of resources does not exceed the amount specified by NHSE for the financial year
- take account of any directions issued in respect of specified types of resource used in a financial year to ensure the CCG does not exceed an amount specified by NHSE
- publish an explanation of how the CCG spent any payment in respect of quality made to it by the NHSE.

CCGs are required to have a governing body by HSCA 2012. It is not a committee of the CCG and the constitution must specify the arrangements made by the CCG for the discharge of functions by the group members or member practices.

The NHS Commissioning Board and Clinical Commissioning Group (Responsibilities and Standing Rules) Regulations 2012 set out the healthcare services that will be commissioned by NHSE and specifies the categories of people for whom CCGs will commission services. They also set out certain financial matters for the governing body, and the standing rules regulations that detail those people who are disqualified from being a chair or member of a CCG. These include:

- a Member of Parliament (MP), Member of the European Parliament (MEP) or London Assembly Member
- a member of a local authority in England, Wales, Scotland or Northern Ireland
- an employee, member, shareholder or partner of an organisation providing commissioning support
- anyone convicted in the prior five years of any UK offence; or offence outside of the UK if deemed illegal at home and convicted to a sentence of three months or more
- anyone subject to (interim) bankruptcy restrictions under insolvency legislation
- anyone dismissed from paid employment (not including redundancy) in the previous five years from any NHS organisation (including Wales, Scotland and Northern Ireland)
- a healthcare professional subject to an investigation or proceedings by a regulatory body resulting in suspension or removal from the register, prevention or conditions on practising from those not removed from the register
- someone subject to an order or undertaking from company directors' disqualification legislation
- a person removed from being a trustee by charities legislation.

Becoming a clinical commissioning group

NHSE set out the application process for becoming a CCG in the October 2012 publication *Clinical Commissioning Group Authorisation: Guide for applicants*. In order to be authorised, CCGs had to meet the following requirements:

- they must have a geographical area
- all of England must be covered without overlaps
- all designated holders of primary care contracts must be members of a CCG
- there must be a governing body, with an accountable officer and a chief finance officer
- the governing body has to have at least two lay members,* who have to take specific responsibility for audit and governance and for public and patient engagement
- the CCG has to have its constitution authorised by NHSE.

* Note: The minimum number of lay members is now recommended as three (*NHSE, Managing Conflicts of Interest: Revised Statutory Guidance for CCGs* (June 2017)).

Other NHS England guidance

The NHSE website hosts a substantial amount of guidance on governance in CCGs. Key publications include:

- Towards establishment: Creating responsive and accountable clinical commissioning groups

- Clinical commissioning group governing body members: Role outlines, attributes and skills
- The functions of CCGs
- Procedures for clinical commissioning groups to apply for constitution change, merger or dissolution
- Best Practice Resource/Practical Toolkit – for the appointment of lay members to Clinical Commissioning Groups
- Maximising the lay member role in CCGs
- Clinical commissioning group guidance on senior appointments, including accountable officer
- Integrated Support and Assurance Process (ISAP)
- CCG Annual Reporting Guidance
- Managing Conflicts of Interest: Revised Statutory Guidance for CCGs (June 2017)
- Patient and public participation in commissioning health and care: statutory guidance for CCGs and NHS England
- Involving people in their own health and care: statutory guidance for CCGs and NHS England
- The Good Governance Standard for Public Services.

Other than the minimum composition and a model constitution set out in HSCA 2012, there are no specific requirements for CCG governance. NHSE advocates adherence with the *Good Governance Standard for Public Services* as the guidance for best practice. It builds on the Nolan principles for the conduct of individuals in public life, by setting out six core principles of good governance for public service organisations as set out in Chapter 4 and illustrated in Figure 13.1.

It is important to note that the standard presupposes a form of leadership that is not based on the principle of a unitary board. This is in stark contrast to most other NHS organisations (such as foundation trusts (FTs)) for whom the unitary board is a core principle of governance. As such, CCGs are unlikely to operate in a way that is entirely consistent with the major codes of corporate governance practice for the NHS (such as the UK Corporate Governance Code, King IV, the Higgs Report and the FT Code).

Nevertheless, the Standard states that organisations should be clear about a number of areas that bear a close similarity to the recommendations in the above codes:

- the responsibilities of non-executives and the executive, and that those responsibilities are carried out (Standard 2.2);
- members of the governing body behaving in ways that uphold and exemplify effective governance (Standard 3.2); and
- engaging stakeholders and making accountability real (Standard 6).

Figure 13.1: The six core principles of the Good Governance Standard

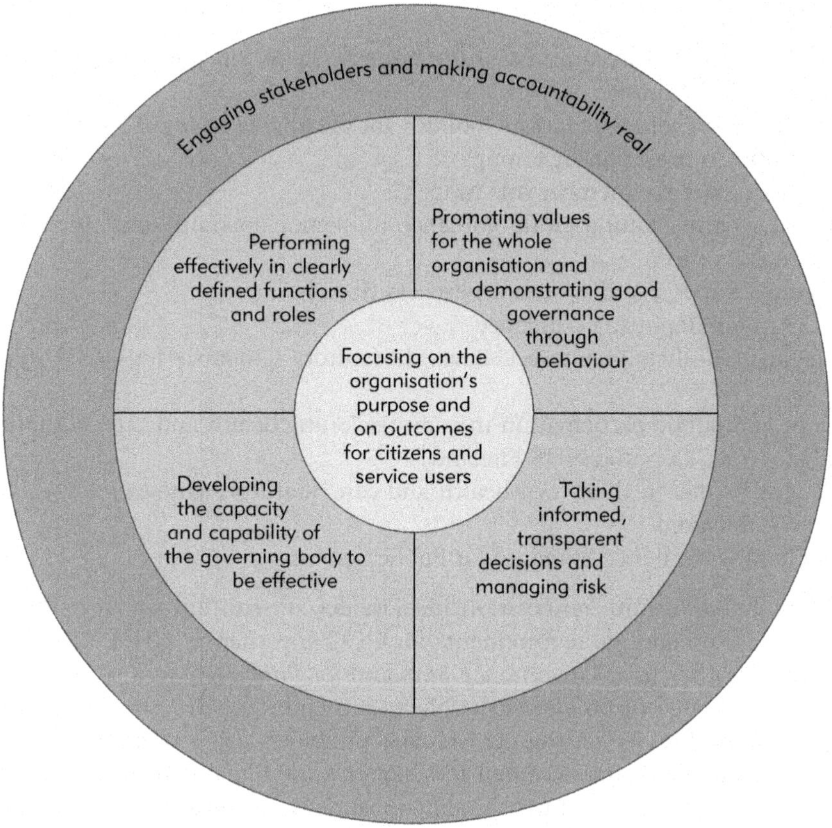

The standard also includes a useful appendix, which sets out questions for members of the public and their representatives to ask if they want to assess and challenge standards of governance.

The clinical commissioning group model constitution

CCG governance and decision-making depends on the form of a CCG's constitution. While every CCG is legally required to have a governing body, audit committee and remuneration committee, there can be some variation between each CCG in the arrangements in place for setting strategy and performing its functions.

The July 2013, the King's Fund and Nuffield Trust publication *Clinical Commissioning Groups: Supporting improvement in general practice?* revealed that:

> 'In-depth knowledge of the constitution was scarce [within CCGs], both in the governing body and the membership ... many GPs who were, nominally, signatories to the constitution expressed little knowledge of its contents.'

All CCG constitutions should contain the following information:

- the title of the CCG and its geographical area of operation;
- the purpose of the CCG and from where it derives its legal duties and powers;
- its powers – the ways in which the CCG can fulfil its duties, the activities it may or may not undertake;
- amendments and variations to the constitution requiring the permission of NHSE;
- membership criteria, list of members, voting rights and responsibilities and details of any removal procedures. It may also include the requirement for any membership rights to be exercised in the best interests of the CCG;
- functions and general duties and an outline as to how those duties and functions will be fulfilled, including any conditions attached to the CCG by NHSE; and
- governance arrangements – the principles to be followed, how the CCG will be administered and how decisions will be made.

Other details should include information about the governing body, other committees and joint working powers (see below); accountability – how the group will demonstrate and effect accountability to its local health economy; and arrangements for engaging with interested parties in commissioning and service re-configuration.

CCGs did not originally have the power to establish joint committees (as PCTs did) with other CCGs. It was recognised that this was a gap in the legislation, which was remedied in October 2014. In the interim period, CCGs established committees (known as 'committees-in-common') that could make decisions on behalf of two or more CCGs. The committee-in-common structure enabled CCGs to make joint decisions based on member and stakeholder engagement as to the implementation of service change. It is now being used to achieve a large-scale service reconfiguration within the health economy within the 5YFV (see Chapter 14). It is important to note that the power to set up a joint committee relates to the CCG and not to its governing body. Any such joint committee can only exercise functions of the CCGs (i.e. functions that have not been delegated to the CCGs' Governing Bodies or to committees or sub-committees of the CCGs).

Further provisions contained in a well-written constitution will include:

- procedures for appointing governing body and committee members
- procedures for appointing the chair
- eligibility conditions for such positions
- re-appointment, tenure, co-option procedures
- procedures for the removal of governing body and committee members

- details of how governing body, committee and member meetings will be run
- the quorum needed to transact business
- frequency of meetings
- a statement and details regarding the management of conflicts of interest
- a clause indemnifying GP member practices and governing body members.

In addition, the model NHS CCG constitution features options to include:

- the mission, values and aims of the CCG
- group committees details
- joint arrangements
- transparency arrangements
- financial policies
- standing orders
- schemes of delegation and reservation
- checklists.

Careful thought should be given as to what material is included within the constitution, as some aspects of administration and strategy are likely to change with time. Such aspects that may be subject to amendment and change and which are not central to the constitution, should not be included in the constitution – such as naming an individual in the constitution as opposed to a role. The constitution forms part of the CCG's authorisation; any changes to the document must be agreed by NHSE. Any amendments to the constitution will not become valid until that permission has been granted.

A CCG can request an amendment to the constitution twice each year. However, any amendments that will impact on the financial allocation for the group have to meet a June deadline. NHSE demands assurance from the accountable officer, on behalf of the CCG, that the constitution will continue to meet legal requirements. There is no appeal process against NHSE's decision to approve proposed changes. As soon as an amended constitution comes into effect, the CCG should make arrangements to ensure the document is available to the public.

ICSA Code of Governance for NHS clinical commissioning groups

ICSA: The Governance Institute published a governance code for CCGs in November 2013. It was developed with the support of an expert panel including NHS leaders and chaired by Lord Hunt of Wirral. There is a commitment to update the code at a future date in an effort to ensure it reflects lessons learned.

The objective of the six principles contained within the code is to:

> 'support clinicians, and those that work with them, to perform their commissioning activities and help to maintain public trust in clinicians and the NHS. [Moreover] application of the principles ... should be proportionate and appropriate for each CCG and its governing body.'

The document outlines some suggestions for how a CCG can achieve each of the six principles and poses a set of questions for consideration (see Table 13.1).

Table 13.1: ICSA Code of Governance for NHS clinical commissioning groups

Principle	Suggestions
Ensure effective decision-making processes to drive improvements in experience and quality	Member practices and the governing body need a working relationship underpinned by trust, with roles and responsibilities established. Among the suggested mechanisms are: open communication between CCG committees, the governing body and members; transparent approach to resolving any disputes; and clear guidance. The CCG should consider how involved their member practices are involved in its work and whether members understand how to challenge decisions.
Co-operation with 'interested provider parties' to enhance outcomes	This could involve: identification and management of both 'potential and real conflicts of interest'; developing relationships with both 'current and future' providers and keeping them under review; and highlighting outcome improvements in a variety of formats. The CCG also needs to consider how it gathers feedback 'from and about' providers and its processes for responding to concerns from regulators regarding local providers.
Develop strong relationships with other CCGs and regulators to support local and national health systems and contribute to wider policy debate	The CCG and governing body need to ensure clarity around 'the form, level and scope of co-operation required' with the various actors within the system. This can include: guidance for authorised individuals; provision of appropriate information to other organisations; and clear information requests. CCGs should 'maintain full records of delegated decision-making' and also keep these under regular review.
Combine collective accountability with 'drawing on the strengths and expertise' from individuals	Governing body members hold equal responsibility for the decisions taken and need to ensure that the CCG invariably complies with relevant legislation and regulation. They must also remain fully aware of relationships and responsibilities with others including patients, member practices and committees. All members should have undertaken a comprehensive induction and clear understanding of aspects such as decision-making and collective responsibilities.

Principle	Suggestions
The CCG should ensure the views of patients, carers and the public are utilised to inform commissioning and consider consequences of decisions	Among the suggested methods for delivering on this principle are: holding governing body meetings whenever appropriate; effective communication; holding consultations 'on significant changes to services commissioned and policies affecting the wider health economy'; and a system that manages complaints 'constructively, impartially and effectively'. Governing body members need to consider target audience identification, the inclusion of public and patient engagement within CCG annual reports and the publication procedure around learning from complaints.
'Robust and effective processes for decision-making' to provide foundations for 'transparency and accountability at every level'	Governing body members are tasked with ensuring their CCG has strong arrangements in place for governance, which could include: adherence to the Nolan principles; promotion of the NHS Constitution's values; and an updated register of interests. Among the areas for governing body members to consider here are: whether an annual summary of information is publicly available; the regular review of Freedom of Information activity; and feedback in relation to procurement.

Clinical commissioning group governance structures, governing bodies and committees

CCGs are clinically led membership organisations accountable to their constituent GP practices. These member practices must decide how the CCG will operate, through developing the CCG constitution within the legislative framework. They must ensure that the CCG is led and governed in an open and transparent way, which allows them to serve their patients and population effectively.

As a membership organisation, it is the CCG members that must ensure the CCG complies with the full range of regulations and legislation to ensure the group is governed appropriately. Whether it is statutory requirements or NHS guidance, CCG members are legally accountable for meeting these obligations though acting in the best interests of the organisation, patients, their carers and the wider CCG community.

Members

All GP practices are required by law to be a member of a CCG. Changes to the General Medical Services Contract Regulations in 2013 made it a contractual requirement for all GP practices to be a member of a CCG and for every GP practice to nominate a practice representative to liaise with the CCG.

The legal requirement for a GP practice to be a 'member' of a CCG means:

- that practices must nominate a practice representative to liaise with the CCG
- that practices should be able to demonstrate that they have engaged with the CCG in line with the requirements outlined in the CCG constitution and subject to the reasonableness of the CCG's requests
- that practices should abide by the contents of the CCG constitution
- that practices should work with commissioning decisions of the CCG and NHSE.

The CCG cannot expel a practice, as they need to have coherent geographical coverage – therefore there should be no provisions within the constitution that give CCGs the power to expel a practice. The HSCA 2012 does give CCGs the power to apply to NHSE to have a member practice expelled from the group in extreme circumstances. Such circumstances might include refusal to engage or participate with CCG activities, failure to demonstrate active effort to address agreed practice/clinical behaviour, failure to support local plans and/or no commitment to supporting other practices or the CCG by sharing expertise and/or delivery where capacity and resources allow.

The model constitution requires each CCG to define the role of their member practice representatives and to ensure that the arrangements made for the discharge of their functions secure the effective participation by each member of the group in exercising its functions. Practice representatives are individuals appointed by a member practice to act on its behalf in the dealings between it and the group, under regulations made under sections 89 or 94 of the NHS Act 2006 (as amended by section 28 of HSCA 2012) or directions under section 98A of the 2006 Act (as inserted by section 49 of HSCA 2012).

Each CCG may also identify a number of other GPs or primary care health professionals from member practices to support the work of the group and/or represent the group rather than represent their own individual practices. Any such role, which is not required by statute, must be set out in the constitution.

CCGs have a statutory duty to ensure the effective participation of member practices in the exercise of the CCG's functions as set out in HSCA 2012. This means that practices can challenge the CCG if they feel that it is not fulfilling its statutory duty to ensure effective member participation. For example, the constitution will include electoral procedures and how member practices can remove a CCG governing body member. The July 2013 King's Fund/Nuffield Trust research mentioned earlier recommends that GP practices should ensure that they understand how to hold their CCG to account and to get involved in the decisions of the CCG.

The model constitution establishes that the CCG is accountable for exercising the statutory functions of the group. It may grant authority to act on its behalf to:

- any of its members
- its governing body
- employees
- a committee or sub-committee of the group.

Like FTs and NHS trusts, the governing body is required by statute to have audit and remuneration committees at a minimum. The extent of each party's authority to act depends on the powers delegated to them by the CCG as expressed through its scheme of reservation and delegation (or terms of reference for committees).

The scheme of reservation and delegation sets out those decisions that are reserved for the membership as a whole and those decisions that are the responsibilities of its governing body (and its committees), the group's committees and sub-committees, individual members and employees. The CCG remains accountable for all of its functions, including those that it has delegated. The CCG's standing orders stipulate that ordinary meetings of the CCG shall be held at regular intervals at such times and places as the CCG may determine. They should provide further detail on frequency, notice and authority for calling such meetings.

Many CCGs have interpreted this as some form of 'member council' comprising either representatives from all practices (in smaller CCGs) or locality representatives (in larger CCGs). The precise responsibilities delegated to these members' councils differ, but often include approving the CCG's constitution and proposed changes to the constitution, such as:

- the powers reserved to the membership and those delegated to the governing body, committees, employees or other persons specified in the CCG's constitution
- the overarching scheme of reservation and delegation
- the membership of the CCG's governing body and committees.

Such a council may also be responsible for:

- the arrangements for members joining and leaving the CCG
- the appointment of the chair and chief officer
- ensuring publication of the annual report and accounts by the governing body.

There is no requirement for the members meetings to be held in public, but some CCG councils have voted to do so.

Details as to how practice representatives are selected should be set out in a group's standing orders and must comply with regulations. Many CCGs have local GP groups, which are often known as 'localities'. According to the King's Fund/Nuffield Trust research, these 'locality' structures have been put in place in approximately 70% of CCGs across England. The locality groups act as an engagement mechanism to pass information between practices and the governing body, as well as a means of identifying local priorities. Some localities may be given a greater degree of autonomy and play a very important role in the organisation. For example, they may be given an annual commissioning budget and allowed to keep a proportion of any underspend for reinvestment in local priorities.

The model constitution requires CCGs that wish to delegate authority to their localities (as a committee of the group) to include in their constitution details of the role of the locality and to whom they are accountable. The locality committee must account to the governing body when it undertakes work which falls within the scope of the functions of the governing body. The CCG is free to determine the scope of the responsibilities delegated to locality committees and to include in the terms of reference for each committee how it will be held to account for its work. Reference should also be made as how the locality committee will relate to the broader membership and the governing body in discharging its functions.

Elections and appointments

The model constitution does not specify exactly how the governing body, officers and committees should be elected and dismissed. Therefore, the accountability structure can vary in the actual details from CCG to CCG.

One version is where the member practices elect a representative to sit on a member council. The member council then appoints the non-officer members of the governing body, and the governing body appoints the specific officers of the CCG (the chair, accountable officer and chief financial officer (CFO)).

An alternative model sees the member practices directly select and elect or appoint their governing body members and chair. Regardless of the structure used, the governing body is always accountable to the member practices for the running of the CCG in accordance with its constitution.

Appointments are usually made in relation to the executive members, lay members and non-GP clinicians of the governing body – AO, CFO, secondary care clinician and so on. Typically, a process of open competition and advertisement is completed. This may be undertaken by the members' council or governing body dependent upon the constitution. These appointments are usually only made on a permanent basis for executive members, with fixed-term appointments for the other roles.

Elections usually take place in relation to GP members and the chair, with nominations being made by the member practices. An election will then take place if there is more than one candidate. The election may be overseen and administered by the members' council or by the local medical committee. If a CCG has localities, then votes can only be cast for one of the GPs standing in their own locality area. Depending upon the CCG's constitution, votes may be available to all GPs providing primary medical services to a registered list of patients (based on a general medical services, personal medical services or alternative provider medical services contract) and practicing within the geographical area of the CCG (one person, one vote). Alternatively, votes may be allocated to each member practice based on the population it serves.

Some CCG member councils have established members' council advisory panels, which are small panels comprising three council members and an independent HR adviser. It oversees the process of appointing members to the governing body – including the chair – by assessing prospective candidates to determine their suitability for the role, then inviting suitable candidates to stand for election. The panel then makes recommendations to the members' council on those appointments.

Governing body

The CCG is required by statute and it is not a committee. The constitution must specify the arrangements made by the CCG for the discharge of functions by its governing body. Details concerning the functions and composition of the governing body should be specified in the group's constitution.

The main functions of the governing body are described in section 14L of the NHS Act 2006 (inserted by section 25 of HSCA 2012). The governing body's principal aim is to ensure that the group has made appropriate arrangements for ensuring that it complies with its obligations to exercise its functions effectively, efficiently, economically and in line with relevant generally accepted principles of good governance.

The model constitution framework sets out that the governing body must not have less than six members, consisting of:

- the chair
- representatives of member practices
- other GPs or primary care health professionals
- a minimum of two lay members – one to lead on audit, remuneration and conflict of interest matters and one to lead on patient and public participation matters
- a registered nurse
- a secondary care specialist doctor
- the accountable officer
- the CFO
- any other individuals as required by the CCG.

CCGs may choose to have more than two lay members and other individual roles on the governing body, but this must be specified in their constitution. As with all such structures, the numerical size of the governing body needs to be considered. It should not be so large as to be unwieldy, but not so small as to lack the necessary skills and experience. As the governing body is not a committee, it cannot have terms of reference and, therefore details about its composition must be specified in the CCG's constitution. The standing orders of the CCG should also set out:

- how the group will appoint such members of the governing body (e.g. will they be elected?)

- the tenure of office
- how such a person would resign from their post
- the grounds for removal from office.

Tenure

Terms of office for all elections and appointments to the governing body are as set out in each CCG's constitution. With the exception of executive appointments, which are made on a permanent basis, there is little consistency as to the terms that are offered – some are for two or three years, while others are for five years. There is no mandated limit set on the maximum term of office. The guidance given elsewhere in this handbook may be considered but is only advisory. Even so, it is critical that CCGs consider how to find a balance between continuity of knowledge and renewal of thinking in the governing body.

Section 13 of The National Health Service (Clinical Commissioning Groups) Regulations 2012 states there is nothing to prevent the re-appointment of a chair or a deputy chair whose term of office has come to an end, or a person's appointment as either chair or deputy chair following a term of office as the other (remembering that the deputy chair must be a lay person).

The remuneration committee

The NHSE guidance *Remuneration Guidance for Chief Officers (where the senior manager also undertakes the accountable officer role) and chief finance officers* makes it clear that CCGs must have a remuneration committee drawn from the CCG's governing body, of whom one member should act as its chair.

Section 15 of The National Health Service (Clinical Commissioning Groups) Regulations 2012 stipulates that the committee chair must be appointed by the CCG for a term to be determined by the CCG. It also states that all members of the governing body other than lay persons are disqualified from being the chair.

The committee should not include full-time employees or individuals who claim a significant proportion of their income from the CCG, nor should member practices be in the majority. The committee will make recommendations to the CCG governing body as to the determination of remuneration, fees, pension and allowances payable to the employees of the CCG. No governing body member or senior manager should be present for discussions about their own remuneration (although it is reasonable for the chief officer, the human resources (HR) lead and other senior managers where appropriate, to attend meetings of the committee during which the remuneration of other staff is discussed). The governing body should approve and keep under review the terms of reference for the remuneration committee, which include information on the membership of the committee and should be available upon request to the public.

In addition, some CCGs have conferred on or delegated to the remuneration committee the authority to make recommendations on remuneration and terms of service for elected governing body members.

CCGs are now subject to the same controls on senior remuneration as NHS providers. Consequently, when a CCG is seeking to appoint a clinical chief officer or chief officer who will hold the AO role, early consideration has to be given to the level of remuneration proposed for the post. Where the remuneration proposed is anticipated to exceed £150,402 pa (pro-rata), under requirements promulgated from time to time, CCGs require approval from the Department of Health (DH) before the role can be advertised. If the appointment does not exceed £150,402 pa (pro-rata), then no further approvals are required and the CCG Remuneration Committee can determine the remuneration in accordance with existing guidance

Annex 2 of the NHSE guidance *Clinical Commissioning Group Governing Body Members: Role outlines, attributes and skills* proposes a number of principles that CCGs may also wish to take into account as they determine the reimbursement or remuneration rates for individuals on the governing body who undertake their roles on a part-time or sessional basis, since many governing body members will continue in their clinical roles.

The principles recommend that all payments should be evidently in line with the individual's current earnings, commensurate with the average rate for their current employment or the specific role or demonstrably required to provide backfill. The guidance goes on to set out what these principles mean for GPs, other practice staff, lay members, the nurse and the secondary care clinician on the governing body. Good practice would also suggest that robust benchmarking information be available to support the remuneration committee in this decision-making process – for example, remuneration could be in line with non-executive director (NED) payments in other NHS organisations, at a rate commensurate with their salary or as needed for replacement costs, or at a rate commensurate with the average rate for their profession and level of seniority.

National guidance has been published with a set fee for the lay members, secondary care doctor and nurse roles but, where the NHS currently employs these postholders, the guidance recommends their fee is based on their existing NHS salary instead of the set fee. Guidance on salary ranges for executive members based on NHS trust executive pay is provided by NHSE and follows the principles set out in the Hutton Fair Pay Review. A survey by NHS Clinical Commissioners (January 2016) outlined the variation across CCGs in terms of lay member contract hours, actual hours worked and allowances paid. The original expectation, based on previous experience in PCT NED roles, was two days a month. However, compared to PCTs who generally had seven NEDs, including the non-executive chair, most CCGs have a much smaller NED capacity. The survey of lay members revealed that on average CCGs contract with lay members for 3.4 days per month, and the average number of days actually worked is 5.7. The survey suggested that primary care commissioning and increasing complexity in CCGs are the biggest reasons for this increase, and that as more CCGs adopt delegated or increased responsibility for primary care commissioning, the overall work commitment for many lay members will continue to rise. The survey recommended more transparency around the methods used to establish lay member allowances.

As with all NHS bodies, the actions of the remuneration committee must be publicly defensible. When advising on the pay of the accountable officer, CFO and so on, the remuneration committee should bear in mind the need for properly defensible remuneration packages. These should be linked to clear statements of responsibilities and with rewards linked to the measurable discharge of those responsibilities.

The remuneration committee is required to make a report of its activities in the CCG's annual report and accounts. This is in line with the reports required of FTs and NHS trusts; likewise, the report must also include the relationship between the remuneration of the highest-paid director in their organisation and the median remuneration of the organisation's workforce in line with the Hutton Fair Pay Review.

The audit committee

Section 15 of The National Health Service (Clinical Commissioning Groups) Regulations 2012 stipulates that the audit committee must have a chair appointed by the CCG (for a term to be determined by the CCG). The chair must be a lay person with such qualifications, expertise or experience as to enable them to express informed views about financial management and audit matters. The chair of the CCG's governing body and the chief finance officer are disqualified from membership of a CCG's audit committee.

The lay member on the governing body, with a lead role in overseeing key elements of governance, is therefore usually the chair of the audit committee. The committee provides assurance and advice to the governing body, and to the AO, on the proper stewardship of resources and assets, including:

- value for money (VFM)
- financial reporting
- the effectiveness of audit arrangements (internal and external)
- risk management
- control and integrated governance arrangements within the group.

The governing body should approve and keep under review the terms of reference for the audit committee, which include information on the membership of the committee. This should be available upon request to the public. It is recommended that CCGs refer to the Healthcare Financial Management Association (HFMA) *NHS Audit Committee Handbook* (2014) and this ICSA handbook for further guidance.

Duties, rights and powers of the governing body members

As a member of the CCG's governing body, each individual will share responsibility as part of the team to ensure that the CCG exercises its functions effectively, efficiently, economically, with good governance and in accordance with the terms of the CCG constitution as agreed by its members.

The NHS guidance *Clinical Commissioning Group Governing Body Members: Role outlines, attributes and skills* describes the various roles that make up the governing body. It sets out a core role for all governing body members and then explains the specific nuances of the different roles as follows:

- The GP or other healthcare professionals acting on behalf of member practices will bring the unique understanding of those member practices to the discussion and decision-making of the governing body as their particular contribution.
- The chair is responsible for leading the governing body, ensuring it remains continuously able to discharge its duties and responsibilities as set out in the CCG's constitution. The chair will have a key role in overseeing governance, particularly ensuring that the governing body and the wider CCG behaves with the utmost transparency and responsiveness at all times.
- The lay member on the governing body with a lead role in overseeing key elements of financial management and audit will oversee key elements of governance including audit, remuneration and managing conflicts of interest. They will need to be able to chair the audit committee. Good practice would also suggest that this person would also have a specific role in ensuring that appropriate and effective raising concerns and anti-fraud systems are in place.
- The lay member on the governing body with a lead role in championing patient and public involvement will help to ensure that the public voice of the local population is heard in all aspects of the CCG's business and that opportunities are created and protected for patient and public empowerment in the work of the CCG. As one of the lay members, they may be asked to fulfil the role of deputy chair or chair of the governing body, if appropriate.
- The secondary care doctor clinical member on the governing body will bring to the governing body an understanding of patient care in the secondary care setting.
- The registered nurse clinical member on the governing body will bring a broader view, from their perspective as a registered nurse, on health and care issues to underpin the work of the CCG, especially the contribution of nursing to patient care.
- The accountable officer will need to be in the position of understanding the fundamentals in order to take on the responsibility of setting strategic direction and making key decisions, which will come with this role.
- The CFO will have a professional qualification in accountancy and the expertise or experience to lead the financial management of the CCG.

The ICSA specimen code of conduct for NHS clinical commissioning group governing body members

This guidance reflects current best practice from across economic sectors and the requirements of NHSE. It is available to ICSA members at www.icsa.org.uk. It should be read in conjunction with the Professional Standards Authority's standards for NHS boards and governing bodies. It sets out a specimen code, which covers the following areas:

- appointment and tenure
- ceasing to be a governing body member
- code non-compliance
- conflicts of interest
- confidentiality
- expenses
- mediation
- meetings
- induction and training
- role and function of governing body members
- stakeholder engagement
- standards of conduct.

Liabilities of governing body members

Guidance issued to the NHS in Health Service Circulars 1998/010 and 1999/104 outlines the extent to which people not employed by an NHS body but taking an active role in decision-making may be personally liable for their decisions and action.

In accordance with this guidance, each CCG confers the following indemnity upon its governing body members who are not employees of the group who are undertaking duties on behalf of the Group as part of its governance arrangements.

> 'Such individuals, who have acted honestly and in good faith, will not have to meet out of his or her own personal resources any personal civil liability which is incurred in the execution of his or her governance functions, save where the person has acted recklessly.'

Such individuals need to ensure they act in accordance with the CCG's constitution (including standing orders, prime financial policies and scheme of reservation and delegation), the CCG's policies and procedure, guidance issued by appropriate regulatory bodies and any appropriate statute or regulations.

The position of employees of the CCG is different to that of governing body members, as the CCG is always liable for the actions of its employees in the course of their employment.

Maintaining an effective governing body

The model constitution requires the governing body to have an ongoing role in reviewing the CCG's governance arrangements to ensure that the CCG continues to reflect the principles of good governance.

The research project *Developing CCGs as High Performing Membership Organisations*, in which Calderdale and Greater Huddersfield CCGs worked with Ashridge Business School, established seven areas of competency that demonstrate a high-performing membership organisation. The research was based on the premise that the CCG existed primarily for the benefit of the community, not for the members, but that it was the members who would secure success or otherwise for the CCG. These competencies would make an interesting yardstick for an annual effectiveness review of the governing body and/or members' council. The seven competencies are:

- the membership contract
- encouraging and promoting best practice
- information and advice to members
- the development of member skills
- promoting the CCG to the membership
- policy and decision-making
- engagement with the wider public.

Though there are no mandated requirements to annually assess/evaluate their effectiveness, CCGs would be well advised to consider the guidance on evaluation given elsewhere in this handbook.

The chair of the governing body

The chair runs governing body meetings and sets the agenda; they are pivotal in creating the conditions for overall committee and individual effectiveness.

The National Health Service (Clinical Commissioning Groups) Regulations 2012 specify that the chair cannot be the accountable officer or CFO, the mandatory secondary care specialist or nurse, or the lay person with a lead role in overseeing key elements of governance.

If the chair is a GP or other healthcare professional, the deputy chair should be a lay member who should take the chair's role for discussions and decisions involving conflict of interest for the chair.

The chair also plays a key role in managing the relationships between member practices, governing body and committee members and staff. The chair's relationship with the accountable officer is particularly critical to the successful functioning of the CCG, its governing body and other committees. This relationship should be clearly defined in writing.

The chair will also have a key role in overseeing governance, particularly ensuring that the governing body and the wider CCG behaves with the utmost transparency and responsiveness at all times. They will ensure that public and patients' views are heard, their expectations understood and, where appropriate, met. The chair will ensure that the organisation is able to account to its local patients, stakeholders and NHSE, as well as ensuring the CCG builds and maintains effective relationships, particularly with the individuals involved in overview and scrutiny from the relevant local authorities.

The chair of the governing body has specific responsibility for:

- leading the governing body, ensuring it remains continuously able to discharge its duties and responsibilities as set out in the CCG's constitution
- building and developing the CCG's governing body and its individual members
- ensuring that the CCG has proper constitutional and governance arrangements in place
- ensuring that, through the appropriate support, information and evidence, the governing body is able to discharge its duties
- supporting the accountable officer in discharging the responsibilities of the organisation
- contributing to the building of a shared vision of the aims, values and culture of the organisation
- leading and influencing clinical and organisational change to enable the CCG to deliver commissioning responsibilities.

The accountable officer

The CCG's AO is charged with ensuring that the CCG complies with its:

- duty to exercise its functions effectively, efficiently and economically;
- duty to exercise its functions with a view to securing continuous improvement in the quality of services provided to individuals for, or in connection with, the prevention, diagnosis or treatment of illness;
- financial obligations, including information requests;
- obligations relating to accounting and auditing;
- duty to provide information to the NHS Commissioning Board, following requests from Secretary of State;
- obligations under any other provision of the NHS Act 2006 specified by the Board for these purposes.

The AO must also ensure that the CCG performs its functions in a way which provides good value for money.

CCGs are responsible for the recruitment and selection process for the appointment of chair of the governing body, AO and CFO. NHS England plays a particular legal role in the appointment of the AO. The NHSE guidance *Clinical commissioning Group Guidance on Senior Appointments including Accountable*

Officers (March 2017) sets out the procedure, which should be followed in appointing a new accountable officer. It also sets out those persons who are disqualified from membership of CCG governing bodies (see the earlier section of this handbook). Under the guidance, CCGs are responsible for ensuring that the recruitment and selection process ensures that any candidate appointed to senior positions can demonstrate the experience and skills required for that post. It is for the chief executive of NHSE and, as the accountable officer for that organisation, to confirm the appointment to this role. This does not create an employment relationship between the accountable officer and NHSE.

The individual who undertakes the accountable officer role is required to be a member of the CCG's governing body and therefore needs to meet the core requirements for governing body members. Once an individual has been successful in the selection process, to carry out the duties of the accountable officer they may be either:

- an employee of the CCG, or an employee of any member of the CCG;
- a member of the CCG (e.g. a GP); or
- a person specified in the constitution.
- Though two or more CCGs may choose to share a single person to undertake their accountable officer roles, it is not possible for a single CCG to appoint two individuals to share this role. The accountable officer may not be the chair of the governing body.

CCGs could decide that their accountable officer role will be held by a clinician supported by an expert manager, or undertaken by a manager with expert clinical leadership support. The term chief officer is used to identify senior managers who undertake the accountable officer role, while chief clinical officer is used for senior clinicians who undertake the role. When the accountable officer role is held by a clinician, the CCG's senior manager is called the chief operating officer.

The individual who undertakes the accountable officer role is required to be a member of the governing body. They will therefore need to meet the core requirements as described for governing body members.

The clinical commissioning group company secretary

While the current legislation does not specify the need for CCGs to appoint a company secretary, good practice from the corporate sector and experience in FTs would suggests that this is also a key role in the governance of an organisation.

ICSA has issued guidance on the role of a CCG head of governance, which encompasses the company secretary role. The CCG head of governance role covers three main areas:

- the governing body and CCG committees
- the CCG itself
- the member practices.

In brief, the head of governance would be responsible for ensuring that the CCG complies with relevant legislation and its authorisation (including any conditions attached to it) issued by NHSE. They would establish procedures for the sound governance of the CCG and would advise the governing body, committees and member practices on developments in governance issues. The head of governance would also ensure that meetings of the governing body, committees and member practices run efficiently and effectively, are properly recorded and that all relevant participants receive appropriate support to fulfil their legal duties.

Clinical commissioning group reporting requirements

CCGs are subject to an ongoing assurance process – the CCG Improvement and Assessment Framework (CCG IAF) – overseen by NHSE regional teams, which also provide developmental support to CCGs as required. This framework replaces the CCG Assurance Framework and the separate CCG performance dashboard. The CCG IAF has been designed to supply indicators for adoption in STPs as markers of success. In turn, those plans will provide vision and local actions that will populate and enrich the local use of the CCG IAF. It draws together in one place NHS Constitution and other core performance and finance indicators, outcome goals and transformational challenges.

The framework is intended to be a dynamic tool; in future NHSE expects to retire indicators for assessment where CCGs have made the greatest strides and to add in new indicators, so that the assessment of CCGs continually focuses on what are the greatest emerging and actionable opportunities facing the NHS in future years. For example, for the 2017/18 assessment, NHSE have included an indicator to measure the role of CCGs in supporting patient safety, and it intends to work to develop a suitable indicator that can better measure how CCGs are focusing on patient and public engagement.

The new framework covers indicators located in four domains:

- **Better health:** this section looks at how the CCG is contributing towards improving the health and wellbeing of its population, and bending the demand curve.
- **Better care:** this principally focuses on care redesign, performance of constitutional standards, and outcomes, including in important clinical areas.
- **Sustainability:** this section looks at how the CCG is remaining in financial balance, and is securing good value for patients and the public from the money it spends.
- **Leadership:** this domain assesses the quality of the CCG's leadership, the quality of its plans, how the CCG works with its partners, and the governance arrangements that the CCG has in place to ensure it acts with probity, for example in managing conflicts of interest.

The 5YFV and accompanying planning guidance set out national ambitions for transformation in a number of vital clinical priorities such as mental health, dementia, learning disabilities, cancer, maternity and diabetes. To reinforce the collective efforts in these areas, NHSE is committed in the government's Mandate to creating a separate clear rating for each of these six clinical areas, on a four point 'Ofsted-style' scale.

In additional to these six areas, the framework will also allow a tailored support package to be created around each CCG. Such support is not synonymous with an NHSE action or intervention, as the main function of the support is to enable a tailored approach to the diagnosis and application of improvement solutions. The framework sets out the categories set out below which are not mandated but instead offered to help conversations around what support means or what support would be useful.

- Forward-looking support:
  - Describes what CCGs need to do and what good and excellent looks like for these ambitions
  - Provides practical solutions to enable CCGs to get there
- Facilitative support:
  - Addresses emerging delivery issues
  - Gets the CCG back to an agreed level of performance
- Bespoke support:
  - Addresses specific poor performance in one or more area(s)
  - May resolve chronic or persistent issues.

The NHSE teams work with CCGs in different ways depending on whether the CCG needs to get back on track or whether it is planning for future development and transformation. A CCG that is particularly challenged requires a much more bespoke support package, tailored to its needs. All CCGs benefit from examples of excellence which they can replicate.

The teams take an approach of enquiry and partnership to review plans and performance data in the form of regular, issue-focused meetings, where wider sources of evidence inform mature conversations on improvement and the support required to achieve it. The scheduling of meetings is primarily to be based on the level of risk a CCG is carrying, although more frequent meetings are held by mutual agreement. The focus is on unlocking improvement and enabling change, rather than an assurance process and giving ratings. Good record-keeping of decisions and actions following these conversations/meetings are important, particularly when improvement actions are required. Articulation of agreed improvement milestones and arrangements for ongoing monitoring should be clear and proportionate.

Conversations around forward-looking support normally forms part of the planning process and year-end assessment conversations, whilst facilitative or bespoke support applies in response to in-year performance against plans or standards. The framework sets out the tone and culture of support by asking CCGs

'What support do you need?' This allows for a multi-disciplinary approach by the NHSE teams, which can include a robust diagnostic is undertaken to ensure the reasons for underperformance are understood and the impact fully assessed. Deep-rooted or serious issues need to be addressed with a more bespoke support solution and in some cases the bespoke support may be described in terms of NHSE's special measures regime.

The NHSE teams may also work through delivery partners, a local structure such as cancer alliances, or be able to recommend suitable resources from other development providers, as well as providing their own guidance, tools, webinars, workshops and other resources. Clinical networks have an important role to play at the local level in cancer, maternity, diabetes, adult and children's mental health, dementia and urgent and emergency care. This support will be co-ordinated through NHSE's teams. The framework recognises that system solutions will increasingly be important and NHSE and NHSI have carried out further work to provide a more joined up approach to supporting local systems.

Previous assurance frameworks have linked a CCG's assurance status with intervention actions. A CCG assessment moving down to limited assurance or not assured in a particular component would signal the need for an improvement plan. An improvement plan could form part of the application of special measures or legal directions. The CCG IAF does not make in-year assessments to provide these triggers. However, the process remains the same. If the data, or wider sources of insight, raise concerns that initiate a discussion between NHSE and a CCG, the outcome could be an improvement plan. If the circumstances match the description of special measures or the statutory definition of directions, these actions may also be taken.

NHSE is supported by legislation in exercising formal powers of direction if it is satisfied that a CCG is (a) failing or (b) is at risk of failing to discharge its functions. Formal intervention action would be proposed, as laid out in section 14Z21 of the NHS Act 2006 (as amended). These interventions include:

- directing the CCG as to how it discharges its functions
- directing the CCG or the AO to stop carrying out any functions for a defined period
- terminating the AO 's appointment and appointing a new AO
- varying the CCG's constitution
- carrying out certain functions on behalf of a CCG or arranging for another CCG to do so
- dissolving the CCG.

Since the use of such formal direction affects CCG autonomy, careful consideration is required before this course of action can be implemented. When considering the use of intervention powers, a number of steps have to be taken in order to establish whether the use of such powers is proportionate and appropriate – see Table 13.2.

Table 13.2

Step	Action
1. Review	If insight raises serious concerns, a discussion between NHSE and the CCG should take place. This is the formal opportunity to raise concerns.
2. Formal letter and request for information	Using powers under sections 14Z18 and 14Z19 of the NHS Act 2006 (as amended), NHSE should formally write to the CCG requesting further information or assurance following the review.
3. Consideration of options	If the formal request for information does not provide sufficient assurance about the CCG's ability to deliver the required improvement, consideration should be given as to whether the CCG can make the required improvement with the intensive support of special measures.
4. Consideration of intervention options	If it is found that the concern is so deep-set or serious that only intervention is appropriate, then the implications of doing so should be considered carefully. The principle must be that the implication of the intervention action for patients is at the very least no worse than the status quo of not intervening.
5. Consistency	Because intervention is being discharged on behalf of the NHSE Board, it is important to ensure that moderation is sought through the CCG improvement and assessment oversight group to ensure that the rationale for intervention is robust.
6. Summary report and directions drafted for commissioning committee approval	Finally, the relevant evidence and legal wording needs to be submitted to NHSE's commissioning committee. Once approved, the documentation, including any directions, will be passed to the chief executive for signature. Where emergency action is required, the chair of the commissioning committee may approve the use of directions prior to a scheduled commissioning committee.

NHSE has a statutory duty to conduct an annual performance assessment of each CCG. The government's Mandate to NHSE specifies the four 'Ofsted-style' headline categories to be used – Outstanding, Good, Requires Improvement and Inadequate. The methodology to apply a year-end assessment is agreed during the year and it also requires regional and national moderation to ensure assessments have been applied consistently across all CCGs.

Clinical commissioning groups' annual planning and delivery cycle

The NHSE publication *NHS Operational Planning and Contracting Guidance 2017–2019* sets out the formal planning process that CCGs will take the lead on. CCGs, as the local leaders of health commissioning, will work with all key stakeholders in line with the STP process to develop the strategic, operational and financial plans required to achieve the prescribed outcomes. The plans need to demonstrate how the CCG will deliver all the aspects of the government's Mandate to the commissioning system in line with the STP process and the growing collaborative approach with providers.

Annual report and accounts

CCGs also have a statutory obligation to develop and publish an annual report. The annual report and accounts is a single document, which presents the story of the CCG's activities during the previous financial year ending 31 March. The form and content of the annual report and accounts is directed by NHSE and must be in line with the DH's manual for accounts (MfA). In practice, this is achieved by following NHSE's annual reporting guidance (ARG3). The CCG's annual report and accounts must contain:

- An annual report:
  - member practices' introduction
  - the strategic report
  - the members' report
  - the remuneration report.
- A statement of the accountable officer's responsibilities
- A governance statement
- Four primary financial statements
- Notes to the accounts
- A report and opinion from an independent auditor.

The member practices' introduction is produced collectively by the GP practices which make up the membership of the CCG. It should include:

- reflections on the CCG's progress and performance in relation to the health priorities of the local community as set out in the CCG's strategy and business plan
- consideration of the impact the council of members and governing body have had in key areas
- a statement which sets out how the annual evaluation of effectiveness of the council of members and/or governing body was conducted and how any recommendations are being taken forward.

The strategic report and members' report are based on the requirements of sections 414A, C and D and section 416 of the Companies Act 2006 tailored to be relevant to CCGs. The strategic report should stand alone, but can include summarised information cross-referenced to other parts of the annual report.

It is the responsibility of the CCG's AO to prepare the annual report and accounts. Usually, the governing body approves the annual report and accounts for submission to NHSE and wider publication, but this may vary depending on the CCG's constitution. In approving the annual report and accounts, the members of the governing body confirm that they are satisfied that they present the CCG's year in an appropriate, comprehensive, balanced and coherent way. Before 30 September, each CCG must present its annual report and accounts to stakeholders, including members of the public, at an annual general meeting (AGM). The HFMA's *Introductory Guide – CCG Annual Report and Accounts* (2014) was published to assist members of the CCG and its governing body through the process of reviewing and approving the annual report and accounts. CCGs do not need to present their annual reports and accounts to Parliament.

The clinical commissioning group governance challenge

Non-executive members and independence

The independence of the governing body currently rests on the role of the lay members, of which there must be at least two, with specified roles to oversee elements of governance and to help champion patient and public engagement. This has the potential to be further strengthened with the appointment of the secondary care specialist and the registered nurse member and a third additional lay member in line with the conflicts of interest guidance.

In considering the current makeup of the governing body, the lay members, secondary care specialist and registered nurse member can all be considered non-executive members. They are defined as such in the model CCG Constitution. However, the GP members are also referred to as non-executive members at times.

The Good Governance Standard (following on from the Higgs Report) sets the role of these non-executive members. It says they should:

- contribute to strategy by bringing a range of perspectives to strategy development and decision-making
- make sure that effective management arrangements and an effective team are in place at the top level of the organisation
- delegate which decisions are reserved for the governing body, and then clearly delegate the rest
- hold the executive to account, by assessing performance in fulfilling their responsibilities, agreeing levels of remuneration and appointment/removal of executives
- be extremely discriminating about getting involved in matters of operational detail.

As a comparison, the Financial Reporting Council (FRC)'s UK Corporate Governance Code (2016) (UK Code) requires a board and its committees to have the appropriate balance of skills, experience, independence and knowledge to enable them to discharge their duties and responsibilities effectively. This ensures that no individual or group of individuals can dominate the board's decision-making. Non-executive members can be either independent or non-independent. Though non-independent non-executives are permissible, the Code recommends that the majority of the board should consist of independent non-executives. If there are non-executives who are considered to be not independent, the Code suggests that it may be necessary to appoint further independent non-executives to act as a counterbalance. Non-executives are not independent if their opinion is likely to be influenced by the senior executive management of the organisation or by a major stakeholder, or for example, if a person personally stands to gain or otherwise benefit substantially from income from the organisation.

The significant governance issue for CCGs relates to the independence of its non-executive members in carrying out this role of independent scrutiny. The independent non-executives would be identified as the lay members and clinical members. GP members would be classed as non-independent non-executives; good practice would suggest their number needs to be balanced with an equivalent number of NEDs to ensure good governance.

The boundaries in CCGs can sometimes become further blurred, however. In a number of CCGs, GP members on the governing body take on clinical project leads or operational roles within the CCG. These roles support the CCG in developing robust clinical pathways and models of care in order to deliver the strategic priorities of the CCG. The GPs who undertake these roles will usually have a specific knowledge and expertise in the field in question.

Managing conflicts of interest

As mentioned in the opening remarks of this chapter, managing conflicts of interest is a critical factor in the success of CCGs. Conflicts can arise in the work of CCGs in a variety of ways: for example, if members of the practice became involved in the process of deciding to commission or awarding a service to a GP provider in their locality or to their own practice, they would be potentially conflicted. It would not be clear that they favoured the decision because of the needs of patients rather than their own financial gain.

For a GP or other clinical commissioner, a conflict of interest may also arise when their own judgment as an NHS commissioner could be, or be perceived to be, influenced and impaired by their own concerns and obligations as a healthcare provider; as a member of a particular peer, professional or special interest group; or those of a close family member. Commissioning decisions that are in the overall best interests of taxpayers and the local population may not always be in the best interests of individual patients for whom GPs are required to advocate, or for the companies and partnerships which they own, manage or work for.

Individual behaviour is a major factor in the effectiveness of the governing body, and also has an influence on the reputation of the organisation, the confidence and trust members of the public have in it and the working relationships and morale within it. Conflicts, real or perceived, can arise between the organisation's interests and those of individual governors; public trust can then be damaged unless the organisation implements clear procedures to deal with these conflicts.

The guidance *Next Steps Towards Primary Care Co-commissioning* (2014) included a strengthened approach to managing such conflicts in co-commissioning decisions. These requirements related to the make-up of the decision-making committee, where the committee must have a lay and executive majority and have a lay chair. Local Healthwatch and a local authority member of the local HWB will also have the right to serve as observers on the decision-making committee in order to secure the external involvement of local stakeholders.

On 16 June 2017, NHS England published revised statutory guidance on managing conflicts of interest for CCGs. The guidance has been updated to ensure it is fully aligned with the recently published cross system conflicts of interest guidance – Managing conflicts of interest in the NHS: Guidance for staff and organisations (see Chapter 7). A small number of changes have been made including:

- Registers of interest: CCGs are required to have systems in place to satisfy themselves as a minimum on an annual basis that their registers of interest are accurate and up-to-date, and to require that only decision-making staff are included on the published register.
- Gifts from suppliers or contractors: In line with the NHS-wide guidance, gifts of low value (up to £6), such as promotional items, can now be accepted.
- Gifts from other sources: the thresholds for such gifts has been revised to under £50 (rather than £10) and such gifts do not need to be declared. Gifts with a value of over £50 can now be accepted on behalf of an organisation, but not in a personal capacity.
- Hospitality – meals and refreshments: the thresholds have ben revised so that hospitality under £25 does not need to be declared. Hospitality between £25 and £75 can be accepted, but must be declared, and hospitality over £75 should be refused unless senior approval is given.

New care models: a new annex providing further advice on identifying, declaring and managing conflicts of interest in the commissioning of new care models: has been included.'

The guidance *Managing Conflicts of Interest: Revised Statutory Guidance for CCGs* (June 2016) recognises that conflicts of interest are inevitable in commissioning and it is how they are managed that matters. The guidance includes a number of strengthened safeguards to mitigate the risk of real and perceived conflicts of interest arising in CCGs. The guidance requires CCG employees and practice staff with involvement in CCG business to complete mandatory online conflicts of interest training annually. NHS England is working with CCGs to develop the training package. Where a CCG has decided not to comply with this statutory guidance, they must include within their next annual self-certification statement the reasons for deciding not to do so.

The general safeguards described in *Towards Establishment: Creating Responsive and Accountable Clinical Commissioning Groups (CCGs)* (2012) include:

- arrangements for declaring interests
- maintaining a register of interests
- excluding individuals from decision-making where a conflict arises
- engagement with a range of potential providers on service design.

The NHSE guidance provides more specific, additional safeguards that CCGs are advised to have in place when commissioning services that could potentially be provided by GP practices. These safeguards are set out in the form of questions which governing bodies are encouraged to ask themselves.

- How does the proposal deliver good or improved outcomes and VFM – what are the estimated costs and the estimated benefits?
- How does it reflect the CCG's proposed commissioning priorities?
- How have the public been involved in the decision to commission this service?
- What range of health professionals have been involved in designing the proposed service?
- What range of potential providers have been involved in considering the proposals?
- How have the HWB(s) been involved?
- How does the proposal support the priorities in the relevant joint health and wellbeing strategy (or strategies)?
- What are the proposals for monitoring the quality of the service?
- What systems will there be to monitor and publish data on referral patterns?
- Have all conflicts and potential conflicts of interests been appropriately declared and entered in registers which are publicly available?
- Why has this procurement route been chosen?
- What additional external involvement will there be in scrutinising the proposed decisions?
- How will the CCG make its final commissioning decision in ways that preserve the integrity of the decision-making process?

Further questions are included for any qualified provider (AQP) or single tender situations.

Other requirements in the 2016 guidance were as follows:

- the strong recommendation for CCGs to have a minimum of three lay members on the governing body;
- the introduction of a conflicts of interest guardian in CCGs undertaken by the audit committee chair as long as they do not have any provider interests;
- the requirement for CCGs to include a robust process for managing any breaches within their conflict of interest policy and for anonymised details of the breach to be published on the CCG's website;
- strengthened provisions around decision-making when a member of the governing body, or committee or sub-committee is conflicted;
- strengthened provisions around the management of gifts and hospitality;

- a requirement for CCGs to include an annual audit of conflicts of interest management within their internal audit plans; and
- to include the findings of this audit within their annual end-of-year governance statement.

CCGs will also need to adhere to relevant guidance issued by professional bodies on conflicts of interest, e.g. the British Medical Association (BMA), the Royal College of General Practitioners (RCGP), and to procurement rules such as the Public Contract Regulations 2015 and other legislation such as the Bribery Act 2010 (as discussed in Chapter 7).

The CCG's public register of conflicts of interest will include information on the nature of the conflict and details of the conflicted parties. The register will form an obligatory part of the annual accounts and be signed off by external auditors. CCGs will also be required to maintain and publish, on a regular basis, a register of all key procurement decisions.

If the governing body is considering a decision in which a member is conflicted, it is good practice for that member must play no part in that decision – normally leaving the room during the discussion of that agenda item. In making the decision as to whether to exclude the member from the discussion, the chair and/or lay member for governance will consider the expertise or insight of the member in relation to the item under discussion. If more than 50% of the members are conflicted then the chair (or deputy) should have the authority to decide whether the discussion can proceed. Where a quorum cannot be achieved, the chair of the meeting could invite other individuals on a temporary basis to make up the quorum. Such an individual may be a member of a relevant HWB or a member of another CCG.

The lay member for governance or conflicts of interest guardian should provide oversight of the management of conflicts of interest and provide impartial, unconflicted advice and judgment to the governing body in cases where it is not obvious whether a material conflict exists or how best to manage it. They should define a reasonable balance to avoid conflicts, though enabling the CCG to harness the knowledge of clinicians and other staff for commissioning in order to improve care to patients and value for money to the taxpayer. The deputy chair of the governing body should deputise for the chair of the governing body where the chair has a conflict of interest.

Further guidance, which will specifically address developments in the new care models and integrated care organisations may cause particular challenges with regard to conflicts of interest.

Being a membership organisation

The King's Fund and Nuffield Trust report *Clinical Commissioning Groups: Supporting improvement in general practice? (2013)* states:

'[T]here are significant disparities between the views of those involved in leading CCGs and member GPs, with the latter being less likely to say that their CCG is 'owned' by its members, that its decisions reflect their views or that it has had a positive impact to date. There is also significant variation in views from one CCG to another, with levels of member ownership and involvement much higher in some areas than others. Larger CCGs may face a particular challenge in engaging member practices and creating a culture of collective ownership.'

There is a significant challenge here to ensure that the member practices are able to play an influential role in setting the direction of the CCG. The balance of power between the members council and the governing body needs to be carefully handled by the chair and the AO.

Procurement

The National Health Service (Procurement, Patient Choice and Competition) Regulations (No 2) 2013 replace the existing administrative rules governing the procurement of NHS-funded services previously set out in the Principles and rules for cooperation and competition (DH, 2010) and the Procurement guide for commissioners of NHS-funded services (DH, 2010).

The substance of many of these principles and rules is still preserved in the regulations. The regulations require commissioners to ensure good practice in relation to the procurement of NHS healthcare services and to protect patients' rights to make choices regarding their NHS treatment. They also prohibit commissioners from engaging in anti-competitive behaviour unless this is in the interests of health care service users.

It is for commissioners to decide what services to procure and how best to secure them in the interests of healthcare service users. The regulations adopt a principles-based approach that is intended to give commissioners flexibility. NHS Improvement (NHSI)'s role is limited to ensuring that commissioners have operated within the legal framework established by the regulations.

CCGs will need to decide, subject to the National Health Service (Procurement, Patient Choice and Competition) (No 2) Regulations 2013 and current procurement rules set out in the Public Contracts Regulations 2006 where it is appropriate to commission community-based services through competitive tender, through an AQP approach or through single tender. In general, commissioning through competitive tender or AQP will introduce greater transparency and help reduce the scope for conflicts.

Good Governance Institute

In 2014, The Good Governance Institute (GGI), with its partner Capsticks, was commissioned by NHSE to carry out a major work programme to assist the ongoing development of CCGs. The work was designed and overseen by a 'task and finish' group of the NHS Commissioning Assembly CCG Development Working Group, made up of CCGs from around the country.

In particular, GGI have developed:

- a consistent language to describe governance that is engaging for clinicians and the public
- a proposed set of outcomes of good governance that can be described and measured
- a series of diagnostic tools with which CCGs can measure the outcomes of their governance arrangements supported by a process that CCGs can employ.

Eleven outcomes for good governance were identified by GGI, CCGs and other relevant stakeholders, and are:

- **Clarity of purpose**, including setting tone at the top, leading by example, living the values etc.
- **Leadership and strategic direction,** including understanding of market and context, balance between operational demands and strategic goals and creating a pipeline of clinical leaders for the future.
- **Effectiveness of relationships**, including co-operative behaviours.
- **Membership and unity,** including member ownership of CCG.
- **Public and community engagement**, including openness and transparency.
- **Quality and safety structures and systems,** including mechanisms to gather patients and carer experience data, adoption of best practice, commitment to research, investment in development, holding each other to account professionally etc.
- **Focus on outcomes**, including understanding what matters to improve health of population, driving quality and safety, co-design with service users, co-ordination of care.
- **Better decision-making**, including development of key performance indicators (KPIs), use of information, data integrity, and ongoing audit etc. used to support sound decisions, mature management of conflict of interest.
- **Control systems**, including clarity of external authority and expectation, risk appetite, internal assurance on resources and quality, effectiveness of governance structures, quality of challenge etc.
- **Legal and regulator compliance**, including fulfilling statutory and other duties such as the duty of candour.
- **Organisational effectiveness**, including resource management, effective procurement, best use of commissioning support, fewer diversions arising from governance failures, etc.

GGI have also now developed a suite of tools that have been tested by more than 40 volunteer CCGs. The tools allow CCGs to self-evaluate the degree to which their governance arrangements deliver on the outcomes of good governance, and include a maturity matrix, a peer review guide, a standards and evidence tool, a board observation guide and a survey that can be administered both online and in hard copy. They are all available for CCGs to use free of charge and can be found at www.ccggovernance.org.

NHS Clinical Commissioners

NHS Clinical Commissioners is the membership organisation of CCGs. It provides CCGs with a strong collective voice and represents them in the national debate on the future of healthcare in England. It facilitates shared learning; and delivers networking opportunities for its members so that local clinicians can commission the best possible services for their patients and populations. It has a democratically elected NHS clinical commissioners board to provide strategic leadership for the organisation and its six networks. The board, which is made up of a blend of clinicians, managers and lay people from its membership, was secured through a democratic election process ensuring it is fully member led and open and transparent.

Governance checklist

- ✓ How clear is the vision and aims of the CCG to the member practices and the governing body? Do they understand the constitution and their role as set out there?
- ✓ Do the member practices and governing body understand the statutory duties prescribed for a CCG? To what extent does the information that they receive help them to make rigorous decisions in line with those duties?
- ✓ What does the size and complexity of the CCG mean for the ways in which they approach each of the main functions of governance set out by the Good Governance Standard for Public Services?
- ✓ How clearly defined are the respective roles and responsibilities of the member practices, the governing body and the individual members?
- ✓ Do all members of the governing body take collective responsibility for the governing body's decisions?
- ✓ How well does the CCG understand the views of the public and service users?
- ✓ How does the behaviour of members, both individually and collectively as a governing body, show that their responsibilities to the CCG and its stakeholders are taken very seriously?
- ✓ Are there any ways in which member behaviour might weaken the CCG's aims and values?
- ✓ Are there formal agreements on the types of decisions that are delegated to the executive and those that are reserved for the governing body and/or the member practices? Is this set out in a clear and up-to-date statement?
- ✓ Is there clarity on the election/appointment processes for the members' representatives and the governing body members? What approach will be taken to finding a balance between continuity of knowledge and renewal of thinking in the governing body?

- ✓ How well does the role of the lay members support independent scrutiny and challenge? What further measures might be considered to strengthen this if required?
- ✓ Is there a process for regularly reviewing the CCG's governance arrangements and practice? Is this independently assessed at any point?

Summary

The governance of CCGs is maturing, and there are clear signs of consistency developing around the principles, if not around the actual governance processes. CCGs were specifically developed as membership organisations; to expect a rigidity of governance more closely aligned to a publicly listed company may not have been appropriate.

It is clear that there is a requirement for robust governance arrangements within the accountability structure envisaged by NHSE, allowing CCGs the flexibility to develop those arrangements. As CCGs seek to integrate and work more closely with their stakeholders, the opportunity to deliver their statutory duties more effectively may present itself. As such, the CCG's role will continue to evolve. As new care models are established, the boundary between what is done by CCGs and by new integrated care providers will shift. However, there will continue to be a need for an effective commissioning function in the NHS. This includes acting as funder, setting local priorities and incentives, oversight of contracts, ensuring best value for the taxpayer, and ensuring the provision of a comprehensive local NHS within the available resources.

CCGs will need to consider the opportunities for establishing new care models, the likely timetable for this and the implications for contracting. CCGs have a key role in the future in defining the scope of services for Multispeciality Community Providers (MCPs) and Primary and Acute Care Systems (PACSs), engaging with local communities and providers over proposals, and running procurement processes. In particular, where the scope of MCP services includes services previously provided in hospitals, CCGs will need to agree revised contracts with the providers of these services. As part of the process for setting up new care models, NHSE will need to work with CCGs to ensure they have the capability and capacity to operate effectively in the changing provider landscape. This will include building on locally-led initiatives up and down the country for CCGs to work together across larger geographical footprints, for example, through joint appointments, integrated management and governance arrangements.

14 Governance and new models of care

New models of care

Many of the new models of care promoted by the Five Year Forward View (NHS England (NHSE), 2014) (5YFV) are underpinned by different legal structures, which would qualify a significant transaction (e.g. acquisitions, mergers, foundation groups, hospital chain, accountable care organisations). Given that the Healthcare Commission had already identified back in 2008 that 'it is clear that, in relation to service failure, problems often occur at the borders between one organisation or team and another' (*Learning from Investigations* (2008)), the good governance of these new models and the relationships that they create is essential. This chapter seeks not only to establish the governance structures for the various models but also explores the key themes that underpin the success of these models.

> 'It is just as important to have good governance between organisations as within organisations. A service that stops at the doors of the hospital or when a partner fails to deliver is not really a service, it's a broken link in the chain of care. In an increasingly complex and interconnected world organisations can no longer operate in isolation. Boards must seek assurances from partners that they have identified the risks to overall strategic objectives and put adequate controls in place.'
>
> *Integrated Governance II: Governance Between Organisations (Institute of Healthcare Management, June 2008)*

Five Year Forward View

Chapter 2 sets out the main implications of this guidance, but all of the new models of care covered there have their origins in the direction of travel set out in this guidance. The challenge for all boards or governing bodies is to recognise that the drivers within the guidance for transformation and sustainability do not necessarily mean large-scale transactions and structural change. Networks and collaboration may be the better option, perhaps lessons learned from earlier major restructures have demonstrated that changing the structural form does not readily lead to the scale of transformation required for sustainable services.

> 'The higher the degree of organisational change, the higher the risk that the benefits will not be delivered (the evidence on mergers and acquisitions is pretty unequivocal that the risks from full-scale organisational change are high).'
>
> *Future organisational models for the NHS. Perspectives for the Dalton review (The King's Fund and Foundation Trust Network (FTN), July 2014)*

What is clear is that, in order to be successful, these new models of care will require a greater clarity of purpose, objective setting and lines of accountability than seen before in the NHS sector. The key principles, then, for any form or structure have to be as follows:

- Ensure each partner to the new structure has the capability to lead and control the agreed objectives
- Explore the culture of the partner organisations to determine cultural alignment and purpose
- Ensure that the founders of the new structure can exert control over the vehicle they have collectively created
- Consider creating a memorandum of understanding between the partners as an indication of the intended direction of travel
- Be clear about how the new structure will relate to its key stakeholders, particularly the regulators (e.g. will a new Care Quality Commission (CQC) registration or provider licence be required)
- Consider the ability of the partners to be able to integrate technology so that information can easily be shared
- Take the appropriate advice, both legal and financial, to ensure compliance with competition laws.

To be clear then, there are various models of care and their associated organisation forms presented within the Dalton Review, however, these are not necessarily clearly defined legal forms. When considering any of the models of care, the board or governing body must consider whether a new corporate legal form is required or whether a contractual legal arrangement would be sufficient. This distinction is helpful as the corporate or contractual form clearly establishes the degree of integration the partner organisations in the new form are trying to create.

The remainder of this chapter will seek to set out the various models that are currently being considered, and will then attempt to define the legal forms that may underpin the model.

Models of care

Buddying, federations and learning and clinical networks

Buddying is one of the least formal approaches to collaborative working and can start as an informal arrangement to share best practice, experience and learning across organisations. It stems from the buddying arrangements introduced for trusts in 'special measures' and the Dalton recommendation was that this should be expanded in a more formal setting to allow organisations in difficulty to benefit from support and improvement that can be offered by successful trusts. His review recommended that those organisations able to demonstrate a track record of high performance should be encouraged to consider managing an organisation in persistent difficulty through a long-term management contract.

A federation is a group of practices and primary care teams working together, sharing responsibility for developing and delivering high-quality, patient focused services for their local communities, which may include developing, providing or commissioning services, training and education, back office functions, safety and clinical governance. The size and legal entity involved will depend on the purpose for which the federation has been developed. For example, for running out of hours or other urgent care services, a larger organisation with sophisticated risk sharing arrangements is likely to make sense, whereas a joint provider of extended primary care services or a clinical governance group might be smaller and operate as a network.

Learning and clinical networks are also an informal arrangement and can be organised horizontally (e.g. across providers) or vertically (e.g. between general practitioner (GP) practices and providers). They may have terms of reference or a memorandum of understanding, but are unlikely to have more substantial contractual arrangements. Learning networks aim to share best practice and may align policies between institutions, but they do not create new integrated delivery structures.

Accountable care organisations

An accountable care organisation (ACO) is a partnership or network (led by providers) that collectively agrees with the commissioner(s) to share a proportion of any savings – on the condition that agreed quality standards/outcomes are met. The ACO provides all of the care for a given population for a defined period of time under a contractual arrangement with set quality standards/outcomes. These standards/outcomes are negotiated and agreed locally between the provider group and the commissioner(s). This model challenges the provider/commissioner split and anti-competition rules established by the Health and Social Care Act 2012 (HSCA 2012) and earlier government policy to deliver a competitive market in healthcare services as the providers work together to both provide and commission services e.g. when the ACO subcontracts to other providers for certain services.

CASE STUDY: ACO in Staffordshire

In Staffordshire two clinical commissioning groups (CCGs) are working with Macmillan Cancer Support to redesign cancer care services for the county. They are co-designing new care pathways with patients and their carers. Care is to be managed and contracted through a single provider, which will be held accountable for the entire patient experience and clinical outcomes. The provider will need to demonstrate that they have achieved a pre-agreed set of quality measures within a given expenditure target. Macmillan will support the selected prime provider for two years to manage the changes and ensure the specified outcomes are achieved.

Examples of this kind of model include:

- Multispeciality Community Providers (MCPs), where primary care (e.g. GP federations) and community care combine together. These can be 'virtual', 'partially integrated' or 'fully integrated', depending upon the level of integration envisaged.
- Primary and Acute Care Systems (PACSs), where secondary care providers pull the entire health and care system together. These, too, can be 'virtual', 'partially integrated' or 'fully integrated', depending upon the level of integration envisaged.
- Acute Care Collaborations (ACCs) where hospital chains, clinical networks, specialty franchises, multi-provider hospital groups or foundation groups combine together to provide secondary care.
- Enhanced health in care homes (EHCH) where care homes provide joined up primary, community, secondary and social care to residents of care and nursing homes, with staff from across health and social care organisations working together as part of multidisciplinary teams.
- Urgent and Emergency Care Networks (UECNs) aim to simplify the urgent and emergency care system to provide better integration between A&E departments and other services that provide and support urgent treatments. Such networks include the development of hospital networks with access to specialist centres, new partnership options for smaller hospitals and greater use of pharmacists and out-of-hours GP services.

Many of these new models have been pooling budgets and integrating services, but they have done so on the basis of informal partnerships – however, others are now opting for more formal governance arrangements. Whatever the form, the models continue to challenge regulators on how to:

- contract for the new systems of care
- work together with emerging partnerships

- allocate funding
- share risk and rewards.

Foundation groups

A foundation group is the joining together of providers, and at present can present in a variety of different forms. The groups use a mixed economy of membership models, ranging from buddying through to full acquisition. Foundation groups may, for example, involve trusts joining together under the umbrella of a successful NHS provider and sharing management skills, clinical expertise and back-office functions. There are, however, common themes principally relating to the governance and management of acute services at different locations.

In October 2016, NHS Improvement (NHSI) published Acute care collaborations – guidance on options for structuring foundation groups, outlining the current statutory framework for such a foundation group, namely, corporate joint ventures (CJVs) or committees in common. These are covered in more detail below.

Accountable Clinical Networks

Accountable Clinical Networks (ACNs) cover a range of acute services, including maternity and paediatrics, cancer, mental health and radiology services. The network aims to deliver rapid and sustained improvements in the systematic delivery of care by optimising patient pathways for the services covered by the network, and by identifying and implementing best practice at each stage along those pathways. The networks bring groups of providers together to consider how best to serve a defined population rather than just focusing on the services provided by their own individual organisations.

Clinical networks have existed for some time across the NHS, sometimes underpinned by contract, but often based on loose collaborative agreements. However, those arrangements have been quite fragile at times and have not been resilient enough to make the relevant services sustainable. The arrangements for an ACN will involve stricter accountability, which in most cases, means a single provider taking on a single capitated budget for the population and services covered by the network, in a similar fashion to that of MCPs and PACSs.

Specialty franchises

A good example of a speciality franchise would be the model developed by Moorfields Eye Hospital NHS Foundation Trust, one of the world's leading eye hospitals, under which they offer a range of specialist and routine ophthalmology services through satellite clinics in hospitals across London and elsewhere.

Corporate forms

Corporate joint ventures

A joint venture (JV) is a strategic alliance where two or more parties, usually businesses, form a partnership to share markets, intellectual property, assets, knowledge, and, of course, profits. A JV differs from a merger in the sense that there is no transfer of ownership in the deal. In a CJV, the companies start and invest in a new company that is jointly owned by both of the parent companies. By comparison, a strategic alliance is a legal agreement between two or more companies to share access to their technology, trademarks or other assets. A strategic alliance does not create a new corporate body, which a CJV does.

As CJVs create a separate corporate body, they are only available to foundation trusts (FTs) as NHS trusts do not have the power to set up or participate in corporate bodies except for income generation. FTs have the power to invest money 'for the purposes of, or in connection with, their functions', so they are able to make investments, which includes forming bodies corporate or otherwise acquiring membership of bodies corporate.

A CJV can be established by either forming a company (whether established by shares or by guarantee) or an LLP. Regardless of the legal structure used, the most important document is the JV agreement, which sets out all of the partners' rights and obligations as well as the objectives of the JV, the contributions of the partners and the rights to the profits (and losses).

CASE STUDY: 3Sixty Care Partnership

Northamptonshire Healthcare Foundation Trust has established a CJV arrangement with 3Sixty Care, an 'at scale' GP federation. The partners have set up 3Sixty Care Partnership – a new, jointly owned company – which will offer NHS health and social care to a population of 272,000 across Kettering, Corby, Wellingborough, east Northamptonshire and surrounding areas. The company plans to bid for contracts and is keen to bid for an MCP contract.

A CJV between FTs could also be described as a public–public CJV as seen in a foundation group that uses the CJV form. Other CJVs could also be created, such as between an FT and a private sector organisation (public–private CJV).

There are a number of issues that a board would need to consider in establishing a successful CJV, all of which would have to be discussed with commissioners, NHSI and NHSE. These issues include:

- how the financial, operational and other risks are shared between the contracting parties, since a CJV is always a separate legal entity
- legal and financial advice on the advantages and disadvantages of using a corporate vehicle – for example, how these vehicles are treated for tax purposes

- whether the investment meets the definition of control or joint control under accounting standards
- the issues of accounting consolidation within the DH's group accounts
- the cultural fit and responsiveness of the chosen partner since these are as important as any considerations about commerciality
- the appropriate governance structure, beyond just the shareholding, which balances taking sufficient control to ensure the FT's requirements are met and allowing the partner the necessary freedom to act to achieve them
- how to work in a partnership rather than solely enforcing a contractual model.

Interestingly, research by Grant Thornton (Better together: Building a successful joint venture company) demonstrates that public–public CJVs can be more successful as they combine common cultures and all profits are returned to the public sector. The research, although focussed on local government, recommends the following relevant considerations which have been adapted here for NHS joint ventures:

- Clear objectives for the CJV e.g. income growth, costs savings etc.
- Readiness to work in partnership as well as contractually
- Robust understanding of own services and opportunities for growth
- Access to professional advice and support
- Effective procurement process to test partnering arrangements
- Effective sharing of profit and risk
- Anticipation of future changes, building in flexibility to contracts, performance monitoring etc.
- Creating a culture of trust and strong working relationship
- Ongoing scrutiny of key outcomes (not inputs or activity)
- Allow the CJV to operate independently not as a division of the FT
- Appropriate corporate structure and governance arrangements – CJV is commercial in its relationship with non-partners and a partnership manner with CJV partners
- Appropriate plans for an exit if and when an exit will be required.

Committees in common

The NHSI guidance on foundation groups also offers committees in common as a possible vehicle for a new model of care. Currently, neither FTs nor NHS trusts have the power to set up legally binding 'joint committees', but it is possible for CCGs, FTs and NHS trusts to delegate to committees in common.

There is no statutory restriction on a director of an FT or an NHS trust or member of a CCG governing body holding more than one directorship, although in all cases fiduciary duties and the management of any potential conflicts of interest will need to be considered. CCGs, FTs and NHS trusts can therefore establish their own committees, which should meet at the same time and with the same remit. Wherever possible, membership should be identical. Each committee can only make a decision in relation to its own organisation but the decisions can be co-ordinated. The committees can be supported by a legally-binding contractual joint venture between the participating partners (see below). The key features of committees in common are:

- they are accountable to their respective boards
- although each organisation appoints its own committee, they can meet at the same time and with the same remit
- co-ordinated decision-making is improved by each committee having, wherever possible, the same membership
- commissioning contracts remain with the respective partners
- assets remain in each organisation's ownership but committees in common can be given responsibility for managing them
- establishing committees in common does not affect the regulatory framework.

Committees in common may be useful where three or more providers, including an NHS trust, wish to form a foundation group. Some provider boards have appointed a joint chief executive and/or a chair as a practical first step in setting up these arrangements. If a foundation group comprises a single FT and a single NHS trust, the NHS trust could appoint a committee whose membership consists of all the directors of the NHS FT.

Mergers and acquisitions

Ultimately, however, the legal forms above are limited in that accountability remains with each organisation's board. Consequently some boards may conclude that the real value of the structural change is to develop clinical and management integration as the first step towards a full merger or acquisition. A word of caution does need to be mentioned here since the King's Fund's review found that, although reconfigurations are sometimes undertaken to produce financial savings, the evidence that these savings are delivered is almost entirely lacking (see Imison, Sonola, Honeyman and Ross, King's Fund, 2014). Trust mergers are often seen as enabling change to services by removing organisational barriers. Again a parallel study of 20 mergers between 2010 and 2015 by the King's Fund found a cost to the DH of approximately £2 billion to support 12 of these mergers. This funding was used for various purposes, including paying off legacy debt, tackling underlying deficits, and investing in new buildings and upgraded facilities to enable clinical services to be reconfigured (see Collins, King's Fund, 2015). There was no clear evidence that these mergers had produced commensurate financial benefits through changes to clinical care or through cutting back on management costs: Delivering Sustainability and Transformation Plans (King's Fund, 2017).

Nevertheless this is still a regularly used vehicle for improving sustainability and delivering transformation, particularly in relation to dealing with poorly performing organisations. In fact, the *Supporting NHS providers: guidance on transactions for NHS foundation trusts* (2015) permits providers, where they acquire or merge with a poorly performing provider, to apply for an investment adjustment to agree relaxations in financial and/or operational standards for a specified period while historical performance issues are corrected through the integration. NHSI has recently confirmed that these investment adjustments, where appropriate, will continue to assure high-performing providers that they can help tackle poor performance at another provider through merger or acquisition without fear of significantly impacting on their own performance. Nevertheless, evidence in the Cass Business School report Mergers in the NHS: lessons learnt and recommendations: Summary (May 2016) states that: 'On the clinical side, improving performance in a failing trust could take two to three years, making the "performance holidays" allowed by the regulators too short.'

Provisions in the National Health Service Act 2006 (NHS Act 2006) govern NHS mergers and acquisitions. There are different provisions (and implications) depending on whether the transaction is structured as a merger or an acquisition. The Single Operating Framework sets out that NHSI is responsible for reviewing mergers and acquisitions to understand their potential impact on both the risk profile of the acquiring FT and its ability to continue to meet its provider licence conditions. NHSI and the Competition and Markets Authority (CMA) also have a role in approving mergers and acquisitions (see Chapter 12). Both the NHS organisations involved in the transaction, as well as commissioners of their services, are also required to consider their obligations under the Public Contracts Regulations 2015, as such obligations may be triggered as a result of the merger or acquisition. And finally, each NHS trust and/or FT must comply with its own internal governance arrangements when making a decision to merge or acquire another organisation.

Contractual forms

Contractual joint ventures

Both NHS FTs and NHS trusts can enter into contractual joint ventures that are legally binding. Such ventures do not establish new bodies but can create legally binding rights and responsibilities, e.g. establishing a contractual joint venture for pathology services. In principle, contractual joint ventures could be used to establish prime contractor/subcontractor arrangements to address changes to commissioning arrangements/proposals for service reconfiguration and financial adjustments/risk share arrangements.

Alliance Agreement

Alliance contracting for delivering projects has grown rapidly since it was first adopted with outstanding results in the early 1990s for the development of the BP Andrew oil field in the North Sea. An alliance contract creates a collaborative environment without the need for new organisational forms. By having one alliance contract, all parties are working to the same outcomes and are signed up to the same success measures. There is a strong sense of 'your problem is my problem, your success is my success'. The parties share risk, collectively own opportunities and are all responsible for the delivery of a contract. Unlike a contract co-ordinated by a prime contractor, there are no subcontractual arrangements. All organisations within the alliance are equal partners and organise their own internal governance to manage the delivery of care.

The Alliance Agreement is a contractual arrangement being consulted upon by NHSE for use by virtual MCPs/PACSs and does not replace or override existing services contracts (i.e. contracts between the commissioner and the provider for delivery of care). Instead, it is intended to bring providers together around a common aspiration for joint working across the system by setting out a number of shared objectives and a set of shared governance arrangements. The governance arrangements establish an alliance leadership team, an alliance management team and an alliance programme manager. The alliance leadership team is a forum, in which the representatives of each provider and commissioner have been given delegated decision-making authority. This allows them to make decisions on behalf of each alliance member. The need for unanimity in decision-making to make such an arrangement effective is set out in the terms of reference for the alliance leadership team.

Integration Agreement

The Integration Agreement is a contractual arrangement being consulted upon by NHSE for use in partially integrated MCPs/PACSs and will ensure that the GPs involved have the necessary commitment to integration for the MCP/PACS to succeed. The Agreement will perform two main functions:

1. to create a framework for shared governance and decision-making between practices and the MCP/PACS; and
2. to set out how the integration of services will be affected, setting out the primary care contribution to the MCP/PACS care model.

MCP/PACS Contract

The MCP/PACS Contract is a contractual arrangement being consulted upon by NHSE to make sure that the contracting and financial environment supports integration and delivery of the MCP/PACS care model. By awarding an MCP/PACS Contract, commissioners can ensure that the integrated working and aligned incentives that providers have built through the model are sustainable and that organisational siloes are truly dissolved. The MCP Contract will be awarded for up to 15 years and NHS bodies (e.g. FTs) and non-NHS bodies (e.g. a GP LLP) can bid for the contract. The PACS Contract will be of longer duration than those that are typically offered to NHS providers at present but with an initial early breakpoint (e.g. after the first two or three years of the contract term).

Bidders will need to demonstrate to commissioners, NHSI and NHSE through the procurement process and the Integrated Support and Assurance Process (ISAP) (see below), that they are capable of holding and delivering the contract. Any bidder for the MCP Contract (fully or partially integrated) will be required to demonstrate how they will work with GPs.

The PACS contract could be held by a new entity, formed (e.g. through a JV between a group of GPs, an acute trust, and other local health and care providers, or held by an existing NHS provider).

Formal agreement

Implementing the EHCH care model does not involve the creation of a single lead provider; nor are care home providers expected to merge with an MCP or a PACS in a new organisational form. Consequently a formal agreement is the contractual arrangement whereby care home providers may, if they wish, enter into an agreement with an MCP or PACS, or existing commissioners and providers, to formalise their commitment to whole-system, partnership working.

NHS Improvement and NHS England – oversight of new models of care

NHSI has indicated that it must be consulted when new care models involve transactions, mergers or raise other oversight considerations. NHSI must also be involved if NHS trusts or FTs are entering into new or novel contracts with their commissioners to deliver a new care model.

For FTs, NHSI will also continue to review transactions that are material, significant or statutory (see Chapter 12). For NHS trusts, NHSI also has a role, on behalf of the Secretary of State, in overseeing and assuring transactions.

NHSI is working with NHSE to develop and implement the ISAP. The Integrated Support and Assurance Process (ISAP): an introduction to assuring novel and complex contracts was published in November 2016 and was designed to be a consistent, streamlined NHSE and NHSI process for supporting and assuring novel procurements.

Summary

There is much technical and legal guidance in this area and it is clear from the wealth of resources being made available by NHSI and NHSE there is still more clarity to be gained on how to implement the new models of care and how to address their implications in terms of the statutory and regulatory frameworks.

Interestingly though, the key to success in all of these structural forms is related to clear governance processes which foster trust and collaboration. Such processes require a new type of leadership which is set out in the NHSI's new national framework, *Developing People – Improving Care. A National Framework* for action on improvement and leadership development in NHS-funded services (2016). High-performing health systems show that compassionate and inclusive leadership behaviours create cultures where people can deliver sustainable quality and efficiency improvements quickly.

> '[A]ny of the arrangements under consideration could bring benefits but it is not the organisational form that will determine the outcome, it is the quality of leadership alongside a culture of excellence in performance and accountability for results.'
>
> *'New organisational models for the NHS won't be built in a day', King's Fund, Blog, 1 July 2014*

PART FIVE

Risk management, assurance and audit

15

Risk management

Introduction

The responsibility of boards for effective risk management came under close scrutiny following the 2007–2009 banking crisis. Many banks were criticised for getting into financial difficulty because of reckless business strategies and failing to recognise the business risks that they were taking. Within NHS organisations, the scrutiny of risk management is also the responsibility of the board; however, there tends to be rigorous external scrutiny as well.

The leaders of NHS organisations are responsible for deciding risk strategies and risk policies, and for ensuring that the systems to support the management of those risks are effective. There are some similarities between a risk management system and an internal control system, but each has a different purpose. It is important to distinguish between them: in essence, the risk management system is the overarching system that is then underpinned and supported by the internal control system.

The boards of publicly quoted companies currently face a step change in their approach to risk management with the introduction of the Financial Reporting Council (FRC) *Guidance on Risk Management, Internal Control and Related Financial and Business Reporting* (2014). This guidance revises, integrates and replaces the previous editions of the FRC guidance *Internal Control: Revised Guidance for Directors on the Combined Code* (formerly known as the Turnbull Guidance) and the *Going Concern and Liquidity Risk: Guidance for Directors of UK Companies*. It also reflects the changes made to the FRC's UK Corporate Governance Code (UK Code) in 2014.

The guidance sets out its aims as 'bring[ing] together elements of best practice for risk management; prompt[ing] boards to consider how to discharge their responsibilities in relation to the existing and emerging principal risks faced by the company; reflect[ing] sound business practice, whereby risk management and internal control are embedded in the business process by which a company pursues its objectives; and highlight[ing] related reporting responsibilities'.

The new FRC risk management guidance has resulted from the economic recession and high-profile failures of risk management in the corporate sector. Many boards outside of the financial sector have delegated most risk matters to the audit committee and then only in a limited fashion – this is now an outdated and untenable model. As we will see in Chapter 16, the introduction of the strategic report now requires boards to report annually on their principal risks and why they are important to the organisation. This new guidance states that board responsibilities for risk include 'financial, operational, reputational, behavioural, organisational, third party, or external risks, such as market or regulatory risk, over which the board may have little or no direct control'.

Consequently, the challenge is to include behavioural and organisational risk into their risk management systems. The FRC's rationale behind this has been the recognition that the root causes of most crises lie in human behaviour and in the way that organisations are led, structured and managed. The guidance recommends that boards should evaluate their skills as to understanding risk as part of the annual board evaluation process so ignorance of risk will cease to be an excuse. Boards therefore need to understand:

- the nature of their principal risks
- the responsibility of the board to decide how much risk the organisation should be prepared to accept in order to achieve hoped-for financial or performance returns
- how much risk the organisation should be able to tolerate.

Exposures to business risk should not exceed the levels determined by the board. The business risk management system should be effective in ensuring that board strategies and policies are implemented and also reviewed.

Risk has a higher profile within NHS organisations with the active involvement of the audit committee in the board assurance framework (BAF) and the regular scrutiny of principal risks, or the existence of specific committees, which consider risk as part of the quality and/or governance agenda. Even so, this new FRC guidance provides a new benchmark for consideration.

The regulatory framework for risk management and internal control

Though not required to follow the UK Code, NHS organisations and health service governance can benchmark best practice against the provisions in the Code in recognition of the connection between good corporate governance and risk management. It is therefore worth setting out these provisions in more detail.

The Turnbull Guidance on internal control

When principles and provisions relating to internal control and risk management were first introduced into the UK (then the Combined Code) in 1998, a working party known as the Turnbull Committee published guidelines to listed companies on how to apply them. This was referred to as the Turnbull Guidance, and was the responsibility of the FRC.

This guidance has now been replaced by the FRC *Guidance on Risk Management, Internal Control and Related Financial and Business Reporting* (2014), which revises, integrates and replaces the Turnbull Guidance and reflects changes made to the UK Code in 2014. The new guidance also links the traditional Turnbull Guidance on internal control with emerging good practice for risk management. However, the Turnbull Guidance still offers helpful insights on the effective working of an internal controls system.

The guidance applied to the entire system of internal control, including operational and compliance controls as well as financial controls. The Turnbull Guidance defined an internal control system as 'the policies, processes, tasks, behaviours and other aspects of an organisation' that, taken together:

- help it to operate effectively and efficiently so that the organisation can respond in an appropriate way to principal risks to achieving the organisation's objectives
- help it to ensure the quality of external and internal reporting
- help to ensure compliance with applicable laws and regulations, and also with internal policies for the conduct of business.

According to the guidance, internal control should be embedded in the business and its operating systems. Controls should not be applied occasionally or from an external source, and they should be applied regularly and automatically as part of established procedures. Controls also have to remain relevant over time. As circumstances change, controls should be altered or adapted to meet the new requirements as controls that are appropriate to an organisation should take account of its particular circumstances.

The Turnbull Guidance also suggested that a system of internal control includes control activities, information and communications processes and process for monitoring the effectiveness of the system. The system of internal control should be embedded in the operations of the organisation and form part of its culture; be capable of responding quickly to evolving risks to the business arising from factors within the organisation and to changes in the business environment; and include procedures for reporting immediately to appropriate levels of management any significant control failings or weaknesses that are identified together with details of corrective action being undertaken.

FRC Guidance on Risk Management, Internal Control and Related Financial and Business Reporting

The guidance aims to bring together elements of best practice for risk management; prompt boards to consider how to discharge their responsibilities in relation to the existing and emerging principal risks faced by the organisation; reflect sound business practice, whereby risk management and internal control are embedded in the business process by which an organisation pursues its objectives; and highlight related reporting responsibilities.

The guidance is primarily aimed at companies subject to the UK Code but provides useful best practice benchmarking for NHS organisations and will be referenced throughout this chapter.

UK Corporate Governance Code requirements

A core principle of the UK Code is that: 'the board should maintain sound risk management and internal control systems'. The board has overall responsibility for the system of internal control, but the responsibility for designing and implementing the system, and for operating it, is delegated to management.

The UK Code also includes the following principle: 'the board is responsible for determining the nature and extent of the significant risks it is willing to take in achieving its strategic objectives'. This is elaborated upon in the following provision:

> '[T]he board is required to conduct a review of the effectiveness of the organisation's system of internal controls at least annually, and should report to the stakeholders that they have done so. The review should cover all material controls, including financial, operational and compliance controls.'

In other words, the board's responsibility for reviewing internal controls (and risk management) extends beyond financial matters to business operations and regulatory compliance.

Within the NHS, this review is known as the Annual Governance Statement (AGS) (previously known as the statement on internal control). It is covered in more detail in Chapter 16.

The nature of risk

Risk refers to the possibility that something unexpected or unplanned for will happen. In many cases, risk is seen as the possibility that something bad might happen. In everyday life, there is a risk of becoming seriously ill, being involved in a road accident, having a house burgled or flooded, having a motorcar breakdown, and so on. This can be described as downside risk, because it is a risk that something will happen that would not normally be expected.

There is also upside risk – the possibility that events might turn out better than expected. In a health service context, an example is the possibility that activity levels will be higher than planned or that working days lost through industrial action will be lower than anticipated. Another example is investment decisions. Every investment is risky, and actual returns could be lower or higher than expected. In deciding whether to undertake an investment, the risks as well as the potential returns should be considered. Some risks are easy to recognise because they are always present and an NHS organisation may have had many years of experience in dealing with them. For example, financial risks include the risk that tariff will be set at a substantially lower level or that the costs of pharmaceutical supplies will increase. Other risks, however, are more difficult to identify and anticipate.

The 2014 FRC guidance describes the board's responsibilities for an organisation's overall approach to risk management and internal control as follows:

- ensuring the design and implementation of appropriate risk management and internal control systems that identify the risks facing the company and enable the board to make a robust assessment of the principal risks;
- determining the nature and extent of the principal risks faced and those risks which the organisation is willing to take in achieving its strategic objectives (determining its 'risk appetite');
- ensuring that appropriate culture and reward systems have been embedded throughout the organisation;
- agreeing how the principal risks should be managed or mitigated to reduce the likelihood of their incidence or their impact;
- monitoring and reviewing the risk management and internal control systems, and the management's process of monitoring and reviewing, and satisfying itself that they are functioning effectively and that corrective action is being taken where necessary; and
- ensuring sound internal and external information and communication processes and taking responsibility for external communication on risk management and internal control.

That said, it is still management's role to implement and take day-to-day responsibility for board policies on risk management and internal control. The board needs to satisfy itself that management has understood the risks, implemented and monitored appropriate policies and controls, and are providing the board with timely information so that it can discharge its own responsibilities.

Risk appetite and risk tolerance

The board has overall responsibility for risk management and for deciding the organisation's risk appetite. Risk appetite is the level of risk that an organisation is willing to take in the pursuit of its objectives. Risk appetite can be defined as the combination of the desire to take on risk to obtain a specific return (financial or quality), risk capacity and risk tolerance. The 'desire to take on risk' refers to the amount and type of risk that the board of directors would like the organisation to have exposure to. Risk capacity is the maximum risk exposures that the organisation can accept without threatening its financial stability. Risk tolerance is the amount of risk that the organisation is prepared to accept to achieve its financial objectives. Risk tolerance is therefore the amount of risk that an organisation's board of directors allows the organisation to accept.

Risk appetite and risk tolerance are closely related. One is the amount of business risk (and types of business risk) the board would like the organisation to have and the other is the amount of risk that the board is prepared to tolerate.

Although the Walker Report made recommendations for corporate boards, which has been picked up by the 2014 FRC guidance, these should also be considered by NHS organisations. The Walker Report recommended that the board should consider risk appetite and risk tolerance, and that much more attention should be given to these issues:

> 'Board-level engagement in risk oversight should be materially increased, with particular attention to the monitoring of risk and discussion leading to decisions on the entity's risk appetite and tolerance.'

The 2014 FRC guidance confirms that the board has ultimate responsibility determining its risk appetite. The board should review risk appetite regularly, and decisions should be taken about the scale of risk that is desired or acceptable. Risk tolerance could be expressed in numerical terms, such as the maximum loss that the board would be willing to accept on a particular venture if events turn out adversely or in terms of the quality of the service that is provided. Alternatively, risk tolerance could be expressed in terms of a total ban on certain types of business activity or behaviour.

The relevance of risk for health service governance

NHS organisations must take risks in order to deliver healthcare. How much risk should they be prepared to tolerate, and would they be able to withstand 'shocks' in the business environment if an unexpected event or development were to occur? The board has the responsibility for strategic decisions on risk, and an important aspect of health service governance is for the board to recognise its responsibilities and ensure that the risk management system in the organisation is effective.

The board has a responsibility to govern the organisation in the interests of the stakeholders. A part of this responsibility is to decide the objectives and strategic direction for the organisation, to approve detailed strategic plans put forward by management, and to monitor and review the implementation of those plans. An important objective of NHS organisations is to make economic, efficient and effective use of public resources in its provision of healthcare, and the organisation's strategies should be directed towards this. However, any business strategy involves taking risks and actual results may be better or worse than expected.

Bad health service governance can result in the collapse of an organisation, and excessive risk-taking is one aspect of poor governance. The board should consider risk when it makes strategic business decisions. It should choose policies that are expected to deliver the key objectives, but should limit the risks to a level that it considers acceptable. For example, when the board takes major investment decisions or decides on a new corporate strategy such as a clinical services strategy, risks as well as expected returns must be properly assessed. The board should also be satisfied that managers take risk as well as expected outcomes into account in their decision-making. The Cadbury Report (1992) described risk management as:

> 'the process by which executive management, under board supervision, identifies the risk arising from business … and establishes the priorities for control and particular objectives.'

The significance of risk management for corporate governance was demonstrated forcibly by the global banking crisis in 2007–2009. In the UK, the government-initiated Walker Report into the failures in the banking industry commented that while there were failures in the regulation of the banking industry, much of the blame for the crisis was attributable to poor governance, and in particular inadequate attention to risk management. The significance of risk management for health service governance has already been well documented in case studies throughout this publication.

Types of risks

A distinction can be made between business risk and internal control risk (sometimes called governance risk). Business risks are risks that occur and arise in the business environment in which an organisation operates. Business risks may also be referred to as strategic risks, as they are determined by the strategies that the organisation pursues. Risks will differ between organisations but may include financial, operational, reputational, behavioural, third party, or external risks, such as market or regulatory risk, over which the board may have little or no direct control. In the NHS, business risks could be risks to patient safety and financial security that arise from factors in their external environment, including competition or government policy, over which management has no direct control.

Categories of business risk

The nature and severity of business risks varies from one organisation to another. Risks change over time: some become less significant, and new risks emerge. Business risks are risks that the actual performance of the business could be much worse (or better) than expected due to unexpected developments in the business environment. For example, when an organisation develops a new service, it will have an expectation of the likely activity level. Actual levels could be higher or lower than expected. With some new services, the risk that activity levels will differ from expectation could be much more severe than with other new services. There are various reasons why activity levels may be less than expected, or may fall unexpectedly. Competitors may take away some of the organisation's market share; an organisation may suffer from bad publicity; there may be new regulations making the provision of a particular service more difficult.

Business risks can be categorised or identified in different ways, but it may help to understand the variety of risks by considering the following sources of risk.

- **Financial risk:** these are risks that financial conditions may change, with adverse changes in tariff or interest rates, higher losses from bad debts or changes in prices from major suppliers.
- **Operational risk:** the risk of losses resulting from inadequate or failed internal processes, people and systems, or external events.
- **Reputational risk:** the risk of loss in customer loyalty or customer support following an event that damages the organisation's reputation.
- **Behavioural risk:** these are risks connected with the workplace and lifestyle behaviours of employees and organisations that have a negative impact on its productivity.
- **Third-party or competition risk:** the risk that business performance will differ from expected performance because of actions taken (or not taken) by other organisations.
- **External risks:** these are risks of significant changes in the business environment from political and regulatory factors, economic factors, social and environmental factors and technology factors (the so-called 'PEST' factors). For example, business performance may be affected by the introduction of new regulations, a change of government, economic decline or growth, environmental issues, unexpected changes in social habits or technological change.

Each industry and each organisation within an industry faces different risks. The questions that management should ask are 'What risks does this organisation face?' and 'How can these risks be measured?' It has to be possible to assess the risk in a business, even one with unpredictable variations in key factors such as activity levels or market prices. High volatility is associated with high business risk.

CASE STUDY: Heart of England NHS Foundation Trust

Heart of England NHS Foundation Trust (FT) was the first FT to acquire another NHS trust, Good Hope Hospital, in 2007. The board realised that making an acquisition was a complex process – especially in the NHS – and had to establish clear governance structures to manage the inherent risk in the project. Key areas for consideration were:

- understanding the strategic imperative to acquire
- appraising options
- how to value a trust
- how to negotiate terms
- handling the actual transaction process and interacting with key stakeholders
- planning for post-merger integration
- organisational development post merger to enhance staff morale.

Large-scale mergers and acquisitions have inherent risks and Monitor's role in this area was to ensure that the trust did not jeopardise its quality of services or financial stability. It did this by providing indicative risk ratings of major transactions, leaving the board to put in place strategies and mechanisms to mitigate any material risks.

- For each of these risks, how would the organisation be affected if the worst outcome came about, or if a fairly bad outcome happened?
- What is the likelihood of a bad outcome for that risk item?
- What is the organisation's risk appetite or risk tolerance?
- What should the organisation be doing to manage the risk, either by avoiding it altogether or planning to deal with the problems that will arise in the event of a bad outcome?

Though all manner of principal risks in the business environment may cause an organisation to fail to achieve its objectives, further principal risks are failures or weaknesses within its own internal systems and operating procedures or human error. These failures and weaknesses could be avoided, or the consequences of failures could be limited, by means of internal controls. Internal controls are measures or arrangements that are intended to prevent failures from happening, limiting their potential effect, or identifying when a failure has occurred so that corrective measures can be taken. The failure or weakness of these controls is classified as an internal control risk.

Internal control is also an aspect of governance, because the board of directors has a responsibility to ensure that the assets of the organisation are not threatened, and that the interests of the stakeholders are not damaged, by making sure that an effective system of internal control is in place.

Internal control risks

An internal control system is the system that an organisation has for identifying internal control risks, applying controls to reduce the risk of losses from these risks and taking corrective action when losses occur. There should be controls to ensure that the organisation, its systems and procedures operate in the way that is intended, without disruption or disturbance. In addition, there should be controls to ensure that assets are safeguarded, such as controls to ensure that money received is banked and is not stolen, and that operating assets such as items of equipment and computers are not damaged or lost. Such controls should include measures to reduce the risk of fraud and financial controls that should ensure the completeness and accuracy of accounting records, and the timely preparation of financial information. Controls should also be in place to ensure compliance with key regulations, such as CQC regulations, NHS Improvement (NHSI) regulations or health and safety regulations.

However, just like risk management, the board needs to be clear on its strategy and corporate objectives in order to assess what internal risks exist and therefore what controls are needed. The Auditing Practices Board says:

> 'Clear business objectives need to be identified before an effective system of internal control can be established. Without clear objectives, management will be unable to identify and evaluate the risks that threaten the achievement of their objectives and design and operate a system of internal control to manage those risks.'

Internal control risks are risks that arise within an organisation because of weaknesses in its systems, procedures, management or personnel. Unless there are controls to deal with them, internal control risks can lead to losses because of operational failures, errors or fraud. The controls for these risks are 'internal controls' and internal controls are applied within an internal control system. It is the responsibility of the board of directors of an organisation to ensure that the internal control system (and the internal controls within this system) is effective in preventing losses from internal control risks, or identifying losses and taking corrective action when they occur.

CASE STUDY: Internal controls weaknesses

A hospital operated from three separate locations in the same city. At one of these locations, a considerable amount of cash had built up following donations from grateful patients. This was kept in a safe in the manager's office. One day, two uniformed individuals came to the building and said that they had instructions to take the safe to the organisation's head office, which was in a different building. They were allowed to take the safe and the security guard actually helped them to put it into their vehicle, parked outside the front door of the building. The two individuals drove off with the safe, containing over £30,000, and were not seen again.

It should be apparent that the organisation lost £30,000 because of basic mistakes, which point to weaknesses in internal controls:

- Why was there was a lot of money in the safe? Why had most of it not been taken to the bank?
- Why were the two individuals allowed to take the safe without checking their authorisation to take it?
- How did they gain access to the building so easily?

There were weaknesses in the procedures for managing donations, banking cash, building security and authorisation of actions. If suitable internal controls had been in place, the loss of the money would not have occurred.

Categories of internal control risks

A useful definition of internal control was given by the US Committee of Sponsoring Organizations of the Treadway Commission (COSO). The COSO Framework defines internal control as 'a process, effected by an entity's board of directors, management and other personnel, designed to provide reasonable assurance regarding the achievement of objectives' in the areas of effectiveness and efficiency of operations (through operational controls), the reliability of financial reporting (through financial controls) and compliance with relevant laws and regulations (through compliance controls).

It follows then that internal control risks can be categorised into three broad types, namely: financial, operational and compliance.

- **Financial risks**: these are risks of errors or fraud in accounting systems and accounting and finance activities. Errors or fraud could lead to losses for the organisation, or to incorrect financial statements. Weak controls may also mean that financial assets are not properly protected. Examples of financial risks include the risk of failure to record transactions in the bookkeeping system, failure to collect money owed by customers, failure to protect cash and misreporting (deliberate or unintentional) in the financial statements.
- **Operational risks:** the Basel Committee for banking supervision gives a helpful definition of 'operational risk'. Although this definition applies to risks in the banking industry, it has a wider application. Operational risk is 'the risk of losses resulting from inadequate or failed internal processes, people and systems, or external events'. Operational risks include the risks of a breakdown in a system due to machine failures or software errors, the risk of losing information from computer files or having confidential information stolen, the risk of a terrorist attack, and losses arising from mistakes or omissions by staff.
- **Compliance risks:** these are risks that important laws or regulations will not be complied with properly. Failure to comply with the law could result in legal action against the organisation and/or fines.

Responsibilities for risk management and internal control

The organisation's risk management strategy should set out how the authority, responsibility and accountability for risk management and internal control is defined, co-ordinated and documented throughout the organisation from individual employees through to board members. This strategy should be reviewed and approved by the board.

The board

The board is responsible for risk at a high level, but responsibilities for the management of risk are delegated to executive management. The board should decide the level of risks that are acceptable at a strategic level, and should ensure that the management team consider risk in the decisions that they make.

The 2014 FRC guidance explains:

> 'The board should define the processes to be adopted for its on-going monitoring and review [of risk management and internal control systems], including specifying the requirements, scope and frequency for reporting and assurance. Regular reports to the board should provide a balanced assessment of the risks and the effectiveness of the systems of risk management and internal control in managing those risks. The board should form its own view on effectiveness, based on the evidence it obtains, exercising the standard of care generally applicable to directors in the exercise of their duties.'

The 2014 FRC guidance goes on to recommend questions that the board should consider throughout the year.

- How effectively have the risks been assessed and the principal risks determined?
- How have they been managed or mitigated?
- Have the necessary actions been taken promptly to remedy any significant failings or weaknesses?
- Do the causes of the failing or weakness indicate poor decision-taking, a need for more extensive monitoring or a reassessment of the effectiveness of management's on-going processes?

In addition to the board's ongoing monitoring and review role, the 2014 FRC guidance recommends that it should undertake an annual review of the effectiveness of the systems to ensure that it has considered all significant aspects of risk management and internal control for the year under review, up to the date of approval of the annual report and accounts. An effectiveness review of should consider:

- the organisation's willingness to take on risk (its risk appetite), the desired culture within the organisation and whether this culture has been embedded;
- the operation of the risk management and internal control systems, covering the design, implementation, monitoring and review and identification of risks and determination of those which are principal to the organisation;
- the integration of risk management and internal controls with considerations of strategy and business model, and with business planning processes;
- the changes in the nature, likelihood and impact of principal risks, and the organisation's ability to respond to changes in its business and the external environment;
- the extent, frequency and quality of the communication of the results of management's monitoring to the board which enables it to build up a cumulative assessment of the state of control in the organisation and the effectiveness with which risk is being managed or mitigated;
- issues dealt with in reports reviewed by the board during the year, in particular the incidence of significant control failings or weaknesses that have been

identified at any time during the period and the extent to which they have, or could have, resulted in unforeseen impact; and

- the effectiveness of the organisation's public reporting processes.

At board level, responsibility for reviewing the effectiveness of the risk management system may be delegated by the board to the audit committee, which is also likely to have responsibility for reviewing the internal control system. Alternatively, the board may prefer to establish a separate risk committee. Where delegation does occur, the 2014 FRC guidance makes it clear that:

> 'The board should be satisfied that the arrangements for the work carried out, for the co-ordination of their work (if more than one committee is involved), and for reporting to the board are appropriate and operating effectively. The board retains ultimate responsibility for the risk management and internal control systems and should reach its own conclusions regarding the recommendations it receives.'

The board should also ensure that the remuneration committee takes appropriate account of risk when determining remuneration policies and awards, and should also ensure that the links between the remuneration committee and the risk and/or audit committee are operating effectively.

Risk committees

The advantages of having a separate risk committee are as follows.

- It can focus on risk issues and reviewing the organisation's risk management system, without having to concern itself with other issues (such as the external auditors). It would give advice to the board on matters such as risk appetite and risk strategy.
- The composition of the board is not restricted by statutory requirements. A risk committee should ideally consist mainly of non-executive directors (NEDs) but should also have the finance director as a member. If the audit committee had responsibility for the oversight of risk management, the finance director could not be a committee member (although they could be invited to meetings of the audit committee to give their views).

However, a separate risk committee is probably more useful for a large public organisation than for a smaller listed organisation. The Walker Report recommended that another risk committee could be established, consisting of senior executives and chaired by the chief executive officer (CEO). This committee would be responsible for risk management at an operational level. The responsibilities of this committee and the board risk committee would be very different as:

> 'The role of the board risk committee is to advise the board on all high-level risk matters and should not extend into operational matters which are for the executive within the overall risk framework determined by the board. The

> NEDs on the committee cannot be expected to be able to replicate the industry expertise of the executive team nor will their capacity to contribute be enhanced by information overload. The materials presented to them should be in succinct format, highlighting major issues.'

This provides an interesting consideration for larger NHS organisations, where a similar structure may be helpful.

Risk officers

In common with larger companies, some larger NHS organisations may also appoint specialist executive managers with responsibility for risk – a chief risk officer (CRO). The Walker Report recommended that the CRO should report directly to the finance director or CEO, but also have direct access to the board. They should also be able to provide advice to the board on all risk issues affecting the organisation. The Walker Report added:

> 'Alongside an internal reporting line to the chief executive officer or [chief financial officer (CFO)], the CRO should report to the board risk committee, with explicit, and what is clearly understood to be, direct access to the chair of the committee in the event of need, for example, if there is a difference of view with the chief executive officer or CFO.'

The report emphasises the need to protect the independence of the CRO from the influence of the CEO or finance director. It also recommends that (like the company secretary) only the board should be able to appoint or dismiss the CRO, and the remuneration of the CRO should be decided by the organisation chair or the remuneration committee.

Again, this provides an interesting consideration for larger NHS organisations where a similar role may be helpful or the function may be appended to the role of the company secretary.

Risk management systems and procedures

To enable the board of directors to carry out its responsibilities for risk management effectively, there are two essential requirements. Firstly, board members should have an understanding of risks and risk management. Secondly, there should be a risk management system in place that the board as a whole or the appropriate board committee can review.

Risk registers

An organisation might use a risk register for recording identified risks, the evaluation of the risks, and the measures that have been taken to deal with them. Executive management maintains the risk register, but it can be used by the risk committee of the board (or the audit committee) as a way of reviewing the effectiveness of the risk management system. At board level, there should be regular programmed scrutiny of the register of principal risks, including:

- the risk score
- mitigation/action being taken
- escalation or de-escalation of risks.

Individual areas or divisions within the organisations should have processes in which the same risk management system operates with the responsibility of escalating risks, which are outside of their resources or authority to manage.

Interestingly, the King III Code is much more explicit about risk management than the FT Code and UK Code. Provisions in the King III Code relating to risk management include the following.

- The board's risk strategy should be executed by management by means of risk management systems and processes.
- The board should ensure that effective and ongoing risk assessments are performed by management.
- Risks should be prioritised and ranked, in order to focus on areas where action is most needed.
- The board should regularly receive and review a register of the organisation's key risks.
- Key risks should be quantified where practicable (e.g. in terms of maximum potential loss or expected loss).
- The board should ensure that processes are in place for anticipating unpredictable risks.
- Management should identify and note in the risk register the responses that have been decided upon and taken.
- Management should provide assurances to the board that the risk management plan is integrated into the daily activities of the business.

Stress testing

'Stress testing' is widely used by major organisations to assess their ability to withstand extreme 'shocks' or unexpected events in the business environment. This can be done by taking the normal business planning or forecasting model used by the organisation and altering a key variable, such as the rate of growth (or decline) in economic growth, a very large increase in a major resource such as staff costs, loss of access to a key market for service provision, and so on. The purpose of stress testing is to assess whether the organisation could survive the shock. If there are doubts about this ability, the organisation should consider measures to reduce the risk, perhaps by developing contingency plans, or taking measures to improve their capital or liquidity.

This is not widely used in individual NHS organisations, although NHSI does make extensive use of downside scenario planning in its FT application process to assess the financial resilience of the applicant NHS trust.

Elements of the risk assessment process

The 2014 FRC guidance does not set out in detail the procedure by which a company designs and implements its risk management and internal control systems. Defining a single approach to achieving best practice would be misguided, as it would lead boards to underestimate the crucial importance to high-quality risk management of the culture and behaviour they promote. However, it still possible to identify some basic elements to a risk management system. These elements are:

- risk identification
- risk evaluation
- risk management measures
- risk control and review.

A further element that might be considered is that of risk training. Risk identification involves an organisation having a procedure in place for reviewing and identifying the risks it faces. Risks change over time, and risk reviews should therefore be undertaken regularly.

Risk evaluation calls for procedures to assess the potential size of the risk. The expected losses that could occur from adverse events or developments depend on the probability that an adverse outcome will occur and size of the loss in the event of an adverse outcome. Where a risk is unlikely to materialise into an adverse outcome, and the loss would in any case be small, no management action might be necessary. Where the risk is higher, measures should be taken to protect the organisation so that the remaining exposure to risk is within the organisation's tolerance level and consistent with its risk appetite.

The 2008 NHS National Patient Safety Agency publication *A Risk Matrix for Risk Managers* was developed to assist NHS risk managers in implementing an integrated system of risk assessment. The guidance sets out a matrix for NHS organisations to score both the probability and the size of the loss. The matrix covers risks associated with:

- adverse publicity/reputation
- business objectives/projects
- environmental impact
- finance, including claims
- human resources/organisational development/staffing/competence
- impact on the safety of patients, staff or public (physical/psychological harm)
- quality/complaints/audit
- service/business interruption
- statutory duty/inspections.

Management should decide the measures taken to deal with each risk and is accountable to the board for these measures. In broad terms, risks can be dealt with by avoiding them or by taking steps to limit the exposure. Some risks can be avoided but many risks have to be accepted as an inevitable feature of business.

For principal risks, an organisation should decide what measures might be necessary to reduce the risk to acceptable proportions. Risks may be reduced through measures such as stakeholder management and collaborative ventures. From a health service governance perspective, it should be a responsibility of the board to make sure that risks are reviewed regularly and that management takes suitable measures to deal with them.

Executive management should establish control systems to monitor risks that include identifying situations that are getting out of control, or where significant events have developed or are developing.

A further consideration for NHS organisations is the requirement of the 2014 FRC guidance that:

> 'the board should consider whether it, and any committee or management group to which it delegates activities, has the necessary skills, knowledge, experience, authority and support to enable it to assess the risks the organisation faces and exercise its responsibilities effectively. Boards should consider specifically assessing this as part of their regular evaluations of their effectiveness.'

This should ensure that they are capable of contributing proactively to board discussions on risk strategy. Training in risk management should be particularly important for members of the board committee (audit committee or risk committee) with responsibility for reviewing the risk management system.

Internal control systems and procedures

The board of directors is responsible for maintaining a sound system of risk management and internal control, as shown earlier in the UK Code and FRC Guidance 2014. They require the board of directors to set appropriate policies on internal control, to seek regular assurance to satisfy itself that the system is operating effectively and to ensure that the system of internal control is effective in managing risks in the way that it has approved.

In deciding its policies for internal control and assessing what constitutes an effective system of internal control, the board should consider:

- the nature and extent of the risks facing the organisation
- the amount of risk and types of risk that it regards as acceptable for the organisation to bear
- the likelihood that the risks will materialise
- the organisation's ability to reduce the impact on the business of the risks that do materialise
- the costs of operating particular controls relative to the benefits to be obtained from managing the risks they control. Controls are not worth having if they cost more than the expected benefits or savings they will provide.

Having identified the responsibilities of the board for maintaining a sound system of internal control, the 2014 FRC guidance adds that it is the job of management to implement the board's policies on control. Management must have procedures for identifying and evaluating the risks faced by the organisation, as well as designing, implementing and monitoring a control system to deal with these risks in a way that is consistent with the board's policies. In addition, all employees have some responsibility for internal control, for example to avoid making mistakes in their work and also to ensure that the control procedures for which they are responsible are properly performed.

The board needs to have assurance that there is a robust and resilient internal control system for managing internal control risks that feeds into and underpins the risk management system. Having established the internal control risks to the organisation's strategic objectives, management needs to identify the internal controls to limit or manage those risks. The controls are an essential part of an internal control system; their nature and extent will depend to a large extent on the organisation's size, what controls it can afford and whether the benefits obtained from any particular control measure are sufficient to justify its cost. The internal control system should be sufficiently robust and effective to minimise the risk of serious losses through error or fraud. In a large organisation, there would be thousands of different financial operational and compliance controls, each designed to prevent particular financial, operational or compliance failures, or to detect them if they occur.

An important aspect of health service governance is to ensure that the system of internal control (and the internal controls within that system) is adequate and effective in preventing or detecting failures in the system. For example, if the system is ineffective, an organisation may be exposed to a high risk of fraud and also to a high risk that its annual financial statements will not be accurate or reliable.

A sound system of internal control should be embedded in the operations of the organisation and form part of its culture. It should be capable of responding quickly to risks to the business as they emerge and develop, should include procedures for reporting immediately to the management responsible and control failings that have been identified and any corrective action that has been undertaken.

The Turnbull Guidance emphasised that a sound system of internal control cannot provide certain protection against an organisation suffering losses or breaches of laws or regulations or failing to meet its business objectives. The possibility will always exist of 'poor judgement in decision-making, human error, control processes being deliberately circumvented by employees and others, management overriding controls and the occurrence of unforeseen circumstances'. A sound system of internal control provides reasonable assurance that risks will be suitably controlled, but cannot provide absolute assurance that there will not be any material losses, fraud, errors or breaches of laws and regulations.

In addition to the internal controls themselves, an internal control system should also have other elements to be effective and achieve its objectives. The

COSO Framework identifies five elements to a system of internal control (also recognised in the Turnbull Report).

- A control environment that describes the awareness of (and attitude to) internal controls in the organisation, shown by the directors, management and employees generally. It therefore encompasses corporate culture, management style and employee attitudes to control procedures.
- There should be a system or procedures for identifying the risks facing the organisation (and how these are changing) and assessing their significance. Controls or management initiatives should be devised to deal with significant risks.
- Controls should be devised and implemented to eliminate, reduce or control risks.
- All employees who are responsible for the management of risks should receive information that enables them to fulfil this task.
- The effectiveness of internal controls and the internal control system generally should be monitored regularly. Internal audit is one method of monitoring the internal control system. Internal controls are also monitored by executive management and (as part of their annual audit) by the external auditors. The board of directors also has a responsibility to review the effectiveness of the system.

Types of internal controls

Financial controls are internal accounting controls that are sufficient to provide reasonable assurance that:

- transactions are made only according to the general or specific authorisation of management
- transactions are recorded so that financial statements can be prepared according to accounting standards and generally accepted accounting principles
- transactions are recorded so that assets can be accounted for
- access to assets is only allowed according to the general or specific authorisation of management
- the accounting records for assets are compared with actual assets at reasonable intervals of time
- appropriate action is taken whenever there are found to be differences.

The maintenance of proper accounting records is an important element of internal control. Effective financial controls should ensure the quality of external and internal financial reporting, so that there are no material errors in the accounting records and financial statements. They should ensure that no fraud is committed (or that fraud is detected when it occurs) and that the financial assets of the organisation are not stolen, lost or needlessly damaged, or that these risks are reduced.

A useful method of categorising internal financial controls was used in an old guideline issued by the UK Auditing Practices Board, using the mnemonic SPAMSOAP. In this guideline (no longer in issue) internal financial controls are categorised as follows.

S: **Segregation of duties:** where possible, duties should be split between two or more people, so that the work done by one person acts as a check on the work done by another. With segregation of duties, it is more difficult for fraud to take place, because several individuals would have to collude in the fraud. It is also more difficult for accidental errors to occur, because when several people are involved in a task, they act as a check on each other.

P: **Physical controls**: measures to ensure the physical safety of assets, such as putting cash in a safe, banking cash receipts immediately, and preventing unauthorised access to computer systems through the use of passwords and internet firewalls.

A: **Authorisation and approval:** all financial transactions should require the authorisation or approval of an appropriate responsible person, and there should be an authorisation limit to how much spending each responsible person can approve.

M: **Management controls:** management should exercise control over financial systems, for example by preparing a budget and then monitoring actual performance by comparing it with the budget. Management controls can also be exercised by reviewing other financial statements, such as a balance sheet, profit and loss account and cash flow statement.

S: **Supervision:** the day-to-day work of employees should be properly supervised. Good supervision will reduce the likelihood of errors or fraud.

O: **Organisation:** everyone should be fully aware of his or her responsibilities, and lines of authority, lines of reporting and levels of responsibility should be clear. Errors and fraud are much more likely where it is uncertain who is responsible for what and who should be reporting to whom.

A: **Arithmetical and accounting controls:** these are procedures in an accounts office to check the accuracy of the records and the numbers. They include the use of control totals and reconciliations.

P: **Personnel:** the quality of internal controls is dependent on the quality of the individuals working in the organisation. Personnel selected to do a job should have the right personal qualities and be properly trained and/or qualified.

This list of different types of control is provided as a guide to the nature of financial controls. Health service governance is concerned with the adequacy of internal controls and the effectiveness of the internal control system; designing and implementing controls is a responsibility of management.

Operational controls are controls that help to reduce operational risks, or identify failures in operational systems when these occur. They are designed to prevent failures in operational procedures, or to detect and correct operational failures if they do occur. Operational failures may be caused by machine breakdowns, human error, failures in the performance of systems (possibly due to human error), weaknesses in procedures and poor management. Operational controls are measures designed to prevent these failures from happening, or identifying and correcting problems that do occur. Regular equipment maintenance, better training of staff, automation of standard procedures, and reporting systems that make managers accountable for their actions are all examples of operational controls.

Compliance controls are concerned with making sure that an entity complies with all the requirements of relevant legislation and regulations. It can be difficult to understand the nature of internal control risks and internal controls to deal with them. There are many different risks and many controls that are applied. The following are simple examples.

CASE STUDY: Risk reporting in an FT applicant trust

A trust had a cumulative deficit of £20 million at 31 March 2012. However, the trust's sights were set firmly on achieving FT status, which meant that the trust's ongoing financial performance had to improve and the cumulative deficit had to be recovered.

Over the past three years the trust had recovered the deficit and was forecasting a £12 million surplus for 2014/15. The trust achieved this in a number of ways, notably with significant improvements in its arrangements to manage performance against budgets.

The trust reorganised its management structure, moving from 13 clinical directorates to five clinical divisions, plus a sixth division covering corporate services. Key to this restructuring was the decision to have a clinician as the head of division, who is then accountable to the chief executive. The head of division is paid to manage the division (four sessions per week) as well as undertake clinical activities.

Another key part of the trust's strategy was to minimise its reliance on non-recurrent measures. The financial strategy allows for non-recurrent measures to account for no more than 1% of turnover. If this limit is exceeded, the director of finance works with divisions to replace non-recurrent with recurrent.

The trust has also improved reporting to the board so that key risks are more readily apparent. A new format of finance report to the trust board has been introduced, which includes traffic light risk indicators for the high level summary and includes commentary on high level details of the main risks in relation to each division's financial performance.

As a result the trust's budgetary control arrangements have improved considerably over the past three years, which has resulted in the trust being well-placed to deliver significant surpluses in the short to medium term and embark on an investment programme to replace all of the trust's facilities that are currently unfit for purpose.

CASE STUDY: Prescribing practice in clinical commissioning groups

Delivering healthcare to satisfy the local population and providing clinically effective treatment requires the extensive use of medicines. External benchmarking suggested that through improved generic prescribing alone, general practitioners (GPs) could save at least £350,000 each year. A clinical commissioning group (CCG)'s medicines management team worked closely with GPs in trying to improve prescribing practice both in terms of clinical effectiveness and the assurance of best value. Education, incentive schemes, practice profiling and local drug formularies all helped to improve prescribing habits, but the decision over which drug to prescribe ultimately rested with the GP during their consultation with the patient.

The CCG completed a business case for the use of a new software package that tied into the GPs' electronic prescribing system. Under the control of the medicines management team, a series of protocols were programmed into the system that automatically raised a flag in response to the GPs' drug selection. Alternative drug choices were offered, giving the GP an option to accept the recommended alternative(s).

After eight months of full implementation, the CCG reported actual savings in excess of £400,000. In addition to financial savings, the implementation of the software had been a successful means of getting important information to GPs at the moment that they made their prescribing decision. The system provides the CCG with an opportunity to realise financial savings in drug prescribing while at the same time influencing good prescribing practice and supporting clinical effectiveness.

Reviewing the effectiveness of risk management and internal control

The UK Code states that the board of directors (or the audit committee) should carry out a review of the effectiveness of the system of risk management and internal control at least annually. NHS bodies, as part of the Department of Health (DH)'s NHS Controls Assurance project, were required to include a statement on internal controls (SIC) in its annual report and accounts. This has now been replaced by the AGS (see Chapter 16).

In order to review the effectiveness of the system, there must be procedures for monitoring and review. The board or audit committee needs to form its own view about the effectiveness of the system, based on the information and assurances it receives. The sources of information about risk management and internal control are management, the internal auditors (if the organisation has an internal audit function) and the external auditors, who notify management and the audit committee about weaknesses in internal controls that they have discovered in their audit. Their roles are set out in more detail in Chapter 17.

The board of directors and the audit committee do not have the time to carry out a detailed review themselves, and they must therefore rely on information provided to them by management and internal auditors. The most regular source of information for the board or audit committee about internal control should be management reports. Additional reporting may be provided, however, by the internal auditors, or by a firm of external accountants or auditors hired to perform a specific internal audit investigation.

In its *Guidance on Audit Committees* (revised 2010), the FRC states that except where the responsibility is retained by the entire board, or delegated to a risk committee:

> 'The audit committee should receive reports from management on the effectiveness of the systems they have established and the conclusions of any testing carried out by internal and external auditors.'

Emergency preparedness and business continuity

Emergency preparedness is a plan of what to do if a disaster that is unconnected with the organisation's business and outside the control of management occurs. Disaster recovery planning goes beyond procedures that should be taken in an emergency, such as a fire or explosion in a building. It is intended to establish what should be done if an extreme disaster threatens the ability of the organisation to maintain its operations. Examples of disasters are natural disasters (such as major fires or flooding or storm damage to key installations or offices), major terrorist attacks and pandemics.

Emergency preparedness plans are vital for NHS organisations, as lengthy or widespread overwhelming demand or shutdown of operations could be catastrophic. While the training of appropriate NHS staff regarding such arrangements in the UK is the responsibility of NHS organisations, the DH fund an extensive training programme delivered by the Health Protection Agency (HPA) to support the NHS in England in planning and preparing for major incidents.

Guidance is given in *NHS Emergency Planning Guidance 2005*, which sets out general principles to guide all NHS organisations in developing their ability to respond to a major incident (or incidents) and to manage recovery whether the incident or incidents has effects locally, regionally, or nationally, within the context of the requirements of the Civil Contingencies Act 2004 (CCA 2004). The guidance contains strategic national guidance for all NHS organisations in England and equivalent guidance is provided by health departments in devolved administrations. The CCA 2004 defines an emergency as:

> 'An event or a situation which threatens serious damage to human welfare in a place in the UK, the environment of a place in the UK, or war or terrorism which threatens serious damage to the security of the UK.'

The definition is concerned with consequences rather than the cause or source. For the NHS, incidents are classed as either:

- Business Continuity Incident
- Critical Incident
- Major Incident

Each will impact upon service delivery within the NHS, may undermine public confidence and require contingency plans to be implemented. NHS organisations should be confident of the severity of any incident that may warrant a major incident declaration, particularly where this may be due to internal capacity pressures, if a critical incident has not been raised previously through the appropriate local escalation procedure.

Business Continuity Incident

A business continuity incident is an event or occurrence that disrupts, or might disrupt, an organisation's normal service delivery, below acceptable predefined levels, where special arrangements are required to be implemented until services can return to an acceptable level. (This could be a surge in demand requiring resources to be temporarily redeployed)

Critical Incident

A critical incident is any localised incident where the level of disruption results in the organisation temporarily or permanently losing its ability to deliver critical services, patients may have been harmed or the environment is not safe requiring special measures and support from other agencies, to restore normal operating functions.

Major Incident

A major incident is any occurrence that presents serious threat to the health of the community or causes such numbers or types of casualties, as to require special arrangements to be implemented. For the NHS this will include any event defined as an emergency as above.

Although not formally described, there may be events occurring on a national scale, such as fuel strikes, pandemics or multiple events that require the collective capability of the NHS nationally. In each NHS organisation, the CEO is responsible for ensuring that their organisation has a Major Incident Plan in place that will be built on the principles of risk assessment, cooperation with partners, emergency planning, communicating with the public and information sharing. The plan will link into the organisation's arrangements for ensuring business continuity as required by the CCA 2004.

The CEO will ensure that the board receives regular reports, at least annually, regarding emergency preparedness, including reports on exercises, training and testing undertaken by the organisation, and that adequate resources are made available to allow discharge of these responsibilities. As a minimum requirement, NHS organisations will be required to undertake a live exercise every three years; a tabletop exercise every year and a test of communications cascades every six months. A review of emergency preparedness plans may therefore be a part of the annual review of the effectiveness of internal control by the board or audit committee.

NHS organisations and providers of NHS funded care must:

- nominate an director level accountable emergency officer who will be responsible for EPRR; and
- contribute to area planning for EPRR through local health resilience partnerships (LHRPs) and other relevant groups.

Business continuity management also forms an important part of risk management arrangements and is a further requirement of the CCA 2004. The aim of business continuity management is to ensure that NHS organisations are able to maintain the highest level of service possible whatever might happen to the infrastructure. There is a range of problems that might affect NHS organisations and services at any time, for example, loss of water or power, flooding, or criminal action. The aim of business continuity planning is to enable planning and reaction in a coordinated manner. While business continuity and major incident planning are usually separate processes within an organisation, a major incident may occur at the same time as a business continuity issue, or be triggered by it.

Business continuity management, including processes for recovery and restoration, should be considered by NHS organisations as part of its everyday business processes. Business continuity should be seen as embedded in the culture of the NHS as principles of health and safety, and there must be demonstrable commitment to the process from the boards of NHS organisations. The skills to develop business continuity plans are complementary to those involved in emergency planning and may therefore need to be undertaken by separate officers. It is critical though that both plans are integrated and complementary to each other.

High reliability organisations

There has been some interesting work carried out in recent years with regard to major hazard organisations such as airlines and oil refineries, who have been attempting to influence the organisational and safety culture at their sites to transform them into high reliability organisations (HROs) with a positive safety culture These are organisations that are able to manage and sustain almost error-free performance despite operating in hazardous conditions where the consequences of errors could be catastrophic.

Descriptions of HROs usually include organisations where failure may have far-reaching, potentially catastrophic consequences. Such organisations will be typically characterised by a high level of interactive complexity: for example, interaction among system components is unpredictable and/or invisible, and there is a high level of interdependence amongst a system's component parts (including people, equipment and procedures). Much like many HROs, the healthcare industry does complex, high-stakes work where mistakes can equal great harm.

A review of the literature published by the Health and Safety Executive (HSE) in 2011 identified key features and characteristics that could be adopted by organisations to achieve ongoing high reliability and safety objectives.

Successful containment of unexpected events by:

- having in place back-up systems in the event of failures and cross-checking of important decisions (redundancy);
- allowing people with expertise, irrespective of rank, to make important safety-related decisions in emergencies, though maintaining a clear hierarchical structure and an understanding of who is responsible for what during routine operations (deference to expertise in emergencies; oscillation between hierarchical and flat organisational structures), investment in training and technical competence; and
- well-defined procedures for all possible unexpected events.

Effective anticipation of potential failures through:

- engagement with front-line staff in order to obtain 'the bigger picture' of operations (sensitivity to operations);
- attentiveness to minor, or what may appear as trivial, signals that may indicate potential problem areas within the organisation; using incidents and near misses as indicators of a system's 'health' (preoccupation with failure); and
- systematic collection and analysis of all warning signals, no matter how trivial they may appear to be, and avoiding assumptions regarding the nature of failures. Explanations regarding the causes of incidents tend to be systemic rather than focusing on individual, 'blame the operator' justifications (reluctance to simplify).

Just culture, characterised by:

- open reporting systems for near misses and accidents without fear of punishment;
- follow-up of accident investigation outcomes by implementing corrective actions;
- empowering staff to abandon work on safety grounds; and
- fostering a sense of personal accountability for safety.

Learning orientation, characterised by:

- continuous technical training;
- systematic analysis of incidents to identify their root causes and accident types or trends within the organisation;

- open communication of accident investigation outcomes; and
- updating procedures in line with the organisational knowledge base.

Mindful leadership, characterised by:

- proactive commissions of audits to identify problems in the system (often in response to incidents that occur in other similar industries);
- 'bottom-up' communication of 'bad news';
- engagement with front-line staff through site visits; and
- investment of resources in safety management and the ability to balance profits with safety.

In addition to this review, further research into the applicability of the characteristics and systems of HROs for the healthcare sector has been carried out to further the safety culture in healthcare services. The most commonly applied resulting principles include:

- attempts to improve safety culture
- checklists and other tools
- initiatives to build teamwork using crew resource management and human factors approaches
- standardised processes using care bundles.

It will be interesting to see how developments in this area can be built into NHS risk management processes.

Governance Checklist

✓ How has the board agreed the organisation's risk appetite? With whom has it conferred?

✓ How has the board assessed the organisation's culture? In what way does the board satisfy itself that the organisation has a 'speak-up' culture and that it systematically learns from past mistakes?

✓ How do the organisation's culture, code of conduct, and human resource policies support the business objectives, risk management and internal control systems?

✓ How has the board considered whether senior management promotes and communicates the desired culture and demonstrates the necessary commitment to risk management and internal control?

✓ How is inappropriate behaviour dealt with? Does this present consequential risks?

✓ How does the board ensure that it has sufficient time to consider risk, and how is that integrated with discussion on other matters for which the board is responsible?

✓ To what extent do the risk management and internal control systems underpin and relate to the organisation's business model?

- ✓ How is the risk management strategy communicated throughout the organisation? How does the board determine whether this is clear, appropriate and effective?
- ✓ How effectively is the organisation able to withstand risks, and risk combinations, which do materialise? How effective is the board's approach to risks with 'low probability' but a very severe impact if they materialise?
- ✓ What are the channels of communication that enable individuals, including third parties, to report concerns, suspected breaches of law or regulations, other improprieties or challenging perspectives?
- ✓ What are the responsibilities of the board and senior management for crisis management? How effectively have the organisation's crisis management planning and systems been tested?
- ✓ To what extent has the organisation identified risks from joint ventures, third parties and from the way the organisation's business is organised? How are these managed?
- ✓ How effectively does the organisation capture new and emerging risks and opportunities? How and when does the board consider risk when discussing changes in strategy or approving new transactions, projects, products or other significant commitments?
- ✓ To what extent has the board considered the cost-benefit aspects of different control options?
- ✓ How does the board ensure it understands the organisation's exposure to each principal risk before and after the application of mitigations and controls, what those mitigations and controls are and whether they are operating as expected?
- ✓ What are the processes by which senior management monitor the effective application of the systems of risk management and internal control?
- ✓ In what way do the monitoring and review processes take into account the organisation's ability to re-evaluate the risks and adjust controls effectively in response to changes in its objectives, its business, and its external environment?
- ✓ How are processes or controls adjusted to reflect new or changing risks, or operational deficiencies? To what extent does the board engage in horizon scanning for emerging risks?
- ✓ How has the board satisfied itself that the disclosures on risk management and internal control contribute to the annual report being fair, balanced and understandable, and provide shareholders with the information they need?
- ✓ How has the board satisfied itself that its reporting on going concern and the longer-term viability statement gives a fair, balanced and understandable overview of the organisation's position and prospects?

Adapted from Appendix C of the 2014 FRC guidance

Summary

The FRC Guidance 2014 is very clear that good stewardship by the board should not inhibit the sensible risk-taking that is critical to growth. However, the assessment of risks as part of the normal business planning process should support better decision-making, ensure that the board and management respond promptly to risks when they arise, and ensure that stakeholders are well informed about the principal risks and prospects of the organisation.

The addition of behavioural and organisational risk into the risk management system highlights the challenge that is embedding risk management processes into an organisation. This seems to be a critical area for boards to consider as part of their ongoing training and development.

11 Assurance

Introduction

In corporate governance, the annual report and accounts is seen as the most important communication between a company and its stakeholders. This is not the case in health service governance. Although significant, the annual report and accounts is not the sole means of communication for NHS organisations. Instead, there are a wide variety of reporting requirements. These primarily focus on reporting to the regulators, as well as providing information to key NHS stakeholders.

These complex reporting requirements seek to provide assurance to the board, regulators and a much wider public audience. Assurance can be understood as the provision of accurate and current information about the efficiency and effectiveness of an organisation's policies and operations, and the status of its compliance with statutory obligations. Assurance is the process of establishing the integrity and validity of disclosures, including statements and reports. Good assurance is confidence backed by sufficient evidence: the board should obtain assurance that performance and quality are as they should be, that risks are properly controlled and that strategy is being implemented successfully and sustainably. Board members, regulators and others need to have information from more than one source in order to be able to validate this evidence.

Regulators are primarily required to provide assurance on the stewardship of public money, as well as the corporate governance and performance of the NHS organisation. By contrast, inspection (by bodies such as Care Quality Commission (CQC)) provides assurance that services satisfy service users and are achieving levels of quality consistent with national standards. Trustworthy reporting and auditing is probably the most significant issue for health service governance. Good health service governance should ensure that quality, performance and financial reporting is reliable and honest, and that the opinion of the external auditors is objective and unbiased.

Performance reporting

Frameworks for the NHS in England are published each year. They describe the national priorities, system levers and enablers needed for NHS organisations to maintain and improve the quality of services provided, while delivering transformational change and maintaining financial stability.

From 2017/18 onwards, foundation trusts (FTs) and NHS trusts will be subject to the same performance reporting framework from NHS Improvement (NHSI) – the Single Oversight Framework. CCGs are subject to an ongoing assurance process overseen by NHS England (NHSE) regional teams, which consists of quarterly assurance meetings and an annual 'health check' assessing organisational capabilities, delivery and support needs under the CCG Improvement and Assessment Framework. Both of these frameworks were covered in Chapters 12 and 13 respectively.

The operational plan of each commissioner and provider will need to be approved by its individual board or governing body. NHSE and NHSI will undertake a joint assurance process, working with local organisations in a coherent and joined-up way. Equally, commissioners and providers are expected to ensure their plans reconcile and are agreed locally prior to submission.

This joint assurance approach will focus on:

- how operational plans set out to deliver the next two years of the system Sustainability and Transformation Plan (STP), covering agreed plans to close the three gaps – care and quality, health outcomes and finance;
- ensuring milestones and deliverables are clear;
- provider and commissioner plans reconcile both to the system STP and to each other and share planning assumptions;
- agreement of robust, stretching and deliverable activity plans by commissioners and providers. They are directly derived from the projections agreed within system STPs and reflect historic growth levels moderated by agreed transformation and efficiency schemes. They enable agreed performance trajectories to be delivered within available financial resources;
- ensuring that finance, workforce and activity projections are fully aligned with activity projections; and
- that risks inside and outside of the direct control of the organisation are identified and mitigated. This involves considering both the assumptions in individual plans and the shared understanding across the system in terms of how the system will work together to manage risks.

To ensure coherence of plans across the locality, activity and finance assumptions made by providers and commissioners should be consistent and must be fully aligned in local contracts. For the 2017/18 and 2018/19 planning rounds, commissioners and providers will provide aligned planning information to NHSE and NHSI respectively.

All of this performance information is publicly available through publications from the regulators and on the UK's biggest health website NHS Choices, which provides a comprehensive health information service.

The performance indicators in this oversight approach form the basis of the quality, financial and sustainability reporting to the board or governing body and its committees.

Quality governance

The growing political agenda for assurance on the delivery of quality services, as well as quality outcomes for patients, has led to the growth of quality governance as a specialised area of governance. While not strictly part of health service governance, many NHS company secretaries or governance practitioners will find themselves involved in the quality agenda purely because the board is required by its regulators to give regular and specific assurance on the delivery of quality within their organisation.

Quality has been part of government strategy for modernising the NHS for many years. *A First Class Service: Quality in the new NHS*, published in July 1998, set out the agenda for quality improvement in the NHS. The framework established:

- clear quality standards, through the establishment of the National Institute for Health and Clinical Excellence (NICE) to provide clear advice on clinical and cost-effectiveness and the development of National Service Frameworks (NSFs) to help raise standards of care and reduce unacceptable variations;
- effective local delivery of these standards through a system of clinical governance;
- strong monitoring mechanisms, including the NHS Performance Assessment Framework, together with a statutory Commission for Health Improvement (CHI) and a programme of national patient and user surveys.

The publication of Lord Darzi's 2008 report *Quality Care for All* revived and reinforced this strategy. He highlighted four key areas that would demonstrate improving quality of care:

- patient safety
- effectiveness, including clinical outcomes and patient reported outcome measures (PROMs)
- user experience
- innovation.

As a result, greater clarity on quality standards was required; metrics had to be developed to measure quality; Quality Accounts were to be published; the delivery of quality was to be rewarded via Commissioning for Quality Improvement (CQUINs); and standards were to be raised with the creation of the National Quality Board.

Since, ultimately, the board of an NHS organisation is responsible for the quality of care delivered across all services that it provides, this has to be achieved through governance arrangements which delegate responsibility down to the operating levels in the organisation. In the case of quality, this means that, although individuals and clinical teams are at the frontline and responsible for delivering quality care, it is the responsibility of the board to create a culture within the organisation that enables clinicians and clinical teams to work at their best. In addition, the board must have in place arrangements for measuring and monitoring quality and for escalating issues, including, where needed, to the board. Boards should encourage a culture where services are improved by learning from mistakes, where staff and patients are encouraged to identify areas for improvement, and where they are not afraid to speak out.

The term quality governance is used to refer to the values and behaviours and the structures and processes that need to be in place to enable the board to discharge its responsibilities for quality. The board's responsibilities for quality are threefold:

- to ensure that the essential standards of quality and safety (as determined by CQC's registration requirements) are at a minimum being met by every service that the organisation delivers
- to ensure that the organisation is striving for continuous quality improvement and outcomes in every service
- to ensure that every member of staff that has contact with patients, or whose actions directly impact on patient care, is motivated and enabled to deliver effective, safe and person-centred care.

The arrangements for quality governance should complement and be fully integrated with the governance arrangements for other aspects of the board's responsibilities, such as finance governance and research governance. The National Quality Board (NQB) has published a new framework *Shared Commitment to Quality* (2016) that will promote improved quality criteria across all national health organisations for the first time. The new publication provides a nationally agreed definition of quality and guide for clinical and managerial leaders wanting to improve quality. The approach has been agreed across NHS and social care organisations to provide more consistency and to enable the system to work together more effectively. The Five Year Forward View (5YFV) confirms a national commitment to high-quality, person-centred care for all; the framework describes the changes that are needed to deliver a sustainable health and care system in key areas which matter most to the users of the service:

- **Safety:** people are protected from avoidable harm and abuse. When mistakes occur lessons will be learned.
- **Effectiveness:** people's care and treatment achieves good outcomes, promotes a good quality of life, and is based on the best available evidence.
- **Positive experience:**
  - Caring: staff involve and treat people with compassion, dignity and respect.
  - Responsive and person-centred: services respond to people's needs and choices and enable them to be equal partners in their care.

The framework goes on to describe the standards required for those providing services as high performing providers and commissioners working together and in partnership with, and for, local people and communities, that:

- **Are well-led:** they are open and collaborate internally and externally and are committed to learning and improvement.
- **Use resources sustainably:** they use their resources responsibly and efficiently, providing fair access to all, according to need, and promote an open and fair culture.
- **Are equitable for all:** they ensure inequalities in health outcomes are a focus for quality improvement, making sure care quality does not vary due to characteristics such as gender, race, disability, age, sexual orientation, religion, belief, gender reassignment, pregnancy and maternity or marital or civil partnership status.

Quality accounts

The significant report relating to quality is the annual quality account, which reports on the quality of services provided by an NHS healthcare service. Quality accounts are not intended as marketing documents, but as an opportunity for NHS providers to enter into an open and honest dialogue with the public regarding the quality of care in the organisation. All providers of NHS services are required to produce a quality account as set out in the Health Act 2009 and supporting regulations. The Quality Account must be presented to the Secretary of State and published on NHS Choices website each June.

According to the Department of Health (*DH) Quality Accounts Toolkit* (2010), Quality Accounts aim to improve organisational accountability to the public and engage boards in the quality improvement agenda. They should enable providers to review services, decide and show where they are doing well, but also where improvement is required demonstrate what improvements are planned. They provide information on the quality of services to patients and the public, though explain how providers respond to feedback from patients and the public, as well as other stakeholders.

NHS trusts and FTs are required to report on a prescribed set of quality indicators in their Quality Accounts. The Health and Social Care Information Centre (HSCIC) Indicator Portal provides the latest data reported for each of the indicators. As trusts use the same data sources, they can easily be compared with each other. Trusts are asked to report the result for each quality indicator by following a prescribed statement, including what actions they have taken, or will take, to improve the results and therefore the quality of care they provide. There are 15 quality indicators, however trusts only have to report on those that are relevant to the services they provide. For example, an ambulance trust will include different indicators to those of a mental health trust as they provide different services.

Organisations must decide on at least three areas where they are planning to improve the quality of their services. They should also provide details about how they prioritise improvements and why and how they are planning to report back on progress to their patients and the public. Patients' views should be taken into account when organisations decide on the priorities for improvement. The Quality Account also reports on the organisation's participation in national, local and clinical audits as well as clinical research. It must also make two statements to the CQC. The first statement gives information on a provider's registration status (either without any conditions, with conditions, or not registered). The CQC can also apply specific conditions in response to serious risks that it finds. For example, it can demand a ward or service is closed until the provider meets safety requirements or that it is suspended or taken off the register if absolutely necessary. Such action must be disclosed in the Quality Account. The second statement provides information on what reviews and/or investigations the provider has taken part in and what the CQC said about the provider.

The accuracy of data is key in being able to measure and compare quality improvements. The Quality Account requires organisations to make statements, which give an indication of the quality and accuracy of the information an organisation collects.

To ensure that the information presented in the Quality Account is accurate and fairly interpreted, and that the range of services described and priorities for improvement are representative of the services delivered, assurance is required to ensure accuracy. The commissioners have a legal obligation to review and comment on the Quality Accounts, while the council of governors, local Healthwatch organisations and OSCs will be offered the opportunity to comment on a voluntary basis.

For June 2017, NHS trusts and FTs were required to include:

- evidence of implementation of the Duty of Candour;
- (where applicable) the patient safety improvement plan as part of the Sign Up to Safety campaign;
- the most recent NHS Staff Survey results for indicators relating to staff experiencing harassment, bullying or abuse from staff in the last 12 months and to equal opportunities for career progression or promotion; and
- the organisation's CQC ratings grid, alongside the plan to address any areas that require improvement or are inadequate, and the timescale for improvement.

For the June 2018 Quality Accounts, providers will be expected to report how their investigation and learnings from deaths have informed their quality improvement plans. There will be an annual summary of the monthly/quarterly trust board reports on reviewing and learning from deaths.

NHSE requires NHS trusts and FTs to gain external audit assurance on their quality accounts and two of their quality indicators. The auditors will issue a limited assurance report on whether anything has come to their attention that leads them to believe that:

- the quality account has not been prepared in line with the requirements set out in the Regulations;
- the quality account is not consistent with specified documentation detailed in section 3 of the annual guidance; and
- one or both quality indicators are misstated.

CASE STUDY: University College London Hospital NHS FT

University College London Hospital NHS FT has published Quality Accounts for a number of years and has developed a format for establishing the quality priorities.

First of all, a long list of contenders are drawn up. Three of the FT's top ten objectives are around improving patient safety, experience and clinical outcomes so the long list contains contenders across all these domains. Possible priorities are derived from three sources: the FT's performance over the past year against its quality and safety indicators; national or regional priorities; and finally, from horizon scanning. The list of contenders has to be in areas that fulfilled most or all of the following criteria:

- where the FT genuinely had a desire or need to drive improvement
- known improvement strategies; so that the FT could hit the ground running in delivering tangible improvement in a defined timeline
- have measures either in place or in development
- capable of historic or benchmark comparison.

The long list plus the rationale for selection was then discussed and consulted on extensively with groups of internal and external stakeholders to develop a shortlist. The FT also asks if there is a good reason to carry forward any of the quality priorities from the previous year. The FT found that the shortlist and final selection became virtually self-selecting following this process in that there was wide consensus on what should be the final priorities.

Once established, the FT has put delivery strategies in place for all the quality priorities. It has also tracked performance against improvement trajectories at all levels from ward to board on a monthly basis using the quality scorecard and priority specific improvement charts.

Quality report

In addition to the Quality Accounts, FTs must also include a report on the quality of care they provide (the quality report) within their overall annual report as set out by FT Annual Reporting Manual (ARM) for the year under review. The quality report specifically aims to improve public accountability for the quality of care.

The quality report incorporates all the requirements of the quality account regulations as well as a number of additional reporting requirements set by NHSI. The additional NHSI requirements are as follows.

- A statement which gives a monetary total for the amount of income in the year under review conditional upon achieving quality improvement and innovation goals, and a monetary total for the associated payment in the previous year.
- An explanatory note for clinical coding stating that the results should not be extrapolated further than the actual sample audited and which services were reviewed within the sample.
- An overview of the quality of care offered by the FT based on performance in the year under review against indicators selected by the board in consultation with stakeholders, with an explanation of the underlying reason(s) for selection. The indicator set selected must include at least three indicators each for patient safety, clinical effectiveness and patient experience. Where the quality indicators are the same as those used in the previous year's report, the data reported should be consistent.
- Performance against the relevant indicators and performance thresholds set out in the oversight documents issued by NHSI.

The FT board is also required to make a statement of directors' responsibilities that the quality report meets the requirements set out in FT ARM for the year under review. FTs are also required to obtain a limited assurance report from their external auditors on the content of the quality report and to include it in the annual report. The limited assurance report has reported on whether anything has come to the attention of the auditor that leads them to believe that the content of the quality report has not been prepared in line with the requirements set out in FT ARM. The auditors must also undertake substantive sample testing on two mandated performance indicators and one local indicator selected by the governors of the FT. The auditors must then provide a report to the FT's council of governors and board of directors of their findings and recommendations for improvement on the content of the quality report, mandated indicators and locally selected indicator.

Financial reporting

As previously mentioned, NHS trusts and FTs provide regular financial reporting to comply with the oversight approach of the NHSI *Single Oversight Framework*. However, the other key financial reporting tool for NHS organisations is the annual report and accounts.

NHS trusts are obliged to comply with the determination and directions given by the Secretary of State in the preparation of their annual report and annual accounts. These directions are set out in the *NHS Finance Manual*, published by the DH. In addition, the government publishes the *Financial Reporting Manual* (FReM), which is the technical accounting guide to the preparation of financial statements. Foundation trusts are required to follow the guidance given by NHSI in the FT ARM; CCGs should follow the guidance in the *CCG Annual Reporting Manual* (CCG ARM).

NHS organisations must publish an annual report and (full) audited accounts as one document and present it at a public meeting, whether or not summary financial statements are also produced. Where an NHS body has dissolved, or taken FT status, an annual report and audited accounts for its final accounting period must still be published and presented at a public meeting by a successor organisation. NHS organisations still have the option to prepare and distribute an annual report and summary financial statements, however, this is additional to the annual report and accounts described above which must be available if requested.

The year-end for all NHS organisations is 31 March and the timetable for the production of the annual accounts is quite constrained. For 2016/17, the deadline for sending unaudited accounts to the NHSI and NHSE was 26 April 2017 and the deadline for submitting audited accounts to DH was 1 June 2017. The annual accounts of each NHS organisation are summarised as part of the NHS Annual Accounts and laid before Parliament in July of each year.

The guidance sets out the minimum content of the annual report. Beyond this, however, the entity must take ownership of the annual report. It should ensure that additional information is included where necessary to reflect the position of the NHS body within the community and give sufficient information to meet the requirements of public accountability.

The financial statements report on the financial performance of the organisation over the previous financial year and the financial position of the organisation as at the end of that year. The directors' report and other statements published in the same document provide supporting information, much of it in narrative rather than in numerical form. Stakeholders use the information in the annual report and accounts to assess the stewardship of the directors and the financial health of the organisation.

Annual report and accounts

The annual report of NHS FTs must, as a minimum, include:

- the performance report, comprising:
  - overview of performance
  - performance analysis;

- the accountability report, comprising:
  - directors' report
  - remuneration report
  - staff report
  - the disclosures set out in the FT Code of Governance
  - NHSI's Single Oversight Framework
  - statement of accounting officer's responsibilities
  - annual governance statement
  - a quality report.

The accounts should include:

- the accounting officer's statement of responsibilities
- the auditor's opinion and certificate
- a foreword to the accounts
- four primary financial statements
- notes to the accounts.

The annual report may, at the FT's discretion, include additional reporting covering equality, the Modern Slavery Act 2015 and the NHS Constitution. FTs are also required to include progress against their sustainable development plan in their annual report.

A model statement of the FT annual governance statement is set out in FT ARM. It is a backwards-looking statement that captures information on risk management and internal control, and includes some specific requirements on quality governance. It replaced and expanded upon the former requirement for a statement on internal control and is signed by the FT's chief executive officer (CEO).

Under the STP process progress is being made in defining system control figures for financial performance. This raises interesting questions as to the reporting requirements for system control totals which will be multi-level across the footprint. At present, each individual organisation will continue to report financial performance through its own governance route and in addition as part of the system control group. NHSE and NHSI will continue to monitor and report the financial performance of individual organisations against their agreed plans.

Accountability and transparency

The annual report and accounts is an important document for health service governance because it is a means by which the directors are made accountable to the stakeholders, and it provides a channel of communication from directors to stakeholders. The report and accounts enable the stakeholders to assess how well the organisation has been governed and managed. It should therefore be clear and understandable to a reader with reasonable financial awareness, and reliable and 'believable'.

The reliability of the annual report and accounts depends on several factors, including those that follow.

- The honesty of the organisation in preparing them: if allowed to do so by accounting regulations, organisations might indulge in window dressing their financial performance or financial position through the use of accounting policies (methods) that hide the true position.
- The care used by directors to satisfy themselves that the financial statements do give a 'true and fair view' and that everything of relevance has been properly reported.
- The opinion of the external auditors, which the stakeholders should be able to rely on as an objective and professional opinion.

If financial statements are produced in a way that is intended deliberately to mislead stakeholders, the persons responsible would be guilty of fraud, which is a crime. Misleading financial statements, however, could only be issued if the audit committee is satisfied with their preparation, external auditors provide a 'clean' audit report, and the board of directors approves the financial statements. In most organisations, this would require deception by a small group of executives, such as the CEO and finance director.

The diverse requirements for reporting in health service governance highlight a number of ways in which the organisation's directors are held accountable to stakeholders. The information given can be used to assess the success of the organisation and the effectiveness of its board. It is therefore essential that the reporting should give a clear presentation of the position and performance of the organisation. In other words, there should be 'transparency' in reporting by organisation, so that the recipients of the reports can see what the organisation has achieved and assess what is likely to happen in the future.

The UK Code states as a main principle that: 'the board should present a balanced and understandable assessment of the company's position and prospects' in its report and accounts, as well as in its interim reports and other public statements. This principle applies to narrative reporting in the annual report as well as to the financial statements. These principles are mirrored in the FReM, the FT ARM and the CCG ARM.

The Companies Act 2006 (Strategic Report and Directors' Report) Regulations 2013 require directors to prepare a strategic report that is separate to the directors' report. It must therefore be separately approved by the board of directors and signed on behalf of the board by a director or secretary of the company. The strategic report has replaced the business review previously required by section 417 of the Companies Act 2006 (CA 2006). In support of these regulations, the Financial Reporting Council (FRC) *Guidance on the Strategic Report* was issued in June 2014 to set out best practice principles.

The overriding purpose of the strategic report is to inform members of the company and to help them assess how the directors have performed their duty to promote the success of the company. The strategic report should include the business model, strategy, objectives and principal risks, a review of the year and future outlook. It should provide context to the financial statements and insight into the main objectives, strategies, and risks and how these might impact future performance. The rules will also require quoted companies to make new disclosures about human rights, gender diversity and greenhouse gas emissions.

The 'principal risks' reference is important as it ties into the 2014 FRC Guidance on *Risk Management, Internal Control and Related Financial and Business Reporting*, which is considered more fully in Chapter 15. Principal risks that are included in the strategic report should be limited to those considered by the organisation's management to be material to the development, performance, position or future prospects of the organisation. They will generally be matters that the directors regularly monitor and discuss because of their likelihood or the magnitude of their potential effect on the organisation or a combination of the two.

Under section 496 of the CA 2006 the auditor is required to state whether, in their opinion, the information in the strategic report is consistent with the accounts. The FReM, FT ARM and CCG ARM have adopted these changes and the previous directors' report (including an operating and financial review) has now been split into a strategic report and a directors' report.

Directors' duties and responsibilities for financial reporting

An organisation's directors are responsible for the preparation and content of the financial statements. The UK Code states that the directors should explain in the annual report their responsibility for preparing the annual report and financial statements. There should also be a supporting statement by the auditors (in their report) about their reporting responsibilities. The UK Code also requires that the directors should include in their annual report an explanation of the basis on which the company generates or preserves value over the longer term (its 'business model'), and strategy for delivering the objectives of the company.

Responsibilities of the directors for financial reporting

There is sometimes confusion and misunderstanding about responsibilities for financial reporting, and a mistaken belief that the external auditors are responsible for the 'true and fair view' in the financial statements. If misleading and incorrect financial statements are produced, it may therefore be supposed that the auditors have been negligent and must be to blame. This view is incorrect. The directors are responsible for the financial statements: they prepare the financial statements and have the primary responsibility for the reliability of the information they provide. Management and the directors are therefore responsible for identifying and correcting any errors or misrepresentations in the financial statements.

The responsibility of the external auditors is to obtain reasonable assurance, in their professional opinion, that the financial statements are free from material error or misstatement. They present a professional opinion to the stakeholders, not to the directors of the organisation, and the directors should not rely on the opinion of the external auditors in reaching their own view.

In UK law, the directors are also potentially liable for any errors or misleading information in the annual report and accounts. Any person (e.g. an investor) suffering a loss because of an error or misstatement in an organisation's report and accounts may sue the organisation, and the organisation may then take legal action against the directors to recover any losses it has occurred from the legal action.

Going concern statement

A key accounting concept is the 'going concern' concept. This is the view that the organisation will continue to trade for the foreseeable future (at least the next 12 months). This is different to an understanding of an organisation's viability.

In the UK Code, the board is required to make an explicit statement in the financial statements about whether the going concern basis of accounting has been adopted and whether there are any material uncertainties about the company's ability to continue to do so in future. It is also required to make a broader statement about the board's reasonable expectation as to the company's viability based on a robust assessment of the company's principal risks and the company's current position. This is developed in the latest FRC Guidance on *Risk Management, Internal Control and Related Financial and Business Reporting* (2014) which states:

> 'A company that is able to adopt the going concern basis of accounting and does not have related material uncertainties to report, for the purposes of the financial statements, is not necessarily free of risks that would threaten the company's business model, future performance, solvency or liquidity were they to materialise. The board is responsible for ensuring this distinction is understood internally and communicated externally.'

The financial statements are therefore prepared on the going concern basis, and assets are valued differently from what their value might be if the organisation went into liquidation. The statement of going concern should also give reasons why the directors have reached their view, and also indicate any doubts there might be. Where there is fundamental uncertainty over the going concern basis (for instance, continuing operational stability depends on finance or income that has not yet been approved), or where the going concern basis is not appropriate, the directors will need to disclose the relevant circumstances and should discuss the basis of accounting and the disclosures to be made with their auditors. Similarly, the UK Listing Rules require the directors to make a statement in the report and accounts that the company is a going concern, together with supporting assumptions and qualifications as necessary. These requirements are mirrored in the NHS Finance Manual, FReM, NHS FT ARM and CCG ARM.

The going concern basis has come under greater scrutiny due to the severe financial circumstances faced by many providers and commissioners. There are continuing significant financial pressures within the sector, with NST trusts, FTs and CCGs requiring additional financial support.

There is no presumption of going concern status for FTs. Directors must decide each year whether or not it is appropriate for the FT to prepare its accounts on the going concern basis, taking into account best estimates of future activity and cash flows. FTs are required to prepare their accounts in accordance with the relevant international accounting rules as interpreted by the FT ARM which sets out that:

> 'An entity should prepare its financial statements on a going concern basis, unless:
> (a) The entity is being liquidated or has ceased trading; or
> (b) The directors have no realistic alternative but to liquidate the entity or to cease trading, in which circumstances the entity may, if appropriate, prepare its financial statements on a basis other than going concern.'

In recent years NHS trusts have been issued letters from their regulator, where required, confirming that the DH would continue to make funding available to the trust. On this basis such NHS trusts in financial deficit have been able to declare themselves as a going concern. Such letters were not issued for 2016/17 which created additional challenges for boards of any NHS trust that could not meet the definition of a going concern as set out in the DH's Group Accounting Manual (GAM) 2016/17, which specifies that unless an NHS trust expects its services to cease to be provided in the public sector the going concern basis should be assumed. If an NHS trust is dependent upon financing which is not confirmed, this would ordinarily be an uncertainty for the going concern basis and the DH GAM requires that these be disclosed in the annual report and accounts. However, while this uncertainty is being disclosed it does not affect the going concern basis itself. The NHS trust should consider preparing a paper for its board and/or audit committee if necessary. If the NHS trust's auditor considers this disclosure to be of sufficient importance they may enter an 'emphasis of matter' as part of their annual report. This does not constitute a 'qualified opinion' and would not cause a concern for NHSI as long as the NHSI was already aware of the matters being disclosed.

The auditor's responsibility is to consider the appropriateness of the use of the going concern assumption in preparing the financial statements. They should also consider if there are material uncertainties about the organisation's ability to continue as a going concern that need to be disclosed in the financial statements.

A typical going concern statement within an annual report might be as follows:

> 'After making enquiries, the directors have a reasonable expectation that the NHS foundation trust has adequate resources to continue in operational existence for the foreseeable future. For this reason, they continue to adopt the going concern basis in preparing the accounts.'

In the UK, disclosures about the assumptions or qualifications about going concern status are becoming more extensive. The directors may be personally liable if they make a statement that the organisation is a going concern without giving the matter careful consideration. Liability could arise if the organisation subsequently goes into liquidation within the next 12 months and stakeholders claim that they relied on the going concern statement when making their investment decisions.

In the strict accounting sense, NHS bodies cannot prepare accounts on any other basis than as a going concern. Various Acts of Parliament prevent NHS organisations from becoming insolvent in the strict accounting sense, as the DH bears the ultimate liability for any debts. Even so, NHS annual reporting requirements still require NHS organisations to include a statement on whether or not the financial statements have been prepared on a going concern basis and the reasons for this decision, with supporting assumptions or qualifications as necessary. The distinction between going concern and viability make for interesting audit committee discussions, particularly in the current financial climate and in the context of shared financial controls across STPs.

The corporate governance statement

In 2006, the European Union (EU) adopted a Company Reporting Directive that required quoted companies to produce a corporate governance statement in their annual reports. The statement must refer to the corporate governance code applied by the company (e.g. the UK Code) and explain whether, and to what extent, the company complies with that code. The statement must also include a description of the main features of the company's internal control and risk management systems in relation to the financial reporting process, and provide a description of the composition and operation of the board and its committees.

In the UK, listed companies were already required to report much of the corporate governance information required by the Company Reporting Directive. The UK Listing Rules require companies to include in their annual report a statement of how they have applied the principles of the UK Code, for example disclosures about the composition of board committees and their work.

However, the Company Reporting Directive required the information to be presented in a separate 'corporate governance statement' and that the statement should include a description of the main features of the company's internal control and risk management systems relating to the financial reporting process, neither of which were contained in the UK Code.

The parallel arrangement for FTs is that they are required to include a statement of compliance with the FT Code.

The annual governance statement

This requirement is in line with the UK Code, which states that the board should report to shareholders each year that it has conducted the annual review of the effectiveness of the systems of internal control and risk management. The Financial Services Authority (FSA)'s Disclosure and Transparency Rules for listed companies also requires companies to report on the main features of their internal control and risk management systems in relation to financial reporting.

All public bodies (including NHS organisations) must provide assurance that they are appropriately managing and controlling the resources for which they are responsible. The requirement for an annual governance statement (AGS) has now been rolled out across all NHS organisations and a template for guidance issued for NHS trusts, FTs and CCGs. The annual guidance from the DH continues to set out the key elements that need to be considered when producing the AGS. While NHS organisations will have risk management, control and review processes in place, the detail of these processes vary from one organisation to another depending on circumstances such as size and the complexity of the risks faced. The annual guidance, therefore, offers a summary of characteristics under six high-level elements to help with consideration of the completeness of the processes that have been put in place in a particular body.

NHS organisations are required to ensure that they have sufficient evidence to demonstrate that they have implemented processes appropriate to their circumstances under the following six high-level elements:

- scope of responsibility
- the governance framework of the organisation
- risk assessment
- the risk and control framework
- review of the effectiveness of risk management and internal control
- significant issues.

The guidance also requires full disclosure of any significant control issues or weaknesses. This is to deliver assurance that significant internal control issues have been, or are being, addressed and that the AGS is a balanced reflection of the actual control position. Although not required, it may help the disclosure in relation to a significant internal control issue if the description of the weakness and its impact is given to provide context for the actions taken. NHS bodies may exercise discretion in such disclosure to avoid further adverse impacts or exploitation of the weakness.

A single definition of a significant internal control issue is not possible and NHS organisations are required to exercise their judgement in deciding whether or not a particular issue should be regarded as falling into this category. The guidance sets out factors that may be helpful in exercising that judgment, including:

- might the issue prejudice achievement of priorities?
- could the issue undermine the integrity or reputation of the NHS?
- what view does the Audit Committee take on this point?
- what advice has the internal or external audit given?
- could delivery of the standards expected of the accountable officer (AO) be at risk?
- has the issue made it harder to resist fraud or other misuse of resources?
- did the issue divert resources from another significant aspect of the business?
- could the issue have a material impact on the accounts? and
- might national or data security or integrity be put at risk?

The audit committee plays a key role in the production of the AGS. It supports the board and AO by reviewing the comprehensiveness of assurances in meeting the board and AO's assurance needs, and reviewing the reliability and integrity of the assurances. The audit committee also advises the board and AO of any control issues that could be considered significant and are therefore appropriate for disclosure in the AGS.

The board assurance framework

In order to sign off the AGS, NHS boards need to be assured that the systems, policies and people they have put in place are operating in a way that is effective, is focused on key risks and is driving the delivery of objectives. There is, however, the potential for a lack of clarity within the board (and beyond) to what is meant by the term 'assurance'. This can extend to uncertainty over the level of assurance required, where that assurance comes from and how the reporting of assurance is managed in a co-ordinated manner.

Although the process of securing assurance has always been a fundamental principle of good management and accountability, the requirement for all NHS AOs to sign the AGS has focused attention on the level of assurance that boards receive. To provide this statement, boards need to be able to demonstrate that they have been properly informed through assurances about the totality of their risks, not just financial, and have arrived at their conclusions based on all the evidence presented to them. Assurance is the foundation of evidence that gives confidence that risk is being controlled effectively, or conversely, highlights that certain controls are ineffective or there are gaps that need to be addressed.

The HM Treasury *Guidance on Assurance Frameworks* (2012) defines an 'assurance framework' as:

> 'A structured means of identifying and mapping the main sources of assurance in an organisation, and co-ordinating them to best effect.'

The board assurance framework (BAF) is a framework that NHS organisations are required to put in place to identify the key risks to the trust's achievement of its strategic objectives and how these risks are being managed. It provides an organisation with a method for the effective and focused management of the principal risks to meeting its objectives. It also provides a structure for the evidence to support the AGS. It identifies which of the organisation's objectives are at risk because of inadequacies in the operation of controls or where the organisation has insufficient assurance about them. At the same time it provides structured assurances about where risks are being managed effectively and objectives are being delivered. This allows the board to determine where to make efficient use of resources and to address the issues identified to improve the quality and safety of care. As a natural extension of risk management, it is reasonable to incorporate the board assurance arrangements into the risk management documentation, therefore ensuring that risk, control and assurance identification and monitoring processes are considered as one and not disparate activities.
It is also a key tool for a well-led organisation and if used as a live and dynamic tool offers significant evidence in the Well-Led assessment (see Chapter 4).

Baker Tilly and NHS Providers issued a toolkit, Board Assurance: A toolkit for health sector organisations – Do we really know what we think we know? in 2015 which explains:

> "[A]ssurance mapping as a key part of developing and maintaining board assurance arrangements and producing a BAF. Mapping provides an organisation with an improved ability to understand and confirm that they have assurance over key controls or where control gaps exist and whether actions are in place to address these gaps. The assurance mapping process and the way of illustrating the results using a BAF can give confidence to management and the board that they "really know what they think they know".'

In documented form, a BAF would include:

- the trust's strategic objectives
- the key risks to achieving the objectives
- the controls in place to manage the risks
- the assurances that the trust used to provide evidence that the controls were operating effectively
- any gaps in the assurances
- an action plan to address the gaps.

There are three types of assurance that can be sought: verbal, written and empirical. All can be of use depending on the circumstances. Each will be valued differently depending on other factors. The governing body has defined the overarching levels of assurance as noted below:

- Level 1 – Operational (Management)
- Level 2 – Oversight functions (Committees)
- Level 3 – Independent (Audits/Reviews/Inspections etc.)

The evidence supporting assurance should be sufficient in scope and weight to support the conclusion and be:

- relevant
- reliable
- understandable
- free from material misstatement
- neutral/free from bias
- such that another person would reasonably come to the same conclusion.

All evidence does not carry the same weight and should be weighted in accordance to independence and relevance. Evidence may be flawed in terms of both quality and quantity, leading to limitations in the assurance that can be provided.

Every NHS organisation must design its own framework, which will relate to the delivery of its own objectives within the context of an understanding of the principal risks that the organisation faces. The BAF should enable the board to:

- establish principal objectives (strategic and directorate)
- identify the principal risks that may threaten the achievement of these objectives – typically in the range of 75–200 depending on the complexity of the organisation
- identify and evaluate the design of key controls intended to manage these principal risks, underpinned by core controls assurance standards
- set out the arrangements for obtaining assurance on the effectiveness of key controls across all areas of principal risk
- evaluate the assurance across all areas of principal risk
- identify positive assurances and areas where there are gaps in controls and/or assurances
- put in place plans to take corrective action where gaps have been identified in relation to principal risks
- maintain dynamic risk management arrangements including, crucially, a well-founded risk register.

The audit committee should not be responsible for creating the BAF; instead, it should satisfy itself that line management is carrying it out appropriately and that the processes and format are valid, relevant and effective. The committee needs to be satisfied that it contains the high-risk areas pertinent to the organisation.

CASE STUDY: Areas of concern within a trust

In 2011, the CQC inspected a service area within a trust and found a number of areas of concern resulting in a series of recommendations for improvement. A year later the trust had failed to make the required level of progress against two of the three recommendations, with some of the recommendations still requiring significant steps in order to be implemented. Two specific problems related to the failure to appoint a consultant and to recruit sufficient staff to ensure the trust operated a service that was safe and effective.

The trust had put in place an action plan to deal with service delivery problems in by the end of 2012. However, the board devoted insufficient effort to ensuring that action plan was delivered in a timely manner and there was insufficient evidence of the board driving improvement forward.

In particular, the effectiveness of board assurance processes, leadership by the board and clinical leadership within the trust was a cause for concern. The trust remained under enhanced monitoring.

Integrated reporting

A reporting initiative from the International Integrated Reporting Council (IIRC) may provide a benchmark for further developments in NHS reporting requirements. The IIRC is a global body established to promote the worldwide adoption of integrated reporting as the main annual report by companies.

The IIRC aims to 'promote a more cohesive and efficient approach to corporate reporting that draws on different reporting strands and communicates the full range of factors that materially affect the ability of the organisation to create value over time'. The IIRC has been working to achieve consensus among governments, listing authorities, standard setters, companies and investors about the use of integrated reporting by listed companies. As its name suggests, an integrated report should bring together into a single report different aspects of a company's activities, which contribute, to the creation of (or destruction of) value. Value is accumulated in the form of six different types of capital:

- financial capital
- human capital
- intellectual capital
- manufactured capital
- natural capital
- social capital.

It is therefore argued that an integrated report should provide information about the company's policies and performance with regard to each of these aspects of capital. It is sufficient at this stage to note that 'capital', as defined for the purpose of integrated reporting, includes aspects of the company's policies and performance with regard to employees, the environment and society. These are issues that quoted companies may be expected to include in their strategic report.

IIRC guidance published in 2013 states that an integrated report should contain eight elements:

1. an overview of the organisation and its external environment
2. how the governance structure supports the company's ability to create value
3. a description of the company's business model
4. risks and opportunities that affect the organisation's ability to create value, and how the organisation is dealing with them
5. material on strategy and resource allocation, outlining the company's strategies and strategic objectives, and how it intends to achieve these
6. performance information covering whether the company achieved its strategic objectives for the period in terms of effects on the 'six capitals'
7. an outlook based on challenges and uncertainties
8. information on the basis of presentation, detailing how the organisation decides what to include in the integrated report and how are these matters are quantified and measured.

Governance checklist

- ✓ Has the board signed off the operational plan, a five-year strategic plan and a development support plan?
- ✓ Does the board have a good understanding of the requirements imposed by the relevant framework for performance reporting? Is the board clear about how this aligns to its overall strategy and corporate objectives for the organisation?
- ✓ Is the board confident that the performance and quality dashboard it reviews is supported by robust and viable data?
- ✓ Has the board signed off the operational plan, a five-year strategic plan and a development support plan?
- ✓ Does the board have a good understanding of the requirements imposed by the relevant framework for performance reporting? Is the board clear about how this aligns to its overall strategy and corporate objectives for the organisation?
- ✓ Is the board confident that the performance and quality dashboard it reviews is supported by robust and viable data?
- ✓ Is the board confident that the annual report and accounts present a balanced and understandable assessment of the organisation's position and prospects?
- ✓ Does the annual report meet the appropriate reporting requirements, including the addition of a strategic report?

✓ Was the annual governance statement signed by the accountable officer?
✓ How regularly does the board consider the BAF? Is it a live, dynamic, document that changes as the organisation changes?

Summary

Assurance can sometimes be hard to find in the NHS, not because of the lack of information but because there is so much information. In addition, the validity and robustness of some of the information can also create difficulties, such as problems with coding. There is clearly a large and complex reporting structure for NHS organisations with NHSE, the NHSI and the CQC responsible for the design of much of its content. Since the publication of the Francis Inquiry findings, there has been a growing commitment for these agencies to work together and align their reporting requirements. This alignment can already be seen; for example, in the use of a Single Oversight Framework, and the commitment to develop the Well-Led Framework.

There is, however, a significant amount of information in the public domain, allowing key stakeholders and the general public to assess whether, indeed, the board is fulfilling its statutory duties. In the context of this highly regulated sector, the work of internal and external audit and the role of the audit committee is a significant contribution to the assurance evidence required by the NHS board to fulfil its statutory duties. This is considered in the next chapter.

Audit

The role of audit

The role of audit is important in ensuring accurate reporting, which is one of the foundations for health service governance. Given the range and diversity of reporting requirements that are imposed on NHS organisations, the role of audit clearly becomes a crucial tool in the reliability and robustness of those reports and provides vital independent assurance to NHS boards.

All stakeholders rely on the quality, performance and financial information that is published by the organisation. It is important, therefore, that the information is objective and robust. As a result, the work of both internal and external audit are vital in making sure that, as far as is reasonably possible, the information is objective and can be relied on. Within NHS organisations the remit of internal and external audit includes the review of quality, performance and financial information. Part of the audit committee's role is to monitor the work of both internal and external auditors and to ensure that the external auditors can place full reliance on the work of internal audit in these three areas of information.

Audit Commission and the independent auditor panel

The Audit Commission used to play a significant role in the provision of audit services to the NHS. However, in August 2010 the Department for Communities and Local Government (DCLG) announced plans to put in place new arrangements for auditing England's local public bodies. The Local Audit and Accountability Act 2014 made it possible for the Audit Commission to close on 31 March 2015 in line with Government expectations, 30 years after it was established. The new approach in this Act means that the regulation of local public audit is the responsibility of the Financial Reporting Council (FRC) and brings the public sector approach into line with that used by the corporate sector.

The Commission's in-house Audit Practice used to undertake the majority of audits for local public bodies. In March 2012 this work was transferred to the private sector following a procurement exercise awarding five-year contracts to four private firms. On 1 November 2012 around 700 auditors transferred to new private sector employers and the Commission's Audit Practice closed. The result of these changes is that Grant Thornton, KPMG, Ernst & Young or the DA Partnership audited all NHS trusts and clinical commissioning groups (CCGs). The newly created Public Sector Audit Appointments Ltd oversees these contracts until they end in 2016/17 or in 2019/20 if the contracts are extended.

The new framework for CCGs and NHS trusts was set out in the Local Audit (Health Service Bodies Auditor Panel and Independence) Regulations 2015. Three other sets of regulations were also issued that are relevant to health bodies:

- Local Audit (Auditor Resignation and Removal) Regulations 2014 (SI 2014 No 1710) which came into force on 1 April 2015
- Local Audit (Liability Limitation Agreements) Regulations 2014 (SI 2014 No 1628) which came into force on 1 April 2015
- Local Audit (Appointing Person) Regulations 2015 (SI 2015 No 192) which came into force on 10 February 2015.

From 2017/18 onwards, NHS trusts and CCGs must appoint their own auditors and directly manage the resulting contract and the relationship just as NHS foundation trusts (FTs) already do. FTs were not required to be audited by the Audit Commission and were free to make external audit appointments from the wider market of audit firms.

NHS trusts and CCGs were required have an independent 'auditor panel' to advise on the selection, appointment and removal of external auditors and the maintenance of an independent relationship for future audit contracts. The panel had to be in place early in 2016 to allow for auditor appointments to be made for 2017/18. The panel can be the existing audit committee (or members of that committee), which fulfils the requirement of independence as audit committees are – by definition – independent and members have the relevant experience and skills.

The aim of the Regulations is to ensure that there is appropriate scrutiny and oversight of the CCG's or NHS trust's relationship with its external auditor. This is achieved through having the auditor panel chaired by an independent member who is not part of the body's management structure (a non-executive), and so can look objectively at the wider public interest, and with the majority of the other panel members also being independent. The full guidance on the role of the auditor panel is set out in the Department of Health (DH)/Healthcare Financial Management Association (HFMA) guidance, *Auditor Panels – Guidance to help Health Bodies meet their Statutory Duties* (September 2015).

The National Audit Office

The National Audit Office (NAO) scrutinises public spending for Parliament. Its public audit perspective helps Parliament hold government to account and improve public services. The Comptroller and Auditor General (C&AG) leads the

NAO and is an officer of the House of Commons. The C&AG and the staff of the NAO are independent of government. They are not civil servants and do not report to a minister. The Public Accounts Commission (PAC), a Parliamentary committee of MPs, oversees its work.

The Local Audit and Accountability Act 2014 makes the C&AG responsible for the preparation, publication and maintenance of the Code of Audit Practice for local auditors (i.e. those auditing public sector bodies including the NHS). The Code sets out what local auditors are required to do to fulfil their statutory responsibilities under the Act. The new Code took effect from 1 April 2015 for audit work relating to the 2015/16 financial year onwards. The Code covers the audits of all local NHS bodies including FTs and CCGs and will supersede the Code of Audit Practice 2010 for local NHS bodies, and the 2011 Audit Code for FTs. The C&AG can also issue guidance to auditors, which may explain or supplement the provisions of the Code.

The Local Audit and Accountability Act 2014 also gave the C&AG the power to carry out examinations into the economy, efficiency and effectiveness with which relevant authorities have used their resources. The NAO recently scrutinised the use of the Better Care Fund to achieve health and social care integration; it concluded that it had not achieved the expected value for money, in terms of savings, outcomes for patients or hospital activity.

> 'Integrating the health and social care sectors is a significant challenge in normal times, let alone times when both sectors are under such severe pressure. So far, benefits have fallen far short of plans, despite much effort. It will be important to learn from the over-optimism of such plans when implementing the much larger NHS sustainability and transformation plans. The Departments do not yet have the evidence to show that they can deliver their commitment to integrated services by 2020, at the same time as meeting existing pressures on the health and social care systems.'
>
> *Amyas Morse, C&AG, 8 February 2017*

The Act also provided for the Commission's data matching powers, and therefore the National Fraud Initiative, to transfer to the Cabinet Office. The Commission's counter-fraud function will transfer to a new public sector Counter Fraud Centre to be established by the Chartered Institute of Public Finance and Accountancy (CIPFA). The C&AG will be a prescribed person to whom whistleblowing disclosures can be made in respect of local public bodies under the Public Interest Disclosure Act 1998 from 1 April 2015. Appointed auditors retain their status as a prescribed person under the Act (see later section on whistleblowing).

Function and scope of external audit

External audit traditionally has been the process by which the annual accounts of public and private sector bodies are subject to external scrutiny to provide independent assurance that they have been prepared in accordance with relevant legal and professional standards and give a 'true and fair' view of the financial performance and financial position of the audited body. More recently, however, external audit has comprised a wider brief including quality and performance audits as well. According to the Public Audit Forum:

> 'It is one of the basic principles of audit in the public sector, that the scope of the audit should be understood to go beyond giving assurance on the accounts, to include examination of aspects of corporate governance and the use of resources.'

External audit in the public sector is characterised by three distinct features:

- auditors are appointed independently from the bodies being audited
- the scope of auditors' work is extended to cover not only the financial statements, but also aspects of corporate governance and arrangements to secure the economic, efficient and effective use of resources
- auditors may report aspects of their work to the public and other key stakeholders.

The statutory responsibilities and powers of appointed auditors for public bodies including NHS organisations are set out in the Local Audit and Accountability Act 2014. In discharging these specific statutory responsibilities and powers, auditors will be required to carry out their work according to the NAO's Code of Audit Practice. Auditors are required to have regard to this guidance under the Act. Key components of the guidance package will include:

- planning local NHS audits
- planning local government audits
- the auditor's work on value for money (VFM) arrangements
- limited assurance engagements at smaller authorities
- the auditor's additional duties and powers
- auditor reporting
- dealing with technical queries.

Schedule 7 to the National Health Act 2006 (NHS Act 2006) provides the C&AG with access rights to FTs that allow NAO representatives to inspect the accounts and any records relating to them, including the auditor's report. Although the C&AG is not the appointed auditor of individual FTs, NAO may wish to examine financial aspects of one or more FTs in the context of its wider role in providing assurance to Parliament over the proper use of public monies.

After completing their annual audit, auditors are required to prepare a report to the stakeholders of the organisation, which is included in the published report and accounts. The audit report has two main purposes:

- to give an expert and independent opinion on whether the financial statements give a true and fair view of the financial position of the organisation as at the end of the financial year covered by the report, and of its financial performance during the year;
- to give an expert and independent opinion on whether the financial statements comply with the relevant laws.

However, in carrying out their audit, external audit must also pay attention to aspects of the organisation's corporate governance and it's securing of economy, efficiency and effectiveness in the use of resources.

Auditors must be appointed by 31 December of the year prior to the relevant financial year. Any public body that fails to do so must notify the Secretary of State, who will have reserve powers to make, or direct the body to make, an appointment.

Function and scope of internal audit

Internal audit is defined by the Chartered Institute of Management Accountants (CIMA) as 'an independent appraisal activity established within an organisation as a service to it. It is a control that functions by examining and evaluating the adequacy and effectiveness of other controls'.

The Chartered Institute of Internal Auditors (IIA) describes the role as follows:

> 'The role of internal audit is to provide independent assurance that an organisation's risk management, governance and internal control processes are operating effectively. Internal auditors deal with issues that are fundamentally important to the survival and prosperity of any organisation. Unlike external auditors, they look beyond financial risks and statements to consider wider issues such as the organisation's reputation, growth, its impact on the environment and the way it treats its employees.'

An organisation might have an internal audit unit or section, which carries out investigative work. An internal audit function should act independently of executive managers, but normally reports to a senior executive manager such as the finance director. The NHS Accounting Officer Memorandum requires all NHS trusts to have an internal audit function. The NHS Internal Audit Standards (or Government Internal Audit standards for Foundation Trusts for FTs) set out the requirements for internal audit and how to assess the service that is delivered. The FT Code requires the FT audit committee to monitor and review the effectiveness of the FT's internal audit function.

In the corporate sector, the FRC *Guidance on Audit Committees* (2012) suggests that the audit committee should ensure that the internal auditor has direct access to the board chair and the audit committee, and is also responsible to the audit committee. This means that the internal auditors maybe in an unusual position within the organisation. For operational reasons they may have a line reporting responsibility to a senior executive manager such as the finance director. Executive managers may also ask the internal auditors to carry out audits or reviews of the systems or procedures (and internal controls) for which they are responsible. However, the senior internal auditor should have some control over deciding what aspects of the organisation's systems should be investigated or audited, and also has a responsibility for reporting to the audit committee and the chair of the board.

Reliance on the work of internal audit

It is expected that the external auditors will liaise with the internal audit function to obtain a sufficient understanding of internal audit activities to assist in planning the audit and developing an effective audit approach. The auditors may also wish to place reliance upon certain aspects of the work of internal audit in satisfying their statutory responsibilities as set out in the NHS Act 2006 and in the NAO Audit Code. In particular the auditors may wish to consider the work of internal audit when undertaking their procedures in relation to the annual governance statement (AGS).

The NAO's Code of Audit Practice (2015) requires external audit to establish effective coordination arrangements with internal audit. External audit should seek to place maximum reliance on the work of internal audit whenever possible.

This all demonstrates the key relationship between internal and external audit as it is vital for the external auditors to be able to rely on the work undertaken by internal audit, not just on financial controls but on quality and performance controls as well.

The role of external audit

Audit report

The audit report is contained in the organisation's annual report and accounts, and is addressed by the auditors to the stakeholders of the organisation. The main purpose of the audit report is to give the users of an organisation's financial statements (and in particular the stakeholders) some assurance that the information in the statements is believable and that the financial statements present a 'true and fair view' of the organisation's financial position and performance. The opinion of the auditors should be the opinion of independent professional experts, based on an investigation of the organisation's control systems, accounting systems and financial/business transactions. The audit report itself provides only limited information to stakeholders, even though stakeholders often assume that an unqualified audit report means that the financial statements of the organisation are accurate and reliable.

An unmodified audit report (sometimes called an 'unqualified opinion') is given when the auditor believes that the accounts give a true and fair view of the organisation's financial position and performance. The wording of an unmodified audit report is usually fairly standard, although reports are longer for public companies (where the auditors might also report on some corporate governance statements) and differ between countries. Such a report may include an 'emphasis of matter' paragraph where, although the audit report is unmodified (i.e. the auditors consider that the financial statements present a true and fair view), there is an item that the auditor wants to bring to the attention of users because it is of some importance for an understanding of the statements, e.g. as specified for NHS organisations, who have to disclose issues with regard to their going concern statement (see Chapter 16).

Alternately, external auditors may present a modified audit report, although this is unusual. If it happens, there is a potentially serious problem with the financial statements and, by implication, the financial condition of the organisation. It also means that the auditors have been unable to agree with the directors of the organisation about what information the financial statements should contain. Because the directors and the auditors cannot agree, the auditors have considered it necessary to give a statement to stakeholders to this effect. There are three types of modified audit opinion, namely, a qualified opinion, an adverse opinion, and a disclaimer of opinion.

A qualified audit opinion is sometimes called an 'except for' opinion. It is given when, in the opinion of the auditor, the financial statements would give a true and fair view except for a particular matter, which the auditor explains.

An adverse opinion is given when the auditor considers that there are material misstatements in the accounts and that these are 'pervasive'. In effect, the auditor is stating that the figures in the accounts are seriously wrong.

A disclaimer of opinion is given in cases where the auditor has been unable to obtain the information that he needs to give an audit opinion. The lack of information means that the auditor is unable to state that the financial statements give a true and fair view, and that there may possibly be serious misstatements that the auditor has been unable to check.

In the rare circumstances that the auditors give a modified audit report to the stakeholders, a situation has arisen where professional accountants have given an opinion that the stakeholders cannot trust the information that has been given to them by the directors. If the stakeholders cannot trust the directors, the quality of corporate governance could hardly be lower.

CASE STUDY: An audit report

Here is a simplified example of a typical unmodified audit report.

Report on the financial statements

We have audited the accompanying financial statements of XYZ Organisation, which comprise the statement of financial position as at 31 December 20XX, and the statement of comprehensive income, statement of changes in equity, and cash flows for the year then ended, and a summary of significant accounting policies and other explanatory notes.

Management's responsibility for the financial statements

Management is responsible for the preparation and fair presentation of these financial statements in accordance with International Financial Reporting Standards. This responsibility includes: designing, implementing and maintaining internal control relevant to the preparation and fair presentation of financial statements that are free from material misstatement, whether due to fraud or error; selecting and applying appropriate accounting policies; and making accounting estimates that are reasonable in the circumstances.

Auditor's responsibility

Our responsibility is to express an opinion on these financial statements based on our audit. We conducted our audit in accordance with International Standards on Auditing. Those standards require that we comply with ethical requirements and plan and perform the audit to obtain reasonable assurance whether the financial statements are free from material misstatement.

An audit involves performing procedures to obtain audit evidence about the amounts and disclosures in the financial statements. The procedures selected depend on the auditor's judgment, including the assessment of the risks of material misstatement of the financial statements, whether due to fraud or error. In making those risk assessments, the auditor considers internal control relevant to the entity's preparation and fair presentation of the financial statements in order to design audit procedures that are appropriate in the circumstances, but not for the purpose of expressing an opinion on the effectiveness of the entity's internal control. An audit also includes evaluating the appropriateness of accounting policies used and the reasonableness of accounting estimates made by management, as well as evaluating the overall presentation of the financial statements.

We believe that the audit evidence that we have obtained is sufficient and appropriate to provide a basis for our audit opinion.

Opinion

In our opinion, the financial statements give a true and fair view (or present fairly, in all material respects) of the financial position of XYZ Organisation as of 31 December 20XX, and of its financial performance and its cash flows for the year then ended in accordance with International Financial Reporting Standards.

Report on other legal and regulatory requirements

[Form and content of this section of the report will vary depending on the nature of the auditor's other reporting responsibilities.]

Signed: (Auditor) ______________________________

Date: ______________________________

Responsibility for detecting errors and fraud

Stakeholders would probably like to assume that if the auditors provide a favourable audit report, the financial statements must be 'correct', and there has not been any fraud or error that has resulted in incorrect use of accounting policies, omissions of fact or misinterpretation of fact. This view is based on the belief that if professional accountants have checked the figures, they must be correct – unless the accountants have been negligent and have failed to do their job properly. However, it is a popular misconception that the auditor is responsible for detecting fraud or error in an organisation's financial statements. This is not the case.

The board of directors is responsible for preventing fraud in their organisation, or detecting fraud if it occurs. The organisation's system of internal control, described in Chapter 16, should be designed to limit the risk of fraud and error, and the board is responsible for monitoring the effectiveness of the internal control system. The responsibility of the board (with delegated responsibility of management) for the prevention and detection of fraud and error is a core principle of corporate governance. The directors are fully accountable to the stakeholders and so are fully responsible for the information presented in the annual report and accounts.

It is not the primary responsibility of the external auditors to detect fraud. The auditors will assess the risk or possibility that fraud or error might have caused the financial statements to be materially misleading. The auditors should therefore design audit procedures that will provide reasonable reassurance that material fraud or error has not occurred, and that the financial statements give a true and fair view of the organisation's financial position and performance. The external audit might also act as a deterrent to fraud, because the auditors will carry out checks of control procedures, documents and transactions in the course of their audit work. They might discover fraud during the course of their audit work, in which case it would be their responsibility to report the matter to the directors (unless the fraud is carried out by the directors themselves).

No matter how well an audit is planned and carried out, there will always be some risk that fraud or error has occurred but not been detected. Given the nature of auditing, for which there is only a limited amount of time and resources, and which is carried out through a process of sampling and testing, it would be impossible to ensure that all errors are detected. Accounting systems and internal control procedures are also vulnerable to fraud and error, arising, for example, from criminal collusion between employees or decisions by management to override the system of controls.

An area for dispute, however, is whether the auditors ought to be able to identify fraud or a significant error during the course of their audit work, whenever a fraud or error occurs. Although they are not responsible for the financial statements, it can be argued that a failure by the auditors to discover a major fraud or material error might be the result of professional negligence. If they are negligent, they should be held liable to the organisation and its stakeholders. In the UK, the Companies Act 2006 (CA 2006) introduced new rules on auditors' liability for negligence, breach of duty or breach of trust regarding the conduct of the audit.

Shareholders of both public and private companies can vote by ordinary resolution to limit the potential liability of the external auditors, by means of a liability limitation agreement (LLA). Such an agreement can limit the liability to the company by the auditor in respect of negligence, default, breach of duty or breach of trust occurring in the course of the audit of accounts. The Act states, that in considering what is fair and reasonable in the circumstances, the court should have no regard to the possibility or otherwise of recovering compensation from other persons who are jointly or partly responsible for the loss that has been incurred. Although the Act provides the possibility of some protection for auditors against liability for negligence or breach of duty with LLAs, it also introduced two new criminal offences for auditors in connection with the auditors' report (i.e. it is a criminal offence, punishable by a fine, to knowingly or recklessly cause an audit report to 'include any matter that is misleading, false or deceptive in any material particular', or knowingly or recklessly cause an audit report to omit a statement that is required by certain specified sections of the Act).

Auditors' liability to third parties

The auditors have a legal duty of care to the organisation and its stakeholders. There is some doubt as to whether they might also have a duty of care to other parties. In the UK, the extent of auditor liability to external parties has been tested in two legal cases: *Caparo Industries plc v Dickman [1990]* and *Royal Bank of Scotland v Bannerman Johnstone Maclay [2002]*. The latter case, crucially, concluded that the absence of any disclaimer of liability to third parties was a significant contributing factor to the duty of care owed to them. In response to this auditors have since included a disclaimer of liability to third parties using its audit reports such as:

> 'This report, including the opinion, has been prepared for and only for the organisation's members as a body in accordance with the Companies Act 2006 and for no other purpose. We do not, in giving this opinion, accept or assume responsibility for any other purpose or to any other person to whom this report is shown or into whose hands it may come save where expressly agreed by our prior consent in writing.'

No firm decision has yet been reached in the UK as to how to protect auditors from the entire burden of liability where others, e.g. directors, may also to be to blame. The consequence of which is a limited competitive market for audit services that is dominated by the 'Big Four' (Deloitte, PwC, Ernst & Young, KPMG). There are an increasing number of advocates for a 'proportional' system of liability replacing the current 'joint and several' one. Under this proposal, the audit firm would accept their proportion of the blame in a negligence case and would pay that proportion of the compensation. This system, as introduced in Australia in 2004, would ensure a fair outcome for the plaintiff without placing the entire financial burden upon the audit profession.

The Local Audit and Accountability Act 2014 requires that any agreements to limit the liability owed to an NHS organisation by the auditor in respect of negligence, default, breach of duty or breach of trust must comply with regulations made by the Secretary of State. These state that:

- a restriction on the duration of an agreement: it cannot cover more than the financial year or years to which the appointment of the external auditor relates, and
- an agreement for limiting the external auditor's liability cannot be less than such amount as is fair and reasonable given the circumstances.

Independence of external audit

The external auditor should be independent of the client organisation so that the audit opinion will not be influenced by the relationship between the auditor and the organisation. The auditors are expected to give an unbiased and honest professional opinion to the stakeholders about the financial statements.

An unmodified audit report is often seen by investors as a 'clean bill of health' for the organisation. However, doubts are sometimes expressed about the independence of the external auditors. It could be argued that unless suitable governance measures are in place, a firm of auditors may reach audit opinions and judgments that are heavily influenced by their wish to maintain good relations with the management of a client organisation. If this happens, the auditors are no longer independent and the stakeholders cannot rely on their opinion. For example, in the corporate sector, an official 2010 report on the collapse of Lehman Brothers in 2008 criticised the external auditors Ernst & Young for allowing the company to account for certain transactions (repo 105 transactions) in a way that misleadingly improved the look of the end-of-quarter balance sheets during 2007 and 2008, in the months before the bank eventually collapsed.

Perhaps the most significant threat to auditor independence is that the audit firm relies on the organisation's management to secure its appointment and re-appointment as the organisation's auditor. Although companies may give their audit committee responsibility for recommending the appointment of the auditors, the opinions of senior management are often decisive in the matter of auditor selection. The auditor is therefore reliant for future audit work from the organisation on the views of the management whose financial statements it is their job to audit. In addition, the audit firm has to rely extensively on management for the information and explanations needed to enable them to carry out their audit work. A UK Ethical Standards Board has commented on this situation, saying:

> 'Any reasonable and informed third party – for example, a shareholder – is likely to regard this as a significant threat to the auditor's objectivity.'

Professional guidelines are given to auditors by national and international accountancy bodies, notably the International Federation of Accountants (IFAC). The IFAC Code of Ethics for Professional Accountants identifies certain ways in which the integrity, objectivity and independence of the auditors might be put at risk. An audit firm should not have to rely on a single organisation for a large proportion of its total fee income, because undue dependence on a single audit client could impair objectivity. IFAC does not specify what amounts to 'undue dependence' on a single client. However, in the UK, the rules of the Association of Chartered Certified Accountants (ACCA) state that where an audit client is a public interest entity and, for two consecutive years, the total fees from the client represent more than 15% of the total fees received by the auditing firm, the firm shall disclose this fact to the client, and discuss safeguards to reduce the threat to independence to an acceptable level.

A risk to objectivity and independence also arises when the audit firm or anyone closely associated with it (such as an audit partner) has a mutual business interest with the organisation or any of its officers. Similarly, objectivity could be threatened when there is a close personal relationship between a member of the audit firm and an employee of the organisation. The audit firm should not have a client organisation in which a partner holds a significant number of stakes. The IFAC Code does not have any objection in principle to an audit firm providing non-audit services (such as consultancy services) to a client, although the auditor should not perform any management functions in an organisation nor take any management decisions.

The audit profession has identified five categories of potential threats to auditor independence.

- **Self-interest threats:** if the audit firm earns a large proportion of its revenue from a client organisation, it may be unwilling to annoy that client by challenging the figures and assumptions used by management to prepare the organisation's financial statements.
- **Self-review threat:** this can arise when the audit firm does non-audit work for the organisation, and the annual audit involves checking the work done by the firm's own employees. The auditors may not be as critical of the work, or prepared to challenge it, because this would raise questions about the professional competence of the audit firm.
- **Advocacy threat:** this can arise if the audit form is asked to give its formal support to the organisation by providing public statements on particular issues or supporting the organisation in a legal case. Acting as advocate for an organisation means taking sides; this implies a loss of independence.
- **Familiarity threat:** a threat to independence occurs when an auditor is familiar with an organisation or one of its directors or senior managers, or becomes familiar with them through a working association over time. Familiarity leads to trust and a willingness to believe what the other person says. The auditor will also be unwilling to think that the other person is capable of making a serious error or committing fraud. A familiarity threat arises through personal association (e.g. family connections) and through long association with the organisation and its management.
- **Intimidation threat:** an auditor may feel threatened by the directors or senior management of an organisation. Both real and imagined threats can affect the auditor's independence. Intimidation may result from a domineering and bullying personality on the organisation's board of directors (e.g. the chief executive officer (CEO)). An organisation may also threaten to take away the audit or stop giving the firm non-audit work unless the auditor accepts the opinions of management.

Threats to auditor independence must be identified, and measures should be taken to limit the threat to an acceptable level of risk. Two areas of debate about how to ensure auditor independence have been whether auditors should be prevented from carrying out non-audit work for clients or whether the amount of non-audit work they do should be restricted, and whether there should be a regular rotation of either the audit firm or the audit partner and other senior members of the audit team.

Non-audit work for a client by an audit firm

The codes of conduct of national professional accountancy bodies are similar to the IFAC Code and lack any clear restrictions on the performance of non-audit work for an audit client. Suggestions for regulatory measures to ensure auditor independence have included proposals to restrict the amount of non-audit work, or the type of non-audit work, that the firm of auditors is permitted to carry out for a client organisation. Non-audit work might include:

- consultancy on taxation issues (helping an organisation to minimise tax liabilities)
- investigating targets for a potential takeover bid
- helping an organisation to construct a bid for a major government contract
- providing advice and expert assistance on IT systems
- internal audit services
- valuation and actuarial services
- services relating to litigation
- services relating to recruitment and remuneration.

The main problem with auditors doing non-audit work is that when the firm audits transactions recommended by its consultancy arm, it is unlikely to take an independent view.

The risk to auditor objectivity and independence from carrying out non-audit work became apparent in the wake of the Enron collapse. Arthur Andersen were the auditors of Enron, and in the financial year before the company's collapse in 2001, Andersen earned more fee income from Enron for non-audit work than from audit work. The audit firm was suspected of failing to carry out a proper audit of the company. It was claimed that the audit firm would have been reluctant to question the accounts of Enron because it would risk losing not just the audit work but also the substantial non-audit fee income. In addition, it was suggested that since the information in the company's financial statements reflected the non-audit consultancy advice given by the audit firm, the firm's auditors would be unlikely to challenge the fairness and accuracy of the statements. In other words, Andersen's auditors would not challenge the opinions of Andersen's consultants.

Audit firms have denied that fees from non-audit work will affect their independence, arguing that the individuals who work as consultants for a client organisation (such as on IT projects) are not the same individuals who work on the audit. Even so, activist shareholder groups continue to challenge this assertion. In the UK, a well-reported attempt was made in 2002 by some institutional stakeholders to vote against the re-appointment of Deloitte as auditors to Vodafone at the AGM of the company. The 'dissidents' argued their case because the audit firm did too much non-audit work for the company and so could not be considered sufficiently independent.

There are three broad approaches to the regulation of non-audit work by audit firms:

- there should be no restrictions at all on non-audit work by the audit firm
- there should be a total prohibition on non-audit work for a corporate client by the audit firm
- there should be a partial prohibition on non-audit work for a corporate client by the audit firm.

A partial restriction could take either of two forms. There could be a prohibition on audit firms from taking on certain types of consultancy work where their independence as auditors could be put at risk, such as tax planning advice work. However, audit firms would be free to carry out other types of non-audit work. The second approach to restricting non-audit work would be to set a limit on the amount of fees an audit firm could earn from non-audit work, expressed perhaps as a proportion of the fees it earns from the audit. For example, a limit might be imposed restricting non-audit fees to, say, 50% of the fees from the audit work.

The difficulty with a partial restriction on non-audit work is that rules have to be devised and agreed as to what permissible and non-permissible non-audit work should be, or what the maximum amount of non-audit fee income should be. In the UK, the audit profession is governed by ethical principles rather than rules and regulations about non-audit work for audit clients. The Institute of Chartered Accountants in England and Wales (ICAEW) has made the following statements about non-audit work:

> 'The most effective way to ensure the reality of independence is to provide guidance centred around a framework of principles rather than a detailed set of rules that can be complied with to the letter but circumvented in substance.'
>
> 'A blanket prohibition on the provision of non-audit services to audit clients can be inefficient for the client and is neither necessary to ensure independence, nor helpful in contributing to the knowledge necessary to ensure the quality of the audit.'

The need for auditor independence when the audit firm does non-audit work is recognised in the UK Code. The code includes a provision that 'the annual report should explain to stakeholders how, if the auditor provides non-audit services, auditor objectivity and independence is safeguarded'.

Another suggestion for protecting auditor independence is that there should be 'rotation' of auditors. There is an important distinction, however, between the rotation of an audit firm, whereby a firm is required to give up the audit for an organisation after a maximum number of years, and the organisation must appoint different auditors; and rotation of audit personnel, whereby the audit engagement partner and other key individuals involved in the annual audit should be removed from the audit after a certain number of years, and new individuals assigned to the work.

Rotation of audit firm

Rotation of the audit firm would enhance auditor independence because a firm of auditors would have little to gain by agreeing with the wishes of the client organisation, and carrying out a less than rigorous audit, if it knows that it will soon lose the audit work anyway. The work of outgoing auditors would also be subject to review – and criticism – by the firm of auditors taking their place.

In 2013 the Competition Commission published a report on the statutory audit services market. The report reached the following conclusions about the restricted nature of competition in the market for audit services.

- Companies are reluctant to switch auditors, partly because it is difficult for them to compare the services of different auditors and partly because the costs of switching would be high.
- Too often auditors focus on the needs of senior management, who are the key decision takers on whether to retain their services.
- Companies and audit firms invest in a relationship of mutual trust and confidence 'from which neither will lightly walk away'.

The report concluded that the Competition Commission would be investigating the following possible combinations of remedies including:

- mandatory tendering for audits (which is already a UK Code requirement)
- mandatory rotation of audit firms
- prohibition of 'Big-Four-only' clauses in loans to companies by banks
- greater accountability of the auditors to the audit committee.

On 1 April 2014, the functions of the Competition Commission transferred to the Competition and Markets Authority (CMA) which made the Statutory Audit Services for Large Companies Market Investigation (Mandatory Use of Competitive Tender Processes and Audit Committee Responsibilities) Order 2014. This Order came into force on 1 January 2015 and applies to FTSE 350 companies. As a consequence of the Order, all such companies must put their statutory audit services engagement out to tender every ten years or earlier. This means that an auditor may not conduct more than ten consecutive statutory audits of a FTSE 350 company without a competitive tender process having taken place. In addition, it required that the terms of the statutory audit services agreement must have been negotiated and agreed between the audit committee and the auditor.

In the UK, the Statutory Auditors and Third Country Auditors Regulations 2016 (SATCAR 2016), has introduced a requirement for all public interest entities (PIEs) to conduct a tender at least every ten years and rotate auditors after at least 20 years. A PIE is defined as follows:

- entities whose transferable securities are admitted to trading on a regulated market of any member state of the EU;
- credit institutions;
- insurance undertakings; or
- entities designated by member states as public-interest entities, for instance undertakings that are of significant public relevance because of the nature of their business, their size or the number of their employees (the application of this fourth criterion varies significantly across member states).

This superseded the UK Code which already recommended that 'FTSE 350 companies should put the external audit out to tender at least every ten years'. The principles of retendering are explored in the FRC *Audit Tenders: Notes on good practice* (February 2017), adds that, apart from the regulatory requirement, feedback from companies that have changed auditors since the change in requirements indicates that there are benefits to be gained from fresh insight. Even if the incumbent firm is reappointed, experience suggests that the tender process itself can reinvigorate the audit approach.

The UK has not designated NHS organisations as PIEs despite their significant public relevance, and so these regulations are not directly applicable to the NHS. Nevertheless, the recommendations for tenders demonstrate best practice.

The FT guidance *Governance over Audit, Assurance and Accountability: Guidance for Foundation Trusts* (March 2015) also sets out good practice for maintaining independence of audit services. It recommends a three- to five-year period of appointment and a market-testing exercise for the appointment of an auditor at least once every five years. The external audit should be subject to a tender process at least every ten years, and in most cases more frequently than this.

The DH *Guidance on the Local Procurement of External Auditors for NHS Trusts and CCGs* (March 2016) states that the contract length can be anything from one to five years, with three to five years being 'normal' and considered an appropriate period for an auditor to develop a strong understanding of the organisation. Contracts can be awarded with an optional extension period, such as three years with an optional two-year extension. Whatever length of contract is chosen, it must be agreed at an early stage. It makes no stipulation as to retendering.

Audit partner rotation

An argument put forward by the major accountancy firms is that the requirement for rotation should apply, not to the firm of auditors, but to the individual partner of a firm in charge of the audit. For example, it might be acceptable for ABC Corporation to retain the services of Ernst & Young indefinitely, provided that the partner in charge of the audit is replaced every, say, five or seven years. Supporters of this argument claim that the independence of the audit is threatened by the personal relationship an audit partner builds up with the client organisation, not the length of association of the audit firm with the organisation.

In the case of large organisations, there is also an argument for a regular rotation of other senior audit managers, as well as the lead partner. Peter Wyman, former president of the ICAEW, stressed the distinction between audit partner and audit firm rotation. Writing in the *Financial Times* on 25 July 2002, he commented:

> 'Improvements could be made in the area of audit partner and audit firm rotation, although it is vital not to confuse the two. Audit firm rotation achieves

the appearance of greater auditor independence but research shows it is likely to produce a reduction in audit quality, particularly in the first two years after the new firm is appointed. Because people rather than organisations are likely to get "cosy" with one another, greater audit independence could be achieved by rotating the audit partner. This approach avoids quality loss, which arises when the entire cumulative knowledge of the audit firm is cast aside when a new firm is appointed.'

A counter-argument, however, is that audit partner rotation would not have prevented the problem that arose between Andersen and its clients Enron and WorldCom. Although Andersen as a whole was not over-dependent on Enron, the company was a vital client for the firm's Houston office, which carried out the audit. Similarly, the Andersen office in Jackson, Mississippi was heavily dependent on the work that it did for WorldCom. To prevent loss of audit independence, audit partner rotation would almost certainly have been ineffective, whereas audit firm rotation might have been much more effective.

Currently, regulations in most countries favour audit partner rotation rather than audit firm rotation. In the UK, for example, the ICAEW's ethical standards require the rotation of various members of an audit team, including the rotation of the audit engagement partner at least every five years.

The role of internal audit

According to CIMA official terminology, internal audit is the:

> 'independent appraisal activity established within an organisation as a service to it. It is a control which functions by examining and evaluating the adequacy and effectiveness of other controls'.

The IIA describes the role as being to 'provide independent assurance that an organisation's risk management, governance and internal control processes are operating effectively. Internal auditors deal with issues that are fundamentally important to the survival and prosperity of any organisation'.

The work done by any internal audit unit is not prescribed by regulation, but is decided by management or by the board (or audit committee). The possible tasks of internal audit include the following.

- **Reviewing the internal control system:** traditionally, an internal audit department has carried out independent checks on the financial controls in an organisation; however, this has now extended to include quality and performance controls as well. The checks would be to establish whether suitable quality, performance and financial controls exist and if so, whether they are applied properly and are effective. It is not the function of internal auditors to manage risks, only to monitor and report them, and to check that risk controls are efficient and cost-effective.

- **Special investigations:** internal auditors might conduct special investigations into particular aspects of the organisation's operations (systems and procedures), to check the effectiveness of operational controls.
- **Examination of financial and operating information:** internal auditors might be asked to investigate the timeliness of reporting and the accuracy of the information in reports.
- **VFM audits:** this is an investigation into an operation or activity to establish whether it is economical, efficient and effective.
- **Reviewing compliance by the organisation with particular laws or regulations:** this is an investigation into the effectiveness of compliance controls.
- **Risk assessment:** internal auditors might be asked to investigate aspects of risk management, and in particular the adequacy of the mechanisms for identifying, assessing and controlling significant risks to the organisation, from both internal and external sources.

Investigation of internal financial controls

Internal auditors are commonly required to check the soundness of internal financial controls. In assessing the effectiveness of individual controls, and of an internal control system generally, the following factors should be considered.

- **Whether the controls are manual or automated:** automated controls are by no means error-proof or fraud-proof, but may be more reliable than similar manual controls.
- **Whether controls are discretionary or non-discretionary:** non-discretionary controls are checks and procedures that must be carried out. Discretionary controls are those that do not have to be applied, either because they are voluntary or because an individual can choose to dis-apply them. Risks can infiltrate a system, for example, when senior management chooses to dis-apply controls and allow unauthorised or unchecked procedures to occur.
- **Whether the control can be circumvented easily:** an activity can be carried out in a different way where similar controls do not apply.
- **Whether the controls are effective in achieving their purpose:** are they extensive enough or carried out frequently enough? Are the controls applied rigorously? For example, is a supervisor doing his or her job properly?

Reports by internal auditors can provide reassurance that internal controls are sound and effective, or might recommend changes and improvements where weaknesses are uncovered.

The objectivity and independence of internal auditors

The manager of a directorate or department should monitor the internal controls within the operation and try to identify and correct weaknesses. They should also report on reviews of the effectiveness of internal control. However, a line manager cannot be properly objective, because they could face 'blame' for control failures in the system or operation for which they are responsible.

In contrast, internal auditors ought to be objective, because they investigate the control systems of other directorates and departments. However, they are also employees within the organisation and report to someone on the organisation structure. If the internal auditors report to the finance director, they will find it difficult to be critical of the finance director. Similarly, if the internal auditors report to the CEO, they will be reluctant to criticise the CEO. In this respect, their independence could be compromised.

In its *Guidance for Audit Committees*, the ICAEW comments that the internal auditors should be separate and independent from line management, but that 'independence' for internal auditors does not have the same meaning as independence for external auditors. To protect the independence of the internal audit function, the FRC's *Guidance on Audit Committees* suggests that the audit committee should have the responsibility for the appointment of the head of internal audit, and his removal from office.

Review of the effectiveness of the internal audit function

The board or audit committee should review the effectiveness of the internal audit function each year. As part of this review, the 2014 *HFMA NHS Audit Committee Handbook* (HFMA Handbook) suggests that the audit committee should make sure that the head of internal audit has direct access to the chair of the board and the audit committee, and is accountable to the audit committee.

There should also be a review and assessment of the annual internal audit work plan along with regular reports on the results of work done by the internal auditors. The review should consider and monitor the responses of management to the recommendations made to them by the internal auditors. The audit committee should also meet with the head of internal audit at least once a year without executive management being present. The HFMA Handbook states that the audit committee should actively review the plans of both internal and external audit and assess the quality of the services that are provided.

The audit committee

The UK Code requires that a board of directors should establish formal and transparent arrangements for considering how they should apply the corporate reporting and risk management and internal control principles, and maintaining an appropriate relationship with the organisation's auditors. These arrangements should be met by establishing an audit committee, which should be given certain responsibilities by the board. This does not detract from the unitary board principle and despite of the work of the audit committee, the board remains responsible for making the final decision.

The FRC has issued a number of guidance notes in 2016 covering audit committees, the revised ethical standard and revised auditing standards.

The FRC *Guidance on Audit Committees* (2016) has introduced the following requirements:

- The audit committee should consider key matters of its own initiative rather than relying solely on the work of the external auditor. It must satisfy itself that the sources of assurance and information it has used to carry out its roles to review, monitor and provide assurance or recommendations to the board are sufficient and objective.
- The board has ultimate responsibility for an organisation's risk management and internal control systems, but the board may delegate to the audit committee some functions to assist the board in meeting this responsibility.
- The need for an internal audit function should be regularly reviewed by the audit committee and where such a function is required then the audit committee should review and approve its role and mandate; approve the annual internal audit plan (which must be aligned to the risks of the organisation); and monitor and review the effectiveness of its work. The audit committee should review and approve annually the internal audit charter to ensure that it is appropriate to the current needs of the organisation.
- The audit committee should ensure that the internal auditor has a reporting line that enables it to be independent of the executive and so be able to exercise independent judgement. The audit committee should ensure that the internal audit function has unrestricted scope and evaluates the effectiveness of the risk, compliance and finance functions as part of its internal audit plan. The audit committee may also wish to consider whether an independent, third party review of internal audit effectiveness and processes is appropriate.
- The audit committee should have primary responsibility for negotiating the fee and scope of the external audit, initiating a tender process, influencing the appointment of an engagement partner and making formal recommendations to the board on the appointment, reappointment and removal of the auditors (reflecting the CMA Order).
- More emphasis is placed on interactions with the external auditor around the areas of significant judgement and risks to audit quality.
- Set and apply a formal policy specifying the types of non-audit service for which use of the external auditor is pre-approved. The guidance reaffirms that such approval should only be in place for matters that are clearly trivial.
- The audit committee has a role in ensuring that shareholder interests are properly protected in relation to financial reporting and internal control. The committee should consider the clarity of its reporting and be prepared to meet investors.
- Remuneration should reflect the responsibility members bear and that a significant extra amount of time needs to be committed.

Reporting requirements for Audit Committees have also been updated to include the following:

- how the audit committee composition requirements have been addressed;
- how the performance evaluation of the audit committee has been conducted;
- the current external audit partner's name and for how long the partner has held the role;
- advance notice of any plans for retendering the external audit;
- the committee's policy for approval of non-audit services;
- the audit fees for the statutory audit of the company's consolidated financial statements and the fees paid to the auditor and its network firms for audit related services and other non-audit services, including the ratio of audit to non-audit work;
- for each significant engagement, or category of engagements, an explanation of the services provided and why the audit committee concluded that it was in the interests of the company to purchase them from the external auditor;
- explanations of how the committee has assessed the effectiveness of internal audit and satisfied itself that the quality, experience and expertise of the function is appropriate for the business;
- the nature and extent of interaction (if any) with the FRC's Corporate Reporting Review team; and
- that the FRC's Audit Quality Review team has reviewed a company's audit, disclosures about significant findings and the resulting actions they and the auditors plan to take. This disclosure should not include the audit quality category awarded.

The changes to the ethical standard set out the principles that underpin high quality, independent audit and, particularly for the audits of PIEs, strengthen auditor independence by prohibiting or restricting a range of engagements that could result in a conflict of interest.

Whilst these changes are not directly applicable within the NHS, they provide a benchmark of good practice and NHS audit committees must consider how the new requirements impact their own practice. There is a formal requirement, however, for every NHS board to establish an audit committee. The role of the audit committee in applying the principles of risk management and internal controls is described in Chapters 15 and 16; this chapter concentrates on the role of the audit committee is applying corporate reporting principles and maintaining an appropriate relationship with the external auditors.

Role and responsibilities of the audit committee

The HFMA Handbook describes the role of the audit committee as 'critically reviewing and reporting on the relevance and robustness of the governance and assurance processes on which the governing body places reliance'. This is a wider role than the traditional role of financial scrutiny, as envisaged by the UK Code, and has resulted from the broad range of stakeholder requirements that exist in the NHS. The two key areas that the audit committee should provide assurance to the board on are the board assurance framework (BAF) and documents that are to be publicly disclosed (the AGS, registration evidence for the Care Quality Commission (CQC), the annual report and accounts and Quality Accounts).

The role of internal audit is addressed earlier in this chapter. However, the role of the audit committee is to review the adequacy of the organisation's internal control system, and in the absence of a separate risk committee to review the organisation's capacity to manage its risk management systems. In NHS organisations there is usually an overlap between the work of the audit committee and the quality committee. Clarity on how these areas will be addressed by the two committees is vital to ensure that duplication of work is avoided and no gaps of assurance arise. The committee should challenge and test the effectiveness of the internal audit function and should promote its role within the organisation ensuring that it has adequate resources.

With regard to public disclosure statements the audit committee has an essential role in reviewing these prior to approval by the board. It should be satisfied with the strength of the processes and the quality of data that has been relied upon to produce the statements.

In addition the UK Code lists the role and responsibilities of an audit committee (excluding those concerned with risk management and internal control set out in Chapter 16) as follows:

- to monitor the integrity of the organisation's financial statements and any formal announcements relating to the organisation's financial performance. In doing so, it should review 'significant financial judgments' that these statements and announcements contain;
- to make recommendations to the board in relation to the appointment, re-appointment or removal of the organisation's external auditors, and for putting these recommendations to the stakeholders for approval at a general meeting of the organisation;
- to approve the remuneration and terms of engagement of the external auditors (after they have been negotiated with the auditors by management);
- to review and monitor the independence and objectivity of the external auditors, and also the effectiveness of the audit process, taking into account relevant UK professional and regulatory requirements;
- to develop and implement the organisation's policy on using the external auditors to provide non-audit services. This should take into account any relevant external ethical guidance on the subject. The committee should report to the board, identifying actions or improvements that are needed and recommending the steps to be taken;
- to provide advice on whether the annual report and accounts, taken as a whole, is fair, balanced and understandable and provides the information necessary

for shareholders to assess the company's position and performance, business model and strategy;

- to review arrangements by which staff of the company may, in confidence, raise concerns about possible improprieties in matters of financial reporting or other matters. The audit committee's objective should be to ensure that arrangements are in place for the proportionate and independent investigation of such matters and for appropriate follow-up action; and
- to report to the board on how it has discharged its responsibilities.

The board should decide just what the role of the audit committee should be, and the terms of reference should be tailored to the organisation's particular circumstances. A separate section of the annual report should describe the work of the committee. The audit committee should review its terms of reference and effectiveness annually, and recommend any necessary changes to the board. The board should also review the effectiveness of the audit committee annually.

The core functions of the audit committee are concerned with oversight, assessment and review of other functions and systems in the organisation. It is not the committee's duty to carry out those functions (e.g. management remains responsible for preparing the financial statements and the auditors remain responsible for preparing the audit plan and carrying out the audit).

However, the high-level oversight function can sometimes lead to more detailed work. For example, in a recent case of a FT where there were concerns over payroll, the audit committee requested a full-scale independent review of payroll services and the director of human resources (HR) was required to attend to give a full response to the recommendations made.

Composition of the audit committee

The specific requirements in respect of composition are set out in Chapter 5. However, the distinctive characteristic of the audit committee is that it comprises only non-executive directors (NEDs).

The FRC *Guidance on Audit Committees* suggests that appointments to the committee should be made by the board on the recommendation of the nomination committee, in consultation with the audit committee chair. Appointments should be made for a period of up to three years, extendable by no more than two additional three-year periods and so long as the director remains independent.

The UK Code states that a separate section of the company's annual report should describe the work of the audit committee. 'This deliberately puts the spotlight on the audit committee and gives it an authority it might otherwise lack.' Similar recommendations are contained in the DH's model standing orders for NHS trusts and in the FT Code.

The organisation's management is under an obligation to make sure that the audit committee is kept properly informed and should take the initiative in providing the committee with information instead of waiting to be asked. The executive directors (EDs) should also have regard to their common law duty to provide all directors, including the audit committee members, with all the information they need to discharge their duties as directors of the organisation. This point is crucial: the audit committee can only do its work properly if it is kept properly informed by the executive management.

Remuneration, induction and training of committee members

Because audit committees carry out wide-ranging and time-consuming work, organisations must make the necessary resources available. This includes making suitable payments to the members of the audit committee in view of the responsibilities they have and the time they must commit to the work. The amount of remuneration paid to the audit committee members should take account of the remuneration paid to other members of the board. The committee chair's responsibilities and time commitments will normally be greater than those of the other committee members, and this should be reflected in their remuneration.

The committee should have the support of the company secretary and should have access to the services of the organisation's secretariat. Audit committee members must also be given suitable induction and training. Ongoing training should include keeping the committee members up to date on developments in quality, performance and financial reporting and related NHS guidance or legislation. It may include:

- understanding financial statements
- the application of particular accounting standards
- the regulatory framework for the organisation's business
- the role of internal and external auditing
- risk management.

Induction and training can take various forms, including attendance at formal courses and conferences, internal organisation talks and seminars and briefings by external advisers.

Audit committee meetings

The audit committee chair should decide the timing and frequency of committee meetings, in consultation with the company secretary. There should be as many meetings as the role and responsibilities of the committee require. The FRC *Guidance on Audit Committees* suggests that there should be no fewer than three committee meetings each year, timed to coincide with key dates in the financial reporting and audit calendar. For example, meetings might be held when the audit plans are available for review and when interim statements, preliminary announcements and the full annual report are near completion. Most audit committee chairs will probably want to call meetings more frequently. In practice, most NHS audit committees meet quarterly, if not bi-monthly, to manage the significant workload carried by the committee. This is reflected in the HFMA Handbook.

Sufficient time should be allowed between audit committee meetings and meetings of the main board to allow any work arising out of the committee meeting to be carried out and reported to the board as appropriate. This is reflected in the HFMA Handbook. Only the audit committee chair and members are entitled to attend meetings of the committee. It is for the committee to decide whether other individuals should be invited to attend for a particular meeting or a particular agenda item. It is expected that the external and internal audit lead partners and the organisation's finance director will be invited regularly to attend meetings.

At least once a year, the audit committee should meet the external and internal auditors, without management being present, to discuss matters relating to its responsibilities and issues arising from the audit.

The audit committee's role in quality, performance and financial reporting

It is the responsibility of management, not the audit committee, to prepare complete and accurate quality, performance and financial statements. It is the responsibility of the audit committee to review the significant reporting issues and judgements that are made in connection with these statements. For example, the audit committee should consider significant accounting policies used to prepare the financial statements, any changes to them, and any significant estimates or judgements on which the statements have been based. Management should inform the committee about the methods they have used to account for significant or unusual transactions, particularly where the accounting treatment is open to different approaches. Taking the external auditors' views into consideration, the committee should consider whether the organisation has adopted appropriate accounting policies and made appropriate estimates and judgements.

The committee should also consider the clarity and completeness of the disclosures in the quality, performance and financial statements. If the committee is not satisfied with any aspect of the proposed reporting by the organisation, it should report its views to the board. The committee should also review related information presented with the quality, performance and financial statements, including the business review and the corporate governance statements relating to audit and risk management.

Appointment and removal of external auditors

Under the UK Code, the audit committee has the primary responsibility for making a recommendation to the board on the appointment, reappointment or removal of the external auditors. FRC guidance recommends that the audit committee should 'oversee' the selection process if it recommends to the board that new external auditors should be selected. The committee's recommendation should be based on the qualification and expertise of the auditors, the resources of the auditors and the independence of the auditors.

Under the FRC guidance, if the audit committee recommends that new external auditors should be selected, the committee should 'oversee' the selection process and its recommendation should be based on the qualification and expertise of the auditors, the resources of the auditors, the independence of the auditors and the effectiveness of the audit process. The assessment should cover all aspects of the audit service provided by the audit firm. In carrying out the assessment the committee should obtain from the audit firm a report on its own internal quality control procedures. If the external auditors resign, the audit committee should investigate the issues that led to the resignation, and consider whether any action is needed.

The audit committee should consider the terms of engagement of the external auditors and the remuneration to be paid to the auditors for their audit services. It should satisfy itself that the fee payable for the audit services is appropriate, and that an effective audit can be carried out for such a fee. The fee should not be too large, but neither should it be too low. A low audit fee creates a risk that the audit might be of an inadequate scope or quality. The audit committee should then make a recommendation to the board of directors (or council of governors in the case of FTs). The committee is not required to negotiate terms and remuneration.

The FRC guidance also recommends that the committee should review and agree the engagement letter issued by the external auditors at the start of each audit, to make sure that it has been updated to reflect any changes in circumstances since the previous year. In addition, the committee should review the scope of the audit with the auditor. If it is not satisfied that the proposed scope is adequate, the committee should arrange for additional audit work to be undertaken.

In FTs, while the audit committee may make recommendations as to appointment, re-appointment or removal of the external auditors, it is the council of governors who make the decision. The FT guidance *Governance over Audit, Assurance and Accountability: Guidance for Foundation Trusts* (March 2015) sets out recommendations for procurement, appointment and selection.

For NHS trusts and CCGs, auditors have been appointed by the auditor panel under the Local Audit (Health Service Bodies Auditor Panel And Independence) Regulations 2015 and the selection/procurement process is set out in the DH *Guidance on the Local Procurement of External Auditors for NHS Trusts and CCGs* (March 2016).

Audit committee responsibilities and auditor independence

The Local Audit (Health Service Bodies Auditor Panel and Independence) Regulations 2015 and resulting NAO Code of Practice gives the audit committee the responsibility for monitoring and ensuring the independence of the external auditors. If the external auditors provide non-audit services to the organisation, the annual report should explain how auditor independence and objectivity are safeguarded. The audit committee should have procedures for ensuring the independence and objectivity of the external auditors annually. The FRC guidance recommends that the committee should:

- seek reassurance that the auditors and their staff have no family, financial, employment, investment or business relationship with the organisation that could adversely affect their independence or objectivity. The committee should seek from the audit firm, annually, information about the firm's policies and processes for maintaining independence and monitoring compliance with relevant requirements, such as those regarding the rotation of audit partners and staff;
- agree with the board the organisation's policy on employing former employees of the external auditor. Particular attention should be given to the organisation's policy on former employees of the auditor who were members of the audit team and then moved directly to the organisation. This policy should be drafted, and the audit committee should monitor its application. The committee should monitor the number of former employees of the external auditor who now hold senior positions within the organisation, and consider whether there may be some impairment (or appearance of impairment) in the auditors' judgement and independence with regard to the audit;
- monitor the audit firm's compliance with ethical guidance in the UK about the rotation of audit partners, and the fees the organisation pays as a proportion of the overall fee income of (1) the firm; (2) the office of the firm responsible for the audit; and (3) the audit partner;
- develop and recommend to the board the organisation's policy relating to the provision of non-audit services by the external auditors. The committee's objective should be to ensure that the provision of such services does not impair the independence or objectivity of the auditors.

Provision of non-audit services

The audit committee should ensure that the provision of non-audit services by the organisation's audit firm will not impair the objectivity and independence of the auditors. The committee should consider:

- whether the skills and experience of the audit firm make it a suitable supplier of the non-audit services
- whether there are safeguards in place for ensuring that there would be no threat to the objectivity and independence of the auditors arising from the provision of these services
- the nature of the non-audit services and the fees for these services
- the level of fees for individual non-audit services and the fees in aggregate for these services, relative to the size of the audit fee
- the criteria governing the compensation of the individuals who perform the audit.

The audit committee should set and apply a formal policy specifying the types of non-audit work from which the external auditors are excluded and for which the external auditors can be engaged without referral to the audit committee. It should be established on a case-by-case basis and in these cases, it may be appropriate to give a general pre-approval for certain classes of work, subject to a fee limit decided by the audit committee and ratified by the board. If the external auditor subsequently provides any of these services, the engagement of the auditors should then be ratified at the next audit committee meeting. The policy may also set fee limits generally or for particular classes of non-audit work.

In deciding its policy on the provision of non-audit work by the external auditors, the committee should take into account relevant ethical guidance. The FRC guidance recommends that the external auditor should not be engaged for non-audit work if the result is that the external auditor would audit work done by its own employees or make management decisions for the organisation or create a mutuality of interest or where the external auditor is put in the role of advocate for the organisation.

The FT Code states that, if the external auditors do provide non-financial services, the annual report should explain to stakeholders how auditor independence and objectivity is safeguarded.

The audit committee and the annual audit cycle

The FRC Guidance on Audit Committees goes into some detail on the annual audit cycle, and the relationship between the audit committee and the external auditors during this process. At the start of each annual audit, the audit committee should ensure that appropriate plans are in place for the audit. The committee should consider whether the auditors' overall work plan (including the planned levels of materiality and the proposed resources to carry out the audit) seems consistent with the scope of the audit engagement. This assessment should have regard to the seniority, expertise and experience of the audit team.

The audit committee should review, with the external auditors, the findings of their work. As a part of this review, the committee should:

- discuss with the auditors any major issues that arose during the audit (and whether these have been resolved)
- review key accounting or audit judgments
- review levels of errors identified during the audit and obtain explanations as to why certain errors might remain unadjusted.

The FRC guidance states that the audit committee should review the audit representation letters from management before they are signed, and consider whether the information provided is complete and appropriate based on the knowledge the committee has. It should also review the management letter from the auditors, and the responsiveness of the organisation's management to the auditors' findings and recommendations.

Representation letters from the organisation's management are a part of the audit evidence collected and considered by the auditors. They contain information from management to the auditors. These deal with matters for which other audit evidence does not exist; therefore, the auditors are relying on what management tell them. Representations are required from the directors, acknowledging their collective responsibility for the financial statements and confirming that they have approved them. These should have regard to matters where knowledge of the facts is confined to management (e.g. management's intention to sell off a division of the business) or where there is a matter of judgement and opinion (for example, with regard to the trading position of a major customer and debtor, or the likely outcome of litigation in progress).

The audit committee should review these representations from management and assess whether (on the basis of the knowledge of the committee members) the information provided seems complete and appropriate. At the end of the audit cycle, the audit committee should assess the effectiveness of the audit process. As a part of this assessment, the committee should:

- review whether the auditors have met the agreed audit plan and consider the reasons for any changes
- consider the 'robustness and perceptiveness' of the auditors, in their handling of key accounting and audit judgements, and in their commentary on the appropriateness of the organisation's internal controls
- obtain feedback about the conduct of the auditors from key people within the organisation, such as the finance director and the head of internal audit
- review the auditor's management letter, to assess whether it is based on a good understanding of the business and to establish whether the auditors' recommendations have been acted on (and if not, why not).

Management reports to the audit committee

Management is accountable to the board (or the audit committee) for monitoring the system of internal control and for providing assurances that it has done so. To be effective, monitoring should be on a regular basis, and management should also provide regular reports to the audit committee (or the board). These regular reports should each deal with a specific aspect of operations and provide an assessment of the significance of the risks and the effectiveness of the system of internal control for dealing with them. They should also report any significant control weaknesses or failings that have been identified, the impact these have had (or may have) on the organisation and the action that has been taken to deal with the problem.

The board or audit committee may also receive independent reports from the internal auditors. In addition to receiving regular reports from management on internal control, the board (or audit committee) should carry out an annual review of the effectiveness of the internal control system. The annual review should consider the following in particular:

- the changes that have occurred since the previous annual review – in what ways have the significant risks for the organisation changed, and how successful has the organisation been in responding to those changes
- the scope and quality of monitoring of the control system by management
- the scope and quality of the investigations by the internal audit function, the weaknesses in the system identified by the internal auditors and the measures taken to implement recommendations of the internal auditors.

Raising concerns procedure

The UK Code states that the audit committee should 'review arrangements by which staff of the organisation may, in confidence, raise concerns about possible improprieties in matters of financial reporting or other matters'.

In other words, the audit committee should be responsible for the review of the provisions and procedures for raising concerns within the organisation. The UK Code specifies that the objective of the audit committee should be to ensure that there are satisfactory arrangements in place for the 'proportionate and independent investigation' of allegations, and appropriate follow-up action. The Code is referring to the adequacy of what the NHS has understood to be whistleblowing procedures within the organisation. This terminology has now changed and the NHS now refers to raising concerns in line with Code.

The HFMA Handbook sets out a similar provision in its recommended terms of reference for an NHS audit committee. Chapter 4 sets out the details of the specific legislation, namely, the Public Interest Disclosure Act 1998 and the Employment Rights Act 1996. This chapter will focus on the development of best practice in raising concerns procedures in the NHS.

The Francis Report

In March 2013, the government gave an announcement in response to the Francis Report, which is designed to create a culture of 'zero harm' and compassionate care. The announcement included a number of items which related to raising concerns:

- the creation of a new post of Chief Inspector of Hospitals and Care Homes, which will be a 'chief whistleblower' with the power to name and shame poorly performing trusts
- the introduction of a statutory duty to be honest about mistakes which harm patients, known as a duty of candour
- the barring of hospital managers who manipulate statistics or who try and cover up cases of poor care from any future role in healthcare
- the banning of clauses gagging ex-NHS staff from raising concerns publicly about patient safety.

The NHS Constitution

As part of a series of measures intended to highlight the importance of raising concerns in the NHS, and in response to the Francis Report, the 2013 Constitution includes:

- an expectation that staff should raise concerns at the earliest opportunity
- a pledge that NHS organisations should support staff when raising concerns by ensuring their concerns are fully investigated, and that there is someone independent to speak to outside of their team
- clarity around the existing legal right for staff to raise concerns about safety, malpractice or other wrong doing without suffering any detriment.

The need for raising concerns

There is a strong connection between health service governance and raising concerns. An employee may honestly believe that there is (or has been, or could soon be) serious malpractice by someone within the organisation, but feel unable to report his or her concerns in the normal way. This could be because the individual to whom he or she normally reports is involved in the suspected malpractice. Serious malpractice or a misdemeanour could be damaging to the organisation, such as:

- it might suffer financial loss if some employees are acting fraudulently
- it might incur severe penalties as a consequence of employees breaking the law or regulations
- there could be damage to the organisation's reputation if the misdemeanour is made public.

The need for raising concerns arises when normal procedures and internal controls will not reveal the illicit activity because the individuals responsible for the activity are somehow able to ignore or 'get around' the normal controls.

However, although raising concerns procedures are an internal control, they are not an embedded control within the organisation's regular procedures. Their effectiveness relies on the willingness of staff to come forward with their allegations. The incidence of illicit or illegal behaviour should be uncommon; therefore raising concerns should be an occasional event. Extensive inquiries into the baby heart unit at Bristol Royal Infirmary, the behaviour of the GP Dr Harold Shipman, and the concerns at Mid Staffs have raised questions about the protection provided to those, who raise concerns within the health service.

Sir Robert Francis QC led an independent review into creating the open and honest reporting culture in the *NHS: The Freedom to Speak Up Review* (November 2014). Following this, NHS Improvement (NHSI) issued the Freedom to Speak Up: Raising Concerns (whistleblowing) policy for the NHS in April 2016. The Freedom to Speak Up (FTSU) policy will ensure that:

- NHS organisations encourage staff to speak up and set out the steps they will take to get to the bottom of any concerns;
- organisations will each appoint their own FTSU guardian, an independent and impartial source of advice to staff at any stage of raising a concern;
- any concerns not resolved quickly through line managers are investigated;
- investigations will be evidence based and led by someone suitably independent in the organisation, producing a report which focuses on learning lessons and improving care;
- anyone raising a concern will be kept informed of the investigation's progress; and
- high level findings are provided to the organisation's board and the policy will be annually reviewed and improved.

All NHS organisations in England have been required to adopt the policy since 31 March 2017 as a minimum standard to help normalise the raising of concerns for the benefit of all patients.

The policy also creates a national guardian role that is intended to support local FTSU guardians and staff who have raised a concern with their NHS organisation and feel the concern has been poorly handled by their employer or other body. The priorities of the national guardian's office include establishing and supporting a strong network of local FTSU guardians, highlighting NHS providers that are successful in creating the right environment for staff to speak up safely and share this best practice across the NHS, and independently reviewing cases where NHS providers may have failed to follow good practice, working with statutory bodies to take action where needed. The national guardian's office is not an arbitration or appeals service and cannot investigate the detailed concerns raised in specific cases.

Local FTSU guardians have a key role in helping to raise the profile of raising concerns in their organisation and providing confidential advice and support to staff in relation to concerns they have about patient safety and/or the way their concern has been handled. They do not have a remit to assist staff who are employed outside of their trust. Guardians do not get involved in investigations or complaints, but help to facilitate the process where needed, ensuring organisational policies in relation to raising concerns are followed correctly and typically report to the trust chief executive.

Raising concerns: best practice

> 'Health and social care professionals have a responsibility to raise concerns if they believe that patients or people who use services are being put at risk. The first course of action should be to raise these concerns within your organisation – but if you feel unable to, or if your voice is not being heard, it's important to know that there are other options open to you.'
>
> *Cynthia Bower, ex-CEO of the CQC*

If an employee has a genuine, honest concern about something happening within the organisation which they believe to be unsafe or improper, there should be a way for the employee's concerns to be brought to the attention of management and dealt with in a constructive way. Having a system for listening to employees' concerns should be a part of an effective risk management system within the organisation, because diligent employees can act as an early warning system of problems.

There are several problems with raising concern procedures and policies. For example, experience in many organisations appears to show that an individual who reports concerns about illegal or unethical conduct is often victimised by colleagues and management. If the allegations are rejected, they might not receive the same salary increases as colleagues, or could be overlooked for promotion. The attitude of colleagues and managers might also be hostile, making it difficult for the individual to continue in the job.

However, employees may deliberately make false claims about their colleagues or bosses, out of spite or a desire for revenge for some actual or perceived 'wrong'. It would be inappropriate to provide protection for individuals making malicious and intentionally false allegations. Organisations therefore need to establish a system that encourages employees to report illegal or unethical behaviour, but discourages malicious and unfounded allegations.

An organisation might state its policy on raising concerns in the following terms.

- An employee is acting correctly if, in good faith, he or she seeks advice about improper behaviour or reports improper behaviour, where it is not possible to resolve the individual's concerns through discussions with colleagues or line management. Raising concerns is appropriate if the employee does it in good faith and is not being malicious, and there is no other way to resolve the problem.
- The organisation will not tolerate any discrimination by employees or management in the organisation against an individual who has reported in good faith their concerns about illegal or unethical behaviour. This is a policy statement that those who raise concerns will be protected if they have made their report in good faith.
- Disciplinary action will be taken against any employee who knowingly makes a false report of illegal or improper behaviour by someone else. Malicious reporting should not be tolerated.
- In practice, employees may feel obliged to take their concerns (possibly anonymously) to someone outside the organisation, risking the anger of the employer for breach of proper procedures if he is identified. An employee can be disciplined for making groundless complaints and allegations in bad faith about his or her employer. However, there is an 'official' raising concerns channel that provides a way of reporting concerns to someone outside the employer organisation provided by the government-funded whistleblowing helpline, which changed to a freephone service in January 2012.

CASE STUDY: Raising concerns at Queen Elizabeth Hospital Trust

At Queen Elizabeth Hospital Trust, consultant Ramon Neikrash was suspended in 2008 after writing a series of letters to management warning about the impact of cost-cutting. An employment tribunal ruled the suspension was unlawful and that Mr Neikrash had been acting as a whistleblower.

Internal procedures for handling allegations

An organisation should have a fair system for dealing internally with accusations or allegations of concern so that an honest individual does not feel under threat. Employees ought to know what those procedures are. Since raising concerns is not a regular event, an organisation may simply try to deal with each case on its merits when it arises, without any formal procedures or channels of complaint being established. The employee will therefore not know whom to complain to, and will probably go to the most senior manager available – possibly the CEO.

A problem with dealing with raising concern incidents on an *ad hoc* basis is that the accusations may relate to senior members of staff or the EDs themselves. An employee who believes the CEO or finance director to be guilty of wrong-doing will have no option other than to resign or take the complaint to an external authority.

It is, therefore, more appropriate to establish a formal internal channel for dealing with concerns that have been raised. This is the remit of the FTSU raising concerns policy which should provide:

- documented internal procedures available to all employees who wish to raise a concern
- the procedures by which an allegation will be investigated
- a named person to whom employees should report their suspicions or concerns
- an independent means of investigation
- a statement that the employer takes malpractice or misconduct seriously, and is committed to a culture of openness in which employees can report legitimate concerns without fear of penalty or punishment
- examples of the type of misconduct for which employees should use the procedure and set out the level of proof that there should be in an allegation (although positive proof might not be required, there should be good reasons for his or her concern)
- that false or malicious allegations will result in disciplinary action against the individual making them
- that no employee will be victimised for raising a genuine concern. Victimisation for raising a qualified disclosure is a disciplinary offence
- an external raising concern route, as well as an internal reporting procedure
- that, as far as possible, anyone raising concerns will be informed about the outcome of their allegations and the action that has been taken

- that anyone raising concerns will be promised confidentiality, as far as this is possible.

Raising concerns procedures and the Bribery Act 2010

In the UK, the Bribery Act 2010 introduced a new offence of 'failure of commercial organisations to prevent bribery' by a person associated with them (such as an employee or agent). However, an organisation could avoid conviction if it can show that, although bribery may have occurred, it has in place 'adequate processes' to prevent bribery. Having a suitable raising concerns procedure is likely to be a sufficient defence against a criminal charge, provided that the organisation can demonstrate that the procedures work well in practice. It would not be sufficient simply to have a raising concerns policy in existence that no one uses.

The majority of trusts should already have an anti-fraud and corruption policy or equivalent policy; the reporting of potential acts of bribery should follow the same procedure. It is important that NHS organisations update their raising concerns policies to cover potential acts of bribery, so employees are aware of what behaviour is unacceptable.

Governance checklist

- ✓ Does the audit committee have the requisite skills, financial experience, resources, time commitment and robust independence to undertake its tasks?
- ✓ Does the audit committee review all financial statements, the Quality Accounts and any supporting audit assurance prior to their release?
- ✓ Does the audit committee control (or, in the case of FTs, support) the process of appointing and assessing the external auditors and is it satisfied as to their independence and effectiveness?
- ✓ Has account been taken of the ten-yearly audit tender requirements (five-yearly for FTs) and is the audit committee involved in the tender process?
- ✓ Is the external audit plan in place? Does the audit committee review and monitor the auditors' performance against that plan?
- ✓ Does the audit committee meet at least annual with the external and internal auditors without management being present?
- ✓ Is the internal audit team effectively and adequately resourced?
- ✓ Does the audit committee regularly challenge and review the effectiveness of the internal audit function?
- ✓ Is the internal audit function used effectively to provide objective assurance to the board on the key risks?

- ✓ Is the head of internal audit appointed by and accountable to the audit committee, and do they have unrestricted access to the audit committee and board chair? Is the management team responsive to their findings and recommendations?
- ✓ What action has the audit committee taken to review the raising concerns policy and procedures in the last 12 months.

Summary

Audit plays a key role in providing assurance to the board and wider NHS stakeholders. This critical role means that ensuring the independence of those functions is high on the agenda of the board and its audit committee. This, however, is only part of the role of the audit committee, which has a broad and extensive role that is not restricted to considering just the financial aspects of the organisation.

Glossary

accountability: the requirement for a person in a position of responsibility to justify, explain or account for the exercise of his/her authority and his/her performance or actions. Accountability is to the person or persons from whom the authority is derived.

accountable officer: the primary authority for providing financial management and accountability for NHS property and services.

annual governance statement: the AGS is a mandatory disclosure for all central government entities that comply with the FReM. All public bodies (including NHS organisations) must provide assurance that they are appropriately managing and controlling the resources for which they are responsible. The AGS replaces the statement on internal control.

apply or explain rule: similar to the comply or explain rule. Companies should apply the principles of a code or explain why they have not done so.

audit committee: committee of the board, consisting entirely of independent non-executive directors, with responsibility (among other things) for monitoring the reliability of the financial statements, the quality of the external audit and the organisation's relationship with its external auditors.

audit firm rotation: changing the firm of external auditors on a regular basis, say every seven years. Not common in practice.

audit partner rotation: changing the lead partner (and possibly other partners) involved with an organisation's audit on a regular basis, typically every five or seven years.

audit report: report for stakeholders produced by the external auditors on completion of the annual audit, and included in the organisation's published annual report and accounts. The report gives the opinion of the auditors on whether the financial statements present a true and fair view of the organisation's financial performance and position.

balance of power: a situation in which power is shared out more or less evenly between a number of different individuals or groups, so that no single individual or group is in a position to dominate.

board committee: a committee established by the board of directors, with delegated responsibility for a particular aspect of the board's affairs. For example, audit committee, remuneration/ compensation committee and nominations committee.

board succession: the replacement of a senior director (typically the chair or CEO) when he or she retires or resigns.

box-ticking approach: an approach to compliance based on following all the specific rules or provisions in a code, and not considering the principles that should be applied and circumstances where the principles are best applied by not following the detailed provisions.

Bribery Act 2010: UK Act of Parliament making it a criminal offence to give or receive bribes, to bribe a foreign public official for business benefit or to fail to prevent the payment of bribes by employees or agents.

business ethics: standards of business behaviour, sometimes set out by companies in a code of corporate ethics.

business risk: the risk from unexpected events or developments in a business or in the business environment, which are outside the control of management. In the NHS, business risks are to patient safety and financial security.

business risk management: the management of business risks within a strategy based on risk appetite and risk tolerance. The board is responsible for business risk strategy and management is responsible for implementing the strategy within a business risk management system. The board is also responsible for monitoring the effectiveness of the business risk management system, at least annually according to the UK Corporate Governance Code.

Cadbury Code: a code of corporate governance, published by the Cadbury Committee in the UK in 1992 (and since superseded).

Care Quality Commission (CQC): the safety and quality regulator for all health services, which is also responsible for the regulation of adult social care services.

chair: leader of the board of directors. Often referred to as the 'company chair' in companies and 'chair' in public bodies and voluntary organisations.

chief executive officer: the executive director who is head of the executive management team in an organisation.

clinical commissioning groups (CCGs): groups of GPs and other health professionals responsible under the Health and Social Care Act 2012 for commissioning most healthcare.

Combined Code: the UK code on corporate governance for listed companies from 1998 to 2010. It was revised in 2010 and re-named the UK Corporate Governance Code.

comply or explain rule: requirement (e.g. in the UK, a requirement of the Listing Rules) for a company to comply with a voluntary code of corporate governance (in the UK, the UK Corporate Governance Code) or explain any non-compliance.

connected person: a person with whom a director has an enduring and direct relationship, such as a family member, including a spouse, civil partner, children and step children (and equivalent relationships arising through civil partnerships) and companies in which the director has an interest of 20% or more.

corporate governance: the system by which a company is directed, so as to achieve its overall objectives. It is concerned with relationships, structures, processes, information flows, controls, decision-making and accountability at the highest level in a company.

council of governors: a council of governors is a several member group that oversees or manages the running of an institution. In the context of an NHS FT it is an elected body of members who hold the board of directors to account.

Davies Review: a government-sponsored report (published February 2011) recommending greater diversity on the boards of companies and in particular a greater proportion of women on the boards of FTSE350 companies.

directors' report: the 'report' in the annual report and accounts of a company or organisation. A report by the board of directors to the stakeholders, contained in the annual report and accounts and containing a variety of reports and information disclosures, such as the business review and remuneration report.

Disclosure and Transparency Rules: in the UK, rules on disclosures that listed companies are required to comply with. The rules (like the Listing Rules) are issued and enforced by the UK financial markets regulator.

downside risk: a risk that actual events will turn out worse than expected. Downside risk can be measure in terms of the amount by which profits could be worse than expected. The expected outcome is the forecast or budget expectation.

duty of skill and care: a duty owed by a director to the company or organisation. In the UK, this has been a common law duty, but became a statutory duty under the provisions of the Companies Act 2006. A question can be raised, however, about what level of skill and care should be expected from a director.

elective care: planned specialist medical care.

emergency preparedness: emergency preparedness is a plan of what to do if a disaster that is unconnected with the organisation's business and outside the control of management occurs.

EU Directive: an instruction, devised by the European Commission and approved by the European Council and European Parliament. The contents of a Directive must be introduced into national law or regulations by all members states of the EU. Some Directives, such as the Shareholder Rights Directive, deal wholly or partly with corporate governance issues.

European Commission: the managing and administrative body of the EU.

executive director: a director who also has executive responsibilities in the management structure. Usually a full-time employee with a contract of employment.

external audit: statutory annual audit of an organisation by independent external auditors.

fairness: impartiality, a lack of bias. In a corporate governance context, the quality of fairness refers to things that are done or decided in a reasonable manner, and with sense of justice, avoiding bias.

fiduciary duty: a duty of a trustee. The directors of a company or organisation are given their powers in trust, and have fiduciary duties towards the company or organisation.

financial risk: a risk of a failure or error, deliberate (fraud) or otherwise, in the systems or procedures for recording financial transactions and reporting financial performance and position, or the risk of a failure to safeguard financial assets such as cash and accounts receivable.

fixed pay: the elements in a remuneration package that are a fixed amount each year, such as basic salary.

going concern statement: a requirement of some corporate governance codes, such as the UK Corporate Governance Code. A statement by the board of directors that in their view the organisation will remain as a going concern for the next financial year.

Greenbury Report: report in the UK in 1995 by the Greenbury Committee, focusing mainly on corporate governance issues related to directors' remuneration.

Hampel Committee: committee set up in the UK to continue the review of corporate governance practices in the UK, following the Cadbury and Greenbury Committee Reports. The Hampel Committee suggested that the recommendations of all three committees should be integrated into a single code of corporate governance, which was published in 1998 as the Combined Code.

health service governance: the system, practices and procedures by which power is shared and exercised by the board of directors (and the council of governors in foundation trusts) and how the holders of that power are held accountable for ensuring that the individual parts of the NHS achieve their objectives and are in line with public sector values such as value for money and providing universal and free healthcare benefits to all those in need.

Higgs Report: the 2003 UK government commissioned review into the role and effectiveness of non-executive directors.

induction: process of introducing a newly appointed director into his or her role, by providing appropriate information, site visits, meetings with management and (where necessary) training.

internal audit: investigations and checks carried out by internal auditors of an organisation. Internal audit is a function rather than a specific activity. However, the work programme of the internal audit team might reduce the amount of work the external auditors need to carry out in their annual audit, provided the internal and external auditors collaborate properly.

internal control: a procedure or arrangement that is implemented to prevent an internal control risk, reduce the potential impact of such a risk, or detect a failure of internal control when it occurs (and initiate remedial action).

internal control risk: a risk of failure in a system or procedure due to causes that are within the control of management. They can be categorised as financial risks, operational risk and compliance risks.

internal control system: a system of internal controls within an organisation. The system should have a suitable control environment, and should provide for the identification and assessment of internal control risks, the design and implementation of internal controls, communication and information and monitoring. In the UK, the board of directors of a listed company has responsibility for the system of internal control.

International Corporate Governance Network (ICGN): a voluntary association of institutional investors that has the objective of raising standards of corporate governance globally, to meet the requirements and expectations of global investors.

King Code: also called the King Report and King IV (because it is the fourth version of the Code/Report, issued in 2016). The corporate governance code for listed companies in South Africa.

lead governor: the lead governor's role is to facilitate direct communication between Monitor and the NHS foundation trust's board of governors in a limited number of circumstances and in particular where it may not be appropriate to communicate through the normal channels.

management board: a board of executive managers, chaired by the CEO, within a two-tier board structure. The chair of the management board reports to the chair of the supervisory board. The management board has responsibility for the operational performance of the business.

modified audit report: audit report in which the auditors express some reservations about the financial statements of the organisation, because of insufficient information to reach an opinion or disagreement with the figures in the statements.

money laundering: the process of transferring or using money obtained from criminal activity, so as to make it seem to have come from legitimate (non-criminal) sources. Companies are often used as a cover for money laundering.

Monitor: the regulator of foundation trusts. Under the Health and Social Care Act its role will be extended to become the sector regulator for health making it responsible for licensing providers of NHS- funded services.

mutual society: a mutual, mutual organisation, or mutual society is an organisation (which is often, but not always, a company or business) based on the principle of mutuality. A mutual is therefore owned by, and run for the benefit of, its members – it has no external shareholders to pay in the form of dividends and, as such, does not usually seek to maximise and make large profits or capital gains.

nomination committee: a committee of the board of directors (or council of governors in foundation trusts), with responsibility for identifying potential new members for the board of directors. Suitable candidates are recommended to the main board (or to the council of governors), which then makes a decision about their appointment.

non-audit work: work done by a firm of auditors for a client organisation, other than work on the annual audit, such as consultancy services and tax advice. In the context of corporate governance, the independence of the auditors might be questionable when they earn high fees for non-audit work.

non-executive director (NED): a director who is not an employee of the company and who does not have any responsibilities for executive management in the company.

OECD Principles of Corporate Governance: general principles of corporate governance issued by the Organisation for European Cooperation and Development, which all countries are encouraged to adopt.

policy governance theory: policy governance theory is an integrated set of concepts and principles that describes the job of any governing board. It outlines the manner in which boards can be successful in their servant-leadership role, as well as in their all-important relationship with management.

postcode lottery: a situation where local budgets and decision-making can lead to different levels of public services in different places especially with regard to health and social services, e.g. access to cancer drugs or quality of education.

primary care: the first point of healthcare such as GPs, dentists, pharmacists and optometrists.

public benefit corporation: a public benefit corporation is usually a corporation created by the government that performs a specific function for the benefit of the public, such as a hospital or public library.

Quality Account: a Quality Account is a report about the quality of services provided by an NHS healthcare service. The report is published annually by each NHS healthcare provider, including the independent sector and made available to the public.

quality governance: the combination of structures and processes at and below board level to lead on trust-wide quality performance including:

- ensuring required standards are achieved
- investigating and taking action on sub-standard performance
- planning and driving continuous improvement
- identifying, sharing and ensuring delivery of best-practice
- identifying and managing risks to quality of care.

remuneration committee: a committee of the board of directors (or council of governors in foundation trusts), with responsibility for deciding remuneration policy for top executives and the individual remuneration packages of certain senior executives, for example, all the executive directors (or non-executive directors in foundation trusts).

reputation risk: risk to the reputation of a company or other organisation in the mind of the public (including customers and suppliers) when a particular matter becomes public knowledge

responsibility: having power and authority over something. A person in a position of responsibility should be held accountable for the exercise of that authority.

risk appetite: the amount and type of business risk that the board of directors would like their organisation to have exposure to. Identifying risk appetite should be a part of strategic planning.

risk assessment: an assessment of risks faced by an organisation, Typically risks are assessed according to how probably or how frequent an adverse outcome is likely to be in the planning period and the potential size of the losses if an adverse outcome occurs. The greatest risks are those with a high probability of an adverse outcome combined with the likelihood of a large loss if this were to happen.

risk capacity: the maximum risk exposures that the organisation can accept without threatening its financial stability.

risk committee: a committee of the board that an organisation may establish, with the responsibility of monitoring the risk management system within the organisation, instead of the audit committee. A risk committee may be established when the audit committee has too many other responsibilities to handle.

risk management: a function of the administration of the NHS body directed toward identification, evaluation, and correction of potential risks that could lead to injury to patients, staff members, or visitors and result in loss or damage.

risk management committee: a committee of senior executive managers and risk managers, whose responsibility is to implement the risk management strategy of the board.

risk tolerance: the amount of business risk that the board is willing to let their organisation be exposed to. Alternatively, the amount of risk that the organisation is able to accept without serious threat to its stability.

Sarbanes-Oxley Act: legislation, largely on corporate governance issues, introduced in the USA in 2002 following a series of corporate scandals such as Enron and WorldCom.

secondary care: acute healthcare, either elective or emergency.

secret profit: a profit that is not revealed. In the context of corporate governance, a director should not make a secret profit for his/her personal benefit and at the expense of the company or organisation.

senior independent director: a non-executive director who is the nominal head of all the non-executive directors on the board. The SID may act as a channel of communication between the NEDs and the chair, or (in some situations) between major stakeholders and the board.

severance payment: payment to a director (or other employee) on being required to resign (or otherwise leave the company).

shareholder value approach: approach to corporate governance based on the view that the objective of its directors should be to maximise benefits for shareholders.

Smith Report: a report concerned with the independence of auditors in the wake of the collapse of Arthur Andersen and the Enron scandal in the US in 2002. It raised the important point that an auditor himself should look at whether a company's corporate governance structure provides safeguards to preserve his own independence.

stakeholder: a stakeholder group is an identifiable group of individuals or organisations with a vested interest. Stakeholder groups in a company include the shareholders, the directors, senior executive management and other employees, customers, suppliers. In the NHS stakeholders will also include patients, employees, the regulators, the general public and the government.

Statement on Internal Control: the SIC is a mandatory disclosure for all central government entities that comply with the FReM. All public bodies (including NHS organisations) must provide assurance that they are appropriately managing and controlling the resources for which they are responsible. This has now been replaced by the AGS.

statutory duties: duties imposed by statute law.

strategic risk: the risks of taking decisions on strategy that will result in exposures to excessive business risk and so could lead to losses or even business collapse.

stress testing: testing the ability of a business to withstand the effects of extreme adverse events or developments in the business environment.

succession planning: planning for the eventual replacement of a senior member of the board (chair, CEO and possibly finance director) by his or her successor.

supervisory board: a board of non-executive directors, found in an organisation with a two-tier board structure. The supervisory board reserves some responsibilities to itself. These include oversight of the management board.

sustainability: conducting business operations in a way that can be continued into the foreseeable future, without using natural resources at such a rate or creating such environmental damage that the continuation of the business will eventually become impossible.

sustainability report: report on the economic, social and environmental performance of a company or organisation.

transparency: openness. Being clear about historical performance and future intentions, and not trying to hide information.

Turnbull Guidance: initially a report of the Turnbull Committee in the UK, giving listed companies guidance on how the directors should carry out their responsibility for the internal control system, as required by the UK corporate governance code. Now the responsibility of the FRC.

two-tier board: board structure in which the responsibilities are divided between a supervisory board of non-executive directors led by the chair, and a management board of executives led by the CEO.

UK Corporate Governance Code: the code of corporate governance issued by the FRC in the UK, which is applied to UK listed companies. Formerly (until 2010) called the Combined Code.

UK Listing Rules: rules that apply to all listed companies in the UK. They include the 'comply or explain' rule on compliance with the UK Corporate Governance Code.

ultra vires: in corporate law, ultra vires describes acts attempted by a corporation that are beyond the scope of powers granted by the corporation's objects clause, articles of incorporation or in a clause in its bylaws, in the laws authorising a corporation's formation, or similar founding documents.

unitary board: board structure in which decisions are taken by a single group of executive and non-executive directors, led by the company chair.

upside risk: a risk that actual events will turn out better than expected and will provide unexpected profits. Some risks, such as the risk of a change in foreign exchange rates, or a change in interest rates, or a change in consumer buying patterns could be 'two-way' with both upside and downside potential.

variable pay: the elements in a remuneration package that vary each year according to the individual's performance, such as annual bonuses, and the grant of shares or share options

voluntary code of governance: a code of governance that is not enforced by law or regulation. However, as in the UK and South Africa, listed companies may be encouraged to adopt a voluntary code by means of a 'comply or explain' or 'apply or explain' regulation.

Walker Report: a report published in the UK in 2009 about corporate governance in banks and other financial services organisations, following the banking crisis of 2007–2009.

whistleblowing: the disclosure by a person, usually an employee in a government agency or private enterprise, to the public or to those in authority, of mismanagement, corruption, illegality, or some other wrongdoing.

window dressing of accounts: applying accounting policies that are just within the limits of permissible accounting practice, but which have the effect of making the company's performance or financial position seem better than it would if more conservative accounting policies were used. For example, accounting policies might be used that recognise income at an early stage in a transaction process, or defer the recognition of expenses.

Women on Boards Report: a report highlighting the poor representation of women on boards, relative to their male counterparts, and raised questions about whether board recruitment is in practice based on skills, experience and performance. This report presents practical recommendations to address this imbalance.

wrongful trading: wrongful trading occurs when a company continues to trade when the directors are aware that the company had gone into (or would soon go into) insolvent liquidation.

Directory

Further reading, codes of practice and guidance

A First Class Service: Quality in the New NHS, Department of Health, 1998.

Audit Code for NHS Foundation Trusts, Monitor, 2011.

Board Governance Assurance Framework, Department of Health, 2011.

Carver, J. *Boards that Make a Difference: A New Design for Leadership in Nonprofit and Public Organisations*, Jossey-Bass, 2006.

Chait R, Ryan W, and Taylor B. *Governance as Leadership: Reframing the Work of Nonprofit Boards*, Wiley, 2005.

Code and Report on Governance for South Africa (King IV), Institute of Directors South Africa, 2016 (see www.iodsa.co.za).

Code of Ethics for Professional Accountants, International Federation of Accountants, 2006.

Code of Governance for Foundation Trusts, Monitor, 2010. See Appendix 2.

Corporate Governance Policy and Voting Guidelines, National Association of Pension Funds, 2011.

Davies Review into Women on Boards, Department of Business, Innovation and Skills, 2011.

Effective Boards in the NHS, NHS Confederation, 2005.

Equity and Excellence: Liberating the NHS, Department of Health, 2010.

The Foundations of Good Governance, Foundation Trust Network, 2010.

Good Governance: a Code for the Voluntary Sector, NCVO, 2010. See: www.ncvo-vol.org.uk/codeofgovernance

Government Financial Reporting Manual (FReM), HM Treasury, annual.

Guidance on Audit Committees, FRC, 2010 (see Appendix 5).

Guidance on Board Effectiveness, FRC, 2011 (see Appendix 4).

Guidance on Risk Management, Internal Control and Related Financial and Business Reporting, FRC, 2005 (see Appendix 6).

The Healthy NHS Board: Principles for Good Governance, NHS Leadership Council, 2010 (see Appendix 3).

High Quality Care for All (Darzi Report), Department of Health, 2008.

Hutton Review of Fair Pay in the Public Sector, HM Treasury, 2011.

ICGN Global Corporate Governance Principles, ICGN, 2009.

The Integrated Governance Handbook, Department of Health, 2006

New Voices, New Accountabilities: A Guide to Wider Governance in Foundation Trusts, Foundation Trust Network, 2005.

NHS Audit Committee Handbook, Department of Health, 2005.

The NHS Emergency Planning Guidance, Department of Health, 2005.
The Nolan Principles of Standards in Public Life, Committee on Standards in Public Life, 1995
Plurality, Stewardship and Engagement, The Ownership Commission, 2012.
Quality Governance Framework, Monitor, 2010.
Quality Governance in the NHS: A Guide for Provider Boards, Department of Health, 2011.
Sonnenfeld, J.A. 'What Makes Boards Great', *Harvard Business Review*, September 2002.
Taking it on Trust, Audit Commission, 2009
The UK Corporate Governance Code, FRC, 2010.
Walker Review of Corporate Governance of UK Banking Industry, HM Treasury, 2009.
Your Statutory Duties: A Reference Guide for NHS Foundation Trust Governors, Monitor, 2009.

Useful websites

Association of British Insurers (ABI)
www.abi.org.uk

Audit Commission
www.audit-commission.gov.uk

Care Quality Commission
www.cqc.org.uk

Chartered Institute of Internal Auditors
www.iia.org.uk

The Chartered Institute of Public Finance and Accountancy
www.cipfa.org.uk

Department for Business, Innovation and Skills (BIS)
www.bis.gov.uk

Department of Health
www.dh.gov.uk

European Corporate Governance Institute
www.ecgi.org/codes/all_codes.php.

Financial Reporting Council (FRC)
www.frc.org.uk

Foundation Trust Governors Association
www.ftga.org.uk

Foundation Trust Network
www.foundationtrustnetwork.org

HM Treasury
www.hm-treasury.gov.uk

The Institute of Chartered Secretaries and Administrators (ICSA)
www.icsa.org.uk

The Intelligent Board series
www.drfosterintelligence.co.uk/thought-leadership/intelligent-board

International Corporate Governance Network (ICGN)
www.icgn.org

The International Federation of Accountants (IFAC)
www.ifac.org

National Association of Pension Funds (NAPF)
www.napf.co.uk

Monitor
www.monitor-nhsft.gov.uk

NHS Confederation
www.nhsconfed.org

OECD
www.oecd.org

The Ownership Commission
www.ownershipcomm.org

Index